THE
ASTROLOG
ORACLE

WHAT WE MAKE OF OUR LIVES CAN BE DONE IN A MOMENT

— AND OF THOSE MOMENTS WE MAKE OUR LIVES

THE
ASTROLOGICAL ORACLE

DIVINING YOUR FUTURE, SECURING YOUR PRESENT, RESOLVING YOUR PAST

LYN BIRKBECK

Thorsons

Thorsons
An Imprint of HarperCollins*Publishers*
77–85 Fulham Palace Road
Hammersmith, London W6 8JB

The Thorsons website address is:
www.thorsons.com

and *Thorsons*
are trademarks of
HarperCollins*Publishers* Limited

First published 2002

1 3 5 7 9 10 8 6 4 2

A catalogue record for this book
is available from the British Library

ISBN 0 00 712766 9

Designed by Claire Brodmann Book Designs, Lichfield Staffs

Printed and bound in Great Britain by
Scotprint, Haddington, East Lothian

✻
CONTENTS

TO MARC, ELSIE AND DANE

INTRODUCTION

ABOUT THE SYMBOLS

The Astrological Oracle is based upon the Sabian Symbols, which are clairvoyantly conceived images for each one of the 360 degrees of the circle that makes up the Zodiac. The images that comprise the Sabian Symbols were psychically received by a sensitive called Elsie Wheeler at the behest of one of the 20th Century's most respected astrologers, Dr Marc Edmund Jones (who was also the founder of the Screenwriters' Guild of America). Marc Edmund Jones took Elsie Wheeler into Balbao Park in San Diego one day in 1925, parked in a quiet spot, and in four sessions noted down all 360 images as Elsie 'saw' them, as was her very special talent. Marc's method here was to prepare blank cards with the Sign degree numbers written on the back of each. He would shuffle the cards face down, select one and present it blank face up to Elsie. As she then described what she 'saw', he quickly pencilled down her description on the card – sometimes questioning, sometimes being corrected by her. They then repeated this procedure for each of the remaining 359 degrees – all in that one day!

The remarkable speed and intensity of this operation, plus the fact that Marc used occult disciplines and rituals to facilitate and validate what was happening, points to the likelihood that he too was involved in the psychic process. His own belief was that they were channelling an occult brotherhood from ancient Mesopotamia (Sumeria), the originators of astrology, who still exist on inner planes.

My own research and intuition leads me to believe that there is also a connection to a group in that time and area called the Sabians who were followers of a religion led by Hermes Trismegistus, whose writings were in the form of the *Corpus Hermeticum*, and to whom is attributed the axiom that perfectly summarizes astrology: 'As Above So Below'. In the light of this, it may be said that the Sabian Symbols come down to us from the same source that has carried and kept through the millennia some of the key mysteries and secrets of life on this planet.

USING THE SABIAN SYMBOLS AS AN ORACLE

The Astrological Oracle is a book that will give you insights into your destiny and answer questions and give advice about problems relating to everyday life. In order to access this advice, you need to identify and focus on a matter that concerns you, and shape a question to put to the Oracle. Then, holding this question in your mind, through randomly selecting one or more of the Sabian Symbols with the use of ordinary playing cards or dice, you will receive guidance, support and feedback regarding your concern.

Each one of us has a unique and natural course that our life is meant to take and the Oracle will help you find the best way of following this course. The answers provided by the Sabian Symbols are given in four sections:

※ General Interpretation
※ Love/Relating/Social
※ Money/Work/Creativity
※ Karma/Attitude/Health

Depending on your question, one section might be more relevant to your situation than the others, giving highly specific advice about a particular problem. At other times, it may be necessary to take a more all-round view of things. In either case, the Oracle will help confirm your place on your path, and at the same time confirm that we always have a link to an all-seeing and compassionate spiritual reality.

✳

HOW TO USE THIS BOOK

Part I of this book begins with a general introduction to the use of oracles, particularly with regard to the sort of help and answers you may hope to receive from them. Attention is then turned specifically to the Astrological Oracle: step-by-step advice is given on formulating questions, how to consult the Oracle, and how to understand the answers. There is a full explanation of each of the key features of the Sabian Symbol pages, and these are backed up with a number of Case Studies to show how it all works in practice.

Part II contains the Symbols themselves. There is an index of the Symbols at the beginning of this section that you may find useful to start with but before long you should easily be able to find your way around. The three chapters in **Part III** take a look at more advanced techniques of using the Sabian Symbols, as well as methods you can use to integrate the Oracle into your life. These may encourage and inspire you to find your own ways of asking the Oracle to be your guide along your life's path. All you have to do is ask!

PART I

✳

THE
ASTROLOGICAL
ORACLE

USING AN ORACLE

'What do you wish to hear and see, and to learn and come to know by thought?'

'Who are you?' I said.

'I,' said he, 'am Poimandres*, the Mind of the Sovereignty.'

'Hermitica' by Hermes Trismegistus
*Poimandres means 'Shepherd of Men'

Life as we experience it – relationships, conscious thoughts and feelings – is like the foliage, flower and fruit of a plant that grows above the surface of the ground. But the plant originates from its seed and roots beneath the surface and even, you could say, from the one who planted it. This subterranean area, the invisible or unconscious realm from which all outer manifestation springs, is what we access when we consult an oracle. The oracle then gives us a view of what is potentially taking shape in our lives or what the 'score' is. Astrologically, the unseen, unconscious realm is governed by the Moon and Neptune. However, what actually accesses or connects us to it is Mercury, the intermediary or go-between. Mercury (the Roman form of the Greek God, Hermes) is the Messenger of the Gods who commutes between the Divine and the Unconscious Realms. The 'Mind of the Sovereignty' could also be interpreted as Mercury, the planet that orbits closest to the Sun, or the Sovereignty, and is the one who is nearest to the all-seeing, all-powerful King or Queen. Mercury/Hermes has also been called the 'Psychopomp', the one who guides us through the Unseen Realms, and he is also the part of us that is asking the questions.

AGREEMENT

A favourable answer from an oracle is one that *agrees* with the subject matter of your enquiry. Like a rhyming word or the right chord being struck, this kind of agreement automatically makes it clear that the oracle's reply is in accord with your thoughts, feelings and actions. Or, to put it the other way around, the oracle is saying that what you are feeling, thinking, intending or doing is aligned with the direction your life is supposed to take. Later on I give a number of examples of what such an agreement can be like in the context of the Astrological Oracle, and explain the case of a 'negative agreement' when what the Oracle is warning you of agrees only too well with your thoughts and circumstances. In any event, the Astrological Oracle will always advise you and shed light upon your situation, rather than just make bald predictions.

LET EXPERIENCE BE YOUR GUIDE

In addition, there is a seemingly perverse aspect to the answers that an oracle gives. Upon consulting an oracle over whether or not to follow a certain course of action or how best to respond to a given situation, and then receiving an unfavourable or unwelcome reading, a person will sometimes feel doubt and carry on with that course of action anyway. If a person is basically averse to following a proposed course, then they will not follow it, even though the oracle says it's a good idea. In such a situation, the oracle is forcing us to register how we really feel about the object of our enquiry. This is because there is an innate drive in most of us to find things out through experience. After all, the responses given by the oracle are technically just theory, and as the poet-genius Goethe wrote in *Faust*: 'All theory, dear friend, is grey, but the golden tree of actual life springs forever green'. And so, sometimes it is only when you act *against* the oracle's advice that you discover what it really means. But, doing nothing at all – avoiding experience – can be the greyest experience on Earth. Eventually, though, we learn to believe and understand the oracle, and take heed of its counsel – possibly after we have 'road-tested' it!

THE ELEMENT OF CHOICE

A good oracle will always give you the choice to follow its advice or not. After all, 'all roads lead to Rome', meaning that you will get where you are supposed to sooner or later, and so the oracle could say 'this way is easier but takes longer' or, conversely, 'this way is harder but quicker'. This issue of choice is explored more fully under 'Fate and Free Will' in the next chapter (see page 19).

NUDGED TOWARDS YOUR DESTINY

A good oracle 'knows' that a yes/no, good/bad answer to your question is not what's required – even though 'on the surface' we might think it is. What is really required is a way of going forward or responding to a situation with an awareness of where you are supposed to be going and what you are supposed to be doing – an awareness that life is a growing and purposeful thing that demands consideration and discernment on your part. Then, whatever happens, a positive outcome is likely, even though it may not turn out as you expected.

Sometimes, an oracle might just give you food for thought rather than a comprehensive answer, nudging you along, like a kindly parent with a young child, in whatever is the right direction for you – towards your destiny. Most of us do not know our destiny, our ultimate reason and purpose for being. Possibly we would try to avoid it if we did! Figures of destiny, such as Jesus Christ, Joan of Arc, Mahatma Gandhi and Martin Luther King, knew that their destiny ultimately involved the violent death of the martyr to their cause. Similarly, ordinary mortals have to be led down the path towards their destiny, step by step, and often in the face of their reluctance to follow that path because they have something 'better' in mind. A good oracle does this leading.

POSITIVE ATTITUDE

A positive life is created by a positive attitude – not by knowing the 'answer', as is a common illusion. Life is a journey, not a quiz show. Things are rarely bound to turn out right purely because of luck or Fate; it is a positive attitude that creates the good luck or happy fate as a result of pursuing and trusting in one's true destiny. A good oracle should therefore give a positive attitude, and also allay doubts and warn of negative attitudes and actions for they would lead one away from one's true path, or simply into unnecessary difficulties.

WEATHERING THE STORM

Sometimes life leads us into highly unpleasant situations. This adversity is always there to teach us something and is not there just for the hell of it! However, if we refuse to confront the reality of the situation, obey the signs and learn our lessons, we will then find that such adversity does become a living hell. This is a bit like being stuck in tailback on the highway, losing one's patience, driving down the hard shoulder, crashing into a police car, being arrested – and by the time you are brooding in jail, the traffic has dispersed.

A good oracle will 'know' that you are headed for a difficult situation, warn you of it, advise you how best to handle it and respond to it, and get you through or around it as swiftly and/or as easily as possible, coming out the other side with the lesson well learned. Incidentally, another 'road to hell' is using an oracle repeatedly to get the answer you think you want, or because you doubt the oracle itself. This 'muddying of the waters' can lead to a very confused state of mind as a result of taking in too much intense and condensed information – psychic indigestion, in fact!

DIVINATION AND SCIENCE

The factor common to both divination and science is Chance. While chance is central to the use of an oracle – such as throwing coins, dice, runes or sticks, or drawing cards – it is the very thing that scientists feel they must banish to the periphery and beyond. The diviner or user of an oracle is using chance as the vital medium between them and the absolute knowledge of the Unconscious or the Divine. The scientist, in order to replicate an experiment over and over again, must eliminate chance altogether. Using an oracle for a particular question at a particular time in a particular mood or frame of mind is a one-off event. A scientific experiment is something that has to be repeated wherever and whenever in order to be regarded as 'scientific'.

And so, divination and science are, strictly speaking, two opposing aspects of life, perfectly represented by the astrological symbol for life, the Sun – ⊙ – that is, a centre and the periphery. The difference between diviners and scientists is that the former accept both aspects, and the latter accept only one. For this reason, science cannot be used to 'prove' the efficacy of divination. To accomplish this we have to turn to psychology, and a psychology of a singularly metaphysical persuasion at that – Jungian psychology.

The psychologist Carl Jung created the concept of the *archetype* as being a major dynamic of the psyche.

An archetype is seen as anything in your being that is highly charged with feeling and significance. Furthermore, all archetypes derive from basic or collective archetypes such as the hero, the wizard, the witch, the monster, the king and the queen. An archetype is so powerful as to *constellate* an external event, meaning it makes things happen in your life – such as attracting a mate, an accident or any chance occurrence. When consulting an oracle, it is archetypes that are activating it because they are talking the same language, operating on the same frequency. This is why, as you will see in the next chapter, an accurate and meaningful answer from the oracle is far more likely when you really feel the need for an answer, because at such times one or more archetypes is being constellated. This is the nature of *synchronicity*, the principle upon which oracles are based. What the oracle says synchronizes with the archetypes at any given time, and what happens in your life depends entirely upon the archetypal or innermost state of your being. A good oracle will help 'school' that state into one that attracts more positive events – good fortune. Put simply, if you *feel* lucky deep in the fibre of your being, then you will *be* lucky.

CONSULTING THE ASTROLOGICAL ORACLE

Did you ever want to be

A sailor on the lonesome sea

Singing a sailor's tune

As you steer by the Stars and Moon

THE NAUTICAL ANALOGY

One of the best ways of looking at and understanding our course through life is by viewing it as a sea voyage, a journey from one land mass to another, from potential and intention to realization and destination. The adventure along the way, your life, can then be interpreted in terms of vessels, ships in the night, favourable winds, your ship coming in, treacherous currents and dangerous reefs, havens and halcyon days and many more significant and enlightening metaphors. The Astrological Oracle itself – in addition to being used as the crow's nest, enabling you to see further ahead than usual; or as a sounding device, helping you detect what lies beneath – can be viewed as the equivalent of that most important piece of the sailor's equipment, the compass.

THE MAGIC COMPASS – BEARINGS AND DIRECTIONS

The Astrological Oracle is a Magic Compass which you can ask to:

- Give you your bearings – shed light upon where you are and who you are with.
- Advise on the course you have been on, are currently on, and where it is taking you.

- Advise on a course or direction you are presently thinking of making.
- Give you a new direction to take, if you are stuck or at a 'crossroads'.
- Help you make choices between one direction/relationship and another.
- Give you a 'lift' in the form of guidance and reassurance at a particular moment.
- Give you overall guidance at regular intervals, such as daily, weekly or monthly, or at key times like New and Full Moons.
- Make psychic connections with others, particularly departed loved ones.
- Give you insights into any subject of your choosing, be it general or personal.

In reality, the Magic Compass is simply the Zodiac, which is very similar to an actual compass – a circle divided into 360 degrees. Each of the 12 Signs is a 30 degree segment of that circle, and 4 of the Signs, the Cardinal Signs (Aries, Cancer, Libra, Capricorn), correspond to the 4 cardinal points of the compass (East, North, West, South respectively). (*See* The Magic Compass, page 8.)

The Astrological Oracle can also be regarded as Poimandres, the 'Mind of the Sovereignty', for the Zodiac is the path that the Sun describes throughout the year and, as such, it symbolizes and is aware of all of life's possible conditions, eventualities and directions.

♈	Aries	♎	Libra
♉	Taurus	♏	Scorpio
♊	Gemini	♐	Sagittarius
♋	Cancer	♑	Capricorn
♌	Leo	♒	Aquarius
♍	Virgo	♓	Pisces

The Zodiac as Magic Compass. The cardinal points are only marked in to illustrate how the Zodiac is orientated – technically they do not have any significance in the use of the Oracle itself. You will notice that the image of the Zodiac is reversed. This is because here it is projected on to the Earth's surface, whereas it is usually set against the sky. If you like you may use this picture as a mandala to gaze upon and focus your concentration while consulting the Oracle.

USING THE ASTROLOGICAL ORACLE

You can ask your question of the Oracle by using an ordinary pack of playing cards or dice. According to the cards that you pick or the dice you throw, you will select one of the 30 degrees of a particular Sign.

In the same way that a 30 degree segment of the Zodiac has a symbolic meaning and set of characteristics, so does each individual degree. The symbols that describe each one of the 360 degrees are the Sabian Symbols, and these are used in serious astrological circles for the close-up interpretation of the positions of the Sun, Moon and Planets. Right now, though, we'll go through the stages of asking a question of the Astrological Oracle. Basically, there are three stages:

- Formulating a Question
- Asking a Question
- Understanding the Answer

FORMULATING A QUESTION

Phrase your question in such a way that it does not simply ask for a yes/no answer, because a good oracle always offers you a choice and demands that you embark on any course with an increased sense of awareness and with a positive intent. For the same reason, the Oracle will sometimes appear ambiguous in its reply because it is reflecting back at you your own ambivalent state of mind, while at the same time stressing the imperative of choosing for yourself. (Ambiguity, a common 'complaint' concerning the answers given by oracles, is dealt with in more depth on page 18).

The most important ingredient in posing your question is that you concentrate on it deeply. Feel the very essence of what your question is about, ponder on it, then focus again on your feelings within and around it. To help you concentrate, make sure that you feel a genuine need for guidance and are not just asking out of idle curiosity or in order to test the Oracle – this does not mean to say that you cannot ask the Oracle about your own doubts!

It is a good idea to regard the Oracle as a Higher Being who is aware of all the pros and cons, and who can see the overall plan of your life, much as the Sun, Moon,

Planets and Stars oversee the whole surface of the Earth from predictable or fixed positions, making it possible to navigate by them. The more you establish this sense of addressing a Higher Being, then the more you will develop a rapport with the Oracle and get clearer answers from it. This is like the immediate under-standing one can have with a close friend or relative whose opinion you hold in high esteem. By the same token, it helps if you are polite and respectful in the manner you put your question, using 'please', 'I would be grateful if …', and suchlike phrases. Visualize this Higher Being as an image that spontaneously comes to you. This can be a classic one, such as a shining angel above the cloud decks, a wise old man in a cave, or a goddess in a beautiful setting in Nature.

To summarize, along with a few more rules for phrasing questions to the Oracle:

- Make sure that you feel a genuine need for guidance, and that you focus upon it deeply.
- The clearer the question then the clearer the answer. If your question is vague or ambiguous then so will the answer be. If you are not sure how to phrase your question, first ask the Oracle for clarity on the matter of your concern. This could be regarded as a 'rangefinder' or 'sighter'. Sometimes the Oracle will give you a rangefinder without your asking, because it knows you need to clarify your question and shows you how to do so. When the Oracle makes it clearer to you what the situation actually is, you can phrase your question more precisely, or zoom in on a certain aspect of the situation with another question.
- Always try to keep questions as open as possible, rather than making a presumption that may be incorrect, for then the Oracle will then have to point this out to you. For example, if I asked, 'What will happen if X carries on behaving so badly?' when, in fact, it was my perception of X's behaviour that was at fault, then the Oracle would be bound to point this out to me. This would be like blaming the sea for my being a poor sailor. Instead, you could try asking 'What am I to make of how X is behaving?'
- Phrase your question in such a way that it does not simply ask for a yes/no answer, but instead asks the Oracle to comment on the relevant possibilities. The Oracle wants you to exercise a degree of judgement and contemplation and not just obey an instruction in

a mindless way. Just like a compass, the Oracle guides you, it does not actually take you there.

- Be aware of any strong thoughts or feelings that you experience while casting the Oracle; it is quite likely to reply to them in addition to, or instead of, your intended question.

- The more complex the question, the more complex the answer. For example, asking, 'What is my destiny?' would be a tall order – not so much for the Oracle, but for you to understand.

- Avoid asking questions like 'When ...?' and 'How long ...?' as the Sabian Symbols do not indicate answers to these as a rule. It is better to suggest a time frame, like 'What will finances be like in three months time?' or 'Where will this present situation have got to by the year after next?' (*see* 'The Timeline' on page 426).

ASKING A QUESTION

Start by opening a log to record all your questions, the date and time that you ask them, and the answers given by the Oracle. This is essential to track how the development of certain issues/questions is matched by the Oracle's answers. It is especially useful to keep your log on a word processor so that you can search with ease for details such as the previous times you have drawn a certain Sabian Symbol or asked a particular question. Now it is time to draw your Sabian Symbol using either the playing card or dice method described on the next page.

USING PLAYING CARDS

Bearing your question steadily and intently in mind, you now pick two cards that will give you a Zodiacal Sign and one of its 30 degrees, which in turn gives you the Sabian Symbol for that degree. Refer to the chart below. Use ordinary playing cards.

1 Separate the deck into two packs, one which comprises just the court cards (Jacks, Queens and Kings – 12 cards in all) and the other which comprises the remaining cards (Ace to Ten of each suit – 40 cards in all). The first pack is the *Sign* pack, from which you will select the Sign. The second pack is the *Degree* pack, from which you will select the Degree of that Sign. Keep these cards in a safe place, only for this purpose. Treat them with reverence, wrapping them in a piece of velvet, for instance, or keeping them in a special container.

2 Focusing intently upon your question, pick up the Degree pack, shuffle and feel the cards until your *hands* (rather than your conscious mind) select one.

- If you draw the Ace to Ten of HEARTS you have picked the 1st to 10th Degree respectively;
- If you draw the Ace to Ten of DIAMONDS you have picked the 11th to 20th Degree respectively;
- If you draw the Ace to Ten of CLUBS you have picked the 21st to 30th Degree respectively;
- If you draw Ace to Ten of SPADES you are 'Void of Course'.

If you are 'Void of Course', this means that the Oracle cannot or will not answer your question at this time because your attitude is incorrect or you are not sufficiently focused on the question. In such a case, put the card back, shuffle, 'dig' deeper with more focus, if necessary rephrasing your question, and then pick again. If you select a Spade for a second time, repeat and then try once more. If you select a Spade for a third time, it's a case of 'three strikes and you're out'. For some reason known to the Oracle, and possibly yourself, the question is inappropriate or irrelevant at this time. Of course, you are free to override this rule, but you probably won't get a satisfactory answer. Sometimes a situation calls for basic common sense rather than the Oracle.

3 Now, pick up the Sign pack, and again concentrating on your question, shuffle and feel the cards until your *hands* (rather than your conscious mind) select one.

King of Spades	=	Capricorn
Queen of Spades	=	Taurus
Jack of Spades	=	Virgo
King of Hearts	=	Aries
Queen of Hearts	=	Leo
Jack of Hearts	=	Sagittarius
King of Diamonds	=	Libra
Queen of Diamonds	=	Aquarius
Jack of Diamonds	=	Gemini
King of Clubs	=	Cancer
Queen of Clubs	=	Scorpio
Jack of Clubs	=	Pisces

To take an example, if the card you draw from the Degree pack is the **Five of Clubs**, then you have picked the **25th Degree**. Next, you draw the **King of Clubs** from the Sign pack, giving you the Sign of **Cancer**. So, you have **Cancer 25 Degrees**.

D	Card	1♥	2♥	3♥	4♥	5♥	6♥	7♥	8♥	9♥	10♥
E	Deg.	1	2	3	4	5	6	7	8	9	10
G	Card	1♦	2♦	3♦	4♦	5♦	6♦	7♦	8♦	9♦	10♦
R	Deg.	11	12	13	14	15	16	17	18	19	20
E	Card	1♣	2♣	3♣	4♣	5♣	6♣	7♣	8♣	9♣	10♣
E	Deg.	21	22	23	24	25	26	27	28	29	30
	Card	1♠	2♠	3♠	4♠	5♠	6♠	7♠	8♠	9♠	10♠
E	Deg.	PICK AGAIN									

S	Card	JACK			QUEEN			KING			
I	♥	Sagittarius			Leo			Aries			
G	♦	Gemini			Aquarius			Libra			
N	♣	Pisces			Scorpio			Cancer			
	♠	Virgo			Taurus			Capricorn			

Now you have established the degree and sign of the Oracle's answer, now go to the Sabian Symbols Index (page 26) to find the Sabian Symbol for that degree and sign, and what page it is interpreted on. Once you know your way around the signs and degrees, you won't need to use the Index – you can simply turn to the appropriate page.

USING DICE

The use of dice to cast the Oracle derives more directly from the bones or stones that were originally employed when oracles first came into existence a long, long time ago. They are not only more authentic, but are more random in their given result, whereas cards can get marked with wear and tear, and shuffling is not always that thorough. Initially, it seems a little more complex than using cards, but ultimately it is simpler and quicker. An aspect to dice that I personally like is that I can invest more psychic energy into the actual throwing.

It is possible to cast the Oracle using 1, 2 or 4 dice. For details about using 2 and 4 dice, *see* page 439. Here we will look at the method using just one, referring to the chart below. You throw the die FOUR TIMES: twice to obtain the Degree number, and twice again to obtain the Sign. As with the cards, it is best to look at this method using an example.

THROWING FOR THE DEGREE

Throw the die. In our example **3** is thrown. Looking at the table overleaf, check against possible throws in the top-left panel headed FIRST THROW for the selection of 6 degrees you are to throw for next.

3 = 13–18 Degrees

[**Note:** If you throw **6** this is 'Void of Course' and you should throw again. *See* 'Using Playing Cards – 2' for what this means.]

Throw die for second time. This time **5** is thrown. Look at the top-right panel headed SECOND THROW and find the number which you have just thrown. Below this there are given five possible degrees (5, 11, 17, 23, 29). Only one of these will fall in the range you achieved with your first throw (13–18). So, your degree number is:

17 Degrees

THROWING FOR THE SIGN

Throw die for third time. Now **4** is thrown. Looking at the table, in the bottom-left panel headed THIRD THROW. If you throw an Odd number (1, 3 or 5) your next throw will be to select from the Yang/Male Signs (Aries, Gemini, Leo, Libra, Sagittarius or Aquarius).

If you throw an Even number (2, 4 or 6) your next throw will be to select from the Yin/Female Signs (Taurus, Cancer, Virgo, Scorpio, Capricorn or Pisces). Since you have thrown 4, you will next be selecting from Yin/Female Signs.

Throw the die for the fourth and last time. You have thrown 2. Look in the panel headed FOURTH THROW in the column headed 2, the corresponding Yin/Female Sign is **Cancer**.

THE RESULT
Put the Degree and Sign together and you have:

    Cancer 17 Degrees

By looking at the Sabian Symbols Index (*see* page 26) you find that the Sabian Symbol for Cancer 17 Degrees is 'The Germ Grows Into Knowledge And Life'.

D	FIRST THROW			SECOND THROW					
E				*1*	*2*	*3*	*4*	*5*	*6*
G	1	= 1–6	→	1	2	3	4	5	6
R	2	= 7–12	→	7	8	9	10	11	12
E	3	= 13–18	→	13	14	15	16	17	18
E	4	= 19–24	→	19	20	21	22	23	24
E	5	= 25–30	→	25	26	27	28	29	30
	6	THROW AGAIN							

S	THIRD THROW		FOURTH THROW					
I			*1*	*2*	*3*	*4*	*5*	*6*
G	Odd number (1, 3 or 5) → Yang/Male		Ari	Gem	Leo	Lib	Sag	Aqu
N	Even number (2, 4 or 6) → Yin/Female		Tau	Can	Vir	Sco	Cap	Pis

✳
UNDERSTANDING
THE ANSWER

The language of symbolism is like the language of dreams. Sometimes it can appear crazy and irrelevant, but with a little close study and an awareness of basic symbols (*see* the reading list on page 471) you begin to discover the wealth of information, insight and support that the Symbol is giving you. Getting a helpful and accurate reply from the Oracle is not as easy as just picking two cards. A cavalier 'just want an answer' attitude is not going to be alive to the details and fuller implications of a given situation. This is what I call 'perfunctory input'. Like with most things in life, with oracles you get out what you put in.

Each page of Sabian Symbols is laid out like a compass heading, with the Degree Position at the top, and with the Sabian Symbol of that degree immediately below it. We then see a keyword or keyphrase for that Sabian Symbol, somewhat in the form of a ship's Nameplate. This suggests that one best navigate this passage – approach or live out the object of your enquiry – in the spirit of the Nameplate.

Following these headings are the interpretations, with the compass symbol set in the middle of them. The interpretations are divided into four sections as follows:

 GENERAL INTERPRETATION

This is usually worded in a non-specific way so that you can apply it to most questions, including issues appertaining to the other three sections. In order to make it general this interpretation is kept closer to the Symbol itself, and does not as a rule get too particular. Sometimes the word 'one' is substituted for 'you' in order to make the reply more generally applicable.

 LOVE/RELATING/SOCIAL

This is an interpretation that caters to all issues that have to do with relating to others, be it one person or society as a whole. It will also describe the nature of a relationship or the person concerned, depending what you asked for. Sometimes the word 'other' is used as a general term to refer to who or what is the object of your enquiry. It usually addresses issues of being alone too.

 MONEY/WORK/CREATIVITY

This interpretation is aimed at anything that has to do with functioning in the material world. The text may be referring to such things as products, projects, plans, ideas, inventions, cash or creative flow, income, expenditure or profitability. It can also refer to questions about people in work or financial situations, such as co-workers and customers, but sometimes these may be better answered in the Love/Relating/Social section. (*See* the Money/Work/Creativity section of Capricorn 29 for a point concerning the use of oracles for material issues).

⑤ **KARMA/ATTITUDE/HEALTH**

This is often concerned with the spiritual dimension of life. It refers to deeper reasons why a situation is like it is, and recommends metaphysical ways of looking at it or resolving it. It also caters to health issues, but solely with the view that physical or mental health is ultimately caused by the overall state of your personality. This health advice is *not* a prediction and *not* supposed to replace conventional or complementary medical care/diagnosis, which you should always seek out if you feel there is something wrong with you.

These four sections are further divided into three approaches.

- Basic
- Keep Focused On
- Watch Out For

The first is a basic or suggested interpretation that describes how the Oracle sees the nature of your enquiry with respect to that section – a bit like the kind of weather you are in or are heading into. This approach can be seen as a description of yourself, or the object of your enquiry.

The second approach tells you what to KEEP FOCUSED ON – like fair winds and calm waters – what is worth using, accentuating or enjoying, a direction to take or maintain, and it is usually about your inherent *strengths* regarding the issue concerned. It indicates what *good fortune* or positive events are likely to happen of their own accord, and how focusing upon them would help. Also, whatever you are recommended to focus upon could simply be a confirmation of what you hope or feel to be the case. You use this approach by reading the heading 'Keep Focused On...' as preceding each of the recommendations which follow, preceded by '...'.

Thirdly, you are told what to WATCH OUT FOR – like dangerous reefs or fog banks – *misfortune* or negative events that are possibly (but not definitely) in danger of happening. Also, where you are simply going in the wrong direction or the wrong way about things, and this usually refers to possible *weaknesses*. It also indicates what the snags are to a given situation. You read this approach in the same way as 'Keep Focused On ...'

Finally, at the bottom of the page is a Quote, chosen to lend a helpful sentiment to the nature of your situation. This quote of reassurance or poetic summation is preceded by a little picture of the dove, symbolizing that a haven is nearby, or that 'a little bird told me'. (The sources of these quotes are given on pages 445–455.)

To look at the answers in more detail, we'll work through an example. In response to the question *'How will the Astrological Oracle be of help to people?'* the Oracle has given the answer Cancer 25 Degrees, *'A Dark Shadow Or Mantle Thrown Suddenly Over The Right Shoulder'*.

THE SABIAN SYMBOL

A DARK SHADOW OR MANTLE THROWN SUDDENLY OVER THE RIGHT SHOULDER

It is important to contemplate this before reading the interpretations given below it. This is because, as with dream interpretation, the Sabian Symbol you have drawn is entirely personal to you. The words, concepts and images it contains or evokes will have associations that possibly only you will know – occasionally they will be found to be quite literal (*see* Case E, pages 22–3). Simply take on board what any word or group of words, or the Symbol as a whole, intuitively suggests to you. Let the image of the Symbol run like a film clip in front of you, weaving its spell, unfolding the outcome, revealing the truth of the matter.

'The night has a thousand eyes/And the day but one', wrote F.W. Bourdillon. The use of intuition (night) as distinct from a purely intellectual appraisal (day) is vital to the interpretation of symbols. Symbols are the language of intuition and the unconscious, and like pictures they are worth a thousand words. Logic and words, on the other hand, are the language of reason and scientific thought. Astrology embraces both these mental functions for it requires a combination of divination and common sense; a certain aspect or interpretation of the Sabian Symbol can *intuitively* be seen to answer or 'fit' your question perfectly. This use of intuition is what enables you to see where and how your question is answered through the Sabian Symbol. You may find that just one line or phrase of the text is sufficient to answer your question, meet your need, or show that you are 'on course'.

As I am writing this book, the Oracle's answer to our example question is clearly of great interest to me. My immediate association is of a time when I saw a thin black cloud passing across the face of the Moon, which was itself framed by cumulus clouds, at the very moment that I looked up at the night sky as I drove along the highway to meet someone for whom, I was reminded, I had strong but confused feelings. It was as if at that moment it was saying something significant to me concerning my situation. So, right away, this Sabian Symbol seems an appropriate answer – it *agrees* with my question – for it suggests a portent of what is to come, or an image or reminder of how I truly feel.

There are other Sabian Symbols which have more obvious associations with the use of an oracle, such as 'A Crystal Gazer' (Aries 9 Degrees), 'A Ouija Board' (Virgo 18 Degrees) and 'A Woman Reading Tea Leaves' (Capricorn 29 Degrees), but this one seems to be more directly and closely allied to signs and omens that appear at critical times – as if the events of the visible world and those of the invisible worlds are synchronously, spontaneously and momentarily linked. So, it is saying to me that the Astrological Oracle is of help to people in much the same way that a sign in the sky or a sign on the road would be to the traveller. Generally speaking, it seems to be saying that the Oracle has a very intimate and immediate connection to the inner world of which the outer world is a reflection. As such, it cannot only be trusted, but must also be respected and not taken too lightly.

Having made this intuitive interpretation, we can now look at the Sabian Symbol more analytically. This Symbol is particularly rich in individual symbols, which again implies and agrees with the wealth of information that symbols, and especially Sabian Symbols, can give you. It is also one of the more enigmatic Symbols, so the Oracle is obliging us with a good example to dissect word-by-word.

A '**shadow**' is symbolic of something from out of the unconscious, or something which has no substance of its own, but has been created by something that does. A shadow crossing one's path warns one or indicates something real and solid approaching or nearby. A '**dark**' shadow implies that it has weight and importance, but not that it is necessarily ominous. Shadows are always relatively dark, the degree depending on how bright the light behind the objects that are making them, and so a dark shadow implies strong light – that is, great love and knowledge.

Next comes an extremely subtle piece of symbolism. The words '**or mantle**' say that it may not be a shadow but something solid and real instead. Or is something being covered up or protected? This again suggests that making use of the Oracle depends upon being discerning and not just 'jumping at shadows', while at the same time appreciating that a shadow is as real as what is casting it.

The word '**thrown**' follows – again what could be a more literal reference to consulting an oracle (throwing coins, stalks and dice). Furthermore, because the shadow or mantle is thrown over the **right** shoulder, it implies that it has been done so from the *left*. As the left side is symbolic of the unconscious this could be seen as

alluding to the importance of selecting the two playing cards or the numbers on the die without deliberately choosing them, but letting your hands do the picking.

All this happening '**suddenly**' corresponds to the fact that the Astrological Oracle is quick and simple to consult and the meaning of the Oracle's answer can suddenly become apparent.

Then we come to '**across the right shoulder**'. 'Right' in symbolic terms always represents our conscious and deliberating side. So, this Sabian Symbol is saying that the Astrological Oracle will swiftly inform the conscious mind of what is taking place in the unconscious. To put it another way, it is saying what is in the process of happening, what is about to happen, or what has already happened (shadows from the past) – so enabling one to act, decide or respond more wisely.

Lastly, the Symbol refers to the '**shoulder**' and this says that whatever you do you must consciously take full responsibility for using the Oracle and for what issues from your unconscious mind, because they *are* powerful and not to be trifled with or shrugged off.

CANCER 25 DEGREES

One final thing to consider at this stage is the actual Sign in which the Sabian Symbol is placed. Preceding each Zodiacal grouping of Sabian Symbols are given some of the various qualities and elements associated with the Sign. In our case, the sign is Cancer and this has to do with such things as Dreams, Care and Protection, Comfort, Feelings, Motherhood, Nurturance, Personal Matters, Subjectivity, and the Unconscious (*see* page 135). From this we can assume that the Astrological Oracle has qualities we can feel safe with, that are in sympathy (another Cancerian quality) with our inner states, and that it cares about us. It is also significant that the Crab is a creature that lives on the shore between the sea (unconscious realm) and the land (conscious realm), and as such can be seen as a go-between, which is what an oracle essentially is – in fact, Cancer governs oracles. Using whatever other knowledge you have of the Sign concerned will further help you understand the Oracle and its counsel.

A selection of further examples is given at the end of this chapter (*see* pages 21–4).

THE KEYPHRASE OR NAMEPLATE

☆ DRAMATIC PORTENT ☆

This puts into focus the meaning of the Symbol as a whole and can be regarded as the name of the 'craft' you are recommended to 'sail' upon for this part of your 'voyage'. Here it is 'Dramatic Portent' which describes the usefulness of the Astrological Oracle in terms of it having the capacity to give signs, insights and forecasts regarding life's dramas in a commensurately dramatic way. The keyword given this Symbol by Dr Marc Edmund Jones, co-creator of the Sabian Symbols, was 'Destiny', which is very appropriate. It is also coincidental because the working title of this book was 'Destiny Astrology'.

THE FOUR TYPES OF INTERPRETATION

These are self-explanatory, but, as in life itself, one area tends to 'bleed' or cross over into another. So, whatever the nature of your enquiry, you will probably gain help and insight from reading all four. With our example question, on the face of it the General Interpretation and Karma/Attitude/Health would appear to be the most apt. At times, it is also important to read between the lines. A symbol, by its very nature, speaks volumes, so the texts given here are necessarily limited in that they will not always apply in a totally literal sense. Reading these interpretations in this way will automatically prompt further interpretations of your own.

✸ GENERAL INTERPRETATION

The power of intuition and of unconscious forces that can exert an influence over the individual in order that he or she might consciously recognize these forces and what they imply, and thereby be guided by them, act upon them and be protected by them.

KEEP FOCUSED ON ... the insight you have that enables you to change dramatically your own or someone else's orientation and so positively transform a situation ... your sense of the mysterious and intriguing, and of 'whodunit', for this enriches and, ultimately, enlightens.

WATCH OUT FOR ... exaggerating or overreacting to signs, omens, innuendoes, suggestive behaviour, alarming rumours, ominous ideas ... dabbling with occult matters and then finding them out of control ... feeling weighed down by responsibilities that are not shouldered gladly.

♥ LOVE/RELATING/SOCIAL

An intriguing or complex emotional situation that has a mystery about it or a shadow cast over it. A set-up where the female, intuitive, nurturing element is holding sway – or is trying to, or ought to be. A sudden passionate development incurring responsibility.

KEEP FOCUSED ON ... your feelings until you have fully understood what they imply ... your sense of the romantic, dramatic and of hidden meaning ... the soul nature of those involved – their karma, longings and sensitivities.

WATCH OUT FOR ... not taking full responsibility for the part that your own dark side plays in the situation ... secrecy, or not coming clean, becoming a block to honesty and understanding, eventually creating a morass of deep and dangerous emotions. Be on your guard against excessive emotions.

♆ MONEY/WORK/CREATIVITY

Intuitive powers are central to your work, bestowed upon you as a great responsibility. Possibly a cloak and dagger scenario, industrial espionage or office intrigue. An unexpected development that has nothing to do with work per se – an emotional or psychological factor could be in play.

KEEP FOCUSED ON ... the less obvious or more emotionally compelling aspects of the object of your concern, for therein lies its main asset – and the answer to any difficulty ... the hidden or mysterious ... trusting intuition and being prepared to take responsibility for your actions.

WATCH OUT FOR ... anything that could be going on behind your back – but avoid being paranoid ... it being a case of 'what you don't know *can* harm you' ... hidden agendas ... the sheer weight of responsibility, especially when unseen by others.

♄ KARMA/ATTITUDE/HEALTH

The importance of balance between reason and intuition, of being able to act upon hunches rather than keeping them at the theory stage and letting them build up into suspicion, dread or disease. A past issue that needs admitting to, coming to terms with and sorting; depression arising from this or excessive reasoning.

KEEP FOCUSED ON ... your deep sense of powerful emotional undercurrents, for it will greatly strengthen your constitution ... the fact that your well-being calls for a swift and effective response born of your willingness to take responsibility for acting upon your gut instincts or whatever is deep-seated ... being guided by signs.

WATCH OUT FOR ... being spooked by superstitious nonsense, possibly born of a religious doctrine ... projecting your shadow onto the world around you and then feeling powerless or intimidated ... karmic weight; offset it with lightness and recreation.

THE QUOTE

'Unless you see miraculous signs and wonders, you will not believe'

The quote here is from St John 4:48, *'Unless you see miraculous signs and wonders, you will not believe'*, which was what Jesus said to a man who asked him to heal his son, followed by *'You may go. Your son shall live'*. Taking him at his word and going back home to his son, he discovered that he had got better at exactly the time Jesus had said these words to him. This quote conveys the idea that if you trust the Oracle it will serve you well, remedy your difficulties and always be synchronous with the issues in question.

FINALLY ...

Ponder and absorb what you have discovered, enter it in your Log and allow the impression the Oracle has made to filter through to you as clear or significant thoughts, ideas and feelings in the time that follows. As time goes by you may find that what the Oracle was telling you turns out to be slightly or very different from what you first thought.

HOW ACCURATE IS THE ORACLE?

It is important that you have some sense of how accurate the Oracle's reply is to your question. By 'accurate' we mean how much the Oracle *agrees* with what you are thinking, feeling or proposing. The Oracle always understands you and your question – but the question can often be 'do you?'. Here is a rough guide to knowing how well you 'scored'.

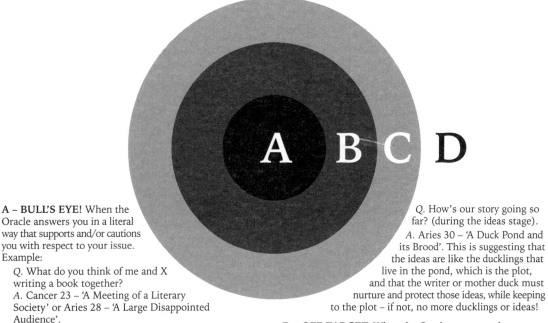

A – BULL'S EYE! When the Oracle answers you in a literal way that supports and/or cautions you with respect to your issue. Example:

> *Q.* What do you think of me and X writing a book together?
> *A.* Cancer 23 – 'A Meeting of a Literary Society' or Aries 28 – 'A Large Disappointed Audience'.

B – INNER BULL. When the Oracle gives a directly encouraging or discouraging reply. For example:

> *Q.* How's our story going so far?
> *A.* Pisces 16 – 'The Flow of Inspiration' which is a general agreement with what is hoped, or Aquarius 10 – 'A Popularity that Proves Ephemeral' which is warning that shallow or ill-thought out material will not sustain either the writers' interest or the readers'.

C – OUTER BULL. When the Oracle gives you advice or reflects on your issue in a helpful but not necessarily obvious way which needs pondering upon. For example:

> *Q.* How's our story going so far? (during the ideas stage).
> *A.* Aries 30 – 'A Duck Pond and its Brood'. This is suggesting that the ideas are like the ducklings that live in the pond, which is the plot, and that the writer or mother duck must nurture and protect those ideas, while keeping to the plot – if not, no more ducklings or ideas!

D – OFF TARGET. When the Oracle appears to be so irrelevant as to imply that either there is a 'radio black-out' (*see* 'Doubting the Oracle', page 20), or your question is too vague, or you are not really concentrating enough upon it, or that the issue at stake is a non-starter and is falling by the wayside. For example:

> *Q.* What do you think of us writing a book?
> *A.* Libra 2 – 'The Light of the Sixth Race Transmuted to the Seventh', which if not irrelevant for one of the above reasons, is either saying you've got a very long way to go, or that you don't really understand what you are doing or asking.

✳
POINTS TO WATCH

AGREEMENT

When you receive your reply from the Oracle, be alive to the ways in which it agrees with the nature of your enquiry. The more accurate or appropriate the reply is, the more likely it is that there is a clear answer concerning your situation. You will feel that the Oracle is definitely 'on your case' and that you are in step with yourself. This in itself is consoling for it engenders a connection with the fact that you are not just a speck floating in space, but a definite entity with a purpose and direction, that something higher and deeper than you is aware of and cares about. (*see* 'How Accurate is the Oracle?', page 17)

It follows that if the positive aspects of the Oracle's reply (mainly the KEEP FOCUSED ON sections) agree with the positive aspects of your situation, then it is giving you a favourable reply. This is when the Oracle's reading can be said to be 'auspicious'. Conversely, when it is the negative aspects (mainly the WATCH OUT FOR sections) that agree, then the Oracle is giving you an unfavourable reply, or it is simply giving you a warning. Alternatively – and this is important – the Oracle is giving you a negative reading because you have asked what is wrong with something, as you might over a question of health. This is called a 'negative agreement'.

IF THE CAP FITS, WEAR IT

Another, highly significant type of agreement is the one that is given spontaneously by your unconscious mind. This is when the Oracle's response triggers what you unconsciously feel to be the best course, even though it may not have actually said so itself in black-and-white. This is particularly noticeable when asking questions concerning two choices, such as '*What is the advisability of A?*' and '*What is the advisability of B?*' Say one's reaction to the Oracle's answer to A is automatically interpreted negatively, whereas the answer to B is interpreted positively, it has thereby revealed one's natural preference and correct course.

PERSON TO PERSON

For the sake of convenience, most of the interpretations are written under the assumption that the question asked is one regarding yourself. However, often one will also be asking about other people, animals and things. If this is the case, you will need to substitute a 'you' for a 'he', 'she', 'it' or 'they', etc.

OCCASIONED OR CALLED FOR

This phrase is often used to introduce an interpretation of a Sabian Symbol. If not for being tiresomely repetitive it could be used in every case because it means that every Oracle reading is either telling what is happening or is about to happen, or what needs to happen.

AMBIGUITY

Ambiguous replies from oracles are very common, and this is usually because the very nature of your enquiry – or rather your own attitude towards it – is ambivalent. Because you are in two minds, the Oracle throws this back at you, but as an 'enhanced' version which should help you get a clearer picture of what is involved.

When I now ask the Oracle to give more clarity on the subject of ambiguity, I receive:

Taurus 17 – 'A Battle Between The Swords And The Torches'

First of all this is strongly *agreeing* with the whole concept of conflict between one thing and another, in this case between swords – often symbolic of the intellectual powers of reason, and duality itself – and torches which can be seen to represent intuition. Putting them together we can say that the Oracle *lights* your way (torch) so you may see more clearly the issues at stake, allowing you to judge them as good or bad, or setting the way out for you. You must *decide* (sword) and *fight* for and towards the *truth* of the matter. Things are not so much fated, but up to you. This is why the Oracle does not simply predict your future, but guides you towards the most positive version of it – your destiny. To put it another way, the Oracle is aimed at helping you relate to what is happening now, because this has everything to do with what is going to happen next. Indeed, one of the great dangers of using any oracle is that of wanting to know the future when you would not be able to handle it if you were actually told, and then filling your head with a number of seemingly conflicting prospective scenarios. As the *I Ching* states, 'Thinking that goes beyond the immediate situation makes the heart sore'.

Another way of looking at this is to be aware that in the everyday world everything is viewed in a dualistic way (sword, two-edged). This means that for any one thing there is always an opposite or an alternative. Intuition (torch), on the other hand, has an all-round illumination and holistic overview of the situation, and can therefore show the right path.

Apart from the Oracle reflecting back one's own indecision, an ambiguous reply can also be presenting you with the mystery of life itself. For example, within a question like 'Will he/she love me forever/soon/when I'm 64' there are too many variables to make a hard and fast prediction. A woman friend was asking if she would ever have a good relationship, and received Cancer 22 – 'A Woman Awaiting A Sailboat'. This could be saying that one day her ship will come in, or that she was hoping against hope. Only time and her faith would tell. Frustrated by this apparent ambiguity, she asked for more clarity – a quite proper course of action, you can always ask the Oracle about what it is telling you – and received: Gemini 9 – 'A Quiver Full Of Arrows', which she took to mean 'You are only given so many shots or chances – unless you create more of your own'.

Ultimately, everything can be viewed as getting where it has to get to – as in the saying 'All roads lead to Rome'. In other words, at all times, *accentuate the positive*.

FATE AND FREE WILL

When using any means of divination, it is not long before the age-old question of 'Is it Fate or Free Will?' rears its head. The immediate answer is 'Both', for very little is entirely fated, and free will is invariably conditioned by forces beyond one's control. No means of divination can state that such-and-such definitely will or will not happen.

The whole issue of Fate and Free Will is perfectly demonstrated with our Nautical Analogy. Your free will is a sailboat that has as its main equipment a compass, a rudder, sails and a chart. Fate is the open sea with its tides and currents, the occasional landmass, and the wind and weather. The boat itself is your personality, with its talents, intelligence, mobility and sensitivity. Its equipment is your sense of direction and purpose (compass), the ability to steer yourself (rudder), some

idea of where you are, where you came from and where it is you are bound (chart), and the means of getting there (sails, oars). The open sea, weather, other boats and any landfalls are what bring you the events, encounters and conditions of your life.

In *The Astrological Oracle* you have as part of your equipment the Magic Compass which is like compass, chart, almanac and weather forecaster all rolled into one.

THE MYSTERY OF IT ALL

'In a symbol lies concealment or revelation'
Thomas Carlyle

It should be borne in mind when using any oracle that by the very nature of divination there can always be something referred to that is outside your scope of expectation or imagination. 'Tomorrow never knows' is a powerful and provocative axiom, and yet the Oracle has a far better idea of what is shaping up than we mere mortals usually do. Moreover, it also has our fear of hearing the truth to contend with. For instance, it may be trying to convey information about some imminent change or unknown circumstances while we insist on interpreting in a way we think suits us. This is not necessarily as ominous as it sounds. I remember asking the Oracle about an idea for a part of a book I was writing – an idea to which I was quite attached. It kept giving me discouraging responses, not least of which was Aries 28 – 'A Large Disappointed Audience'! In the event, it turned out that my publishers at the time were already in the process of producing an entire book on the same subject, but, as it was being dealt with by a separate department of the publishers, I had not been informed. So, the Oracle was not criticizing the idea itself – something to which I was naturally sensitive – but was alluding to the timing and circumstances that had a direct bearing upon its realization. The way to be attuned to the 'mystery' is to keep as open a mind as possible, to trust the Oracle, and to be alive to the signs around you that concur with its indications.

Above all, an out-and-out, straightforward course through life is unlikely. This is why sailors say that they are *bound for* somewhere, not that they are *going* to it. Anything can happen along the way.

SOME NAVIGATION TIPS

Here are a few more points to bear in mind while using The Astrological Oracle. Take these on board and then you are ready to cast off!

- Providing you are asking genuine questions in a focused fashion, then you are advised to trust the Oracle. It can see more than you. This is like Christopher Columbus (C) crossing the Atlantic for the first time. He knew that if he kept a certain star (★) in a certain position in relation to his ship he would get where he wanted to get to. His crew, on the other hand, did *not* trust this method. Needless to say, *they* would never have got to America (A)!

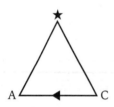

- Tacking. One's ego tends to want to go in a straight line to what it thinks it wants. As any genuine oracle is there to guide your *soul* rather than your ego, it will sometimes appear to be leading you away from your supposed goal as it takes you on a zigzag course towards it. It has to do this because the prevailing conditions of your life (the wind and current) are against you, or because there are obstacles in your path that you are unaware of, or because where you think you want to go is not where your soul wishes you to go.
- Often the Oracle will not reply to what you think you are asking. The Oracle, being a phenomenon of the unconscious realm, will detect what you are *really* asking. Either you should be aware of this and realize what the Oracle is actually referring to, or you should be a lot clearer about what you are asking in the first place. This subtle point has been responsible for the self-imposed confusion of many an oracle-user. Strange things happen at sea!
- Emphasize the positive part of the reading (mainly the KEEP FOCUSED ON sections). However, if the negatives (the WATCH OUT FOR sections) seem to

be predominantly agreeing with your situation, then this would imply an unfavourable reply to your question.

- Making choices. If you have a number of choices to choose between, you can ask the Oracle 'Which one is right for me?' but you would then have to be clear which option the Oracle was referring to. It can be better to enquire about each choice individually – and then make an informed choice.

RECOMMENDED QUESTIONS OR REQUESTS

It is often difficult to know how actually to phrase a question. Apart from pondering upon the issue long and hard enough in order to find this out, there are a few simple formulas that make this easier. For example, just preface your situation with the word(s) *'Concerning ...'*, *'Regarding ...'*, *'Please advise on ...'* or *'Please give me a Reality Check on ...'*. It could also help to use these:

- *'What does the path immediately ahead look like?'*
- *'Please give me a lift/encouragement.'*
- *'Please give me something that will empower me.'*
- *'Help!'*
- *'What is my situation?'* (see 'rangefinder', page 9)
- Symbols like '→?' (*'Where is this headed?'*) '←?' (*'How did I get here?'*) or '*' (*'Clarification please'*, which is useful following a reply from the Oracle you do not quite understand)
- *'What is good about my situation?'* (pay heed to KEEP FOCUSED ON sections)
- *'What is bad about my situation?'* (pay heed to WATCH OUT FOR sections)

DOUBTING THE ORACLE

Because of all the subtleties and quirks regarding oracles and the use of them, it is natural at times to question the Oracle's worth and accuracy. The actual writing of this book, because I had to be so exhaustive in testing and researching the Oracle – as well as using other oracles to check things out – gave rise to many a slough of despond, doubt and despair as my logical left-brain insisted on more literal and easy-to-understand answers.

When I asked the *I Ching* concerning my doubt, I received Hexagram 61 – Inner Truth. This is expressly about the connection between the inner and outer worlds and how doubt cuts you off from the truths that the Oracle or Sage make available to you. Carol Anthony's comment on line 1 of this hexagram in her highly-recommended book *A Guide To The I Ching* is totally to the point, 'These doubts ensure failure; the negative power is not quiescent, it is an actively destructive force'. This was all confirmed, and the dilemma created by my own doubt finally resolved, when such doubt reached an extreme in the early hours of one morning. Somehow frustration gave rise to a question to the Oracle of startling clarity. I simply asked it *'Who are you?'* I got Taurus 16 – 'An Old Man Attempting Vainly To Reveal The Mysteries' which not only answered that question clearly but also the one regarding the difficulties of writing of the Oracle itself.

Also worth considering when doubting the Oracle's efficacy is the 'radio black-out'. At times, and possibly for mystical reasons, one's questions or the Oracle's answers just don't 'get through' clearly or at all. This is just the way things are.

EXAMPLE READINGS

To give a further idea of how the Astrological Oracle can best be used, here are some examples taken from real-life cases. Note not only the significance of the Sabian Symbol itself and its interpretation, but also the types of question that can be asked, as well as how the questions are phrased to elicit an understandable response from the Oracle. These examples also demonstrate how the Oracle operates by responding to the whole of you, rather than just the question you think you are asking. It also shows itself to have its own conditions. This is similar to any sage-like or higher being who will not dance entirely to the tune of the inquirer. After all, it has a mind of its own – the Mind of the Sovereignty, no less!

CASE A – PRACTICAL ADVICE AND ENCOURAGEMENT

A female client had recently found herself freed from certain responsibilities and was now wanting to do something more meaningful in the rural area where she lived. Some woodland that had been open to all had recently been bought up by a business concern and it was no longer open to the public. My client had the idea of campaigning to purchase a plot of land and plant a wood for her village's future and the new millennium. However, she was beset with doubts about it being 'a crazy, unlikely idea' and so asked the Oracle for its advice concerning the plan.

She drew 2♦ and K♣ which is the 12th Degree of Cancer – 'A Chinese Woman Nursing a Baby with a Message' (*see* page 147). This is a plain approval from the Oracle regarding her idea, especially the line under the General Interpretation '… the rare, even divine, qualities you possess that can serve the community where other more conventional means fail … nurturing your ideas; they are saying something new and important.' She was suitably encouraged by this and before long met someone, by chance, who knew how to get funding for such things as tree-planting!

CASE B – WHAT THE ORACLE CAN AND CANNOT TELL YOU

A friend who was very nervous before sitting an examination relatively late on in her life asked the Oracle what attitude of mind to adopt towards the terrifying prospect. She selected 3♦ and Q♣ which is the 13th Degree of Scorpio –'An Inventor Experimenting'. She found this extremely consoling because it was suggesting she sit her exams in the spirit of experimentation, that she was finding out a formula for living and was not under pressure to 'get it right' first time. She would also possibly discover something other than what the exam subject itself was about. As it happened, apart from reducing her nervousness considerably, she found out that how she felt was just as important as what she knew, and that braving the academic environment for which she held bad memories laid a ghost that had been haunting her for years.

Later on, after having sat two of the three exams, she asked the Oracle if she was 'on course for a pass'. I told her that the Oracle was being asked for a yes/no answer which it was unlikely to give because we are supposed to think for ourselves, contemplate issues, exercise positive discrimination, and not expect the answers to problems to be served up on a plate. In the event, she drew 10♥ and J♣ which is the 10th Degree of Pisces – 'An Aviator in the Clouds'. This was telling her that she was already airborne – taking the exams – but there was no way of knowing how she was doing until she came out of the clouds – got her results. Then again, it could also be saying that the 'clouds' represented her doubts by which she was being blinded.

What she did next further demonstrated what could be called the *integrity* of the Oracle. She had had a dream in which she was again seeing the exam papers and it looked as if she had done better than she thought she had, and so she asked the Oracle if this dream was a reliable insight. She then drew exactly the same Sabian Symbol, stressing the fact that she would know when she knew.

Finally, she asked it how best to sit her third and final exam. Incredibly, she received the same Symbol yet again. The odds of this happening by chance are astronomical (360 × 360 × 360 to 1) and one cannot help but be impressed by the sheer fact of the Oracle, that it was being deliberately emphatic about something. In this case it was stressing that she was still in the clouds of not knowing outcomes and being beset by doubts, and all she could do was keep to her course and she would eventually come out into the clear. Perhaps, more subtly, it was also making it plain that its advice had already been given to her and that she was expecting life's lessons to be taught by using the Oracle alone rather than through actually living through them.

She then remembered that she had asked the Oracle about how well-prepared she was for her exam about a week before. To this she had received Taurus 20 – 'Wind, *Clouds* and Haste' (the only other reference to 'clouds' in the Sabian Symbols). This was saying that such a thing was by its very nature unpredictable (wind's classic symbolism), entailed her doubts haunting her (clouds again) and that she would have to get a move on (haste) with more studying (she was behind). Later, she decided that she had taken on too much with the exams in trying for other subjects as well, and so she postponed sitting exams for them until later. As it turned out she did pass her exam, but only just – true to the 'Flying by the seat of one's pants' reference in the Money/Work/Creativity section of Pisces 10.

CASE C – SAME SYMBOL, DIFFERENT ANSWERS

This was a case of two quite different questions being asked some distance apart in time but receiving the same answer. The first question concerned an error of judgement that the inquirer had made some time before as a result of not sticking to his guns. He could not really do anything about it but was still fretting over the issue. He asked the Oracle if he thought he had made a real mess of things and he received 15♦ and K♦, 15th Degree of Libra – 'Circular Paths'. Essentially, this told him that he was going over the same old ground more than was necessary merely to learn from his mistake and know and trust himself more next time. This immediately let him off the hook because he *knew* the Oracle was telling him the truth. This is a very important aspect of using any oracle – to know subjectively that its counsel is good and true because you can sense it speaking directly to you in a way which a third party might not appreciate.

Some time later he had a very serious row with his partner and was quite distraught, feeling that everything had been blown away. He asked the Oracle, simply by saying '*Help!*' It came back with Libra 15 – 'Circular Paths' again. This time, though, he understood it to mean that a well-established relationship such as he had would soon revert to normal. This came out to be true for he and his partner were making up within a very short time.

CASE D – THE REALITY CHECK

This is an example of using the Oracle for a 'Reality Check'. This is when you want to know where you are at, but are not quite sure how to phrase a particular question. In my line of work – that is, advising people – you often wonder if you have the right to advise anyone on anything! So I asked the Oracle to give me, as an astrological consultant, a Reality Check. I drew Aries 11 – 'The President Of A Country'. This made it clear to me that firstly I had a position of great responsibility, and that secondly the effective executing of such responsibility hinged upon making certain personal sacrifices (which I do), and doing a lot of hard work and soul-searching (which I also do). Consequently, I took the Reality Check to be saying that I still qualified for the job, provided I kept up the payments, so to speak.

CASE E – EMOTIONAL DISCLOSURE

Earlier I referred to the importance of association, that if possible you should initially interpret a Sabian Symbol purely through what it brings to mind straightaway. A client of mine was at a loss for what direction her life was taking, and what she was supposed to be doing in the world. First of all I explained to her that this was because she was, owing to previous life experiences, in the habit of disconnecting from her deeper and more profound feelings, thereby cutting herself off from her true motivations. You have to feel where you are coming from to know where you are going. So she wisely asked for a clue to her direction/purpose, as distinct from asking for an actual description of it. She selected Gemini 15 – 'Two Dutch Children Talking'. She immediately became emotional and explained that her late paternal grandmother used to have two figurines of Dutch children on her mantelpiece. On asking her how she got on with grandmother, she said she was 'her best friend' and the tears began to flow. The Sabian Symbol was confirming the importance of her staying attuned to her deepest feelings, while giving her a personal example/demonstration of this at the same time. There was also the likelihood (as was evident in her astrological chart) that my client had a 'hotline' to discarnate spirits. Such would be a guide to her finding her purpose, and possibly that purpose would involve being a medium.

CASE F – THE ORACLE AS MEDIUM

Here is a good example of how the Oracle may be used as a medium, as a way of communicating with inner planes or with people who are no longer living in their physical incarnation. A female client felt perennially insecure, especially since the untimely death of her mother, and whenever she turned to other women for support she always felt let down or taken advantage of. So she asked the Oracle if her mother was still aware of her and her plight, and whether she could help her to feel more secure in the world. She received Cancer 18 – 'A Hen Scratching For Her Chicks' (Cancer is the Sign of Mother and Comfort). This was a strong communication that had a favourable emotional effect upon my client, all the more because her mother's actual pet name for her was 'chick'. She immediately asked for another message and got Gemini 4 – 'Holly and Mistletoe' (Gemini is the Sign of Communication). This is a strong symbol of

Immortality and the Everlasting; it also recommends the importance of sincere ritual. She knew her mother was saying that she was not gone forever and would always be there for her, and that she should make it a regular ritual to stay in touch with her in this and other ways. When my client had recovered emotionally, her doubts crept back in and she wanted confirmation that she had interpreted these symbols correctly, that she wasn't just being fanciful. To this she received Pisces 19 – 'A Master Instructing His Pupil'. Message received and understood – and believed!

CASE G – A COLLECTIVE QUESTION

This is an example of a General or Collective question where you ask about something to do with the world and mankind as a whole. The difficulty with this is that you are setting yourself up as a soothsayer, where you have to put aside your personal or subjective feelings and issues. It helps if you already have some existing material or version concerning your question, as this allows the Oracle to add to it, confirm it or disagree with it.

Being greatly interested in the Mayan Calendar, I wanted the Oracle to shed light upon the End Date of the Winter Solstice of 2012. This has posed a number of 'end-time' scenarios, but the one I wanted to look at concerned the idea that at this time there would be an alignment with our Galaxy's centre, affecting everything in our Solar System, especially the Earth and the consciousness of Humanity. This would supposedly entail a kind of upgrade effect upon human consciousness that would benefit those who had freed themselves of egoism (false centredness), seeing themselves and acting as expressions of God, a Higher Power or the Hunab Ku (the Mayan supreme God). Those still ego-centred and overly materialistic would, as it were, have their fuses blown, giving rise to death, illness or insanity. The former would then become stewards of the upgraded Earth, and look after the incapacitated, while those who died would be reborn on another Earth-type planet at an earlier epoch of evolution.

I decided to use a 'rangefinder' first (see page 9), and got Sagittarius 12 – 'A Flag That Turns Into An Eagle That Crows'. The salient part seemed to be from the Karma section '… if one has a strong sense of something coming into being, like a "new age" or some such vision of the future, then it needs to be broadcast far and wide.' Eagles symbolize vision and prophecy because they have amazing eyesight and, flying high, can see the coming day before anyone or anything else. So, taking my cue from the imagery of this rangefinder, I asked what the Eagle was crowing or saying. I received Capricorn 22 – 'A General Accepting Defeat Gracefully' which is expressly about the relinquishment of the ego's control being the way forward. Encouraged by this I then asked about the Winter Solstice 2012 being the actual time of major change. To this I received Gemini 4 – 'Holly And Mistletoe' which refers straightaway to the Winter Solstice, and the Nameplate of this Symbol is 'Ritual and Renewal'. (I asked these questions at the final stage of writing this book, when all of the Sabian Symbols interpretations had been written.)

THE THREE GOLDEN RULES
FOR USING THE ASTROLOGICAL ORACLE

1 The question you ask should be as clear, focused and genuine as possible – if it is, then so will the answer. Meditate, pray, still yourself, and then visualize or contemplate your situation/question with a minimum of intrusion of other thoughts or feelings.

2 Before and during the reading of the interpretations, attempt to understand the Sabian Symbol itself as an answer to your question by visualizing and analysing it, and freely associating with what the images mean to you personally, much as you would interpret a dream. This is vitally important because the Symbol is like a magical, multi-faceted jewel that is capable of giving you a very personal answer when you use it in this way. The given interpretations are, after all, only facets or suggestions, common meanings and catalysts to your own thinking and feeling processes, much as you'd get in a list of meanings for dream images.

3 Bear in mind that the Oracle will often answer the question you are *really* asking, as distinct from (and sometimes in addition to) the question you *thought* you were asking. Be alive to this possibility or make your question as open and free from agenda and presumption as possible. The ultimate open question is *'What is happening?'* or *'What should I do?'* or just *'?'* while feeling that deep and genuine need for help or enlightenment.

PART II

THE
SABIAN
SYMBOLS

THE SABIAN SYMBOLS INDEX

Note that the nature of Sabian Symbols is varied in that although they are largely universal by way of reference, they are sometimes characterized by the time (1920s) and by the American culture in which they were psychically received. Occasionally they are of an esoteric nature.

To use the Index find the Sign section and Degree number you have selected with the cards or dice and you will find the Sabian Symbol the Oracle has used to reply to your question, along with the number of the page where you will find its interpretation.

THE SABIAN SYMBOLS OF ARIES

The **Sign Subject Matter** is given on page 39.

※

THE SABIAN SYMBOLS OF TAURUS

*The **Sign Subject Matter** is given on page 71.*

THE SABIAN SYMBOLS OF GEMINI

*The **Sign Subject Matter** is given on page 103.*

THE SABIAN SYMBOLS OF CANCER

*The **Sign Subject Matter** is given on page 135.*

THE SABIAN SYMBOLS OF LEO

*The **Sign Subject Matter** is given on page 167.*

THE SABIAN SYMBOLS OF VIRGO

*The **Sign Subject Matter** is given on page 199.*

THE SABIAN SYMBOLS OF LIBRA

*The **Sign Subject Matter** is given on page 231.*

THE SABIAN SYMBOLS OF SCORPIO

*The **Sign Subject Matter** is given on page 263.*

THE SABIAN SYMBOLS OF SAGITTARIUS

*The **Sign Subject Matter** is given on page 295.*

✳
THE SABIAN SYMBOLS OF CAPRICORN

*The **Sign Subject Matter** is given on page 327.*

THE SABIAN SYMBOLS OF AQUARIUS

The **Sign Subject Matter** is given on page 359.

THE SABIAN SYMBOLS OF PISCES

The **Sign Subject Matter** is given on page 391.

THE SABIAN SYMBOLS OF
ARIES

Either directly, or in a subtle way, all these Symbols are concerned with the following qualities, or with situations that involve or call for them:

BEGINNINGS

CHAMPIONING

COURAGE

DIRECTNESS

FORCEFULNESS

THE HEAD

HEROISM

HONOUR

INDEPENDENCE

THE MILITARY

RAW ENERGY/ANGER

SELF-ASSERTION

SIMPLICITY

STARTING THINGS UP

WEAPONS AND TOOLS

A WOMAN RISES OUT OF WATER, A SEAL RISES AND EMBRACES HER

☆ EMERGING POTENTIAL ☆

✳ GENERAL INTERPRETATION

The soul emerging from primordial or unconscious realms, spontaneously attracting an allegiance with Nature herself. Birth. The emergence of potential – no more, no less. This is a very fitting Symbol for the very beginning of the cycle of life which is the Zodiac. It may be referring to an actual birth. Paradoxically, although this is a time of coming into a new and more conscious life, we are not aware of it at the time, hence the need to …

KEEP FOCUSED ON … plunging into any new experience with a straightforwardness that is typical of the Sign of Aries. There has to be an innate enthusiasm for life because there is no turning back any more than a baby can retreat into the womb.

WATCH OUT FOR … abortive attempts to assert oneself due to an inability to free oneself from past attachments.

⚜ MONEY/WORK/CREATIVITY

You are on the brink of a new venture, perhaps after a time of stagnation or inactivity. Everything in you is pressing forward to create and busy yourself in the world. If the actual nature of your work has to do with innovation or renewal, this is very auspicious. It is only inertia and self-doubt, or a fear of change and the unknown, that can scupper your plans.

KEEP FOCUSED ON … all the advantages of making a success of your plans and intentions. This Symbol describes a very powerful 'will to be' that can overcome any obstacle, as long as you stay mindful of its essential nature – the impulse to win, win over or win through.

WATCH OUT FOR … seductive offers, bribes or compromises that have selfish or fearful interests that would keep you from realizing your potential as a creative and productive individual who has something of value to offer the world.

♡ LOVE/RELATING/SOCIAL

Here is a relationship that promises renewal and heralds a new chapter in life. You become more aware of what you are and can be, and possibly of your sensual or animal side. Yet, by virtue of the new you emerging, the old can try to claim you back; this could take the form of a previous or dying relationship which is seemingly revived.

KEEP FOCUSED ON … the natural fact that life and yourself have to move ever onward, evolving and developing … the importance of freeing yourself from the tired and outworn, otherwise this is what you will actually feel and eventually be.

WATCH OUT FOR … not grasping the opportunity to break away from what you know to be stale, even though you are still pulled back by it because it is the devil you know.

☯ KARMA/ATTITUDE/HEALTH

You are in the throes of becoming greater and better than you ever were. However, the past and what you were acts like an 'undertow' that tries to suck you back and down when you should be rising up and forwards. There could be seen to be two 'entities' here – the urge to evolve and the fear of doing so. You may need help, possibly of a professional psychological kind, such as Rebirthing, to sort out any conflict.

KEEP FOCUSED ON … the fact that you are experiencing a crucial and natural point of development. Nothing should be allowed to get in the way of evolution and this is not a time for what might seem to be a worthy sacrifice.

WATCH OUT FOR … the fact that the mean alternative to not moving on is stagnation and regression, and possibly health problems, such as constipation and reproductive problems, or with any other part of the body or being that has to do with elimination, renewal or creation.

'Our birth is but a sleep and a forgetting:/The soul that rises with us, our life's Star …'

A COMEDIAN ENTERTAINING A GROUP

☆ RAISING A LAUGH ☆

✹ GENERAL INTERPRETATION

A time to be alive to the fact that life has an inherent joke running through it. Significantly, the Sabian Symbol following the one that symbolizes the birth of the whole cycle is to do with comedy. It is as if the Zodiac is saying 'Once you have got yourself a body to travel in, the first thing to pack is a sense of humour'. Indeed, one of the first things babies do, apart from cry and make a mess, is laugh.

KEEP FOCUSED ON ... your ability to appeal to your own and other people's sense of the absurd ... literally laughing it off; the physical act of laughing removes stress and puts you in a better and lighter frame of mind.

WATCH OUT FOR ... an unhealthy irreverence that masks and overlooks issues of serious concern ... laughing *at* rather than *with* someone.

♡ LOVE/RELATING/SOCIAL

Humour is probably one of the most enduring and attractive qualities one can have, both romantically and socially. Less popular is making fun or light of others' emotions on a personal level, especially one-to-one. Often we make inappropriate jocular responses in situations which are actually pushing our own emotional buttons, in the hope that those emotions won't be noticed. But this can so upset the other person that they passively or actively take it out on that part of our emotional make-up we are trying to suppress.

KEEP FOCUSED ON ... the funny side of love and relating, without losing sight of the serious side, either regarding yourself or somebody else.

WATCH OUT FOR ... inappropriate humour or use of humour ... making light of what is heavy – particularly where sexuality or looks are concerned.

♒ MONEY/WORK/CREATIVITY

If what you do for a living is supposed to be funny or entertaining, then the Oracle is laughing with you – truly auspicious. Hopefully, it is not implying that you are kidding yourself in some way, as in 'You've got to be joking!' As a rule, humour has little place in the world of money and business, but everyone everywhere warms to someone who is amusing. Humour sells. And the workplace joker is a vital element as they keep spirits up in the face of workaday pressures.

KEEP FOCUSED ON ... discerning the difference between a situation that calls for gravity, such as where you still have a lot to learn, and one that calls for levity, where you might have too much to learn – or that it is just too late to worry about it.

WATCH OUT FOR ... taking things lightly that require greater earnestness, for the last laugh will be on you ... labouring the joke.

☯ KARMA/ATTITUDE/HEALTH

A seeker asked a wise man why there was so much boredom, restlessness and emptiness in life. The wise man promptly yanked a water pistol from under his chair and squirted the seeker in the face. This anecdote speaks volumes, and made everyone, including the seeker, laugh heartily. We never really know the answer and so we sense that there is something we are missing – and humour fills that gap.

KEEP FOCUSED ON ... not taking oneself too seriously, for ultimately the joke is on us.

WATCH OUT FOR ... covering up with jokes and laughter when you are afraid of having a good look at a serious issue or shortcoming ... the clown syndrome where you allow others only to see your bright side because you think no one will accept or love your darker, sadder side. Wit offsets serious matters, but it should not eclipse them. Consciously seek out people who accept all of you.

'A sense of humour is a sense of proportion'

A CAMEO PROFILE OF A MAN IN THE OUTLINE OF HIS COUNTRY

✧ CHARACTER IS DESTINY ✧

 GENERAL INTERPRETATION

A time to identify with your allegiances and place of belonging, and the sense of purpose that this imbues you with. This Symbol could also describe something that is self-contained, someone quite egocentric or a person very much in their own right – the 'man (or woman) of the moment'.

KEEP FOCUSED ON ... the wholehearted commitment that you have and show for what you believe in, that in itself displays how worthwhile such commitment is. If you believe in something enough, then so shall it be ... taking the responsibility, rather than the blame, for whatever is happening to you; in this way you become stronger and more influential.

WATCH OUT FOR ... a blind adherence to some external value system that ultimately proves to be hollow and unimaginative.

 LOVE/RELATING/SOCIAL

One way or the other, consciously or unconsciously, you are the architect of your social and emotional life. If you are not that keen on mixing, you won't attract much of a social gathering; if you feel unfit or disinclined to have a partner, then you won't easily attract one, or you'll feel put upon even if you do. Conversely, if you are gregarious and amorous, then you'll need a big diary and a big heart.

KEEP FOCUSED ON ... honestly defining to yourself, and others, exactly what you require out of life socially and emotionally.

WATCH OUT FOR ... your socially orientated parts and the anti-social parts, your affinities and aversions, for they'll be the key that opens, or doesn't open, the door – depending upon whether or not you want others access to yourself, or to others by you ... not fitting in.

MONEY/WORK/CREATIVITY

Your work is a direct expression of who you are as a person – or it ought to be. Furthermore, you act as an agent for, or personification of, something greater – be that your local environment, your company, country, creative vision, speciality, or whatever – so that others may see themselves as a part of that greater whole, or be moved by what they see in you and your activities. Your rewards are in direct proportion to how well you live up to this, and the financial status of that greater whole.

KEEP FOCUSED ON ... being open spontaneously to be what you see as an extension of your own thoughts and feelings; this could entail the necessity of being your own boss – or having a boss with whom you closely identify, sharing similar goals and values.

WATCH OUT FOR ... getting swallowed up in the greater whole, unless you and it have become one and the same.

KARMA/ATTITUDE/HEALTH

What is important here is your integrity. This means knowing your position in the situation in which you find yourself, and then being true to that position. It also means accepting that whatever that situation is has everything to do with your personality and karma. Health depends upon this integrity, otherwise parts of your life that you neglect or disassociate from will manifest as suffering parts of your body. You *are* your body, for it is the most direct and basic expression of you.

KEEP FOCUSED ON ... the issue of your concern as part of your whole being, a part which must be included ... the fact that all concerned are dependent on feeling a part of a whole, be it a home, a family, a neighbourhood or a race.

WATCH OUT FOR ... being overtaken by someone or something else's negative regime, while avoiding imposing your own regime unless it is benevolent, and it is recognized and accepted as such.

'What you are is what you're going to be'

TWO LOVERS STROLLING THROUGH A SECLUDED WALK

☆ BE TRUE (TO YOUR PATH) ☆

 GENERAL INTERPRETATION

Love in bud. Life and Nature stimulating us to take steps into deeper and richer experiences by somehow disguising the fact that these will most probably be difficult at times. Romance can be seen as 'Love's Calling Card', in that it entices us into the business of loving and being loved through the soft sell of its allure. This Symbol may also be alluding to an illicit affair that has to be kept secret, which suggests that there is something about you that you are unaware of or wish to conceal from others.

KEEP FOCUSED ON ... a spontaneous belief that all things are destined for something good and true, which helps ensure that they actually are so.

WATCH OUT FOR ... a loss of sense of reality and of self-potential through indiscriminate surrender to illusion or the spell cast by desire and romance.

 LOVE/RELATING/SOCIAL

This could point to a literal expression of this Symbol. However, as pointed out in the General Interpretation, such exclusive and intertwined bliss often tends to have a hidden agenda. After all, romantic involvements have filled millions of books with their highs and lows, intrigues and implications. There are also many books that aim to guide lovers, but, in the main ...

KEEP FOCUSED ON ... what and who you really are to one another, rather than falling prey to unreal expectations ... the positive feelings you feel or first felt for one another and continually cherish and preserve them ... spending time alone together, neither influenced nor compromised by the presence, opinions or machinations of others.

WATCH OUT FOR ... being blinded by 'love' ... falling in love with love.

 MONEY/WORK/CREATIVITY

A close partnership or finding a kindred spirit in your workplace is what is imaged or advised here. Both of you could be treading a path that is little known by others, possibly even scorned. Alternatively, it could be pointing to your having to take a route through work and material matters that is very personal, and this tests you to be true to it.

KEEP FOCUSED ON ... finding the career path that you feel drawn to for reasons that go beyond strictly material interests or, if you already have or perceive one, finding the resolve and support to help you stay the course.

WATCH OUT FOR ... assuming that you are entirely alone in what you do and how you are ... falling prey to some illusion around your idealistic values concerning money or work. After all, to a certain extent you are being tested to see if you can remain true to those ideals.

KARMA/ATTITUDE/HEALTH

The love and closeness between you and another are gradually getting you where you wish to be. Alternatively, or additionally, it could be saying that soon you will at last be alone with a certain person with whom to enjoy and progress through life. Generally speaking, you can rest assured that events are moving along at a measured pace and in the right direction, just so long as you ...

KEEP FOCUSED ON ... taking your time and taking it easy, while trusting and drawing maximum benefit from any close bond you have ... staying with the 'process of love', that is, recognizing and accepting that the lows are just as important as the highs to gaining whatever it is you are after.

WATCH OUT FOR ... being too exclusive or reclusive, blaming others or the way of the world for things not being just as you would like.

'Two's company, three's a crowd'

A TRIANGLE WITH WINGS

☆ ON STANDBY ☆

✺ GENERAL INTERPRETATION

You are in a situation where you are called upon to be centred and stable, impassive and self-contained, but ready to move or take off at a moment's notice. The fact that you drew this Symbol implies that you have the potential to abide in a state of readiness for something. Could be a starting point of astral travel.

KEEP FOCUSED ON ... merely being, rather than jumping to conclusions, be they hopeful or dismal. Drawing an image of the Symbol itself and concentrating on it can be of great help here ... the independence of your choice in this matter, and what a simple, yet subtle and relative thing, choice can be.

WATCH OUT FOR ... getting lost in abstract concepts, or mistaking potential for reality.

♡ LOVE/RELATING/SOCIAL

The Eternal Triangle? If this is the case, freeing yourself from such a dilemma is usually desirable. But if it seems impossible, you are hung if you do and hung if you don't. The trick lies with letting it free *itself* up. This means that you need to ...

KEEP FOCUSED ON ... the fact that you are stuck in this triangle because you are stuck with whatever the 'third point' of it is. The third point need not necessarily be another person in the present – it could be a figure from your past, or your car, your job, or your computer. The 'wings' are telling you that you will lose nothing that you do not really need. Just *be* with that idea and see what happens. Let it go. (*See* also Cancer 24.)

WATCH OUT FOR ... being too conceptual about your own or others' emotions; denying something is not the same as being free from it.

⚜ MONEY/WORK/CREATIVITY

This Symbol bodes well for any enterprise, but it has to be remembered that it is very much a 'symbol' in itself. This means that everything is in the right position, is stable and free – potentially. So, whatever the matter concerning you ...

KEEP FOCUSED ON ... establishing a balanced viewpoint or position that in itself is compensated for by a readiness and ability to move on if need be ... stabilizing your finances by making them more fluid, negotiable or accessible ... stilling your mind, freeing it of all expectations, then letting your imagination take flight; this is the way to create now.

WATCH OUT FOR ... the very fact the Symbol has wings on something that does not normally have them (a triangle) suggests that the object of your enquiry could take flight just like that – unexpectedly ... having too fixed an idea of what you wish to create, or having too many ideas and not being able to give them substance.

☯ KARMA/ATTITUDE/HEALTH

In symbolism, three is a trinity such as Mental–Emotional–Physical, Mind–Soul–Body or the Christian Father–Son–Holy Ghost. But what does three mean to you? The 'wings' represent the potential for flying – reaching higher states of consciousness; levitating; seeing things from an overview; freedom. Taken together we could see the Symbol as freeing oneself mentally, emotionally and physically – or at least, the potential or need to do so.

KEEP FOCUSED ON ... creating a state of equanimity with regard to the object of your enquiry ... the fact that all is stable and free, exactly as it should be – one only has to accept this.

WATCH OUT FOR ... neglecting the very real and practical necessities of life, or, conversely, ignoring the transcendental and symbolic side of it.

'Be here now'

A SQUARE BRIGHTLY LIT ON ONE SIDE

☆ ACCENTUATE THE POSITIVE ☆

⚙ GENERAL INTERPRETATION

Occasioned or called for is a strong sense that one side of a given issue is being given or needs to be found, especially in the realm of logic and analytical thought. Focusing attention on one facet or direction of a specific material object or situation. Obtaining very real information, as distinct from being satisfied with a mere notion, possibility or implication.

KEEP FOCUSED ON ... the daemonic conviction that enables you to see something through to its conclusion, or to make one aspect of an issue very clear.

WATCH OUT FOR ... a bias and partiality that leaves you vulnerable to what you have rejected or do not (wish to) know or see ... overlooking the possibility of snags, or seeing snags where there aren't any because of an obsession.

♥ LOVE/RELATING/SOCIAL

This could indicate a one-sided relationship or the occurrence of partiality, for good or ill. Then again, it could mean the 'only have eyes for you' situation that often occurs during the early romantic stages of a relationship. Or just seeing one side, the obvious side, to a person, relationship or thing.

KEEP FOCUSED ON ... what or who you have set your sights on and you will probably attain it ... the best side of yourself or another, rather than the negative or shadowy side ... the true reason for not getting what you want, because that alone will relieve your discomfort.

WATCH OUT FOR ... going after what you want too passionately because you may discover later that it wasn't really that desirable.

⚘ MONEY/WORK/CREATIVITY

If you give very focused attention and energy to the object of your concern, you will achieve what you are after. One side of your business or interest is doing, or is going to do, very well.

KEEP FOCUSED ON ... the most positive and creative aspects of what you are doing; a case of life becoming what you see it to be and wish it to be.

WATCH OUT FOR ... neglecting those things that do not interest or delight you as much as your major objectives. Such a practice could eventually comprise a sizeable problem, simply because these things have been left in the shade.

☯ KARMA/ATTITUDE/HEALTH

Life is unequivocally calling your attention to something of great importance. You must obey this call and read the writing on the wall; it probably is not what you fear – it is more likely to be something very positive coming your way. Anyhow, what you fear is more likely to be what you do not wish to see, and so have not looked at properly. Complaints coming from a biased or vague viewpoint.

KEEP FOCUSED ON ... shedding love and light wherever there is darkness, doubt or disease ... concentrating on what ails you with a positive attitude, until you see its underlying cause.

WATCH OUT FOR ... philosophies and beliefs (and those who espouse them) that are 'polarized in the light', that is, ones which totally fail to consider the shadow side of any person or thing ... those who see only what they wish to see, and would have you see only that also.

'Always look on the bright side of life'

A MAN SUCCESSFULLY EXPRESSING HIMSELF IN TWO REALMS AT ONCE

☆ DIVISION OF LABOUR ☆

✸ GENERAL INTERPRETATION

The fact that this Symbol contains the word 'successfully' makes it appear a wholly positive image of holding or enjoying two stations in life. However, this could be referring to the intention rather than the accomplishment and it does not give any assurances as to sustaining such success.

KEEP FOCUSED ON ... developing or using the ability to divide your time and labour in order to pursue more than one goal or responsibility, expressing possibly conflicting parts of your personality with ease.

WATCH OUT FOR ... the illusion of successfully keeping two areas of life separate, only to find at some stage that they are intruding upon one another ... living a double life ... falling between two stools through taking on too much, being too clever.

♥ LOVE/RELATING/SOCIAL

Keeping strictly within the realms of relationships, this Symbol could suggest having more than one on the go at the same time. Whether or not everyone is enjoying this situation, or even knows about it, could be a question. Apart from this, another interpretation could be that of simply and satisfactorily fulfilling an emotional role on the one hand and, say, a work role on the other.

KEEP FOCUSED ON ... how your social or love life would benefit from having an interest apart from it ... the fact that you are fortunate in having a balanced lifestyle ... giving whatever is due to the various elements of your life.

WATCH OUT FOR ... putting too much energy into one person or relationship, for this could be overloading it, giving rise to problems later.

⚒ MONEY/WORK/CREATIVITY

Here is a plain indication that multifarious talents are in evidence. Although this Symbol could be regarded as an unalloyed seal of approval or a prediction of dual or multiple success, in order to fulfil the promise of such talents or maintain the success they breed, it could be necessary to ...

KEEP FOCUSED ON ... managing your resources and delegating time and responsibilities in a judicious and disciplined fashion ... keeping more than one iron in the fire ... performing functions other than just what you have been led to believe you are capable of – such as getting rid of the middleman.

WATCH OUT FOR ... spreading yourself too thinly, possibly as a result of greed, conceit or over-ambition ... dithering between alternatives or not being organized enough to satisfy both/all of them ... putting all your eggs in one basket.

⚘ KARMA/ATTITUDE/HEALTH

An appreciation of the dual nature of your own being or of existence is occasioned or called for here. When a teacher was asked by a seeker if he should do more on the spiritual side or the material side of life, he was told, 'Do more on both!' Likewise, it is unavoidable and advantageous to follow both the orthodox and esoteric paths in life. Health-wise, the use of both conventional and complementary medicines is suggested.

KEEP FOCUSED ON ... what else you can do with your life; having another string to your bow improves how you use the first one ... seeing how the other half lives; this will enrich your experience and open doors you did not even know were there.

WATCH OUT FOR ... being trapped or fixed in a singular interpretation of life or of yourself ... getting stuck in a rut for fear of branching out into some untried avenue of expression.

'Delegation is the secret of success'

A LARGE HAT WITH STREAMERS FLYING, FACING EAST

☆ INSPIRED VIGOUR ☆

 GENERAL INTERPRETATION

Here is a positive prospect of what the future has to bring, born of a strong sense of the ideals that must and shall be made real. At the same time being protected from harmful elements, so long as one protects the very ideals that one sets out to espouse.

KEEP FOCUSED ON ... an enthusiastic or joyful attitude of mind towards what lies ahead ... the fact that you are aware of the forces of Evolution itself, and that you only need to turn towards the challenges you have before you, and you will have those forces propelling forwards ... the idea that courage is its own reward.

WATCH OUT FOR ... naive optimism or brittle flamboyancy for such would repel or annoy what or who you wish to find favour with ... false confidence born of spiritual pretension.

LOVE/RELATING/SOCIAL

Either a relationship or social set up that is in its earliest, freshest and most enthusiastic stage, or one that includes young or young-at-heart people who are set upon maintaining that initial spark. A party, an occasion or an atmosphere with a party feel. Upbeat.

KEEP FOCUSED ON ... the very first things that appealed to you when you first got involved ... the most romantic or gallant aspects of yourself and another ... what it is in you and another that each of you looks to and admires – or initially admired.

WATCH OUT FOR ... quixotic behaviour; being carried away by an unlikely goal or neurotic feeling that is acting as a compensation for something, such as a past failure or upset, that you are not really facing up to.

 MONEY/WORK/CREATIVITY

The object of your concern depends or thrives on your innate inclination to take on a challenge with a heroic or pioneering orientation. Your great asset is your sense of predominant trends with regard to certain issues.

KEEP FOCUSED ON ... your original aims and motivations for they have the power to steer you towards your objectives and be met with like enthusiasm ... your championship of a cause ... your vision ... striking out for what you see as being more 'you' ... making things fun and appealing, rather than merely making sense.

WATCH OUT FOR ... losing sight of your ingenuousness for then you would be in danger of contriving. Bear in mind that contrivances require more time and energy to maintain than you can afford or than comes naturally to you.

KARMA/ATTITUDE/HEALTH

A positive outlook that engenders an equally healthy physical disposition. The (past) use of subtle, passive, possibly oriental, means of looking at life and maintaining well-being. The consequences of great ideas/ideals.

KEEP FOCUSED ON ... the fact that leaders also need to have something or someone to follow ... your God, positive vision, sense of joy, role model or whatever it is that 'crowns' you – is seen to be your best quality or that which has most authority/authenticity ... looking to oriental health methods, such as yoga, acupuncture, Reiki and tai chi.

WATCH OUT FOR ... fooling yourself into thinking that all is well on all fronts because things look good on one or two of them ... the fact that mistaking gusto for faith is like so-called 'healthy irreverence', when reverence itself is the main basis for health.

'He who binds to himself a joy doth the wingéd life destroy.
But he who kisses the joy as it flies, lives in Eternity's sunrise'

A CRYSTAL GAZER

✶ INSIGHT THROUGH CLARITY ✶

✸ GENERAL INTERPRETATION

The possibility of seeing into the future or into areas normally closed to us. This is highly dependent upon one's skill, sense of discrimination, and upon one's field of vision not being clouded by one's hopes and fears. Receiving this Symbol could also be the Oracle telling you that you are treating it too much like a fortune-teller. It is not.

KEEP FOCUSED ON ... visualizing the course of events according to an intuitive or divine scheme of things ... imagining yourself as a crystal – strong and symmetrical ... trying Guided Imagery (*see* page 427).

WATCH OUT FOR ... losing your sense of the present reality as a result of being consumed by what is naively craved or fearfully anticipated ... believing that determining the future is as simple as 'gazing into a crystal ball'.

♥ LOVE/RELATING/SOCIAL

So often we want to know how a relationship is going to turn out – or when one is going to turn up. The fact is that, short of going to see a genuine clairvoyant (a very rare individual), we can only discover this by looking hard and deep into the here and now. Then, if you ...

KEEP FOCUSED ON ... the positive aspects of a relationship or another person; you'll be making the best investment for a good future. If you are on your own, then focus upon the advantages of being in such a state, or why you happen to be in such a state if it is unacceptable to you.

WATCH OUT FOR ... looking to the future in the hope that 'things will get better' because someone said they would change. Only when changes actually occur, mainly in your own attitude, will you see the future in the making.

♟ MONEY/WORK/CREATIVITY

On a strictly material level this Symbol is recommending or referring to such things as projections, futurology and feasibility studies. On a creative level it is saying that what is required is an intuitive sense of the way things are going to be, culturally or artistically. If the object of your enquiry is concerned with the above in some way, then this is an auspicious oracle.

KEEP FOCUSED ON ... current trends and as comprehensive and complete a view as possible of the overall picture ... being as still and unemotional as one can, in order to achieve maximum clarity of forward vision.

WATCH OUT FOR ... exactly what kind of 'crystal' or lens you are using to view your future and prospects. Beware if it is wildly hopeful, ignoring or rationalizing away any snags, or wanting a finite answer.

☯ KARMA/ATTITUDE/HEALTH

A true seer is able to 'pierce the veil' that separates one time from another. There are many who can do this to a degree, but this is like intermittently tuning into a radio station. It is not very reliable, and is unpleasant, even disturbing, to listen to. A genuine seer can 'hold the signal' and mask out the static.

KEEP FOCUSED ON ... anything, inwardly or outwardly, that resembles a blank screen, if you wish to receive a true impression, image or message with regard to the object of your concern.

WATCH OUT FOR ... just seeing what you want to see, or don't want to see. It is only when one is free of hopes and fears, or the need to make an impression or money, that one is sufficiently open to receive the truth. Quite simply, if you do not want to see the truth, then you won't ... not being earthed in the here and now, for this can lead to devitalization and other health problems.

'Only a man devoted to complete inner sincerity can know the future'

A MAN TEACHING NEW FORMS FOR OLD SYMBOLS

☆ UPGRADE AND RE-PRESENTATION ☆

 GENERAL INTERPRETATION

Learning or teaching that life is, presently at least, a process of finding a new take on life and/or yourself. More literally, presenting and interpreting age-old wisdom and intelligence, or anything at all that has some history, in a way that is more understandable, accessible and appreciable to people today.

KEEP FOCUSED ON ... your special talent for doing things another way when the old way is proving ineffectual, or worse ... the constantly evolving process that is intrinsic to the object of your enquiry – it is designed to evolve and renew itself naturally ... repositioning yourself.

WATCH OUT FOR ... trying too hard to teach old dogs new tricks ... being intimidated by the fear of not getting things right straightaway or sooner than is possible.

 LOVE/RELATING/SOCIAL

Something that should never be underestimated when considering relationships is how one actually relates to the relating! In other words, before being able to understand an individual relationship, the issue at stake is often what one thinks relationships are all about generally. Nowadays, there are many new ways of looking at relationships and this Symbol is advising that attaining a new 'relationship paradigm' is essential to you now – or that someone is already showing you this.

KEEP FOCUSED ON ... the idea that through a relationship, or the lack of one, you are first learning about yourself, then about another, and then about psychological projection ... new ways of looking at and expressing old feelings.

WATCH OUT FOR ... staying stuck with traditional gender roles and, above all, denying how you feel.

 MONEY/WORK/CREATIVITY

Your enquiry is concerned with a new way of presenting to others or yourself whatever has been your line up to now, possibly for quite a time. This may involve retraining, a fresh approach free of preconceived ideas, or the injection of something entirely new and revolutionary. It may also refer to reforming price structures, how you evaluate things, or to putting a new spin or interpretation on something from the past.

KEEP FOCUSED ON ... the essence of what you are endeavouring to achieve, kicking out the old and inefficient ways of trying to do this, then doing or getting whatever is necessary to redesign and reform.

WATCH OUT FOR ... throwing the baby out with the bathwater, that is, inadvertently or indiscriminately getting rid of the good at the same time as eliminating the bad or introducing something new.

KARMA/ATTITUDE/HEALTH

The whole concept of reincarnation, of having one lifetime after another – or simply the progress within one lifetime – is summed up in this Symbol. The 'old symbol' is one's timeless soul looking for better ways of expressing and looking at itself and life through the 'new form' of one's personality of the time – or of whatever it is that requires renewal.

KEEP FOCUSED ON ... the fact that this process is a natural one, in that you are supposed to keep renewing yourself and your expressions of self, so simply by stepping in that direction you will sooner or later attract the new form you are after.

WATCH OUT FOR ... any part of you that is resisting new experiences and avenues of expression, for that part is born of a fear of your own unknown, yet-to-be self that would be revealed if you allowed yourself to unfold.

'They that drink of the old wine have no place for the new'

THE PRESIDENT OF THE COUNTRY

☆ SOVEREIGNTY OF BEING ☆

⊛ GENERAL INTERPRETATION

Now is the time for a total focus of ego upon itself in order to achieve and maintain (worldly) position, possibly at the expense of what could be termed normal personal interaction and lifestyle.

KEEP FOCUSED ON ... organizing your life and affairs in the knowledge that it is entirely down to you to do so and entirely up to you how you do this ... your willingness to make sacrifices indefinitely in order to fulfil your duty or destiny ... being single-minded.

WATCH OUT FOR ... ultimately destructive ego-centricity and arrogance, or being a puppet or victim of it.

♡ LOVE/RELATING/SOCIAL

Here is stressed the importance of being in charge of your own space to avoid being entrapped in, or vulnerable to, someone else's, or that of society as a whole. Then there is the decision as to how much you bend your energies towards establishing your own social position in order to further this end.

KEEP FOCUSED ON ... what you do and do not have control over with regard to a partner or society ... building up inner independence, that is, having a strong enough sense of your own inner core that you do not need-lessly react emotionally to another's words and deeds ... being in command of all facets of your own personality.

WATCH OUT FOR ... trying to control another's life and personality because you do not feel in control of your own ... taking liberties, for there will be payback time sooner or later.

♆ MONEY/WORK/CREATIVITY

Whoever is in charge, or is supposed to be, must really be cut out for the job, otherwise disaster can strike. Drawing this Symbol implies that you are the one in charge, if that is relevant to your enquiry, or that you should look to the one who is in charge and follow and assist them if they measure up, or part company with them if they don't.

KEEP FOCUSED ON ... the fact that the buck stops with you, and take any necessary steps or privileges in order that you may live up to that status ... what sacrifices have to be made to your personal life, and willingly make them ... the power you have to success-fully manage your affairs.

WATCH OUT FOR ... sycophants who would seek to further themselves through flattering you, yet would put the knife in when it suited them.

♋ KARMA/ATTITUDE/HEALTH

Of paramount importance in life is the assuming of responsibility for your own life and personality if you wish to be successful as a person. This rule also states that it must be recognized, understood, believed and put into practice that nothing and no one other than yourself is ultimately responsible for you.

KEEP FOCUSED ON ... the belief that pursuing this rule will, through time, attract and earn you all the power you need to attain any objective, conquer any foe, overcome any weakness and meet any challenge.

WATCH OUT FOR ... worrying too much about what others think or make of you; it is what you make of yourself that matters. Otherwise, you run the risk of erecting defences against imagined foes and these defences then become impediments to your own freedom.

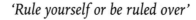

'Rule yourself or be ruled over'

A FLOCK OF WILD GEESE

☆ NATURAL TIMING AND SENSE OF DIRECTION ☆

 GENERAL INTERPRETATION

The situation involves the natural phenomenon of living things operating in a way that is both instinctively organized at a group level and also connected to seasonal cycles and even subtler influences with regard to when and where to relocate, gather or do anything significant.

KEEP FOCUSED ON ... proceeding in a manner that feels right, that follows a natural course of events ... utilizing the powers and combined intelligence of a group to which you belong or feel drawn, or would like to form.

WATCH OUT FOR ... isolating yourself as this can be confusing, counterproductive and even self-destructive ... being too dependent upon anybody and everybody else ... making off before the time is ripe or right; escapism.

 LOVE/RELATING/SOCIAL

So often in our emotional lives we are beset by elements that we seem to have no control over. This is because, much as we like to think we have some control over the comings and goings of relationships, there is another deeper factor at work that determines what happens and when. The times of arrival, departure or reuniting are, for the most part, definite in one respect but unfathomable in another, particularly with regard to what actually prompts major turning points. All we can do is ...

KEEP FOCUSED ON ... the history, nature and course of our relationships and any signs or intimations of where our emotional lives are going, and respond and act as appropriately as possible ... letting things unfold as they will.

WATCH OUT FOR ... frustration as a result of trying to force things when they are not ready.

 MONEY/WORK/CREATIVITY

Follow your instincts, particularly in conjunction with the instincts of others with whom you feel some sort of working bond. Teamwork. Creatively, you need to organize all the elements of your enterprise to head in the same direction and at the right time; ask again about this. Financial issues are also entirely dependent upon the group and time factors.

KEEP FOCUSED ON ... what direction it is most suitable to take in terms of conditions, supply and timing ... something that is best arrived at through a form of group consensus ... giving and gaining reassurance and inspiration from close colleagues ... the fact that the time will arrive for things to take off financially.

WATCH OUT FOR ... trying to go it alone. You may just make it this way, but the stress would prove hard to bear. Being 'lord of all you survey' is not desirable when your 'kingdom' is in disarray.

 KARMA/ATTITUDE/HEALTH

You are not alone with respect to your situation, but are assisted by others in your Soul Flight, that is, the group of individuals who share the same spiritual intent or mission. You can be in touch with them psychically and/or physically. The experience of this, or of crossing the flight path of some other Soul Flight, is very poignant and significant, and in tune and in time with subtle currents, interactions and deep inner promptings.

KEEP FOCUSED ON ... who the members of your Soul Flight might be, and honour and help them as they do you; you have probably been 'in flight' together for a very long time ... which member is currently leading the whole Flight, and follow them until it is another's turn – possibly yours.

WATCH OUT FOR ... leaderless groups; they can be detrimental to health and survival ... taking off when the time is not right.

'To everything there is a season, and a time to every purpose under heaven'

AN UNSUCCESSFUL BOMB EXPLOSION

☆ AVERTING DISASTER ☆

✷ GENERAL INTERPRETATION

The intentions of evil, violence or plain misfortune thwarted, nullified or minimized through one means or other. Goodness wins through, be it as a consequence of a specific act against destructive forces, or a more imponderable factor such as 'luck' or 'coincidence' or even divine intervention.

KEEP FOCUSED ON ... an intrepidity that enables you to rescue others from danger or distress, that ultimately redeems your own soul ... getting through a tricky or difficult situation with non-action or not reacting.

WATCH OUT FOR ... the inevitable failure or pointlessness of brute force or mere impetuosity, as a way of life ... short fuses; things could blow up in your face.

♥ LOVE/RELATING/SOCIAL

The explosion (blow-up) or implosion (void/loneliness) you fear is not really an issue – it could have been, or you just think it is. However, considering the persistence and strength of destructive impulses, do not expect the results of them always to be defused by fortune or a helping hand. Alternatively, you may be frustrated by being denied some form of social or sexual excitement, but despite your lack of better judgement, Fate is seeing to it that it never happens, because you ultimately wouldn't like it.

KEEP FOCUSED ON ... being grateful for what you have got, rather than craving something that would be a lot more trouble than it is worth.

WATCH OUT FOR ... looking or pushing for any kind of reaction, simply to get an emotional response – you'd regret it.

♆ MONEY/WORK/CREATIVITY

On the one hand, if you are hoping to make a big splash with a 'great' idea or product, then expect to be disappointed. On the other hand, if your intention is to defuse a situation, or divert excess energy or resources, then success is assured. Then again, if what you have in mind has something that parallels or reflects this Symbol in a more literal sense – such as averting disasters or defeating antisocial forces – then take this as a green light.

KEEP FOCUSED ON ... accomplishing anything that is in aid of promoting peace ... an objective that does not have to create a crisis in order to be reached ... acting as if the heat is off.

WATCH OUT FOR ... damp squibs, non-starters. Anything that does not take off after a few good attempts is not worth the time and effort.

☯ KARMA/ATTITUDE/HEALTH

The disaster you fear is being defused, or already has been. The real disaster is more likely to be an impetuous, excitable or explosive temperament that is being curbed or is having to be curbed or let go of. A need to control could also be an issue, born of a fear that no one but you is taking care of things.

KEEP FOCUSED ON ... the idea that there are agencies, be they in this world or another, that are continually striving to remove potential problems from our lives before they even occur. One only has to continue to *allow* them to do this.

WATCH OUT FOR ... being unnecessarily anxious, yet at the same time do not leave everything to God or someone else to take care of; energy is at a premium everywhere.

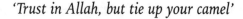

'Trust in Allah, but tie up your camel'

A SERPENT COILING NEAR A MAN AND A WOMAN

☆ THE URGE TO EVOLVE ☆

✱ GENERAL INTERPRETATION

Apart from the obvious Biblical one of temptation, a more esoteric interpretation of this Symbol is that it is sex and the desire for union (or reunion) that precipitates us into a more intense, challenging and meaningful phase of experience – indeed, into life as we know it. The ultimate goal, and the older symbolism of the serpent, is the evolution of consciousness and the healing of splits and old wounds.

KEEP FOCUSED ON ... what it is about you or another that powerfully draws you into closer intimacy with each other – and possibly the so-called darker side of yourselves – with the ultimate aim of reaching a higher and more complete sense of yourselves and what life on Earth means.

WATCH OUT FOR ... mindless enticement or submission with regard to passing urges and carnal pleasures ... being a victim of basic instincts.

MONEY/WORK/CREATIVITY

That sex sells is only too well-known. The question is *what* it sells. If your business, idea or product uses or is involved with sex with a view to putting people more in touch with the joy of sex or making them aware of the dangers of sex, then this is an auspicious oracle. If, however, your employment of sex is gratuitous, then, owing to the current state of sexual awareness, you will probably profit from it to some degree, but you would be contributing to the problem rather than providing a solution. The problem being the monumental one that much of this interpretation of this Symbol is alluding to.

KEEP FOCUSED ON ... doing what you can to enlighten, facilitate and alleviate whatever negative sexual attitudes or practices rear their heads.

WATCH OUT FOR ... the likelihood that sexual truths are often unacceptable because of sexual taboos.

♡ LOVE/RELATING/SOCIAL

Most likely you are in the process of becoming sexually involved with someone – or you are about to be so or are contemplating it. Or you are in need of reminding yourself how and why you got involved in an existing relationship in the first place.

KEEP FOCUSED ON ... ritualizing your relationship – that is, seeing it as being something more than just a means of meeting sexual, social or emotional needs – and conducting it in a manner that is mindful of the alchemy of bodies and souls merging and coming together. Recommended here are Tantra, Taoism or other methods that take one out of one's sense of separateness into that of divine congress.

WATCH OUT FOR ... such things as guilt, a need to control and a fear of intimacy – and what lies behind them – for they are what destroy or prevent union.

⑤ KARMA/ATTITUDE/HEALTH

Having to address and resolve longstanding issues such as original sin, loss of innocence and sexual shame which have arisen because of a basic misinterpretation or misrepresentation of what desire is for and about. The idea that one has something to lose through revealing one's inner self to another human being insinuated itself into the collective unconscious. Making people feel guilty and sinful about the profoundly natural process of *re*-union effectively keeps them in bondage and alienated.

KEEP FOCUSED ON ... identifying and letting go of the inhibitions and fears that you feel have taken hold in your beautiful and innocent self ... how great personal power and liberation from fear would arise from touching each other's souls via our bodies.

WATCH OUT FOR ... the belief that truly loving or friendly sex is wrong ... passion laced with design.

'Life is a sexually transmitted disease'

AN INDIAN WEAVING A BLANKET

☆ THE THREADS OF LIFE ☆

 GENERAL INTERPRETATION

Occasioned or called for is a natural or inherited ability to make use of resources in a way that stabilizes and integrates the various strands of the story of life, and which gives rise to a pleasing, practical and therapeutic result.

KEEP FOCUSED ON ... fashioning things in a way that reaches its goal through a quiet persistence that does not allow you to be pressured ... occasionally taking a step back from what you are doing and seeing how it is shaping up ... how the pattern, future or fabric of your existence is created by every thought, word and deed that you weave it into, or into it.

WATCH OUT FOR ... settling for a poorly rewarded and humdrum existence born of low self-esteem ... inactivity; if you do not 'weave' you get no 'blanket'.

❤ **LOVE/RELATING/SOCIAL**

The two people or sides involved here are like the warp and weft of the threads of life, going this way and that. As you get to know one another, you 'interweave', forming a fabric and a pattern. In this way it is discovered what the relationship is made of – and what it means. It's handmade by you both.

KEEP FOCUSED ON ... the fact that you both have an equal part to play, and that 'it takes two to tango' ... the fact that it takes care, skill and patience to make something worthwhile, that you can be proud of ... the pattern that emerges as you 'interweave' or come together, for this will tell you what the relationship is about and/or what it is developing into ... basing your 'design' on a preconceived template, tradition or vision.

WATCH OUT FOR ... how fine and delicate each thread can be, what pains you must take at times.

 MONEY/WORK/CREATIVITY

The essential nature of your work is that it has to be a personal expression of the fabric of your own being or of some tradition, be it spiritual, familial or tribal – just so long as it is something 'in your blood'. Drawing this Oracle says that it most probably is, and that material reward is secondary to this.

KEEP FOCUSED ON ... the roots of the object of your concern, or the nature of your work, and if you recognize something great and longstanding about it, then you will also be aware that it has an energy and influence that goes beyond your own little self. As such, it has great power, possibly more than you have noticed or are utilizing ... being assisted, inspired and encouraged by this.

WATCH OUT FOR ... signs that you do not 'have it in you', that your work does not come naturally to you. You must persist until it is plainly seen that your efforts do not have that inborn quality.

KARMA/ATTITUDE/HEALTH

The warp and weft of a traditional blanket is symbolic of the interaction of yin and yang, passive and active, female and male energies as they go to make up your current reality and state of health.

KEEP FOCUSED ON ... how well they are balanced and conform to a definite philosophy, regimen or diet ... being laid back, taking things in one's stride, seeing things through thoroughly, recognizing the energies in play ... any healing process whereby tissue has to knit together; Nature gets it to do so, but you can help it along by visualizing the process involved (such as bone cells proliferating).

WATCH OUT FOR ... the possibility of 'dropped stitches', how one has to 'unpick' back to where one went wrong and correct it ... webs of deceit, which usually result from an ignorance of how they will eventually come back on one.

'Upon our dignity's seed we weave and gaze away,
With 'voidance vanquished we no longer plead or dwell in our dismay'

DEVAS DANCING IN THE SETTING SUN

☆ SUPERNATURAL ATTUNEMENT ☆

✦ GENERAL INTERPRETATION

Imaged here is the subtle and symbiotic bond that exists between the human realm and that of the devas or nature spirits, particularly at times when darkness is nigh, twilight. This is a good time to commune with Nature. The Sun setting is symbolic of the daylight or ego consciousness of logic and mundane awareness ebbing or being absent, thereby making one's mind more conducive to the perception of the devic, mystical or unseen realms.

KEEP FOCUSED ON ... any inclination to show a delight in living that can magically affect those around you ... any sense you might have of being in touch with nature spirits, for they will help you and inspire you.

WATCH OUT FOR ... being prey to seductive images and false values, to artificial or risky highs.

♡ LOVE/RELATING/SOCIAL

The magic of being in love and all that it entails. Conversely, if there is one thing that gets in the way of love and harmony it is the ego. When we can put our selfish interests, sense of importance and need for attention aside, we then let subtle thoughts and feelings infiltrate our psyches, adding a touch of the magical or mysterious to our interactions.

KEEP FOCUSED ON ... what it is that entrances you about another, and remember this, for it is the essence of your love and connection ... the most delightful and dreamy, enchanting and otherworldly aspects of one another. In this way, the 'invisible menders' can set to work, putting things right overnight – literally.

WATCH OUT FOR ... trying to make this magic of love present all day long. You do have to get up and go about the mundane business of living as well!

✦ MONEY/WORK/CREATIVITY

Success or personal fulfilment here depends on not being too consumed with attaining such things. At hand there is something or someone to guide or inspire you, but they are more likely to be noticed or contacted when you are not looking so hard, or when you simply open your mind to them. So ...

KEEP FOCUSED ON ... keeping very still so that they can notice and favour you. Such a connection is like people receiving significant ideas or solutions in their dreams or upon waking – perhaps when they have asked for such before going to sleep ... what appeals to children or the children in adults. Fairy tales perhaps.

WATCH OUT FOR ... material reward as being your main objective. This does not mean to say that there will be no reward, but that using it as a main incentive would blind you to the very idea or thing that would point you in the right direction.

☯ KARMA/ATTITUDE/HEALTH

This Symbol is saying that contact with nature spirits or elemental beings is possible when the energies of the ego are waning or at a low ebb – which mostly occurs between being awake and asleep, if ill or fevered, or when in an altered state of consciousness. Such devas are usually seen as small points of coloured light, as floating lights, or sometimes as strange shapes or creatures. As soon as one tries to rationalize or analyse them, make something out of them that is not to their liking, they vanish! However, the time and you are ripe for a contact of this kind, providing you ...

KEEP FOCUSED ON ... using them for the most spiritual or healing of reasons. Or, if it is your fate, being a go-between for them and humanity.

WATCH OUT FOR ... exposing yourself to such beings in a reckless fashion, for this can be physically or psychologically disturbing.

'Those who cannot see the Unseen are like radios stuck on one waveband'

TWO PRIM SPINSTERS

☆ SOBRIETY OR DENIAL? ☆

✸ GENERAL INTERPRETATION

A sedate security can be or is being achieved, but possibly at the expense of exploring and satisfying more exciting urges. The doubling of an image in symbolism can mean that you (and others) are currently coming into an awareness of how this duality or conflict figures in your life. The point is that right now it is going into the 'restrained' end of the spectrum. So …

KEEP FOCUSED ON … getting your facts right … the safe and proper dimensions of life and you will find out what being that way does for you – or does not … faithfully adhering to whatever is seen as a serious inner reality of self or life.

WATCH OUT FOR … having a partially informed or too narrow a view of your situation … an insulation from, or disapproval of, emotional or physical interaction born of a fear of confronting the so-called darker side of yourself.

♥ LOVE/RELATING/SOCIAL

A time of necessary sexual abstinence, possibly stemming from a fear of encountering what, for some reason, has come to be regarded as difficult, unpleasant or unattractive. Or, as this Symbol depicts two people of the same sex, it is implied that having to relate to someone of the opposite sex has never happened, has a negative connotation, or both.

KEEP FOCUSED ON … the fact that the time has come for you to consider that your relationship status is compromised by fear of intimacy. If you can accept or are quite happy with the situation, then all well and good, but asking the Oracle usually implies a question mark … playing it safe as a 'period of adjustment', but …

WATCH OUT FOR … accommodating your fears to the point of either hating your own company or that of the person you originally felt so safe with or turned on by.

♟ MONEY/WORK/CREATIVITY

If your work is of a pure or clinical nature, then this Symbol is saying that you have the discipline and attitude to carry things through successfully. On the other hand, your idea, product or practice may be too narrowly conceived to have that much appeal. Or maybe the work environment is very orderly but lacks verve or creativity – so it does not really progress. Financially speaking, being economical is a strength – or a need. Then again, parsimony may be the problem.

KEEP FOCUSED ON … being utterly realistic about what concerns you. This means that you need to consider in what ways you are being too hard or tight – as well as too soft or loose – either financially or creatively, or about your situation generally.

WATCH OUT FOR … letting the Protestant work ethic get the better of you.

☯ KARMA/ATTITUDE/HEALTH

Down through the ages the battle has raged between restraint and licence, the sacred and the profane. More recently, healthy eating habits and lifestyle have become the index of being 'wholesome'. The point is that, beyond being merely harmless, the situation, like this Symbol, may simply smack of a fear of living.

KEEP FOCUSED ON … honestly assessing whether your withdrawal or restraint is born of better judgement or of a censorious and fearful view of the object of your enquiry. If it is the former, then you are to be commended for your self-control … loosening up somewhat.

WATCH OUT FOR … being 'sober' (diet, weight and health conscious) to the point of finding life impossibly narrow and restrictive, with no fun to make it worth living … taking oneself so seriously that others find it hard to take you seriously at all – find you laughable even.

'Moral indignation is jealousy with a halo'

AN EMPTY HAMMOCK

☆ MUCH NEEDED REST ☆

 GENERAL INTERPRETATION

There arises the necessity or need for rest and recuperation. The ever-present opportunity to take a break – if you care to look. The promise of rest. Being still in a turbulent situation. Conversely, this Symbol could also be pointing to the need to be up and about the business of living. It should be obvious what this is a case of. Ask the Oracle again if it isn't.

KEEP FOCUSED ON … finding a healthy balance between activity and inactivity … looking at this Symbol through the 'nautical analogy' and raising the question of where the 'sailor' is; busy on deck? In the mess? Overboard? Jumped ship? In other words, what does the image of that Empty Hammock evoke in you? … letting the matter rest if it feels tiresome thinking about it or trying to 'put it right'.

WATCH OUT FOR … an inability to take it easy.

 MONEY/WORK/CREATIVITY

Working hard is probably what you are doing – either because you like to or you have to, or both. Maybe the Oracle is pointing out that it is necessary to work even harder and not take time off or laze around. But it is far more likely that you are not taking the time out that you should or would really like to.

KEEP FOCUSED ON … telling yourself that a task is often better accomplished by taking the occasional break from it, taking a step back … the fact that ideas come when they will, or after you have prepared the ground – you cannot force seeds to germinate … finding a job or schedule that is more amenable to your own rhythms.

WATCH OUT FOR … 'workaholism' creeping up on you. This is created by a need to salve one's conscience without actually listening to it, or by a need to avoid emotional interplay.

 LOVE/RELATING/SOCIAL

You need a break from whatever your social or domestic set-up happens to be – maybe your relationship itself needs a break from it all. Alternatively, you and your partner need a break from one another. Unless such a recourse can be easily taken – and it is strongly recommended – there is the possibility that it just isn't that simple. Much as you need the break, you have not got the place, time or facility, or even the will, to take one. So …

KEEP FOCUSED ON … finding a time and a place where you can be alone, together or on your own, every so often … the old truth that a change is as good as a rest … learning to withdraw, be still or detach – even when in the presence of others … just letting things lie, go their own way.

WATCH OUT FOR … exhausting yourself and others and making matters worse by trying to force a resolution or agreement.

 KARMA/ATTITUDE/HEALTH

This strongly suggests that widespread scourge of modern life, insomnia, whether it is a case of not being able to get to sleep, waking up in the middle of the night, sleeping fitfully, or a combination of these. There are many reasons for it, such as anxiety, depression, worry, insecurity, an over-active left-brain, bad conscience or over-conscientiousness. There are also many recommended cures, but very few of them work for long or at all, otherwise the problem would decrease, whereas it is increasing.

KEEP FOCUSED ON … finding the root cause of your particular case, perhaps using the Oracle to help track it down … knowing, like a tired traveller, that the knowledge that a resting place lies ahead is relieving in itself … adjusting to the pattern, or breaking it with the *temporary* use of medication.

WATCH OUT FOR … being too hard on yourself.

'Sleep/Come unto me/Stay/While I might mend/My violated vehicle.
O sleep/Stay with me/Until dawn'

THE MAGIC CARPET

☆ ELEVATED OVERVIEW ☆

 GENERAL INTERPRETATION

Offered or needed now are the means to see the overall layout of things, and thereby provide a more all-inclusive view of whatever one is looking at. The possibility of taking off to visit realms quite different to those of the everyday world and observe and wonder at them, but not necessarily get involved. Astral travelling.

KEEP FOCUSED ON ... any means at your disposal with which to get a better idea or view of the overall situation ... adventures that can make a life for you that others would merely dream about ... the fact that there is more in your imagination than there is in the physical world.

WATCH OUT FOR ... forming opinions or making decisions when you are not aware of the whole picture, or are looking at a whimsical or neurotic version of your situation ... impossible flights of fancy and the disaster they can bring.

♥ LOVE/RELATING/SOCIAL

Here we have the heady romance that can take you on a wonderful journey, or for a ride. Whichever the case, everything depends upon gaining a more objective perspective, one way or the other, sooner or later.

KEEP FOCUSED ON ... where such elated or deluded feelings are taking you; do they make you feel happy yet still aware of the everyday aspects of life, or do they have you hoping against hope and not connecting with where the other person is coming from? ... being ruthlessly honest with yourself in answering these questions.

WATCH OUT FOR ... being romantically or socially deluded ... being so aloof or alienated that you cannot expect to have a 'normal' social life ... not coming down to earth to meet your emotional responsibilities.

 MONEY/WORK/CREATIVITY

The object of your concern either has to do with an overall, comprehensive view of things, or is in need of it. It could well be both.

KEEP FOCUSED ON ... the possibility that there is a way of attaining this comprehensive, aerial view. This could be the use of creative imagination or astral projection, conducting or obtaining some kind of survey – or both ... introducing a bit of wonder into people's lives ... having a more commanding view of whatever it is you are dealing with ... considering the whole or world-market situation, rather than just your limited or immediate sphere.

WATCH OUT FOR ... losing sight of the everyday needs and concerns of people, while at the same time giving or getting the false impression that you are aware of them ... rambling on and losing the plot.

☉ KARMA/ATTITUDE/HEALTH

This is a serious case of two choices. You can carry on living the 'high life', which can mean anything you want it to mean, but it usually amounts to some form of escapism. Or you are at a point in your development when the adoption of some more transcendent means of living and perceiving is on the cards. Rising above an issue.

KEEP FOCUSED ON ... using meditation or creative visualization to 'see' what can be seen from an elevated, detached viewpoint, and to 'image forth' a better situation or state of health for all concerned ... finding out how to do this if you do not already know ... inner flight.

WATCH OUT FOR ... letting your imagination get the better of you as you assume that either the worst or the best is going to happen, when more likely than not it is taking place purely in your head ... 'wonder' drugs, treatments or doctrines.

'We carry within us the wonders we seek without us'

A YOUNG GIRL FEEDING BIRDS IN WINTER

✵ NURTURE OF THE NEEDFUL ✵

 GENERAL INTERPRETATION

Here and now Nature looks after Her own, particularly during times of need. Sustainment through hard times thanks to the kindness of soulful or natural people, or through a matter-of-fact generosity born of innocence.

KEEP FOCUSED ON ... the simple pleasure and sense of communion that is gained from giving food and attention to others of the animal kingdom – or giving to the spiritual or physical welfare of any beings ... your naive genius for seeing to immediate needs in an admirably straightforward fashion ... doing whatever you do out of innocence; God, if not society, looks after the innocent.

WATCH OUT FOR ... the devotion of too much time and energy towards a pet concern, maybe in order to avoid normal social interaction ... being motivated by guilt or dubious motives.

 LOVE/RELATING/SOCIAL

Even though love or social life may not be all you hope, either you are sustained through it and by it, or you are the sustaining influence yourself. Implied is the possibility that there is someone who is in need of such care, a care that is, or should be, given as a joy in itself.

KEEP FOCUSED ON ... the beauty of such simple care and love that is made available to you or by you ... the idea that virtue is its own reward ... the fact that emotionally lean times do not last forever ... handing out love, support and affection wherever and whenever you find the need for it.

WATCH OUT FOR ... emotional poverty consciousness, that is, collapsing into the belief that you are only worth 'crumbs' of support and affection; or just doling out same as a means of 'treat 'em mean, keep 'em keen'.

 MONEY/WORK/CREATIVITY

You receive enough to tide you over while you prepare for the Spring of more fruitful or creative times. Or, if you are in the business of helping out those who are deprived, or dependent on those better off, then the Oracle smiles upon you.

KEEP FOCUSED ON ... exercising economy and you will not want for anything that is essential to your progress and welfare ... entertaining the idea of non-profit making whenever necessary or possible ... the whole concept of mutual or symbiotic sustainment, such as bartering and knowing that generosity generates generosity.

WATCH OUT FOR ... opportunists who take advantage of hand-outs when they have no need of them ... big ambitious enterprises without due fore-thought, or get-rich-quick schemes, because you are not personally suited to them or do not have the appropriate ideas or resources – yet.

 KARMA/ATTITUDE/HEALTH

Innocence and a closeness to Nature attract support and guidance – possibly in the form of spiritual messengers, something of which birds are symbolic. Furthermore, you and others are living through a time that could be regarded as 'spiritual winter', in that egoism and materialism are to the fore. There is a great need for those who are able to keep the spirit fed through such times, in whatever way one can, and no matter in what form one encounters such a need. So ...

KEEP FOCUSED ON ... helping anything or anyone that is natural and innocent and feed it with whatever it requires ... the fact that the health of the whole planet depends upon the conservation and respect of the natural world and the inner world of the soul.

WATCH OUT FOR ... leaving it to others to do all such caring; as many as possible must do so.

'He rained down manna for the people to eat, He gave them the grain of heaven'

A BOXER ENTERING THE RING

☆ FIGHT THE GOOD FIGHT ☆

✳ GENERAL INTERPRETATION

Your situation poses the raw desire to win and this necessitates having an uncompromising attitude, being prepared to suffer personal damage, and to be fit to cope with what you have in mind. Without being thus equipped, you are in danger of suffering a beating or taking a fall.

KEEP FOCUSED ON ... the realization of your talents in a concentrated attempt at establishing yourself ... affirming to yourself regularly 'I can, I must, and I will' – but make sure you really are cut out for what you are after.

WATCH OUT FOR ... thinking that you can get what you want merely by asking; you have to train and prepare for it, and then go for it and fight for it ... a blinkered and selfish pushiness, or shyness, both of which inevitably encounter defeat ... cowardice, for this leads to even harder lessons.

🏆 MONEY/WORK/CREATIVITY

Whatever your chosen field of activity might be, you have to take on something or someone in order to win, whatever position, reward or honours you are after. That something or someone could be external, such as a professional rival or the state of the market, or internal, such as your own inner doubts, lethargy and indecisiveness. As for the 'prize money' or financial aspect to all this, you have to fight to win it because it won't just be given you. But it *is* there to be won.

KEEP FOCUSED ON ... gathering around you a team – in the form of discipline, talent and effort – that supports and encourages you ... taking on someone or something that is the same 'weight' as you, that you are equal to, otherwise you'd be either asking for defeat, or you'd just be cheating.

WATCH OUT FOR ... taking unnecessary punishment; throw in the towel if need be.

♥ LOVE/RELATING/SOCIAL

Nearly every relationship has conflict within it and battles that have to be fought out. If this is not to degenerate into violent words or actions, a set of 'rules' is needed in the form of self-control born of an enlightened perception of such conflicts.

KEEP FOCUSED ON ... being firm and standing your ground rather than having to attack or defend ... seeing another as your 'worthy opponent', someone who is there to test or force you to forge your assertiveness, mettle, principles and, most of all, independence ... using 'gloves' (softening the blow) ... fighting fair ... boxing clever.

WATCH OUT FOR ... 'foul punches' – avoid or ignore them, otherwise things could go from bad to worse ... fighting another's fights for them ... getting into fights you cannot win; back off.

☯ KARMA/ATTITUDE/HEALTH

The fighting spirit, as distinct from mere aggression and violence for its own sake, is very real. In essence, it is the yang or male energy within us that has to find its proper measure and expression. This started purely as the hunter or survival instinct, but as we evolve, it evolves too.

KEEP FOCUSED ON ... what you are actually, or should be, fighting for, and go about it in a straightforward way ... assertiveness training, or fighting off your own negativity.

WATCH OUT FOR ... suppressing the fighting spirit, for a reason such as past abuse, feeling a victim or a loser, or not recognizing that anger and stress – in yourself or those around you – are signs that your Mars or red energy is not being properly expressed through a physical or creative activity, or by fighting your own corner.

'Courage is not simply one of the virtues, but the form of every virtue at its testing point'

THE GATE TO THE GARDEN OF DESIRE

☆ THE PLEASURE – PAIN PRINCIPLE ☆

 GENERAL INTERPRETATION

The prospect of sexual experience, physical or material pleasure, or whatever delights and longings, anxieties and doubts this might present one with. There is a pronounced female phallic symbolism here as well.

KEEP FOCUSED ON ... seizing the opportunity that is presenting itself to you, while at the same time not giving in to temptation or else you could get more than you bargained for ... your strong awareness or possession of whatever people find irresistibly attractive ... the profits, pleasures and responsibilities that accompany this.

WATCH OUT FOR ... forever dallying with what appeals to others' or one's own most basic needs and urges, but never taking the plunge into the joys and sorrows of closer intimacy.

LOVE/RELATING/SOCIAL

Although the General Interpretation applies here well enough, in the context of relationships the prospect of sensual or sexual experience needs to be explored to a greater degree. Issues of satisfaction and frustration, of real experience and mere fantasy, can be a small or great distance apart, depending on your physical and emotional state.

KEEP FOCUSED ON ... what is practically attainable and avoid making yourself sore chasing what is not ... the clarity and opinion of those you trust to give you a clearer idea of where you stand ... making as sure as possible what you want before taking what could be a fateful step.

WATCH OUT FOR ... allowing your feelings to build up into a red mist through which you cannot see the situation clearly ... feelings of rejection; their cause is bound to go back to childhood.

MONEY/WORK/CREATIVITY

You are very close to what you are after – or at least close enough to see it. The nature of your work should be concerned with the basic appetites and drives of human nature – anything from food to sex – or simply the concerns of womanhood. Financially, you are near to getting or receiving what you are after, but be very careful what else the 'deal' might involve because you could wind up having to pay something that you can't afford.

KEEP FOCUSED ON ... following your most obvious ambitions through to a point of realization or accomplishment ... keeping headed in the same direction and you will achieve your objective.

WATCH OUT FOR ... letting your desires get the better of you to the point of blinding you to the best way of satisfying them. Ambition must always be tempered with patience and prudence.

KARMA/ATTITUDE/HEALTH

We are presented here with the age-old question of what place desire has in the spiritual or greater scheme of things. Some say that it is our desires that get us into trouble in the first place, so they should be avoided or sublimated at all costs. Then again, there are spiritual disciplines that have the controlled and informed expression and experience of desire as their central theme. In the end, everything depends on what level you as a unique individual are functioning in this lifetime.

KEEP FOCUSED ON AND WATCH OUT FOR ... who or what is associated with your desires, in all their respects, and if you find any of them beneath you, then pursuing them will take you down; if they are above you, then they will take you up. If they are some of both they will take you round and round in an ascending or descending spiral, depending on which has the greater influence ... health issues, for they originate from difficulties with sexual expression.

'Strange, the desire for certain pleasures is a part of my pain'

A WOMAN IN PASTEL COLOURS CARRYING A HEAVY AND VALUABLE BUT VEILED LOAD

☆ IMPORTANT BURDEN ☆

❂ GENERAL INTERPRETATION

You are carrying out important and weighty responsibilities but, because of the need for privacy or secrecy, others might erroneously see you as being superficial or as shirking those responsibilities.

KEEP FOCUSED ON ... making sure you do your best to bear your load with dignity and with a lightness of heart. Your hidden strength of character is all the stronger for having to remain so ... the fact that modesty is a thoroughly desirable and character-building trait.

WATCH OUT FOR ... complicated subterfuges that sabotage your ultimate objectives ... superficial displays that conceal deeper feelings, thereby isolating you even more.

♥ LOVE/RELATING/SOCIAL

A relationship or individual whose emotional sensitivity or vulnerability has to be camouflaged or given the lie to in some way, because it is unlikely that it will be appreciated or understood. This Symbol could also image an apparently superficial person with a heavy heart.

KEEP FOCUSED ON ... presenting a 'light' and uncontroversial image in order to avoid awkward confrontations or heavy atmospheres ... letting things pass unless there is something critical at stake ... trusting that your weight of personality alone will carry the day, make the point.

WATCH OUT FOR ... being challenging or provocative; you are in too vulnerable a position to be this way ... sweeping heavy and important issues under the carpet, solely because you are afraid to face the inevitable consequences.

⚜ MONEY/WORK/CREATIVITY

The object of your concern is probably harder than it looks, or than it first appeared. Or, more subtly, its nature is such that it has to be given a light and easy image in order that others will initially be drawn to it and then, ultimately, to its heavier and harder content. This could be referring to the 'packaging' of your product or idea.

KEEP FOCUSED ON ... the fact that you do indeed have something of great value to offer, but that its success depends upon its presentation ... making sure you are appreciated for your hard work.

WATCH OUT FOR ... whether or not you really do have what it takes to carry your issue through all the various stages of its development ... things that are just not going to make it until the world is ready for them; if this is the case, you will have to decide whether or not to continue carrying that load.

☯ KARMA/ATTITUDE/HEALTH

This sounds as if you are carrying some kind of karmic weight, or it could be an internal complaint (which might amount to the same thing), or, then again, it could be a baby! In any event, you need to pierce or remove anything that is obscuring the fact that this is a karmic burden or simply your fears. While keeping others in the dark is sometimes advisable, keeping yourself in the dark is not.

KEEP FOCUSED ON ... the fact that you will feel the better for getting to the truth of the matter, for the chances are that the suggestion of something ominous is usually far worse than the thing itself ... the possibility that the object of your concern is important enough to merit special consideration from those that matter.

WATCH OUT FOR ... situations in which it is prudent only to let those you really trust into your 'secret' ... carrying anything that you are not prepared to take ultimate responsibility for.

'Thus does the superior man live with the great mass: he veils his light but still shines'

AN OPEN WINDOW AND A NET CURTAIN BLOWING INTO A CORNUCOPIA

☆ RECEPTIVE TO REWARD ☆

✿ GENERAL INTERPRETATION

Here is the openness of mind and heart that welcomes every experience, be it a challenge or a blessing, with equal faith and enthusiasm, and in doing so receives the very best that life, chance and change have to offer. This Symbol could also be alluding to the womb – or to a blessing in disguise.

KEEP FOCUSED ON ... your sense of the direct and immediate link between your own being and life itself, giving rise to spontaneous and uncontrived successes, even though they may at first seem an unwelcome intrusion.

WATCH OUT FOR ... good fortune that seems merely to amount to naivety or prodigality ... trusting too much in luck ... shutting out what at first looks intrusive but is actually good fortune.

♥ LOVE/RELATING/SOCIAL

A relationship, group or individual is open to being influenced in a subtle or suggestive manner. Such input will benefit them and, consciously or unconsciously, they are aware of this. Equally, the individual could be you.

KEEP FOCUSED ON ... sending out good thoughts and feelings and they will be picked up and reciprocated ... reading between the lines as to what someone is trying to convey to you, even though, or especially because, it is vague or awkward.

WATCH OUT FOR ... shutting someone out because what they are or what they are offering is insubstantial or superficial. It can still amount to something if you give it a chance to develop ... what is just hot air (insincere words).

♟ MONEY/WORK/CREATIVITY

Sometimes we have to undergo a disturbance or invasion of privacy if we wish to make a success in the public domain or gain some kind of inspiration. Advertising or putting yourself about, which is what this Symbol could be alluding to, will attract both good and bad reactions. Crucially, it is a point of determining what, on balance, you are laying yourself open to.

KEEP FOCUSED ON ... what is the worst and the best that your accessibility or imagination is going to pull in. If it is likely to be troublesome to the point of not justifying what you could gain, then withdraw. Bear in mind that this Symbol is basically one that anticipates good fortune.

WATCH OUT FOR ... exposing to the world anything that you feel would make you vulnerable, or to anything and anyone that does not respect your private world.

☯ KARMA/ATTITUDE/HEALTH

This is a Symbol of receptivity to Spirit and the abundance and wonders that It can bring. It also refers to the way in which the wind, as Nature's means of spreading things around, affects us personally. What is 'blowing in the wind' is something that one can pick up and make something of, or be lifted up by.

KEEP FOCUSED ON ... allowing whatever veils or protects your inner being to be blown aside and transformed into something of value. For example, inhibitions can prevent good things from happening to you; so, loosening up and being more transparent would improve your lot.

WATCH OUT FOR ... being too open psychically, thereby making yourself vulnerable to bad input such as negative emotions. Learn to seal your chakras.

'Tis an ill wind that blows nobody any good'

A DOUBLE PROMISE

☆ EVERYTHING IS GOING TO BE ALL RIGHT ☆

⊛ GENERAL INTERPRETATION

Assurance here is backed up by belief. Or, for example, one could be saying to oneself, 'not only will I accomplish so-and-so, I will also be healthy enough to enjoy it'. Things will work out right as long as you keep your promises to yourself.

KEEP FOCUSED ON ... any means at your disposal with which to maintain an inner conviction, coupled with a practical ability that assures you of every success.

WATCH OUT FOR ... fooling yourself or others without having the slightest clue that one is doing so. The 'Walter Mitty syndrome', living a fantasy life; or being on the receiving end of such ... making or believing promises that can't be kept.

♡ LOVE/RELATING/SOCIAL

Indicated here is a particularly positive and reliable situation. Such is the level of love and commitment, you will overcome whatever challenges or difficulties may assail you and yours. This is saying that any promises are very unlikely to be broken because they are 'double-strength'.

KEEP FOCUSED ON ... maintaining ongoing faith in whatever or whoever is the object of your concern for it is this that instils faith and trust. In turn, this is what encourages faith and trust in the other person, for they have been shown through you that such genuine qualities exist. The roles could be reversed, with you the one being shown and taught to trust by someone else.

WATCH OUT FOR ... believing at face value promises that are not borne out by experience, especially when there is a poor track record.

⚑ MONEY/WORK/CREATIVITY

Faith backed up by action is the formula for success here. Any doubts or tensions would be signs that one or both of these vital ingredients were missing, for faith and action are respectively the opposites of doubt and tension (action held back).

KEEP FOCUSED ON ... making some kind of promise (in the form of a target or reward) for efforts made – for yourself or others. The carrot-on-a-stick method is a valid one.

WATCH OUT FOR ... making impossible promises to yourself or others out of a misguided need to make an impression. Also, be on your guard against others who are promising more than they can deliver ... conflicting promises made to more than one party, thereby making one or both of them impossible to make good.

⊛ KARMA/ATTITUDE/HEALTH

Promises made by you or to you is the karmic issue here. Previously, you may have repeatedly made a promise. Now you are having to make that promise good. Alternatively, a string of promises were made to you that were broken, and so you now are having a hard time trusting and believing. There may be other variations on this theme, but essentially ...

KEEP FOCUSED ON ... the ins and outs of pledges given or received (possibly unconsciously), and ascertaining who should be living up to what. Basically, you cannot force anyone but yourself to make or keep a promise – so what is your promise to yourself? 'Doubling' in symbolism means that the relevant issue is coming into the consciousness to be addressed and acted upon.

WATCH OUT FOR ... how promises (to yourself or another) that are not kept can affect your well-being.

'A promise made is a debt unpaid, and the trail has its own stern code'

A MAN POSSESSED OF MORE GIFTS THAN HE CAN HOLD

☆ SPOILT FOR CHOICE ☆

GENERAL INTERPRETATION

This would seem to be a case of being endowed with more than one knows what to do with – which is a perverse sort of problem. Implied then, is the challenge to discriminate between what is of pertinent worth and what is not. Or it could be a case of feeling or having more than one can express or satisfy.

KEEP FOCUSED ON ... whatever it is that you have that you need or appreciate most ... your un-compromising independence and the support that it gives to others in the form of spin-offs ... giving away what you do not need for yourself ... only on what you have, not what you cannot have.

WATCH OUT FOR ... being incapacitated through indecision, or being greedy for more than you can use or enjoy ... spreading yourself too thinly ... feeding your frustrations.

❤ LOVE/RELATING/SOCIAL

This describes a number of scenarios or types of people: someone who has too much going on in their lives to make it possible to commit to another person; someone who is indulged or desired so much by others or one other so they are not that appreciative – too full a social life. Whatever the case, the problem is one that is not necessarily apparent until later, when some of the 'gifts' fade, fall away or lose their value, or when one recognizes that 'a bird in the hand is worth two in the bush'.

KEEP FOCUSED ON ... eventually settling for what is solid and reliable rather than frothy or unpredictable ... withdrawing your attention or involvement until everyone knows which side their bread is buttered.

WATCH OUT FOR ... falling between two stools; trying to have your cake and eat it.

♟ MONEY/WORK/CREATIVITY

You probably have a lot going for you, but it needs management and direction. Otherwise, there is, so to speak, the danger of putting in the front window what should be kept in the back, and vice versa. Failing to appreciate what you have can also lead to issues around remuneration – where you are under- or over-charging, or just being plain wasteful.

KEEP FOCUSED ON ... itemizing what you have going for you and then allocating worth and significance to each. This will give you a healthier perspective on your assets, revealing areas of underestimation and overestimation ... whatever you have that is needed or appreciated most by others, and make sure that it is priced accordingly.

WATCH OUT FOR ... feeling you are on a roll and not noticing that some snag is developing outside your line of vision.

☯ KARMA/ATTITUDE/HEALTH

Finding yourself with more than you can manage, as a result of not having done so previously or of accumulating and not sharing as you did so. Also, for human beings, sensitivity is a great gift that we may find a burden because we do not know how to handle or express it well. Physically, an example of this mismanagement can be when the immune system goes into overload as one fights against oneself, or over-defends oneself.

KEEP FOCUSED ON ... a regimen of relaxation that quells the desire nature, dampens down the fight-and-flight impulse thereby stopping you from overreacting to external stimuli ... processing past traumas and other experiences that you no longer have the room to contain.

WATCH OUT FOR ... biting off more than you can chew ... entertaining or being overwhelmed by too many possibilities.

'Stop wanting, start having'

A LOST OPPORTUNITY REGAINED IN THE IMAGINATION

☆ THE POWER OF VISUALIZATION ☆

GENERAL INTERPRETATION

You can regain what appears to have been lost through the use of thoughtful reflection and visualization. If you have mislaid or forgotten something, if you wish to recapture an experience or in some way turn the clock back in order to rerun or recall something important to you, then turn your attention inwards and play back the scenario in question. Then, as you …

KEEP FOCUSED ON … your issues in an intent fashion, you will find what you are looking for … maintaining a creative attitude that transcends or sees a way through confusion and dismay … going through all the steps that led up to the situation; you will then discover the answer.

WATCH OUT FOR … idly pondering or just losing yourself in feelings of hopelessness, impotence or self-pity.

MONEY/WORK/CREATIVITY

The situation calls for a long ponder, a brainstorming session, or time out to reflect upon the pros and cons of something again in the offing. Creatively speaking, this Symbol could be referring to the resurrection of an idea or project, the potential of which was not made enough of previously, or it could simply mean that you need to get your thinking cap on in order to get something off the ground.

KEEP FOCUSED ON … any profitable scheme that has been lying around waiting to be regenerated … reviewing your situation with an eye for any opportunity or item you may have missed … making the best of another chance that is presenting itself.

WATCH OUT FOR … wasting too much time or resources on something that is hypothetical or merely at the theory stage, or that you simply cannot remember no matter how hard you try.

LOVE/RELATING/SOCIAL

Your emotional life or present situation can now benefit from concentrating upon the object of your love or concern. In particular, if there has been some kind of upset, it can be repaired, or the ground made ready for reconciliation.

KEEP FOCUSED ON … an image of the other person in your mind's eye and hold it there with loving and caring attention, allowing your feelings to respond freely towards this image. This sends a positive message that, unless you are merely hoping against hope, will attract a welcome response from the other person.

WATCH OUT FOR … trying to imagine someone into doing what you think you want them to do; active visualization such as recommended here does not work – or can backfire – if a selfish will is involved in this way.

KARMA/ATTITUDE/HEALTH

Now a connection can be made with invisible helpers such as Angels or friendly spirits by building a bridge to them with your imagination. Also, health matters can be aided or facilitated in this way, be it by visualizing healthy tissue or growth (or a baby in the womb), or an image of an area the condition of which you wish to diagnose.

KEEP FOCUSED ON … an image or idea of some divine or metaphysical entity and this will invoke them, literally a mental construct … the actual physical nature or process of the relevant part or function of the body (by looking it up in a book, for example) and then 'see' it being there or happening. Listen to what your body is telling you … performing these visualization techniques frequently and regularly.

WATCH OUT FOR … only making a few attempts at this; for success one has to persist.

'Happiness is not an ideal of reason but of imagination'

A LARGE DISAPPOINTED AUDIENCE

☆ WHO TO BE TRUE TO? ☆

✲ GENERAL INTERPRETATION

Being in the doldrums or an unsatisfactory situation as a result of bad timing or inappropriate behaviour. The transience of popularity, the fickleness of the masses. The inadvisability of relying on the crowd for approval, when inner values should be the only criteria. All this poses the basic balance or decisiveness that this Symbol calls for – being true to yourself and pleasing others.

KEEP FOCUSED ON ... developing an inner independence that is your true security and centre, rather than playing to the gallery all the time. Paradoxically, this in itself has the ultimate appeal ... being clear what your pitch is.

WATCH OUT FOR ... the downward spiral of despondency caused by a dependence on the passing whims of society ... in what way, if any, you expect too much or aim too high.

♥ LOVE/RELATING/SOCIAL

This indicates an unpromising relationship, or a way of relating that is unlikely to get what is wanted or that invites a distinctly negative response. In astrological terms, the 'synastry' (planetary connections between one person and another) is not compatible or conducive to harmony and pleasure, or to security and commitment.

KEEP FOCUSED ON ... what your illusions are with regard to the situation, as they hold the key to why you are in it – or not in it, as the case may be. You will have to be very honest with yourself here. A fairly reliable sign that an illusion is on the loose is that one person wants what the other does not, or that what both or all parties initially thought looked great starts to show cracks.

WATCH OUT FOR ... unrealistic expectations or thinking something is desirable when it's not.

♔ MONEY/WORK/CREATIVITY

A lack of the common touch, or awareness of where the public is at, is the most likely problem, unless you are prepared to carry on regardless with a project simply to please yourself. In any event, material success is not to be expected, at least, not if you stick to the same formula.

KEEP FOCUSED ON ... what is the 'inscape' of your public, customers or audience. Inscape is the internal landscape of needs and predilections that is present in all people, and tuning into this is the key to commercial success – rightly or wrongly.

WATCH OUT FOR ... being attached to any kind of pet idea for this will only breed success in your eyes if you have them closed to what is *really* going on ... the possibility that your idea/product/style is not bad but just out of sync with what is happening. So, don't scrap it, put it on the back burner.

♄ KARMA/ATTITUDE/HEALTH

Being out of sorts or off course, or a case of 'bad karma' – something negative that was done previously is revealing itself now, or is about to. Collectively, it could be referring to something that was culturally acceptable once but is no longer so. Then again, the 'disappointed audience' could well be mistaken, for what is hated today may be loved tomorrow.

KEEP FOCUSED ON ... your conscience and obey what it is telling you ... what is currently acceptable in your culture ... what your beliefs, ideals or principles are, and if they are worth going it alone for, waiting for the world to catch up with, or catch on to ... recuperating.

WATCH OUT FOR ... going against the current out of a sense of righteousness that is more likely to be bloody-mindedness born of past failure or maltreatment. This could prove most unhealthy.

'Commercialism is doing well that which should not be done at all'

A CELESTIAL CHOIR SINGING

☆ COSMIC ATTUNEMENT ☆

☀ GENERAL INTERPRETATION

Here is the Music of the Spheres: the idea or reality that Creation is akin to music in that everything and everyone has a note, part or piece to play that contributes to a symphonic whole, and that Evolution is a process of development analogous to a musical theme with its movements, stanzas and rhythms. The Angels are Divine agencies intoning such Music that we might more easily hear it, and live our individual lives in accordance with it.

KEEP FOCUSED ON ... your genius for aptly expressing the poetic and harmonious themes that permeate the fabric of reality, thereby enabling yourself and others to experience their individual place in it ... astrology itself as the celestial 'score'.

WATCH OUT FOR ... having an inflated, high and mighty sense of self that is out of tune with the everyday world. There is only one way to go from there – down.

♡ LOVE/RELATING/SOCIAL

This could be a marriage made in Heaven that you have or are after – but bringing it down to Earth could be a problem. You like or want your social life to be something that is closely knit and concerted, rather than a haphazard mingling of people. Such tall orders for these areas of your life require that you ...

KEEP FOCUSED ON ... the spiritual rather than the exclusively mundane, sexual or emotional side to relationships ... creating or joining a group of people that pursues specific rituals that have a metaphysical interest.

WATCH OUT FOR ... having your social, sexual or romantic expectations frustrated by looking or dwelling among people and places that do not cater to your appetite for the lofty or divine.

MONEY/WORK/CREATIVITY

Your work, and/or its functioning, is all about harmony and being attuned to a higher frame of reference. Music itself, maybe. Whatever career or money problems you might have are down to a part of you or yours being out of tune with the whole. This is rather like an orchestra or band having to practise and practise until they get it right.

KEEP FOCUSED ON ... discovering or being true to whatever greater whole, organization or movement that you are, or want to be, a part of ... putting in the time and effort to 'get it right' ... the fact that there are higher forces that are helping you, but you must tune into that high-frequency waveband ... that goal of success through the harmony that you can see or hear in your head.

WATCH OUT FOR ... settling for less than your best ... forgetting you are helped from on high.

☯ KARMA/ATTITUDE/HEALTH

This Symbol is saying that your life or soul has reached a point where it can and must be attuned to a greater pattern of existence. Yours is the quest for harmony leading to the attainment of true spirituality. Each part of your being has ultimately to be in harmony with every other part, utilizing a form of cosmic attunement such as astrology, Angels, or any cosmology that appeals to you.

KEEP FOCUSED ON ... anything and anyone that has an unmistakable beauty or harmony about them – be they animal, human or divine, or in Nature ... taking time to develop an ear for your inner voice, through such methods as chanting, meditation, yoga and tai chi.

WATCH OUT FOR ... any part of your body playing up, for this would be a sign that it, and the aspect of your personality that corresponds to it, is out of tune with the whole.

'A band of angels coming after me, coming for to carry me home'

A DUCK POND AND ITS BROOD

☆ MOTHER NATURE'S BOSOM ☆

 GENERAL INTERPRETATION

At hand is a complete and natural system of security and peace. Even though there are external dangers that may threaten, there is here the image and sense of something eternal and ordered.

KEEP FOCUSED ON ... your innate awareness of how best to take care of you and yours, which has something to do with accepting limitations as an integral part of the stability. If you are at a distance from those others, regularly and frequently visualize those you wish to protect as being in a safe place.

WATCH OUT FOR ... fussing and fretting because this would only create or attract the very disturbance you are anxious about ... a smug and narrow conception of life and what it has to offer.

 LOVE/RELATING/SOCIAL

There is a strong indication here of the significance of family and family-making, or of being 'in the fold', so consider what this might mean in the context of your question.

KEEP FOCUSED ON ... the importance of the family unit, perhaps making it a priority ... the fact that if you wish to have security, then there have to be limitations and not too much, or perhaps very little, excitement ... emphasizing the essentially caring, passive and instinctual nature of the situation.

WATCH OUT FOR ... allowing your relationships to be subsumed with *too much* concern for safety and security. Insisting on a quiet life can make you blind to the very things you fear might disrupt it – this could simply amount to boredom.

 MONEY/WORK/CREATIVITY

Seeing and managing your project or situation in terms of the natural scheme of things can be very helpful and profitable. Essentially, we have here the individual items, people or ideas (brood), the situation, environment, plot (pond), and the one who is making it productive and secure (duck). Tailor your concern to this image of organic order.

KEEP FOCUSED ON ... giving everything in your interest, and everyone under your care and control, an equal chance; then see what or who naturally survives the test of time, for they have, or will create, a strong future ... creating a secure base of operations or source of information and inspiration.

WATCH OUT FOR ... any kind of 'predator' who could steal away what you have invested so much time, care and energy in ... limiting yourself, owing to a fear of the outside world.

KARMA/ATTITUDE/HEALTH

From a background of natural order, peace and safety, springs something equally wholesome and reassuring. Conversely, a negative karma here could be quite the opposite – a background lacking in love and/or boundaries. A 'fox' or some predator could have appeared on the scene.

KEEP FOCUSED ON ... giving liberally to those less fortunate, who have not got the sense of belonging bestowed by a sound lineage ... whatever it is that gives you a sense of constant reliable security.

WATCH OUT FOR ... 'agoraphobia' or 'claustrophobia' induced by an overly restrictive regime or set-up ... whatever is breeding or accumulating where it should not ... interfering with the natural order of things for it knows better than you what constitutes security, peace or productivity.

'From troubles of the world/I turn to ducks/Beautiful comical things'

THE SABIAN SYMBOLS OF
TAURUS

Either directly, or in a subtle way, all these Symbols are concerned with the following qualities, or with situations that involve or call for them:

CONSUMERISM

FARMING AND GARDENING

FECUNDITY

INERTIA

MONEY

NATURAL BEAUTY AND HARMONY

THE NECK AND THROAT

PHYSICAL SENSATION

POSSESSION

PRODUCTIVENESS

STABILITY

TALENT

WORTH

A CLEAR MOUNTAIN STREAM

☆ NATURAL INCLINATION ☆

GENERAL INTERPRETATION

Here is a purity of intent, or a pure sense of being, that naturally finds a path through life from source to source. Obstacles are simply gone around, or time is taken to overcome or rise above them. Similarly, depressions are just filled up and then the path is continued upon.

KEEP FOCUSED ON ... the sureness of direction that you have, even though you may not be aware of what it is. It is your instinctive sense of coming from where you came from, and going where you will, that is the essential thing ... following the line of least resistance with innocent and trusting intent.

WATCH OUT FOR ... a simplistic attitude that is blind to the complications and convolutions of life and others ... meandering aimlessly.

LOVE/RELATING/SOCIAL

Here is a healthy relationship or way of relating that, as long as it remains true to itself, will eventually find what it wants and needs. This does not mean that it won't encounter difficulties, for there will almost certainly be times when it isn't that clear what move to make without making compromises.

KEEP FOCUSED ON ... your most wholesome needs and natural feelings. You are bound to get through any difficulty while at the same time refreshing others with a fresh and bubbling personality ... always showing how you feel.

WATCH OUT FOR ... influences that could pollute your innocent and straightforward nature ... anything that tempts you to hold back from spontaneously expressing how you feel ... allowing feelings to build up or be blocked.

MONEY/WORK/CREATIVITY

Here is cash or creative flow. Something or someone that perennially revitalizes and inspires. The inner certainty of reaching your destination or goal.

KEEP FOCUSED ON ... your beginnings, what has gone before and behind you. This should tell you how matters will or should now proceed for there is a reliable continuity or tradition to your working life and earning or creative power. There will be times when there is a danger of drying up or losing direction, but in time you will always be replenished and regain that sense of where you are supposed to go.

WATCH OUT FOR ... getting bogged down in side issues or feelings of doubt ... trying to go faster than you need or are able to ... anyone or anything that could deflect you, particularly with offers or means that go against Nature and wholesome practices.

KARMA/ATTITUDE/HEALTH

This Symbol can be interpreted as the Life-Stream itself. Your soul can be seen as proceeding through various forms of terrain (lifetimes) as it journeys from source to source. Health is maintained by never clinging to anything for longer than is necessary; likewise, many complaints will simply pass, especially if you don't fuss over them.

KEEP FOCUSED ON ... life as being a stream, flowing ever onward, visualizing the sea as that great freedom and mystery that you are bound to get to one day, which is also the womb of life ... finding a way around obstacles, the path of least resistance ... feeling buoyed up by the Life Force.

WATCH OUT FOR ... losing touch with the natural flow of events, through skipping over issues or dwelling too long on anything.

'Flow like a flower, fall like a shower'

AN ELECTRICAL STORM

☆ DISCHARGE OF TENSION ☆

 GENERAL INTERPRETATION

What is happening, or needs to happen, is some form of impressive impact on the environment that clears the air by discharging pent-up energies. It also makes one aware of the power of Nature, or the object of your enquiry. The element of surprise.

KEEP FOCUSED ON ... your special talent for dramatizing a situation and thereby catalysing those involved into realizing their true potential ... the fact that such shocks cannot last forever, which should help you to remain placid and in control ... releasing what tension you can through physical exercise or exertion.

WATCH OUT FOR ... an explosive temperament that creates more tension than it releases ... staying around dangerous or threatening places and people.

 LOVE/RELATING/SOCIAL

It may need a shock or bolt from the blue to get things moving or sorted out on the emotional front. A breakthrough may also occur as a result of such a disruption, possibly through deep or long-buried feelings being forced to the surface. A fuse may have to be blown before you know what the fault is – or that there even is one. Sexual tension.

KEEP FOCUSED ON ... not being afraid to experience hairy or emotionally embarrassing situations for they open the way to greater closeness and understanding, and thereby peace ... how you become stronger through emotional storms and shocks – shockproof, in fact.

WATCH OUT FOR ... overreacting or going over the top and then finding you have a runaway train on your hands. Just let off enough steam so as not to blow up the boiler.

 MONEY/WORK/CREATIVITY

Lightning responses and intuitive decision-making are now called for. Brilliant ideas could be at hand or in play. Something surprising or spectacular occurring that makes everyone concerned sit up and take notice. If your work or actions involves such an effect then this is an auspicious oracle. However, it is very important that you ...

KEEP FOCUSED ON ... being accurate and precise ... keeping a cool head in the midst of any crisis or disruption ... interpreting shocks or unforeseen difficulties as being a spur to action.

WATCH OUT FOR ... being sensational for its own sake, or just making sparks and loud noises that mean nothing or merely upset others rather than draw their attention or make them aware ... anything apparently good or advantageous that happens suddenly, for it cannot necessarily be relied upon, or you must strike while the iron is hot.

KARMA/ATTITUDE/HEALTH

Pressure has been building up for some time, perhaps even lifetimes, and must now find a form of release. A catharsis, that is, a purging of the effects of pent-up emotions and repressed thoughts through them being quickened by shock and made conscious.

KEEP FOCUSED ON ... whether you are the one who is having to 'earth' the shock, or the one through which the shock is being delivered. In the first case, this means that you must be earthed, in touch with your body and centre. Literally, standing barefoot on the ground or hugging a tree for as long as it takes can work very well here. In the second case, it has fallen to you to wake others up to something, for spiritual and/or health reasons.

WATCH OUT FOR ... knee-jerk reactions of freezing with fear rather than earthing or conducting.

'A little alarm now and then keeps life from stagnation'

STEPS UP TO A LAWN BLOOMING WITH CLOVER

☆ COMING UP ROSES ☆

⚙ GENERAL INTERPRETATION

You can be sure that abundance or whatever you are after will eventually be attained through making the right steps at the right time. With this ascent one's values become higher and more refined, so that what was originally envisaged becomes clearer, but possibly more demanding.

KEEP FOCUSED ON ... the certainty that with effort and vision you will get where you are bound – 'in clover'.

WATCH OUT FOR ... a manic optimism that is forever insisting that, no matter what, success will be reached – this would be asking for a fall ... thinking you will get where you want to without taking the necessary steps.

♥ LOVE/RELATING/SOCIAL

Here is one of the most positive of outlooks, especially seeing that clover has an auspicious connotation with regard to love and lovers. Generally, taking positive steps and holding a positive outlook improves relationships and social life.

KEEP FOCUSED ON ... proceeding and relating in the same manner as you are now, or in the way you have in mind – be it difficult or easy. Harmony and happiness will eventually be yours.

WATCH OUT FOR ... giving up on this promise of contentment because occasionally the going gets rough, or the hill too steep a climb.

⚛ MONEY/WORK/CREATIVITY

Whatever you see as being the level you want to reach, the stage you wish to mount, the recognition you long to win, the affluence you are working to attain – these can definitely be yours, as long as you ...

KEEP FOCUSED ON ... that very goal ... feeding yourself and co-workers with positive encouragement and practical advice ... ignoring or silencing any negative influence; identifying its source and recognizing its falsehood.

WATCH OUT FOR ... giving up when confronted with any step that seems too hard to mount, or whenever a negative voice whispers 'who are you kidding' or 'you're just not good enough' ... being afraid of failing, for that is the only way that you will.

☯ KARMA/ATTITUDE/HEALTH

Through progressing and striving, possibly lifetime after lifetime, we attain a plateau of independence and freedom from fear and doubt. Any difficulties are seen as the natural effect of gravity as we struggle upwards and onwards, with the scent and vision of what lies ahead making it all worthwhile.

KEEP FOCUSED ON ... your goal as a vision of a far better time and place than this one ... holding to this vision, and the absolute certainty of reaching it ... bringing forward a piece of that beautiful vision into the present moment, giving it some reality in the way you live and relate ... evolving and ascending stage by stage.

WATCH OUT FOR ... despairing of the time it all takes, or being too tough on yourself and others; grant yourselves periods of deserved rest and recreation along the way.

'I'm taking one step at a time/And I'll rest every seven,
For it's a mighty long climb/On your way up to heaven'

THE RAINBOW'S POT OF GOLD

☆ PROMISE OF REWARD ☆

GENERAL INTERPRETATION

You cannot actually get to the end of a rainbow where the pot of gold is supposed to be; it is an optical illusion that is only made possible by being at a distance. So, this Symbol is expressly about the promise of reward, of it ultimately being all worthwhile as long as you are true to your own colours and to the laws of Nature and Life itself. A positive outlook based upon a sense of ultimate glory. In a word, hope.

KEEP FOCUSED ON ... inner assurance that enables you to keep headed in the direction you know to be worthy of your efforts and imagination ... distinguishing between a quick, ill-thought out and unreal objective and an ongoing, constantly reconsidered and spiritual one.

WATCH OUT FOR ... hoping against hope; chasing rainbows.

MONEY/WORK/CREATIVITY

If you are or have been striving to reach an important goal, then one day you will hit the jackpot. The burning question is 'When?' This is a trick question because it is the getting there that is more real than the arriving.

KEEP FOCUSED ON ... what you have got and are doing now rather than what you think you ought to have or be doing somewhere down the line. It is essential you have a dream that you want to make real, but expecting it to happen when and how you imagine can be misleading and frustrating. You are destined always to have something better and further distant that you want to achieve or create, and so you will consistently achieve and create a great deal. Just look behind you and see what you have done so far.

WATCH OUT FOR ... being dazzled and misled by unrealizable or unreachable prospects and projects.

♥ LOVE/RELATING/SOCIAL

Our idea of emotional harmony or romantic bliss is imaged by this Symbol, but one must be careful not to take it as a literal prediction or an assurance of such. You are in the process of creating and discovering it, but it could go sour or not happen if you insist on getting what you fantasize as being the 'pot of gold', or that you should have it right now. This is a patently spiritual Symbol for it refers to an ideal we are striving after, longing for. The sheer fact that we have this sense of something beautiful and wonderful ahead of us is the point here. So, whatever your situation ...

KEEP FOCUSED ON ... the 'gold' of love and goodness that you make with every act, word, thought or feeling of love and goodwill.

WATCH OUT FOR ... confusing the target with the arrow, the ideal with the means of realizing it.

☯ KARMA/ATTITUDE/HEALTH

This Symbol images the essence of what the spiritual life is ultimately all about: bringing spiritual values and reality down to Earth. In some ways, this is its *only* meaning that can be relied upon; a purely materialistic interpretation is indicative of either a pie-in-the-sky fool's errand or an eternal carrot on a stick. Karmically, we have lifetime after lifetime in order to integrate our spiritual selves into our earthly lives. This is also how we attain perfect health – by our bodies being aligned with our spiritual intent.

KEEP FOCUSED ON ... the idea that the 'path is the goal', what you are aiming for is what makes the journey towards it worthwhile ... realizing ideals and aspirations.

WATCH OUT FOR ... assuming you have arrived when you haven't, because you never will. The Soul is, after all, Eternal.

'Hope springs eternal in the human breast'

A WIDOW AT AN OPEN GRAVE

✫ A NEED TO LET GO ✫

 GENERAL INTERPRETATION

Although having to cope with the loss of someone or something could be the literal interpretation of this Symbol, it could be more generally regarded as the imperative of accepting the loss of what can no longer be had or enjoyed physically, or letting go of what seems to concern you so.

KEEP FOCUSED ON ... getting a grip on what it is that you are so attached to; only then will you be able to let go of it ... your innate ability to transcend loss or disappointment as this in turn creates an enrichment of spirit ... mourning or grieving out of respect rather than out of desperation ... letting time tell and do the healing.

WATCH OUT FOR ... over-attachment – or attachment without enough psychological awareness – to anything or anyone; the despair that this can attract.

♥ **LOVE/RELATING/SOCIAL**

If there is a relationship or issue that you have been hanging on to when in your heart of hearts you know it is finished, then now is the time to make that break, tear yourself away from what has been emotionally draining you, and move on. If you find this impossible to do then you have some serious soul-searching in front of you.

KEEP FOCUSED ON ... asking yourself which is the greater difficulty: painfully hanging on to someone or something you are addicted to, or looking deep into your past and finding where you first felt that yawning gap in your life. Whatever is going on now is related to that time and is calling your attention to it, urging you to lay it to rest once and for all.

WATCH OUT FOR ... neurotic attachments.

 MONEY/WORK/CREATIVITY

Some idea or project or product has come to an end – or at least, it seems that it will. Then again, possibly you are giving up on something that was close to your heart. It could be a tough call as to whether it is 'dead' or not.

KEEP FOCUSED ON ... the object of your concern with a view to consigning it to the scrap heap and note how you feel about this. If you feel there is life in the old dog yet, then give it another crack. If on the other hand it smacks of something that is past its sell-by date, then let it go. Ask the Oracle again about this.

WATCH OUT FOR ... giving up the ghost on everything simply because something has not turned out as you hoped it would. For example, writers are advised to 'kill their little darlings', their pet ideas that have appeal only to them and few others.

☯ **KARMA/ATTITUDE/HEALTH**

The harsh truth that the death of one person usually leaves one or more others behind. Or possibly, the prospect or idea of death is becoming morbid and obsessive.

KEEP FOCUSED ON ... the transitory nature of physical life, thereby recognizing the eternal nature of the spiritual life ... grieving 'properly' where the grave is symbolic of the hole of loss inside oneself that should be seen as a receptor for an influx of spiritual energy or awareness ... death and its trappings as reminders of what does and does not matter in your life. According to Carlos Castenada's sorcerer, Don Juan, your death is always stalking you, and can be sensed by darting your eyes momentarily (without moving your head) to where he hovers just off your left shoulder. This is strangely comforting and guiding.

WATCH OUT FOR ... hanging on to what is dead and gone, it could prove harmful to you.

'O death where is thy sting? O grave, where is thy victory?'

A BRIDGE BEING BUILT ACROSS A GORGE

☆ HEALING SPLITS ☆

 GENERAL INTERPRETATION

You are in the process of resolving some conflict, be it inside or outside your head. Creating a link between two separate entities, possibly where there is some steep risk involved – or at least where deep and dark fears loom.

KEEP FOCUSED ON ... what or who you owe your loyalty or allegiance to at this time, and seek to make or maintain your link with them ... your qualities of being that act to span divides, be they between cultures, languages, sexes, races, or whatever.

WATCH OUT FOR ... being neither one thing nor the other, split loyalties, not knowing which way to turn – all probably owing to some division or confusion of values within you.

 LOVE/RELATING/SOCIAL

Your relationship, social life, or ability to relate, is proceeding healthily and constructively, leading ever onwards to a satisfying state of affairs. If you are estranged from someone, then this too is in the process of being reconciled; or at least, steps should be taken to that end, for the time is right for healing splits. If you are on your own and hoping for a relationship, one is forming (even though you may not be aware of it), because you are becoming ready for one.

KEEP FOCUSED ON ... the nature and needs of yourself and the other person, in equal measure.

WATCH OUT FOR ... any divisive traits in yourself and eliminate them, or, if they belong to another, make them aware of them in as neutral a way as possible; they will respond positively in due course.

 MONEY/WORK/CREATIVITY

This could be some kind merger imaged here, a joining of departments or forces, or the improving of communication and operation between one entity and another, internally or externally. This is happening, needs to happen or continue to happen until a definite sense of mutual involvement is experienced. Then again, such a bridge could be a loan, funds or a mental construct that is enabling you to reach a certain creative objective, possibly between the inspired and the inspiration, the creator and the created, idea and form.

KEEP FOCUSED ON ... making sure that every person or part knows what role they are playing, what function they are performing and, most of all, that everyone is aiming for the same thing.

WATCH OUT FOR ... any dangers and risks involved in your operation, and take the necessary precautions and measures.

KARMA/ATTITUDE/HEALTH

There is a longstanding rift, be it natural or otherwise, that is being healed. Or the endeavour that you are involved in could be the process of going from one state to another. This could be, for instance, going from unhealthy living to healthy living, from a materialistic lifestyle to a more spiritual one, from danger to safety, even from this world to another. This Symbol may also refer to the Rainbow Bridge that is said to join the soul to the personality; that is, that your Earthly, everyday life is influenced and guided by the higher dictates of your finer feelings and spiritual values and inner promptings.

KEEP FOCUSED ON ... the difficulties involved in accomplishing any of the above in as objective a way as possible; bridges do not, as a rule, get built overnight.

WATCH OUT FOR ... trying to do it all yourself; it is impossible without help – possibly divine help.

'Why did the chicken cross the road? Because it wanted to get to the other side'

A WOMAN OF SAMARIA

☆ ABSENCE OF AGENDA ☆

✦ GENERAL INTERPRETATION

Here there is no issue to answer, or an absence of opportunism and dogma that in turn attracts revelation of profound truth where more intent seekers fail to do so. The Woman of Samaria was the first person to whom Christ revealed that he was the Messiah, simply because she had no vested interest in knowing this, one way or the other.

KEEP FOCUSED ON ... your unselfconscious generosity of spirit which lights your way and auto-matically that of others too ... being open to whatever presents itself as the new order of things ... being free of desire and you will be free of fear, in direct proportion.

WATCH OUT FOR ... a self-effacing nature that meekly justifies itself with the notion that there is nothing to be done about one's meagre circumstances.

♥ LOVE/RELATING/SOCIAL

This images a person to whom one can relate to with the assurance that they will not judge you in any way. It could even point to a relationship of this nature, where neither person judges the other. As such, one or both has the inner man or woman drawn out. Also, any repressed feelings in forms such as anger, fear and frustration can be vented, giving rise to a new and refreshed sense of being. This clearing of repressed feelings will also prevent them from wreaking social, emotional or even physical havoc. Or there is a need for this.

KEEP FOCUSED ON ... maintaining as unstructured a view as possible of the object of your concern; from kindness and openness an unconditional love and deep intimacy will grow.

WATCH OUT FOR ... fearing or insisting that things develop in a preconceived way.

♛ MONEY/WORK/CREATIVITY

Stressed here is the importance of emptiness and of being open to whatever course presents itself. Creatively speaking, this is the blank piece of paper which one can either wait to be written upon by your inspired hand, or that frustrates you so much that you give up. Knowing the Lord alone provides.

KEEP FOCUSED ON ... doing whatever you are doing with as little expectation or forethought as possible, strong in the faith that what needs to turn up will do so when the time is right ... the possibility that your worth, ideas or product, because they are unusual, are as yet unrecognized, but will one day be hailed as something of great significance and value.

WATCH OUT FOR ... having set plans or fixed agendas for they inhibit the flow of money or ideas, and blind you to new opportunities.

☯ KARMA/ATTITUDE/HEALTH

Yours could be said to be a strange fate. This is because it is your unsureness and unworldli-ness that marks you out for an unusual and, possibly, momentous role. However, the paradox is that if you deliberately look for this role it will elude you. This does not mean to say that you cannot dream of it and remain open to it in a decidedly non-specific way. This is the karma of innocence and of taking no particular side. Better still ...

KEEP FOCUSED ON ... eliminating any grand or detailed plans, while sensing what draws you on, much as a compass needle points to magnetic North ... seeing disruptions as timely course corrections.

WATCH OUT FOR ... preoccupying yourself with what could or should have been, or what might or should happen, for this would confuse you horribly, possibly giving rise to complaints of congestion or needless anxiety.

'In transparency, worlds are created'

A SLEIGH WITHOUT SNOW

☆ THE NEED TO GET UNSTUCK ☆

 GENERAL INTERPRETATION

Although this Symbol could be referring to a means of getting somewhere if conditions become difficult or different, it is more often than not an indication that the object of your enquiry is in the wrong place at the right time, or the right place at the wrong time. Or it could simply be saying that, for one reason or another, your attitude or question is inappropriate or irrelevant. Inertia.

KEEP FOCUSED ON ... what it is you really want, need, think and feel ... mobilizing yourself in spite of circumstances ... finding a way of shifting what needs shifting ... waiting for conditions to be right ... relinquishing any idea or course of action as soon as you realize or admit to its fruitlessness.

WATCH OUT FOR ... a fear of the unexpected that is born of a mistrust of spontaneity.

♡ **LOVE/RELATING/SOCIAL**

A relationship that is at a standstill for want of being in the right environment. The relationship itself may be perfectly fine, but until it finds its rightful place, physically or socially, then it will have a hard time of it. Alternatively, this could be referring to a lone individual who is in a location or situation that is not conducive to finding a mate/company.

KEEP FOCUSED ON ... why you are in this difficult, apparently unsuitable, situation. If there is a good reason, like it is forcing you to change or improve in some way, then all well and good, and read the writing on the wall ... putting yourself in a more fruitful environment for satisfying your needs; otherwise, accept your situation for what it is and look within for satisfaction, and just wait.

WATCH OUT FOR ... wanting to have it both ways ... burying your head in the sand.

 MONEY/WORK/CREATIVITY

Your idea, product or project is in need of different conditions in order to function or prosper. Otherwise it will be hard going, probably leading to a standstill – if it is not already at one. Alternatively, this Symbol speaks of a concept without substance, or that has yet to be substantiated.

KEEP FOCUSED ON ... looking either for a different vehicle for what you want to say or achieve, for a new area of endeavour, or looking for someone or something that has the necessary means to get you moving again.

WATCH OUT FOR ... investing time or energy in anything which is now dead in the water ... whatever it is that is keeping you stuck, and then negotiate it.

☯ **KARMA/ATTITUDE/HEALTH**

Something or someone has left you high and dry, and you now feel stranded and immobilized. This may have bred in you a feeling of impotence or hopelessness, which may in turn create an attitude and state of being that keeps you stuck in that place. This is a dire situation which must either be changed or looked at differently. Constipation or stiffness.

KEEP FOCUSED ON ... what exactly got you into such a plight, in terms of what attitudes and actions *of your own* created the state of affairs that led to this. Without honestly digging deep for these causes, you are going to remain stuck ... the possibility that you have been 'grounded' for some reason, and will just have to sit it out until you have learned your lesson.

WATCH OUT FOR ... becoming inured to a life situation that is unsatisfactory because you cannot see beyond the devil you know.

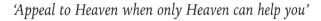

'Appeal to Heaven when only Heaven can help you'

A CHRISTMAS TREE DECORATED

☆ TIME TO CELEBRATE ☆

GENERAL INTERPRETATION

Whatever may be going on in your life, this Symbol is calling you to 'be of good cheer' for salvation or good news is at hand, even though you may not be that aware of it. This is seen in the symbol that marks a time that combines both the birth of Christ and the Winter Solstice or Yuletide. On the one hand, goodwill to all, and on the other, that once maximum darkness has been reached, things can only get brighter.

KEEP FOCUSED ON ... or search for a genuine feeling within you of goodness and that all will eventually be all right as long as an inner sense of goodwill is maintained and expressed.

WATCH OUT FOR ... thinking that superficial displays of merriment or positivity (tinsel) will last ... dressing things up to the point where the original and natural quality is not visible or is even lost.

♥ LOVE/RELATING/SOCIAL

Every relationship has positive ties, otherwise it would not have come together in the first place. The trouble is often that the mundanities of life and our personal complexes can obliterate the pure and simple bond that was initially made and felt. It therefore becomes necessary to ...

KEEP FOCUSED ON ... celebrating the fact that you are in a relationship, and in so doing become mindful of the essential reason why. This should be done frequently (the word *celebrate* means 'frequented') so that that essence of the relationship is never lost sight of.

WATCH OUT FOR ... empty shows of emotion or lack of sincerity. This does not necessarily mean there is no genuine feeling; it is just that it needs quickening ... dressing down too much.

MONEY/WORK/CREATIVITY

Good news on the career and/or money front! Or this may also refer to a seasonal renewal or time when business or creative endeavour is more fruitful. A time of 'gifts' being received and given. Any kind of work that brings joy and wonder is very auspicious.

KEEP FOCUSED ON ... ensuring that whatever is on offer is being given freely ... the goodwill that is necessary or present in any current transactions ... doing your work for the joy it ... how effectively anything is presented.

WATCH OUT FOR ... reducing what is sacred to something blindly traditional or downright materialistic ... anything that is all show and of no substance or worth.

☯ KARMA/ATTITUDE/HEALTH

This is to remind us that there is something perennially good and magical that persists through life eternally. There is always life and renewal in the midst of death. As legend has it that the lights on Christmas trees were originally put there to simulate the stars shining through the branches at night, this Symbol could also be said to represent our Earthly connection with the Heavens, and that we are of cosmic origin.

KEEP FOCUSED ON ... your strong sense of a common belief in and reliance on humanity's most cherished and basic qualities ... something bright and good and everlasting; this will cheer up yourself and others, and good spirits promote good health ... any celebration your culture has of the above.

WATCH OUT FOR ... not connecting with the deeper sentiments of any tradition or symbol.

'Oh Christmas Tree, oh Christmas Tree, with faithful leaves unchanging'

A RED CROSS NURSE

☆ SELFLESS SERVICE ☆

 GENERAL INTERPRETATION

Selfless service to others. Ultimately, this is service to the planet as a whole and all who live on it, and so implies that all is one. Furthermore, because the Red Cross is a worldwide organization, this Symbol implies the possibility of having more weight and substance than someone doing good on their own. Structure and discipline being imposed by the organization may prevent selflessness becoming a curious form of self-indulgence, but, on the down side, red tape may inhibit the noble intentions of the Red Cross!

KEEP FOCUSED ON ... dedicating yourself to what-ever your heart holds dear, healing and uniting wherever it is needed. This may entail having to transmute anger (red + cross) into positive energy and effective action.

WATCH OUT FOR ... being blinded to one's shadows and shortcomings by a veil of worthiness.

 LOVE/RELATING/SOCIAL

Someone needs healing and attending to here, and it looks as if aid is at hand. On the other hand, someone is trying too hard to be a 'ministering angel' to all and sundry, and not paying enough attention to themselves or those closest to them. More generally, imaged here is a relationship or social set-up that is healing and mutually supportive. But then, it might need to be.

KEEP FOCUSED ON ... the fact that the surest way to emotional happiness and fulfilment is living for the welfare of others or another. For this to be genuine however, one needs to have gone through and beyond one's own need for attention. So ...

WATCH OUT FOR ... being the 'saviour' to others when really it is yourself who is the victim; displacing this on to others who you see as being in need of your attention.

MONEY/WORK/CREATIVITY

Most obviously this Symbol could be referring to some kind of healing work and approving of this, while at the same time stressing what it involves. In any event, help or supply is here or on its way, be it for you or from you. With regard to what the actual work involves, it will be testing and gruelling at times. You have not chosen an easy path, which is a testament to the fact that it is a very worthwhile one – a vocation, no less.

KEEP FOCUSED ON ... what greater whole or tradition your work is a part of. The principles and power of such a body should stand to guide and support you, morally and materially ... being non-profit making – or at least de-emphasizing the material gain – this will ensure that the essential aims of customer service and satisfaction are (continued to be) met. But ...

WATCH OUT FOR ... being taken advantage of.

KARMA/ATTITUDE/HEALTH

True spirituality could be said to be what one is seeking through lifetime after lifetime, until one is liberated from the Wheel of Fate or Karma. One of the surest expressions or ways to this spirituality and liberation is through selfless service. Whatever is the nature of your question, the Oracle is either confirming that you are on this path or that you are being considered for it. The second option means that, as with any healing or helping ministry, you have to qualify to be part of it – it is not sufficient merely to want to do it. The dreamy idealists have to be separated from those who genuinely feel the call to help others.

KEEP FOCUSED ON ... your deepest motivations with regard to your question. For instance, have you truly considered what it involves in terms of hard work and inconvenience?

WATCH OUT FOR ... any doubts about your goals.

'He who would do good to another, must do so in minute particulars'

A WOMAN SPRINKLING FLOWERS

☆ CULTIVATION OF WORTH ☆

⚙ GENERAL INTERPRETATION

Enjoyment and profit deriving from the natural inclination to nurture whatever it is that is growing around or within you. Providence smiles upon those who interact with Mother Nature in this way.

KEEP FOCUSED ON ... your innate sense of how life gives as it receives; this ensures that you are never really wanting for anything, be it of material or spiritual value ... viewing or treating the nature of your concern in the same way that a gardener would his garden ... tending all in your sphere that needs tending, and 'see how your garden grows'.

WATCH OUT FOR ... instinctual nurturing on a hand-to-mouth basis; without a sense of how it fits into the greater scheme of things; this is unsatisfactory or hard to maintain.

♥ LOVE/RELATING/SOCIAL

Keeping love alive with simple and frequent acts of care and kindness. Being in a relationship and nurturing it in this way is something that is its own reward. If you are seeking to find a relationship then foster any little shoots of encouragement or signs of interest that come your way.

KEEP FOCUSED ON ... causing love or lovability to bloom through loving thoughts and deeds ... making sure that you are not just flirting/dallying or being flirted/dallied with.

WATCH OUT FOR ... the practice of keeping people sweet just in case they might become preferable, more interesting or useful.

MONEY/WORK/CREATIVITY

Regularly and frequently feeding, refreshing and tending your projects and products will ensure their future development, as well as keeping them fresh and appealing in the present. Without such care they could wither and die, or just be lacklustre.

KEEP FOCUSED ON ... developing your ideas, style and ability on a daily basis ... encouraging yourself and others ... giving attention to whatever or whoever needs attention ... seeking out whoever or whatever can be 'fertilizer' or 'fertilized'.

WATCH OUT FOR ... over-watering, under-watering or not watering the object of your concern. In other words, do not try to force things to fruition, expect things to get on with little funding and effort, or leave things entirely to whatever Fate will dish out.

♨ KARMA/ATTITUDE/HEALTH

Your lifestyle includes, or needs to include, a natural and down-to-earth pastime that keeps you in touch with Nature or whatever replenishes you in an organic way – literally, this could be gardening, the pleasure and connectedness you get from seeing things grow. This is the karma of returning to the simple life, being free of practices and attitudes that are divorced from natural processes.

KEEP FOCUSED ON ... nurturing the physical and spiritual welfare and development of yourself and others on a regular basis as a matter of course.

WATCH OUT FOR ... for being hurried and forced into the rat race of meeting targets and being over-governed by schedules.

'Let us cultivate our garden'

WINDOW SHOPPERS

☆ JUST LOOKING ☆

 GENERAL INTERPRETATION

Taking time out to examine what is on offer before making a decision to buy, commit, speak or act. Or killing time by indulging in the contemplation of what one would like but cannot or will not afford or attain; the compensation that this bestows. For the time being, at least, you can just observe and not engage with, or buy into, anything that you do not like the look of or are not sure about.

KEEP FOCUSED ON ... your well-conceived sense of what is necessary and desirable, for this ensures eventual satisfaction ... researching, then deciding.

WATCH OUT FOR ... being a spectator of what life has to offer, rather than experiencing it ... poverty consciousness – believing you are worse off than you actually are.

 MONEY/WORK/CREATIVITY

This patently material and Taurean Symbol has a plain and obvious meaning here. Essentially, this Symbol is saying that the time for buying or selling has not quite arrived, but that the product or the customer is out there.

KEEP FOCUSED ON ... (if you are buying) taking your time to see what is on offer and to assess what you can afford ... (if you are selling) appreciating that success has a lot to do with your display, shop window or advertising ... what the crucial ingredient is that clinches a deal, makes a sale, or appeals to the public – then making your move.

WATCH OUT FOR ... the truth of the saying 'nothing ventured, nothing gained'. The notion or mere intention of selling, buying or creating something does not actually produce anything at all – except frustration and confusion.

 LOVE/RELATING/SOCIAL

A case of observing what is happening or available on the social or romantic scene with a view to 'investing' oneself in a relationship. This Symbol could also be describing someone who is looking but not yet ready to become involved, who is waiting for when they can 'afford' to involve themselves.

KEEP FOCUSED ON ... what and who you are interested in (or already involved with) while bearing in mind what you have to offer them and what they have to offer you ... looking around while at the same time improving your eligibility until you find what you feel right about.

WATCH OUT FOR ... always being alone owing to a reluctance to commit, possibly due to a under- or over-estimated idea of oneself or another ... thinking that love is something that can be bought.

KARMA/ATTITUDE/HEALTH

A well-known esoteric concept is that of the soul 'choosing' the life it wants or needs before incarnating. One 'shops around' until a suitable life or personality is found or is available. However, the fact that you are reading this means that you have already made that choice. Possibly you have forgotten this and need to be reminded that this life, and the one that lives it, are what you 'chose' or were drawn to, even though it may have been an 'impulse buy' or the 'best available'. Health-wise, you could be prevaricating about what to do for the best.

KEEP FOCUSED ON ... comparing one thing to another until you know what is best, and then give it 100% ... looking around for the best health care or remedy.

WATCH OUT FOR ... putting off interminably making a decision or a commitment, for in that way you will never really know.

'Are we in fact, more accurately speaking, condemned to choose?'

A MAN HANDLING BAGGAGE

✵ CARRY THAT LOAD ✵

GENERAL INTERPRETATION

Occasioned or called for here is the strength and know-how needed to deal with the everyday practical or emotional challenges of life, and perhaps more importantly, a sense of joy in doing so.

KEEP FOCUSED ON ... the cheerful way of working that constitutes your sense of normal living and that attracts the admiration and dependence of others ... the fact that life at present is unavoidably hard work, and that you just have to get on with it.

WATCH OUT FOR ... submitting to a life of meaningless drudgery for the sake of not being prepared to put one's talents to the test or to discover and develop them.

♥ LOVE/RELATING/SOCIAL

Certain relationships at certain times are a trial and a burden and just have to be borne. This is such a case.

KEEP FOCUSED ON ... your emotional situation in as an objective fashion as possible, which means that you best avoid emotional reactions and evaluations, and view what has to be done as just what has to done ... bearing your load with a sense of joy of service, for this will lighten that very load – you might even get a tip!

WATCH OUT FOR ... comparing what you've got with what you want for this will only aggravate a situation in which you are carrying something that you cannot drop (if you think you can, look at the Karma section below); the more you grudge, the more you drudge ... carrying more than you can genuinely bear.

MONEY/WORK/CREATIVITY

Material matters will be all right as long as you (continue to) manage them in a conscientious manner. There is no promise of great good fortune here, unless it happens to be a 'burden of wealth', where the sheer responsibility of having a lot, materially or creatively, is a burden in itself!

KEEP FOCUSED ON ... finding the means and methods that lighten your load. This may mean renegotiating a financial agreement, working longer or different hours. Or it could be a case of getting someone to help you, in spite of a disinclination to let go of the reins.

WATCH OUT FOR ... carrying more than you have to, once you are absolutely sure it is not or is no longer your responsibility ... for the reason why you might be doing more than your share – for example, you may need to appease a feeling of guilt that relates to another area entirely.

KARMA/ATTITUDE/HEALTH

'Baggage' is a symbol for karmic weight, what you are carrying around from something that happened previously. It could be a good idea to ask the Oracle about the nature of the karmic burden you are having to carry, and why you are having to carry it.

KEEP FOCUSED ON ... the actuality of karma: every one of us is a package of energy, and energy is never born or dies but just changes form. So 'karma' could be termed your 'energy history' and what you are having to bear now relates to what you previously did not carry well or long enough, or at all; accepting this puts more strength in your 'arms' and a spring in your step.

WATCH OUT FOR ... attempting to avoid or excuse yourself from what circumstances or your conscience are now forcing upon you. This would be like putting your bags down, walking on, then having to turn around and fetch them later.

'... an affirmation of things as they are; an unconditional "yes" to that which is, without subjective protests'

SHELLFISH GROPING AND CHILDREN PLAYING

☆ PRIMAL PLAYPOWER ☆

GENERAL INTERPRETATION

This suggests a beach scene, which in itself is symbolic of the shifting boundary between the conscious and unconscious realms. In this place then, we see the most primitive and instinctual outreaching for basic sustenance, and the natural delight that is a part of being in an area of spontaneous discovery. The juxtaposition of, or conflict between, the thrill of experience and sheer existence.

KEEP FOCUSED ON … your innocent sense of what life has to offer at a basic or physical level of experience, and the simple enthusiasm that allows you to leap in and feel your way.

WATCH OUT FOR … any signs of a repressed or retarded sense of what one would really like to be doing, and the confusion or dissatisfaction that this amounts to … merely playing at things; groping for answers (especially with the Oracle).

♥ LOVE/RELATING/SOCIAL

Here is a situation – or the call for one – that could be regarded as a return to first principles where relating is concerned. This centres mainly on the discovering or rediscovering of what could be called 'innocent sexuality'. There is almost an 'I'll let you see mine if I can see yours' feel about this. So much confusion and frustration is created by the 'shoulds' and 'shouldn'ts' that have been handed down by repressed sources such as parents, church and state. This Symbol invites you to …

KEEP FOCUSED ON … creating an openness to emotional and sensuous experience with an absolute minimum of expectation or design … a kind of Return to the Garden where spontaneity, experimentation, a gentle expression of the animal side of one's nature, and a lack of self-consciousness are to be encouraged.

WATCH OUT FOR … the poisons of guilt and envy, jealousy or abuse.

⚘ MONEY/WORK/CREATIVITY

Creatively, this Symbol urges one to get in touch with the unconscious mind that inspires in a direct and uninhibited way. Such expression as issues forth from this is spontaneous, unpretentious and vibrant. It can also be profitable because it readily appeals to basic levels in the public at large. It also stresses the validity of a working environment where people can interact naturally with one another.

KEEP FOCUSED ON … what it is that wants to be naturally expressed through using 'automatic' techniques, where there is no intention other than to write, paint or play what is 'there', and to silence to the utmost the internal critic or censor. This has been called Stream of Consciousness.

WATCH OUT FOR … contrivance or censure as this would inhibit any natural flow of expression … being too immature materially.

☯ KARMA/ATTITUDE/HEALTH

This Symbol portrays something which modern society thinks on the one hand it has left behind, yet on the other hand is instinctively, and sometimes rather coarsely, trying to re-establish. Mythologically, this is the domain of Pan, Bacchus or Dionysius – the realm of the expression of natural urges, stripped of the veneer of so-called civilization. The unconscious mind has its own patterns, laws and agendas which, when given some rein (but not too much) have a liberating effect, and put one more closely in touch with oneself and others at a fundamental level.

KEEP FOCUSED ON … finding harmless outlets for libido and adventure, and any pursuit that puts you more in touch with Nature.

WATCH OUT FOR … lustful or selfish behaviour that smacks of crudeness or naivety rather than innocence and natural curiosity … dangerous loss of control, possibly due to intoxicants.

'Lo, I receive the gifts thou bringest me – Life, and more life, in fullest ecstasy.
… Come unto me, Great Pan, come unto me!'

A MAN MUFFLED UP, WITH A RAKISH SILK HAT

☆ STYLE AS PROTECTION ☆

GENERAL INTERPRETATION

The combined stylization and protection of self, that one should cut a dash *and* be practical, whatever the season or situation. A case of emotional security having to take precedence over vanity and sex, or having to be incorporated into it.

KEEP FOCUSED ON ... a personal style that moves with the times yet remains ever your own ... attaining or retaining whatever gives you both security and a pleasant lifestyle.

WATCH OUT FOR ... a self-conscious affectation that betrays a more profound sense of significance ... risking insecurity for the sake of trying something that (you feel) would expose you too much to the unknown ... letting appetites jeopardize health and security.

LOVE/RELATING/SOCIAL

As far as it goes, style, be it of character or fashion, is a highly effective and accepted means of keeping one's sensitivity under wraps. But unless one can distinguish one's 'body armour' from the person inside it, relating and making oneself understood can be severely impeded; the Houdini Syndrome, where you can't get out and they can't see that you are trapped. This is often the 'male', butch, hard or repugnant/punk look. And, of course, whole sections of society subscribe to the wearing of such uniforms.

KEEP FOCUSED ON ... determining how one's armour affects a relationship, and finding a way of shedding it, penetrating it, or letting it be so ... the actual way in which you come across, and ...

WATCH OUT FOR ... how this can protect, mislead or impress, but make one unreachable.

MONEY/WORK/CREATIVITY

The issue here is one of balance between image and content. Your idea or product must pay special attention to this and satisfy both requirements if it is to meet with success. A great idea that is unattractive or lacks public appeal is unlikely to get started; something that is all looks but no practical function will not last very long.

KEEP FOCUSED ON ... determining a way of accomplishing the balance between style and content; find a way where the one can complement the other, then success will most surely be yours ... bestowing credit on a good idea by investing a suitable amount on its production and promotion ... putting an appropriate amount of spin on the object of your concern, but ...

WATCH OUT FOR ... being seduced by packaging and presentation, only to find that there is little of substance contained therein, or that the image or packaging detracts from it.

KARMA/ATTITUDE/HEALTH

This Symbol suggests the relationship between Soul and Personality. The soul is the essential or inner being that clothes itself in the outer appearance of the personality – one's character, style, image, and the rest of the physical–emotional–mental equipment. Viewed in this way, it can be seen how the way we wear our personality can be a suitable or creative expression of what lies within, or as deceptive, constrictive and suffocating to the inner dwelling being.

KEEP FOCUSED ON ... the actual nature of your soul – What does it feel? What does it wish to say and do? Where has it been? Where is it bound? The more these questions are properly addressed and answered, then the more successful and satisfying will be the expression your personality gives your soul.

WATCH OUT FOR ... losing sight of who you are or who someone else is because of the outer show.

'May I address myself to me/So the eye inside my head might see'

AN OLD MAN ATTEMPTING VAINLY TO REVEAL THE MYSTERIES

☆ NO QUICK FIX OR EASY ANSWER ☆

✳ GENERAL INTERPRETATION

An answer to your question involves going deep into issues that are foreign to everyday thinking. Such knowledge can threaten security, 'the devil you know', and so is difficult to put across – even though such awareness would make life far better and easier.

KEEP FOCUSED ON ... summoning a dogged determination to grasp what at first evades you ... your persistence in helping others to grasp what is vitally important – even if they do not appreciate it until much later. Do you appreciate it yourself?! Hold or heed your own counsel until you do.

WATCH OUT FOR ... expecting a pat answer to your question because you would then fail to understand any answer the Oracle gave ... failing to accomplish much as a result of a preoccupation with abstractions at the expense of the practical.

♡ LOVE/RELATING/SOCIAL

This could describe an individual who is well-versed in intellectual matters but has trouble getting across emotionally. Or it could be saying that you are encountering a relationship issue that has long confused people through the ages, and so there is no conventional or superficial answer.

KEEP FOCUSED ON ... learning/teaching how to make a point through emotional or sensual means, rather than through some doctrine or theory. Then again, you may need to familiarize yourself with a more profound reason for your situation in order to see your way through it.

WATCH OUT FOR ... lecturing because you think you have the 'answer' or being lectured by someone else who does ... having access to deeper explanations, but not listening to them or acting on them ... frustration from trying too hard.

MONEY/WORK/CREATIVITY

Your work entails a type of information that is as difficult to put across as it is for the average person to understand. Such technical/esoteric knowledge needs to be couched in everyday terms in order to be accepted and understood. Alternatively, you could be in need of information that is not easily acquired or assimilated, but which is important to your financial or career situation.

KEEP FOCUSED ON ... the fact that it is through your own efforts that others may be better educated and informed, especially in areas where 'dumbing down' has become the norm ... being a living example of the value of what you know and believe, for it is through this that you will grab others' attention, which is the prerequisite for success.

WATCH OUT FOR ... being disheartened by the failure of others to appreciate what you are trying to say or do ... being out of touch with the person in the street ... casting pearls before swine.

☯ KARMA/ATTITUDE/HEALTH

The reasons for your predicament are available to you but you cannot recognize or digest them, possibly because you do not want to accept what they pose. The Oracle itself is often beset with the problem of giving a reply that the enquirer does not want to hear or does not take in because of what they *want* as an answer. This Symbol may be pointing to an area of your personality or past that you are afraid of, or averse to, for some reason. Left unattended for long enough, such 'no-go areas' can eventually manifest as a condition that is as hard to understand or diagnose.

KEEP FOCUSED ON ... summoning the courage and desire for the truth that enables you at last to grasp what has so long evaded or haunted you. By bringing it into the light it cannot then harm you, but you should ...

WATCH OUT FOR ... pleading ignorance or disbelief for this ultimately proves to be no excuse.

'Genius is only a greater aptitude for patience'

A BATTLE BETWEEN THE SWORDS AND THE TORCHES

☆ LEFT BRAIN VERSUS RIGHT BRAIN ☆

GENERAL INTERPRETATION

A situation posing ambiguous or conflicting messages or values. More specifically, the ongoing struggle between thinking/logic (Swords/left brain) and feeling/intuition (Torches/right brain), and the need to find a balance between the two. Also, to get the two functions to co-operate rather than cause difficulties owing to left- or right-brain dominance, or inertia caused by one side cancelling out the other. (*See* page 18 about ambiguity when using oracles.)

KEEP FOCUSED ON ... using art and visualization exercises to strengthen the right brain ... learning anything that concerns lists, order, numbers or any linear subject such as mathematics and the sciences to strengthen the left brain.

WATCH OUT FOR ... stalemates created by a failure to reconcile one's sense of reason with one's passions, or vice versa.

MONEY/WORK/CREATIVITY

Here the left-brain/right-brain conflict can give rise to problems of motivation or lack of co-operation between workers of different biases. There is also the issue between the practical necessities of life and the mettle and decisiveness that is needed to cope with them on the one hand, and the motives and meanings that give them direction on the other.

KEEP FOCUSED ON ... the fact that ideas are as nothing without action, and actions are blind without ideas and vision behind them ... giving persistent attention to immediate issues while never losing sight of a goal that serves a greater purpose ... introducing professional management skills that organize work roles to interface rather than conflict ... grasping the nettle.

WATCH OUT FOR ... paying too much attention to what accountants say on the one hand, or what 'visionaries' say on the other.

LOVE/RELATING/SOCIAL

This Symbol points to the basic conflict that is the Battle of the Sexes. How men, who are usually left-brain dominant, and women, who are usually right-brain dominant, so often fail to understand one another because of these different biases.

KEEP FOCUSED ON ... learning from the opposite sex or those different from you, for this will make you more complete as a person, and also make for a happier relationship or social life.

WATCH OUT FOR ... passionate reactions as signs that you do not listen to your feelings (because you are left-brain/logical) ... numbness or confusion because you follow your feelings to excess and do not use your head enough (because you are right-brain/feeling orientated).

KARMA/ATTITUDE/HEALTH

The basic flux between one pole/extreme and another (yin and yang) out of which Creation itself came and continues to come about. Seeing this as a 'battle' is historically accurate in that mankind has always subscribed to an 'if you are not with me you must be against me' attitude. However, this is wrong thinking and the Age of Aquarius is about putting right this ancient Taurean bias born of possessiveness and a fear of the unknown.

KEEP FOCUSED ON ... (if left-brain/logical) suspending disbelief in whatever is illogical, and endeavouring to incorporate it into your life – or at least accept it ... (if right-brain/intuitive) making the effort to think things through.

WATCH OUT FOR ... health issues arising from complaints such as insomnia (left-brain over-emphasis) or sticking one's head in the sand (right-brain overemphasis) ... brain chemistry imbalance.

'Jack Spratt could eat no fat, his wife could eat no lean
And so between them both they licked the platter clean'

A WOMAN HOLDING A BAG OUT OF A WINDOW

☆ CLEARING AIR AND GETTING RID ☆

 GENERAL INTERPRETATION

A time to state your case plainly, thereby clearing and cleaning out whatever needs it, or showing the outside what is carried on the inside, or simply making some weighty issue known.

KEEP FOCUSED ON ... ascertaining whatever it is in your life that could do with such clearing out, refreshment or exposure ... anyone who is trying to unload or express their grievances, and helping to facilitate this – then everyone will be the lighter and happier for it.

WATCH OUT FOR ... making fatuous attempts to gain attention through peculiar or indirect behaviour; this could give completely the wrong impression and have the opposite to the desired effect ... the first thing to come out of an unblocked pipe is dirty smelly water – eventually it'll run clear and sweet.

MONEY/WORK/CREATIVITY

Your way of working or making money can be hampered by hanging on to outworn or habitual practices. This may simply amount to clearing up your workspace, ordering and filing. Creatively, one often needs to express the dross in one's mind, purely for the sake of getting rid of it, with no intention of anyone else seeing it. This having been done, the 'scum' removed from the surface, you then have clear water to drink, some fresh ideas to express.

KEEP FOCUSED ON ... getting co-workers to gather round and express their grievances; such 'clearing' can have a miraculous effect upon the efficiency and morale of all concerned.

WATCH OUT FOR ... overlooking the emotional dimension of work and money. For example, a fear of having a weakness exposed can lead to that weakness becoming a serious block or error.

 LOVE/RELATING/SOCIAL

Here we have an individual or relationship that has a number of issues that need airing, otherwise they could clog or make communication worse. Possibly such 'airing' is already in process.

KEEP FOCUSED ON ... expressing or accepting what comes to the surface naturally, rather than forcing issues or bringing up long-past problems and creating even more fall-out ... expressing what is concerning you to someone outside of the relationship, thereby getting a more objective view.

WATCH OUT FOR ... being misled, frustrated or confused by what at first may appear to be hard to understand about yourself, the other person(s), or the relationship itself. The more you give things a chance to express themselves or find the light of day, then the clearer things will become.

KARMA/ATTITUDE/HEALTH

Past issues are inclined to build up if unattended to, and have now reached a point where they are being dealt with, or need to be. Stale attitudes and negative habits need to be refreshed or eliminated. Health-wise, the retention of unregenerate or unlooked at issues can eventually give rise to problems with the body's circulation or eliminatory systems. Flatulence.

KEEP FOCUSED ON ... employing whatever means you can to clear out or creatively express what is weighing you down, inhibiting you, causing feelings of guilt, or anything else that is beginning to 'smell' a bit off. This having been done, blockages and discomfort will eventually melt away; it may already be under way.

WATCH OUT FOR ... making only token attempts to clear yourself of old memories and feelings. Continuing emotional, verbal or physical blocks would be a testament to such partial or superficial clear-outs.

'Slowly the poison the whole blood stream fills ...
The waste remains, the waste remains and kills'

A NEWLY FORMED CONTINENT

✵ VIRGIN TERRITORY ✵

GENERAL INTERPRETATION

You have before you or within you the raw materials, with the challenges and adventures that they present. Following this can be imagined long and dramatic developments which may or may not be noticed or appreciated on first impressions. Envisioning a new life for yourself.

KEEP FOCUSED ON ... your powerful and basic sense of innovation and origination, be it of your own character or someone or something else ... what is fresh and full of potential, for this will naturally replace what is decadent and spent ... exploration and your sense of adventure.

WATCH OUT FOR ... a rough and ready nature that is in need of refinement if success and satisfaction are to be attained ... the fact that however new the territory you enter, you still take your baggage with you.

MONEY/WORK/CREATIVITY

You have the basic ingredients in terms of materials, talent, contacts or experience, which you may work on and cultivate. Eventually you will come up with something quite impressive, provided you ...

KEEP FOCUSED ON ... a regular and disciplined procedure whereby, like a sculptor, you take your lump of raw clay, mould it into the rough shape you have in mind, and then refine it with details and finishing touches ... the natural pace that things want to develop at, keeping in time with the 'seasons' of idea, experimentation, waiting, things taking form, resting.

WATCH OUT FOR ... being impatient for growth and results ... spoiling the rough and ready nature of whatever or whoever you are working on or with.

♡ LOVE/RELATING/SOCIAL

A young or barely formed individual or relationship. There is great potential here, and the free choice to do many things. The sheer wonder of it can be enthralling, intimidating, or both.

KEEP FOCUSED ON ... exercising enormous respect for the uncharted mysteries and proclivities of who or what you have in mind ... the nature of your concern by stepping back from it, seeing how it operates over a period of time, and getting its true measure ... leaving behind stale habits and attitudes, or self-destructive patterns of behaviour.

WATCH OUT FOR ... presuming on someone or something because you see no obvious signs of warning or difficulty. They are bound to be there ... jumping in with all guns blazing, simply because everything seems up for grabs.

KARMA/ATTITUDE/HEALTH

This suggests a life that is a 'clean slate' in that it lacks sophistication, but has a purity and beauty all of its own. Success is ultimately assured, but a great deal depends upon identifying and respecting its natural inclinations, and allowing the personality or situation to develop at its own healthy pace.

KEEP FOCUSED ON ... the original potential contained within whatever or whoever is the object of your concern. Through focusing upon this you are made aware what is required; it teaches you what to do, rather than the other way around ... the wonder of the new.

WATCH OUT FOR ... unexpected, hidden aspects that could be no danger in themselves, but when coming into contact with others who are unaware, harm could arise ... unwanted growth ... not growing or developing when the situation calls for it.

'Atlantis will rise, Babylon will fall'

WIND, CLOUDS AND HASTE

☆ THE TRANSITORY ☆

 GENERAL INTERPRETATION

Change and uncertainty, and the pressures these two hands of Fate mete out, seemingly forcing us to hurry things to a conclusion or resolution. The comings and goings, the ups and downs, and the rushing hither and thither, which are the lot of most people, but which provide an inexhaustible supply of interest and enthusiasm – and needless anxiety. The ephemeral.

KEEP FOCUSED ON ... accustoming yourself to living with uncertainty, letting things unfold as they will, in their own time ... your lust for life that is ever able to maintain its poise and hold its course amidst the hustle and bustle of the everyday world, enjoying every moment as being sufficient unto itself ... keeping cool, stable and unruffled.

WATCH OUT FOR ... squandering time or wasting energy on what is inconsequential or very unlikely.

 LOVE/RELATING/SOCIAL

We have here a passing relationship, interlude or feeling within a lasting relationship. Notwithstanding a more mystical or philosophical approach to this (see Karma below), it should be, or become, obvious which it is for you. In either case ...

KEEP FOCUSED ON ... letting go of the experience, while at the same time cherishing or noting the experience for what it is – or was – because it could soon be gone ... the positive moments for they are the seeds of a positive future ... the negative moments as the husks of past negative experiences needing to be discarded.

WATCH OUT FOR ... clinging on to anxieties and making them into future events ... trying to fix, contain or possess someone for this will surely hasten the loss of whatever it is you wish to keep.

 MONEY/WORK/CREATIVITY

The object of your enquiry is either of passing concern, or the critical point has already passed and the answer is 'blowing in the wind'. Alternatively, the nature of your work is concerned with ephemera, such as a daily newspaper, for example, and encompasses all that this Symbol represents. Financial matters would also be concerned with or dependent upon such passing affairs and daily rounds.

KEEP FOCUSED ON ... and work on what you can change easily and swiftly; if not, just let things go as they will ... what is in the air for whatever it is you wish to have, know or use ... appreciating and utilizing the relatively superficial mind-set of the general public in order to fashion your common touch.

WATCH OUT FOR ... getting in too deep or being too profound, for circumstances probably do not merit it. Things are currently in a state of flux.

 KARMA/ATTITUDE/HEALTH

Change is the only constant. This paradox is suited to the stable and unchanging nature of Taurus: trying to keep all as it is or 'should be' can have you chasing your tail; or the whirlwind of life can have you as the still eye observing it from the centre. The regular and predictable movement of the planets in their courses is stability and duration itself. A true grasp and control of life's passing show is attained by letting go of it and trusting things to come and go as they will, when they will.

KEEP FOCUSED ON ... the idea that there is great freedom and wisdom in learning how to allow life's moments and events to fly by, at the same time appreciating and being part of their timelessness.

WATCH OUT FOR ... impatience with or doubts concerning life's patently intelligent processes.

'All things must pass'

A FINGER POINTING IN AN OPEN BOOK

✫ AND SO IT IS WRITTEN ✫

☀ GENERAL INTERPRETATION

A situation in which you are made aware of what is significant and important. A critical point in the proceedings. Something that can be found on the printed page (or screen), and the authority, justified or not, that this implies. Issues of relevance; the salient factor.

KEEP FOCUSED ON ... giving the situation the attention it merits, deducing its full implications ... researching and discovering whatever it is you wish to know, for it is available somewhere ... your sense of precision and enduring meaning that guides and enriches your own life and the lives of others.

WATCH OUT FOR ... being misguided by the letter of the law for want of being able to appreciate the spirit of it ... taking things too literally.

♥ LOVE/RELATING/SOCIAL

A significant point has been reached in a relationship or your social life. You are aware, or are being made aware, of some particularly important aspect to this and it is imperative that you take it on board and not disregard it. A defining moment.

KEEP FOCUSED ON ... guiding principles that either have been published or in some other way have weight and approval ... moving onwards rather than lingering too long over an experience because it is was so good or bad.

WATCH OUT FOR ... conducting your emotional life according to a doctrine or theory; it is not that simple. A reference point can be very useful, but it should not be regarded as an all-round guide to the vagaries of the human heart and soul, not to mention the sex drive, which cannot 'read' at all!

⚘ MONEY/WORK/CREATIVITY

The Oracle is simply saying 'carry on' or 'look where you have got to', especially if your enquiry has anything to do with books or writing. Generally, the answers or facts are there to be seen. With regard to finances, it is saying for you to look to your accounts and you will discover what you need to know there.

KEEP FOCUSED ON ... the figures appertaining to your situation, taking heed of what they tell you, and making plans accordingly.

WATCH OUT FOR ... ignoring, hard facts or written evidence and information ... fixing the books.

☯ KARMA/ATTITUDE/HEALTH

You are being shown, or you have to show someone, the writing on the wall. Fully digesting and understanding it will equip you for the next phase of your journey or situation. Health matters may require research before coming to any conclusion.

KEEP FOCUSED ON ... whatever is set before you, deal with it, and then be ready for the next issue or question. In this way you will successfully reach a conclusion.

WATCH OUT FOR ... believing that the written word is final. Every book was written by another fallible human being.

'The moving finger writes, and, having writ, moves on'

WHITE DOVE OVER TROUBLED WATERS

☆ PEACE AND GOODWILL ☆

 GENERAL INTERPRETATION

Whatever is giving you cause for concern is either groundless or there is relief or supply close at hand. Right now, whatever is disturbing you is being removed, allayed or cancelled – or is about to be.

KEEP FOCUSED ON ... the ultimate healing power that the tranquillity and order of Creation has over all the vicissitudes of life, especially on the plane of feeling ... your skill in bringing solace to those around you with a sense that everything will be all right in the end, and how this feeling immediately begins to improve the nature of experience in the present moment, even though it may be fraught and distressed.

WATCH OUT FOR ... well-intentioned but wishful thinking, the effect of which is temporary and superficial, if not downright ineffectual.

 LOVE/RELATING/SOCIAL

Any disturbance or strife in your love or social life is about to be quelled, or it already has been. It is also possible, or necessary, that your relationship or way of relating attracts peace and goodwill, and bestows them upon others.

KEEP FOCUSED ON ... whatever it is in you or another that has a healing and reassuring effect, for this will in turn create or awaken the same talent in others. This is how world peace is created ... your own heart and the hearts of others ... the fact that selfless love is the only real answer.

WATCH OUT FOR ... any possible snags or pitfalls in your love or social life and, with your strong sense of understanding and kindness, remedy them before they have time to cause any damage.

 MONEY/WORK/CREATIVITY

There is a sound and caring element in play that is bringing goodwill and ease of expression, so there is no need to feel anxious about anything because matters will eventually go well or be sorted out successfully. Auspicious endeavours are concerned with helping people with difficulties; effective troubleshooting.

KEEP FOCUSED ON ... whatever or whoever it is that has the true welfare and vision, for it will be them who create the solutions, open up the way ... surveying with a sense of generosity and compassion what it is that is giving you cause for concern, and in your heart you will know that all is well, or is going to go well.

WATCH OUT FOR ... being too laid-back for this dulls your edge ... mistaking weakness for kindness, or being too easygoing, for you could be taken advantage of.

KARMA/ATTITUDE/HEALTH

Whatever ails you, or has been like a shadow cast over you from the past, is now being healed or lifted – or, at the very least, is in a position to be so.

KEEP FOCUSED ON ... your heart as the seat and ultimate creator of good health, both physically and psychologically ... the fact that there is such a thing as the Divine, as Angels, as plain goodness, always seeking to heal, bring peace, offering a resting place ... a feeling within you of surrender and peace to a transcendental force for the good ... that peace which surpasses human understanding.

WATCH OUT FOR ... not trusting that all the above is true, and then attempting to 'fix' your problem in a 'clever' or manipulative fashion.

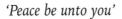

'Peace be unto you'

A JEWELLERY SHOP

☆ STORE OF GREAT WORTH ☆

✺ GENERAL INTERPRETATION

The displaying of the finest and most valuable that one has to offer, and making it available – at a price. This could also be saying that something very valuable is in store for you, be it of material or spiritual worth – or whatever it is.

KEEP FOCUSED ON ... your ability to dazzle others with your best qualities, and to show them theirs as well ... what could be called 'prosperity consciousness', that is, you act and feel as if you have a lot to offer, that you are a class act, that you are worth a great deal.

WATCH OUT FOR ... knowing the price of everything and the value of nothing ... putting out an image that you cannot hope to live up to.

♥ LOVE/RELATING/SOCIAL

'If you've got it, flaunt it!' could be one interpretation here. Hiding your light under a bushel because you are afraid of being put down or overlooked would really be missing the point. This Symbol is confirming that you *do* have something of great value to offer, or being offered to you, physically, emotionally, mentally, and maybe spiritually too.

KEEP FOCUSED ON ... rating yourself rather than expecting or waiting for someone else to do it for you ... being more sparkly, more feminine if you are female, more male if you are male, or just more of whatever you are ... what is best in others, and one other in particular, for they are a reflection of your own worth.

WATCH OUT FOR ... being flashy, brassy or a show-off – at least, not for too long ... being superficial or insincere, merely for effect.

⚚ MONEY/WORK/CREATIVITY

The obvious interpretation in this material context is one of good fortune. Resources and talents in abundance.

KEEP FOCUSED ON ... the fact that what you have in mind or on offer is of substantial worth – even the tackiest jewellery shops have some gems in stock! ... putting a decent price and value upon whatever you are considering.

WATCH OUT FOR ... being greedy or, conversely, undervaluing yourself and everything associated with you ... fakes or cheap imitations.

☯ KARMA/ATTITUDE/HEALTH

Spiritually this looks very promising, considering how diamonds and jewels figure in the symbolism of certain religions, especially Buddhism. Because you have a pure desire to be enlightened you will follow the right path. Health matters also look favourable, possibly because you are getting the best treatment. Healing through crystals. Karmically, there appears to be some great store of talent and goodwill present, or on its way.

KEEP FOCUSED ON ... the glory and wonder of whatever your situation, for it is there, even though it may be hidden by external settings or trappings that do no credit to the inner worth.

WATCH OUT FOR ... spiritual pride, or for allowing material considerations or status symbols to get in the way of seeing things clearly.

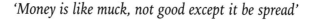

'Money is like muck, not good except it be spread'

A MOUNTED INDIAN WITH SCALP LOCKS

☆ SEIZING POWER ☆

GENERAL INTERPRETATION

This primitive Symbol engenders a symbol in itself. Through grasping the 'crown' of someone or something, one is taking possession of their powers, mastering or overcoming whatever it might mean, pose or threaten. Or possibly something or someone is seizing yours or 'crowning' you.

KEEP FOCUSED ON ... maintaining or developing your control over a situation, born of a willingness to grasp the nettle and make something your own ... going for it with desire, will and passion, then see what you have and how you feel.

WATCH OUT FOR ... avaricious and intimidating usage of others ... macho behaviour or male chauvinism.

LOVE/RELATING/SOCIAL

When taken too literally, such a Symbol of primitive instincts and caveman-type aggression has little place in modern-day relating and social behaviour. However, we are not as 'civilized' as we like to think we are, for we still like to express and experience raw feelings and signs of being the 'property' of one another. In fact, at certain times where it is critical that feelings be made more definite, we need to ...

KEEP FOCUSED ON ... showing unequivocally our feelings and intentions towards others ... recognizing such signs from another as basic evidence of their interest, rather than seeing them as being crude or pushy, although it is a fine line that separates directness from being brutal.

WATCH OUT FOR ... shilly-shallying around in the guise of being 'considerate' or politically correct.

MONEY/WORK/CREATIVITY

A powerful and impressive, but dangerous idea or commodity. Possibly your situation is either one that cannot move or improve unless aggressive, decisive and even ruthless action is taken, or one which has become excessively competitive and powermongering to the point of destabilizing the whole.

KEEP FOCUSED ON ... whatever is the object or source of power in terms of wealth, position, ideas and resources, and on finding a genuine and justifiable means of attaining it; this Symbol is telling you that it is there for you to claim as your own.

WATCH OUT FOR ... getting in over your head – somebody could 'scalp' you, take you for more than you can afford ... the dog-eat-dog world of business and commerce; prepare yourself for this if need be.

KARMA/ATTITUDE/HEALTH

Something primitive and possibly brutal is present in your past or karma, either as a perpetrator or victim of such. More particularly, it is the Seizing of Power that could allude to anything from ritual abuse to insensitively invasive surgery or some such act where one person is violated or at the mercy of another. To heal or deal with the wounds caused by this, be they yours or another's ...

KEEP FOCUSED ON ... the fact that it is all to do with power, whether it is used, abused, misused, unused or lost in some way ... how power figures, or has figured, in your life, determining how you may regain your power if you have lost it (which probably includes discovering how and why you lost it), or how having stolen or abused someone else's is affecting you now.

WATCH OUT FOR ... any use of power other than what evidently promotes the general good ... being afraid of using power, for it could then be used against you.

'Carpe diem' (Seize the day)

A LARGE WELL-KEPT PUBLIC PARK

✧ PLEASING ORDER ✧

❂ GENERAL INTERPRETATION

On the face of it, everything is in order, is being admirably and regularly tended to. Overall, here are the fruits of social integration and order that allow people to enjoy facilities that they probably could not achieve on their own. In a word, civilization, something that should act as steward to Mother Earth herself.

KEEP FOCUSED ON ... exercising your practical concern for the general welfare, leading to a satisfying sense of organization ... making full use of what your society has to offer, especially with regard to recreation and relaxation.

WATCH OUT FOR ... a superficial or cosmetic arrangement of things that ultimately attracts abuse. Pretentiousness ... letting things fall into a state of disuse or disrepair.

♡ LOVE/RELATING/SOCIAL

Here is a healthy relationship where each person knows their role and place. Things are planted and grown, admired and enjoyed. The basis for a good family life or social centre that others can draw and benefit from. Also, facilities are available to you to improve your social or love life.

KEEP FOCUSED ON ... seeing yourself and your relationship as part of the fabric of society; in this way it will feed and support you, while you contribute towards it ... frequenting places that have a civilized atmosphere that is conducive to meeting and engaging with others.

WATCH OUT FOR ... making you and yours too accessible, for this would leave insufficient time for the fostering and maintaining of your private concerns, and find you too stretched for comfort ... selfishly imposing just your idea of order.

♛ MONEY/WORK/CREATIVITY

All appears to be working well, plans for growth implemented, excellent facilities made available or utilized. Alternatively, this Symbol could be pointing you towards an organization that knows how to accomplish such things.

KEEP FOCUSED ON ... making sure that matters are laid out properly, include all that is necessary, and meet the public's needs ... ensuring that all is maintained and maintainable ... providing amenities that serve to improve the work and environment, and thereby the quality of work itself.

WATCH OUT FOR ... abuse or misuse. This can be prevented by everyone feeling they have a valid role to play, but mainly through imaginatively creating an atmosphere that evokes respect and a feeling of being a part of something.

☯ KARMA/ATTITUDE/HEALTH

Imaged here is something or someone of great peace, sublime beauty and cosmic order. Whatever or whoever this is acts as a guiding star or waymark as you follow the path of life, leading you on towards your destiny. Health-wise, all is in order, or is in a position to be restored to order.

KEEP FOCUSED ON ... an image (like this Symbol) or feeling that gives rise to a state of order ... what the system or another organization has to offer by way of health care ... making the best of what you've got.

WATCH OUT FOR ... an impersonal attitude or 'official' form of tending and caring that can never substitute for the more private and personal kind. Each one of us is a little garden that needs individual attention within that greater garden of life as a whole ... any kind of abuse, including that of neglect.

'... and happy as the grass was green'

A SPANIARD SERENADING HIS SEÑORITA

☆ PASSION AND SKILL ☆

 GENERAL INTERPRETATION

A passionate and creative means of attaining objectives is in evidence here. Or if not, it needs to be, because that objective expects and depends on such a display in order to make an impression, to win someone or something. The power of feeling has to be coupled with skill and control.

KEEP FOCUSED ON ... your ability to immerse your feelings utterly into an experience. Through such wholehearted pursuit, the object of your desires is won over ... giving out hot-blooded and unmistakable emotional messages ... music and song as possible means of putting something across or creating a certain atmosphere.

WATCH OUT FOR ... corny or egocentric ways of making an impression that are doomed to failure or ridicule ... feeble expressions or overtures.

 MONEY/WORK/CREATIVITY

Apart from being auspicious for any creative, particularly musical, pursuit, this Symbol is saying that in order to attain what you are after, or to resolve any difficulty, you would have to make some sort of 'overture'. This means that you ...

KEEP FOCUSED ON ... exactly what appeals to or is required by the object of your concern and pour yourself heart and soul into the matter; then ambitions will be satisfied, solutions realized ... enthusiasm as being the key to success, as well as making work a joy rather than a drudge ... using charm to get what you are after.

WATCH OUT FOR ... being over-the-top in a tasteless fashion. Although this might feel good from your end, it may seem inappropriate or outmoded at the other ... mixing business with pleasure unwisely.

 LOVE/RELATING/SOCIAL

Here you have a traditionally ardent relationship, with the suitor throwing his all into charming, impressing and captivating the object of his love. But this points to a possible downside, for such an 'object of love' can be or become simply a 'love object', with ultimately disappointing results for both parties.

KEEP FOCUSED ON ... the sense that creative courtship should be followed by deep devotion, followed in turn by commitment and respect, all giving rise to such traditionally stable products of relationships as home and family. This is the way to emotional ful-filment.

WATCH OUT FOR ... male (or female) chauvinism ... hollow displays of interest or affection that are really directed at what is wanted rather than loved ... being insipid when fiery emotions are called for.

KARMA/ATTITUDE/HEALTH

Sincerely connecting with and creatively expressing what is in one's heart is possibly what life is all about. Or at least, your present state has everything to do with being true to such a passionate feeling and intent. Implied here is the probability of suffering as being part and parcel of this because genuine courtship is in itself symbolic of the drama of life being the self-perpetuating pursuit of the satisfaction of the heart's desire, for, by its very nature, it continues to create more to pursue as it pursues. Likewise, the health of the heart depends upon it being open and its contents sought after and expressed.

KEEP FOCUSED ON ... the ultimate object of desire which is encoded in the word 'serenading'. It comes from the Latin *serenus*, meaning 'bright clear sky' ... giving from the heart.

WATCH OUT FOR ... suppressing or controlling what lies in the heart – that way lie *dark* skies.

'If music be the food of love, play on'

A SQUAW SELLING BEADS

✰ MODEST OR MENIAL? ✰

✸ GENERAL INTERPRETATION

Basic practicality, particularly of the female variety. Skills learnt as part of the natural or cultural process of development are best capitalized upon in a modest and non-exploitative way.

KEEP FOCUSED ON ... your talent for profiting from your most fundamental gifts, not least because you have detached from superficial status symbols ... selling, making a profit from, what you do, make or are ... how simple, natural and bright things have perennial appeal, often over and above the more glamorous and technological.

WATCH OUT FOR ... accepting the least that you are because that is all that life and society have appeared to have recognized or validated ... underselling or undervaluing yourself and others.

♥ LOVE/RELATING/SOCIAL

Here is pictured a person (possibly female but could also be a 'soft' male) or a relationship that has an issue with regard to being or feeling downtrodden or unappreciated – or the fear of being or feeling so. This may really be the case, or purely in one's head, in which case it could become a reality. Such a person could at first appear merely willing and easygoing, if not actually subservient.

KEEP FOCUSED ON ... the probability that there are always humble tasks to be done and lowly positions to be held in any relationship, but this does not mean that one person is worth less than the other ... standing up for yourself.

WATCH OUT FOR ... making sure that no one is taking or going to take a menial, undignified role in the relationship, and that you or they are not a victim just waiting to be dominated or trapped.

♟ MONEY/WORK/CREATIVITY

This is either saying that your work or income does not have to be sensational to make it worthwhile or acceptable, or it is saying that you are undervaluing yourself and what you do to the point of putting yourself in that position – 'There's no success like failure'. The Oracle could also be favouring a natural, homespun line of work.

KEEP FOCUSED ON ... whatever your 'beads' are and then making them or seeing them as the best beads of their kind ... finding the best pitch to sell your 'beads' ... being modest in what you do and how you charge, concentrating upon the job satisfaction rather than great material reward.

WATCH OUT FOR ... the fact that there is some necessary drudge involved in most occupations, as there are slumps and times when things are slow ... being too ambitious for this could set you up for disappointment.

☯ KARMA/ATTITUDE/HEALTH

Here is stressed the value of being humble and modest as opposed to being wretched and self-pitying, and how a 'squaw' (in the sense of being someone who accepts unquestioningly an inferior position) is simply the polar opposite of a 'brave' (in the sense of someone who has the courage to stand their ground and face/take on the world).

KEEP FOCUSED ON ... in what way you might be a 'squaw' and either change it, or humbly and gracefully accept it ... in what way you are being a 'brave' and make sure that, while being in command of yourself and others, you are not being domineering to those weaker than yourself.

WATCH OUT FOR ... falling into any inferior role your culture or background has allotted you, rather than discovering and establishing your own unique and special qualities – qualities that may have been branded inadequate or not recognized at all.

'Before enlightenment: chop wood, carry water. After enlightenment: chop wood, carry water'

A WOMAN PURSUED BY MATURE ROMANCE

☆ TIMELY REWARD ☆

 GENERAL INTERPRETATION

Fate, or one's openness to Providence, brings about a 'maturing of one's assets or investments', in the form of something rounded and reliable appearing on the scene.

KEEP FOCUSED ON ... your seasoned sense of what gives life uplift and meaning, leading to ever more satisfying scenarios.

WATCH OUT FOR ... a false assumption that deprivation is final, or foolishly jumping at superficial signs of interest in yourself or from another ... assuming that such offers will always be there ... looking a gift horse in the mouth. Basically, this Oracle is favouring what is being offered to you.

 LOVE/RELATING/SOCIAL

Whether you are male or female, here is (at last) an enjoyable and possibly lasting involvement. If it isn't yet visible, it is a little way over the horizon. This probably happens owing to your attractiveness that is ever-present and always capable of taking itself to a new level of expression, regardless of age or physical appearance. You can also improve your romantic/social chances as long as you ...

KEEP FOCUSED ON ... being open to a suitor through accentuating or developing your more receptive and attractive qualities. If you are a woman, then classic female traits should be stressed ... maturity being the key to success.

WATCH OUT FOR ... emotional opportunists who are adept at giving the impression that it is you they are after when really it is merely something you have got or can supply – like sex or money.

 MONEY/WORK/CREATIVITY

You have something of great worth, or an investment that is paying off or will do so. The object of your concern does not need to be touted around or dumbed down, for it has its own ability to draw attention and acclaim based solely on its merits and pedigree. However ...

KEEP FOCUSED ON ... getting your idea or product seen in the right places in a low-key manner, rather than using a hard sell ... stressing the high class or 'quality' aspect, and aiming for the older or more intelligent/discerning customer.

WATCH OUT FOR ... undervaluing yourself and whatever you have created or are working at.

KARMA/ATTITUDE/HEALTH

The Oracle is entreating you to depend upon Fate to resolve your difficulties, to bring you what you want or need, rather that angling and worrying after such things. In the fullness of time, your patience and efforts will be rewarded.

KEEP FOCUSED ON ... the idea that something good is after you as well as you being after it ... relying on, or developing a reliance on, compassion over passion, and using your heart combined with your head.

WATCH OUT FOR ... wearing yourself out pursuing something that is not yet ready to be 'caught'.

'A woman is like a man's shadow. Walk away from it and it will follow you;
follow it and it will walk away'

TAURUS 29 DEGREES

TWO COBBLERS WORKING AT A TABLE

CO-OPERATION

GENERAL INTERPRETATION

Simple co-operation and the highly practical and lasting results that it can produce. Synergy. Stable togetherness. Shaping or trying things out until they fit, until they are capable of taking you somewhere.

KEEP FOCUSED ON ... being aware of the usefulness of what you are doing ... your integrity and industry that is a sign of your fundamentally sound and wholesome personality ... the possibility that sometimes we have to 'make do and mend'; in these days of 'take, make and throw away', this is quite desirable and environmentally friendly ... breaking in whatever needs to be so.

WATCH OUT FOR ... an inclination to waste your time and energy on tasks or commitments that provide bread but little else.

LOVE/RELATING/SOCIAL

Before two or more people can work together as one there has to be an understanding, and often this understanding can only be arrived at by thrashing things out 'across the table' or knowing what it's like to 'stand inside their shoes'. It may not be a case of 'working together as one' but reaching an understanding where you agree to differ. It takes two to tango.

KEEP FOCUSED ON ... meeting one another halfway ... having a shared goal or task ... pointing out and protecting each other's sensitive spots ... the other as being a 'worthy opponent' against whom you develop emotional strength and self-awareness, if or because you hold very different perspectives on life and love.

WATCH OUT FOR ... being oversensitive to other's opinions, ways or habits. This is like forcing yourself to wear shoes that don't fit.

MONEY/WORK/CREATIVITY

Here is a straightforward image of two (or more) people working together at something, complementing each other's skills and benefiting from having more than one view of the job in hand. The management of staff and resources.

KEEP FOCUSED ON ... sharing knowledge or pooling resources and thereby reaching a target or solving a problem ... allocating various tasks to the appropriate individuals or parts ... the possibility that specialization could be a path worth taking ... hammering out plans or agreements ... bouncing ideas off anyone whose opinions you respect ... preparing for later advances.

WATCH OUT FOR ... professional jealousy or over-competitiveness, for this is ultimately counterproductive ... discord between workers and management (mismanagement) for this could be a disaster in the making.

KARMA/ATTITUDE/HEALTH

The goal of the individual is to become an 'integrated personality'. This is like doing a jigsaw of yourself or getting a pair of shoes to fit you perfectly. You are in the process of doing just this, and it will produce positive results as long as you ...

KEEP FOCUSED ON ... some overall vision or shape that everything and every part of you must cleave and be true to ... reshaping or refashioning anything about you that does not fit, further or conform to this goal, or that sees no goal at all.

WATCH OUT FOR ... making life harder for yourself than it need be because of some minor part of your personality (such as a habit or attitude) that does not 'fit' your personality as a whole. Identify it, and get it in line or eliminate it. Such an inner conflict of interests can create indecisiveness, emotional stress, physical tension, pressure or discomfort.

'Life without industry is guilt, and industry without art is brutality'

A PEACOCK PARADING ON AN ANCIENT LAWN

☆ INHERENT WEALTH AND PRIVILEGE ☆

✷ GENERAL INTERPRETATION

On the face of it, there is a promise or prospect here of wealth and opulence, or at least the show of it from someone else. More subtly, though, this Symbol implies that you have a background or sense of splendour and elevated position. How you use this, or how relevant it is to the more ordinary, day-to-day world, could be a question.

KEEP FOCUSED ON ... what can profit from a show of style and grandeur, rather than assuming that this is enough in itself ... your inner sense of style and richness.

WATCH OUT FOR ... pretentious aspirations or dwelling on previous glories for they divorce one from, rather than connect one with, the situation in hand ... egotistical displays that attract scorn or damage rather than the admiration that it expects ... what is bright but brainless.

♡ LOVE/RELATING/SOCIAL

A romantic or glamorous image of relationships. The burning question is whether this can be realized and maintained as something gracious and ordered, or whether it is just a fantasy born of an immature dream that acts as a compensation for real life and 'ordinary' love. Showing off could also be an important element here, its validity depending upon whether or not the goods are delivered.

KEEP FOCUSED ON ... what you have to give to another, which is considerable, rather than what you can get from them.

WATCH OUT FOR ... the 'prince or princess syndrome' where you believe you are entitled to more than you actually are ... outmoded or inappropriate ways of relating such as macho strutting or being coquettish or a femme fatale.

MONEY/WORK/CREATIVITY

You or the object of your concern certainly has the potential and vision to be successful. There is a sense of what is grand and impressive. What is required is that you ...

KEEP FOCUSED ON ... creating or maintaining a product that matches the advertisement or intention. Also, the sheer abundance of your plans and ideas necessitates good ordering and management. An English stately home, for example, takes a lot of expertise and resourcefulness to give the impression that it runs itself.

WATCH OUT FOR ... having titanic aspirations while not putting in the spadework that is essential to making something out of the real potential that you have.

KARMA/ATTITUDE/HEALTH

This harks back to a previously held position of grace and privilege. The critical thing is how that sense or memory is now applied or experienced. Could it be an attempt to simulate Heaven on Earth, to blend natural beauty with man-made order? Or a frustrated and misguided hankering after past glories and advantages?

KEEP FOCUSED ON ... taking pride in your health and well-being, and in helping others to attain or maintain the same. From this you create and maintain dignity or grandeur with respect to the external or formal side of life with your inherent knack for making the most out of whatever constitutes your background, inner life or history, and thereby introducing to the world a palpable sense of what is fine and great.

WATCH OUT FOR ... flaunting wealth or privilege, whether real or faked, for it can elicit scorn, loss or injury.

'True style and pedigree need never vaunt themselves; they are plain for all to see'

⚥

THE SABIAN SYMBOLS OF
GEMINI

Either directly, or in a subtle way, all these Symbols are concerned with the following qualities,
or with situations that involve or call for them:

COMMUNICATION
⚥

CONTACTS
⚥

EVERYDAY OR PASSING AFFAIRS
⚥

HUMOUR
⚥

LEVITY
⚥

LOCAL TRAVEL
⚥

LUNGS, ARMS AND HANDS
⚥

NEIGHBOURS
⚥

NERVES
⚥

NIMBLENESS
⚥

PRIMARY AND SECONDARY EDUCATION
⚥

QUICKNESS
⚥

SIBLINGS
⚥

WRITING AND SPEAKING
⚥

A GLASS-BOTTOMED BOAT IN STILL WATER

☆ LUCIDITY THROUGH TRANSPARENCY ☆

✹ GENERAL INTERPRETATION

An ability, need or opportunity to see the unconscious or underlying realities of the situation or life in general – possibly only when one feels safe and calm. A certain transparency of being that can be elucidating or naive. This is also one of the Symbols that sometimes refer to the use of the Oracle itself.

KEEP FOCUSED ON ... an openness to the infinite possibilities that life has to offer ... the possibility that the Oracle is trying to tell you something obvious which you cannot see for the looking ... being emotionally still enough to see clearly and with great insight.

WATCH OUT FOR ... getting nowhere as a result of indecision or a reluctance to become genuinely and emotionally involved.

♥ LOVE/RELATING/SOCIAL

This Symbol, like all Sabian Symbols, can mean whatever you choose it to mean by way of association. For instance, does it mean that in a relationship you feel like an open book to one another, trusting one another? Or does a relationship provoke in you a fear of being seen through, of having what you think of as your shameful or unattractive parts exposed? If it is the latter, this poses a difficulty in connecting emotionally.

KEEP FOCUSED ON ... your innermost feelings in an as calm and detached a manner as possible, allowing the inner truth of your being to come into view, acknowledging, accepting and caring for it as you do so. Then allow others to see this part of you also. This is healing and bonding ... being seen.

WATCH OUT FOR ... feeling bad about being excluded when you yourself are excluding, aloof or backward in coming forward.

MONEY/WORK/CREATIVITY

With an open mind and an absolute minimum of expectation or agenda, you are able to see what underlying trends, opportunities or incipient problems are in play. On seeing whatever catches your curiosity or enthusiasm, you can then make a decisive dive for it and thereby attract what you need or desire.

KEEP FOCUSED ON ... whatever arena is most likely to present you with what you are searching for, like a seabird soaring in the sky looking for fish. A casualness and apparent lack of intent is what makes the target visible and available.

WATCH OUT FOR ... being lulled into inactivity by indecision or fear of getting your feet wet; otherwise significant others, ideas or solutions will consistently fail to come your way.

☯ KARMA/ATTITUDE/HEALTH

This emphasizes that you have the ability or opportunity to see clearly into the mysteries of life. However, it also stresses the necessity of stilling your own thoughts and emotions to the extent that they do not obscure those insights.

KEEP FOCUSED ON ... whatever strikes you as being wonderful, beautiful, transcendental, otherworldly, unfamiliar or strange, for therein lies the way ahead ... looking deeply into the issue; this will reveal what you wish to see.

WATCH OUT FOR ... making whatever you are looking at – the object of your enquiry – seem bleak or chaotic simply because you are viewing it through an agitated lens. Don't rock the boat! ... giving too much away in a naive desire to be accepted ... looking too hard; give it a rest if necessary.

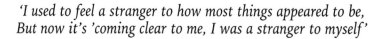

'I used to feel a stranger to how most things appeared to be,
But now it's 'coming clear to me, I was a stranger to myself'

SANTA CLAUS FILLING STOCKINGS FURTIVELY

☆ GOODNESS UNSEEN ☆

 GENERAL INTERPRETATION

Occasioned or called for is the endearing tradition or belief that innocence is looked after and appreciated by spiritual forces or the elders, even if they have to employ some artifice to do so.

KEEP FOCUSED ON ... your simple faith that magic and care is always in the air, bringing ultimate joy and goodwill ... that if you are open to receive, then it shall be given ... the fact, that although you may not be aware of it or believe it, goodness is coming (out of this, the issue of your concern).

WATCH OUT FOR ... a naive expectation that others are as good-hearted as you would like to believe ... doubts, for they are born of the ego's fears, and they must 'go to sleep' for the 'stockings' to be filled, for Goodness Unseen to be given a chance to put things right, to restore faith.

 MONEY/WORK/CREATIVITY

Apart from a literal case of referring to something to do with Christmas trade, this is more likely to be saying that goodwill and generosity in business are now required, especially since it is often sadly lacking. More subtly, though, the chance or advisability of exercising a covert scheme in order to succeed – so long as it is in the best interest of all concerned.

KEEP FOCUSED ON ... the probability that something is being given – be it ideas, funds, abilities or custom – in a roundabout way, secretly ... doing what you do for altruistic reasons. Philanthropy: expressing it or receiving it.

WATCH OUT FOR ... making the object of your concern into just another transaction or commercial/political manoeuvre.

 LOVE/RELATING/SOCIAL

On the face of it, this Symbol seems to be referring to and counselling the kind of unconditional love that can be shown by parents to children, or that is supposed to be shown to one another during the 'season of goodwill'. There is also a sexual connotation regarding the conflict that can arise from not being open about the object of one's desire or affections.

KEEP FOCUSED ON ... good-heartedness and generosity as the eternal mainstay of love between individuals and amongst society as a whole ... the idea that wherever there is love, one should not have to go as a 'thief in the night'.

WATCH OUT FOR ... denying yourself the love and goodwill of others because you feel undeserving of it yourself – the 'Scrooge' complex ... shyness subverting goodness.

KARMA/ATTITUDE/HEALTH

Remember that virtue is its own reward. Bearing goodwill to others makes you feel good too – especially when the recipient of your goodwill does not know where it came from. Do not be put off or become disheartened by the ill will of others; have faith that your goodwill will penetrate their hearts in the fullness of time, and that there is a goodness that originates from an 'invisible realm'.

KEEP FOCUSED ON ... the fact that often the most effective means of helping or healing someone is to do it in such a way that they do not know about your help. A person's ego is well-known for resisting even what is good for them.

WATCH OUT FOR ... playing at there being an 'invisible realm', acknowledging it in theory, but giving it no practical expression or allowing it into your life; this demands a suspension of those ego-generated doubts and fears.

'Blessed be'

THE GARDEN OF THE TUILERIES

✧ CLASSICAL STYLE AND FORM ✧

✷ GENERAL INTERPRETATION

In representing the order and wealth resulting from the acquisition of position and power following the Renaissance in Europe during the reign of King Louis IV of France, this Symbol suggests 'The Golden Mean', a device whereby the man-made is put in harmony with Nature, making for a healthy and pleasing environment.

KEEP FOCUSED ON ... your unmistakable and unerring sense of the stately and gracious that gives rise to a heightened sense of life's material or emotional possibilities, and sets an example to others ... the best becoming available to the many ... devising or observing a formal layout, rules or plan with regard to the situation.

WATCH OUT FOR ... a privileged or exclusive attitude or position that puts one dangerously out of touch with what is going on at street level.

♡ LOVE/RELATING/SOCIAL

Often there is an inclination to have a preconceived ideal in mind where relationships and social activity are concerned. One then tries to get what actually happens to fit this template of 'how things ought to be'. Marriage is possibly the most common manifestation of this, and as such it serves to both guide and limit, reassure and disillusion. And so ...

KEEP FOCUSED ON ... the guidelines and precepts that you have decided upon that will keep you on the straight and narrow ... the fact that true beauty dwells within ... being gracious.

WATCH OUT FOR ... keeping to certain rules that are either outmoded or inappropriate to your standing or means ... any dyed-in-the-wool ideas or values that suffocate spontaneity and ingenuousness, and that prevent you from being natural and relaxed with one another.

⚘ MONEY/WORK/CREATIVITY

You have a heightened sense of the object of your concern, but in order to make it a reality you need to organize yourself or it according to an elegant formula that has been seen to work, and to make sure that it is relevant to the ordinary world around you. Also, limits are set on your time and availability when you have business to attend to.

KEEP FOCUSED ON ... what has significance, and what pleases the masses, yet at the same time satisfies your inner vision of something better ... the fact that this will take a lot of time and effort to accomplish ... simplicity taking preference over complexity.

WATCH OUT FOR ... an overly exclusive way of going about your business, unless of course, you are aiming to make whatever it is just that – exclusive ... letting form overtake content.

☯ KARMA/ATTITUDE/HEALTH

Deep within you lies a notion of a perfectly proportioned life, a life of grace and order, where everything and everyone has its proper place and time. It is up to you whether this translates into a rigid and exclusive world that is all form and little content, or whether it serves as an image of grace and harmony to which you and others may aspire.

KEEP FOCUSED ON ... visualizing what creates such order and harmony, rather than insisting it be there or complaining because it is not. Love or ill health will sometimes challenge you to live up to your model of harmony.

WATCH OUT FOR ... laziness or fecklessness born of previous riches or times of ease and privilege ... thinking that it should all be laid out for you or fall into your lap ... trying to control what should be left to itself because of a neurotic need for perfection ... hubris.

'Art follows Nature'

HOLLY AND MISTLETOE

☆ RITUAL AND RENEWAL ☆

 ### GENERAL INTERPRETATION

Here promised or suggested is the magic of renewal as symbolized by the celebration of the Winter Solstice when the days at last begin to lengthen again. Now is a good time to perform an act of renewal for yourself or for anyone or anything else. But, while mistletoe is symbolic of renewal, holly represents the suffering involved (Christ's blood and crown of thorns); it also represents the everlasting and spiritual protection of one's life force.

KEEP FOCUSED ON ... using your gift for imbuing certain moments with a deep sense of meaning and occasion that fellow beings can instinctively identify with and be inspired by.

WATCH OUT FOR ... pre-occupation with superficial formalities while failing to appreciate their underlying significance.

 ### MONEY/WORK/CREATIVITY

In the material world this Symbol has a sharply divided significance. Of late, Christmas has come to mean an opportunity to sell more goods. Traditionally, however, it was a time of goodwill and renewal. So, the Oracle is saying that you can prostitute whatever is the object of your concern in a bid to make a material profit, or you can respect your idea or product for its inner value and not pander to the marketplace.

KEEP FOCUSED ON ... honestly making the ends justify the means. If you cannot do this, because it compromises your values, then resist commercialization. If commercialism still manages to satisfy some inner value or need for renewal, then all well and good.

WATCH OUT FOR ... leaching off anything or anyone that you depend on or utilize – biting the hand that feeds.

♥ LOVE/RELATING/SOCIAL

This is pointing to a relationship that brings about renewal, or is in need of renewal. It could also mean that you or another needs to be renewed by a relationship, or to renew their role in a relationship. Or there is the possibility of a parasitic or opportunistic presence implied, but this may have some subtle role, so be careful not to condemn it out of hand.

KEEP FOCUSED ON ... devising a simple ritual whereby you revere your pain and dependencies for what they are. It is only when you offer up and solemnly admit to your vulnerability that a transformation can occur ... the beauty and significance of your pain and need, and you will see that there is a holy quality about it.

WATCH OUT FOR ... how you or somebody else might be protecting themselves to the point of preventing another getting close to them.

KARMA/ATTITUDE/HEALTH

This is a message that says that there is something eternal, and that there is always somebody there for you, on this plane or another one. It is saying that life itself is eternal, that we renew ourselves lifetime after lifetime, and can also do so within a lifetime. Also, where Pagan and Christian meet.

KEEP FOCUSED ON ... the image of Holly and Mistletoe, for it is a powerful symbol having an ancient significance as well as a personal one. What do the holly prickles remind you of? Pain, defences and prickliness? The holly berries? Blood, menstruation and life? The mistletoe? Parasitism, stolen kisses and eggs/sperm? Let the images work upon your mind to reveal truths about your current state, especially your health. Whatever it evokes, strive to revere its significance.

WATCH OUT FOR ... giving up, or thinking that anything is final and unalterable.

'The magic and the beauty are still to be found/If you can spy a bluebird's wing'

A RADICAL MAGAZINE

☆ ROOTING OUT AND ROOTING FOR ☆

⚙ GENERAL INTERPRETATION

The Oracle suggests a composed or packaged way of presenting or communicating something extraordinary, unorthodox or rebellious. Also, dealing with or exposing anything in a radical manner, if need be.

KEEP FOCUSED ON ... an inner conviction that ignores external convention. Approaching the object of your concern in an unusual or unconventional way.

WATCH OUT FOR ... a reactionary urge to take issue, for this means that you have not worked out that the consequences might be worse than what you had before ... knee-jerk reactions to anything that appears to be unjust when it is really just different from you or not to your taste.

♥ LOVE/RELATING/SOCIAL

Here is imaged a person or relationship that departs from the norm and espouses a morality that is shocking or challenging in some way. Whether you agree with it or not, it or they are still demanding that you have a good look at what you believe is right for you, emotionally and morally. You need to ...

KEEP FOCUSED ON ... aligning yourself with your own set of values, otherwise you will be led from pillar to post, with security often giving way to unpredictability ... forging together the rules that work for you as a couple or group rather than being confused by conventional standards.

WATCH OUT FOR ... just being politically correct, 'liberal' or 'open' when really it is a case of you being afraid of confronting your own emotional truth or committing to something long-term – and being left alone with your principles.

MONEY/WORK/CREATIVITY

Your work and finances should subordinate themselves to an underlying policy of reform, to find their direction and character by departing from the norm, and possibly by being outspoken. The Oracle favours anything that makes people aware of something they need to know in a way that is easily accessible. Perhaps this can also refer to a need for a radical change in expenditure and money management.

KEEP FOCUSED ON ... the essence of the point you wish to make, believing and living by that point yourself ... perfecting the 'sound bite' by making your point in a punchy, precise and economical fashion.

WATCH OUT FOR ... being glib or trite, for although there might be some initial appeal, it'll wear off like water-based graffiti.

☯ KARMA/ATTITUDE/HEALTH

The call of this Symbol is finding a voice for what you and your kindred spirits believe in. It also refers to health, as much can be done to heal with the use of words that reach into the very root of a condition. When something is unhealthy at a structural level (as distinct from a functional one), this Symbol could be referring to something more radical, such as surgery.

KEEP FOCUSED ON ... putting time and energy into whatever the *cause* is, be it in the sense of something you pursue or crusade for, or the fundamental reason for something being the way it is. If you are not definitely connected with and aware of the cause, then any effect you wish to create will be superficial and short-lasting.

WATCH OUT FOR ... complacency, for such an attitude will eventually undermine all you stand for, or put you out of touch with current trends.

'Today's radicals are tomorrow's conservatives'

DRILLING FOR OIL

☆ PROBING AND PROSPECTING ☆

GENERAL INTERPRETATION

Having to delve as deep as necessary in order to find what you are after. This involves hard and 'dirty' work and investment of time and resources, but its potential rewards are very great. Sometimes we might tap into something we'd rather not be involved with.

KEEP FOCUSED ON ... maintaining a depth and intensity of resolve, yet at the same time taking only calculated risks ... the faith that there is something worthwhile at the end of it all – and there will be, because that is what keeps you going ... 'capping' or forestalling troublesome events or possibilities.

WATCH OUT FOR ... just hoping for the best, stabbing around in the dark in erratic attempts to make an impression or profit ... wasting time and resources in the wrong area.

LOVE/RELATING/SOCIAL

Relationships, especially in their early stages, are rather like prospecting in that we sound one another out, or play the field, then become more deeply involved – or not, as the case may be. Then again, we may suddenly have a 'gusher', like falling head over heels in love or getting more than we can cope with. But cope we must.

KEEP FOCUSED ON ... the fact that, at present, you may be just looking to see what might be emotionally available. If you do 'strike' though, remember that what you get at first is just 'crude' or raw emotion; it'll need refining as time goes by ... how deep you really want to go.

WATCH OUT FOR ... just 'drilling' with little or no preparedness for a deeper commitment should it become necessary ... just wanting a 'bit on the side'; you are likely to get more than you bargained for.

MONEY/WORK/CREATIVITY

You are in the process of discovering what you are after. Sometimes you may wonder if you are getting anywhere, in which case you may need to take a step back and survey the area of your endeavour with a fresh eye.

KEEP FOCUSED ON ... the supremely obvious fact that you never know what you are after or going to get until you actually get it. One can only do all that is necessary – and make sure that others do so too ... believing that one day you will make that 'strike', for doubt is the very thing that could stop you short of making it ... doing things in an informed and researched way ... knowing the drill.

WATCH OUT FOR ... looking too long for profit or results when time and experience tell you there is none to be found. Cut your losses.

KARMA/ATTITUDE/HEALTH

The answer lies within. Our present day lives rest on the strata of all that has gone before – our memories, feelings and experiences. We can go consciously probing for what lies within, or have it 'accidentally' brought to the surface by an event or relationship. Such probing can be very difficult, especially when we hit the bedrock of a hard and apparently impenetrable emotion or locked-away memory. It is then that we must ...

KEEP FOCUSED ON ... the fact that what we are after is worth the pain, effort and discomfort, and that we must see things through, sooner or later ... always living to dig another day, and to access that reservoir or resource eventually.

WATCH OUT FOR ... the probability that the time or place is not something we can be sure of, and that it is only through digging down deep that we really find out what's what.

'Seek and ye shall find'

GEMINI 7 DEGREES

AN OLD-FASHIONED WELL

SOURCE AND REFRESHMENT

GENERAL INTERPRETATION

Here is where one may obtain emotional, spiritual, intellectual or physical nourishment. The meaning of Hexagram 48 in the Chinese oracle, *I Ching*, is identical to this. Water or nourishment is always there at some level, yet its accessibility is the crucial issue. There is also the symbolism of the possibility of luck that is drawn from a past good deed.

KEEP FOCUSED ON ... friendly and refreshing words and sparkling ideas that constantly replenish others ... making full use of whatever is clear, fresh and good ... digging down deeper if necessary.

WATCH OUT FOR ... what there is to be given drying up from disuse or a lack of faith in its infinite supply (like the Oracle) ... denying yourself what you need through an act of self-punishment, misguided asceticism or fear.

LOVE/RELATING/SOCIAL

This suggests a person or relationship that is deep, reliable and possibly of a conservative or traditional disposition. But you should 'test the water' first.

KEEP FOCUSED ON ... the fact that a relationship is only as good as what you are bringing to it or accepting from it ... that you 'divine' and draw upon the wellspring of goodness in one another ... the better, purer, longstanding qualities of yourself or another, for such form the basis of a healthy relationship.

WATCH OUT FOR ... relationships and people that do not nourish that part of you that you feel needs nourishing ... taking to a new relationship the problems you had in an old one ... you or another being stuck in the mud, unwilling to be 'sluiced' – to acknowledge and remove emotional blockages and fearful attitudes.

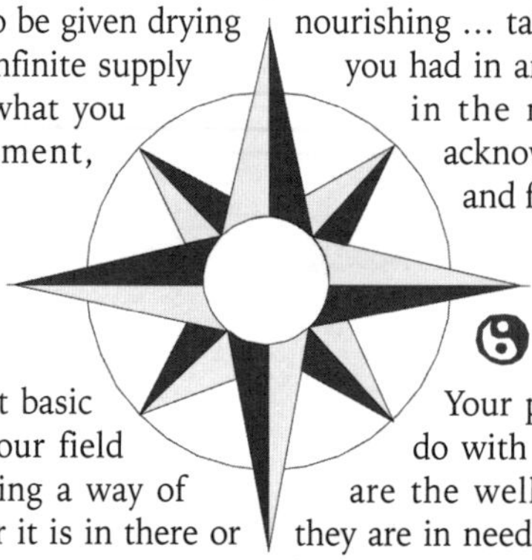

MONEY/WORK/CREATIVITY

You are dealing in or with what is most basic to your requirements, depending on your field of endeavour. The issue is one of finding a way of accessing or maintaining this supply, for it is in there or out there somewhere.

KEEP FOCUSED ON ... the fact that what you are after is now available, and that you might have to dig for it, divine for it, pray for it, make way for it or work harder for it ... the belief that what you know to be truly good is accessible ... traditional or tried-and-true methods that blend in with existing surroundings.

WATCH OUT FOR ... products, people or ideas that are tainted for they will get into the 'food chain' and become troublesome and hard to eliminate at a later date ... sources of supply that are limited, unpredictable or dubious.

KARMA/ATTITUDE/HEALTH

Your past and background have everything to do with how things are in the present, for they are the wellspring of your being. Ask yourself if they are in need of purification or clarification, or if you have cut yourself off from them, or should have done so in order to leave a negative past behind; this could bear significantly upon the object of your enquiry and state of affairs. Also, you will eventually get what you truly wish for – for good or ill.

KEEP FOCUSED ON ... the very best in terms of your sources of energy, information and emotional sustainment ... what you feel deep inside of you as being good and true – for it is!

WATCH OUT FOR ... impure thoughts, feelings and foodstuffs, for no matter where you are or what you may be doing, these will always be with you, influencing your life and well-being.

'The town may change, but the well does not'

AN INDUSTRIAL STRIKE

✵ ORGANIZED PROTEST ✵

GENERAL INTERPRETATION

A time or need to use powerful means of righting wrongs. When the 'system' is taking advantage of its position of power to get as much as possible for as little as possible from the individual, then drastic measures have to be taken – even if it means greater deprivation and suffering for a time.

KEEP FOCUSED ON ... a well-thought out and justifiable stand that you make in the face of an abuse of power or a negative condition ... rallying others to whatever cause you regard as important, that moves you to action ... creating and maintaining solidarity with those who share your cause and condition ... suing for something better in life ... taking issue before leaving or capitulating.

WATCH OUT FOR ... displacing one's own shortcomings on to the general situation, and impotently making a fuss about it.

MONEY/WORK/CREATIVITY

Here this Symbol could be taken literally, with all the obvious connotations that go with suing for better pay, conditions, deals, benefits, marketing strategy and promotion.

KEEP FOCUSED ON ... holding out for what you want and believe in ... establishing better lines of communication as a preliminary to doing anything more drastic – if it's not too late for that already ... the worth of what you are standing for; you will then know how far any sacrifices should be taken ... the bigger reasons for taking drastic action to get justice ... resisting or throwing over what is holding you back.

WATCH OUT FOR ... your own weaknesses and shortcomings before pointing a finger at anyone or anything else. After all, you'll need to be in as strong a position as possible if push comes to shove.

💗 LOVE/RELATING/SOCIAL

All too often there is someone 'in charge' in a relationship, in that they have the power – be it money, sexual favours, emotional security or anything that holds the other person to ransom. They play on the other's fear of losing something important to them, or on the other feeling the threat of losing it if they protest.

KEEP FOCUSED ON ... the fact that, consciously or unconsciously, you have given that power to them. The time has come for the 'oppressed' to make a stand and confront the very thing that they feel weak about, rather than just taking things lying down. Either they get stronger (perhaps by joining forces with others) or accept their weakness and make some sort of deal.

WATCH OUT FOR ... protesting when you are not prepared to take the consequences.

☯ KARMA/ATTITUDE/HEALTH

Apart from the government or status quo, the 'system' can mean many things. The law of cause and effect is a system that we are all caught up in, and we must recognize our individual 'cause' or actions if we wish to understand, or have the right, effect. There are many systems that govern and contribute to our health; one of the least understood is the autoimmune system as it is so closely involved with our psyches that it baffles conventional science. Then there is the Solar System of which we are all a part.

KEEP FOCUSED ON ... the 'system' in which you usually operate; if necessary, change the way you relate to it, and you will then get it to behave differently towards you.

WATCH OUT FOR ... how you relate to any particular system; are you abusing it or is it abusing you, or is one abuse the result of the other?

'A riot is at bottom the language of the unheard'

A QUIVER FILLED WITH ARROWS

☆ EQUIPPED TO CONQUER ☆

✳ GENERAL INTERPRETATION

Present here are versatility and potential or real talents; whatever is necessary in order that we may go to meet life with confidence. In days of yore, bowmen would make their own arrows with great care, reflecting the concentration and precision needed to ready oneself for making one's mark in this world. This Symbol would seem to belong to the opposite sign of Sagittarius, but then a quiver is worn on the back, arrows made with deft Geminian hands!

KEEP FOCUSED ON ... your acquisition of knowledge and technique that furthers and accomplishes your aims ... 'loading, drawing, aiming, shooting, and hitting' the target, whatever that might be.

WATCH OUT FOR ... a reluctance to make full use of latent abilities, or giving a plausible show of them that masks a basic ineffectuality.

♥ LOVE/RELATING/SOCIAL

On one hand this can mean a relationship that challenges one or both people to muster their talents and sharpen their weapons in order to overcome or resist whatever the other person assails them with. On the other hand this can be a relationship that has a formidable arsenal of qualities with which it can 'shoot' at whatever is seen as the 'target'. It may be a case of both, possibly with the first case developing into the second.

KEEP FOCUSED ON ... what are the real objectives of, or obstacles to, a healthy relationship, and then using your talents and awareness; aim at and 'hit' them ... the relationship's assets.

WATCH OUT FOR ... seeing enmity where there is little or none, for you are in danger of making external a war that is going on inside yourself.

⚚ MONEY/WORK/CREATIVITY

You are in possession of the necessary talents, co-workers, materials or equipment to achieve whatever you wish to achieve.

KEEP FOCUSED ON ... your objectives, and you will attain them ... obstacles to those objectives, and you will overcome them ... ways and means to replenish your 'quiver'; you only have a number of shots at whatever you are aiming at ... developing or attaining the means to deliver or put across what you have.

WATCH OUT FOR ... running out of materials, ideas, personnel or customers – or whatever is fundamental to your continued progress or survival. Look to your back every so often.

☯ KARMA/ATTITUDE/HEALTH

Being forced to make full use of the talents that God or Nature has given you, and through developing them, creating more of them. Helping others toward the same end. More esoterically, this Symbol refers to Zen archery, where the target is one's own self-importance (and therefore, fear), that which gets in the way of achieving self-mastery.

KEEP FOCUSED ON ... life's obstacles and objectives, and what you have in your personality's equipment to pierce through the one and attain the other ... keeping this process going rhythmically, for this is what truly gives you the power to attain your goal and fend off any attacks upon you.

WATCH OUT FOR ... resting on your laurels or using your talents without seeking to create new ones; this would find you at a serious loss when the chips are down at some later stage.

'Bring me my arrows of desire'

AN AEROPLANE FALLING

☆ TO TAKE OR NOT TO TAKE CONTROL ☆

 GENERAL INTERPRETATION

Suggested here is a plunging into a situation or environment that is prompted by intuition and faith alone, or an irresponsible devil-may-care attitude. An act of being that attracts ridicule or admiration, or possibly both. Flying by the seat of your pants.

KEEP FOCUSED ON ... your preparedness to seize the moment, trusting in your wits and poise to ultimately better position yourself in a totally unexpected way.

WATCH OUT FOR ... a blind and aimless way of living that smacks of a criminal lack of care ... chancing it just because you cannot be bothered to read the lie of the land ... giving up the ghost.

 LOVE/RELATING/SOCIAL

Here we have a relationship or manner of relating that is on the way down, or appears to be. Either you must take immediate action to rectify it or, failing that, succumb to the way things are going, allowing Fate to unfold as it will. It could also mean falling in love, with all that such loss of control implies!

KEEP FOCUSED ON ... the present moment, rather than seeking to blame the situation on some past deed or words as this would ensure disaster ... letting the dust settle once the crisis has passed, then look into the pros and cons of why it happened ... handing over the controls to the other person, or a third party, if you genuinely feel unable to do so yourself ... taking the plunge.

WATCH OUT FOR ... repeating the irresponsible ways that led to this state of affairs, but only when you are out of immediate danger.

 MONEY/WORK/CREATIVITY

On the face of it, the object of your concern appears to be in a precarious predicament. It is unwise just trusting to Fate and leaving things as they are; you must seize control immediately and use your wits and intuition – 'pull it out of its dive', direct or pitch things right – then, hopefully, happy landings!

KEEP FOCUSED ON ... doing things entirely your own way if you choose to take the bull by the horns and wrest matters away from disaster. Do not expect anyone else (to be able) to synchronize with the lightning responses and freedom of movement that you, or someone you choose, has to exercise in such a situation ... only what is necessary to bring it off, after quickly assessing that you have what is necessary.

WATCH OUT FOR ... dithering in your decision-making, because timing is critical here.

KARMA/ATTITUDE/HEALTH

Imaged here is something or someone in decline. Whether or not this can be changed depends on the will to do so, to being in a position to do so. There is also a possibility of a certain aimlessness or irresponsibility that led to this state of affairs. If nothing can be done, then succumb to this fate as gracefully as possible; if it is someone or something else that is in decline, do what you can do to help them 'up', but avoid being sucked down as well.

KEEP FOCUSED ON ... keeping stable and in a place that will act as a 'landing strip', a philosophy or attitude of mind that will explain or accommodate whatever is the dilemma.

WATCH OUT FOR ... getting caught in a downward spiral of recrimination or regret; better to hand over the controls to God or some Higher Power – a wing and a prayer, no less.

'I claim not to have controlled events, but confess plainly that events have controlled me'

A NEW PATH OF REALISM IN EXPERIENCE

☆ TOMORROW NEVER KNOWS ☆

⚙ GENERAL INTERPRETATION

Here we have a departure from what was previously considered the norm. Life is very much identified through what actually happens rather than through merely thinking about it. There is no substitute for experience.

KEEP FOCUSED ON ... your ability to appreciate the newness of anything and to make full use of the power inherent in what is new ... gaining a fresh grasp on what is happening now, or will happen, as a result of studying what has gone before.

WATCH OUT FOR ... an inability to see things through when an alternative catches your attention ... giving into an excuse to stay where you are, thus causing you to evade life's challenges.

♡ LOVE/RELATING/SOCIAL

The maxim that there is no substitute for experience is especially true with respect to emotional life and dealing with people. This is because our feelings are like wells – we only experience the nature of them by having drawn from them, and as a result of drawing out the feelings of others.

KEEP FOCUSED ON ... the fact that all emotional experiences enrich our lives and those of others – providing we see it that way ... the idea that you will only find out how you really feel by taking the plunge into intimacy.

WATCH OUT FOR ... missing out on the opportunity for experience by holding back emotionally; missing out on such key experiences as are on offer here could seriously inhibit your ability to relate or attract at a later date ... resenting others for *your* choices.

⚙ MONEY/WORK/CREATIVITY

Whatever idea or venture you have in mind will only reveal its real value and nature when you have embarked on making it a reality. Projections, surveys, feasibility studies and oracles can only tell you so much. Sooner or later you have to see how it runs in real terms. You may have already made a move, and this Symbol affirms it.

KEEP FOCUSED ON ... how the way will open to you, helping you develop as you go once you have decided to move forward with the object of your enquiry. If you are already in process, then be quick to learn from, and respond to, whatever happens ... the fact that you are now really finding out what's what – or are about to – and this is priceless; it will serve you in the future one way or the other.

WATCH OUT FOR ... doubt clouding the way ahead ... newness merely for the sake of it.

⚙ KARMA/ATTITUDE/HEALTH

Life is forcing you or obliging you with a new way of experiencing your reality, thus making it sharper and more vivid.

KEEP FOCUSED ON ... appreciating this new era and what it is showing you about your life on Earth ... the fact that everything that happens to you now is to do with the real you – not what you think you could be or ought to be – and it is your future in the making ... the feeling that you are more 'you' now than you have ever been – the you of now ... the belief that much of life is about acquiring raw experience as opposed to expecting assurances ... the experiences you are having rather than the ones you fear you might have.

WATCH OUT FOR ... anxieties about your future; they exist only because you lack faith in your own path and how it is now asserting itself, expressing its need to embark on a new chapter, strike across virgin territory.

'The proof of the pudding is in the eating'

A TOPSY SAUCILY ASSERTING HERSELF

☆ RIGHTEOUS SELF-EXPRESSION ☆

✿ GENERAL INTERPRETATION

A 'topsy' or black female house-slave strongly represents any underprivileged or suppressed person or group. It also suggests that she has been allowed into 'the home of her masters', meaning that she is believed to be tamed or harmless when really she has got herself into a position of influence and onto a stepping stone to power and freedom.

KEEP FOCUSED ON ... seizing the initiative and daring to become more your own person ... the good-humoured nerve that is able to win apparent superiors over to your worth as an individual ... standing up for yourself and your rights.

WATCH OUT FOR ... playing at making a blow for freedom and consequently not being taken seriously ... giving in to anyone or anything that merely appears to have power or does have power but abuses it.

♥ LOVE/RELATING/SOCIAL

The 'weaker' person in a relationship or group at last owns some of the power they have been hitherto giving away and puts their foot down. This may be in a small way or in a revolutionary one.

KEEP FOCUSED ON ... the fact that you are now in a position to step out and be more independent, to state your case, to refuse to take it any more ... the fact that the time has come for the worm to turn ... those things that you feel very strongly about – and come right out with them; after all, it is your strongest feelings that are your power base.

WATCH OUT FOR ... allowing yourself to be browbeaten or to feel captive to the situation ... being fooled by the illusion that someone else is superior to you because they are stronger in a more obvious or conventional way.

⚜ MONEY/WORK/CREATIVITY

The time has come for the so-called under-lings to make themselves felt, or for that part of you that has so far felt inferior to stop feeling that way and for you not to be afraid to show so-called superiors what you are made of, what you have to say and offer, and demand what you are really worth.

KEEP FOCUSED ON ... going for it until you get it ... the fact that history proves that it is often the 'little man or woman' who makes their mark against all odds – simply because their time had come ... speaking your truth, doing your thing.

WATCH OUT FOR ... falling back into self-doubt and self-criticism, which are largely a product of negative events and programming from the past ... blaming those above you for your own inability to deliver the goods ... not taking responsibility for your own actions.

☯ KARMA/ATTITUDE/HEALTH

Karma here is bound up with the whole system that makes out that one person has to be in the thrall of another. If your karma has to do with being a 'have', then you are now having to contend with something or someone rising up against you or the part of society you belong to. If your karma is that of a 'have not' then the time has come to demand your rights and claim the power that is your birthright. Psychologically, this Symbol is referring to intuition at last believing itself and no longer swallowing the idea that it is stupid.

KEEP FOCUSED ON ... coming forward with your opinions and enacting your desires in the face of what was once totally in power but is now having to learn to accept your value and identity.

WATCH OUT FOR ... being aggressive or obstreperous, for although this may have a dramatic effect it would probably invite further repression.

'No one can make you feel inferior without your consent'

A GREAT MUSICIAN AT HIS PIANO

✵ VIRTUOSITY ✵

GENERAL INTERPRETATION

The creative focus of all that one is, which in turn inspires others to strive towards a fuller expression of what and who they are. Displaying such talent to the world at large so as to validate them, rather than just being an 'unsung genius'. The importance of faith.

KEEP FOCUSED ON ... the strong connection that you have with your soul's intention to amount to something in life and so give it meaning ... keeping in practice for this is what keeps you at your best and improves you ... knowing your 'instrument' ... putting your money where your mouth is, for how else will Fate smile upon you.

WATCH OUT FOR ... a need or desire to be the centre of attention taking precedence over whatever or whoever is the object of your concern ... thinking that inspiration is enough; it is, as they say, only 1% genius – the rest is perspiration.

MONEY/WORK/CREATIVITY

It seems more than likely that you have something wonderful to offer. The critical factor is one of 'putting on a performance' that proves this point. Often there can be a great talent or product, but it fails by not 'reaching' its 'audience'. Financially, there is great worth here, but it needs to be managed well to be made the most of.

KEEP FOCUSED ON ... finding a suitable 'stage' or outlet for what you have or are working on ... the fact that you may have to 'suffer for your art' while you and your public work towards finding a place and time where you meet ... how any creation or product needs to be 'played in' or aired before it is ready for greater exposure or investment.

WATCH OUT FOR ... being too highbrow if you wish to reach the masses; being too lowbrow if you wish to reach a critical and select few ... presentation without sufficient preparation.

LOVE/RELATING/SOCIAL

A relationship or the other person is like an instrument upon which one plays. This presupposes that each person knows what 'part' they are playing, and what they are bringing to the relationship and each other that inspires, soothes, accompanies, supports and delights. A creative attitude to a relationship is the best thing to adopt here. This Symbol could also describe someone who is very accomplished in the art of love, relating or socializing.

KEEP FOCUSED ON ... getting the best out of a relationship or person by putting your very best into it or them ... the probability that you are expecting a lot from yourself and the other person.

WATCH OUT FOR ... playing too many 'bum notes', that is, making emotional *faux pas* when you ought to know better. If this happens too often you might be forced to improve your act.

KARMA/ATTITUDE/HEALTH

People who have some great gift to give are often sorely tried in their inner or personal lives, almost as a counterpoint to whatever their genius is. Then there is the 'Van Gogh Syndrome' where one's 'genius' is not recognized during one's lifetime. In both cases, it can be one's karma to suffer in order to bestow something of great worth upon a world that is not yet ready to appreciate it. This does not mean to say that it will not do so in your lifetime, but that you ...

KEEP FOCUSED ON ... performing and putting out whatever it is you feel to be so important and close to your heart, believing that your time will come ... your body as your instrument; play it and look after it as any self-respecting musician would theirs.

WATCH OUT FOR ... hiding your light.

'Genius does what it must, and Talent does what it can'

A CONVERSATION BY TELEPATHY

☆ PSYCHIC RAPPORT ☆

GENERAL INTERPRETATION

The means through which we can communicate, individually or collectively, without risk of misinterpretation or negative manipulation. Such points of contact constitute a web of transcendental intercommunication and are arrived at through a love of truth and a literal sympathy.

KEEP FOCUSED ON ... a connectedness you have with certain areas, levels or beings that enables you to be in touch with what is happening, unless you wilfully and misguidedly block out what is currently happening.

WATCH OUT FOR ... innuendo or wishful thinking disguising a reluctance to say what is felt ... being closed to subtle communication or subtle forms of communication ... paying heed to negative, troublesome or conspiratorial 'voices' that create fear and factions.

MONEY/WORK/CREATIVITY

Work that involves a higher or more efficient form of communication is well-starred. So too is anything that improves communication by making it less likely that anyone will be uninformed, misinformed or disinformed. This could also describe a creative partnership where little needs to be said, where you are on the same wavelength, or an ear-to-the-ground, connecting one with what is going on, what appeals and is of the moment.

KEEP FOCUSED ON ... what your 'antennae' or sixth sense tells you about the object of your concern. In this way, you will be in touch with the minds of others and have your finger on the pulse of Humanity, without having to resort to more mechanical means of 'market research'.

WATCH OUT FOR ... placing hearsay, rumour or currents fads above your own intuition; in time your hunches will prove accurate and reliable.

LOVE/RELATING/SOCIAL

The relationship or relationships in question are blessed or cursed by you being in touch with one another on a psychic or emotional level. Blessed, when you trust that the truth of the matter will make itself known in a subtle but effective way. Cursed, when you find it hard to get out from under each other's skin because it is uncomfortable and claustrophobic.

KEEP FOCUSED ON ... the fact that what anyone needs to feel or know will eventually be felt or known without having to do so verbally or physically ... deliberately sending your thoughts and feelings to the other person by visualization or in meditation; receiving in the same way.

WATCH OUT FOR ... saying what need not or should not be said, for egos will only get in the way ... misusing psychic powers for selfish reasons.

KARMA/ATTITUDE/HEALTH

Karmic interplay between two or more people who have connections that go beyond a conscious awareness of the present. Consequently, at any one time there are 'lines' between each person that can be filled with love or hate – depending upon what thoughts and feelings are currently 'in transit'.

KEEP FOCUSED ON ... what these 'lines' are telling you or making you feel, without evading or trying to explain them away, for they are the untarnished truth of the matter – your own true state of being conveyed to you along these 'lines' ... the notion of spiritual agencies on higher planes of communication helping you to deal with the situation, or to get the most out of it.

WATCH OUT FOR ... controlling or blocking the 'lines' of emotional and mental interplay, for they are like the nervous system of your body, and must be kept open to ensure a healthy mind and body.

'[Without telepathy] A lie will go round the world while the truth is pulling its boots on'

👬

TWO DUTCH CHILDREN TALKING

☆ **OPEN DISCUSSION** ☆

✸ GENERAL INTERPRETATION

Offered here is a simple and ingenuous means by which one can familiarize oneself with whatever milieu is currently of interest or whatever issue needs attention. Becoming aware of the significance and importance of communication, or a specialized form of it. Everyone making an equal contribution.

KEEP FOCUSED ON ... spontaneously promoting free discussion and open and innocent involvement with all and sundry, thereby resolving problems, dispelling intrigue and suspicion ... calling a spade a spade ... going 'Dutch'.

WATCH OUT FOR ... talking but communicating little or not at all – 'double Dutch' ... excluding anyone – this is divisive and precludes connection with the greater whole ... others being censorious of your openness ... negative internal dialogue.

♥ LOVE/RELATING/SOCIAL

A sign of people being closely and successfully connected is that they can communicate with one another in a special language, a kind of shorthand or through intuitive understanding. This Symbol describes a relationship that has such a familiarity, or it is stating that this is what needs cultivating or seeking out.

KEEP FOCUSED ON ... finding areas of interest or contact where there is a free and easy flow.

WATCH OUT FOR ... where there is a racial, cultural or intellectual difference that is getting in the way of successful communication. Without having or creating such points of common interest and opinion, your interaction can become such hard work it leads to separation ... situations where the hurt inner child in one person reacts to the same in the other person.

⚚ MONEY/WORK/CREATIVITY

Exchanging ideas and talking things out across the table, with no holds barred, is one form of advice this Symbol offers in order to resolve current difficulties. Or what is needed is for you to take steps towards discovering what it is that you want to say or do. Then again, it could be referring to the fact that you have in your possession a medium or device that is concerned with improving communication – in which case it is well-starred.

KEEP FOCUSED ON ... what is of immediate interest to you, without getting bogged down in doubts or agendas, or in personal complexes and preconceived ideas of what you think should be said or done. Just say it or do it – let things unfold from there.

WATCH OUT FOR ... having only a limited appeal owing to an exclusivity or open-mindedness that the world is not yet ready to understand or accept ... crossed lines.

☉ KARMA/ATTITUDE/HEALTH

This Symbol suggests the free association that is important when it comes to getting in touch with whatever it is you are after – including what the Symbols mean to you personally. Also implied here are two dimensions to your personality that are now in communication with one another; because they see each other as equals, a new balance and wholeness is established.

KEEP FOCUSED ON ... getting in touch with your private, inner processes of thought and feeling. This can be done by freely associating with this Symbol on tape or paper, or with a friend or counsellor who allows you to share or 'ramble on' until you make the right connection.

WATCH OUT FOR ... blocks within your own being, for they effectively create blocks on the outside – and vice versa. Ultimately, no one except a professional therapist will understand you if you do not understand yourself.

'Nothing is closed to openness'

A WOMAN SUFFRAGIST HARANGUING

EMANCIPATION

GENERAL INTERPRETATION

The effort of expression that is required in order to make known and gain appreciation for what is by nature passive and responsive. The danger here is that sometimes one has to step outside of one's natural or traditional role in order for it to be noticed and valued. A subtle point here is that 'suffragists' used political and verbal means to make their point, whereas 'suffragettes' were more drastic and provocative in their style.

KEEP FOCUSED ON ... your dedication towards creating a world of equal rights and fair play, or getting the 'still small voice' heard ... giving yourself a pep talk on a regular and frequent basis ... the certainty of success ultimately being achieved – women *did* get the vote!

WATCH OUT FOR ... climbing on a bandwagon in an act that blinds one to personal inadequacies.

LOVE/RELATING/SOCIAL

A relationship where one or both people are looking to get their say, to attain their rights, to sue for equality. Such a person does not have to be a female, for 'woman' in this context symbolizes any part of one's nature that feels downtrodden or overlooked as the result of a history of taking a back seat, being suppressed, being too accommodating, or only seeing things intuitively rather than rationally.

KEEP FOCUSED ON ... being fair, accepting the inevitability of change, listening to the other person ... valuing gentleness, receptivity, adaptability, intuition, sympathy and awareness of relationships.

WATCH OUT FOR ... hiding personal failings behind a social cause, political correctness or sheer superficiality ... just being a nag, diminishing someone else rather than increasing them/yourself.

MONEY/WORK/CREATIVITY

Any work that is concerned with liberating the oppressed is favoured by this Symbol. It may also be calling you to liberate yourself from a regime, drudge or style that you have been enduring for too long. Financial difficulties will be down to any such self-deprivation. Financial success will be up to any self-liberation.

KEEP FOCUSED ON ... what you could gain by taking a chance, emphasizing your strengths and talents, and a bit of self-advertisement ... finding any organization that can assist in the struggle against harassment, underpay or poor conditions ... remedying any lack of appreciation (for yourself).

WATCH OUT FOR ... how you do yourself down by playing it safe, emphasizing your weaknesses and failings, and hiding your light ... looking for promotion because of your 'position' rather than because of what you are and what you can do.

KARMA/ATTITUDE/HEALTH

A highly significant evolutionary impulse at this time is to cut the ties to any form of past subjugation, repression or enslavement. This could also refer to stress resulting from trying too hard, or not trying at all, to get out from under someone or something's thumb.

KEEP FOCUSED ON ... identifying and asserting your rights in a firm, forceful, and just way ... realistic equality, positive change and challenging established views and preconceptions ... winning freedom for a reason, rather than for its own sake.

WATCH OUT FOR ... losing sight of your individual nature in a fervour to become something or someone of 'social significance'; leaving behind the 'person' in you can wear out the soul, with deleterious effect upon your health ... allowing the female or emotional side to become too strident, thereby destabilizing the whole.

'The argument of the broken window pane is the most valuable argument in modern politics'

THE HEAD OF HEALTH DISSOLVED INTO THE HEAD OF MENTALITY

✫ MIND OVER MATTER ✫

⚙ GENERAL INTERPRETATION

The interaction between psyche and soma, the emotional and the physical. Also, a coming together of innate wholesomeness and conscious intent, producing a fine example of the best in human nature, and of how one individual can reflect and embody the qualities of many.

KEEP FOCUSED ON ... using your ability to appreciate and detect the connections between mind and body, along with the health and psychological issues that they imply ... filling your mind with spiritual, life-affirming thoughts and ideas.

WATCH OUT FOR ... wrong-headedness that makes you feel so bad that you really do have something to worry about ... letting certain notions make you feel unwell; if a thought rattles you, change the thought.

♥ LOVE/RELATING/SOCIAL

A karmic relationship, probably one that involves a deep and entrenched emotional fixation on two people's parts, that at some time created, or is now in danger of creating, actual physical disturbance or damage. This Symbol is saying that this can now be, or is already being, healed through loving thoughts, feelings and actions.

KEEP FOCUSED ON ... the good, the true and the beautiful in yourself and others ... being open to new ideas concerning the creation of positive relationships; accepting that we create our own emotional and physical reality by the way we think and relate.

WATCH OUT FOR ... diseased and negative attitudes towards others or each other; they are the cancer that you must eliminate ... ignoring danger signs before it is too late.

⚘ MONEY/WORK/CREATIVITY

What is favoured here is anything that promotes healthy minds and bodies. This is saying that the 'health' of your idea, product or project depends upon the attitude of mind that is behind it.

KEEP FOCUSED ON ... the welfare of your customers, audience or anyone involved with your enterprise, for it is their state of being that determines its success ... whatever means you have to promote health generally, and then it will go from strength to strength ... the whole of your being, company or enterprise – not just the parts that are easiest or more favoured ... healthy principles concerning money.

WATCH OUT FOR ... dubious or polluting practices, connections or outlets – although there could be a short-term profit, ultimately things would take a serious downturn.

☯ KARMA/ATTITUDE/HEALTH

Possibly a physical condition or event in the present is the result of a state of mind or personality at an earlier time, and this is still persisting, crystallizing into health problems. This physical state in turn affects one's mental state.

KEEP FOCUSED ON ... right thinking – honest, positive and unbiased by ego or neurosis – for this creates healthy being ... the philosophy of health that espouses that personality traits and conditions are what create one's state of health ... the idea that certain parts of the body have symbolic meaning, for instance, throat troubles meaning problems communicating or feeling understood.

WATCH OUT FOR ... hare-brained ideas about what constitutes health and well-being. So, check out serious conditions with a doctor, even if only with a view to eliminating your worst fears.

'Look to your health; and if you have it, praise God, and value it next to a good conscience'

TWO CHINESE MEN TALKING CHINESE

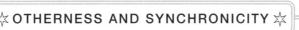

☆ OTHERNESS AND SYNCHRONICITY ☆

✳ GENERAL INTERPRETATION

To get a handle on your situation you need to view it in a manner that is different from the norm, even alien to you. Unlike conventional or Western thinking that views events as causal (A makes B happen, B makes C happen, etc), Chinese thinking asks: 'What tends to happen together in time?' So ...

KEEP FOCUSED ON ... what else is going on in your life at this time, along with the object of your concern, and you will gain an insight into what it means and poses. If you have asked about a number of issues at once, then looking for the connection between them will reveal the answer – or maybe the right question! ... taking on board something you don't know, even though it seems illogical or incomprehensible.

WATCH OUT FOR ... ridiculing or ignoring what you don't know much about.

♡ LOVE/RELATING/SOCIAL

Here is a relationship that has its very own language or connection. Consequently, other people may not understand where you are coming from or what you are about. This may not matter; the point is that you can make yourselves understood by one another in a way that others cannot, because it is tailor-made to and by your respective personalities. So ...

KEEP FOCUSED ON ... that special connection you have, and see how it keeps the two of you constantly and subtly in touch with your mutual needs and states ... finding a new or different means to express what needs expressing to one another; or putting it another way.

WATCH OUT FOR ... any attitude or language that alienates rather than communicates – unless, perversely, you want to be alienated.

⚑ MONEY/WORK/CREATIVITY

Special means of communication are auspicious here. Or you need to familiarize yourself with an area of work or finance that is alien or unique in order to deal with the current issue. Without tackling a learning curve or taking a step into the unknown, those in the know won't be able to put *you* in the know.

KEEP FOCUSED ON ... the fact that to achieve your objectives, you have to own up to a blind spot that is preventing you from getting there. For example, if you wish to improve or maintain your position in your career, you need to be wise to what those in authority wish to hear or see, how it should be presented, or what they are trying to tell you.

WATCH OUT FOR ... failing to connect as a result of unclear thinking or poor communication.

☯ KARMA/ATTITUDE/HEALTH

This could be referring to the language of the psyche or unconscious and to the importance of understanding it. Dreams are the most obvious example of this language, but any kind of sign or symbol comes under this heading. Also, there is the classic Chinese sage–pupil relationship. The Astrological Oracle naturally applies here, and so ...

KEEP FOCUSED ON ... applying yourself to an oracle, striking up a special rapport with it through frequent and assiduous use. The *I Ching* is recommended here and, if health is an issue, a form of holistic medicine ... giving, for it attracts being given to.

WATCH OUT FOR ... going too far into the alternative way of thought, and disregarding common sense or conventional medicine.

'A paradox is the truth standing on its head to attract attention'

A LARGE ARCHAIC VOLUME

☆ ANCIENT WISDOM ☆

 GENERAL INTERPRETATION

The persistence of knowledge and the timeless truths that exist as a source of illumination in the present. They may be handed down through the ages in legends, mythology and esoteric literature, or be the accumulation of personal study and experience.

KEEP FOCUSED ON ... and draw upon past experience to disentangle yourself and others from current difficulties and establish a better path for the future ... what the past tells you as known and established; depend upon your inner knowing.

WATCH OUT FOR ... slavish worship of tradition and authority – the letter of the law rather than the spirit of it ... what is obsolete or irrelevant, and then eliminate or disregard it ... being overly concerned about 'getting it right'; the experience and knowledge you have will suffice and, if not, that is what you are in the process of acquiring.

MONEY/WORK/CREATIVITY

Your work or financial situation has a long track record and this should tell you all you need to know. You just have to study it properly. If the work you are involved in has to do with writing or information technology, or deals with history or wisdom, then this is an auspicious oracle.

KEEP FOCUSED ON ... using or referring to anything that has a good pedigree, in that it has stood, or can stand, the test of time ... the sources and origins of the object of your concern ... keeping a journal or record, for this will help you in a practical and creative way ... wisdom born of your own experience.

WATCH OUT FOR ... stuffy, academic, incongruous or abstruse material, or ways of presenting material. The word 'archaic' means ancient, which can mean either venerable or outmoded.

LOVE/RELATING/SOCIAL

This Symbol refers to a relationship or emotional situation that goes way back. What is both good and bad about it has its roots deep in the past. Everything depends upon looking at that past history, observing its patterns and drawing an inference from all this that can help the present situation. Such 'history' can be deeply reassuring or deeply disturbing – probably a combination of both.

KEEP FOCUSED ON ... the fact that the deeper the history, the longer it will take to sort out any difficulties – if it is a relationship that is the object of your enquiry, the more mileage there will be in it ... the knowledge and experience of both, or all, people involved.

WATCH OUT FOR ... dredging up old issues for the sake of justifying the present, it won't, it'll just perpetuate it.

KARMA/ATTITUDE/HEALTH

The volume in this case is the Book of Your Life – or Lives, rather. This great tome of experiences is your main resource for information and insight, but everything depends upon your willingness and ability to dip into it. It also depends on your memory, or what you think of as your memory.

KEEP FOCUSED ON ... memory being like as on a hard disk in a computer. It is all there, but you have to know how to access it. Some accessing occurs automatically – that's the memory we are all conscious of having. Other areas of memory are accessed on a 'need-to-know' basis. Apply yourself to the job in hand and, although your memory may creak a bit at times, you will access all you need to know. For deeper access, try regression or rebirthing.

WATCH OUT FOR ... worrying about the future, for it is unknown. Your memory banks are known, or at least knowable, as is all you need to know.

'What's past is prologue'

A CAFETERIA

☆ THE CHOICE IS YOURS ☆

 GENERAL INTERPRETATION

The great choice that is available to everyone in a modern society or, more particularly, that the situation presents you with. The combination of equality and efficiency that characterizes anything that is functioning naturally and economically.

KEEP FOCUSED ON ... your knack for perceiving how everyone can get the most out of a situation when they are shown what they are capable of ... whatever course the object of your enquiry prompts you to take intuitively (because of a hunch) or aesthetically (because you like or dislike it) ... what you choose to think, feel or do – this will become your reality ... giving others a choice.

WATCH OUT FOR ... a confusion or drabness of outlook born of fearful lack of commitment.

 LOVE/RELATING/SOCIAL

Whatever you want socially or romantically is laid out before you. You only have to go forth and select what you like the look of and, in the end, pay the price. Help yourself.

KEEP FOCUSED ON ... your freedom of choice being the central issue, within the bounds of whatever is available, and considering your own eligibility ... the probability that there are plenty more fish in the sea ... that people make their own choices and you cannot be held responsible for them; when it comes to the 'check-out', we must all pay the price (and this applies to Karma too).

WATCH OUT FOR ... expecting what you want to be dished up on a plate to you – at least, not until you have waited for your turn ... confusing what is seemingly available with the ability actually to get it.

MONEY/WORK/CREATIVITY

The nature of what you are doing, or what you are supposed be doing, centres upon availing yourself of whatever avenues of expression, training or investment that the world has on offer. Alternatively, it could be offering this kind of service to others – for example, online shopping, or any kind of self-service. Or, literally, catering.

KEEP FOCUSED ON ... carefully taking your pick ... the possibility that you'll know what you want when you have tried several other 'dishes' (jobs or methods) or when you are 'hungry' (when needs must) ... selecting or rejecting whatever is necessary to ensure satisfaction for yourself or your customers/public.

WATCH OUT FOR ... prevaricating so much that the 'dishes' go cold, nothing seems to appeal to your tired view of it all, or certain choices are no longer available.

KARMA/ATTITUDE/HEALTH

The essential quality of being human is the power of choice, as distinct from plain instinct, sheer necessity and immutable fate that characterize lower life forms. The trouble is that one can be 'spoilt for choice'. So ...

KEEP FOCUSED ON ... making any choice rather than none, and then giving that choice a good run to see how it fares. Otherwise, it would be a case of nothing ventured, nothing gained, or of spreading yourself too thinly or in too many directions.

WATCH OUT FOR ... making choices on a whim, letting someone else make them for you, or assuming that because it was all right for someone else, it'll be all right for you ... what foods you consume or beliefs you accept; are they good for you?

'Help yourself, and heaven will help you'

A LABOUR DEMONSTRATION

☆ RIGHTFUL REWARD ☆

✳ GENERAL INTERPRETATION

The power that one has or needs to muster in order to win justice and reward for one's position and efforts. The fact that the individual can, and sometimes must, enlist the support of the masses to rail against the system.

KEEP FOCUSED ON ... a sense of social justice and the courage and willingness to make sacrifices to attain it ... the practical results regarding the object of your enquiry, for they will be a testament to its worth ... developing your skills, ever-expanding and growing; this simultaneously shows your worth and proves it.

WATCH OUT FOR ... idleness combined with a personal dissatisfaction that conceals a need to try harder or retrain.

♡ LOVE/RELATING/SOCIAL

This Symbol is stressing the importance of working on a relationship or your social or love life in order to make it a success. There may be an oblique reference here to the significance of work as it bears upon relationships, perhaps showing one's love by working hard to provide for one's loved ones. A labour of love.

KEEP FOCUSED ON ... the emotional reason for your efforts ... doing something practical and/or profitable that proves you care.

WATCH OUT FOR ... thinking that practical results are the only valid expression of how someone feels ... how your working life may be damaging, or at least affecting, your social or private life, for if left to its own devices such a habit could attract a crisis ... work being a substitute for relationships ... one person doing all the loving and caring.

⚒ MONEY/WORK/CREATIVITY

This Symbol can be taken fairly literally here, in that it refers to the need and necessity of the 'workers' to rally together in order to obtain what they believe their labour is worth. Alternatively, it could be in the sense of demonstrating what you are worth through your efforts or creations. In both cases, the value of work done is the critical issue.

KEEP FOCUSED ON ... appealing to those who have the power and the sympathy to recognize your validity, and who have a vested interest in seeing that you are properly rewarded ... creating and maintaining solidarity with co-workers.

WATCH OUT FOR ... empty displays of self-justification when you have not achieved that much, leaving you on shaky ground ... working too hard; it's counterproductive.

☯ KARMA/ATTITUDE/HEALTH

If you are working well, then you will feel healthy, and if you are healthy you will be working well. Also implied here is the fact that one 'works off' bad karma. You are being seen, by those who matter, as to how you rid yourself of something negative, or to earn yourself something of value, or as an example of the value of working hard at something.

KEEP FOCUSED ON ... recognizing your own worth and the efforts you make to accomplish something ... doing a worthwhile job, one that serves the whole ... believing that you will be taken care of in proportion to how well you fulfil your (spiritual) duties.

WATCH OUT FOR ... undervaluing yourself ... feeling weighed down by the way of the world, when really such a feeling should be interpreted as a challenge to getting yourself up and doing something about it – first for yourself, and then the world.

'By their works you shall know them'

A BARN DANCE

☆ COMMINGLING ☆

GENERAL INTERPRETATION

Offered or imaged here is social function at its most enjoyable; an occasion to look forward to. Each individual finds their place in the dance of life through a give-and-take that is set against a prearranged order, thus creating a pleasing blend of formality and spontaneity, all taking place in a natural fashion. Organized wildness and hilarity.

KEEP FOCUSED ON ... expressing or developing a flair for showing others how to act and behave together in a mutually rewarding way, while doing the same yourself ... having fun, abandoning self-consciousness.

WATCH OUT FOR ... losing yourself in the whirl of social interaction ... feeling inhibited by what other people might think, or how you might appear.

LOVE/RELATING/SOCIAL

The whole process of social and romantic interaction. One avails oneself of whatever the world has to offer – and when, where and how it offers it. Firstly, there is the opportunity to meet and get to know others, then the choosing of a partner and friends, the formal or free style of interacting. Then there could be the feeling of being left out, having two left feet, sitting and watching, or never having the courage to 'join the dance' at all.

KEEP FOCUSED ON ... the sheer naturalness of being a social animal, letting your hair down, celebrating ... being taken up in the social or emotional whirl.

WATCH OUT FOR ... negative associations and self-consciousness concerning this Symbol – such as being a wallflower; let them go and give yourself up to the 'call of the dance'.

MONEY/WORK/CREATIVITY

Whatever the nature of your profession or business, its success depends on getting into the swing of things, to see if it catches on in the normal and natural setting of everyday life.

KEEP FOCUSED ON ... whatever appeals at a street level, or has some down to earth feel about it. This has to be simple enough or traditional enough for it to catch on ... the 'spirit of the dance' or the sheer enthusiasm you feel for what you do – providing you do not step on too many toes.

WATCH OUT FOR ... ethnic chic gone mad, or being in fashion purely for fashion's sake. This may achieve momentary success, but then you would be eternally climbing from one bandwagon to another ... being too boisterous or hard-selling and winding up repelling instead of attracting.

KARMA/ATTITUDE/HEALTH

In this context, this Symbol suggests the Cosmic Dance where all and sundry come together, do what they have to do together, then peel off to 'dance' with one another, sit one or more out, or eventually depart altogether. Also, there is the 'caller', the Inner Voice or Fate itself, that calls the tune, prompts us what to do, who to grab.

KEEP FOCUSED ON ... life as a dance, with the space, drama, opportunity, fun, the letting go and taking hold, the sexual interplay, the innocence and naturalness of it all ... the 'caller', the 'inner voice' or a set of guiding principles.

WATCH OUT FOR ... not really *being* with whoever you are with, but just going through the motions, or thinking/wishing you were with someone else or being somewhere else ... refusing to hear the 'call' of what steps to take and when.

'Will you, won't you, will you, won't you, will you join the dance?'

THREE FLEDGLINGS IN A NEST HIGH IN A TREE

☆ PRE-FLIGHT NERVES ☆

✴ GENERAL INTERPRETATION

The number three usually symbolizes completion or integration (of mind, feelings, senses), so here it is saying that you have reached a stage when you can and should take things into a radically new phase. Not surprisingly, this can be a nerve-racking time. As ever, in using the Sabian Symbols, you need to ponder what 'three' might mean in your particular case, and what future possibility is creating the anxiety and why.

KEEP FOCUSED ON ... developing the ability to make the best use of the advantages that are naturally present at the start of any venture ... staying put and not taking any chances unless you are certain it is reasonably safe to do so. Then you *will* be relatively safe ... Keeping *stum*.

WATCH OUT FOR ... a false sense of security that gives rise to precipitous acts.

♥ LOVE/RELATING/SOCIAL

This could be referring to a 'two's company and three's a crowd' scenario. If this is the case, it is clear that it is not going to stay that way for too long. A certain sense of competition is implied, along with an apprehension caused by the uncertainty of what lies ahead. It would be well to ...

KEEP FOCUSED ON ... trusting that the time will come when everything will be transformed or liberated and that that the weak or inadequate may have to take a fall ... the situation in an unselfconscious, animal way where pecking and squawking are the natural means of making a space for oneself or asserting ones rights.

WATCH OUT FOR ... getting so upset about the situation that you do something that precipitates you into a situation you are not ready for ... being intimidated by those close to you.

⚚ MONEY/WORK/CREATIVITY

Matters have reached a point where they are almost ready to be launched, exposed or tested. For the time being though ...

KEEP FOCUSED ON ... making sure that all the elements to your enterprise are given what they need, that they are as ready as they could ever be for what lies ahead ... what your choices or assets are, and assess the value or potential of each individually on their own merits. Use the Oracle to do this if you wish, or do a feasibility study.

WATCH OUT FOR ... presenting or launching the object of your concern prematurely; it could have disastrous consequences.

☯ KARMA/ATTITUDE/HEALTH

For the time being the object of your enquiry is safe and out of harm's way, barring any far-fetched ideas or beliefs that could take advantage of naivety, a hunger for freedom, spiritual enlightenment or a release from tension. A departure into the unknown is inevitable, reflecting the karmic process whereby things always reach a point that presages a new phase, or even a new life. How that goes is anybody's guess, all you can do is ...

KEEP FOCUSED ON ... the fact that what lies before you is a natural progression and, barring accidents and foolishness, you are more likely to make it than not. Practise breathing exercises.

WATCH OUT FOR ... letting anxiety rob you of the concentration and centredness necessary to the success of your new venture. Precariousness is usually caused by staying too long at a point where you are not supposed to be.

'When you gotta go, you gotta go'

CHILDREN SKATING ON ICE

☆ YOUTHFUL EXUBERANCE ☆

⚙ GENERAL INTERPRETATION

Here is the combination of speed and danger that Nature has to offer to those who feel the faith and exuberance of youth. Importantly, though, the conditions (ahead) should be carefully checked out first.

KEEP FOCUSED ON ... developing or enjoying an ease of accomplishment born of uninhibited movement and a sound sense of reality ... finding ways of doing things that are efficient and fun ... entering into the situation with a flourish and a sense of style and ease – for success lies this way ... using your circumstances to your advantage, trusting to your skill and common sense.

WATCH OUT FOR ... immature risk-taking that may prove harmful to others as well as yourself. Be mindful of that part of you that can indulge in childish irresponsibility.

MONEY/WORK/CREATIVITY

Ideally, work is now best done for the pleasure of doing it. This particularly refers to creative activity, because having some specific goal or objective can often detract from the quality of what is being created. In any event, if going about your business does not amuse or please you, then it is unlikely to appeal that much to others.

KEEP FOCUSED ON ... injecting your work, work environment or co-workers with a sense of the joy of labour and accomplishment ... including recreational activities in your business calendar ... getting your skates on as soon as you have prepared the ground ... skating around problems.

WATCH OUT FOR ... going into things with more enthusiasm than ability, or without first knowing your pitch and techniques ... any signs that things are on or are approaching thin ice (precarious or untested conditions).

♥ LOVE/RELATING/SOCIAL

Although this images a light-hearted and thrilling kind of relationship or person, it could also point to a superficiality or artificiality that skims over the deeper feelings involved. Such immaturity and impetuosity is likely to suffer a fall or, worse still, hit a thin patch and get an icy dunking. In other words, this kind of childishness tends sooner or later to invite cold treatment from those who tire or disapprove of it.

KEEP FOCUSED ON ... enjoying any emotional or physical highs, gliding along in entwined bliss, for as long as and as frequently as you can, but ...

WATCH OUT FOR ... crashing into sensitive emotional areas and then getting the opposite of what you were so happily in the swim of. You would then need to thaw or dry out before the previous intimacy could be resumed.

☯ KARMA/ATTITUDE/HEALTH

Skating is one of those earthly activities that can transcend the usual limitations of physical life – or at least it seems to. It somehow suggests how souls would move around in a swifter and more graceful way than in the physical world, and is reminiscent of dreamy, snowy scenes and winter wonderlands. Perhaps your situation could or should be seen in this frosty sparkling light, thereby lending it a poignant and liberating quality that could be just what is needed to promote physical and psychological well-being.

KEEP FOCUSED ON ... the joy of having a soul, of being a soul, of being close to another soul.

WATCH OUT FOR ... losing track of what is happening in the real world; such flights of fancy as you are capable of enjoying are meant as a respite or inspiration. It is okay to build castles in the air, just so long as you do not attempt to move in!

'Hail to thee, blithe Spirit!'

A MAN TRIMMING PALMS

☆ NECESSARY ERADICATION ONLY ☆

GENERAL INTERPRETATION

Palm trees are not actually 'trimmed' in the sense of being pruned, for if they were then they would die. To maintain healthy growth, only dead or dying matter is removed. It is particularly important that the topknot or crown is kept open to the Sun.

KEEP FOCUSED ON ... removing only that which is outworn or superfluous and that could be destabilizing the whole, stifling the growth of whatever is the object of your enquiry ... what is most important to vitality and growth and pay attention primarily to that.

WATCH OUT FOR ... ill-conceived or neurotically motivated projects resulting in a waste of time, at best, or a deterioration of what was perfectly all right in the first place, at worst ... doing something more radical or drastic than necessary for you would regret it later.

LOVE/RELATING/SOCIAL

The relationship(s) you are involved in has to be regularly attended to and maintained with a view to improving matters – and this bodes well, as long as this 'duty' is kept up. Very few, if any, relationships come 'ready-made'; both people have to make adjustments, work on or remove unsociable traits. This Symbol could also refer to a situation where inappropriate social or emotional interests have to be eliminated, otherwise you could be compromised or disappointed. You may have to be quite ruthless in this, especially if you have not rid yourself of old and outworn attachments.

KEEP FOCUSED ON ... what are the healthy parts of your relationship and manner of relating, attenuating or getting rid of those parts which stifle or suffocate the relationship.

WATCH OUT FOR ... hedging your bets.

MONEY/WORK/CREATIVITY

If your work is concerned with improving what has already been created, like an editor, for example, then this is an auspicious reply to your question. Apart from that, though, it is saying that the object of your concern is in need of having dead wood removed. In this way, success will inevitably be achieved. Financially, it plainly stresses a need to get rid of unnecessary expenditures.

KEEP FOCUSED ON ... eliminating whatever is excess to requirements, that is, everything that is not the essential elements of your product, idea or situation. You will then be able to see the wood for the trees, and healthy growth and development can proceed from there.

WATCH OUT FOR ... inadvertently removing anything or anyone that is vital to your work or finances. Be careful not to throw the baby out with the bathwater.

KARMA/ATTITUDE/HEALTH

Basically, you are a healthy person, psychologically and physically, unless you have allowed old memories and bad habits to clog your life force. It could be said that our lives themselves are like organisms that need to be consciously and consistently encouraged towards a better and more desirable end simply by nipping out anything that is not actually growing, or is getting in the way of growth.

KEEP FOCUSED ON ... getting rid of what you do not need or what does not serve you or others ... gaining clarity and vitality through concentrating on opening your crown chakra.

WATCH OUT FOR ... cutting away or interfering with healthy matter, be this personally or environmentally, for this would obviously give cause for regret.

'What's green is growing, what is not is dying'

WINTER FROST IN THE WOODS

☆ DORMANT POWER ☆

 GENERAL INTERPRETATION

The time when the normal and familiar concerns of life are arrested and when the powers of Nature must take their course – no matter what human interests there may be. A call for individual reorientation during a phase of minimal external change and activity, or of stagnation and want.

KEEP FOCUSED ON ... maintaining your grasp of the moment in a way that allows the old to give way to the new ... conserving energy for the time which will arise naturally and spontaneously, right for action ... the 'spring' of a better, warmer time that is sure to come.

WATCH OUT FOR ... becoming uselessly frozen between what was and what shall be ... thinking a bad or cold time will last forever.

 LOVE/RELATING/SOCIAL

Sometimes, emotionally or socially, things are unavoidably frosty. We are inclined to view such situations as being fearful or depressive and react in a way that makes things worse. This is possibly because cold people and moods are reminiscent of rejection, awkward moments in childhood or the past.

KEEP FOCUSED ON ... the certainty of a thaw coming, that matters will improve, that Spring will come ... maintaining one's cool, for such is an appropriate response to coldness, rather than being forcefully upbeat and jolly, for this can make matters worse. Internalize your 'heat', warm yourself to fend off the 'cold'.

WATCH OUT FOR ... trying to interact intimately when the mood isn't right, or you could get a frosty reception or be unnecessarily discouraged.

MONEY/WORK/CREATIVITY

A hard time that you are going to have to sit out and make do with the minimum, in the knowledge that not only will it not last forever but that it can be used creatively to reflect upon the nature of your position and aims. Assets or cash flow may be frozen, but they will be released ultimately. Do not expend what you have not actually got right now.

KEEP FOCUSED ON ... the possibility that what you need in order to make a success of things has gone into a state of suspended animation. So, use the minimum to maintain what is currently and unavoidably minimal.

WATCH OUT FOR ... and prepare for any material or creative matters being put on ice for a while. Do not presume upon business being as usual – unless it actually is seasonal.

KARMA/ATTITUDE/HEALTH

Things are currently cold and stuck, but they will thaw out and free up eventually.

KEEP FOCUSED ON ... 'hibernating', withdrawing and storing up your energies for a time when you will need them to respond to fresh stimuli ... discerning a beauty in difficult times, because they are a necessary and unavoidable part of the process of getting from one time of fruitfulness to another.

WATCH OUT FOR ... succumbing to the belief that you cannot take the cold, a time of scarcity or hard conditions. At the same time, do not allow yourself to be needlessly left out in the cold because of a masochistic desire to punish yourself or prove that the worst is true ... making an ice age out of a Winter.

'The darkest hour is just before dawn'

A GYPSY COMING OUT OF THE FOREST

☆ INGENUOUSNESS ☆

⊛ GENERAL INTERPRETATION

This could mean coming 'out of the woods', at least regarding the issue in hand, or leaving the 'natural', traditional, instinctual life to immerse oneself in the hurly-burly of 'civilization', bringing to it a freshness of attitude that can prove enlightening – or misleading.

KEEP FOCUSED ON ... keeping intact your native wit and imagination; in this way you are able to show the world what it has been missing ... how utterly appropriate lack of guile can be ... doing your own thing at your own pace ... being true to your heart, amidst those that are not.

WATCH OUT FOR ... a naivety that is in danger of becoming crass, inept and taken advantage of ... feeling too constricted by the conventions of society, for this could prove too great a strain.

♥ LOVE/RELATING/SOCIAL

Coming out of a period of being emotionally lost or out of circulation, and once more immersing oneself in a relationship or the possibility of a relationship. There is also the suggestion of someone who is naive or crude in some way, who is now beginning to gain experience, maturity and sophistication with respect to relating or simply being in the world.

KEEP FOCUSED ON ... the fact that the 'wanderer' has a wild or freedom-loving streak that they do not want tamed - at least, not too much or too soon ... preserving your natural, innocent, even primitive, qualities, for such are love, pure and simple.

WATCH OUT FOR ... biting off more than you can chew, or making someone else do so ... forcing someone, or being forced, to be what they or you are not, or are not ready for.

⚑ MONEY/WORK/CREATIVITY

Going back into the fray. Possibly what you are dealing with here is not quite ready for the world at large, or the world is not ready for it. Then again, it may be its very naivety or simplicity that has appeal. In any case ...

KEEP FOCUSED ON ... the unspoilt soul or essence of whatever is being produced, planned or promoted ... using the sixth sense ... always trusting your wits to 'turn a penny'.

WATCH OUT FOR ... commercialization that misses the point of the very thing being promoted ... initial interest that soon wanes ... allowing the judgement of the world, your inner critic or anyone else to intimidate or discourage you.

⊛ KARMA/ATTITUDE/HEALTH

The gypsy in us is the wanderer who is free to follow his or her heart or nose, unconstrained by the conventions of the society. 'Coming out' in the sense of revealing one's seemingly dark or hidden side.

KEEP FOCUSED ON ... creating a balance between being the 'barefoot' boy or girl, and being the 'civilized', intellectual person. They both need one another to create a whole being. The one has native, intuitive awareness; the other the means of managing and interacting with the modern world.

WATCH OUT FOR ... denying your roots, even though they may be unsophisticated and wild, for they are a part of you and will cause trouble if neglected ... classing worldly ways as 'bad' or too 'clever'; they are like a suit of clothing that needs to be accepted and worn, even though they are not actually you.

'O born in days when wits were fresh and clear ... before this strange disease of modern life'

A MAN DECLARED BANKRUPT

☆ HONEST ADMISSION ☆

❋ GENERAL INTERPRETATION

By honestly admitting to a state of hopelessness, failure or ineptitude, breathing space is attained and a new start is made possible. The point where true values are laid bare, or have to be distinguished from false ones, or socially or financially imposed ones. With regard to using the Oracle, this Symbol may be saying that you are 'bankrupt' in the sense that are overusing it and/or it cannot see any further or give any more information than it already has.

KEEP FOCUSED ON ... your preparedness to own up to any deficiencies that you may have, thereby attracting assistance of the right kind, at the right time ... your inner 'emptiness' – then you will eventually (find a way to) be fulfilled.

WATCH OUT FOR ... evasion of responsibility with the expectation that handouts and get-out clauses will go on forever.

⚘ MONEY/WORK/CREATIVITY

If this is literally a case of bankruptcy, insolvency or an inability to get credit, then you can be sure that either you got something very wrong in your business or with respect to your judgement, and that this was the extreme way you chose to learn your lesson: only an undeniable demise could make the point. Alternatively, you may have such a thing threatening or be suffering a deficit of ideas or supplies. Then you must ...

KEEP FOCUSED ON ... reading and interpreting the writing on the wall before it falls on you ... the consoling fact that real bankruptcy has a kind cleansing or renewing effect, allowing you to start again because you have admitted to the need for that very thing.

WATCH OUT FOR ... bluffing your way or robbing Peter to pay Paul. Disaster this way lies.

♡ LOVE/RELATING/SOCIAL

An individual or a relationship that has exhausted trust and credibility, or is about to. It can also refer to any aspect of a personality or a relationship that has to reach rock bottom before it is realized which way up is. When such a state is admitted to, the point of 'bankruptcy' has arrived. Only then will there be any chance of recovery or closure. Either way, only time will tell which is the case.

KEEP FOCUSED ON ... making an honest person out of yourself or another person ... realizing that all that is or was ever wanted is honesty and sincerity, as opposed to pretence and image.

WATCH OUT FOR ... giving or asking for 'just one more chance' when everyone else can see that is just prolonging the agony and perpetuating weak aspects.

☯ KARMA/ATTITUDE/HEALTH

Sooner or later there comes a point in an individual's life or lifetimes when a fundamental flaw or delusion has to be owned up to, when some karmic debt has to be accepted and (begun to be) paid. Any problem is the result of a past sin of commission or omission. It is only at this point of confession that the upward turn in one's fortunes can genuinely begin.

KEEP FOCUSED ON ... your secret or not-so-secret failing, as this is what is at the root of your problem, and very possibly the problems of others too ... any illness or complaint as being life's way of telling you that there is something wrong with you (not merely the illness itself, but what caused it) that needs seeing to ... the idea that salvation often follows a crisis ... paying what you can.

WATCH OUT FOR ... unattended symptoms.

'Sometimes one has to get to zero before you know the score'

THE FIRST MOCKINGBIRD IN SPRING

✲ ECLECTICISM ✲

GENERAL INTERPRETATION

Suggested here is a spontaneous and creative response to the emergence of new life; celebrating it, giving voice to it. This is not a mere mimicking, but a wonderful combining and weaving of impressions received from the environment. Synthesis.

KEEP FOCUSED ON ... your ability to tune into the emotions and urges of the collective, thereby producing something creative, or literally musical, that meets its needs and elevates its values ... what appeals to others and yet, at the same time, what you make of it personally; it is ultimately up to you, and your choices, skills and predilections ... playing it by ear.

WATCH OUT FOR ... a superficial aping of what is going on around you that has little or no lasting effect ... forming opinions or making plans based upon gossip or second-hand information.

MONEY/WORK/CREATIVITY

An original idea or product that is an outgrowth or evolution of an existing one, but has the advantage of being this first; getting in at the ground floor. There is also a 'when in Rome do as the Romans do' aspect here, in that people like what is familiar to be re-presented in a different way, like a 'cover version' of a record.

KEEP FOCUSED ON ... the spirit of the phrase 'the singer not the song'; the format, interpretation or spin you give to something can make all the difference to the original material, giving it an appeal, accessibility and authority it originally lacked.

WATCH OUT FOR ... plagiarism or copyright infringement, and the fine line between being guided or inspired by what has gone before and copying it word for word, literally or so to speak.

LOVE/RELATING/SOCIAL

This images someone or a way of relating or expressing oneself that is gleaned from other sources, such as friends, public figures or anyone/anything else that has something fresh and attractive to offer. This works well in the early stages of a relationship, especially in the creation of one, but later the lack of any real personality of one's own can become a serious block to genuine intimacy. Alternatively, just 'going through the motions' can be an effective social mask or means of getting through difficult social or emotional situations – but again, not for long.

KEEP FOCUSED ON ... who it actually is within you that is adopting such an image or style, and then expressing *that*.

WATCH OUT FOR ... where it becomes more uncomfortable concealing your true self than it does simply being it.

KARMA/ATTITUDE/HEALTH

The first signs and atmosphere of a new time (maybe Spring itself) are making themselves felt and you are called to respond to them in a fresh and personal way. Health-wise, if relevant, this can be referring to the initial symptoms of something, to which one should respond appropriately. Something that repeats or replicates itself.

KEEP FOCUSED ON ... being spontaneously appropriate and open to whatever happens; do not think about it too much, just respond, lightly ... something like a magical bird with bright plumage that is calling you to the new day.

WATCH OUT FOR ... reacting mindlessly or fearfully to whatever is coming into being, or appearing to do so ... falling prey to or making the same old responses, creating the same old problems.

'All originality is simply an improvement or variation upon an ancient or natural theme'

BATHING BEAUTIES

☆ ATTRACTIVE DISPLAY ☆

 GENERAL INTERPRETATION

This Symbol is saying that the object of your concern has a definite degree of charm about it. Or it would benefit from applying some, but this might only have a short-lasting or superficial effect. In either case, you would be paving the way for eventual success.

KEEP FOCUSED ON ... utilizing or developing what has proven appeal. Developing content rather than just form for maximum or lasting satisfaction ... enquiring more deeply of the Oracle, if not satisfied.

WATCH OUT FOR ... a distortion or perversion of what is simply attractive, for this would lead you down a false and, ultimately, unrewarding path ... superficial value judgements.

 LOVE/RELATING/SOCIAL

Most obviously, this refers to the role and importance of physical looks and personality where relating and socializing are concerned. On the face of it, the Oracle is saying that you or someone else most certainly has such assets. But how you actually use or relate to this could well be an issue.

KEEP FOCUSED ON ... what lasts if you want something that does last ... taking pride or pleasure in appearances, but not as a salve for a sense of inner inadequacy, which is something that would need to be worked upon in its own right ... what has emotional appeal and value.

WATCH OUT FOR ... superficialities such as viewing partners, real or prospective, or other people generally, merely in terms of looks or social position for this would be likely to lead to frustration or embarrassment.

 MONEY/WORK/CREATIVITY

You have something that has obvious appeal, yet at the same time there is probably stiff competition. You could be looking at an opening for success in a far wider market. If your field is concerned with beauty, particularly of the feminine kind, then this is an auspicious oracle.

KEEP FOCUSED ON ... putting out into the world what you have to offer for it to be assessed and made more of ... making sure that what you have to offer looks, performs or sounds the very best that it can ... making sure that there is an immediate appeal, for without that it would be unlikely to go much further.

WATCH OUT FOR ... descending into a 'meat market' mentality where you ignore your deeper principles merely for the sake of material gain ... the ruthlessness, cut-throat nature of the business in which you are involved.

KARMA/ATTITUDE/HEALTH

Could this be a bevy of girls in swimsuits or a school of dolphins? This poses the question of beauty being in the eye of the beholder. Karmically, here is an indication of beauty, style and sexual appeal being a predominant theme. Whether or not this is healthy could be an issue, considering how this poses a possible ignorance of inner values – and the possibility of being tossed aside when of no further use.

KEEP FOCUSED ON ... developing inner worth and practical skills against a future time when age will make physical looks harder to maintain or win others over with.

WATCH OUT FOR ... going only by outer or sensual appeal for they are as nothing when there is no love, care or virtue present.

'Love built on beauty, soon as beauty, dies'

THE SABIAN SYMBOLS OF
CANCER

Either directly, or in a subtle way, all these Symbols are concerned with the following qualities, or with situations that involve or call for them:

BREASTS AND STOMACH

CARE AND PROTECTION

COMFORT

DREAMS

FAMILY AND FAMILIARITY

FEELINGS

THE FEMININE

FOOD AND CATERING

HOME AND SECURITY

THE (INNER) CHILD

INSTINCTS

MOTHERHOOD

THE NATURAL WORLD

NURTURANCE

PERSONAL MATTERS

SUBJECTIVITY

THE UNCONSCIOUS

A FURLED AND AN UNFURLED FLAG DISPLAYED FROM A VESSEL

☆ TURNING POINT ☆

☼ GENERAL INTERPRETATION

As this degree is where the Sun stands at the Summer Solstice, this Symbol can be seen as representing a position of maximum confidence of expression (longest day) that feels it has to guard against its inevitable demise (lengthening nights) until it again comes to fullness. Yet no matter what turning point has been reached, one thing is being folded away, another is unfolding. Ask the Oracle, if need be, what these things are.

KEEP FOCUSED ON ... keeping one's options open or using a 'now you see me, now you don't' way of presenting oneself, enabling one to adjust to matters so that a secure situation is assured.

WATCH OUT FOR ... the fact that nothing physical lasts forever, so be prepared to replace that which is no longer functioning (well or at all).

♥ LOVE/RELATING/SOCIAL

There comes a time when, if you are male, you have to succumb and adapt to the emotional situation in which you find yourself (which means recognizing that the female side is now in the ascendant) and, if you are a female, realizing that you now have the power and must find out how to use it wisely. Mutual caring is the theme here.

KEEP FOCUSED ON ... what exactly it is that is in a process of change from one emphasis to another, from one policy to another or from one set of values to another – and then following it and adapting to it. This is the way to keep a relationship healthy.

WATCH OUT FOR ... hanging on to old sentiments or glories for they will destabilize the relationship. A sea change is occurring, not a minor alteration.

⚱ MONEY/WORK/CREATIVITY

This is a time of success mixed with what would appear to be its opposite. Something new is coming into being which cannot be easily controlled, only followed and adapted to. At the same time, something old and outworn is having its last moment of glory before it fades or folds. Possibly, a state of flux that needs resolving.

KEEP FOCUSED ON ... adapting and keeping your ear close to the ground while you assess which way things are going ... maintaining tenacity in the face of uncertainty or during a state of transition.

WATCH OUT FOR ... vacillation, born of trying to hang on to the devil you know while also trying to be innovative; this could lead to falling between two stools ... anxiety as a result of trying to stay put in the face of inevitable change.

☯ KARMA/ATTITUDE/HEALTH

The issue here is one of 'giving over to the night', for a moment of fullness has been reached that is short-lived, and for the moment the power of your mind and ego is in decline and must surrender and adapt to increasing forces over which you have no real control.

KEEP FOCUSED ON ... the light within yourself that is a sure sense that something is always looking after you, even though you cannot see it or prove it ... caring and letting yourself be cared for.

WATCH OUT FOR ... serious inner doubts or irrational fears for the future, because they could cause you to be over-protective or over-defensive. This, in turn, can attract the very things you feared, or, on a physiological level, provoke your defence system into being over-zealous, giving rise to diseases of the immune system.

'As one door closes, another one opens'

A MAN SUSPENDED OVER A VAST LEVEL PLACE

☆ HUNG UP OR ON HOLD? ☆

✸ GENERAL INTERPRETATION

The need or opportunity to view matters as if from above, seeing all things as equal, thereby allowing the time and space to assess the nature of one's involvement in the situation. Also implied, a contemplative attitude or position – or the need to take one. You may be thinking or feeling that you are stuck or lost, when really you are waiting for things to free up of their own accord.

KEEP FOCUSED ON ... your exceptional breadth of mind with its ability to see things in their entirety, enabling you to make a satisfactory appraisal of the situation.

WATCH OUT FOR ... a disinclination to come down to earth and commit yourself to what truly requires a commitment ... feeling 'out of it' when you are simply pausing to view.

❤ LOVE/RELATING/SOCIAL

There is little or nothing you can actively *do* at present. Emotionally, socially and sexually you are in a position to survey what is going on but, as yet, cannot change it or influence it – at least not in a way that is obvious.

KEEP FOCUSED ON ... trying to see the situation as a whole. You are where you are expressly to take in the complete picture, and then, when the time is right or you see an opening, things will move on ... trusting this 'wait and see' process which is like water filling up a depression before it overflows and flows onward and freely again.

WATCH OUT FOR ... focusing on only the part or parts of the situation that preoccupy you, for this would only frustrate you ... 'kicking against the pricks' or struggling with the way things are, for you will only feel more trapped or desperate.

♛ MONEY/WORK/CREATIVITY

What might feel like a 'quiet patch' or outright recession is actually the necessity to have a good look at what you have been doing or aim to be doing. Financially, cash flow is more or less frozen, so that you are forced to review matters. It is sometimes necessary to withdraw, or be withdrawn, so that the matter can be seen for what it is, or so that it can right itself. Only by looking at the whole layout or plan will you know what is what and which is which. Creatively, you are either experiencing a block or having to step back from what you are doing for long enough to get a fresh take on the subject. These two positions could be one and the same.

KEEP FOCUSED ON ... everything being of equal importance until you know otherwise.

WATCH OUT FOR ... abandoning responsibilities.

☯ KARMA/ATTITUDE/HEALTH

Here is a state of being that can be seen in two distinct ways. Either as a standstill, created by a reluctance to come down to Earth and into the business of living (as in a state of limbo or dissociation), or as a position in which you can be free of the weight and pressure of 'being in the world', seeing it from a detached and more comprehensive or transcendental perspective (as in meditation or an out-of-body experience).

KEEP FOCUSED ON ... emptiness as a positive feeling, as the precursor to being filled up ... the suspension of something as the route to healing.

WATCH OUT FOR ... filling yourself with negative feelings because you are afraid of feeling empty ... feelings of not being accepted by the world, when really it is more a case of you not accepting *it*.

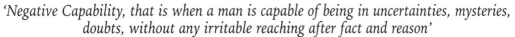

'Negative Capability, that is when a man is capable of being in uncertainties, mysteries, doubts, without any irritable reaching after fact and reason'

A MAN ALL BUNDLED UP IN FUR LEADING A SHAGGY DEER

☆ RUGGED INDIVIDUALITY ☆

✸ GENERAL INTERPRETATION

Suggested here is the rugged pioneering instinct that stems from and empowers the most basic drive or need to root oneself in Nature's processes. Also indicated here is a 'rough diamond' personality, a good heart wrapped up in a gruff countenance. A certain toughness is required when sensitivity ventures forth into the unknown.

KEEP FOCUSED ON ... the unlimited self-reliance that is a product of the good-heartedness which springs from a primitive faith in needs being met ... simply being yourself, in spite of so-called civilized or politically correct opinions ... pushing on through, despite appearances or tough conditions.

WATCH OUT FOR ... an emotional unavail-ability born of a distrust of the genuine existence of tenderness and supply.

♥ LOVE/RELATING/SOCIAL

Outright independence has an important and critical role in relationships. On both sides of a relationship it can be the very thing that prevents it from becoming co-dependent, but if one or both people are *too* independent, that is, actually afraid of relationships, then the relationship can break down or be prohibitively or uncomfortably one-sided.

KEEP FOCUSED ON ... your own values and needs as much as those of another ... who you are as an individual, but without losing sight of your heart's feelings and needs ... being true to your heart, despite difficulties ... blending sentiments of the heart with feelings in the loins.

WATCH OUT FOR ... sacrificing yourself needlessly in a mistaken sense of selflessness ... mistaking defensiveness or a fear of intimacy for sexual licence or independence.

⚙ MONEY/WORK/CREATIVITY

You have to invest your most real and trusted assets, to gird your loins and forge on through to your objective, impervious to any discouraging elements you encounter. All the while, keep your dearest ideas, values and associates close by you.

KEEP FOCUSED ON ... the reasons for your venture and what you actually stand to win or lose ... the hidden or personal aspects of what or whom you are involved with. These will guide you in how to deliberate ... persevering, for this will ensure eventual success ... inspiring those you lead with tenacity of purpose.

WATCH OUT FOR ... any hardship or difficulties that lie ahead, and make provision for them now ... assuming that what appears rough and ready has no value or integrity. You only need to see what someone holds dear to see that their heart is in the right place – or not, as the case may be.

☯ KARMA/ATTITUDE/HEALTH

The experience of isolation and hardship is indicated here, yet at the same time the sentiments of the heart have not been lost. In fact, they could have been the very reason for the hardship, for seeing something through.

KEEP FOCUSED ON ... whatever it is in your personality that has a natural, weathered and stoical feel to it, for this will win through to better circumstances ... what it is that you are protective of, for that is what makes you carry on ... shielding yourself and others from possible infection or hazardous health conditions.

WATCH OUT FOR ... staying in a state of self-denial when something has either served its purpose or because it has become a habit, the devil one knows ... being unapproachable because you are not sure how to handle an awkward situation, for this will only perpetuate or complicate it ... hypochondria; being neurotic about health.

'My heart is a lonely hunter that hunts on a lonely hill'

A CAT ARGUING WITH A MOUSE

☆ NO CONTEST? ☆

✹ GENERAL INTERPRETATION

An absurd situation arising out of one element or force not recognizing or owning its superior power in the face of another patently inferior power. However, an inferior power can remind the superior power of an inner weakness, and so, paradoxically, the inferior can have power over the superior.

KEEP FOCUSED ON ... your gift for bearing with others of less ability or perception, thereby enabling them to evolve ... acting with dignity and respect ... following your instincts rather than interminably talking around the issue ... the fact that the decision is yours if you are the 'cat'.

WATCH OUT FOR ... being a 'mouse around the house', a pushover or feeble in whatever the situation is. And don't give in to bullies ... a discomforting and annoying reluctance to concede defeat or claim victory.

MONEY/WORK/CREATIVITY

If you are the 'cat' you are the one with the power or creativity; if you are the 'mouse' you are not at all sure of what you are or have, or if you have anything at all. Everything depends upon knowing which you are, or rather what you *see* yourself as. It also depends on the situation: for example, as far as taxes go, it is the tax man that is the cat and the taxpayer that's the mouse; for the artist, inspiration is the cat whereas just contriving is the mouse.

KEEP FOCUSED ON ... where your power or talent lies and where it does not, and then take it from there ... take your prey; if you hesitate too much you could lose it (an opportunity).

WATCH OUT FOR ... wasting time and energy on trivia, ineffectual people or matters of no consequence ... using unfair advantage ... any sense of inferiority, for it is preventing success.

♥ LOVE/RELATING/SOCIAL

An unequal relationship, possibly with one person being at the mercy of another who, for reasons of their own, prefers not to have someone of 'equal weight'. Or a situation where someone is trying to be kind but in truth is being cruel because they do not want to hurt them; they are actually prolonging the agony.

KEEP FOCUSED ON ... deciding once and for all whether you are the cat or the mouse in this relationship or situation – otherwise the *game* of cat and mouse will continue ... honestly discerning what the apparently 'weaker' person has going for them that the 'stronger' person does not.

WATCH OUT FOR ... arguing the toss because you are compromised by, say, a fear of being unequivocal or cruel to be kind, or by pandering to the victim in someone. Avoid letting them down so slowly that they don't get the point.

☯ KARMA/ATTITUDE/HEALTH

Why should a cat be arguing with a mouse in the first place? It is a bit like *Tom and Jerry*. What has the physically weaker one got that the physically stronger one has not? Quicker wits? Powerful friends? Inside information? Intuition?

KEEP FOCUSED ON ... what is small but powerful in your situation. This could be one of the talents described above, or it could be something small, such as a stone in one's shoe (niggling doubts, a guilty conscience or physical weakness) slowing one's progress. Most of all though ...

WATCH OUT FOR ... the ego's argument with the Spirit. We are inclined to harbour the illusion that we have control over things when we do not, and consequently get caught in a deadlock until we surrender to the superiority of the Spirit, Higher Power or Fate ... feeling threatened.

'Actions speak louder than words'

AN AUTOMOBILE WRECKED BY A TRAIN

☆ SUPERIOR POWER ☆

GENERAL INTERPRETATION

This apparently horrific Symbol is best not taken literally. Essentially, we see here a situation in which the lesser will or individual must subordinate itself to the greater will, or to the group, officialdom or world at large, if a disaster is to be avoided.

KEEP FOCUSED ON ... your flair for distinguishing between matters of lesser and greater importance, acting accordingly, and saving the day ... letting matters take their course rather than getting in the way of them due to a misguided sense of priorities.

WATCH OUT FOR ... reckless self-interest or lack of self-care ... disregarding or not seeing warning signs ... being presumptuous ... wearing oneself out needlessly.

♡ LOVE/RELATING/SOCIAL

When an individual cannot abide by the conditions of society, or surrender to the emotional truth as rendered in a close relationship, then that individual may be socially ostracized, emotionally devastated, or seen or felt as 'unfit'. This Symbol could also be interpreted as the power of love conquering all lesser considerations, or taking one over.

KEEP FOCUSED ON ... pursuing what is for the good of the relationship or group, not just yourself ... what you have to give up in terms of selfish or egotistical traits in order for emotional satisfaction or social integration to occur.

WATCH OUT FOR ... allowing yourself to be steamrollered in to anything, by anyone, or by your own passions and needs ... anyone who finds it impossible to relate; they'll destroy you.

🏆 MONEY/WORK/CREATIVITY

It is a hard fact of life that institutions and corporations have power over the individual. Depending on your situation or attitude, this can be seen as favourable or unfavourable. Market forces and local/global economics invariably hold sway over one's personal material condition. Creatively, lesser ideas and considerations must give way to the more important ones.

KEEP FOCUSED ON ... the advantages that powerful organizations have to offer the individual; the influence and clout they have may outweigh the significance of individually held personal principles ... what or who has priority, and give them right of way.

WATCH OUT FOR ... trying to buck or beat the system, for though it may not always win, it will in this case.

☯ KARMA/ATTITUDE/HEALTH

Much as a little boat riding a great wave on the open sea, the individual must succumb to his or her fate. Fighting it would mean being or feeling wiped out. Conditions such as ME and nervous exhaustion can be seen as originating in resisting of Fate.

KEEP FOCUSED ON ... what Fate is trying to tell you and go with it ... what the Superior Power is in your life and surrender to it, align yourself with it. A form of meditation or worship is recommended here, or any means that makes one mindful of being a lesser power caught up in a superior one, be it the ego and God, the surfer and wave, or climber and mountain.

WATCH OUT FOR ... wearing yourself out trying to control or avoid Fate or the inevitable ... anything or anyone who takes over individual rights in the name of God, spirituality or salvation.

'Woe be to them that resist their fate'

GAME BIRDS FEATHERING THEIR NESTS

☆ MAKING PROVISION ☆

 GENERAL INTERPRETATION

As 'feathering one's nest' is a well-known phrase, it could be said that this Symbol is not in need of much interpretation. However, 'game birds' implies the possibility of manipulating Nature to human ends and needs, rightly or wrongly. In any event, it means making ready the comfort and safety for those who will need them.

KEEP FOCUSED ON ... your instinct for sensing future needs, and an ability to meet them thoroughly ... making allowances for the young in mind or body.

WATCH OUT FOR ... fussing over details and needs that are naturally met ... mollycoddling others – or being mollycoddled – to the point of never learning or growing up ... overreacting for fear of being smothered by something or someone.

♡ LOVE/RELATING/SOCIAL

Quite simply, the situation calls for or involves the creation of comfort and security, preparing for eventualities such as having a baby, setting up or buying a home, or any future occasion that is more or less inevitable or is desirable. Alternatively, doing whatever is necessary to make one attractive to a prospective mate. There is also an allusion here to 'keeping up with the Joneses', for good or ill.

KEEP FOCUSED ON ... your future requirements as a couple. If alone and looking, determine, develop and acquire what would make you more attractive – not just materially but also as a person, not just externally but also emotionally.

WATCH OUT FOR ... making security such a priority that life becomes restrictive and boring ... assuming what you need is what the other person wants.

 MONEY/WORK/CREATIVITY

A fairly straightforward case of planning for the future, including aftercare. Also implied, the foolhardiness of neglecting this.

KEEP FOCUSED ON ... what product, project or talent you wish to make ready for, or securing your position for the future; the imperative of making this kind of provision ... the fact that something new is definitely on its way, and that you must determine what that is, and allow and prepare for it ... what you have in mind as being a preparation for something beyond it, rather than just that thing in itself.

WATCH OUT FOR ... ambling along without any thought of what tomorrow will bring, or rather won't bring ... putting in a lot of time and energy into something that may not be of benefit to you, and may even cause you harm.

♋ KARMA/ATTITUDE/HEALTH

From a karmic point of view, this Symbol refers to the idea that one life is a preparation for the next one being more accommodating and secure than the current one. Health-wise, this Symbol plainly suggests that tomorrow's well-being has a lot to do with today's lifestyle.

KEEP FOCUSED ON ... and utilize the awesome time factor that may be involved in view of this karmic process, through any kind of preparation, practice or improvement. Have you ever wondered why some people are born lucky?

WATCH OUT FOR ... being mean with yourself and others as you sacrifice too much for future security; this is not good karma ... fear of future insecurity stressing you, giving rise to health problems, especially of the stomach, gut or breasts.

'Hasten to the needs of our children's children's children'

TWO FAIRIES ON A MOONLIT NIGHT

☆ SUPERNATURE ☆

✸ GENERAL INTERPRETATION

Magic in the air, possibly born of the conscious awareness of the existence of realms, activities or species that are not perceivable to the ordinary or limited senses. Nature spirits or devas. The uplift and wonder that the connection with such beings and planes can bring.

KEEP FOCUSED ON ... your ability to transcend the mundane and reach spirit or devic realms and so receive inspiration and healing for yourself and others ... your childlike or childhood perception of things, for it can see what others cannot and is both useful and enchanting.

WATCH OUT FOR ... being out of this world and of no earthly use ... hoaxing or being hoaxed ... tricks of the light ... allowing a lack of acceptance of an unconventional view or perception to invalidate that view or perception. Such are modern-day witch-hunts.

♡ LOVE/RELATING/SOCIAL

Astrologically, emotions are ruled by the Moon, so this Symbol describes a particularly emotional situation between two people. This can pose anything from them becoming aware of the emotional state that exists between them, to being in a highly romantic relationship. It is probably obvious which it is, and it could be a combination of the two. There is a connection here that depends on emotional relating, on the feelings that are in play rather than the words or actions.

KEEP FOCUSED ON ... the invisible aspects to your relationship(s), those elements that are sensed with the heart or gut rather than the head or body ... believing in and allowing an unseen agency to help and guide you towards harmony and integration.

WATCH OUT FOR ... emotional fantasies.

⚒ MONEY/WORK/CREATIVITY

Your work is one that is mainly concerned with the use of intuition and imagination – or it should be. Rational or material standpoints that want scientific explanations or predictable results have to take second place, otherwise they can get in the way of the process that 'delivers the goods'. Disbelief in fairies usually precludes seeing them. Similarly, money or resources can be forthcoming from quite unexpected quarters and in quite unexpected ways if one is open to this possibility.

KEEP FOCUSED ON ... the female element in the area of your concern for direction, support and inspiration. This could be women themselves or any psychic or sixth sense that is available ... furthering anything that is softly nurturing, magically uplifting.

WATCH OUT FOR ... being too immersed in the tangible world of business, economics and hard facts, or being too out of touch with it.

☯ KARMA/ATTITUDE/HEALTH

In the esoteric tradition there is much written about fairies – devas/elemental beings as they are more properly called. Whereas human evolution is about growing ever finer and skywards, the devas (the 'shining ones') are the agencies that build and keep stable the physical world. Therefore, they have a great deal to do with health and healing. Spiritual or energy healers employ their psychic connection with the devas to help repair damaged or diseased tissue.

KEEP FOCUSED ON ... your connection with and experience of the supernatural realm, using it to heal, enchant or help in any way that it can ... finding ways to improve one's spiritual connection through trance, animals, chanting, drumming, dancing and invocation, and prayer, meditation and shamanism.

WATCH OUT FOR ... faking or faked connection.

'There never was a merry world since the fairies left off dancing, and the Parson left conjuring'

RABBITS DRESSED IN CLOTHES AND ON PARADE

☆ CHILDREN IN THE WORLD ☆

 GENERAL INTERPRETATION

Having to wear the mask or outfit that passes muster in the outside world. This can also clothe our inner fears or feelings of inadequacy.

KEEP FOCUSED ON ... only using a conventional display as a means to an end rather than seeing it as an end in itself ... who or what is wearing the outfit rather than the outfit itself. Be kinder and supportive to yourself, the person on the inside ... the more playful or surreal aspects of existence where you are allowed to be silly or less serious.

WATCH OUT FOR ... trying to regiment what is naturally spontaneous ... losing sight of your essential nature in a bid to live up to something or somebody ostensibly more advanced or powerful ... condemning yourself as 'not good enough' ... 'suits' or hiding behind a uniform.

 MONEY/WORK/CREATIVITY

The instinctual and possibly frightened part of you is looking for your true vocation. It may have to do this by stepping into the role or situation that goes with this position in order to find out if it feels right – if the cap fits. Finances would depend on how successfully you got in step with whatever this might be, and how well-turned out you are. Another aspect to this Symbol is that of childlike or immature elements having to get in line with, or influence, the adult world of money and work.

KEEP FOCUSED ON ... the nature of that 'parade' or professional avenue and you will get the feel of it more and more, and whether it's for you ... using your endearing qualities.

WATCH OUT FOR ... having your spontaneity and imagination constrained by conventional rules and expectations ... being dazzled by glamorous prospects and going against your own instincts, or signing up for longer than you can stand.

 LOVE/RELATING/SOCIAL

In the world at large we are generally made to conform to its ways. But in emotional relationships, the child in us is forced to the surface, or it is unless one is caught in a stiff and controlled relationship, or one where both people pretend to be what they are not. This Symbol is saying that your issue is based on one or more of these scenarios; a feeling of constriction, wanting to escape or unreality, will be evidence of this.

KEEP FOCUSED ON ... the fact that the child or victim in you has been 'found out' by the relationship or set-up you are in, or that it is still being kept down. Make a priority of sorting this out and seek professional help if necessary.

WATCH OUT FOR ... being victimized by victims, which reveals the tragedy and absurdity of being a victim ... forming negative sexual habits.

 KARMA/ATTITUDE/HEALTH

Rabbits can be seen to represent victimhood, and the speed with which such a complex can proliferate. Collectively and karmically, victimhood is rife on this planet; the wicked barons and oppressed serfs of the past are still with us, but they are now called the 'haves' and 'have-nots'. On a personal level, this victimhood is often sublimated by wearing the disguise of a 'normal member of society' as we sit on our real feelings and pains for fear of them being seen to be weaknesses. It is sometimes supposed that men don't cry – but of course, they do.

KEEP FOCUSED ON ... expressing in some way your innermost feelings, especially those of helplessness and vulnerability.

WATCH OUT FOR ... suppressing these feelings for this could lead to health complaints, such as congestion or inexplicable physical pains ... being harsh upon the inner child (see Self Talk, page 463).

'If the cap fits, then wear it – but do not if it does not'

A TINY NUDE MISS REACHING IN THE WATER FOR A FISH

✢ EMOTIONAL APPEAL ✢

❂ GENERAL INTERPRETATION

What is still innocent, inexperienced and vulnerable, or not yet fully formed, is instinctively reaching out for whatever will bring what is necessary for growth and knowledge – especially in the emotional sense. A first tentative groping into mystical, psychic or just strange realms of experience.

KEEP FOCUSED ON ... your appealing and irresistible yearning for feeling experiences that bring you ever closer to where and to whom you belong ... caring for and nurturing those who need it, even though it stretches you to the utmost ... trusting your innate ability to tune into what is going on within or around you, then you will become more attuned to what you need to know.

WATCH OUT FOR ... naive and precarious attempts to grasp what is elusive.

♡ LOVE/RELATING/SOCIAL

A vulnerable or inexperienced person who is embarking upon, or involved in, a relationship or entertaining the prospect of having or not having one. Such naivety or lack of experience can lead to emotional disappointments and pain. But ...

KEEP FOCUSED ON ... the fact that it is these very experiences which will equip you with what you need ... finding and getting what you are after, such as emotional sustenance and security – even if at first it keeps slipping away ... sometimes clothing yourself with a bit of reserve.

WATCH OUT FOR ... emotional insecurity causing you to either deny your own or another's feelings, or to be overly emotional by way of compensation. Either of these can create the emotional vacuum or crisis that you fear.

♛ MONEY/WORK/CREATIVITY

Everything you require for professional and material security can be found within your own emotional and imaginative depths. And your freshness and innocence attracts and equips you with what and who you need to guide and support you.

KEEP FOCUSED ON ... the possibility that you can get by on very little for as long as you need to, and as long as what you are after is spiritually worth it – that is, it meets a collective need and is consoling and helpful ... your openness, inexperience and lack of guile, for it is these that attract the support you need ... the saying 'give them a fish and feed them for a day; teach them how to fish and feed them for a lifetime'.

WATCH OUT FOR ... being an innocent abroad for too long, because there comes a time when we are supposed to be a bit more streetwise; that fish might be a shark!

♋ KARMA/ATTITUDE/HEALTH

Somewhere along the line you may have lost touch with the most sensitive and creative parts of yourself, so you are now having to regain and integrate them, by exercising these very parts through exposing them to emotional life and the world at large.

KEEP FOCUSED ON ... the beauty and value of what you have lost, and identifying whatever form that loss is currently taking. For instance, being without emotional understanding is symptomatic of emotions not being sufficiently available or perceivable ... finding within yourself, rather than without, that part you feel is missing.

WATCH OUT FOR ... being unaware of just how sensitive you really are, and blundering impetuously into situations where you are hit back at or simply avoided ... being an emotional junkie dependent on others, because of a refusal to look at your own emotional state; health conditions that stem from such a dependency.

'The innocent and the beautiful have no enemy but time'

A LARGE DIAMOND NOT COMPLETELY CUT

☆ ALMOST THERE ☆

 GENERAL INTERPRETATION

Enormous raw potential about to be realized. Great reward or simply what you are after is within your reach; you just need to take that critical step and, more importantly, prepare for that step. More generally, the potential of the human soul to reach perfection, which in turn highlights the fact that there is careful work to be done in bringing something of value to completion. The eleventh hour.

KEEP FOCUSED ON ... getting your 'angle of approach' dead right before acting ... your feeling for potential in everyone and everything that enables them and you to get one step nearer making that potential real.

WATCH OUT FOR ... mistaking potential for reality, or overlooking the care and skill that is needed to make that transition ... work left unfinished ... losing concentration.

MONEY/WORK/CREATIVITY

You have been working on something for a long time and it now requires that final push and effort. But you have to be very careful how you go about this; get it wrong now and there would be a lot of time and energy wasted. For this reason you may be putting it off or holding back; you may have 'forgotten' what 'it' was altogether.

KEEP FOCUSED ON ... what your ideals are, what your original impulse was to get involved with the object of your enquiry, for this will be the key to what you have worked on for so long and must now bring to completion, or, at least, take to the next stage of the process ... making the necessary preparations for the final 'cut' ... getting the best person for the job; don't spare the expense.

WATCH OUT FOR ... hurrying things to completion; paradoxically, this is not a time to be cutting corners!

 LOVE/RELATING/SOCIAL

This images a relationship or person who is not 'quite right' or ready for some final commitment. In any event, there is enormous potential for happiness and success here; all that is needed is patience and care.

KEEP FOCUSED ON ... what it is in yourself or the other person(s) that is wanting or just short of 'perfection' and ponder on how it can be helped or complemented ... the great value of what is already there, as well as the potential of what could be ... being up to the challenge; it takes a diamond to cut a diamond.

WATCH OUT FOR ... giving up on someone because they are not Mr or Mrs Right. This would smack of fantasy-ridden emotions, or looking for a get-out-clause ... giving up on yourself or someone else just when a corner is about to be turned.

KARMA/ATTITUDE/HEALTH

This sounds like 'unfinished karmic business'. This means that you have been striving for perfection is some field over lifetimes. This lifetime – and this time in particular – is when you are very close to making the breakthrough. Esoterically, we could be talking of the 'diamond soul' that is attempting to create a personality to match its divine intention. There are some special personal qualities that you have and need, in order to live up to enormous ideals.

KEEP FOCUSED ON ... every detail and condition concerning the object of your concern.

WATCH OUT FOR ... skipping anything, for this could be disastrous. Be wary of branding what bothers or preoccupies you as being an imperfection. It is not – it is the very thing that you must change, transcend or understand completely in order to turn that corner. Such branding could even manifest as a health condition.

'Spirituality completes us. The idea of a search for the soul presumes that the ordinary man and ordinary woman are, in a manner of speaking, "unfinished"'

A CLOWN MAKING GRIMACES

☆ SEEMING INSINCERITY ☆

 GENERAL INTERPRETATION

Through the humorous use of gesture, behaviour and other forms of expression, one is able to make a point, submit an idea, get through a bad patch, but without it being taken too much to heart. A sense of the ridiculous is infectious, and many things can be said or done that normally could not be got away with. The Oracle may be grimacing at your question itself – like 'yuk!' or 'poor little you!'

KEEP FOCUSED ON ... using your personal style in a way that can have an impact on others that is quite beguiling ... the possibility that the Oracle itself is responding to your question in a slightly mocking fashion – perhaps because you are taking it all too seriously, are overcome with self-pity or are missing the point. 'Lighten up!' it is saying.

WATCH OUT FOR ... sidestepping important issues through a misguided sense of levity.

 MONEY/WORK/CREATIVITY

Unless you are in the business of making people laugh or another area of theatre – something which the Oracle obviously approves of here – then you are getting bogged down in the heavy and earnest side of your work and finances to the point of losing the lightness of touch that will afford you success.

KEEP FOCUSED ON ... convincing yourself that raising money is like raising a laugh – you have, in a way, not to care. People tend to shy away from and have no confidence in someone who appears to be desperate or overwrought. But ...

WATCH OUT FOR ... flippancy and tomfoolery when they are inappropriate, like when meeting deadlines and paying dues. This Symbol is not about out-and-out buffoonery, but about using a ploy that prevents the serious side of life getting you to the point of incapacitation.

LOVE/RELATING/SOCIAL

Often we make hard work out of a relationship by taking certain things that happen in it *too* seriously. We do this because someone can press our 'no one takes me seriously' button, a common agenda from childhood. The Oracle is showing you how to respond to difficult people or situations by adopting a theatrical, almost vaudevillian, response to them. This neatly defuses situations or puts the ball back in the other person's court.

KEEP FOCUSED ON ... how this ploy is typically Cancerian for it adapts to situations in such a way that protects one from further hurt or stress.

WATCH OUT FOR ... going over the top with such parodying for this reveals the fact that you have been got to, that you can't handle not being taken seriously, because you cannot see your own truth, or your own joke.

KARMA/ATTITUDE/HEALTH

You have a history of showing yourself as either the clown or the 'serious person' – whatever you see as the side of you that you feel others will accept or respect. This can mean that the heavier or lighter, and more powerful or appealing, side of your personality is relegated to your shadow. So people do not see you entirely for what you are – something which may have happened right from the start.

KEEP FOCUSED ON ... the idea that you can creatively parody what you see as that shadow, hard-to-accept side to yourself. The comic Barry Humphries does this brilliantly in the guises of Dame Edna or Les Patterson. He is that popular because he is making funny what most of us have a horror of. This is healthy.

WATCH OUT FOR ... taking self-parody to a point where it is deluding or insulting. This is unhealthy – and health is a serious matter.

'Very sorry can't come. Lie follows by post'

A CHINESE WOMAN NURSING A BABY WITH A MESSAGE

✫ UNIQUE PROMISE ✫

❋ GENERAL INTERPRETATION

Apart from being literally an unusual case or the prospect of a baby, this Symbol is about drawing upon and being nurtured by, or tending to, what might be regarded as alien, unusual or far-flung in order that potential be realized and something useful, beautiful or profound be created and made known. Put simply, nurture and it shall be delivered, nurse it and it shall get better.

KEEP FOCUSED ON ... the rare, even divine, qualities you possess that can serve the community where other more conventional means fail ... nurturing your ideas; they are saying something new and important.

WATCH OUT FOR ... missing the point by refusing to accept the unlikely – or mindlessly indulging in it.

♥ LOVE/RELATING/SOCIAL

A complex and intricate situation that requires unusual awareness and subtle attention. Through such devotion, something new will come about that will be pleasing, welcome and stimulating.

KEEP FOCUSED ON ... your rare talent for recognizing what needs your special tenderness; matters will greatly improve if you do so ... the care you take to get or put across a message and convey feelings ... maintaining a detachment with respect to who you (have to) care for; this may be the only way to do it without getting dragged down in the process.

WATCH OUT FOR ... being brusque, insensitive or alienating ... going about things in too soppy or conventional a manner.

♛ MONEY/WORK/CREATIVITY

A project or issue that is in its early stages and requires or attracts specialized treatment to get it up and running or to bring it to fruition.

KEEP FOCUSED ON ... the small, tender and fragile aspects of the issue, and then the whole will eventually meet with success and show you something about yourself you needed to know ... the conscientiousness you possess that makes sure you are clearly saying or doing what you really mean to say or do ... the fact that there is something special coming into being, and that you best nurture it in a subtle fashion.

WATCH OUT FOR ... ham-fisted, unsubtle methods that try to force things to a quick result or conclusion; this would have an adverse and unwelcome effect.

☯ KARMA/ATTITUDE/HEALTH

The issue – possibly in its early stages, and promising to supply vital information – needs an unusual or foreign remedy (possibly acupuncture or Chinese medicine) in order to identify and resolve it. The very old helping the very young to express themselves, and vice versa.

KEEP FOCUSED ON ... the fact that your concern is of a tender disposition and so requires an equally subtle, detached, viewpoint for a happy outcome ... the humility that you have in order to accomplish this ... the possibility that it is the 'baby' in you that needs looking to and after, and that will then tell you something important.

WATCH OUT FOR ... indulging in unlikely ideas and possibilities, for they will only aggravate and alienate ... impatience – you only learn what you need to know when you are ready to learn it.

'The hand that rocks the cradle/Is the hand that rules the world'

ONE HAND SLIGHTLY FLEXED WITH A VERY PROMINENT THUMB

☆ ACCEPTANCE AND ASSERTION ☆

⊛ GENERAL INTERPRETATION

The appropriate assertion of one's will where it is necessary, coupled with an acceptance of Fate as a superior means of dealing with and approaching the business of living, particularly at this time. This Symbol may also refer to how to get the best out of the Oracle itself, by using a combination of a strong sense of what you are asking (thumb) and an openness to what the Oracle tells you (hand).

KEEP FOCUSED ON ... your sense of personal effectiveness, in a relaxed and alert manner ... the exact nature of your issue or question for what it is, not so much how your fears see it.

WATCH OUT FOR ... a destructive wilfulness born of an ignorance of the part others have to play ... having a pre-conception of what you think the Oracle ought to be telling you, for then you won't understand what it *does* tell you.

⊛ MONEY/WORK/CREATIVITY

The art of business or correctly playing any field of endeavour is the issue here. In other words, being firm but flexible, intent but receptive, or speculative but cautious, are just some of the winning combinations that you have at your disposal – or need to have.

KEEP FOCUSED ON ... being true to your own vision but keeping an ear to the ground ... pushing something through but being ready to make key concessions if need be ... 'Speak softly and carry a big stick; you will go far'.

WATCH OUT FOR ... being too wilful, aggressive or sure of yourself, for this would blind you to what you are, or soon will be, sorely in need of ... being too much of a yes-person, for this could mean getting overloaded or pushed around, being too suggestible, or never being seen or heard.

♥ LOVE/RELATING/SOCIAL

This points to the give and take that is necessary to the success of any relationship. The Symbol is confirming or questioning that this is present with each person recognizing and accepting their respective strengths and weaknesses. If this is so, by the very nature of the relationship both or all of you would agree it to be the case. If there is dissension, then it implies that one person could be exercising their will over another. Then again, a successful relationship could be one where it is accepted that one person has the active role and the other the passive.

KEEP FOCUSED ON ... maintaining this balance or agreement, or redressing the balance of power if it is uneven. For example, does one listen enough or say too little?

WATCH OUT FOR ... pushing when you should be pulling back, or vice versa.

⊛ KARMA/ATTITUDE/HEALTH

One's fate or karma could be seen as the hand you are dealt in life and the 'One Hand Slightly Flexed' symbolizes how best to receive this – that is, readily and willingly. The 'Very Prominent Thumb' shows that a strongly motivated will is a vital part of your 'hand'. Whatever the nature of your predicament, matters will fare well or better as long as you ...

KEEP FOCUSED ON ... doggedly pursuing whatever it is you are after, while always being open to advice and ready to adjust to what Fate might bring ... knowing what matters and what does not, and consequently what should be stressed or changed and what should be left as it is.

WATCH OUT FOR ... forcing issues when it is obvious that letting things be is the better course ... giving in when yours is the 'power of attorney'.

'Life is not a case of either Fate or Free Will – but a case of Both'

A VERY OLD MAN FACING A VAST DARK SPACE TO THE NORTH-EAST

☆ DESOLATION TO CONSOLATION ☆

✸ GENERAL INTERPRETATION

The eventual confrontation, after a considerable length of experience, that one has with what appears to be a desolate prospect, but when seen with a deeper understanding is actually a source of great consolation. The north-east is traditionally the direction of spiritual truth and guidance, but it could equally have a more personal significance.

KEEP FOCUSED ON ... the inner maturity that enables you to reflect upon the deeper and graver issues of life and your role in it, and then discover something uplifting on the other side of it ... seeking spiritual guidance as to a path through current difficulties, for it is possible that nothing else will suffice ... earnestly seeking.

WATCH OUT FOR ... giving in to a sense of remorse and pointlessness; don't ... flippancy.

♥ LOVE/RELATING/SOCIAL

A heavy and difficult relationship or time of relating has within it the potential to reveal strengths and truths that you would not otherwise have found. Such episodes serve to bring out our better and wiser parts.

KEEP FOCUSED ON ... the truth that there is a 'prize' waiting for you beyond whatever is blocking or depressing you. Facing up to despair, hopelessness, loneliness or other negative feelings, is the light that penetrates and guides you through such darkness ... finding, if necessary, someone who can help you do this.

WATCH OUT FOR ... collapsing into 'easy' ways out of emotional problems – such as losing your rag or evading issues – for they will only come back to haunt you at a later, possibly more inconvenient, date.

♆ MONEY/WORK/CREATIVITY

You could be going through a seemingly bad patch here, or you could be in a position to help those that are. In either case, you are gaining or using hard-won knowledge and experience that will serve you and others well in the future.

KEEP FOCUSED ON ... finding the most experienced in your field of concern, or drawing hard on your own experience in the midst of current difficulties, thereby turning them to your advantage ... putting experience before academic knowledge ... a sense of purpose that sees blocks to progress as being par for the course ... seeing beyond immediate problems.

WATCH OUT FOR ... leaving grave and pressing problems to those who are not really equipped to deal with them, either because they are past it or have no experience of it.

♄ KARMA/ATTITUDE/HEALTH

At certain points along one's path of spiritual striving and discovery, one is inevitably confronted by what is theosophically called 'The Dweller on the Threshold', the accumulation of all one's past sins of commission and omission. Then, having finally overcome negative traits and redeemed oneself through such confrontation, one is blessed by the 'Angel of the Shining Presence', representing the truth, beauty and goodness of one's Higher Self.

KEEP FOCUSED ON ... the fact that it is through your darkest hours, the Night of Soul, that true light, strength and goodness are found ... facing your void, aloneness or dark origins, for this will eventually lead to spiritual insight and good health, at least on a psychological level. Be ever hopeful.

WATCH OUT FOR ... giving into despair as if it is going to last forever; it is actually a Rite of Passage.

'Nil desperandum' (Never despair)

A GROUP OF PEOPLE WHO HAVE OVEREATEN AND ENJOYED IT

☆ POSITIVE INDULGENCE ☆

☀ GENERAL INTERPRETATION

A very real acknowledgement or celebration of there being more than enough to go round. An indulgence in Nature's supply. Taking joy in the fruits life has to offer ensures their continuance.

KEEP FOCUSED ON ... your flair for summoning up a communal sense of well-being and affluence – thereby attracting these very things ... the possibility that just when you think you have had all you can take, you then start to like it, or that it just doesn't matter ... what being excessive has shown or given you, and then be wiser and better for having overdone it.

WATCH OUT FOR ... irresponsible indulgence merely for the sake of it, with no sense of significance other than one of being better off than most ... indulging in your 'hangover' rather than getting back to normal.

♥ LOVE/RELATING/SOCIAL

You are or have been experiencing an extreme high or low regarding a certain relationship or your social life in general. As you are asking the Oracle about it, it is more likely to be a low, but then again it may be a high but you feel guilty about it or worried that it won't last. In any case, the Oracle entreats you to embrace all experience, and to ...

KEEP FOCUSED ON ... the very nature of emotional life, which is characterized by its phases, its ups and downs. As long as one rides this roller coaster and does not 'freeze' at any point, be it very good or very bad, we move on, enriching ourselves and our lives in the process.

WATCH OUT FOR ... recriminations or any other negative feelings, for they would perpetuate a problem ... trying to hang on to or repeat good times; they'll come again of themselves.

♛ MONEY/WORK/CREATIVITY

You have enjoyed a good spell with regard to your finances or career – possibly you have been celebrating it – but a return to normality inevitably looms. Alternatively, such good times have been presumed upon, indulged in, and now there is little 'in the pot' for times of scarcity.

KEEP FOCUSED ON ... the fact that the 'wisdom of excess' is that one learns to moderate outgoings, unless you are absolutely sure how much you can afford to blow, or you live in the faith that there is plenty to go around and that 'something will always turn up' ... the idea that creativity thrives on excess, be it low or high.

WATCH OUT FOR ... always expecting matters to work themselves out when experience tells you that controls and restraint have to be employed, that luck is created, not just given.

☯ KARMA/ATTITUDE/HEALTH

Previously, which could mean last week or during another lifetime, you were overindulgent or hedonistic and had no guilt or doubt about being so. This was okay for you felt it was all part of the wealth of your experience. If that spell of excess gave rise to wastefulness or harm to others in any way, then now the piper is having to be paid. This may simply be a case of health or weight problems created by overdoing it.

KEEP FOCUSED ON ... how what is happening now could relate to past profligacy or damage done through excess or debauchery ... considering that the time has come to 'fill the gap' in a more spiritual or creative way – or to make amends ... what any (want of) indulgence is a substitute for.

WATCH OUT FOR ... punishing yourself or others too much for past excesses – an indulgence in itself!

'The road of excess leads to the palace of wisdom'

A MAN IN FRONT OF A SQUARE WITH A MANUSCRIPT SCROLL BEFORE HIM

☆ MORPHOGENETIC FIELD ☆

✸ GENERAL INTERPRETATION

Having or needing some version, plan, model or scheme on which one may map out or create a given thing or situation; constantly trimming or comparing reality and experience to this. At a more fundamental and unconscious level, this can be described as one's morphogenetic field (*see* Karma below).

KEEP FOCUSED ON ... what you feel or think you are 'putting out' in terms of desires and fears, because a response to or manifestation of these is what you will get back sooner or later ... your ability to shape or attract whatever life puts before you, towards a natural or productive end.

WATCH OUT FOR ... being restricted by your own viewpoint, or by the rules or conditions you have chosen or have allowed to be imposed upon you.

❤ LOVE/RELATING/SOCIAL

The nature of our partners and social milieu is not just determined by what we want, but by what we fear. The trouble is that we tend to have a superficial idea of what we want, and then go looking for what may appear to match those desires; as time goes by we see that our fears and aversions are also manifest in our partner and social milieu. Then again, those fears may be so powerful as to preclude us finding what we want at all. So, what are those fears?

KEEP FOCUSED ON ... what you are as a person, and accept that you get what you deserve; only then will you be able to relate lovingly, and understand and appreciate what you've got.

WATCH OUT FOR ... having a 'want/don't want' attitude, for all you'll get are partners with equally mixed feelings or unacceptable inconsistencies.

MONEY/WORK/CREATIVITY

First you have your idea, then you draw up your plan, then you make it real. This intention–formulation–production process is at the root of all life, and cannot be altered or avoided. So, whatever the nature of your enquiry, if each of these stages has been satisfactorily accomplished, then all should be well. However, if any one of them is insufficient, then the others will suffer or will have been in vain. Therefore ...

KEEP FOCUSED ON ... making sure that your intention is clear, your formulation is thorough and your production sound. Then you will have success ... overseeing all stages and processes ... the idea that good workmanship is its own reward.

WATCH OUT FOR ... dubious or fanciful intentions, poorly thought-through plans, sloppy workmanship. Failure lies this way.

☯ KARMA/ATTITUDE/HEALTH

Everything that has ever happened to us, collectively or personally, is stored in the unconscious mind. In turn, these experiences produce in us beliefs, preconceptions and expectations that we try to make happen, or not happen, as the case may be. This is known as the morphogenetic field. Your birth chart is a map of all these intentions and conditions at the time of starting out in life. And at any given time, we have an intention we want to make real or an object we wish to avoid. So ...

KEEP FOCUSED ON ... identifying and eliminating any thought or feeling that could be preventing you from realizing your goal or creating better health ... visualizing intently what you want, for this will further its realization ... getting your birth chart properly interpreted.

WATCH OUT FOR ... dwelling upon your fears, for this will contribute to their manifestation.

'What you are is what you get'

THE GERM GROWS INTO KNOWLEDGE AND LIFE

☆ QUICKENING PROCESS ☆

⚙ GENERAL INTERPRETATION

You are involved in a natural process of development – anything from the expression of your own will to having a baby. The seed has been fertilized and now proceeds towards making something more of itself, multiplying exponentially.

KEEP FOCUSED ON ... the fact that this process is happening even though on the surface it may appear that nothing is happening at all ... nurturing any visible signs of development or an awareness of it ... seeing obstacles as challenges to growth, not as blocks to it.

WATCH OUT FOR ... trusting too much in instinct alone as a guide to self-development, rather than augmenting it with sufficient mental deliberation and discrimination ... interfering or trying to make things happen faster than they are supposed to, for that way you could stymie the whole process.

♡ LOVE/RELATING/SOCIAL

It may help here to see the start of a relationship as being like the successful interaction between a sperm and an egg. Once the one has fertilized the other, the relationship then grows. The critical point is whether it is allowed to grow into what it is supposed to become, owing to interference by one or both people due to their illusions of love and sex, loyalty and harmony. To avoid this ...

KEEP FOCUSED ON ... what the relationship itself seems to give or demand of you, for these are indications of what the germ wants to grow into ... nurturing one another through stages of growth.

WATCH OUT FOR ... signs that one or both of you is not happy with the way things are going. Do not assume that things are all right because no one says they are not. Be honest with each other ... critical stages of growth, and adjust to them.

♛ MONEY/WORK/CREATIVITY

This Symbol very much images the creative process, meaning that if your concern is to do with the creation or production of something, then trust that your initial idea or product will come to fruition and meet with success so long as you nurture it through all its necessary stages. Generally speaking, you are heading towards success if you ...

KEEP FOCUSED ON ... staying with the process and keeping mindful of what your original idea or target is ... 'quickening' the process through genuine encouragement and judicious investment.

WATCH OUT FOR ... expansion for expansion's sake, for this could lead to something unmanageable or cumbersome, leading to eventual collapse ... overlooking important parts of, or people involved with, the process.

⑨ KARMA/ATTITUDE/HEALTH

The acorn and oak tree analogy: that everything and everyone has a seed or destiny which, according to one's karma and intrinsic nature, will eventually develop into what it, and it alone, is supposed to be (dharma). By the same token, you may now be experiencing the growth or critical development of something that originated some time ago. Healthwise, we could be talking about any kind of cell proliferation, including the growth of a baby.

KEEP FOCUSED ON ... thinking positively, even though you might feel a dark empty hole inside. Nature abhors a vacuum, so think and act creatively; what Nature fills your emptiness with will be good ... what's happening now as an indication of your true path, unlikely as it may seem.

WATCH OUT FOR ... dwelling upon your fears, for this will contribute to their manifestation.

'Large streams from little fountains flow/Tall oaks from little acorns grow'

A HEN SCRATCHING FOR HER CHICKS

☆ BASIC SURVIVAL ☆

✷ GENERAL INTERPRETATION

This vividly Cancerian Symbol does not need much interpreting: a mother providing for her young or a hand-to-mouth lifestyle. There is a feel of a matter-of-fact selflessness born of the feeling that one is part of a natural process where needs are mutually met.

KEEP FOCUSED ON ... an unassuming and natural ability to cater to the needs of those in your care ... attending to your own welfare as well as everyone else's, for where would they be if you went down.

WATCH OUT FOR ... a mindless and automatic response to whatever is demanded of you ... 'poverty consciousness', that is, living on the breadline habitually, or denying your own needs and feelings.

♥ LOVE/RELATING/SOCIAL

An ongoing relationship that is so because of an instinctual meeting of each other's needs. A naturally protective and nurturing person.

KEEP FOCUSED ON ... what or who needs caring for in a basic fashion, looking out for the other person, or appreciating everyday acts of care and attention, even though (or because) they appear to be automatic.

WATCH OUT FOR ... a one-sidedness where one person is doing all the caring and supporting – unless it is certain that they are happy to do this ... being a mother hen, fussing around others when they do not want it ... dubious motives for being so 'caring', such as not being inclined to care for oneself.

♛ MONEY/WORK/CREATIVITY

This could mean lean times financially or creatively. However, any projects that serve to meet the basic needs of others are well-starred. In any event, it is a time to ...

KEEP FOCUSED ON ... cutting back or finding the most economical methods ... whatever or whoever really keeps things going, and make sure that they are maintained, rewarded and recognized ... how, one way or another, you receive what you need to survive or keep afloat.

WATCH OUT FOR ... carelessness or misuse of funds and resources.

☯ KARMA/ATTITUDE/HEALTH

Someone or something is always looking out for you, seeing to your welfare so that you do not go without at a basic level. Spiritually speaking, it is often the simplest everyday things that have the most significance and value. Health, too, is best maintained by good, regular and earthy habits. So ...

KEEP FOCUSED ON ... those small details and natural things that bear witness to living in a caring universe, such as a cat licking her kittens, small acts of kindness, and the symbiotic nature of life ... digging around a bit to find what you are after.

WATCH OUT FOR ... expecting sustenance to fall into your lap, unless you are evidently and justifiably in the care of something or someone.

'Back to basics'

A PRIEST PERFORMING A MARRIAGE CEREMONY

☆ JOINED IN HEAVEN ☆

✳ GENERAL INTERPRETATION

The appropriate acknowledgement of the sanctity of, and need for commitment in, a personal relationship. But this Symbol can be seen as the approval or machination of Fate or a Higher Power, or just another well-intentioned act of commitment that fails to deliver. Everything depends that you …

KEEP FOCUSED ON … your reverence for any relationship that has been seriously and religiously thought through. Short of 'luck', this is the only thing that will ensure that unity and security will follow. Then again, if a relationship is destined to happen or last, then it will. 'What God has joined together, let no man put asunder.'

WATCH OUT FOR … being deceived into thinking that merely subscribing to convention will ensure stability and mutual respect.

♥ LOVE/RELATING/SOCIAL

Is this predicting marital bliss? No more than any wedding ceremony does. But it *is* saying that there is something that wants to lead you to the altar or to a public recognition of your relationship. A fated relationship – for better or worse.

KEEP FOCUSED ON … creating or identifying the vows that you are making towards one another, and being true to them … creating or identifying the vows concerning relationships generally, and being true to them.

WATCH OUT FOR … vows you have made that you are not really suited to, for you will naturally find it hard to keep to them. However, it is these vows (and the relationship itself) that may be needed to strengthen your personality, to force you to be more moral and responsible.

MONEY/WORK/CREATIVITY

You are joined to your work, or a work partner, in a way that is binding, be it legally or morally. This may be a strength or a weakness, but the fact remains that you are. Alternatively, the Oracle could be saying that a partnership or official joining of forces is what is required or what is on the cards. Mutual profit born of mutual commitment.

KEEP FOCUSED ON … being true to your first principles or intentions concerning the object of your enquiry. This may be very difficult, but it will ultimately breed and attract the respect and support that you need.

WATCH OUT FOR … courting something or someone outside what you are already committed to – at least, not without being sure that you are prepared to take the flak that such a course of action might attract.

☯ KARMA/ATTITUDE/HEALTH

On the Inner Planes, one person (or thing) and another, are being or have been joined. It is as if a power is bringing or forcing the two together. But, it would be foolish to presume that this is all there is to it, or that it is the end of the story. Indeed, it is only the beginning. A coming together at a spiritual level is calling for a mental, emotional or physical bonding, which has to attain a point of recognition and joining. Health depends upon this balancing or melding.

KEEP FOCUSED ON … any issue, relationship or pairing of opposites that is difficult, but won't go away, for it is likely that this is the very thing that is calling to be taken up, or healed and resolved.

WATCH OUT FOR … not taking seriously something that you are committed to karmically.

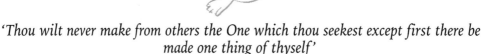

'Thou wilt never make from others the One which thou seekest except first there be made one thing of thyself'

GONDOLIERS IN A SERENADE

☆ LIVING THE MYTH ☆

 GENERAL INTERPRETATION

Occasioned or called for here is a glorious and exuberant sense of the ongoing drama and meaning of the emotional life. It could be rather over the top, though. This Symbol is auspicious for anything to do with singing or performing.

KEEP FOCUSED ON ... your flair for lending a sense of occasion to significant and prominent feelings, which in turn sustains them and gives them direction and purpose.

WATCH OUT FOR ... succumbing to glamour or romance with the consequence that the inevitable return to reality is painful to the point of looking for yet another high, and so on ... naively thinking that life should all be plain sailing ... getting too carried away by feelings because you could go overboard.

♡ **LOVE/RELATING/SOCIAL**

Entering into the spirit of romance, with all the fervour, expectation, fantasy and, sometimes, cliché, that goes with it. Giving oneself up to the feeling of the occasion, as going back to a comparatively drab existence at a later date is more than likely.

KEEP FOCUSED ON ... letting your feelings of high romance and high emotion, be they happy or sad, flow over you and through you, thereby carrying you along ... being ever mindful that although security is what we need of relationships, romance is what we want. Romance may depart but it should at least enrich the heart.

WATCH OUT FOR ... regret and emptiness as a result of expecting too much and being taken for a ride, or of never having taken the plunge and given romance a chance.

 MONEY/WORK/CREATIVITY

The fate or the nature of the object of your concern has everything to do with believing in its value. Others may ridicule or frown on such wholehearted involvement, but one day you could be the one who is laughing, rather than crying, all the way to the bank.

KEEP FOCUSED ON ... believing in your own vision, work, earning power, because belief is the essential ingredient that bears you up ... 'whistling while you work' – injecting work with a sense of being involved in something momentous or marvellous.

WATCH OUT FOR ... discarding or branding what you have or are as worthless or of little value; this makes it seem that way to others, and so your negative assessment is thus confirmed ... that everything has to decline, temporarily or permanently.

⊙ **KARMA/ATTITUDE/HEALTH**

What we all need to carry us through life's ups and downs is a sense of a wonderful story – running through our veins, buoying us up, propelling us onwards. Without such feelings we can become too serious, staid, cynical or inhibited.

KEEP FOCUSED ON ... finding or connecting with something within you similar to the feeling of being lifted up and transported by a song you love ... abandoning yourself to the feelings of the moment, and letting boring considerations, such as safety and mundane reality, come when they will, for they will soon enough.

WATCH OUT FOR ... worrying what others think of you as you live your myth, for the alternative is them thinking of you little or not at all ... suppressing romantic senses, for this inhibits flow and suppresses vitality itself.

'Gather ye rosebuds while ye may'

A PRIMA DONNA SINGING

☆ FERVOUR PLUS CONTROL ☆

❄ GENERAL INTERPRETATION

The full-bodied and red-blooded expression of self, with the passionate and all too human intensity that produces it, coupled with discipline and training.

KEEP FOCUSED ON ... creating a combination of command and receptivity that allows you access to the deepest potentials in yourself, and the deepest feelings in others ... holding that 'note' – that is, whatever you are trying to put across, attract or maintain.

WATCH OUT FOR ... affectation driven by self-importance and a subsequent neurotic need for attention ... expecting people to do what you want them to do.

♡ LOVE/RELATING/SOCIAL

This pictures a passionate relationship, but also one where one or more people are trying to outdo each other, possibly in terms of being centre-stage or dominant. Often there will be emotional scenes and outbursts as one hurt (inner) child reacts to the other. To prevent drama becoming a crisis ...

KEEP FOCUSED ON ... how such interactions intensify the power of one's emotions ... how one's deeper potentials are activated by being in this situation. Then try to channel them into something useful or creative ... how a drama queen is a challenge to the strength of one's own personality.

WATCH OUT FOR ... anger – control it and use its energy constructively, rather than having it use you ... lust – if it is not contained by love or understanding you could be kindling a fire that is hard to put out.

⚘ MONEY/WORK/CREATIVITY

If this is not directly confirming your, or someone's, power as a star performer or a leading player, then it is saying that you must either see yourself more in that light – that is, act like you got it – or you have an overly subjective idea of your talents. In either case ...

KEEP FOCUSED ON ... seeking out the advice and opinions of those who really matter within the field of your endeavour. If you have talent it will be recognized – but you must put it out there if you feel unsure, otherwise you'll always be unsure ... justifying any feelings of possessing superior talent.

WATCH OUT FOR ... flatterers and sycophants for they will mislead you and misuse you ... being precious about yourself and your abilities; a careless abandon is a sure sign of real confidence and star quality.

☯ KARMA/ATTITUDE/HEALTH

Here is suggested the karma of privilege. You or someone else is used to being considered before and above everyone else, and tends to attach more importance to things than is appropriate. But such conceit and melodrama also betoken a powerful sense of life on an emotional level. What is really important now is that you ...

KEEP FOCUSED ON ... directing your powerful energies into something that does them justice, such as healing or uplifting others, rather than letting them do an injustice to yourself or someone else, or wasting energy on what cannot be changed or influenced.

WATCH OUT FOR ... thinking that you deserve preferential treatment when there is nothing that obviously merits it. Doing so will eventually attract harsh and apparently unjust treatment.

'Prosperity doth best discover vice, but adversity doth best discover virtue'

A WOMAN AWAITING A SAILBOAT

☆ PATIENCE AND COMPOSURE ☆

GENERAL INTERPRETATION

The inherent faith and patience that are the original qualities of the human soul: 'one day my ship will come in'. Being becalmed is a call to be calm.

KEEP FOCUSED ON ... the inspiration and reassurance that emanates from your certainty that all will be well ... any details you may have overlooked regarding the object of your concern; one or more of those details could be preventing what you are hoping to happen from doing so, or these details could tell you that you are waiting or wanting in vain.

WATCH OUT FOR ... a gullible trust in the patently undependable ... reluctance to face the unknown – if this is bound up with what you want, then it won't happen; paradoxically, if it is bound up with what you fear, then it will happen.

❤ LOVE/RELATING/SOCIAL

Most likely this is a case where someone is waiting for someone else to come round, become available, get themselves into gear or come into their life as a partner with whom they can go on a voyage, a voyage which could be life itself. Such expectation can often be fraught with anxiety, but there seems no choice in the matter; what's to be done?

KEEP FOCUSED ON ... what such solitary waiting is doing to you emotionally, and you will discover that it is forcing an awareness to develop within you, such as what a person really means to you, or what it is you must first learn about yourself before you can share yourself with another; hence the pain.

WATCH OUT FOR ... becoming obsessed with who you are waiting for; it could delay their arrival; if they are meant to come, then they will.

♆ MONEY/WORK/CREATIVITY

Waiting for a result or for someone to come up with the goods or money. It could also mean waiting for the Muse or inspiration. This is like a farmer who must clear the ground of rocks and unwanted vegetation, plough the earth, sow the seed, and then wait. So, as long as you ...

KEEP FOCUSED ON ... fulfilling these tasks – that is the preparation of whatever field is your concern – then what you are striving for will eventually become a reality.

WATCH OUT FOR ... being tried in your waiting because of unexpected hitches. Such trials are part of the process of testing your resolve to succeed, forcing you to put together whatever is necessary for that success; or they may be a sign that you are throwing good money after bad ... 'chasing the bid' as it puts off the buyer.

☯ KARMA/ATTITUDE/HEALTH

This Symbol has poignant associations karmically for it stresses the fact that certain things will happen only when the time (or lifetime) is appropriate – a boat cannot set sail or come ashore until the tide is right. There is nothing one can physically do to speed their arrival, other than to ...

KEEP FOCUSED ON ... cultivating in yourself the faith that your ship will one day come in if you live your life in the certainty that it will, performing whatever tasks and duties are set before you in the meantime, and then prepare for that arrival.

WATCH OUT FOR ... clinging to fantasies or regrets, as they are the only things which can make your waiting so painful that your physical and mental health suffers.

'Time and tide wait for no man'

A MEETING OF A LITERARY SOCIETY

OF LIKE MIND

GENERAL INTERPRETATION

A communal sharing, enjoyment and quickening of the powers and fruits of the intellect. An interchange of ideas and views. A 'meeting of minds' providing stimulation, security and intelligence – it attracts such people and situations.

KEEP FOCUSED ON ... your mental or literary skills and connections for they should be your passport to a place in the scheme of things ... finding a group that practises and promotes whatever is the area of your concern; such support and encouragement may be the only way to get you going ... being discerning about who you mix with.

WATCH OUT FOR ... an unreal and academic sense of what life is about. Intellectual snobbery can put you out of touch with the very things and people you wish to influence or know ... similarities because these can be negative.

LOVE/RELATING/SOCIAL

Here is great mental accord and communication, be it between two people or a group. Because of this cerebral connection many an emotional problem can be overcome. There is always an area of common ground, no matter what the circumstances. It is as if you are 'scheduled' to meet up or agree again, despite prevailing circumstances or current rifts. One only has to wait for it to come round when it is 'due'.

KEEP FOCUSED ON ... those areas and subjects where you and another unfailingly find mutual harmony and interest, and there will always *be* harmony and interest – at regular intervals, if not constantly.

WATCH OUT FOR ... overlooking the emotional aspect of your relationship, and of your own nature too. Mental accord only goes so far.

MONEY/WORK/CREATIVITY

The key to success here is being a part of a form of 'club' where new contacts can be made, information gleaned and, most of all, where a forum is available that has more punch than just being out on your own. Whether one agrees with the 'not what you know but who you know' aspect of the world of art and commerce, it is a fact of life. If you are strongly against this, then either form your own 'society' or be prepared for the difficulties that can be the lot of a loner. If not ...

KEEP FOCUSED ON ... identifying and getting in with whatever body or society is central to or concerned with your line of business or endeavour.

WATCH OUT FOR ... sacrificing your principles for the sake of being in with the in-crowd. You could find yourself trapped and compromised, obliged to veer away from your chosen path.

KARMA/ATTITUDE/HEALTH

Here the Literary Society can be seen as how matters of the mind have an energy and history of their own, bringing about meetings of like minds as you go through life. Furthermore, such minds keep meeting up over and over again, such are the mental rails that you are running on.

KEEP FOCUSED ON ... immersing yourself in groups and pursuits that have much in common with whatever is your concern, be it a spiritual practice, philosophy, art or health, for this will greatly further your interests, answer queries and morally support you.

WATCH OUT FOR ... isolating yourself from stimulating contacts; cutting off your nose to spite your face. But then again, intellectual competition is stimulating up to a point, beyond which it is petty, blind and destructive.

'If you steal from one author, it's plagiarism; if you steal from many, it's research'

A WOMAN AND TWO MEN ON A BIT OF SUNLIT LAND FACING SOUTH

☆ THE ETERNAL TRIANGLE ☆

✸ GENERAL INTERPRETATION

The situation highlights the necessity of making the distinction between any two possibilities or choices, thereby being able to make a lasting decision. This distinction may lie between the real and the fanciful, the true and the false, or between any other duality. This Symbol suggests the eternal triangle, which is a manifestation of a split in the unconscious mind of the one, and an incomplete sense of the self's emotional requirements of the other two. Or it could be a species of stability.

KEEP FOCUSED ON ... your unusual ability to manage complex situations in a fair and upfront fashion ... the fact that the optimum time has come to sort out the situation.

WATCH OUT FOR ... hopeless and indulgent dithering that confuses all and sundry – even when the truth of the matter has been made plain.

♡ LOVE/RELATING/SOCIAL

An eternal triangle, be it confusing or enlightening, is indicated here. Apart from the valley of decision that it involves, there are also issues such as feeling crowded and restricted, or a lack of privacy and independence to be addressed. As the word 'eternal' indicates, these are problems that have dogged human relationships for ages – probably because the only real answers can be found if you ...

KEEP FOCUSED ON ... what the other two represent to you, what you represent to them, and the fact that the situation will not change until your ties to them have been understood, let go of, accepted.

WATCH OUT FOR ... ignoring the above for then things could carry on interminably, unbearably or, at worst, cause real grief.

♗ MONEY/WORK/CREATIVITY

It should be clear that there is either a conflict of interests dogging your progress, or you have the necessary resources as long it is known who or what does what.

KEEP FOCUSED ON ... what it is that needs doing and can be done, while refusing to be distracted by side issues or considerations that have no immediate impact or relevance ... what your assets are, for they should be plain to see ... making your choice and sticking with it, believing in it – then success.

WATCH OUT FOR ... trying to satisfy too many requirements at once; this will find you overstretched and possibly not accomplishing anything at all ... being preoccupied with problems and weaknesses while your strengths are overlooked.

♋ KARMA/ATTITUDE/HEALTH

Much of what has been written in the other sections again applies, but in this context is emphasized the possibility that the roots of the set-up go deep and a long way back, and that the people or issues involved belong to an ongoing karmic relationship. It also stresses that the time is now right for putting the situation to rest, or taking it forward, once and for all, simply because it should be obvious – if one looks – why things are as they are.

KEEP FOCUSED ON ... spending some time completely on your own, free of anyone else who you could blame or be influenced by ... the effect that one kind of 'eternal triangle' – that of mother, father and child – is having or has had upon the proceedings ... seeking out a third party to help you get a handle on your predicament.

WATCH OUT FOR ... being dominated or intimidated by the others. Stand up for yourself.

'There were three of us in this marriage, so it was a bit crowded'

A DARK SHADOW OR MANTLE THROWN SUDDENLY OVER THE RIGHT SHOULDER

☆ DRAMATIC PORTENT ☆

⚙ GENERAL INTERPRETATION

The power of intuition and of unconscious forces that can exert an influence over the individual in order that he or she might consciously recognize these forces and what they imply, and thereby be guided by them, act upon them and be protected by them.

KEEP FOCUSED ON ... the insight you have that enables you to change dramatically your own or someone else's orientation and so positively transform a situation ... your sense of the mysterious and intriguing, and of 'whodunit', for this enriches and, ultimately, enlightens.

WATCH OUT FOR ... exaggerating or overreacting to signs, omens, innuendoes, suggestive behaviour, alarming rumours, ominous ideas ... dabbling with occult matters and then finding them out of control ... feeling weighed down by responsibilities that are not shouldered gladly.

♥ LOVE/RELATING/SOCIAL

An intriguing or complex emotional situation that has a mystery about it or a shadow cast over it. A set-up where the female, intuitive, nurturing element is holding sway – or is trying to, or ought to be. A sudden passionate development incurring responsibility.

KEEP FOCUSED ON ... your feelings until you have fully understood what they imply ... your sense of the romantic, dramatic and of hidden meaning ... the soul nature of those involved – their karma, longings and sensitivities.

WATCH OUT FOR ... not taking full responsibility for the part that your own dark side plays in the situation ... secrecy, or not coming clean, becoming a block to honesty and understanding, eventually creating a morass of deep and dangerous emotions. Be on your guard against excessive emotions.

♛ MONEY/WORK/CREATIVITY

Intuitive powers are central to your work, bestowed upon you as a great responsibility. Possibly a cloak and dagger scenario, industrial espionage or office intrigue. An unexpected development that has nothing to do with work *per se* – an emotional or psychological factor could be in play.

KEEP FOCUSED ON ... the less obvious or more emotionally compelling aspects of the object of your concern, for therein lies its main asset – and the answer to any difficulty ... the hidden or mysterious ... trusting intuition and being prepared to take responsibility for your actions.

WATCH OUT FOR ... anything that could be going on behind your back – but avoid being paranoid ... it being a case of 'what you don't know *can* harm you' ... hidden agendas ... the sheer weight of responsibility, especially when unseen by others.

☯ KARMA/ATTITUDE/HEALTH

The importance of balance between reason and intuition, of being able to act upon hunches rather than keeping them at the theory stage and letting them build up into suspicion, dread or disease. A past issue that needs admitting to, coming to terms with and sorting; depression arising from this or excessive reasoning.

KEEP FOCUSED ON ... your deep sense of powerful emotional undercurrents, for it will greatly strengthen your constitution ... the fact that your well-being calls for a swift and effective response born of your willingness to take responsibility for acting upon your gut instincts or whatever is deep-seated ... being guided by signs.

WATCH OUT FOR ... being spooked by superstitious nonsense, possibly born of a religious doctrine ... projecting your shadow onto the world around you and then feeling powerless or intimidated ... karmic weight; offset it with lightness and recreation.

'Unless you see miraculous signs and wonders, you will not believe'

CONTENTMENT AND HAPPINESS IN LUXURY, PEOPLE READING ON SOFAS

☆ RECREATION AND RELAXATION ☆

✵ GENERAL INTERPRETATION

This Symbol speaks for itself; civilized, relaxed living conditions and intellectual sophistication. Better times ahead, ease, a coming together of like minds. And luxury is not just material or external, but can be the luxury of being kinder to yourself by taking time to relax, feed your mind with what it wants or needs.

KEEP FOCUSED ON ... your sense of ease, and an accompanying attitude of mind that puts others at ease ... making the most of the simple pleasures of life ... regeneration through relaxation whenever you feel stressed or overwrought.

WATCH OUT FOR ... a loss of life's meaning through excessive comfort and softness, or through indulging in 'brain candy'.

♡ LOVE/RELATING/SOCIAL

Apart from the possibility that this Symbol is referring to 'emotional sloth', being backward in coming forward, here we see a rosy and comfortable relationship or social scene. Quite simply, you have the civilized and contented life. Or at least, you can if you ...

KEEP FOCUSED ON ... enjoying what you have, and ensuring its continuance through making what you have available to others also ... finding new challenges and activities that keep your relationship alive and vibrant.

WATCH OUT FOR ... complacency, for this could turn contentment into meaninglessness ... laziness in emotional relating, or just learning or talking about relating but not actually doing it.

MONEY/WORK/CREATIVITY

Apart from being one goal of working itself, this Symbol of happiness and ease could be seen as the antipathy of productivity. Then again, it could be stressing the need for taking a break from a busy schedule. Purely on a money level, this Symbol seems to be saying that material security is assured. Regarding actual areas of endeavour, catering and literature are well-starred.

KEEP FOCUSED ON ... approaching your work in as a relaxed and comfortable fashion as possible, especially where study and research are concerned ... making whatever you are doing easy to understand. Easy reading.

WATCH OUT FOR ... taking it too easy, or over-indulging in what ease you have rather than doing what is necessary to maintain it ... oversubscribing to the work ethic.

☯ KARMA/ATTITUDE/HEALTH

The importance of feeling at peace within oneself, and of taking in whatever information is necessary in order to enlighten oneself towards that end. Also, providing others with the facilities to relax or gain the information they need.

KEEP FOCUSED ON ... what it is that makes you feel at ease and right with the world – then sink into this, make more of it. Enjoy it ... finding a place and time where you and others can take a break from the hurly-burly of life.

WATCH OUT FOR ... an overly ascetic or earnest attitude for that would simply be wearing a hair shirt or making a rod for one's back – a product of guilt ... overindulging in whatever your poison is, for any excess can lead to problems ... idle or perfunctory behaviour getting you nowhere.

'Trahit sua quemque voluptas' (Everyone is dragged on by their favourite pleasure)

A STORM IN A CANYON

☆ NECESSARY INTENSIFICATION ☆

 GENERAL INTERPRETATION

Here you have a dramatization of a life situation in order that the full force of it may be experienced, appreciated and satisfactorily expressed or dealt with. Sometimes our sense of an issue has to be heightened and intensified to bring it to a head and resolve it once and for all.

KEEP FOCUSED ON ... making sense of intense feelings or any disruptive event, then setting about defusing it, or identifying and containing the troublesome element ... Oracle Storming to sort your issue (*see* page 424).

WATCH OUT FOR ... 'storm in a teacup' scenarios where you attach far too much importance to an issue. You will know this to be the case when either you understand this (after due consideration) or when the issue eventually comes to nothing ... being in the wrong place.

 LOVE/RELATING/SOCIAL

A stormy relationship or something has arisen that has been brewing for quite a while and needs to be given serious attention, or it is just a passing hiccup which is part of being in an emotional relationship – or *not* being in one. Then again, a fuss could be being made about nothing. However, 'there's no smoke without fire', so ...

KEEP FOCUSED ON ... what it really is that is giving you cause for concern, possibly with the help of a third party. Also, it may have nothing to do with another person or society in general but is related to an earlier disturbance in your life.

WATCH OUT FOR ... making a crisis out of what may only have been a dramatic episode where you needed to let off steam or make something known.

 MONEY/WORK/CREATIVITY

A crisis in your affairs that is an unavoidable and natural necessity. It is probably not so alarming as it appears, but needs due consideration all the same. It could be a disturbance in one department only, but that could knock on to other departments if left unattended to. Damage limitation could also be an issue or option. Or the object of your concern could be a disruptive or revolutionary idea that is aimed at a specific area. Creatively speaking, you are having to wrestle with an intense feeling or idea that needs an outlet.

KEEP FOCUSED ON ... brainstorming any problem or question until it is resolved or answered ... finding ways to open closed minds.

WATCH OUT FOR ... making an issue out of something that does not merit it ... overkill – throwing too much money, time or energy at something that does not deserve it. But you would still have to work this through to find out if this was the case.

KARMA/ATTITUDE/HEALTH

A lifetime, a period in it or a particular incident could be seen as an inescapable confrontation with what had been mounting for some time. It is as if Fate decrees that the best way for something to be brought to awareness, then dispersed and transformed, is by making it impossible to ignore.

KEEP FOCUSED ON ... what event from your past is still creating disturbances such as those you are currently experiencing. This event could take the form of a health issue, such as a build up of pressure in a part of the body. In any event, there is stress and tension behind it ... staying earthed and keeping cool.

WATCH OUT FOR ... going from one 'storm' to another in life without tracking down where they all began – the 'mother' storm, so to speak. There is an allusion here to what went on in the womb ... panicking, over-reacting or hypochondriac behaviour.

'Most human beings are too lazy, fearful or enclosed to wake up without the help of some kind of alarm'

A MODERN POCAHONTAS

☆ RADICAL HUMANITARIANISM ☆

 GENERAL INTERPRETATION

The bold crossing of cultural barriers and the breaking of taboos that truly advances the deepest human interests – even if, or because, such accord lasts for a very short time. Pocahontas, the Powhatan Indian woman who helped maintain peace between English colonists and Native Americans during the early part of the 17th century, married one of the white settlers and then went to England, dying there at around 24 years of age.

KEEP FOCUSED ON ... your strength of character and passionate charm that permits and promotes harmony and understanding, even between the most divergent groups and in the most unfavourable of environments.

WATCH OUT FOR ... an ill-timed or ill-conceived idealism that hinders more than it helps.

 MONEY/WORK/CREATIVITY

Your work entails, or should entail, a form of idealism. This is smiled on by God or Higher Powers, but the material side has to take second place. This does not mean that what you have going for you will not prove profitable, but that such considerations are secondary, and may be taken care of as long as you stick faithfully to the expression of your ideals.

KEEP FOCUSED ON ... promoting whatever goes beyond the limited idea of what appeals to the general public. Your work is, or should be, in aid of expanding the hearts and minds of others, whereas conforming to them would prove too difficult or counterproductive.

WATCH OUT FOR ... throwing yourself away on something that is only out to sap you and use you, to take advantage of your better nature ... being made into a political puppet, lever or propagandist, while your real significance gets overlooked.

 LOVE/RELATING/SOCIAL

Cutting through prejudices, mindsets and defence systems such as denial is a perennial challenge of relating. Left to their own, negative emotional ploys like these cause a relationship to go from bad to worse, or just stagnate. Here we have or need someone who has the heart and intuition to disregard or pierce through these blocks to harmony and understanding, and who also has the courage to stake their own welfare on achieving this objective.

KEEP FOCUSED ON ... trusting utterly in your own and another's better nature and sense of truth, while making the minimum of compromises.

WATCH OUT FOR ... duplicity, bigotry, emotional blackmail, hypocrisy or anything that is a block to human openness and acceptance of differences; they should never be tolerated (but *see* Karma below).

 KARMA/ATTITUDE/HEALTH

Pocahontas serves as an icon for humanitarianism, particularly the female aspect of it – something that tolerates and does not tolerate at the same time. Like so many icons, her life was cut short, but possibly this as it should be – short and sweet. This Symbol is calling your attention to the ongoing need for acts of human kindness, understanding and justice. Perhaps a *Modern* Pocahontas can, and is supposed to, make everyday bids for peace and goodwill – and live to tell the tale. Generally, the seemingly odd or unlikely.

KEEP FOCUSED ON ... using everything you have got, including sexuality, in order to attain the overall humanitarian objective ... being prepared to be held hostage or suffer hardship for the sake of your convictions and to have them tested.

WATCH OUT FOR ... notoriety or egoism, for they could expose you to dangers that cut you down in your prime ... wanting 'normal' explanations.

'Her ways are ways of gentleness and all her paths are Peace'

A MUSE WEIGHING TWINS

✵ DIVINE ARBITRATION ✵

 GENERAL INTERPRETATION

Your issue is in the process of being 'assessed' at a higher level. Then again, you could reconcile one aspect of it (such as the inner, dark or passive side) with its opposite (the outer, light or active side) according to some aesthetic and subjective criterion – such as 'I like it/don't like it' or 'It feels/tastes good/bad', so 'I want it/don't want it'.

KEEP FOCUSED ON ... your judgement of the situation, unconfused by pious or petty motives ... the object of your concern as being 'in the balance' and out of your hands, and then endeavour to view it all with equanimity ... being a balancing influence, for it falls to you to be so.

WATCH OUT FOR ... capriciousness, or immorality posing as amorality ... trying to 'fix the scales' in the sense of thinking you can cheat Fate and Her judgement.

 MONEY/WORK/CREATIVITY

Your career and material security is in the lap of the Gods, or at least, your better judgement. This is because your effectiveness and ultimate success is assessed and determined by a power or value system above and beyond the material world. Your creativity depends upon your being moved by and attuned to the Muse – that is, something entirely of the Spirit and beyond material and personal considerations.

KEEP FOCUSED ON ... the belief that in being true to your finest and most noble intent, success will ultimately be achieved, and the books balanced. All the ups and downs, the blocks and the flow, the swinging to and fro, are a necessary part of the process.

WATCH OUT FOR ... expecting everyday affairs such as details, duties and accounts to sort themselves out. They won't, they are very much the human side of the business.

❤ **LOVE/RELATING/SOCIAL**

In any relationship or individual there is a process or story going on. This includes the ups and downs, the confusion or clarity, the straight and the crooked, or any other duality that emotional life is subject to. The point is to ...

KEEP FOCUSED ON ... the fact that things will turn out as they will as a result of this swinging back and forth between whatever extremes you find yourself. Something beyond our conscious awareness is weighing this up and deciding how it is going to pan out ... tuning into this process and enjoying the ride.

WATCH OUT FOR ... rocking the boat because of doubt, impatience or frustration; this will only serve to disrupt the very back and forth process that is getting you there, carrying you forward to a more balanced relationship.

☯ **KARMA/ATTITUDE/HEALTH**

The process of karmic balance, where everything in life is subject to the Law of Cause and Effect, being kept in a state of balance, and every action attracting an equal and opposite reaction. Being a Cancerian Symbol, this points to the emotional aspect of this process, the ebb and flow, the swings and roundabouts of fortune, that characterize it.

KEEP FOCUSED ON ... trusting your aesthetic or higher senses to evaluate the situation, to reconcile any conflict that is creating disease or distress ... looking to God for justice or a decision ... how one experience or lifetime compensates for the one preceding or following it.

WATCH OUT FOR ... going to extremes of hope or despair, for although higher or autonomic intelligences are governing your health and equilibrium, your excesses are capable of destabilizing them – albeit temporarily.

'Oh, East is East, and West is West, and never the twain shall meet,
Till Earth and Sky stand presently at God's great Judgement Seat'

A DAUGHTER OF THE AMERICAN REVOLUTION

☆ THE FEMININE UNBOUND ☆

 GENERAL INTERPRETATION

Possibly you or someone else is experiencing the result of a struggle to be free and independent. Receptivity to change. The next stage in the future of the human race. Being aware of one's emotional rights, to verbally and physically express one's intuitions.

KEEP FOCUSED ON ... an attractive means of heralding what is to be ... what a liberated female, liberated femininity or anything else, actually is ... being young and alive to the New Time.

WATCH OUT FOR ... brashness, where privilege and conceit give rise to a limited perspective that leads to frustration and the shattering of ideals ... getting caught up in the politics of a situation rather than the feelings and customs involved.

 LOVE/RELATING/SOCIAL

Here we have a relationship or individual that is taking a step further, or at least upholding the part women play in society and, more to the point, their rights within it. Then again, you may have to express such values, accept them, help them or be a counterpoint to them.

KEEP FOCUSED ON ... being upfront, open and honest, as well as being unfettered by past conflicts, and so free and future-oriented ... identifying anything that is out to suppress your right to be yourself, and finding a peaceful way of dealing with it.

WATCH OUT FOR ... holding double standards – for instance, espousing or insisting upon freedom of speech yet at the same time not listening to what someone else is saying and feeling.

 MONEY/WORK/CREATIVITY

You are someone, or are involved with someone or something, that is in the forefront of human and social evolution. The hard years, the actual change of direction or revolution, are behind you, but your beliefs and principles concerning this new way now need refining and putting into practice. A giant step has been taken; now we have the steady walk ahead of us.

KEEP FOCUSED ON ... the original tenets, causes or objectives that started you on your road to freedom or achievement in the first place ... non-action as a possibly effective strategy.

WATCH OUT FOR ... losing sight of what you were fighting for, or that you *were* fighting for something ... getting too comfortable now that you feel a battle or two has been won.

KARMA/ATTITUDE/HEALTH

This Symbol is highly significant because it is referring to the shift from male-dominated society and world, to one where long-suppressed or repressed female qualities, such as intuition, care, passivity, receptivity, attunement to Nature and the Moon, motherhood, and all feeling-based qualities (including randomness and irrationality) are progressively surfaced, expressed and established. This equally applies to such qualities that have been locked up within a male being.

KEEP FOCUSED ON ... the fact that this liberation of the feminine is a see-saw process as there is a natural inhibition on it going too far, because then it would be aping the very thing it is supposed to replace. So ...

WATCH OUT FOR ... any signs of strident materialism, or outlandish expressions other than those that are getting rid of bad feelings from the past ... becoming too self-absorbed.

'Men do, women are'

THE SABIAN SYMBOLS OF
LEO

Either directly, or in a subtle way, all these Symbols are concerned with the following qualities, or with situations that involve or call for them:

CHILDREN

CREATIVITY

DRAMA

EGO

GENEROSITY AND PATRONAGE

THE HEART AND SPINE

PARTIES AND FUN

PLAY

RECREATION

RULERSHIP

SELF-EXPRESSION

SEX

WILLPOWER

A CASE OF APOPLEXY

☆ FIT TO BURST ☆

☀ GENERAL INTERPRETATION

The internal pressure to express oneself and realize one's potential can be so great as to overwhelm one's ability to do so. A neurotic need for control brought on, ironically, by a fear of incapacitation.

KEEP FOCUSED ON ... your day-by-day, minute-by-minute creative style that is a testament to how profound a thing human personality can be ... letting things be, through believing that there is more than just you keeping everything together.

WATCH OUT FOR ... insensitively taxing others or damaging oneself in the pursuit of one's desires ... ambition, the 'Devil's own sin', because it can be a substitute for feeling loved, becoming a ruthless and bottomless pit, leading to a crisis such as panic attacks, or worse ... desperation; it is self-defeating.

♥ LOVE/RELATING/SOCIAL

Sometimes it is best just to let people go their own way, and do this with good grace. This is one of those times. Seeing another as someone who needs to be supervised may be true up to a point – in the sense of caring and looking out for them. But to be preoccupied constantly with where someone's at is asking for trouble and puts everyone in a tense position. Taken to the extreme, it can lead to blow-ups with considerable resulting fall-out, or fallings out.

KEEP FOCUSED ON ... what your responsibility is, in and to a relationship, and keep only to that.

WATCH OUT FOR ... getting worked up by a neurotic need to keep tabs on everything and everyone; people must learn by their own mistakes, making things come to a head and resolving them in a natural way, rather than on your own terms, which would be to your eventual discomfort.

MONEY/WORK/CREATIVITY

Ambition and control run rampant. Although passion for gaining an objective is a necessary ingredient, there comes a point where one is like an automobile being driven with the choke constantly out. What is more, you are probably driving others like that as well. Alternatively, *you* could be the one on the receiving end of a control freak, possibly a boss or authority figure. Finances may also be under too tight a control.

KEEP FOCUSED ON ... learning how to delegate, the secret of this is that by trusting others they become trustworthy, or if they do not, exercise a 'three strikes and you're out' rule ... taking it easier, pacing yourself and others better.

WATCH OUT FOR ... signs that you or someone else is stretched to breaking point, and then do something about it. The Oracle is saying that this is precisely what the danger is.

☯ KARMA/ATTITUDE/HEALTH

This Symbol should not be interpreted as predicting a stroke (apoplexy) itself. Rather, it is alluding to the negative outcome of needing to be too much in control. This is itself caused by a distrust of Fate, of allowing things to unfold as they will, and of others being able to do what you believe only you can do.

KEEP FOCUSED ON ... telling yourself that you can only do so much to control outcomes ... what it was in your past that set you on a path of feeling that everything was down to you, and that all hell would break loose if you lost/relinquished control.

WATCH OUT FOR ... tensions and headaches or any other signs that you are not relaxing enough into the way things are. Whatever your physical condition might be, you are advised to see it as being related to tension caused by a fear of losing control brought on by that distrust of Fate.

'An atheist is a man who has no invisible means of support'

AN EPIDEMIC OF MUMPS

☆ LOSS OF POWER ☆

 GENERAL INTERPRETATION

There is something in the air, a 'bug' going around, that can debilitate you and others. There is the danger of letting deep and powerful emotions build up unattended to, which can give rise to a crisis that robs you of the power of feeling or confidence when it's most needed. It may have already happened. Either way, your priority is to …

KEEP FOCUSED ON … dealing with, and finding the reasons for, powerlessness or disempowerment in any shape or form … not allowing yourself to get down or go under, for one disempowerment could lead to another … creating an aliveness to the importance of drama and crisis as an opportunity to develop, mainly emotionally.

WATCH OUT FOR … falling victim to collective fears when a stout belief in one's own sovereignty of being is the vital thing … viruses and infection.

♡ LOVE/RELATING/SOCIAL

Apart from the obvious (but unlikely) case of sexually or socially transmitted diseases, this Symbol is possibly referring to how we 'catch' psychological things off people we are close to. Falling in love, or being infatuated, is like catching something – the love bug. Being 'infected' by one another can be very pleasurable, but it can also disempower us if we become too dependent or insecure when the temperature cools.

KEEP FOCUSED ON … what it is about one another that you have been 'infected' with, and then make sure that it is not going to take you over, or find out what containing or curing it entails. We can become intimately involved not only for romantic reasons, but because one or both needs emotionally healing in some way.

WATCH OUT FOR … being seduced in any way.

MONEY/WORK/CREATIVITY

If your work is about dealing with disease then the Oracle is approving of it, or saying that you are about to have your work cut out. Apart from this, your capability or working environment may have something 'infecting' it, diminishing efficiency.

KEEP FOCUSED ON … what you know to be the source of the trouble – the carriers – and isolate, inoculate or do whatever it is that you know to be necessary … what it is that is negatively affecting your concern and simply cater to the healing or mending of that … establishing a stout belief in your own worth and enterprise, for this will go a long way to repelling negative influences.

WATCH OUT FOR … anything or anyone that can spoil what you are trying to accomplish or have already achieved, and take steps to prevent any intrusion or sabotage … computer viruses.

KARMA/ATTITUDE/HEALTH

There is something about your fate that is infected and this may translate into a physical condition. At a more subtle level, it may be a case of 'future-shock', that is you may be psychically picking up something that is affecting, or is going to affect, a lot of people. On a broader level, there are distorting rumours and notions circulating, either globally or locally, be it psychologically, physically or electronically.

KEEP FOCUSED ON … what it is about you or your life that often seems to go awry, for this will originate from a negative attitude or habit that needs eradicating … protecting yourself from the woes of the world through psychic protection … taking what you hear with a pinch of salt.

WATCH OUT FOR … anyone or anywhere that is obviously unhealthy – stay away if you can.

'I get my energy by getting rid of it, by constantly expending it, by not hanging on to it'

A WOMAN HAVING HER HAIR BOBBED

☆ MAKEOVER ☆

 GENERAL INTERPRETATION

External stylization or alteration as a means to feeling part of an ongoing trend (remember the Sabian Symbols were conceived in the 1920s), and the willingness to undergo these adjustments in order to make the most of the opportunities that modern life presents. A change of image.

KEEP FOCUSED ON ... a way of presenting yourself which is the key to opening many doors ... how a change in image can create a change at deeper levels of yourself and life ... how the outside can be an indicator of what is going on inside ... making changes in and around you, then other people and things will change too ... treating yourself to something.

WATCH OUT FOR ... missing the self's true significance for the sake of following fashion, or of scorning it.

❤ **LOVE/RELATING/SOCIAL**

A change of image that makes one more attractive or fashionable. This could also be a sign of a new person in one's life; an attempt to fit in more with the people around them, which could amount to a superficial relationship; trying to gain someone else's attention. Or it is saying that a change is needed in the way one presents oneself?

KEEP FOCUSED ON ... whether such an image is seen as being superficial or as a mask to conceal what is really going on. Superficiality is just what it appears to be, and need not be taken too seriously one way or the other. But a mask that is a device employed to veil how you really are on the inside can be very useful.

WATCH OUT FOR ... superficiality that is hiding self-doubt or a fear of being known properly ... a mask that confuses more than it veils.

 MONEY/WORK/CREATIVITY

All businesses and arts, unless they are patently traditional in nature, have to keep abreast of the times in order to achieve or maintain success. Also, looking as if you are making it can be a prerequisite for doing so. If your business has to do with fashion or anything cosmetic, then this could be said to be an auspicious oracle.

KEEP FOCUSED ON ... what it is that most appeals to people about your field of endeavour ... the importance of image for catching people's attention; then you can deliver or offer something of more substance or depth if need be ... making sure that you have a product that lives up to the image.

WATCH OUT FOR ... getting stuck with an image that does not allow one to move and develop in line with one's true intentions.

☯ **KARMA/ATTITUDE/HEALTH**

Changes in our external images occur over time, either naturally or artificially. The question arises as to what changes occur on the inside. Trying to keep up appearances for fear of being seen for what one really is smacks of a need for a change on the inside, then the outer appearances become irrelevant, or more suitable. In this context, the Symbol is alluding to superficiality and glamour as being things of passing importance, except when they have been *given* undue importance. In terms of health, it is ill-advised to go solely by how one looks rather than how one is on the inside.

KEEP FOCUSED ON ... giving or finding for oneself a spiritual lift ... looking and acting in accordance with one's circumstances, but ...

WATCH OUT FOR ... losing oneself in the masquerade.

'Change what is on the inside and you change what is on the outside'

A MAN FORMALLY DRESSED AND A DEER WITH ITS HORNS FOLDED

☆ STIFF UPPER LIP? ☆

⚙ GENERAL INTERPRETATION

An effectiveness in the outer world that can be dependent upon being wrapped up in a conventional or formal package, and on displayed 'trophies' that bear testament to that effectiveness. A more esoteric interpretation could see the deer's horns as being symbolic of the vagus nerve that serves the heart, meaning that externals should always be accompanied by interior or feeling values. Or seeing that the horns are 'folded' would suggest that sentiments of the heart are having to be closed off or protected from the outside world – maybe in order to conform to it.

KEEP FOCUSED ON ... your breadth of character that both appeals and commands respect.

WATCH OUT FOR ... contriving a means to gain what is deemed by others to have worth, only to find that it makes one a slave to their expectations.

♡ LOVE/RELATING/SOCIAL

What price baring your soul or wearing your heart on your sleeve? This is the age-old problem of relating, be it to one or many people. Wearing a social mask may protect you and get you by, but this can be at the expense of feeling isolated and inhibited. On the other hand, letting it all hang out can be liberating and entertaining, creating intimacy, but there is the risk of being wounded or wounding. To discover your personal formula here ...

KEEP FOCUSED ON ... who or what really matters to you. If anything doesn't, then do not bother seeking its approval ... sticking to convention only if you have to.

WATCH OUT FOR ... trying to normalize a person or relationship whose appeal is that they are out of the ordinary ... expecting much fun when you are having to behave and keep your feelings in.

⚛ MONEY/WORK/CREATIVITY

This Symbol challenges you with a question: Are you the type whose work or endeavour is dependent upon giving it a form acceptable or appealing to the world at large, or are you the type who is happy to express what is inside you, regardless of public opinion? To help you decide ...

KEEP FOCUSED ON ... what resistances you have to satisfying or fitting in with conventional tastes. If you have none or can overcome them then you are the first type; if you cannot then you are the second type ... finding a compromise that satisfies both your heart and your pocket book ... toughing it out.

WATCH OUT FOR ... ignoring what your heart tells you for the sake of profit or fitting in – you will come to regret it ... sticking to 'principles' that are only a disguise for an inability to deliver the goods.

☯ KARMA/ATTITUDE/HEALTH

This images a heart that is closed or blocked off for a reason probably to do with the conditioning it has been subjected to by way of upbringing or karma – which are one and the same. However, receiving this Symbol indicates that the time is right for opening the heart, expressing what lies within it. In so doing ...

KEEP FOCUSED ON ... identifying or contacting any block in the heart for only then will a way be found to release it. This means that you must summon the courage to break through any embarrassment or fear of being judged inadequate or odd. After all, the first thing to appear from out of an unblocked pipe is dirty water. But it runs clear eventually ... your heart chakra as a lotus or water lily, and visualize the petals opening one by one ... letting things unfold, as they will.

WATCH OUT FOR ... losing heart. It's your life!

'God and devil are fighting there, and the battlefield is the heart of man'

LEO 5 DEGREES

ROCK FORMATIONS AT THE EDGE OF A PRECIPICE

☆ ON THE BRINK ☆

⊛ GENERAL INTERPRETATION

See how Nature and Life conspire to bring things to a point of crisis, thereby demanding a decision, or a change in attitude or direction. Personality achieves its true significance when driven to its limits, when it is prepared to take risks or has to live on the edge. You are possibly in such a character-building situation. Issues of the past coming up when on the verge of something new.

KEEP FOCUSED ON ... living both consciously and cautiously on the edge; then establishing yourself as a power to be reckoned with, standing as a guide and testament to others ... the possibility that a rocky situation precedes something new.

WATCH OUT FOR ... a dangerous mixture of obstinacy and provocation, giving rise to a danger of going off half-cock ... inhibitions preventing you from experiencing what life offers.

♥ LOVE/RELATING/SOCIAL

This sounds as if you are playing with the idea of entering into some form of relationship – one that is outside your usual emotional remit, or one that is regarded as unusual or even foolhardy from a conventional standpoint. Alternatively, an existing relationship has the prospect of trying something new, with similar reservations abounding.

KEEP FOCUSED ON ... the fact that what you do is still your choice, but that carrying on as you are will eventually take you to the point where something has to give ... what you and others stand to gain, or lose, through taking the plunge ... that you never know until you have tried, but ...

WATCH OUT FOR ... tipping yourself into a situation that could harm or threaten others involved.

♆ MONEY/WORK/CREATIVITY

Whatever you are entertaining involves high risk. Or is it a case of brinkmanship? Naturally, the danger of the enterprise depends upon how capable and equipped you are. If your financial situation is in any way precarious, then think more than twice about committing yourself further.

KEEP FOCUSED ON ... gathering as much information as possible from anyone who has already tried what you are about to. If it is virgin territory you are thinking of entering, then make provision against the unexpected, but without weighing yourself down with something that could slow you down or endanger you further.

WATCH OUT FOR ... any structures and methods that are in danger of crumbling or proving unreliable. This is a priority check – for without making it you could fail before you'd hardly begun.

♋ KARMA/ATTITUDE/HEALTH

You are being precipitated into a new chapter of your life, where the adventure and the unknown yawns like a chasm before you. You can still retreat back to the world you know if you wish, but this may mean missing out on important and enriching experiences. So ...

KEEP FOCUSED ON ... what your heart desires ... the probability that successful negotiation of the first stages of this new chapter will either qualify you for the rest, or show that you're not up to it. So, climb up to the edge and have a peek! ... living dangerously as being one way of conquering fears.

WATCH OUT FOR ... where you put your feet, that is, being equipped with clear intentions and a sense of your own limitations. Being impulsive in a precipitous situation is irresponsible, but part of the exercise is finding your 'growth edges' or the areas of your personality that are ripe for development.

'Nothing ventured, nothing gained'

AN OLD-FASHIONED WOMAN AND AN UP-TO-DATE GIRL

☆ THEN AND NOW ☆

 GENERAL INTERPRETATION

Present or called for is a sympathetic and intuitive blending or understanding of the values of the past and those of the present or future in the making – or making a distinction between the two. Conventionality and innovation seen as complement and competition to one another.

KEEP FOCUSED ON ... your ability to synthesize the best from two or more value systems ... appreciating that the demands of the present may need to take precedence over the standards or habits of the past ... the possible need to loosen up, let your hair down – or be more mature ... the inevitability of the old having to give way to the new ... these two aspects of your situation/nature.

WATCH OUT FOR ... an inner and self-cancelling conflict between conservative and radical elements.

 MONEY/WORK/CREATIVITY

You are addressing or catering to two divergent value systems. Old style or new, or a blend of both. Creatively, a combining of the sentimental with the modern. Alternatively, it could be a case of bringing something up to date or changing a schedule. In any event, you probably need to ...

KEEP FOCUSED ON ... finding a formula or plan that satisfies both contingencies ... determining whether your preference or most profitable course lies with one or the other. A combining of wisdom with the common touch.

WATCH OUT FOR ... jeopardizing the present situation or future plans by hanging on to outmoded practices or values ... discarding the traditional and reliable merely for the sake of being new or trendy.

 LOVE/RELATING/SOCIAL

Here you are having to relate to a situation that has differing ages, backgrounds, standards or interests – or to a person who is a mix of the traditional and the modern. That person could be you. A relationship that has moved on, or needs to move on.

KEEP FOCUSED ON ... finding common ground in order to establish harmony or enjoyment ... balancing extremes within one's personality, or balancing one's reactions to such extremes in someone else ... finding new ways of relating and new things to do together.

WATCH OUT FOR ... confusion arising from conflicting needs and values ... being too staid or too progressive; the idea here is the need or potential to blend and balance while avoiding bad social mixes that give rise to discomfort and a waste of time and energy.

KARMA/ATTITUDE/HEALTH

With Symbols that include a twofold image, two sides to one's make-up should be considered and balanced. Here it seems there is a conservative as well as a radical dimension to one's personality. This may be a case of a young person being inside an older body, or vice versa. Your karma is essentially about going forwards.

KEEP FOCUSED ON ... both of these aspects as being equally valid, rather than letting one eclipse or inhibit the other. If you feel held back in some way, then expose the rebel in you or whatever is trying to get out. If you are outlandish to the point of repelling people, then rediscover the traditional, and remember why you rejected it as being passé.

WATCH OUT FOR ... conflicts of interest; they could give rise to complaints born of tension.

'Si jeunesse savait; si viellesse pouvait' (If youth knew; if age could)

THE CONSTELLATIONS IN THE SKY

☆ COSMIC ORDER ☆

GENERAL INTERPRETATION

Looking, or a need to look, to the ordering of your life or situation according to a higher scheme of things. Evoking the wonder and the mystery of life, this Symbol also patently refers to astrology itself. If you are using this subject in any way, including this book, then seek to understand and obey what it tells you regarding timing, character and interaction – and the nature of things generally.

KEEP FOCUSED ON ... your constant trimming of personality towards a cosmic or spiritual order, for this makes you a fine example of harmonious and dynamic living.

WATCH OUT FOR ... confusing notion with reality, or intention with action, and the chaos that this can bring ... imposing your own, possibly misguided, 'cosmic' or neurotic ideas onto others and the situation in hand.

LOVE/RELATING/SOCIAL

This images a relationship that is meant to be – but possibly for a reason that escapes a more rational or ego-based idea of compatibility. After all, the word 'compatible' means being able to suffer together, so in this context it is saying that you have to ...

KEEP FOCUSED ON ... the fact that you have chosen to suffer in the name of something greater than the short-sighted idea of relationships to which most people subscribe ... the higher and longer-term reasons for being together – or for being on your own.

WATCH OUT FOR ... thinking you have a marriage or family 'made in Heaven', in the sense of imposing your ideals upon others, or being smug.

MONEY/WORK/CREATIVITY

Either your ideas, products or finances fit into, or depend upon, some greater scheme of things – or if they don't, they will. And this 'greater scheme of things' could be market forces or a spiritual philosophy. It is important that you ...

KEEP FOCUSED ON ... the backdrop against which you are operating. If you see the backdrop as purely populist/commercial, then *be* populist/commercial. If you see it as something spiritual, in the sense of having a subtle or long-term purpose, then adjust your expectations accordingly and be true to your ideals. You may even 'score' in both arenas, but if it isn't 'written in the stars', destined, then ...

WATCH OUT FOR ... being disappointed on both counts. As they say, you cannot serve two masters – or at least, it is very difficult to do so.

KARMA/ATTITUDE/HEALTH

Every race that has ever been has had their own interpretation of what the Heavens mean. It has been said that this is purely a projection, born of the unconscious idiosyncrasies of the observers. So, this Symbol could be referring to 'constellating', how one's psychological make-up and agendas manifest in the world around you. This Symbol therefore urges you to ...

KEEP FOCUSED ON ... the largest frame of reference available to you; one that simultaneously incorporates a physical reality and a mystery, and to divine patiently and religiously what it tells you and means to you.

WATCH OUT FOR ... being 'spaced out' through identifying too much with 'Heavenly' realities at the expense of losing touch with Earthly ones ... how your own psychological agendas get played out through events happening to and around you.

'As above, so below'

A BOLSHEVIK PROPAGANDIST

☆ SOWING REVOLUTION ☆

 GENERAL INTERPRETATION

Occasioned or called for is the deliberate spread of revolutionary ideas and concepts, be they political, social, sexual or whatever. A conviction that stems from a deep sense that the crystallizing forces of the state or status quo must not suppress the human spirit.

KEEP FOCUSED ON ... your desire to promote your humanistic ideals and thereby improve the lot of the common person.

WATCH OUT FOR ... manipulating the thoughts of others in order to obscure one's own shortcomings ... bolshie reactions, even though they spring from a basic grievance that needs identifying and addressing.

 LOVE/RELATING/SOCIAL

Here is the call or opportunity to revolutionize any relationship, or the way you or another relates. You may be the one who does this, or it may be someone else – but it's in the air. It could be spontaneous or sudden. A third party?

KEEP FOCUSED ON ... making necessary changes, but only those that are in the interest of all concerned, not making waves purely for your own ends or just for the sake of it ... the probability that a radical idea or a new way of relating will create a much needed change in the emotional landscape.

WATCH OUT FOR ... getting unexpected, indignant or bolshie reactions from those you try to influence or are involved with. But then no kind of breakthrough can be made without eliciting some kind of reaction.

 MONEY/WORK/CREATIVITY

There is an inclination in those in charge – and this can mean your own ego – to lose sight of the interests of the masses or those below them. In order to avoid a breakdown in productivity, or in creative appeal to those you wish to reach, it is necessary to make a connection with whatever is close to the hearts and minds of those people. Alternatively, if the nature of your work is concerned with spreading revolutionary ideas, or is a radical way of getting a point across to the downtrodden, then this is a favourable oracle.

KEEP FOCUSED ON ... what changes or ideas really benefit ordinary people, or must be made in order to improve the object of your concern.

WATCH OUT FOR ... what it is that you are stirring up. If it is something destructive in you, it'll be many times more destructive when it gets around. Remember Trotsky and Goebbels!

 KARMA/ATTITUDE/HEALTH

It is significant that this Symbol appears in Leo, the Sign of royalty. You would think it more suited to the opposite, 'republican' Sign, Aquarius. But then it is in the 'royal' camp that a revolutionary *would* position himself – like Rasputin in the Romanoff household before the Russian Revolution. What all this says is that when things get too rigid and stuck, a disruptive element needs to make itself felt to loosen things up. But it is important to ...

KEEP FOCUSED ON ... accepting or finding a benign means of making changes, otherwise violent ones could arise ... what it is in you that is screaming for change. This may show up as a complaint such as nervousness or constipation ... using some kind of laxative, literal or psychological.

WATCH OUT FOR ... the call to revolution being ignored or misunderstood, then such blockages or misuse of power will lead to crisis and downfall.

'Stir It Up!'

GLASS BLOWERS

✫ THE BREATH OF LIFE ✫

GENERAL INTERPRETATION

The breath of life made personal, and given form through dexterity, effort and control. The effect of mind and spirit on the base materials of existence. This means that the ideas you have concerning the object of your enquiry have a direct effect on its outcome. So, it is important to …

KEEP FOCUSED ON … the most positive aspects of your state, believing in the best of possible outcomes in terms of what is realistically available or possible … making a contribution, positively participating in society … (discovering) the medium through which you express yourself best.

WATCH OUT FOR … thrusting upon others unwelcome or distorting ideas … blowing things out of proportion … making a mess of things through not concentrating enough.

♡ LOVE/RELATING/SOCIAL

The shape that your relationships take depends almost entirely on you. This also includes the shaping of a relationship that only exists in your mind. This is like the power of wishing, but you must be careful what you wish, because negative expectations and established patterns of relationship tend to be like bad breathing habits – or like bad breath!

KEEP FOCUSED ON … what you want from a relationship, and with care and control, make it happen – and keep it warm, don't let it get cold.

WATCH OUT FOR … blowing it, by succumbing to negative attitudes, habits and expectations, or by feeling that what you think, say or do won't make any difference … imposing your will on another.

⚘ MONEY/WORK/CREATIVITY

This poses the effort and skill that is needed to create something – or breathe new life into it. This is a Symbol of how mind (air) and will (blowing) can be given physical expression (glass). What is important is that you …

KEEP FOCUSED ON … drumming up or maintaining enthusiasm (heat) for the object of your concern … preparation – that is, making sure that conditions are right before making the effort or a blow for freedom … sustaining a steady pace and input … how your thoughts affect the situation, and vice versa.

WATCH OUT FOR … leaving something too long for it will go cold, and then you would have to start all over again … trying to create something when you are not yet ready or able; this would be like trying to blow glass that had not yet reached melting point.

☽ KARMA/ATTITUDE/HEALTH

You could regard your life and physical body as the 'glass'. You make your life into something useful and pleasing, and you vitalize and maintain the body that lives it with breathing (blowing).

KEEP FOCUSED ON … the idea that you have a life, which is like a blob of raw material, which you learn to fashion into something positive. If it should grow cold for any reason, this means that you have to regenerate it or go on to another life or 'a fresh blob of glass' … learning and practising correct breathing.

WATCH OUT FOR … any complaint caused by weak vitality, anxiety, poor circulation or lack of enthusiasm. Such can be helped considerably by yogic breathing, or any other breathing technique … holding too much in and not letting it out for fear of saying or doing something 'wrong'; this can lead to digestive, reproductive or skin issues.

'Life is what you make it'

EARLY MORNING DEW

☆ STARTING AFRESH ☆

 GENERAL INTERPRETATION

Here, or coming soon, is the freshness that accompanies the beginning of a new phase or chapter of experience, reminding us that life blesses – often unexpectedly – those that trust in its ever-renewing cycles of growth and change.

KEEP FOCUSED ON ... your talent for perceiving the best in people and situations, thereby attracting the saving graces needed when setting off into the unknown ... starting this time or each new day with a refreshing thought or ritual ... the fact that after a time of doubt and darkness – or of rest and withdrawal – a clearer and fresher outlook will spontaneously arise.

WATCH OUT FOR ... leaving things at the potential or idea stage, so that no material result confirms or invalidates them ... being cold rather than cool, sharp rather than fresh.

 MONEY/WORK/CREATIVITY

Imaged here is the energizing and inspirational nature of a new project or idea. Or, if some task or problem is presenting itself, you could benefit from sleeping on it, seeing it in the new light of a new day, refreshed by sleep, informed by dreams. If this is not possible, you will be given the necessary boost or lift purely because, with a fresh start, new ideas and angles will occur to you. The early bird catches the worm.

KEEP FOCUSED ON ... allowing matters to settle for a while, then you will see them in a new light ... getting started at first light, as soon as you wake, or before most others are at work.

WATCH OUT FOR ... labouring too hard and over-preparing for this could rob you of the freshness and intuition that is born of spontaneity, trusting the unknown ... trying to sort everything out too soon.

♡ LOVE/RELATING/SOCIAL

This could be the first refreshing bloom of love in a new relationship, or the refreshment of an ongoing relationship. Seeing and appreciating the ever-present possibility of emotional renewal.

KEEP FOCUSED ON ... introducing into a relationship new ideas and attitudes, new places to go and people to meet, new interests and feelings ... surviving the 'night' of doubt, dread or loneliness, for eventually you will experience the 'dew' of emotional release, relief and realization.

WATCH OUT FOR ... hanging on to resentment or other negative emotions for any longer than is needed. It is the nature of such things to recede and be replaced by something fresh and new – one needs to be alive to this fact. It is easy to persist in feeling bad.

☯ KARMA/ATTITUDE/HEALTH

Here is the sparkle and freshness that is a natural part of the process of renewal, the very making of which occurs during the darkest and most unpleasant phase of that renewal. *'En ma fin git mon commencement'* (In my end is my beginning).

KEEP FOCUSED ON ... any pain and discomfort while at the same time letting go of them; this is the surest way to healing and enlightenment ... the fact that the first flush of new beginnings does not last forever; it is there to get you going and through to the activities of a new day ... being in touch with your feelings so you may process them.

WATCH OUT FOR ... holding on to old emotions and anxieties, or being assailed by them when caught off guard, because they have not been processed and got rid of earlier. Bladder complaints can be down to this – another kind of 'early morning dew'!

'Tomorrow to fresh woods, and pastures new'

CHILDREN ON A SWING IN A HUGE OAK TREE

☆ FREEDOM FROM CARE ☆

✺ GENERAL INTERPRETATION

Here given or available is the safety and pleasure, especially for the young or young at heart, that is provided by a stable foundation or institution that has its roots planted in the natural order of things. Possibly trying to reach for the sky. Getting into the swing of things, accepting the toing and froing of life – swings and roundabouts.

KEEP FOCUSED ON ... your healthy sense of fun that brings out the best of the child in others ... whatever connects the swing to the tree – the critical link in the process that relates to the object of your concern ... what is dependable, having proved itself through time ... taking care.

WATCH OUT FOR ... aimless toing and froing owing to a reluctance to grow up or get down to things, thereby putting a burden on others ... disrepair – it could mean disaster.

♥ LOVE/RELATING/SOCIAL

The enjoyment of the senses and feelings of familiarity that accompany a healthy relationship, or, at least, a relationship in its initial stages. A happy, fun relationship or social whirl. More literally, childlike happiness, well-supported, or the prospect of such.

KEEP FOCUSED ON ... what you definitely have (between you) that is rock steady, for this is what will carry you through love's or society's inevitable ups and downs.

WATCH OUT FOR ... giddy-making involvements that could wind up causing you to feel bad, or to take a fall ... going over the top; childish enthusiasm that loses sight of what is providing the wherewithal, threatening its continued supply.

MONEY/WORK/CREATIVITY

A playful style is essential to any creative process, and to prevent work from becoming a drudge. However, a childish, immature disposition that will not get on with the job in hand, and just wants to 'stay out and play' must be guarded against.

KEEP FOCUSED ON ... what you regard as having sound roots, that is, services, ideas, products or practices that have consistently bred good results; these will continue as long as you maintain connections, oil the moving parts, and replace anything outworn ... a rhythm to your efforts in terms of time or any other medium.

WATCH OUT FOR ... losing yourself in pleasurable or time-wasting activities, evading responsibilities ... getting so carried away when you feel on a roll that you do not notice that a vital element has started to weaken.

☯ KARMA/ATTITUDE/HEALTH

This images a healthy background or history that is steeped in a longstanding, ancient, tradition. This provides and protects, enabling one to enjoy good health and further self-expression. It should also foster a feeling of security, creating a positive attitude that things will continue to hold up.

KEEP FOCUSED ON ... the shelter, foundations and wherewithal at your disposal in order to get into the swing of things, to get things into a self-sustaining mode ... the abundance of childhood dreams and happy memories that serve to support, inspire and warm you in the present.

WATCH OUT FOR ... being disheartened by the 'downs' of life, for they are always followed by 'ups' ... inertia, allowing things to stagnate, for the despondency caused by this could prove hard to shake out of and get things moving again.

'Rhythm and rhyme make a dance out of time'

AN EVENING LAWN PARTY

☆ SOPHISTICATED EASE ☆

❀ GENERAL INTERPRETATION

Here is a sense and occasion of everyday grace and passing enjoyment that acts as a tonic and relief to the stresses and strains of workaday existence. It could also take one beyond them. However, there is also a suggestion of the affluent and superficial that may preclude anything more than idle chitchat.

KEEP FOCUSED ON ... your urbane talent for creating a situation where an easy air of social interaction prevails, giving rise to an agreeable mood among the people concerned.

WATCH OUT FOR ... approaching the object of your concern, and using the Oracle itself, with insufficient earnestness ... a failure or a reluctance to see the less pleasant side of life, and so an inability to connect with what matters to many people.

♥ LOVE/RELATING/SOCIAL

No doubt a pleasant person or relationship, but not necessarily one of much depth or sincerity. The ordinariness of day-to-day existence is left behind, which can mean a denial of the more pressing needs of the emotions, or a break from them. Everything depends on what one thinks one wants or will settle for. For some, such social ease is just the ticket, for others it is emotional anathema. Then again, being superficial is sometimes necessary if things are not to get too turgidly soul-searching.

KEEP FOCUSED ON ... what your 'lawn food' is and is not, what is your social or sexual poison. Cultivate what feeds, stimulates and relaxes you, and avoid what doesn't.

WATCH OUT FOR ... getting caught up in a meaningless round of social occasions that are a substitute for a proper sense of intimacy.

♆ MONEY/WORK/CREATIVITY

This images two things mainly. Firstly, in order to further oneself professionally, it is often necessary to entertain and make the right connections, probably outside of work itself. Secondly, the Symbol is saying that your public or customers are of the middle-class variety and not from a grass roots level. And so your idea or product should be tailored to amuse or interest them, yet take them to a more sublime or cultivated level.

KEEP FOCUSED ON ... cultivating contacts that could be useful to your career ... ironing out any bumps; weeding out anything that spoils the overall effect of your product or situation ... spontaneous creativity.

WATCH OUT FOR ... being seduced by how things seem to be on the surface, or considering your issue in too shallow a way. Conforming or catering to bourgeois values may only have so much mileage.

♄ KARMA/ATTITUDE/HEALTH

Typically, a scene such as this Symbol portrays represents a release from the toil of living. So here is a respite from it all – be it for an evening, a longer period or even a lifetime. But the question arises whether or not such an apparently de-stressing pastime is all it appears to be. There could be areas of great stress as people withhold their truer feelings, or where they don't but are expected to.

KEEP FOCUSED ON ... finding the right blend of ease and stimulation, or establishing which it is that is required at any given time. Tension can be the result of an excess of either – ease and small talk can create stress for someone who is bored; stimulation can create it for someone who is overwrought.

WATCH OUT FOR ... getting lost in the pleasantries or inconsequentialities of life; meaning and direction could fall by the wayside, go to seed.

'Recreation should be an invitation to inspiration'

AN OLD SEA CAPTAIN ROCKING

☆ RESTLESS CONTEMPLATION ☆

⚙ GENERAL INTERPRETATION

This Symbol is similar to Libra 17 'A Retired Sea Captain', but the emphasis here is that he may be old but he is not ready for retirement. A restless desire to get back to the adventures and business of living is in evidence. Although there is a reflecting upon past joys and sorrows, victories and failures, leading to wisdom, there arises out of this a readiness and eagerness for the moment when new dramas and battles arise.

KEEP FOCUSED ON ... your innate maturity of spirit that enables you to deal with the highs and lows of life in a seasoned and philosophical fashion, to dive back into the fray as soon as the opportunity presents itself, which it will.

WATCH OUT FOR ... getting lost in outmoded thinking, or trapped in the past and consequently frozen in the present.

MONEY/WORK/CREATIVITY

You are presently having to step back from what you are doing, even though you are champing at the bit and wanting to resolve an issue or achieve an objective. This Symbol could also be referring to, and agreeing with, anything that involves memoirs, history and recollections.

KEEP FOCUSED ON ... your experiences so far with respect to the object of your concern. Through pondering them you will get an idea of what the next move should be, or why you are not moving forward right now ... calming yourself, and then taking time to consider matters.

WATCH OUT FOR ... getting trapped in old ways of doing things or in circumstances that have no real bearing on the present and its requirements ... putting anything or anyone out to grass when there is evidently 'life in the old dog yet'.

♡ LOVE/RELATING/SOCIAL

The object of your concern is, or will be, a thing of the past which you may look back upon with a discomfort – either because you long for it or regret it, or both. You may need to find some way of absorbing any restlessness you have concerning your situation. 'Rocking' can have a sexual connotation, yet in this context it could be masturbatory.

KEEP FOCUSED ON ... waiting for whatever Fate may bring while doing something to take your mind off the matter. Desperation doesn't like or attract good company.

WATCH OUT FOR ... descending into a spiral of emotional and physical frustration or remorse through becoming preoccupied with something rather than actively doing something about it. If you cannot do anything about it, then do something else entirely. Or nothing at all.

☯ KARMA/ATTITUDE/HEALTH

In between lifetimes or any periods of activity there are periods where one is 'ticking over' while one gets ready for a new cycle of activity. The rocking back and forth is symbolic of both the ticking over and the pendulum-like nature of experience. The Old Sea Captain indicates that we all have a great store of experience of sailing the Seven Seas of the life of the soul. So whatever your situation ...

KEEP FOCUSED ON ... the fact that a new cycle will come in its own time and that you only need to bide your time ... getting into a rhythm of living, for this will harmonize and synchronize you with the flow of life, making for periods of rest and productivity, rather than just restlessly waiting.

WATCH OUT FOR ... neither accepting inactivity nor making a move, for this could cause internal distress and possible health problems.

'The mass of men lead lives of quiet desperation'

THE HUMAN SOUL AWAITING OPPORTUNITY FOR EXPRESSION

☆ INNER CERTAINTY ☆

GENERAL INTERPRETATION

Because the soul is, by its very nature, looking for first a means of expression (a personality) and then a form to give whatever the personality desires, this Symbol could appear to be all too obvious and of no personal significance. However, the significance is in the word 'awaiting'. This implies a state of anticipation and preparation for that 'expression' of whatever is the object of your enquiry, and it also suggests that the manner in which one waits is crucial to the process.

KEEP FOCUSED ON ... the primary assumption that there is a meaning and ultimate purpose to your life. This ensures that it becomes clearer and clearer what that meaning and purpose are.

WATCH OUT FOR ... idly hoping that 'something will turn up' without investing any thought or effort into it doing so ... giving up.

MONEY/WORK/CREATIVITY

The inspiration, idea or wherewithal is not yet available or it has not reached the point where things can actually take form. The potential is there but not the reality.

KEEP FOCUSED ON ... working at whatever it is you are aiming at to manifest, because the essential or creative impulse is there – it is just that it will take time to develop ... keeping an eye on the main chance ... investing in the future.

WATCH OUT FOR ... counting your chickens before they've hatched ... presenting something to the world or an authority before it is ready ... attempting to give form to an idea before that idea has accumulated enough weight, detail or depth ... throwing yourself away on the first offer that comes along – this would indicate that you do not yet have enough faith in yourself or your product to bide your time.

LOVE/RELATING/SOCIAL

Here is a relationship that calls up the deepest and most feeling parts of yourself or all concerned. The nature or objective of the relationship is to connect with the most profound feelings of those involved. In this way the relationship finds its way and its fate is satisfied.

KEEP FOCUSED ON ... waiting for the right moment for making yourself felt, or for becoming aware of how the other person(s) feel(s) ... letting time and the flow of emotions bring about a natural resolution or explanation.

WATCH OUT FOR ... being impatient to make yourself felt or noticed, or to get something; this would have a negative or unwelcome effect.

KARMA/ATTITUDE/HEALTH

Whatever your concern, it is still a time of waiting for a change or for that desired window of opportunity. Consciously or unconsciously, you are making yourself right and ready for when that moment arrives. Life itself is moulding you into a shape that will know how to best use that springboard into the future.

KEEP FOCUSED ON ... how the very process of waiting, in whatever your situation, is breeding in you special or spiritual qualities that are precisely what are required for when the right time comes – including the ability to recognize that time ... listening to your inner voice.

WATCH OUT FOR ... impatience, jumping the gun, getting ahead of yourself – along with the legion of complaints, such as heart and nervous problems, that they can give rise to. These are caused by a lack of faith in the sure process and purpose of Nature, the Cosmos or God.

'Call the world if you please "The vale of soul-making"'

A PAGEANT

☆ ONGOING STORY ☆

GENERAL INTERPRETATION

Your situation is best viewed as a part of the parade of history and experience, of the toings and froings of ancestors, descendants, friends and all and sundry – and of one's own place in this, small or large. The sense of meaning and even glory, that is or can be given to such a display.

KEEP FOCUSED ON ... what your background has to offer, be it of name, worth, tradition, or whatever serves to give a sense of continuity or a place and a time to all who become involved with you ... the ups and downs, squalls and doldrums, as just all being part of the story of your life.

WATCH OUT FOR ... pure ostentation ... pretentiousness that can be dangerously deluding and economical with the truth.

LOVE/RELATING/SOCIAL

If you look back you will see that your emotional or social life, your relationships, form a pattern or continuum. There is also a pattern, like a storyboard, regarding any relationship you might be asking about. This Symbol entreats you to ...

KEEP FOCUSED ON ... the predominant stages or features of your relationship(s) or emotional development, and make out what the 'plot' is. Then you will have some idea of where things are headed and what to make of what is going on right now ... emphasize the positive or joyful aspects of your relationship(s) for they hold the essence of healthy relating.

WATCH OUT FOR ... over-romanticizing your love life or dismissing the more ordinary side of it. The former is asking to be disappointed, the latter is sabotaging what gives relationships stability.

MONEY/WORK/CREATIVITY

Any form of work that has to do with history or story-making is auspicious here. Advertising is also well-starred, but in more ways than one, for this Symbol encourages you to ...

KEEP FOCUSED ON ... your CV, portfolio or career as something positive and colourful, where the best is emphasized and the not-so-brilliant is edited or polished up. It is important that you convince yourself that you amount to something – if you do not think so, nobody else will. However ...

WATCH OUT FOR ... straying into a Walter Mitty world where you make yourself out to be more than you can live up to, or prove if challenged ... being tacky in any way, for this would have the opposite of the desired effect.

KARMA/ATTITUDE/HEALTH

This Symbol is beautifully representative of the procession of lifetimes, and of how certain lifetimes, or episodes within a lifetime, can be given a bit of a spin to emphasize the wonder of one's own existence, and of the soul that lives it.

KEEP FOCUSED ON ... viewing matters in this light and from this perspective, and then the object of your enquiry need not be seen as insignificant or too heavy, too long or too short ... the 'story so far', and then you will gain a greater or clearer idea of the present situation and of what lies ahead.

WATCH OUT FOR ... glamorizing or dramatizing anything, be it positive or negative, to the point that it becomes either manic or depressive ... attaching the wrong sort of meaning to your situation by seeing it in isolation from the bigger picture, or from the ongoing process of karma.

'Trailing clouds of glory do we come/From God, who is our home'

SUNSHINE JUST AFTER A STORM

☆ ALL'S WELL THAT ENDS WELL ☆

☼ GENERAL INTERPRETATION

There is a natural and perennial return to health and goodness, peace and stability, after any crisis or necessary release of tension.

KEEP FOCUSED ON ... an optimism and better nature that endures any upset ... weathering the storm in the knowledge that it will pass, finding you feeling lighter, relieved and refreshed.

WATCH OUT FOR ... making crises unnecessarily; manic behaviour ... trying to avoid crises, for in that way one may have to endure an interminable but uneasy peace or boredom, all in the name of safety or conformity.

♡ LOVE/RELATING/SOCIAL

Rest assured that whatever difficulties you experience, they will pass away and once again you will love and feel loved. It may have happened already – in which case bask in its glory – or you may have a wait on your hands. But love and union will one day shine on you and yours.

KEEP FOCUSED ON ... making your own 'sunshine' in the face of the 'clouds' of another person or the lack of one ... that you might have to endure conflict or confrontation in order to clear the air and thereby make way for positive, loving feelings to break through.

WATCH OUT FOR ... casting shadows with negative judgements and unreal expectations ... avoiding the duller or darker side of relationships – you would also forestall the brighter and better aspects.

MONEY/WORK/CREATIVITY

After a bad patch, your luck turns, or will turn, for the better.

KEEP FOCUSED ON ... what comprises the nature of good fortune, and endeavour to create it ... thrashing out any problems or disagreements, for success will follow upon this.

WATCH OUT FOR ... what presaged the bad patch in terms of morale, market forces and working practices; through improving the awareness and nature of such things, hard times can be avoided or, at least, be viewed constructively ... letting unattended problems accumulate to a level that creates a malaise.

☾ KARMA/ATTITUDE/HEALTH

The cycles of night and day, dark and light, sorrow and joy, illness and health, proceed eternally. They are also interdependent and each serves positive roles in the natural or greater scheme of things. You can survive the darkest periods if you ...

KEEP FOCUSED ON ... even a single chink of light in the image of a loved one, a kind word, a worthy cause or anything else with a bright image ... the fact that it is challenges and pressures that foreshadow a time of great lightness and relief ... trusting and being open to the natural process of crest and trough, tension and release, high and low.

WATCH OUT FOR ... clouds on the horizon, or resting on your laurels when it's plain sailing.

'Take away my demons and you take away my angels'

A NON-VESTED CHURCH CHOIR

☆ NATURAL HARMONY ☆

❋ GENERAL INTERPRETATION

Suggested here is a more natural and free expression of what is traditionally the realm of something more ordered and stuffy. Letting people and things come together informally, naturally and spontaneously. A harmonious group.

KEEP FOCUSED ON ... the quickening of a warm sense of being a part of something as a result of playing an unselfconscious role in your community ... casual and informal ways of attaining your objective. Playing it by ear, for opportunities to create harmony will arise. Doing it for the love of it.

WATCH OUT FOR ... a false sense of exclusiveness that serves no one ... making a big deal out of things – this would only serve to create anxiety and therefore not lead to a pleasing outcome.

♥ LOVE/RELATING/SOCIAL

What is favoured here is a relaxed and informal style of relationship and relating. Conversely, this Symbol counsels against seeing, say, marriage as something that auto-matically makes a relationship work and be more stable. It urges one to tap into the original spirit of a relation-ship, making oneself heard for the good of the whole.

KEEP FOCUSED ON ... who you and another are as unique individuals, and then you and they will behave naturally and respond freely, unfettered by rigid rules and the fear of being yourselves ... playing all romantic, social or family scenarios by ear rather than according to a formula or convention.

WATCH OUT FOR ... preciousness and rigid expectations ... holding fixed ideas, especially negative ones, about another, for they will then rebel under such pressure or live out your fears.

MONEY/WORK/CREATIVITY

This Symbol advocates a movement away from being 'professional' in the sense of the 'suit' who has left behind or has never had sight of their own personality, or toeing the commercial or company line to excess. Such gloss may, in the end, cost more than it makes. Funds shall arise naturally in due course.

KEEP FOCUSED ON ... finding a means of bonding at a personal level for maximum work efficiency and satisfaction ... developing interpersonal skills between staff members and co-workers ... letting creative juices flow unchecked as in a 'stream of consciousness'.

WATCH OUT FOR ... office glamour and executive perks ... sticking to rigid roles or job descriptions for this makes the whole brittle and repels customers ... letting content be dictated to by form and fashion ... being *too* lax or laid back.

☯ KARMA/ATTITUDE/HEALTH

A return to natural and informal ways of being. Your spiritual path is to do with aligning and attuning yourself to natural energies or *chi*, rather than your cultural norm.

KEEP FOCUSED ON ... the necessity of, or advantage gained by, letting it all hang out so that a familiar ease exists ... informal group prayer, meditation, healing, singing and playing. This will promote or cater to whatever is the object of your concern ... finding your way back into the 'fold'.

WATCH OUT FOR ... letting any spiritual or health practice become too regimented – or, for that matter, too open-ended. Return to first principles if ever things should become too woolly or too much like hard work ... imbalances caused by being too left-brained/logical, giving rise to right-body complaints.

'It's the singer not the song'

A TEACHER OF CHEMISTRY

☆ THE SCIENCE OF INTERACTION ☆

 GENERAL INTERPRETATION

Imaged or recommended here is a perception of all forms of reality that provide an understanding of the deeper workings of nature and life, and the course things take. This can make for a means of controlling them or predicting outcomes. There is also a connection to the precursor of chemistry – alchemy – which in symbolic terms has to do with the transmutation from a basic expression to something far more refined.

KEEP FOCUSED ON ... your flair for making it clear to yourself and others what you have learned through close examination of your surroundings and experiences ... what you can teach and/or learn that would improve the situation.

WATCH OUT FOR ... a clinical or detached attitude that affords little real reward for your efforts and that may even be destructive.

 LOVE/RELATING/SOCIAL

Here is a relationship where one is having to teach or learn about what the 'chemistry' between two or more people poses and creates. Someone knows, or is supposed to know, more about this than others.

KEEP FOCUSED ON ... what parts of your life and personality are stimulated or quickened by another, and vice versa, for you can be sure that those parts are in need of another being more aware of them; also, that those parts need to be purified and transformed in some way ... taking responsibility for your own part in the interaction.

WATCH OUT FOR ... not recognizing the fact that we all have different effects upon one another, and that 'it takes two to tango'. Missing this point for long enough would find you left alone to your own devices or having things blow up in your face.

 MONEY/WORK/CREATIVITY

If you are a teacher of any kind, this Symbol is affirming your position as one, and also emphasizing certain aspects to being one, for the teacher must always be learning too. Apart from this, it is demonstrating that the material world operates in ways that have to be obeyed. There is no fast or easy route to where you want to get to; you have to know the rules of the game and keep to them. Money, in particular, is made through adhering to a process of work and observation. Then, if you ...

KEEP FOCUSED ON ... how the various elements and people involved in your situation interact with one another, you will eventually come up with an insight or creative idea that will transform the situation for the better.

WATCH OUT FOR ... exhausting yourself, others and resources by attempting the patently impossible.

KARMA/ATTITUDE/HEALTH

Your situation is pointing to the fact that life is dependent upon and governed by definite natural laws, whether one knows what they are or not. Moreover, it is saying that it is now imperative that you become more aware of these natural laws; if you already are, it is incumbent upon you to show and tell others how everything is caused by the effect of one thing upon the other.

KEEP FOCUSED ON ... discovering or making known the processes and stages that everything and everyone have to go through on their way to and beyond any kind of transformation – and that transformation is what life is all about ... accepting the nature of these stages, for then the whole process of life is lived in a progressive, purposeful and appreciable way ... life itself as being the teacher.

WATCH OUT FOR ... vainly trying to cut corners.

'Transformation, that's the name of the game'

A HOUSEBOAT PARTY

☆ CREATIVE CO-OPERATION ☆

 GENERAL INTERPRETATION

You have here the vitality and wherewithal to keep moving and having fun, but without disturbing those close to you. There is also the freedom to do as you wish with those who have a similar purpose in life.

KEEP FOCUSED ON ... the importance of being aware that co-operation with others helps keep the party afloat ... your flair for creating an original atmosphere that caters to people's need for the familiar *and* the unusual ... how limitation affords security.

WATCH OUT FOR ... the inevitability that there comes a time when we have to disembark from something that is fun, realizing that though we are disappointed, there will always be other happy times to embark upon ... thoughtless self-indulgence that is of no use or, at worst, antagonizes others.

LOVE/RELATING/SOCIAL

A congenial, if somewhat exclusive, sense of fun and adventure. Such a relationship, person or group can also have its limitations, though at first the novelty of it all is everything. But then this defined network of habits and haunts is what provides the security to complement the fun.

KEEP FOCUSED ON ... the advantages of such a relationship, such as variety, mobility, unusualness or a gypsy-like lifestyle ... what your distinct role is in the relationship, be it a family or group, for there is no room for mere passengers or onlookers.

WATCH OUT FOR ... any signs of emotional or physical claustrophobia; whenever possible, take some time out from such 'closeness' ... feelings of being enthralled and over-committing yourself, only to find that you have become a 'captive audience'.

 MONEY/WORK/CREATIVITY

Self-contained teams or partnerships that have clear ideas of their routes and channels of expression or supply are particularly well-favoured here. Financially, flotation is a possibility – recommended even. A celebration of liquidity, perhaps. Some form of co-operative with the accent on the traditional, unusual or tightly knit is also auspicious.

KEEP FOCUSED ON ... knowing the layout or lie of the land with respect to your being aware of your limitations is what gives you your freedom ... establishing what your channels of supply and distribution are, and how they function best ... devising set methods and routines to promote stability and productivity.

WATCH OUT FOR ... creating more than you can use, sell or distribute ... getting stuck with anything because it is hard to move.

KARMA/ATTITUDE/HEALTH

We are all in the same boat, is what this Symbol is saying. A houseboat is representative of a place where you live in close proximity to others, either permanently moored or going somewhere, with the route or mooring rigidly defined by certain facts of life, and by inescapable laws of physical reality. Likewise, we inhabit and travel in our bodies within similarly defined limits of healthy living.

KEEP FOCUSED ON ... who you are as a member of the crew – finding your place in the scheme of things is vital to you ... those people and pastimes that give you a sense of both belonging and going somewhere, for this is available to you now.

WATCH OUT FOR ... being too independent or too dependent, for you will get into difficulties when any change comes your way.

'Recipe for life: Enjoy where you are and who you are with'

THE ZUNI SUN WORSHIPPERS

☆ CREATING FAVOUR ☆

 GENERAL INTERPRETATION

Living a healthy and meaningful life because of a passionate, instinctual awareness of, and reverence for, the source of all life.

KEEP FOCUSED ON ... creating a sound sense of what is essentially important in yourself and others, giving rise to a rich and mutually rewarding lifestyle ... creating what you want or need as an 'offering' to your God or whatever you hold to be of importance over your petty or personal interests. This also sets a good example.

WATCH OUT FOR ... admiring what is bright or impressive without understanding its real significance; always depending on something on the outside to warm you on the inside ... making unnecessary sacrifices of oneself or others because of a faulty attitude to life ... depending on externals to cheer you up; find your inner light.

 LOVE/RELATING/SOCIAL

Fundamentally, the best way to relate to anyone is with respect, and the best way to get them to relate properly to you is through gaining their respect. Respect means considering someone, over and over again.

KEEP FOCUSED ON ... recognizing and acknowledging the most important person(s) in your life, and initially respect them just for that, then take on board why they are so important ... appeasing the egos of others, but only as a necessary expedient rather than at the expense of your own dignity.

WATCH OUT FOR ... seeing someone as being the centre of your universe, or allowing yourself to be seen as such by them, for ultimately this cannot be lived up to; one must find and be one's own centre ... expecting to be flattered or appeased yourself; this does not command respect, but quite the opposite.

 MONEY/WORK/CREATIVITY

Having a central figure or purpose is the key to success here. Also, material reward will eventually come, but when times are hard having such a figure or purpose close to one's heart makes it tolerable – worthwhile even.

KEEP FOCUSED ON ... following or being true to whatever or whoever truly impresses and influences you as long as this also engenders mutual respect and self-respect ... making an impression upon such a figure (who could be yourself) through an act of creativity or service.

WATCH OUT FOR ... centralization, when failing to recognize people and things on the margin. The centre should be like the good father who encourages independence while always being a guiding principle, and who is, within reason, available at all times.

KARMA/ATTITUDE/HEALTH

The state and health of everything ultimately depends on its central cause. It could also be said that everything and everyone is looking for its centre – throughout life, or lifetime after lifetime. Both spiritually and physically, this centre is the heart, and universally it is the Sun. The solution lies in connecting and identifying with this central source of energy and awareness. This can be done by finding a way to ...

KEEP FOCUSED ON ... whatever that centre might be for you. This can be done by meditating upon your heart or heart chakra with a view to opening it, or by practising Sun worship (*see* pages 467–8 for the Mayan version of this).

WATCH OUT FOR ... mistaking the ego for the centre; it is a temporary pretender until the real thing is found.

'The Sun is God'

CHICKENS INTOXICATED

☆ GETTING IN A FLAP ☆

✳ GENERAL INTERPRETATION

Fear feeding on itself. This Symbol, although it has humorous undertones, is essentially a warning of the upset or ridicule that arises from being too exposed to or involved with anything that is poisonous or unsuitable to you. This would include any inclination one might have to overreact, panic or dramatize a situation out of all proportion.

KEEP FOCUSED ON ... the fact that the situation is fundamentally harmless – It is only one's reaction to it that could make it otherwise.

WATCH OUT FOR ... provoking and relying upon sensation at the expense of developing inner peace and worth, so having a hard time of it or not being taken seriously.

♥ LOVE/RELATING/SOCIAL

This Symbol is warning about allowing yourself to be overcome with your own or someone else's emotions or hormones. Getting carried away by fears or desires, pleasure or pain.

KEEP FOCUSED ON ... staying cool and centred when emotions are running high ... allowing oneself some squawking, but only enough to release tension.

WATCH OUT FOR ... letting mere cluck-clucking from others faze you unnecessarily ... cluck-clucking back, for this could escalate into a lot of fuss and feathers ... being a mother hen and getting in a state about it.

♔ MONEY/WORK/CREATIVITY

Overcome with success or failure, there is a danger of losing control and regretting it later. Alternatively, this Symbol could be referring to others losing their head while you remain cool and take the prize. In any event, the world can be a very unforgiving place for a loss of control, be it over your faculties or your material situation.

KEEP FOCUSED ON ... distilling something creative or profitable from what might appear to be frothy, excitable or chaotic ... maintaining self-control ... doing what you want or have to do without being distracted by the dramas, hesitation and disapproval of others.

WATCH OUT FOR ... getting carried away by the mood of the moment and not considering the longer term effects.

☯ KARMA/ATTITUDE/HEALTH

Chickens could be said to represent a vulnerability to attack by predators, maybe as a result of drawing attention to oneself due to a fear of those predators. Looked at from an animistic or totemic standpoint, this Symbol could be referring to the possibility of being taken over, voluntarily or otherwise, by a spiritual entity. In this respect, something often has to be sacrificed in order to attain an altered state of consciousness. Karmically, the situation could be the result of some such practice, like voodoo. More literally, this Symbol is spelling out the plusses and minuses regarding alcohol or drugs.

KEEP FOCUSED ON ... having some centre or base you can return to should things get giddy.

WATCH OUT FOR ... giving yourself over to anything or anyone you do not trust. Avoid anything that you know to be toxic to you.

'Whatever you do, don't panic'

A CARRIER PIGEON

☆ THE MESSAGE ☆

 GENERAL INTERPRETATION

Suggested here is a way of conveying information or feelings that trusts in the natural order of things. The message and the messenger are inseparably intertwined, which means that the messenger has to put their heart and soul into believing and delivering the message they have been entrusted with – no matter what 'weather conditions' of doubt and difficulty they have to contend with.

KEEP FOCUSED ON … a comfortable assurance that your most wholesome traits will win through, giving rise to a steady increase in your sense of satisfaction … that once the message has been delivered properly, then the messenger is free to return to their usual state of security (home to roost) … the probability that there will be 'fair winds' as well as ill.

WATCH OUT FOR … a message not getting through, or doubting its value/importance.

 MONEY/WORK/CREATIVITY

Your work is all about conveying messages – and also receiving them. This has been, or is in the process of being, achieved. If not, then get the message and work out how you are going to put it across.

KEEP FOCUSED ON … delivering the message, what has to be said as you see it … the possibility of it being a while for the message to get across, so keep on pitching … talking turkey.

WATCH OUT FOR … blocking, twisting or diluting the message until you are no longer clear what it is, and are then unable to understand what it meant or how to convey it … 'shooting the messenger' instead of going for the real perpetrator.

♡ **LOVE/RELATING/SOCIAL**

As is so often the case, successful relationships and social events depend upon clear communication. This includes being able to detect what someone is saying to you non-verbally, or what a situation is spelling out for you.

KEEP FOCUSED ON … saying what is in your heart to the person who is in your heart. If they are not in your heart, then say what is in your head. If you do not know what is in either, then have a long and deep conversation with yourself until you get the message and find out … how you say something, as much as what you say.

WATCH OUT FOR … putting things across in a way that is contrived to give a certain impression. A contrivance conveys little if nothing at all – and they'll know it.

KARMA/ATTITUDE/HEALTH

Here is the image of a message that is persisting through time – maybe lifetimes. Possibly it is a message from the 'other side'. Or something that has long remained unsaid, and now must be said. It could also be referring to a biological or neurological messenger (that must get through/be understood).

KEEP FOCUSED ON … giving, receiving and interpreting any communication that comes your way; this may mean appreciating that you have been given a message, that you are a go-between, messenger or medium … the possibility that it is a coded or hidden message.

WATCH OUT FOR … dismissing any communication that you do not at first understand or that does not have 'message' written all over it.

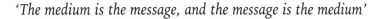

'The medium is the message, and the message is the medium'

A BAREBACK RIDER

☆ FEEL THE FORCE ☆

GENERAL INTERPRETATION

You are involved with or contemplating something that requires a deep and natural connection with what is powerful and forceful in you, or in something or someone else. This requires a spontaneity born of a willingness to develop special skills or give dramatic displays, but that avoids violence.

KEEP FOCUSED ON ... the fact that, although training and preparation are necessary, at some point one has to leap on and grab hold of whatever it is you are intending to do. Otherwise you will only be known for your intentions rather than your achievements. Grasp the nettle.

WATCH OUT FOR ... a rough and readiness that plays to a need for raw sensationalism, disregarding the care and technique required for a relatively 'safe ride' ... violent emotions, for they could inflict harm.

MONEY/WORK/CREATIVITY

The situation requires boldness, balance and skill, but above all it requires confidence. Confidence is something that is either built up (brick by brick) or inborn, but in this case it is something that is won through simply by believing with every fibre of your being that it can be done.

KEEP FOCUSED ON ... keeping your seat, not letting any violent twists or turns interfere with your concentration or equilibrium ... knowing your business or art intimately well, for then even if you do suffer a fall, you will be able to remount and carry on ... going for it.

WATCH OUT FOR ... being frightened of falling off, that is, failing or looking a fool. This would mean that you either failed because you let your fears intrude upon your concentration, or because you never really started or got going at all.

♡ LOVE/RELATING/SOCIAL

Here is a relationship or individual that either has to be taken by storm or given a wide berth. This is because it is dangerous at some level – probably sexual. If you are already involved, then you will just have to ride it out, keeping your balance and poise as best you can, or even enjoy it – or jump free.

KEEP FOCUSED ON ... what it is in you that is looking for danger, and why. Bear in mind that 'danger' can mean anything that bothers, frightens, frustrates or exercises an exciting pull on you. So, you may be confronted with something impossibly challenging because you are trying to avoid something more normal or realistic; or you may choose a rough ride because that is how you get to know how to handle your own feelings and urges.

WATCH OUT FOR ... 'unsafe sex' ... treating another as a sexual object.

KARMA/ATTITUDE/HEALTH

Danger and the exhilaration of living close to Nature or your animal drives is the issue here; conversely, you are shy and out of touch with these drives. In other words, previously you have allowed your passions to take you over and now you are having to tame and control them or learn to be on better terms with them.

KEEP FOCUSED ON ... being aware and attuned to your libido in order that you can harness it to do what you have now got to do. The libido is like the engine that drives one's being, and it has to be given rein or hitched to whatever needs setting in motion. Or reined in and unhitched, as the case may be. Either way the libido has to be harnessed, got a hold of consciously.

WATCH OUT FOR ... playing with fire, getting too involved with energies beyond your control.

'Life is like riding a bicycle; keep going or you fall over'

AN UNTIDY, UNKEMPT MAN

☆ PAUPER OR KING? ☆

✳ GENERAL INTERPRETATION

A rejection of the world and its formal ways and preconceived ideas based upon appearances. Paradoxically, a person can be clean and well turned out, but feel a mess inside. Conversely, a dishevelled appearance can conceal a positive, even aristocratic, individual.

KEEP FOCUSED ON ... creating and maintaining an inner sureness that needs no outer affectation. At the same time, be aware that maintaining a good image helps improve one's inner state; pride in appearance can be an antidote to self-neglect, much as physical yoga raises the spirits.

WATCH OUT FOR ... self-neglect dramatized into something supposedly meaningful ... allowing ones external being or affairs to become rundown because that's how one feels on the inside – this only makes matters worse.

♥ LOVE/RELATING/SOCIAL

This describes someone who has a poor opinion of themselves emotionally, which may or may not be apparent from the outside. Because of this, they doubt anyone really wanting or loving them. It could even describe the state of a relationship – both parties feeling unlovable. Consequently, the relationship could come to grief because of this negative expectation.

KEEP FOCUSED ON ... what is really making you or the other person feel unsure, instead of hiding behind a mask of self-pity. Perhaps you are afraid of having to live up to something, or of showing how you really feel, or of dealing with a negative pattern of behaviour that sabotages relationships.

WATCH OUT FOR ... making a negative self-image into a self-fulfilling prophecy ... self-pity.

⚕ MONEY/WORK/CREATIVITY

Like it or not, the world of commerce and art goes primarily by appearances. It also has little time for anyone who is cap in hand, self-effacing. Like a game of poker, the market place is where you must 'bet like you got 'em', make out you are already successful as a prerequisite of actually being so. This Symbol is pointing to the likelihood that the opposite is currently the case, so you need to ...

KEEP FOCUSED ON ... making and maintaining a good impression upon those with whom you wish to find or keep favour ... *feeling* wealthy, lucky and gifted, for ultimately you are as successful as you feel ... the area you feel most confident in.

WATCH OUT FOR ... getting into a downward spiral of self-criticism and feelings of worthlessness. This would undermine your confidence and diminish your effectiveness, projecting an aura of failure that would attract this very thing.

☯ KARMA/ATTITUDE/HEALTH

This speaks either of a situation where one has to reach or catch sight of rock bottom in order to find out which way is 'up', or where one is learning how reliable or important appearances are or are not.

KEEP FOCUSED ON ... developing an inner peace and self-esteem ... how subjective the state of one's being actually is. What you have on the outside is nothing if you feel worthless on the inside. What you possess can be appreciated more in comparison to the conditions of those less well off ... the possibility that things might not be as they appear.

WATCH OUT FOR ... 'poverty consciousness', a species of victimhood that believes that a feeling or display of unworthiness is proof against harm or disappointment, when in fact it unerringly attracts it ... thinking that external self-neglect makes the inner person somehow more 'spiritual'.

'I was unhappy because I had no shoes. Then I saw someone who had no feet'

A LARGE CAMEL CROSSING THE DESERT

☆ STAYING POWER ☆

☀ GENERAL INTERPRETATION

What concerns one here distinguishes itself by its persistence and fortitude, which others may also rely on, even if there is the occasional grumble. Contending with adversity by drawing upon reserves of strength.

KEEP FOCUSED ON ... what it is in you or around you that can stay the course and reach the destination ... making a firm and lasting commitment to whatever is the object of your concern and then you'll win through or be able to say that you tried your very best ... the resourcefulness that gets you to where you have to get to, no matter what wildernesses may lie before you. Believe in this.

WATCH OUT FOR ... pointless hardship and the grumbling that it generates ... the straw that breaks the camel's back.

♡ LOVE/RELATING/SOCIAL

Although this could indicate a durable and longstanding relationship or social set-up, it does imply that it is something of a test of endurance too. It also suggests that it is going, or trying to get, somewhere, or it is just getting through a difficult patch.

KEEP FOCUSED ON ... the 'oases', that is, whatever it is that keeps you going, that justifies the loyalty and commitment ... the fact that you have what it takes to see things through if you really want to ... the fact that you have what it takes to go it alone, if needs be ... believing that you will find what you need when you need it ... being strong as opposed to hard ... doing without if need be.

WATCH OUT FOR ... putting up with emotional stress merely because you are able to. Only do this if there really is no other option open to you.

⚘ MONEY/WORK/CREATIVITY

Sometimes a hard slog or a thin patch is unavoidable when funds or ideas are in short supply. Such times teach us the worth of things and people, promoting a more realistic and economical view of matters.

KEEP FOCUSED ON ... the fact that no desert lasts forever – unless you are going around in circles! ... whatever reserves or alternatives you have, even if it takes some hard looking and thinking ... whatever it is that got you into difficult straits in the first place, so as not to get caught out again ... making any necessary cutbacks.

WATCH OUT FOR ... spending time, energy or resources until you can see an 'oasis' – that is, whatever input, finances and opportunities you have been waiting or looking for ... 'mirages' – that is, false hopes, pie-in-the-sky prospects or projects that won't last the distance.

☯ KARMA/ATTITUDE/HEALTH

Here is imaged a situation where endurance is a key factor. Health matters could relate to conserving body fluids or hanging on to them unnecessarily (water retention and bladder problems, symbolizing the hanging on to stale emotions or past attachments), or to the feet (treading the same old ground and getting nowhere).

KEEP FOCUSED ON ... life as a wilderness that has to be crossed – making you all the stronger, and the arrival all the sweeter (for instance, the lager scene in the classic war film *Ice Cold in Alex*.) ... making a virtue out of your commitment to reaching some far-off goal for this increases your resolve.

WATCH OUT FOR ... wasting energy and resources in the mistaken idea that the time and place you are living in should be a picnic, for this would only serve to exacerbate the difficulties.

'Human life is everywhere a state in which much is to be endured, and little to be enjoyed'

A RAINBOW

☆ THE COVENANT ☆

 GENERAL INTERPRETATION

Behold the guidance and the assurance of no harm coming to those who follow the good and pursue life's more enduring (spiritual) goals; those who have endured the storms of hardship and tests of faith. The Divine is not simply looking after us, it is ourselves as seen through the right medium and perspective as a rainbow is light manifest as the spectrum through water droplets.

KEEP FOCUSED ON ... your real sense of spiritual presence in your life, leading and encouraging yourself and others, forever on ... the possibility that this Symbol may be a sign or agreement or meaningful coincidence in itself.

WATCH OUT FOR ... blind dependence on fanciful or egotistical notions. Chasing rainbows.

 LOVE/RELATING/SOCIAL

This images a relationship or individual of great significance or promise. It is quite likely that you will have to bear storms – emotional and otherwise – in order to obtain such a realization. Furthermore, such wonderful things may be transient, leaving you with just a wonderful memory. Then again, if you ...

KEEP FOCUSED ON ... what is so colourful and wonderful, and hold it in your heart or mind's eye, then it could last and last – either in the mundane reality of whoever you are with, or as a memory to cherish forever or recall whenever you need to be reminded that there is something special about life, love and other beings.

WATCH OUT FOR ... romanticizing or making someone into more than they are or can be, for there is only one way they can go from there.

 MONEY/WORK/CREATIVITY

Any kind of work that is concerned with physics or metaphysics is favoured here. For instance, we could be looking at how physical phenomena interact, or how the colours of the spectrum esoterically represent dimensions of life (as in Colour Psychology). More generally, anything that reassures, guides or fills one with promise and wonder is auspicious. Financially, better times are ahead, or there will not be any more disasters.

KEEP FOCUSED ON ... making your idea, product or situation as colourful as possible, or a comprehensive 'range' of some kind ... any positive signs around you with regard to direction or approval.

WATCH OUT FOR ... flaky projects or people – given time they will be seen to fade into nothing.

KARMA/ATTITUDE/HEALTH

By living through crises we are treated to a sign that everything is worthwhile or is for a divine, far-flung purpose that escapes our understanding. At other times, out of the blue comes an occurrence or encounter that fills us with wonder or restores our faith.

KEEP FOCUSED ON ... the fact that the Divine is like a rainbow, for it is not physically there, depending entirely upon how you are looking at life ... maintaining that magical link between yourself and the sky of your sense of wonder and imagination, the link that is the Rainbow Bridge that connects Heaven and Earth, soul to personality.

WATCH OUT FOR ... thinking that one sign of divine or coincidental reassurance is going to apply to every situation from hereon in – as the Negro spiritual goes, 'God gave Noah the rainbow Sign,/No more water, the fire next time'.

'My heart leaps up when I behold/A rainbow in the sky./
So it was when my life began;/So it is now I am a man'

DAYBREAK

☆ NEW BEGINNINGS ☆

 GENERAL INTERPRETATION

You have before you one of those new beginnings that are perpetually and regularly offered to us in order that we might make a better life.

KEEP FOCUSED ON ... your healthy sense that life always offers us a clean slate if we are prepared to leave behind the 'night' of old habits and doubts, thus making way for a fresh approach, understanding or offering.

WATCH OUT FOR ... procrastination; always thinking in terms of what could be done tomorrow rather than actually doing it today ... hoping for the best without doing anything to ensure that the best, or anything good at all, happens.

 LOVE/RELATING/SOCIAL

Some kind of breakthrough is occurring in your love or social life. This could take the form of a new relationship or social scene, or something that has 'dawned' on you that puts a whole new complexion upon things. Then again, it could be a case of 'not letting the Sun go down on your wrath', that is, the Oracle is asking you to consider how you will feel tomorrow morning if you part or go to bed on bad terms.

KEEP FOCUSED ON ... how a relationship is the healthier and happier for appreciating that there is ever the possibility of renewing it through an awareness that there is always something new to be found in one another, and that we should ...

WATCH OUT FOR ... misguidedly fixing the other person in a rigid mould of one's own making.

 MONEY/WORK/CREATIVITY

Here is another day, fresh hope; here are new ideas and influences, chances and opportunities that endlessly come around like the rising Sun. Or the Oracle could be telling you that your dull or bad patch is bound to 'break'.

KEEP FOCUSED ON ... being up and about the business of living ... the truth of the saying, 'the early bird catches the worm' – the late one gets little or nothing at all ... making way for the light of a new day by letting go of stale or outmoded ideas, methods and products ... how things can look different in the morning.

WATCH OUT FOR ... the fact that a new beginning or idea will have to be more than just that if it is going to breed a positive result. The passing of the 'day' or 'tomorrow' might not find it quite so wonderful or promising. So, don't invest too much into anything until it has stood the test of time.

 KARMA/ATTITUDE/HEALTH

One of the most important things to remember is that there is always another morning, a dawning of new awareness. Even your whole life could be a new beginning. But there has to be a night before that new day, a period where one is in the dark, cannot see one's way, is frightened and insecure. This Symbol is reminding you of all this, but it is also saying that this night is about to end, or has already done so. Health-wise, you now have the chance to leave behind the bad habits or negative attitudes that have been bringing you low.

KEEP FOCUSED ON ... how 'hope springs eternal', but like a spring you need to go *to* it, drink *from* it.

WATCH OUT FOR ... allowing the 'darkness' or 'phantoms' of the night bedevil you; shake them off, rouse yourself, get up and leave them behind.

'Morning has broken'

MANY LITTLE BIRDS ON THE LIMB OF A LARGE TREE

☆ THE GREAT AND THE SMALL ☆

✸ GENERAL INTERPRETATION

A case of how the many are so often dependent upon the one – for support, nourishment and security. A natural and hierarchical system. Also, the point which the less developed parts of someone or something reach when they have to take off and develop.

KEEP FOCUSED ON ... what is the nature of your relationship to the greater whole that you are part of; this will tell you the best way of being a part of it or extricating yourself from it ... paying fine attention to the potentials in yourself and others; this will give you the necessary lift to make more of them.

WATCH OUT FOR ... being distracted with minor issues when a major one is at hand.

♡ LOVE/RELATING/SOCIAL

Here is a picture of the relatively weak being dependent upon the relatively strong. The strong person is the one who is stable and rooted, secure because of certain assets or resources. You could be the happy or unhappy being, either the 'strong' or the 'weak'. The strong can feel put upon or, simply, strong. The weak can feel safe and looked after or feeble and dependent. Whether you are weak or strong, you may need to ...

KEEP FOCUSED ON ... and maintain respect for whatever it is that is giving you support and security. In this way you can continue to grow or learn to 'fly'. This is a natural symbiotic system. We are supposed to 'use' one another, just so long as we do it with respect and gratitude.

WATCH OUT FOR ... thinking that dependency or co-dependency is always bad.

MONEY/WORK/CREATIVITY

The big fish/little fish set-up that characterizes the material world of commerce and ambition. Statistically, it is more likely that you are a little fish (or bird) rather than a big fish (or tree). This Symbol is emphasizing that you are up against a lot of competition as you try to find a foothold on whatever the large tree happens to be.

KEEP FOCUSED ON ... tailoring yourself or your idea to appeal to the large tree ... making your little bird stand out from the large tree in some way; this is like trying to get a website on the Internet noticed and used ... finding a middleman, agent or contact.

WATCH OUT FOR ... being put off by the competition, for this would put you out of the competition straight-away ... trying to fly when you are not yet ready.

☯ KARMA/ATTITUDE/HEALTH

Little Birds are symbolic of the early stages of liberation or of leading a spiritual life. The Large Tree is the family tree of humankind, its traditions, ancestors and roots. The limbs are branches that, like all religions, stem from one godhead, and then divide further and further in to sects and cults until eventually there is just the individual walking a unique path, flying solo for the first time.

KEEP FOCUSED ON ... what your spiritual tradition is for this will give you the support and direction needed for your solo flight ... progressively developing your own code and philosophy, based upon that tradition and your individual experience ... how the Spirit is supported by and given a means of expression through Nature ... finding God within you.

WATCH OUT FOR ... clinging to dogma and then mistaking it for devotion when really it is doubt.

'Pecking order is universal'

A MERMAID

☆ OTHERWORLDLINESS ☆

⊛ GENERAL INTERPRETATION

This Symbol poses a choice between being either dreamy, creative and fascinated, awash with disconcerting emotions, or dropping your 'tail' and getting down to the business of living in the real world.

KEEP FOCUSED ON ... an awareness and creative use of the powers of the imagination and of the unconscious realm ... being attuned to your soul-nature and its mission on the Earth-plane, for only in this way will you be able to keep your feet firmly planted on the ground while at the same time maintaining a sense of mystery.

WATCH OUT FOR ... getting nowhere by oscillating between being practical and mystical, or being neither for long enough ... being undone by fantasy, temptation or the abuse of intoxicants.

♡ LOVE/RELATING/SOCIAL

More likely than not, this Symbol is describing an unreal or fantasy-prone relationship or person. They may be real for some of the time, but it is quite hard to know when that is. This means that you are involved with an aspect of your unconscious that is demanding your attention through 'bewitching' you in some way. These 'sirens' are often characterized by a preoccupation with themselves (mermaids combing hair in mirrors) rather than with you. Of course, the 'mermaid' here may *be* you.

KEEP FOCUSED ON ... what your 'dream-lover' is about and look to see if the person in question is really like them. Then interpret what they are doing in your life in the same way that you'd interpret (a figure in) a dream.

WATCH OUT FOR ... falling in love with love.

⚒ MONEY/WORK/CREATIVITY

Here this Symbol's meaning is decidedly split, depending on whether your issue is related to business matters or is concerned with art and imagination. With respect to business, be very wary of anything on the table right now for it is probably not what it appears or promises to be; betrayal is a possibility. Creatively, you may be attuned to something quite spellbinding and appealing.

KEEP FOCUSED ON ... what is currently the issue for you. If you want straight facts, hard cash and a business head then be on your guard; if you want to inspire or be inspired, then jump right in.

WATCH OUT FOR ... anything that finds you not questioning; this is a sign that you are headed into danger.

☯ KARMA/ATTITUDE/HEALTH

On the one hand, here is a past or karma of succumbing to passion and temptation, of dreaming impossible dreams – literally drowning even. On the other hand, this could be a karma of having encountered rarefied creatures and explored mysterious places.

KEEP FOCUSED ON ... your otherworldly connections as an aid to viewing and understanding better the 'real world', bringing a beautiful mystery *to* it or of gaining a temporary respite *from* it ... being *in* the world even if you feel that you are not *of* it ... feelings about the sea, fish and swimming, for they could provide clues to your state of being ... being positively enigmatic.

WATCH OUT FOR ... health complaints that may be related to not being 'in your body' enough, or to a preoccupation with escapism or the irrelevant.

'I guess I don't know really who I am,/A struggling bard or a king from Iran,
But there's no one else I'd rather be,/I'd just like to be a better me'

AN UNSEALED LETTER

☆ TRUST OR NAIVETY ☆

GENERAL INTERPRETATION

An innate assumption that others will have respect for what is private even though it is accessible. This is all about trust, something that is so important in life, but takes some defining or knowing, because it can be easily confused with foolishly assuming that something or someone is all right. This Symbol could also be saying that your situation is an open secret – or would like to be.

KEEP FOCUSED ON ... appreciating and respecting in others those delicacies of personal life and being that they are prone and entitled to – and then you will be treated likewise ... looking into the truth of the matter rather than labouring under anxiety or an illusion.

WATCH OUT FOR ... naive openness, born of a lack of experience.

❤ LOVE/RELATING/SOCIAL

Trust is the issue here. On the face of it, it is saying that you or the person of interest are open and trusting, and are in line for an open and trusting relationship. The point is, do you trust this to be the case? Or do you suspect that some other agenda is going on.

KEEP FOCUSED ON ... coming right out with what you think and feel; then you will know the score or be the wiser ... being candid, for this shows you have nothing to hide, and can put others at their ease too.

WATCH OUT FOR ... being too open and getting taken advantage of; being too available does not attract love or respect ... not trusting because of being let down previously ... inviting being let down because of holding back emotionally.

MONEY/WORK/CREATIVITY

Something is waiting to be used, accessed, publicized, published, invented, released or expressed. What you want to find out – be it good or bad – is readily available.

KEEP FOCUSED ON ... introducing or maintaining a policy of openness and trust in your endeavours. This would promote better relations and efficiency or, creatively speaking, it would promote creative flow as each idea is expressed and worked through, honestly and vibrantly, making way for the next.

WATCH OUT FOR ... being reluctant to discover what is waiting to be made use of, perhaps for fear of it being something you might have to take responsibility for, or work harder at. This would be like closing off a house full of possibilities because you dared not enter the front door.

♄ KARMA/ATTITUDE/HEALTH

Nothing to hide or, at least, the intention of showing that you *have* nothing to hide. Such openness and honesty is very liberating, but it can often mean that you have to trust whoever it is you are disclosing to. The release of one secret reveals another. Or perhaps the secret is not so secret. The Symbol is saying that such information is now readily available, asking to be released. Health-wise, being open is usually good for you.

KEEP FOCUSED ON ... communicating whatever is inside of you ... trusting that all will be well as long as you keep trusting the process.

WATCH OUT FOR ... being indiscreet or open with *other* people's secrets ... difficulty with physically retaining or releasing (such as having a weak or inhibited bladder) as a sign of wanting or not feeling able to disclose something inside.

'With nothing to hide, you are free to express who you truly are'

THE SABIAN SYMBOLS OF
VIRGO

Either directly, or in a subtle way, all these Symbols are concerned with the following qualities,
or with situations that involve or call for them:

ANALYSIS

BEING EXACTLY WHO YOU ARE

DISCRIMINATION

DOUBTS

HEALTH

IMPROVEMENT

THE INNER OR ETERNAL FEMININE

INVIOLABILITY

METHOD/TECHNIQUE

NEGATIVE THINKING

PROBLEM MAKING/SOLVING

PURITY

SERVICE

WORK

A MAN'S HEAD

☆ THE IMPORTANCE OF IDENTITY ☆

✹ GENERAL INTERPRETATION

Identity, made consciously clear and asserted, is what this time or situation is about. Through time, experience and introspection, the image that you want to project is established.

KEEP FOCUSED ON ... developing and promoting an effective statement of yourself that is forever to be relied upon ... keeping your head.

WATCH OUT FOR ... vanity or vagueness concerning your image or place in the world – the former will not be taken seriously and the latter cannot be taken seriously ... living solely in your head; this might make sense to you for a while, but eventually you need to be in touch with your body and feelings if you wish to have happy and healthy relationships ... dominating others with your strengths while ignoring your weaknesses.

♥ LOVE/RELATING/SOCIAL

A relationship or person that forces or helps one to gain a stronger sense of one's own identity is what is imaged here. We can often get absorbed by or taken over by a personality stronger than our own.

KEEP FOCUSED ON ... what is unique about your own or another's personality, and strengthen and affirm it. This may be a subtle or indirect quality of being, but its strength lies in its actual presence, and an *awareness* of its presence.

WATCH OUT FOR ... thinking that obvious and outward displays of 'personality' are a testament to someone being strong through and through. Avoid being intimidated by such displays or feeling that you have to be like such people to be strong ... blaming another for being 'overbearing' when in effect they are challenging *you* to be stronger.

⚘ MONEY/WORK/CREATIVITY

That singular piece of advice to the writer 'Write what you know' applies to all walks of life. We are only any good at what we are best suited to. More often than not, we are trained, conditioned or forced into roles that do not have much to do with our natural capabilities. This Symbol is saying that it is critical that you do what you are personally cut out to do, or discover what that is.

KEEP FOCUSED ON ... what interests you most, and what you have enthusiasm for, and develop things from there ... obtaining training or education for your chosen field of endeavour ... finding or being the right person for the job.

WATCH OUT FOR ... being a square peg in a round hole – nothing but frustration will come from it.

☯ KARMA/ATTITUDE/HEALTH

Virgo is the Sign of Health and so, as with all Signs, the first degree makes an essential statement concerning its qualities. Here it is saying that being exactly what you are, no more and no less, is the key to health on all levels – spiritual, mental, emotional and physical.

KEEP FOCUSED ON ... what is essentially 'you', whether this is great or small, bright or plain, complex or simple, and express these traits to the full.

WATCH OUT FOR ... trying to be something that you are not for this will give rise to unnecessary strains or ineffectiveness. Two extreme examples of this would be a model damaging her back trying to lift a great weight, or a weightlifter losing face selling beauty products.

'I am that I am'

A LARGE WHITE CROSS UPRAISED

☆ THE UPHOLDING OF FAITH ☆

⊛ GENERAL INTERPRETATION

Overcoming doubts and withstanding the hardships of life with an inner faith that sees one through. At the same time, these beliefs need constantly purifying, being kept free of distorted or egotistic interpretations. Life is Eternal.

KEEP FOCUSED ON ... the essence of your soul that enables you to inspire, refresh and serve others through their hour of darkness – and your own too ... something sacred as a sign of protection against evil or negative forces; wearing or utilizing this.

WATCH OUT FOR ... negative beliefs that cause you to believe only what can be proved ... self-justifying piety and being opinionated for this repels rather than attracts ... mistakenly making suffering a way *of* God rather than seeing it as just a way *to* God.

♡ LOVE/RELATING/SOCIAL

Quite simply, the love and commitment that enables one to make a success of any personal relationship, social occasion or situation. Love and harmony are won through seeking the truth – the reason for being, or not being, with someone – and being prepared to suffer in the name of it.

KEEP FOCUSED ON ... what is essentially human in yourself and another, for here lies the key to human love and understanding ... the fact that suffering is as essential to love as pain is to relief, and that it denies the illusion of self-interest, thereby bringing forth the highest form of love – compassion.

WATCH OUT FOR ... judging another in any way, shape or form ... dogma or rigidity – they have no place in a healthy relationship or social set-up.

⚒ MONEY/WORK/CREATIVITY

The cross can be symbolic of the material realm, suggesting the process of establishing something, of raising the wherewithal to build or create. So, maintaining the faith to bring something to fruition or completion, to amount to something in the world.

KEEP FOCUSED ON ... your highest goals and principles, while making them abundantly clear to all and sundry ... the idea that anything is possible as long as you truly believe in it ... the furthest reaches of what concerns you, for these comprise the theatre for your endeavours; consider them all carefully with this in mind.

WATCH OUT FOR ... serving two masters – condemning certain forms of behaviour while capitalizing on them at the same time.

☉ KARMA/ATTITUDE/HEALTH

Making it abundantly clear what you stand for, and that you mean to make sure that there is no backsliding. Carrying a heavy load for a good reason. Everything ultimately rests on the 'anatomy of faith': the bones of reality and the flesh of vision.

KEEP FOCUSED ON ... what you know to be virtuous in yourself and others through observing what gives rise to whatever traits have a good and lasting effect ... keeping the faith.

WATCH OUT FOR ... your doubts becoming more than the healthy awareness that one can sometimes be wrong ... unnecessarily making a rod for your own back ... being weighed down by guilt ... adopting moral or psychological principles that you have not studied carefully, or arrived at through your own experience.

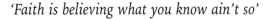

'Faith is believing what you know ain't so'

TWO ANGELS BRINGING PROTECTION

☆ TAKEN CARE OF ☆

✺ GENERAL INTERPRETATION

Take solace in the fact that there is here the absolute certainty of spiritual guardianship, which can either be seen metaphorically as a psychological assurance born of high morals and positive thinking, or literally as heavenly or discarnate entities that have the express intention of guiding and caring for physical life forms – human or otherwise. Indeed, both these ways of regarding 'angels' are valid – which is why there are two of them.

KEEP FOCUSED ON ... the idea that the more you extend yourself into the realms of trust and faith, the more you acquire trust and faith and inspire others with them.

WATCH OUT FOR ... a dogma or bias that is assumed to afford special privileges for the worthy, but in fact eventually undermines itself.

♥ LOVE/RELATING/SOCIAL

This may just be saying that the two of you are a couple who do very well in helping and supporting others. But before jumping to this conclusion it would be better to see this Symbol as telling you that you have 'help from on high', looking over and after your relationship or whatever relationship issue is concerning you. Do not worry, matters will work out all right. Then again, it could be a combination of these two possibilities.

KEEP FOCUSED ON ... calling on help and protection in your hour of need, and they will come to you, through simple, unlikely or mysterious means.

WATCH OUT FOR ... presuming on or disrespecting angelic protection by thinking you can overindulge, take liberties or be in any way arrogant.

⚕ MONEY/WORK/CREATIVITY

Whatever you are working on, or whatever your financial situation, it is being looked after by those 'upstairs' – whatever that might mean to you. Any work that is expressly about helping or healing others is very well starred.

KEEP FOCUSED ON ... practising what you are doing, or seeking what you want to do, in the knowledge and awareness that there is something or someone helping you and looking after you ... the positive feelings and good works that you feel prompted to promote, for this actively enlists continued assistance from 'upstairs' ... the Muse.

WATCH OUT FOR ... treating anything of a spiritual or divine nature as just another commercial twist or gimmick; this effectively disengages you from any connection to the spirit world.

☯ KARMA/ATTITUDE/HEALTH

As the doubling of an image in symbolism means that one is becoming consciously aware of whatever that image represents, this is saying that because you are now connecting with the existence of angels, they are now more able to help and protect you. They are not allowed to intrude upon one's life unless one allows them to by acknowledging their reality. Such divine protection is also at hand with regard to health matters.

KEEP FOCUSED ON ... the fact that whatever happens will be for the best as it is being watched over by beings, influences or agencies who, although outside normal physical perception, have your best interests at heart.

WATCH OUT FOR ... leaving *everything* to the angels to take care of. They too have finite energy and resources; all the same, they are definitely on your case.

'Talk of angels and you hear their wings'

A BLACK CHILD PLAYING WITH WHITE CHILDREN

✲ INTEGRATION ✲

☀ GENERAL INTERPRETATION

Occasioned or called for is the integration of minority with majority in the spirit of equality and brotherhood, while at the same time preserving the right to individuality. Discriminating non-discrimination – that is, integration based upon an appreciation of differences, rather than the mistaken insistence that there aren't any.

KEEP FOCUSED ON ... the human factor, first and foremost. Making someone feel at home or included ... your unselfconscious flair and enthusiasm for participating, or bringing others into participation, in a greater creative whole.

WATCH OUT FOR ... being unable to fit into environments different from your accustomed ones, or overcompensating for this inability with blind and mindless political correctness ... tokenism.

♡ LOVE/RELATING/SOCIAL

For a relationship to work each person has to accept the other for what they are. If you can accept everything about someone and the relationship, and about yourself and your part in it, then you are 'loving' rather than merely 'needing', 'wanting', 'missing', 'regretting' or 'putting up with'.

KEEP FOCUSED ON ... the both desirable and achievable objective, which is that through accepting and loving, everyone can be happy.

WATCH OUT FOR ... excluding anyone so that they feel unloved and threatened, as they are then likely to pose a threat ... any feelings or fears of rejection from childhood, for they are sure to find repeat performances later in life if left unattended to ... projecting what you dislike or disown about yourself onto anyone, making them into your *bête noire*.

⚜ MONEY/WORK/CREATIVITY

Successfully incorporating something or someone regarded as less powerful into something, ostensibly or materially, more powerful. Financially, this is going to be to everyone's advantage. Creatively, including what might have seemed not to belong, this is now seen as a good idea because it has depth and contrast, light and shade.

KEEP FOCUSED ON ... finding a place for anything or anyone that initially seems inferior, for this would be born of a distorted perspective ... seeing yourself as having the potential for success, even though prevailing trends are discouraging – such trends are changing.

WATCH OUT FOR ... any prejudices, racial or otherwise, in the workplace or in one's idea of what is marketable. Such erroneous conclusions can only undermine the whole.

☯ KARMA/ATTITUDE/HEALTH

You are now finding, or you need to find, that through accepting, loving, valuing and welcoming what you have regarded as a part of you that is unacceptable, unlovable, unattractive or unwelcome, that the world too will treat them this way. In terms of health, this refers to the importance of caring for all aspects of your being, not just the obviously valid ones; parts disliked could eventually manifest as a physical problem. (*See also* 'Self Talk', page 463.)

KEEP FOCUSED ON ... identifying what you do not like in yourself, and giving it a place in your life. It will then transform into something positive and powerful. When you first unblock a blocked pipe, all you get is dirty smelly water; let it run and it clears to fresh and clean.

WATCH OUT FOR ... leaving that 'pipe' blocked; there'll be no water (poor self-worth or health).

'We must learn to live together as brothers or perish together as fools'

A MAN DREAMING OF FAIRIES

☆ IN YOUR DREAMS ☆

❋ GENERAL INTERPRETATION

Being placed in Virgo, possibly the most logical of all the Signs, this Symbol is saying that despite the dominance of reason in our world, there is an equal and compensatory force that defies rather than deifies logic. The most fiercely logical type is still prone to fancy and fantasy – perhaps even more so. At present, you are being exposed to something that doesn't make sense, makes you ask 'Why?' but it is profoundly influential all the same. It is necessary for you to …

KEEP FOCUSED ON … sustaining your belief in a more magical realm of being that lends a sparkle and mysterious appeal to the everyday world and that attracts help and understanding … your inner world.

WATCH OUT FOR … self-delusion as a result of wishful thinking … rationalizing things away.

♥ LOVE/RELATING/SOCIAL

Is what seems to be happening actually happening? Will what you want to happen really happen? Nowhere are we more likely to fool ourselves than with romantic or sexual matters. Outer reality here is best seen as what everyone concerned agrees upon. Sexual fantasy is as valid as sexual reality, as long as one can tell the difference. Dreams can come true if you are true to your dreams, and understand what they are saying.

KEEP FOCUSED ON … simply asking the other if such-and-such is the case … the situation as if it was a dream, and then interpret it as such. Through relating to your reality in this way, you will connect with your true, inner reality.

WATCH OUT FOR … fooling yourself … disagreement or misunderstanding, for these are based on delusions, and vice versa … homophobia.

⚗ MONEY/WORK/CREATIVITY

The inner planes where the likes of dreams and fairies come from have long been known to produce creative and profitable ideas. They may be the source of them. Alternatively, this Symbol could be referring to some hard-to-fathom aspect of the market place, for it could be as mysterious as your dreams. Or again, your idea or product could be too personal or subjective for it to be successful in the outside world – unless your project is to do with your inner world.

KEEP FOCUSED ON … suspending inner criticism or dispelling external doubts long enough for something to take form in your imagination; *then* criticize, reject or modify it.

WATCH OUT FOR … letting your imagination get the better of you. Get someone in the know to put you straight.

☯ KARMA/ATTITUDE/HEALTH

When dreamy or mystical issues are looked at and experienced on their own terms, then great insights and ecstatic experiences can be achieved. In other words, one has to know the language of dreams and the esoteric in order to interpret what they truly mean and to get the best out of them. The alternative is reading what one wants into things and getting lumbered with distorted or dangerous versions of the reality in question.

KEEP FOCUSED ON … having your interpretation of the situation corroborated by another, impartial and disinterested party … any reputable psychological or metaphysical means of interpreting and comprehending the matter, preferably one that has stood the test of time … measuring any findings against how things pan out in physical reality.

WATCH OUT FOR … glamorous spiritual ideas.

'A dream not considered is like a letter from God left unopened'

A MERRY-GO-ROUND

☆ PROGRESS THROUGH REPETITION ☆

GENERAL INTERPRETATION

Indicated or recommended here is the enjoyment of the daily round. Another turn of the Wheel of Fortune or Karma, meaning that circumstances have changed or will change and you are advised to bear this in mind with respect to the object of your enquiry.

KEEP FOCUSED ON ... making full use of patterns set in time, and steadily and calmly you will achieve a happy outcome ... creating or maintaining any cycle that retains its original sense of health and rhythm, meaning and efficiency.

WATCH OUT FOR ... allowing one's life to devolve into dull and meaningless routine, or into a circuit of giddy-making indulgences that go nowhere. There is nothing wrong with non-violent perversions, other than that they do not lead anywhere except to boredom and frustration, and the need for a new perversion.

MONEY/WORK/CREATIVITY

'It is through repetition that we make the material our own,' says the *I Ching*. In other words, the creation of anything, be it money or a piece of art, depends upon a positive and rhythmic input of time and energy. Earth Herself produces Nature Herself through her daily round of night and day, and her yearly orbit of the Sun, the central generating station of all life and creative forces.

KEEP FOCUSED ON ... how it is only through gradual accumulation that the creation of anything significant is achieved – at least, in the context of your query and situation. Keep pitching.

WATCH OUT FOR ... getting stuck in a rut simply because it ensures security while all the time you feel unsatisfied and unfulfilled. It may be time to get off this not-so-merry-go-round.

♡ LOVE/RELATING/SOCIAL

Basically, you have a harmonious relationship or social life – or the prospect of one – and as such it'll probably right itself after any upset. If you know this is not the case, or do not feel quite sure that it is, then there are a number of ways of looking or dealing with it, so ...

KEEP FOCUSED ON ... the pattern of the relationship, love or social life so far. Is it stuck somewhere you are not happy with? If so, change it. Could you be happy with things just going on as they are? Do you get off the roundabout or enjoy the ride? Remember that looking at your situation positively will make it more enjoyable, and that a certain rhythm to a relationship is healthy, but may need developing.

WATCH OUT FOR ... allowing security and predictability to eclipse meaning and stimulation ... restlessness sabotaging a good relationship.

KARMA/ATTITUDE/HEALTH

We are all on the Wheel of Karma or Fortune. This means that by going through or over certain issues time and time again we can learn our lessons and create health and stability. Seeing life in this way is very positive, but we are inclined to succumb to the blur of activity/boredom that going round and round seems to induce. But if we ...

KEEP FOCUSED ON ... what exactly it is that life is presenting to you over and over again. You can either accept, change, or act on whatever this is ... regularly trying health regimens or treatments until you find the one that is effective.

WATCH OUT FOR ... going through the same old things over and over and just moaning about them rather than reading the writing on the wall. This is like falling asleep while watching a film of your own life.

'If at first you don't succeed, try, try, and try again'

A HAREM

☆ SUBJUGATION OR SECURITY ☆

✹ GENERAL INTERPRETATION

The question of whether or not an arrangement (possibly sexual) based upon a tradition or inclination is appropriate in the present time and circumstances. Sexual license that is biased, posing a need for equality and reformation. This could apply to any situation where there is a (male) dominance, such as between doctor and nurses.

KEEP FOCUSED ON ... understanding and therefore possessing the freedom that keeping to well-defined limits can bring ... the fact that being a part of something that limits you but may also further you at the same time.

WATCH OUT FOR ... self-betrayal resulting from a lack of respect for the value of oneself or another as an individual human being ... giving away one's power, or allowing it to be taken away. This applies to males too (eunuchs!).

♥ LOVE/RELATING/SOCIAL

The important but prickly issue of sexual balance of power is raised here. There can, for instance, be a trade-off between desires met and protection provided, between favours granted and gifts bestowed, or any other exchange of possession or power. This *can* be okay if all parties agree that it is.

KEEP FOCUSED ON ... arriving at a scrupulously fair and honest awareness, and an understanding or agreement as to who is giving what to whom ... creating mutual respect.

WATCH OUT FOR ... signs that someone, possibly yourself, is setting themselves up to be a (sexual) slave – something which might at first feel comfortable or exciting, or both. This could lead to being a prisoner of one's own weaknesses or appetites ... being abusively dominant or dominated ... compromising situations.

♆ MONEY/WORK/CREATIVITY

This could mean anything from having a captive audience to taking advantage of the lusts or limitations of others, or of institutions. Such a set-up could possibly be agreeable to all concerned. Being looked after by someone or something in return for your input, services or good deeds.

KEEP FOCUSED ON ... there being one person or body that is rightfully and agreeably in charge of operations or proceedings ... the creation and maintenance of mutual respect at all times ... playing ball with them only as they play ball with you.

WATCH OUT FOR ... one person wanting it all their own way without the others being willing to follow ... there being too many 'chiefs' as this would lead to chaos and collapse.

☯ KARMA/ATTITUDE/HEALTH

Memories or feelings of subjugating or subjugation – possibly but not exclusively in a sexual sense – are playing upon how you function, and what is happening to you now. There is also the esoteric idea that one may be, or is in the process of being, chosen from a number of others for a specific task by a superior spiritual force, depending upon one's talents and position.

KEEP FOCUSED ON ... ways in which you can re-empower yourself or whoever is in need of it or calling for it. This would necessitate someone having less of their own way, so a battle of wills might be unavoidable.

WATCH OUT FOR ... giving yourself over to any person or feeling that gives you absolutely no say in the matter. Always maintain your self-respect and free will ... complaints born of guilt, possibly of a sexual nature.

'It is a strange desire to seek power and to lose liberty'

FIRST DANCING INSTRUCTION

☆ TENTATIVE MOVES ☆

 GENERAL INTERPRETATION

The beginning of a process whereby the subtleties of life or the object of your concern are mastered. The give and take, knowing when to lead or follow; all in accord with the various patterns and rhythms that constitute the dance of life or your particular situation. A basic lesson is being learnt.

KEEP FOCUSED ON ... any natural disposition toward perfecting an art or ability to the point of being in total command of your chosen field of endeavour ... who is teaching; be prepared for someone who normally follows to take the lead if the activity is something they happen to be good at or naturally suited to.

WATCH OUT FOR ... giving up just because of the faltering first steps ... forgetting that you have only just begun to learn something.

♥ **LOVE/RELATING/SOCIAL**

In the early stages of relationships one is bound to make mistakes and this should be allowed for, otherwise you'll never get into step together. Such initial difficulties can also apply to one or both of you encountering an aspect of relating that is new to you. Again, it is vitally important to be mindful that one or both of you is learning something new. After the initial burst of enthusiasm it can come as a shock that you are awkward with one another in certain areas. No one said you had to get it all right straightaway. This applies particularly to sexual interplay.

KEEP FOCUSED ON ... the prospect of arriving at a point when you can do well together what at first was difficult ... getting into the swing of things.

WATCH OUT FOR ... overreacting when stepping on one another's toes.

 MONEY/WORK/CREATIVITY

You are involved with, or are contemplating, a job of work or business investment that you are not entirely familiar with, and so you are unsure as to how to proceed or whether to do it at all. The Symbol could also be referring to something that must have definite steps and a sense of rhythm, or that involves working closely with someone else.

KEEP FOCUSED ON ... taking your first steps cautiously, seeking professional advice if necessary ... first getting the feel of what you are doing or considering, and then following up with the technicalities, rather than the other way around.

WATCH OUT FOR ... there being a time factor that prevents you practising or researching; in such a case it may be best to decline or withdraw ... expecting too large a return too soon, as this would frustrate and distort your overall plan.

☯ **KARMA/ATTITUDE/HEALTH**

No one likes being told what to do. That is, unless they really appreciate that they need and want to learn something that will enable them to get into the flow and rhythm of life – thereby enjoying it more and putting a spring in their step. Or you may need to learn something in order to get back on track or into a better state of health.

KEEP FOCUSED ON ... being persistent and patient ... the joy of (one day) 'tripping the light fantastic', of being in step with yourself.

WATCH OUT FOR ... comparing yourself to others who are better at doing something than you; they have been doing it a lot longer ... the possibility that you may have to admit to not being naturally gifted with respect to the issue concerned; this does not mean that you cannot begin to develop skills that one day will make you at least proficient.

'Let's face the music and dance'

A MAN MAKING A FUTURIST DRAWING

✲ FORWARD VISION ✲

❄ GENERAL INTERPRETATION

A vision of the future is needed or being shown so that there is a feeling of things progressing somewhere. This is especially important if the current circumstances are difficult or intolerable.

KEEP FOCUSED ON ... a faith in the inevitability of achieving your goals through an ever-developing process whereby those goals are clarified and eventually realized ... drawing up all your options, then you will have a clearer idea of where you stand in the present moment.

WATCH OUT FOR ... endeavours that are unrealizable or that have so little relevance to the present moment that they can only dwindle to nothing or create confusion.

♡ LOVE/RELATING/SOCIAL

A relationship or individual of the future rather than the present, or having some goal or ideal to aim for within a present relationship. Alternatively, one half of a relationship could be traditional and opposed to change, making the other half acutely aware of how things must and will change. Unless one party gives in or a compromise is made, there is bound to be a parting of the ways.

KEEP FOCUSED ON ... where you *see* the relationship going, not so much where you *want* it to go – take your cue from this, relate to this. If you are in accord with that future vision, then well and good, but if you are not ...

WATCH OUT FOR ... pushing for what you want as this will probably elicit resistance from the other person(s) ... deadlock leading to 'bloody revolution'.

♛ MONEY/WORK/CREATIVITY

Apart from the literal case of an idea or product that is of the future, what is important here is an originality that springs from the urge to express the promptings of intuition and idealism, and that breaks away from traditional or conservative ways of doing or looking at things. This may involve making a clean sweep, but be careful not to throw the baby out with the bathwater.

KEEP FOCUSED ON ... projections or feasibility studies, but only those that have been carefully and creatively prepared ... what you are doing with a sense of what must and will *be*, rather than what you must *have*.

WATCH OUT FOR ... the possibility that what you are working on is just a prototype, not the finished article ... discarding traditional methods and values prematurely, or just because that is what they are.

♄ KARMA/ATTITUDE/HEALTH

What lies ahead, or rather how you experience it, depends almost entirely upon your attitude now. If you go into it with an anxious or fixed idea of what is to come, then the anxiety or inflexibility will colour what happens, or your perception of it. But if you go to meet the future in an open and humble frame of mind, then you make yourself available to the truth of what is unfolding. In other words, you are a part, but only a part, of the future in the making. One drop in a stream contributes to where that stream is flowing, but it cannot control its course completely.

KEEP FOCUSED ON ... having a positive vision of the future, despite or because of the past.

WATCH OUT FOR ... and avoid painting grim scenarios for yourself or anyone else – particularly with respect to health ... egotistical expectations.

'No fate but what you make'

TWO HEADS LOOKING OUT BEYOND THE SHADOWS

☆ TROUBLESHOOTING ☆

✹ GENERAL INTERPRETATION

Two heads are better than one. The advantage of two viewpoints is stereoscopic vision that enables you to gauge what and how far away anything is, thereby seeing beyond current problems and difficulties. Alternatively, the same can be achieved by utilizing a balance between logical and intuitive perception.

KEEP FOCUSED ON ... your ability to assess all the various elements of a situation and synthesize them into an efficient whole or enterprise, or a healthy and stable future ... the fact that there is a better time ahead, but you may have to rid yourself of any doubts about this.

WATCH OUT FOR ... hopelessness, indecisiveness and inertia resulting from trying to satisfy too many considerations or opinions at once, or trying to find an 'answer' when in fact you are going through an emotional process or experience.

♥ LOVE/RELATING/SOCIAL

This describes a relationship or social set-up that is generally positive because the fact that you are together enables you to help and support each other. Often we cannot see our way through a dark patch without the added perspective of someone else. This Symbol is saying that this 'someone' is very good at giving you a sense that things will be all right eventually, that there is light at the end of the tunnel, and that you have company in that tunnel. You also do the same for them.

KEEP FOCUSED ON ... the mutual benefit that you afford one another ... how as a team you are able to help and heal others who are in the dark or overcome by their own shadow.

WATCH OUT FOR ... being smug or aloof, for this could put you both in a shade all of your own.

♆ MONEY/WORK/CREATIVITY

If problem solving is your game, and it involves some kind of partnership, then the Oracle is smiling on your venture. It is also saying that an answer to any creative, financial or employment problems can be thrashed out by getting your heads together. Furthermore, it is a good idea to have more than one string to your bow – to have two or more lines of work, or two or more approaches to what is essentially the same goal or issue.

KEEP FOCUSED ON ... the fact that there is a solution waiting to be discovered as long as you look hard and long enough ... getting assistance from someone who specializes in sorting out your particular dilemma, such as a lawyer or accountant.

WATCH OUT FOR ... putting all your eggs in one basket ... making unilateral decisions ... going it alone.

☯ KARMA/ATTITUDE/HEALTH

The Oracle may be saying that we all have 'two heads', the thinking head (left brain) and the feeling head (right brain). Whatever stage of the game you are now at, it requires that you consider it from both of these perspectives. The Love/Relating/ Social section above may manifest as someone else being the left-brain to your right-brain, or vice versa. But in this context, it is more a case of attaining or using your own dual perspective. Health-wise, it is probably just saying that you should seek a second opinion before drawing any final conclusions.

KEEP FOCUSED ON ... the belief that all conflict and duality is essentially a trick of the light. Or rather, it is a trick of there not being *enough* light, in the sense of not wanting to see the better side of something or someone, or doubting that there will ever be an answer or an improvement.

WATCH OUT FOR ... mental deadlock.

'A problem shared is a problem halved'

A BOY MOULDED IN HIS MOTHER'S ASPIRATION FOR HIM

☆ CHICKEN AND EGG ☆

✸ GENERAL INTERPRETATION

Firstly, the soul chooses for itself the life conditions that are exactly suited to its purposes. Secondly, a mother (or father) usually has her own idea of what her offspring is going to be like and sets about making it become a living reality. Finally, and most significantly, these two forces influence and interact with one another. It should be born in mind how much a parent might mould a child of the opposite sex when they find they can no longer influence their mate, making them into mummy's nice/tame little boy or daddy's nice/tame little girl – or the opposite may happen when they react to this.

KEEP FOCUSED ON ... personal success as a result of being true to a predetermined blueprint of what you feel you are destined to be ... freeing oneself from negative parental influences.

WATCH OUT FOR ... unconscious obedience to someone else's values.

MONEY/WORK/CREATIVITY

Ultimately, the measure of one's success in the outer world is determined by the degree to which you are being yourself rather than the puppet or slave of someone or something else. This Symbol is also saying that any job that helps people to develop their individual potentials is a job worth doing.

KEEP FOCUSED ON ... whatever your 'childhood dream' was and check to see how much your career is related to that. If you cannot remember a childhood dream it is probably because it was nipped in the bud, and therefore you must rediscover it and revive it.

WATCH OUT FOR ... sacrificing your soul for a regular pay cheque or some other security trap ... trying to become something you are not, to fulfil a dream that belonged to your father or mother that they themselves failed to realize or became very successful in realizing.

♥ LOVE/RELATING/SOCIAL

The all too common practice of getting someone to fit one's idea of what is 'right' as a partner. The fact that so many people do try to fit their partner's idea of them is a testament to the deeper reasons for this phenomenon. To make this more complex, an individual who is unselfishly aware of another's potential is indeed often the 'making' of that person. The critical factor is whether one is being a slave or a protégé, a benevolent hand or a selfish one, and this is all about the presence or absence of choice. One must therefore be very honest and ...

KEEP FOCUSED ON ... whether or not you have enough independence in what you say or do when around your partner ... whether or not you grant your partner independence of thought and action.

WATCH OUT FOR ... any kind of coercion.

☯ KARMA/ATTITUDE/HEALTH

Down through the ages the more powerful human beings have subjugated less powerful ones, letting them be exactly and only what they want them to be. An extreme, but not uncommon, example from ancient times was the practice of rulers to have their entire household buried with them when they died, their only identity and purpose being that of servant to their master or mistress. Many of us are still affected by such past lives, giving rise to a fear of 'being oneself' as a unique individual, always needing someone else's yea or nay.

KEEP FOCUSED ON ... tracking down and expressing what you know and feel to be you and only you – even though it might take a long time.

WATCH OUT FOR ... not questioning the values and ideas of other people simply because they appear to be more powerful or developed than you do.

'A slavish bondage to parents cramps every faculty of the mind'

A BRIDE WITH HER VEIL SNATCHED AWAY

☆ THE TRUTH OF THE MATTER ☆

❂ GENERAL INTERPRETATION

As the veil is itself symbolic of the hymen (or 'maidenhead' as it was once graphically called), this Symbol is only too Virgoan. Looking at this further, it implies that the 'virginity' – that which is purely and exclusively that person – has to be seen to be believed. Any pretensions of being other than what and who one is are inevitably exposed. The real thing remains in all its pristine glory, or there is shame-faced embarrassment. Innocence – lost or proven. Where there is guilt, innocence is not.

KEEP FOCUSED ON ... a genuineness about you that cannot fail to stand all tests of time and at last achieve recognition and respect ... the possibility of being stripped down to who you really are.

WATCH OUT FOR ... false claims of honour being laid bare ... inviting exposure of mis-leading behaviour and what lies behind it.

🜨 MONEY/WORK/CREATIVITY

As you have or are about to have your true colours exposed, the genuineness of your work, or of your interest in it, is what is at stake here. Pretending to be something you are not could attract discomfort or ridicule, or eventual loss of position; living up to high standards will attract merit and reward. Similarly, financial dealings have been, are, or will be open to scrutiny. Any project that is expressly about laying bare the inner truth of anything is well-starred – but it could cut both ways.

KEEP FOCUSED ON ... on your works and motiv-ations, until you have a clear idea of their impeccability, or want of it. Then again, this will get done for you, one way or the other ... getting your books straight ... expressing what is closest and dearest to your heart – the real you.

WATCH OUT FOR ... fancying yourself to be, do or get something which you are not really cut out for.

♡ LOVE/RELATING/SOCIAL

The literal interpretation here – finding out that a partner is not as (pure as) one initially thought – may seem rather outmoded. But in fact it is all the more applicable now because we are bombarded with glamorous ideas of what a desirable or acceptable mate should be. So, when we begin to see their true colours, or have our own seen, disillusionment and discontent can loom.

KEEP FOCUSED ON ... the advantage of having laid bare one's illusions and superficial values, painful though this may be ... seeing if you yourself are genuine, that the real person is more truly loveable than the false impression.

WATCH OUT FOR ... reacting to the truth of who someone is, or rather to the shock of how they are compared to how you imagined they ought to be ... violating someone's space or self-respect.

☯ KARMA/ATTITUDE/HEALTH

This Symbol can be seen as representative of violation or rightful exposure. Either way, we are looking at a delicate matter – possibly because one party thinks the first case, and the other the second. Everything depends upon how we view the situation.

KEEP FOCUSED ON ... the fact of the matter, which is that no one should be intruded upon if they have not given permission, and that someone should only be exposed as a confirmation of something that has been established beyond reasonable doubt.

WATCH OUT FOR ... sitting in judgement on yourself or others, or presuming on what they deserve. 'Do not judge, or you too will be judged' or 'Why do you look at the speck of sawdust in your brother's eye and pay no attention to the plank in your own eye?' Leave karma itself to dole out karma.

'Every harlot was a virgin once'

A STRONG HAND SUPPLANTING POLITICAL HYSTERIA

☆ EMOTIONAL CONTROL ☆

✵ GENERAL INTERPRETATION

Here is, or needs to be found, the superior personality that intervenes in the affairs of their milieu, when direction or leaders are failing them, or when emotionalism or panic is in danger of taking over and being destructive.

KEEP FOCUSED ON ... dramatizing the real potentials around you, and championing the truths that they embody; you will then be able to transform confusion into vibrant energy and meaning ... the possibility that actual physical strength could remedy matters.

WATCH OUT FOR ... an excitable and volatile nature that creates more problems than it encounters ... resorting to brute force for this would ultimately make a bad situation worse ... knee-jerk reactions to anything or anyone that seems more powerful than you; you could regret it.

♥ LOVE/RELATING/SOCIAL

There is the distinct possibility of matters getting blown out of all proportion and creating the very situation that is feared. What is needed to forestall this is just one person who has enough power of personality to stem or diffuse this potentially harmful tide of emotion. This person is at hand, and it could be you. Whoever they are, they would need to ...

KEEP FOCUSED ON ... the underlying fear that is threatening to cause emotional or physical damage. Such a fear will most likely originate from a feeling of not being loved, and so the 'strong hand' will, if needs be, first have to control their own feelings of not being loved or understood, and then show love to the person(s) who is emotionally disturbed and disturbing.

WATCH OUT FOR ... merely suppressing emotions rather than controlling or expressing them.

♆ MONEY/WORK/CREATIVITY

Whether it is in your own work/financial situation or that of the world at large, there is an atmosphere of panic or unease that needs to be quelled, or is in the process of being so. It could be either or both, but it would be better to set about calming or restoring order to your own sphere first.

KEEP FOCUSED ON ... adopting and putting out a positive attitude and confidence-building message, which would mean having to identify the key trouble spots ... nipping negative influences in the bud ... any figure in professional or public life that may be the 'strong hand', and draw your confidence from them.

WATCH OUT FOR ... allowing panic or anxiety to generate the very disaster or strife you fear ... false promises from those in high places that are only a means of creating a bogus sense of calm and confidence.

☯ KARMA/ATTITUDE/HEALTH

Things have reached a pass where something or someone has taken, or has to take, matters in hand. If emotions or a state of health is allowed to go unchecked, there could be cause for regret. However, the Symbol seems to suggest that this is already under way or soon will be. All the same ...

KEEP FOCUSED ON ... containing potentially troublesome elements, be they internal or external, by gaining an awareness of their nature, what makes them tick, but most of all what their grievance is deep down ... employing a talent that appeals to others' better nature and their still centres ... intervening where weakness rules, or is in danger of doing so.

WATCH OUT FOR ... misuse of power and influence, and strong-arm tactics ... over-zealousness, for that could provoke trouble in itself ... letting your fears rule you ... giving in to blind emotional reactions.

'You're either part of the solution or you're part of the problem'

A FAMILY TREE

☆ BACKGROUND AND INHERITANCE ☆

❋ GENERAL INTERPRETATION

Your roots – be they biological or spiritual, real or adopted, are the issue or answer here. Family concerns. Many things are produced from one beginning. Making a family. A sense of belonging.

KEEP FOCUSED ON ... a deep inner feeling of a long-evolving quality which, by staying alive to it, you ultimately perfect a lasting expression of something truly worthwhile ... what it is that you have inherited that guides and supports you, and gives you the talents you possess ... establishing your origins, roots and birthright.

WATCH OUT FOR ... a misguided or deluded idea of lineage, or self-esteem claimed on account of name or appearance only ... depending too much on family for approval, for they may have an agenda that inhibits seeing who you are and what you've got ... rootlessness or denying your roots.

🛡 MONEY/WORK/CREATIVITY

If your business is a family one, then this can be a good or bad thing. In the general workplace, shaping the environment into a family-like structure, ethos and atmosphere is a good thing. Generally speaking, the object of your concern is as good as its roots or origins.

KEEP FOCUSED ON ... any and all growth and development so far, for this is a reliable indication of future progress ... what is growing well and cultivating it further ... pruning or cutting back, where and when necessary ... what has continuity, for that is healthy ... the fact that 'from little acorns, great oak trees grow' ... what are strong 'branches' and cultivating them.

WATCH OUT FOR ... what is not growing, or infecting what is; then cutting it out, root and branch.

♡ LOVE/RELATING/SOCIAL

Family relationships, and that somehow you have to do your best to make them work, only breaking away from them when every way and means has been exhausted. Or there could be an issue of how your family, or that of another, is affecting your relationships and social life. That they all integrate can be an issue here.

KEEP FOCUSED ON ... what is giving you the greater sense of *belonging*, and then give preference to this in terms of time and energy ... including each other in your family circles, for this would further mutual growth and support ... putting down and establishing common roots.

WATCH OUT FOR ... allowing any negative family or background issues – of your own or those you are involved with – from becoming so much a part of a relationship that they destroy it.

☯ KARMA/ATTITUDE/HEALTH

The continuation and furtherance of whatever has been previously set in motion, and the many ways in which it spreads and proliferates. Issues of family karma; attitudes that have been created by the family; healthy or dysfunctional families.

KEEP FOCUSED ON ... the better traits of your family and the 'good blood' in your line, and make the most of them ... past life issues that have positive and loving qualities. Regression techniques ... the idea that we are all one family.

WATCH OUT FOR ... 'the sins of the fathers' – or of mothers, uncles, aunts – because they could constitute a rot that it is up to you to stop ... prejudices or fixed ideas that are your family's rather than your own, for they are holding you back ... making fantasies out of 'past lives', while not seeing to very real past issues of concern.

'The family – that dear octopus from whose tentacles we never quite escape'

AN ORNAMENTAL HANDKERCHIEF

☆ FINENESS AND FINESSE ☆

✸ GENERAL INTERPRETATION

This is a Symbol of whatever is finest and most noble. In days of chivalry, a lady's 'bit of lace' acted as a mascot for her knight or champion that reminded him of what and who he was fighting for. So …

KEEP FOCUSED ON … what or who is worth fighting for … displaying or developing a sense of refinement, purity and rightness that will eventually attract an equally gracious response or compliment. Sense and sensibility … attending to the finer details or refinements of the object of your concern.

WATCH OUT FOR … entertaining an impossibly fastidious nature that attracts frustration, pretentiousness or nothing at all.

♥ LOVE/RELATING/SOCIAL

What has to be considered here is delicacy of feeling or, when carried too far, over-sensitivity. By the same token, any relationship that gravitates towards intimacy must sooner or later take into account finer feelings once the fun or passion has given way to the sentiments and aversions that are common to all.

KEEP FOCUSED ON … whether or not a sensitive person treats others sensitively, for only then can they be trusted with a closer intimacy … refinement, gallantry and reserve as being your guiding principles here.

WATCH OUT FOR … over-sensitivity born of pride or a superficial awareness of any given issue. Such contrary characteristics are best met with a minimal emotional response, an economy of words, and certainly nothing of a deeper nature for this will not and cannot be appreciated.

♆ MONEY/WORK/CREATIVITY

What you might lack in dynamism or confidence you make up for with precision and finesse. The quality of your work is everything here, and money has to take second place to the job satisfaction that you have to have, whether you know it or not. But then the Oracle is saying exactly that.

KEEP FOCUSED ON … attention to detail and those finer points that most others miss … maintaining that 'certain something' which sets you above and apart from others in similar fields to your own … what it is you believe in and are working so hard for, and you will win the day.

WATCH OUT FOR … not seeing the forest for the trees by allowing these finer points and details to blind you to the obvious … being too much of a specialist; step back occasionally and take a general, and possibly more conventional, view of the matter.

☯ KARMA/ATTITUDE/HEALTH

Here is imaged a genteel or finer point from the past that needs identifying and treating with care. What is it about the current situation that would benefit from such a memory or quality from the past, possibly from one's grandparents' days or before?

KEEP FOCUSED ON … what it is in life that is fine and gentle, for this is what must be preserved and upheld now. Finding the dignity and valour to do so … the 'feminine' qualities, such as forbearance, subtlety and soulfulness, of yourself and others, for they will enable you to see your way through current circumstances.

WATCH OUT FOR … affectations and trivia getting in the way of more profound concerns … being effete, precious or fussy, for these traits would fail you – particularly with regard to health matters.

'If a job is worth doing, it is worth doing well'

AN ORANG-UTAN

☆ WILD POWER ☆

 GENERAL INTERPRETATION

Animal wit and cunning combined with manual dexterity. Also, we have here humour, innocence and a combination of gentleness and great physical strength. An impressive package of raw abilities that is highly dependent upon there being a lack of agenda.

KEEP FOCUSED ON ... the lack of self-consciousness that results from your absorption in a given task or subject, enabling you to master it with ease and aplomb ... finding a fun aspect to the object of your concern or, failing that, to life in general ... educating natural potential so that it becomes useful and fulfilling.

WATCH OUT FOR ... resorting to childish tantrums, violence or boredom when a thing is not handled as easily as first imagined ... suppressing playfulness and spontaneous childlike behaviour ... bottling things up inside.

LOVE/RELATING/SOCIAL

What we have here psychologically are energies from the *id*, the primitive part of an individual's make-up that lies beneath the pleasure–pain principle. So we are talking about raw emotions such as desire, fear, rage and protectiveness, and what they can give rise to.

KEEP FOCUSED ON ... finding ways of expressing your deepest and most powerful feelings, or connecting with someone else's in a playful and harmless way; just admitting to them would be a good first step ... laughing at life or lightening up in order to de-stress the situation ... identifying and socializing any antisocial instincts.

WATCH OUT FOR ... repressing your deeper feelings, for they will either build up to explosion point, or find someone else expressing them against you ... emotional strength that is inhibited by feeling you have to 'behave properly'.

 MONEY/WORK/CREATIVITY

Taming raw energies, ideas and talents so that they amount to something substantial, composed and profitable. Being in touch with what appeals to people at a basic level.

KEEP FOCUSED ON ... developing or catering to anything in a direct fashion, such as providing the public with what they need right now ... being creative in a spontaneous, amusing and unconsciously driven way, such as in automatic writing, rather than contriving something; you can always refine raw material later, whereas being too critical first off wouldn't allow anything to get off the ground at all ... positive 'hand-to-mouth' living which is a trust that supply will eventually and always meet demand.

WATCH OUT FOR ... having good ideas, but being unable to communicate them or put them into an appreciable form. This can be down to having too much sophistication – or not enough of it.

KARMA/ATTITUDE/HEALTH

Whether or not one believes we are descended from apes, at some level of our being there is something both wild and powerful. The question arises as to how this force should be used or expressed. It gives us the raw drive to make ourselves felt in the world and to maintain our health through uninhibited physical and emotional expression. But these primitive instincts can also be destructive or compromising with regard to others or to our own more evolved qualities of character.

KEEP FOCUSED ON ... giving primitive urges a form of expression where it is appropriate, measured and controlled – such as wild sex with a willing partner, sports, drumming, dancing, and surviving in the wilderness.

WATCH OUT FOR ... problems associated with the inhibition of natural behaviour or expressiveness – such as, stuttering, sexual dysfunction, fearfulness, poor survival instincts, body neurosis and dirty habits.

'There's only one golden rule/Let outside what's inside of you'

A VOLCANO IN ERUPTION

✵ A NEED FOR EMOTIONAL RELEASE ✵

❄ GENERAL INTERPRETATION

The repressed feelings at the very core of one's being that every so often have to come to the surface – with force.

KEEP FOCUSED ON ... the urge to be true to your innermost self that will brook no interference or suppression from others, or for that matter, from your own inhibitions ... finding a way of releasing the tension while exercising maximum damage limitation.

WATCH OUT FOR ... destructive temper and meaningless bluster, unless it is in the presence of someone who recognizes the need for it and does not take it personally – if they do, it has something to do with their own inner tensions ... suppressing powerful feelings as this can prove harmful.

♡ LOVE/RELATING/SOCIAL

An explosive relationship, or an explosion that has just happened or is about to happen within a relationship. Such explosions occur when one or both people have kept a lot under for too long – possibly since before the relationship began. It is critical how you relate to the 'volcano' itself ...

KEEP FOCUSED ON ... allowing each other to blow their top until spent; then let it be without provoking further eruptions ... the original cause for the upset; if need be, seek professional help to release hard and entrenched feelings ... detecting any 'rumblings' in future, and tactfully confront, discuss and defuse them straightaway.

WATCH OUT FOR ... keeping any grievances to yourself, unless they subside naturally ... what first appears as intense passion; it could be a sign that trouble is not far behind.

MONEY/WORK/CREATIVITY

That your working life or place of work is in a state of turmoil could be seen as a dire situation or as a creatively stimulating one. If it is the former then you have to decide whether you can do anything to bring things under control or, if not, get as far away from it as possible. If it is a case of the latter, then this is fine as long as you can ride it without burning yourself out.

KEEP FOCUSED ON ... stabilizing whatever can be stabilized ... calming down your own reactions to the situation as you could be making a volcano out of a molehill ... harnessing the powerful energies that are abounding along a useful or creative channel.

WATCH OUT FOR ... the possibility that the strife and disruption around you has something to do with you and your own deep-seated problems.

☯ KARMA/ATTITUDE/HEALTH

This Symbol refers to anything from your past that is erupting into the present. This could manifest as strife in your home, health or any other area of your life. Unless you track down the roots of what is disturbing you, then this inner turmoil will continue to waste and disrupt your body or surrounding circumstances.

KEEP FOCUSED ON ... admitting to having inner or external turmoil, then finding ways of releasing it, such as talking it out with someone who you trust with your heavy or dark side, through artistic expression, or just living out your emotions in a healthy and honest relationship.

WATCH OUT FOR ... signs of suppressed emotion, like grief erupting as anger, irritability or health problems, such as skin complaints, toxicity, tension and chronic catarrh.

'And then more torrents of fire and shit/A feast of blaming and resentment/
Framed in Honesty's great expanding infinity/Accommodating all our dread'

AN OUIJA BOARD

✶ DANGEROUS DIVINATION ✶

❊ GENERAL INTERPRETATION

Without a sound anticipation of what shall be, or the correct divination of the inner meaning of things through the judicious interpretation of the information at one's disposal, there is a danger of making oneself vulnerable, suggestible and open to questionable ideas and destabilizing influences. This Symbol often questions the very way in which you are using *The Astrological Oracle* – or any other oracle.

KEEP FOCUSED ON ... your uncanny sense of the wisest course to take when you truly know what you want ... using common sense.

WATCH OUT FOR ... being intimidated by superstitions or being misguided by fancy ... being willing to take anything on board because of a reluctance to make up your own mind ... getting confused by asking again when you already have the answer.

♥ LOVE/RELATING/SOCIAL

The essential thing about using an ouija board is that it attracts any spirit that happens to be resonating with you emotionally – often down at the lower end of your emotional scale, such as lust, a need for excitement or false security, or wanting easy answers. Imaged here is someone who offers themselves to be trusted far too easily, promising more than they can or will eventually deliver, except if it's just plain trouble.

KEEP FOCUSED ON ... identifying that part of yourself that is attracting such offers – or making them for that matter – and *then* decide what to do.

WATCH OUT FOR ... what appears to be a chancy situation, and resist the temptation – finding a way of declining as gracefully as possible.

♛ MONEY/WORK/CREATIVITY

Your approach to the material or creative sphere of life is of the pot luck variety in that you are given to hunches and fancies rather than feasibility studies, professional advice or plain hard work. You are expecting luck to play a larger part in your enterprise than it actually will. Or the luck is more likely to be bad than good.

KEEP FOCUSED ON ... treading carefully and employing only the means or people that you trust personally from hard experience or that have good and reliable references ... checking the fine print ... creatively using your imagination rather than letting it get the better of you.

WATCH OUT FOR ... 'wing and a prayer' schemes that have an exciting but frothy, insubstantial feel about them – with people and prospects to match.

☯ KARMA/ATTITUDE/HEALTH

This refers to a hit-and-miss way of living that depends upon the undependable. It may also refer to anything or anyone that preys on those who live in such a fashion. The element of fascination, danger and unpredictability is a heady mixture that smacks of adventure, but it also presumes on more luck and ability than one may actually possess.

KEEP FOCUSED ON ... the more conservative, traditional or safe means of getting in touch with 'the other side' or dealing with any plane of being other than this one ... more than yes/no answers.

WATCH OUT FOR ... what it is in you, or someone else, that craves 'psychic excitement', for this is probably psychically unstable or damaged ... playing with psychic forces and having your scepticism or ennui blown away by stark terror or hard-to-manage occurrences ... so-called 'predictions'.

'Be careful what you wish for – you might just get it!'

A SWIMMING RACE

☆ EMOTIONAL EXERTION ☆

✸ GENERAL INTERPRETATION

Here is competitiveness, especially with regard to gaining a strong position emotionally, such as being the stronger half of a relationship, or feeling 'in the swim' socially and culturally. Until you have perfected your art or ability, you are bound to make mistakes, but you'll ultimately win through.

KEEP FOCUSED ON ... your desire and strength to plough on through any setbacks to achieving personal satisfaction and success ... any sense of pressure as being the stimulus to urge you onward, rather than as something that intimidates and weakens you ... relaxing into your stroke.

WATCH OUT FOR ... strenuous effort for little reward ... trying too hard, rather than relating correctly to the particular environment in which you are operating ... being tense, for this will inhibit or slow you down.

♥ LOVE/RELATING/SOCIAL

Attracting or being involved with people who want to see you succeed, or challenge you to do so. This can be quite arduous, but it is in aid of developing the 'wind and muscle' that enables you to relate better and be more resilient emotionally. It may also entail a competition for emotional attention or favours.

KEEP FOCUSED ON ... another as being a 'worthy opponent', that is, someone who brings out the best and the worst in you – the best to be realized and confirmed, the worst to be eliminated or accepted ... getting stronger, developing emotional stamina and awareness.

WATCH OUT FOR ... regarding another as being someone who is hostile; they are simply what life and your unconscious mind has put there to test your resolve and intention ... indulging in your weakness or distress.

♆ MONEY/WORK/CREATIVITY

Work and emotions are a vital but tricky mixture. We need passion and enthusiasm to perform our tasks and pursue our goals, but these very emotions can set us up, making us feel un-realistically pressured, even panicky. Also, this Symbol simply alludes to professional competition, and all that implies.

KEEP FOCUSED ON ... distinguishing an inner feeling from an external reality ... the rhythm and technique that is required to reach your goal ... how pressure improves performance ... the real nature and strength of your adversaries, rather than assuming that they are out to get you, sink you, or drown you ... keeping true to your aims or products, rather than being distracted by competitors and their tactics or lines.

WATCH OUT FOR ... predatory types (sharks) for these are just your own fears and desires coming back at you on a material level.

♁ KARMA/ATTITUDE/HEALTH

Imaged here is a feat of determination spread out over a period of time – possibly quite a long one and in a number of 'heats'. This may involve 'a race against time', or a natural or biological function, likes sperm racing to fertilize an egg.

KEEP FOCUSED ON ... doing whatever has to be done in a way that is technically effective and aesthetically pleasing, for the 'race' is really *through* time rather than against it ... the fact that the 'winner' is the one who successfully negotiates the currents of life at the times when it is called for, rather than always striving against the current ... being in flow with the quality and demands of the time ... just doing your best.

WATCH OUT FOR ... letting the pressure get to you, for that is precisely what will weaken you and undermine your chances of success, rob you of buoyancy.

'Es irrt der Mensch, so lang er strebt' (*Man will err, while yet he strives*)

AN AUTOMOBILE CARAVAN

☆ THE GYPSY SOUL ☆

 GENERAL INTERPRETATION

A modern and possibly acceptable way of being a nomad, or more generally speaking, a free spirit. Organizing things in such a way as to be ready to go out and meet the world, while having safety and privacy close at hand. This can attract meetings that normally would not occur.

KEEP FOCUSED ON ... your sense of practicality and adventure that makes for an effective creation of opportunity whenever it is needed or desired ... mobility as a species of safety ... what can attract significant chance meetings that would not normally have arisen ... the advisability of 'When in Rome do as the Romans do.'

WATCH OUT FOR ... a self-containment that is used merely to evade responsibility ... assuming airs and graces.

LOVE/RELATING/SOCIAL

Here we have a relationship whose security and meaning are gained and maintained by always seeking, being on the move. If just one person is into this sort of lifestyle then a parting of ways would seem inevitable. Then again, perhaps we are dealing with a person who is like this, who comes and goes where chance takes them.

KEEP FOCUSED ON ... keeping a balance between respective needs for privacy and security on the one hand (or in the one person) and for excitement and adventure on the other (or in the other person).

WATCH OUT FOR ... a sense of 'adventure' really being a reluctance to commit – unless the adventure is more important than, or intrinsic to, the relationship ... being too hard to pin down; one day that open road could be a very lonesome one.

 MONEY/WORK/CREATIVITY

You have the means of getting somewhere, and to sustain you and yours on the way there. Profit, advantage and opportunity are attained through going out to meet the world, while at the same time taking your own life essentials with you, allowing you a base of operations wherever you may be.

KEEP FOCUSED ON ... the fact that as you travel, you discover ... taking what you have to offer to the world, rather than expecting it to come to you ... uncertainty as being an adventure that will bring you, or force you to find, what you would not otherwise have discovered.

WATCH OUT FOR ... being so unreachable that it undermines your efforts to achieve, learn or accumulate the very things you are after.

KARMA/ATTITUDE/HEALTH

Keeping on the move, and the result of having been on the move, breeds a seasoned and philosophical world-view. This may be something you may be in need of, or something you have taken to excess. A 'rolling stone' gathering no moss can mean either that it does not accumulate much of any worth, or that it does not amass a baggage of negative or frustrated emotions.

KEEP FOCUSED ON ... whatever opportunities or talents you have that can bring the world to your doorstep, or vice versa ... getting around and getting to know the world and yourself, for this broadens and enriches your personality.

WATCH OUT FOR ... escapism posing as adventurousness ... taking off when the going gets tough; you could miss out on a really important adventure.

'A rolling stone gathers no moss'

A GIRLS' BASKETBALL TEAM

✫ EMOTIONAL CO-OPERATION ✫

❂ GENERAL INTERPRETATION

Group effort, with the accent upon being emotionally and intuitively attuned. The sense of solidarity and integration that this brings. The kind of interaction that is special between females. Girl power.

KEEP FOCUSED ON ... the success that you achieve through a precise awareness of your particular role in any co-operative venture ... the fact that female issues are 'in the ascendant', are receiving due and concerted attention from whatever the relevant quarter may be.

WATCH OUT FOR ... subscribing to the lowest common denominator of conformity; being limited by the weakest link in a chain ... being outnumbered by females or the female element, for this is just as undesirable as an overemphasis of masculinity ... being too competitive instead of co-operative.

♥ LOVE/RELATING/SOCIAL

Yours is a situation where the female element has the upper hand – or should have. This can mean that relationship issues hinge upon what the female or females concerned want and need, or it could stress the importance of compassion, tolerance and emotional understanding. It could also mean that whatever the situation, it is best to be 'actively passive', which means that you deliberately and consciously allow things to unfold as they will, without pushing.

KEEP FOCUSED ON ... the fact that there is an element involved in your social or romantic life that is organized within itself, and will develop naturally if you let it.

WATCH OUT FOR ... matters becoming *too* emotional – a loss of objectivity or a common goal could lead to chaos and hysteria.

♛ MONEY/WORK/CREATIVITY

Here is stressed the importance of female or emotional rights and solidarity in the workplace or professional arena. The Symbol implies that this is the issue, or is under way, but whether it is a 'good' or 'bad' team is another question – literally. Financially speaking, co-operation and the pooling of resources are essential.

KEEP FOCUSED ON ... anything that promotes the 'female cause' for this is favoured by the Oracle, both generally and with regard to the object of your enquiry in particular ... getting together with others, and in a fashion that operates on a personal rather than strictly professional level ... finding your team, because you cannot do it all on your own.

WATCH OUT FOR ... using feminist issues as a blind to being simply not up to the job ... misusing feminine wiles in the workplace, for this backfires and damages the female cause ... losing sight of the male role.

☯ KARMA/ATTITUDE/HEALTH

This Symbol is stressing the need for a greater emphasis on the female element in life, in terms of being in tune with Nature, Mother Earth, intuition and emotions, and generally being softer, more caring and tolerant. For the same reason, it is vital that women integrate with one another and operate more as a whole, and that men get in touch with their female sides. In order to do this it is important to ...

KEEP FOCUSED ON ... the essence of being female, and applying this to the situation at hand ... giving or seeking out sisterly assistance.

WATCH OUT FOR ... being too female, as in being too accepting, too passive and not asserting one's male energies, such as being pro-active and bold. Being 'too female' can manifest physically with hormonal problems, for hormones are chemicals in the body that must balance and co-operate as a team.

'I do not wish them (women) to have power over men; but over themselves'

A ROYAL COAT OF ARMS

☆ A MATTER OF HONOUR ☆

❂ GENERAL INTERPRETATION

The 'divine right of kings' or the eternal authority that issues from a long and carefully preserved line of values. Also, the stability and dignity that accompanies such a tradition.

KEEP FOCUSED ON ... how the way in which you embody a longstanding ideal can bring together others who work hard and make sacrifices to further that ideal ... how that ideal serves to reassure others in a world that lacks honour ... devising a picture or symbol, or composing a motto, that represents what you feel your life is about – and live up to it.

WATCH OUT FOR ... leaning on tradition and privilege to the point where it becomes not only meaningless, but makes one vulnerable ... being so 'honourable' that you are never allowed to be ordinary – merely human.

♡ LOVE/RELATING/SOCIAL

Honour and integrity are essential to a healthy relationship – especially now. You may have a relationship where these are present, or you wish they were, and that your own honour and integrity were recognized. In respect of all this, it could be a good idea to adhere to the motto of the Order of the Garter (the British royal family): *Honi soit qui mal y pense* (Evil to him who evil thinks). In other words ...

KEEP FOCUSED ON ... the idea that if anyone thinks ill of you for an undeserved reason, they will pay for it without your having to doing anything about it.

WATCH OUT FOR ... thinking ill of others as a blind to, or in defence of, one's own shortcomings, for such a ploy would only attract more difficulties later.

♔ MONEY/WORK/CREATIVITY

You need to ask yourself, does your 'product' match your 'advertisement'? This Symbol also means that honesty is now an issue regarding rights, royalties, agreements and such like.

KEEP FOCUSED ON ... conceiving an image that properly represents what you create, sell or promote; this will serve to guide and remind you and others of what you are doing or setting out to do.

WATCH OUT FOR ... false pretences or sharp practice, on your own or anyone else's part. Even though this may at first appear profitable or convenient, it will ultimately prove to be more of a loss than a profit.

♆ KARMA/ATTITUDE/HEALTH

Your fate or well-being is, or will be, as good as the esteem in which you are held by whatever or whoever truly matters to you, be that your conscience, your peers or a Higher Power. For example, you may expect preferential treatment as long as you feel you have earned it.

KEEP FOCUSED ON ... your past record of conduct or welfare, for this will act as a reliable indicator of what you may expect in the future ... what the nature of your 'bloodline' is, for this will tell you a great deal about your health, character and destiny ... whatever gives you a sense of belonging or tradition.

WATCH OUT FOR ... resting on your laurels, depending solely on what you or those before you have achieved and established.

'Truth is the cry of all, but the game of the few'

AN ANIMAL TRAINER

☆ A NEED TO TAME OR TRAIN ☆

⚙ GENERAL INTERPRETATION

Occasioned here are the raw power of Nature and base drives of human nature that must be brought under control and made good use of. Children or childish behaviour could also be seen as 'raw power', as are energies blocked in the past that eventually agitate to be released.

KEEP FOCUSED ON ... the balance that you need to strike between desire and restraint, between strength and justice, which enables you to promote and sustain progress in a healthy fashion. As every lion tamer knows, kindness succeeds where harshness fails. Being made to wait is often most effective.

WATCH OUT FOR ... using cruelty or brute force to deal with difficult situations or people, for this either makes things worse, destroys something good, or elicits an even more violent reaction.

♥ LOVE/RELATING/SOCIAL

Base desires and raw emotions are the very things that many relationships begin with or bring out in us, and they need restraining and properly expressing – otherwise they can inflict damage or prevent one from getting the very thing one wants. This Symbol could also be referring to someone whose primitive or anti-social instincts have to be handled.

KEEP FOCUSED ON ... taming wilder energies, be they in yourself or others ... these energies being 'animal' drives that can be handled quite simply. For example, good behaviour gets a reward, whereas bad behaviour doesn't.

WATCH OUT FOR ... suppressing raw emotions as opposed to processing and controlling them, expressing them in a safe or creative fashion, or through physical activities such as sex, sports and exercise.

♛ MONEY/WORK/CREATIVITY

You have the basic raw materials needed for performing your task or meeting a need. Alternatively, your work could or should be one of dealing with the wilder or untrained qualities in others. Both of these promise success, as long as you ...

KEEP FOCUSED ON ... the essential nature of your raw materials or subjects, thereby enabling you to fashion them into a better and more profitable expression of what they are, rather than turning them into what they are not – something which, being neither fish nor fowl, would fail in its purpose ... treating yourself and others kindly.

WATCH OUT FOR ... being limited merely to your own little arena of endeavour, that being the area where you feel that you are 'in control'. This could leave valuable potentials unrealized or let them break out in a manner that is dangerous.

☯ KARMA/ATTITUDE/HEALTH

Until certain raw or undeveloped traits of character in yourself or others have been refined or better expressed, then circumstances will remain as they are. The lower natures of those concerned are being tested and trained, and so they need to be confined. Such wild or unruly elements could also be expressing themselves on a physical level in the form of complaints which are based in unexpressed or unexamined drives such as anger, desire or the need to produce something.

KEEP FOCUSED ON ... telling yourself that you are, or can be, in charge of whatever elements are giving cause for concern. Potentially, at least, your mind can control and direct anything going on inside your body or life, but you do have to tame your ego and its fears to do so.

WATCH OUT FOR ... and deal with antisocial or unhealthy instincts in yourself before branding or caging others because of theirs; we all have them.

'Let him that hath understanding count the number of the beast: for it is the number of a man'

MARY AND HER WHITE LAMB

☆ PURITY OF INTENT ☆

 GENERAL INTERPRETATION

Here stressed is the inseparability of purity and innocence – 'and everywhere that Mary went the lamb was sure to go' – along with the importance of cherishing and maintaining such qualities wherever they are found. Purity is being all and only what one is, and innocence is something that is directed and guided by doing anything purely for its own sake, that is, without expectation.

KEEP FOCUSED ON ... your sure and unself-conscious sense of who you are that gives rise to highly appreciable creations, along with a modesty concerning them. As long as your intentions are pure, you get what is truly your due – even when no one else thinks it possible.

WATCH OUT FOR ... naive and empty posturing ... a tweeness that is annoying and ineffectual.

♥ **LOVE/RELATING/SOCIAL**

Here is a relationship or personality that is essentially innocent with all the childlike appeal and naivety that goes with it. In any event, there is a strong bond here because there is a soul connection, with all the highs and lows that this can entail. But there is no guarantee, simply because at the moment one or both of you may find such an unworldly connection not to their liking. To make the best of what is really quite special ...

KEEP FOCUSED ON ... cherishing the bond of innocence and purity that you have between you ... if you are alone, the innocence and purity you have as an individual, trusting that it will eventually attract a mate who mirrors and appreciates it.

WATCH OUT FOR ... being taken advantage of.

🏆 **MONEY/WORK/CREATIVITY**

Your course or fortunes concerning the object of your enquiry are highly dependent on whether or not what you are doing comes naturally to you, that you are simply being yourself rather than what the market, material needs or ambitions urge you to do.

KEEP FOCUSED ON ... what you are concerned with long enough to realize whether it comes easily or at least feels right. If it does not then abandon it, cutting your losses if necessary ... enjoying what you are doing for its own sake, rather than because you feel you have to.

WATCH OUT FOR ... feeling despondent, off-course, directionless or in the wrong place, for this would suggest that you are trying to be what you are not, or that your thinking was wrong concerning the issue at stake ... a naive or subjective approach when an informed and objective one is called for.

☯ **KARMA/ATTITUDE/HEALTH**

This is referring to what could be called The Soul's Own Course Through Life, that your personality could no more avoid or miss its destiny than there could be a mother (Mary) without there being a child (Lamb). It means that if you should ...

KEEP FOCUSED ON ... some goal that has the purest and fairest of motives; there is then nothing on Earth that can stop you from attaining it ... believing that you and your fate are inseparable, then your sense of being on course with yourself will increase in proportion to that belief.

WATCH OUT FOR ... cutting corners or using artificial means to attain your goal, for this would oppose or confuse the innate sense you have of who and what you are. Innocence and purity are paradoxical in that they are very powerful, but also easily overlooked in favour of something more glamorous, obvious or fashionable.

'He who departs from innocence, what does he come to?
Heaven's will and blessing do not go with his deeds'

A FLAG AT HALF MAST

☆ REVERENCE AND RESPECT ☆

⚙ GENERAL INTERPRETATION

At first this may seem a morbid symbol. It signifies the death of someone relatively important – originally at sea. However, the point is that respect is being shown for someone who has lived their life 'before the mast', which means to say that a positive reputation or outcome is earned through facing the sea of troubles that life consistently confronts us with. One could say that a sense of immortality remains, or at least a sense of poignancy.

KEEP FOCUSED ON ... your ability to accomplish far more than is usually expected because of your service to a higher cause than yourself ... the fact that something has passed out of existence, or is in the process of doing so.

WATCH OUT FOR ... a neurotic or overblown sense of one's victories, losses or anxieties.

♥ LOVE/RELATING/SOCIAL

You are in a relationship with someone where some loss might have occurred, or will occur. Alternatively, something has happened that requires mourning or reverence. It is not too morbid to say that one day you or the other person will be no more, and this inevitability should conjure up a rare and poignant emotion.

KEEP FOCUSED ON ... what you have the deepest respect for in each other and about your relationship; what you will cherish until death ... paying respects to whatever a dead or dying relationship means to you, and then getting on with your life, making way for a new relationship.

WATCH OUT FOR ... crying over spilt milk, nursing old wounds or hungering after times that no longer apply to your state of being or relationship.

🏆 MONEY/WORK/CREATIVITY

Probably a natural end of a certain line, activity or pursuit has been reached. Pay it your utmost respects and then move on to what now calls you to set sail once more. You may not quite know what is calling you until you have made that final goodbye to whatever has served its purpose.

KEEP FOCUSED ON ... whatever has young life in it ... regenerating anything that is close to you that is merely flagging rather than that has breathed its last ... whatever or whoever it is that you respect, would die for.

WATCH OUT FOR ... wasting time, energy and resources mourning over what is past its sell-by date, or, worse still, trying to breath new life into it.

☯ KARMA/ATTITUDE/HEALTH

Everything and everyone must pass away, be no longer in physical manifestation. One can take this, the most undeniable of facts, as a comfort or curse, as cause for gloom or celebration. In the end, though, the end will come. This could also mean the death of something in oneself.

KEEP FOCUSED ON ... whatever negative thing it is that you wish to see the back of, and you will. Let go of it ... the eternal nature of the soul; everything and everyone lives its life, and then goes on to a new manifestation when this one has done all it can in that form.

WATCH OUT FOR ... any attitude to death that regards it as unfair or unnatural, when patently it is not, although it may have a subtle reason that is beyond one's comprehension.

'Though lovers be lost, love shall not; and death shall have no dominion'

A BOY WITH A CENSER

☆ DISPELLING NEGATIVITY ☆

✸ GENERAL INTERPRETATION

Here is a time or need for the performance of something in a divine presence (or as if in one) that vanquishes any negative or demonic presence, for this is what is behind any difficulty.

KEEP FOCUSED ON ... your sense of self-dedication and service, which heralds and blesses everything that you do ... finding and using a means to purify any space or situation, such as smudging, exorcism or a banishing ritual.

WATCH OUT FOR ... sanctimoniousness, without any real sense of what the true issue or worth of a given thing is ... going through a ritual without any real sense of what it means ... being put off or out of touch with your true beliefs as a result of an alien doctrine or policy – possibly by way of a cen*sor* rather than a cen*ser*.

♥ LOVE/RELATING/SOCIAL

There is likely to be something that is spoiling an otherwise healthy relationship or social scenario. This could simply be a case of needing to clear the air after an argument, or a more serious and deep-seated emotional or psychic energy that is polluting a relationship, or the manner in which you actually relate. Such feelings as guilt, jealousy, resentment, lust and anger have to be identified and dispelled with innocence, understanding, forgiveness and refinement.

KEEP FOCUSED ON ... the positive values of your relationship and yourself; openly expressing them to one another and to yourself ... regarding your relationships as sacred ... psychically protecting you and yours ... making loving actions.

WATCH OUT FOR ... fretting and worrying for they can attract the very thing you fear.

♣ MONEY/WORK/CREATIVITY

There are problems to be ironed out, programs to be debugged and a positive working environment to be created or maintained. You have the people and methods on hand to perform these functions – or at least they are readily available if you look.

KEEP FOCUSED ON ... whatever you can do to improve quality, create a good and productive atmosphere, further moral welfare. This will go a long way to achieving success in the long run ... purifying your intentions. Making or clearing the way for something of importance ... redecorating or cleaning up the workspace ... approaching matters positively as this will attract the best results.

WATCH OUT FOR ... entertaining or introducing unpopular policies or techniques, for they have the potential to create widespread discontent and inefficiency.

☯ KARMA/ATTITUDE/HEALTH

Innocence in any situation has the power to dispel or keep at bay negative influences. Innocence is basically an absence of guilt or of a devious design or agenda. Left unchecked, negative qualities can eventually toxify the body as well as the mind, no matter what you eat or drink.

KEEP FOCUSED ON ... thinking the best you can of everyone and everything you come into contact with ... regularly and ritualistically cleansing the body and spaces you inhabit, the views you hold ... imbuing your life with the good, the true and the beautiful.

WATCH OUT FOR ... pretending to be pure when really you are being false, falsity being one of the most insidious pollutants of all ... an attitude of mind that is fussy or puritanical because of fear rather than principle.

'Yea, though I walk through the valley of the shadow of death, I will fear no evil'

GRANDE DAMES AT TEA

✫ NOBLESSE OBLIGE ✫

✸ GENERAL INTERPRETATION

Grace and privilege combine to give an aura of respectability, possibly coupled with a narrowness of outlook. But good works can spring from such cosy and exclusive gatherings or types of people, providing they are not out of touch with common emotions.

KEEP FOCUSED ON ... providing advantages to those less blessed than yourself, or being in a position to benefit from those who are more so ... the meaning of *noblesse oblige*, that rank imposes obligations, that wherever or whenever anyone is in a position that is awkward or wanting, it can be resolved by forbearance or generosity from those better off.

WATCH OUT FOR ... a complacent and indulgent ignorance of those worse off than yourself; for this can give rise to depression as the result of an unconscious impulse to put yourself in their shoes.

♥ LOVE/RELATING/SOCIAL

We see here a sedate or exclusive relationship or person, possibly one that is somewhat stiff or out of touch with ordinary life. The critical point is whether or not they promote or demand a finer understanding, means of expression or standard of living; in this way everyone benefits or is supported. Or a case of someone deigning to help another who is viewed as beneath them.

KEEP FOCUSED ON ... thinking kindly of others, even though they might be using you while you are trying to help ... how your good fortune or personal advantages and skills can benefit others, but without being condescending.

WATCH OUT FOR ... setting any kind of price on favours given, or looking on these as 'charity' ... gossip and character assassination ... complacency and indulgence.

♆ MONEY/WORK/CREATIVITY

Either you are in a position to be a patron to someone worthy of your support or investment, or you are the recipient of such patronage or investment. In either case, a measure of respect on both sides ensures a happy continuation and outcome.

KEEP FOCUSED ON ... pursuing whatever you are doing that has some nobility of purpose, for then it is bound to prosper eventually ... creating goodwill and a nicety of feeling.

WATCH OUT FOR ... abusing any kind of advantage, whether you are the one giving or receiving it. Ultimately, this can only create bad feeling and an all-round loss.

♇ KARMA/ATTITUDE/HEALTH

Some people have a more elevated or refined position than most, and such advantage may be used in several ways: an indulgent, wasteful or meaningless life, or one where those advantages are used to help those less well-off to prosper and evolve. Such refinement or patronage can be on a purely financial level, a social or spiritual one, or on a ritualistic one where forms of behaviour are handed down as a means of maintaining a certain type of order in life. This order might appear to have little or no meaning in the modern or material world, but it is actually symbolic of a more subtle and essential human reality.

KEEP FOCUSED ON ... practising whatever bestows meaning, furthers any cause or supports any individual – and all will be well.

WATCH OUT FOR ... falling prey to a sense of superiority, killing off a healthy social perspective.

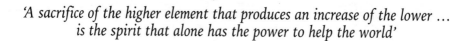

'A sacrifice of the higher element that produces an increase of the lower ...
is the spirit that alone has the power to help the world'

A BALD-HEADED MAN

☆ RESISTING THE FLOW ☆

GENERAL INTERPRETATION

Baldness is congenital, as the male hormone that causes it is active at the embryonic stage, possibly as an overreaction to an incipient surfeit of female energy. Fundamentally, male drive has to express itself in a way other than the showy or vain – baldness hides nothing – and express itself in a more honest and less egotistical way, that is a more direct and spiritual expression of male energy. But the inverse of this is usually the case, so this Symbol is depicting a need to control or predict events owing to a sense of personal inadequacy born of the mistaken idea that one had to be in control in the first place.

KEEP FOCUSED ON ... learning to allow and trust things to unfold as they will.

WATCH OUT FOR ... wearing oneself out trying to get things to go according to some 'plan'.

MONEY/WORK/CREATIVITY

Male energy, proactivity and assertiveness, are usually essential to getting somewhere in the material world. Although the overall interpretation of this Symbol is about unacknowledged female energy, passivity and adaptability, and overcompensating for it, in the dog-eat-dog world of business and commerce, it can be a different story. Unless you are happy and willing to 'wait and see', you'll need to ...

KEEP FOCUSED ON ... putting more energy and effort into being an effective and successful individual than others do ... pushing for what you want until you attain it ... not letting the current of events put you off.

WATCH OUT FOR ... giving up or tearing your hair out when the going gets rough ... pushing so hard that you overstep the mark, getting your timing wrong, or making more enemies than friends.

LOVE/RELATING/SOCIAL

An important aspect of relationships can be vanity based on personal appearance and virility. 'Resisting the Flow' could be expressed here as one's need to cover up what is believed to be insufficient or unattractive, with the result that awkward and embarrassing situations are attracted rather than avoided, or one lives in fear of them happening.

KEEP FOCUSED ON ... giving a frank portrayal of all that you are, think and feel, for this elicits a genuine and uncomplicated response from others ... the inner man (or woman) as being what is important; if this is not recognized and appreciated by you, it may not be so by anyone else.

WATCH OUT FOR ... fighting for advantages that are dubious in themselves ... denial of sensitivity.

KARMA/ATTITUDE/HEALTH

If you are male – bald or not – you have a strong female side that you may or may not understand or accept. Your female side can be felt as a powerlessness that seems to prevent you from getting what you want in life. This is because you are learning to accept things, and go with the flow of events and Nature. If you are female, it is saying that either you are attracted to this sort of man, or that you have a lot of male energy that has to find expression through being more proactive in the world, but then again, you too could be trying to 'push the river' rather than going with the flow.

KEEP FOCUSED ON ... going with the flow.

WATCH OUT FOR ... forcing issues as this will only increase frustration. Ask yourself why you are so desperate to 'make it'; you probably have what you need to proceed. Health-wise, problems arising from excess female energy (too yielding), or male energy (too aggressive), if you are overcompensating for one of them, which is the theme of this Symbol.

'You Don't Pull No Punches, But You Can't Push The River'

A MAN GAINING SECRET KNOWLEDGE FROM A PAPER HE IS READING

☆ INSIDE INFORMATION ☆

✵ GENERAL INTERPRETATION

This could indicate the coming into possession of hitherto unknown facts concerning the object of your enquiry. Such information or wisdom is often attained through accessing what many would regard as unavailable or inaccessible, and which they might be ignorant or fearful of. There are taboos concerning the gaining of a deeper awareness of life and of the ones who live with it.

KEEP FOCUSED ON ... your determination and ability to access those more significant, powerful and useful sources of information.

WATCH OUT FOR ... losing your place in the practical world in the pursuit of the arcane, irrelevant or fanciful ... information that others in the know may have about you.

♥ LOVE/RELATING/SOCIAL

You are involved, or have the prospect of being involved, in a relationship or with a person with access to emotional and psychological truths regarding yourself and regarding relating in general. This person could be you. This will take you to deeper and more profound levels of feeling and intimacy.

KEEP FOCUSED ON ... any means or device you have to find the truth of the matter ... being careful with confidential information, respecting it and not misusing or abusing it ... using the intimate details you possess only when you know it would further the interests of all involved, or you could get your fingers burnt.

WATCH OUT FOR ... being too suspicious, or finding out more than you can handle ... getting sucked into intrigues that you want no part of; make this clear as soon as possible.

♛ MONEY/WORK/CREATIVITY

Being in the business of researching or procuring information that is not available in the usual way is well-starred. However, this Symbol implies that such investigative facilities can just as easily be directed towards you and yours. So ...

KEEP FOCUSED ON ... anything or anyone in your sphere that might be vulnerable or questionable, for this could be a problem waiting to happen ... getting an informed and professional opinion, if you are in any doubt. This could apply to something like a feasibility study, a tax return, editing, professional credentials, private motivations or disinclinations ... the source of whatever you know to be historically reliable.

WATCH OUT FOR ... doing anything illegal; the spies are possibly being spied on ... overlooking the obvious as you delve too deep.

☯ KARMA/ATTITUDE/HEALTH

You are on the trail of discovering the deep reason or cause for something. This could be an aspect of your life or personality, or someone else's, or it could be the root of an illness that you are tracking down. It would be wise to forestall or not entertain any radical course of action until you are in possession of these facts. More generally, the clue you are after concerning the nature or cause of the object of your concern is either in your hands or not far off. This Symbol could also describe someone who is involved with the secret workings of things, such as a psychologist, occultist or astrologer – or using an oracle!

KEEP FOCUSED ON ... seeking and you shall find what you are after. The truth is out there or, rather, *in* there. Meditate (or learn to).

WATCH OUT FOR ... trying to 'audit' your life or that of another. It could get very unreal.

'The answer lies within'

A FALSE CALL UNHEARD IN ATTENTION TO IMMEDIATE SERVICE

☆ A SENSE OF PRIORITY ☆

🌑 GENERAL INTERPRETATION

Nothing will distract or defeat you now because, as long as you maintain an attitude of complete concentration or utter devotion. So …

KEEP FOCUSED ON … what has an immediate relevance to your situation – anything that is on your plate right now or the job in hand … your destiny, and you will be okay in every respect.

WATCH OUT FOR … jumping to involvements that have not yet arisen … wasting time and energy on side issues that are competing for your attention – your question to the Oracle may even be one of these! … single-mindedness that achieves what it sets out to do, but fails to see other issues mounting in importance to a point that they might seriously undermine your overall welfare.

♥ LOVE/RELATING/SOCIAL

You know what or who is most important to you right now – or you certainly ought to. This could also be referring to a one-girl-guy, one-guy-girl type of person, but only the test of time would prove this one way or the other. Alternatively, this being a Virgo Symbol, relationships may not be the priority. Have you or they got some other 'love' in their life, such as work?

KEEP FOCUSED ON … what duty tells you to do, rather than anything more romantic, sexual or volatile, or you will eventually regret it … what exactly you want and need from a relationship.

WATCH OUT FOR … any 'grass is greener' ideas sneaking into your own or someone else's mind; quite simply, it isn't … for anyone whose head is easily turned – it will be turned and turned again.

🏆 MONEY/WORK/CREATIVITY

There may be apparent avenues of opportunity or endeavour presenting themselves to you now, but you must be careful as to whether they are that real or wise to pursue. In other words, now is a time when it is very important to have a firm sense of what you are doing or intend to be and do, otherwise you could get confused and taken advantage of, or waste resources.

KEEP FOCUSED ON … the main chance … following your own star, no matter what advice more conventional voices might be offering you … what your duty is … what will most likely bring results, and make that a priority.

WATCH OUT FOR … looking over others' shoulders or thinking that you should be like them or do what they are doing … making excuses for not doing what you know in your heart of hearts you have to do … being blown off course.

☯ KARMA/ATTITUDE/HEALTH

One's fate or destiny is like the bull's eye of a target. One has to get it into one's sights, concentrate and hold steady. At present, you have a priority that calls you on towards your destiny, and so it is likely that lesser considerations or 'static' may intrude upon your consciousness, trying to deflect you from your path. Your karma might be that of someone who previously lost their way and so now has to keep to the straight and narrow more than most.

KEEP FOCUSED ON … determining what is central and essential to your life as a whole, and dedicate yourself primarily to that, letting all other matters either cleave to it, or dropping them … what matters and what doesn't matter health-wise.

WATCH OUT FOR … being *too* earnest, puritanical or perfectionist because this can create a rigidity that is a distraction or complaint in itself.

'Concentration is the secret of success'

♎

THE SABIAN SYMBOLS OF
LIBRA

Either directly, or in a subtle way, all these Symbols are concerned with the following qualities,
or with situations that involve or call for them:

AESTHETICS
♎
APPEARANCES
♎
BALANCE
♎
DEMOCRACY
♎
EVALUATION
♎
GRACE
♎
HARMONY
♎
INTEGRATION
♎
JUSTICE
♎
OTHERS
♎
PELVIS AND HIPS
♎
PLEASURE
♎
RELATIONSHIPS
♎
SOCIAL VALUES
♎
SOCIETY
♎

♎

A BUTTERFLY MADE PERFECT BY A DART THROUGH IT

☆ THERAPEUTIC PAIN ☆

✸ GENERAL INTERPRETATION

The beauty and significance of the spirit is being made effective and substantial through commitment to a task or relationship that unavoidably involves a degree of pain. But it is this pain that acts as a sharp reminder that one is caught up in a process of transformation and healing – much as a dentist's drill or hypodermic needle might hurt. When the Sun is on this degree it is the Autumnal Equinox, a perfect moment when night equals day.

KEEP FOCUSED ON ... a willingness to forsake the lesser in favour of something greater and this makes you acutely aware of the true significance of your state and being.

WATCH OUT FOR ... a vacillation between elusiveness and capture, between a fear of commitment and devotion, that amounts to nothing but meaningless pain and confusion.

♡ LOVE/RELATING/SOCIAL

You are involved in a highly important and significant state of feeling or relationship. The pain or vulnerability you feel is the very thing that connects you to the other person and thereby to your own heart. And in doing so, you and the other person are transformed.

KEEP FOCUSED ON ... any incident or experience that puts you more in touch with how you actually feel, as distinct from how you think you feel or think you ought to feel.

WATCH OUT FOR ... wallowing in pain while not allowing its meaning to fully penetrate ... not allowing another their pain and so their transformation, because of your own fear of pain and change, and a need to keep things 'just as they are'.

♆ MONEY/WORK/CREATIVITY

Unless you are totally committed to the process of achieving your ambitions, you are in danger of stagnating or being brought to a halt by a world that fails to appreciate what you have to offer or what you are trying to do. Financially, this could be referring to frozen assets.

KEEP FOCUSED ON ... enduring through the ups and downs of your enterprise ... capturing and preserving the essence of what you hold to be so important ... whatever hardships you encounter as being necessary to acquiring what ensures your further progress ... freeing up funds – you can't take it with you.

WATCH OUT FOR ... getting stuck in any situation that does not allow you to change or progress ... inertia brought on through not allowing something that wants to 'die' to do so, carrying around the 'corpse' of some outworn idea or practice.

☯ KARMA/ATTITUDE/HEALTH

This Symbol has enormous significance because it represents being pinned to the Wheel of Karma or Fortune as the spirit is thrust into the body and trapped in it, having to go through transformations that are the whole point of Earthly existence. It is also highly relevant to health, because through pain we are made aware of health conditions, and through the condition we can become aware of what change in lifestyle or outlook is necessary in order to overcome that complaint. A 'complaint' is so called because the body is *complaining* about the way we are expressing our spirit.

KEEP FOCUSED ON ... what pain is telling you. This means going *into* the pain rather than trying to avoid or suppress it. Pain is a messenger and so one must listen to it until you *know* what is causing the problem.

WATCH OUT FOR ... deadening the pain and halting the healing process. But avoid being masochistic.

'What does not kill me makes me stronger'

♎

THE LIGHT OF THE SIXTH RACE TRANSMUTED TO THE SEVENTH

✧ LONG-TERM VIEW ✧

✤ GENERAL INTERPRETATION

In esoteric teachings, the Sixth Race is the one that Humanity has ahead of it and which could be described as a global society with world government. The Seventh Race may be a society that has a galactic frame of reference. So this Symbol suggests that in order to make our next step forward, we should develop a sense of the step beyond that.

KEEP FOCUSED ON ... your imaginative sweep of vision, and upon your eagerness to fulfil its promise ... believing that everything will happen at its appointed time ... considering or making long-term plans, perhaps with a master plan in mind.

WATCH OUT FOR ... an otherworldliness, abstruse to the point of being no earthly use, or trying to fit in too much or plan too far ahead and finding yourself at 'sixes and sevens'.

♡ LOVE/RELATING/SOCIAL

This describes a relationship or a group that is quite advanced in terms of love and understanding, and is ever aspiring towards higher expressions of relatedness or teamwork, holding a 'new society' as its goal. There is a spiritual emphasis here. Alternatively, it is imaging a generation gap, or a rift in a longstanding relationship.

KEEP FOCUSED ON ... interests, considerations or visions that put the current situation into perspective ... visualizing what the greater future holds, or realizing that everything is so indeterminate there is no point in worrying about it unduly ... a sexual discipline such as you'd find in Tantra or Taoism.

WATCH OUT FOR ... you and the others being on different wavelengths, and that trying to find harmony and agreement can lead to the opposite. Beg to differ or minimize contact.

♉ MONEY/WORK/CREATIVITY

Your enterprise or material situation is invested in something far off, but you have to begin somewhere, otherwise it will never happen. This Symbol is also suggestive of the Internet in that a global society is being birthed by that global communication network. Any positive ventures of this nature are favoured.

KEEP FOCUSED ON ... the probability that, at first, ideals and distant goals will be your lot. You are building for the future ... the certainty of making it when you are convinced that with time you can achieve anything you wish ... time as being your instrument, and the inevitability of there being a better time ahead, though it may be far off.

WATCH OUT FOR ... being discouraged by a lack of immediate progress ... procrastinating, for this would be a negatively self-fulfilling prophecy ... hurrying things, for this would frustrate your aims, distort your plans.

☯ KARMA/ATTITUDE/HEALTH

This is like a piece of music that is felt to be the prelude to a change of key, leading up to another movement. Every player, especially the conductor, has to be aware of this, to feel it.

KEEP FOCUSED ON ... any major changes in your life that are imminent or have recently occurred, for they are signalling this change in your life's 'key' ... the 'conductor', or whatever it is in you or your life that directs and leads ... there being a need for con-certedness, and being mindful of the 'score' or karma regarding the situation ... taking a leap of faith ... any need for closure.

WATCH OUT FOR ... not completely moving with change as this would be like one part of the orchestra playing in one key and the other in another, creating dissonance. This would queer your pitch for some time into the future ... hanging back with the 'devil you know', being afraid of the unknown.

'A thousand mile journey begins with the first step'

♎

THE DAWN OF A NEW DAY, EVERYTHING CHANGED

✵ FRESH HORIZONS ✵

☀ GENERAL INTERPRETATION

After a 'night', either of rest or restlessness, the chance that one is able to see things in an entirely new light, and thereby go about the business of living with a renewed sense of what life is all about. Things that previously frightened us now seem ridiculous; shadows that we found threatening now recede into nothing, as they are dispersed by the light of day, the light of conscious awareness.

KEEP FOCUSED ON ... a self-perpetuating confidence created by the knowledge that each new day is yours alone to make of what you will – or for it to make of you what *it* will.

WATCH OUT FOR ... an inability or fearful reluctance to meet the unexpected and grasp the innate promise of life.

♡ LOVE/RELATING/SOCIAL

Your love or social life has been renewed, or is about to be. Someone is turning over a new leaf. Past relationships, or the past state of a current relationship, are seen as belonging to yesterday – making way for a whole new set and setting. Or a new relationship could be here or on its way, heralding a new type of love and social life altogether. Or, with the passing of some old order, a new and vibrant lifestyle and social scene is brought into being.

KEEP FOCUSED ON ... the present with an awareness of the promise of a bright future, possibly after having endured a time of confinement, aloneness or social vacuum.

WATCH OUT FOR ... taking exception to new feelings and traits, people and situations ... thinking that 'new' always means 'good' – it may just mean 'different'.

♛ MONEY/WORK/CREATIVITY

You are enjoying, or are about to enjoy, a renewal in your material affairs. This could be a new job or idea, a cash injection, or simply a new light in which to look at the financial or professional side of your life or of life in general. Then again, a constantly innovative style or improved method could be what is essential to your ongoing or coming success.

KEEP FOCUSED ON ... the fact that you are made to be forever revolutionizing and updating what you make or do ... seeing things in a new light, perhaps literally by waiting to see what the next day will bring ... finding pastures new when the present ones fail to nourish or inspire you.

WATCH OUT FOR ... resting on your laurels or letting the grass grow under your feet. The material or professional sphere you have chosen always needs to be self-renewing and innovative.

☯ KARMA/ATTITUDE/HEALTH

In ancient times people would wonder if the Sun would once again rise in the morning, and so they would do all manner of things to propitiate it. Now we know with virtual certainty that the Sun is bound to come round again, which is analogous to saying that life will go on, no matter what. All we need to do is ...

KEEP FOCUSED ON ... the fact that nothing needs be stagnant for long; it is natural for life to renew itself regularly ... thinking of life as being one constant round of renewals, especially with regard to issues of health and attitude ... some statement, prayer or meditation that is an affirmation that your life will steadily improve from now on with regard to whatever you wish.

WATCH OUT FOR ... leaving things undone today that should have been done yesterday ... hanging on to the past out of guilt, bloodymindedness or a sheer refusal to see that things have taken, or are about to take, a turn for the better.

'The ebbing tide of night gave place to the flood of daybreak and all creation rejoiced'

A GROUP AROUND A CAMPFIRE

COMMON CENTRE

GENERAL INTERPRETATION

The illumination and warmth that arises out of any familiar gathering, allowing individual members to express their true selves without judgement or restriction. Something or someone whose warmth and brightness attracts others or whatever is needed, like a beacon beckoning. This is usually made possible by having an elemental or burning issue that is relevant and familiar to all concerned. The importance of warmth and comradeship.

KEEP FOCUSED ON ... a real quality about you which gives heart and focus to any group or project you choose to apply yourself to ... the common ground or goal, and this will encourage and reassure all involved ... whatever provides warmth, light or centredness.

WATCH OUT FOR ... woolgathering or chewing the fat ... a vague sense of togetherness.

LOVE/RELATING/SOCIAL

Every relationship, be it between two or more people, requires a burning issue, warm feeling or illuminating belief that each person can refer to as a common centre and reason why there is this coming together. If you feel cold or left out, it is because you have yet to find that centre, or, more simply, love.

KEEP FOCUSED ON ... whatever it is that has meaning and significance for all concerned, and keeping this alive by feeding and respecting it – then all concerned will be happier ... discovering what and where your 'fire' or love is, then you will find your kindred spirits and lifestyle.

WATCH OUT FOR ... being averse to sharing what you have with others. Unless you show or seek out what has emotional meaning or social significance for you, you won't have anyone to share it with and keep it going and growing.

MONEY/WORK/CREATIVITY

Gathering your ideas, creations or co-workers around a central theme is what the Oracle blesses or suggests here, as are group efforts and get-togethers. Cash flow benefits from keeping irons in the fire.

KEEP FOCUSED ON ... whatever it is that inspires and encourages individuals to operate as one, and to discuss matters around an ideal that acts as a touchstone for all concerned ... making others aware of what you have to offer ... foraging for and fuelling your central and most important ideas and interests.

WATCH OUT FOR ... leaving any ideas, considerations or individuals 'out in the cold'. This could mean that it is not enough to come to an agreement or devise a plan that only involves what is already in front of you; you may have to look around and see what or who it is you have not included. That could be the reason why you have a problem or no success.

KARMA/ATTITUDE/HEALTH

The state of the 'central generating station' of your life and personality is the issue here. This can be your heart, spirit, passion or anything that burns within you, that is centrally important to you. This 'fire' is like any other fire in that it has to be tended and not left to go out or substituted with an artificial version of it. Psychological and physical health depends upon this fire more than anything else, so it is vitally important that you ...

KEEP FOCUSED ON ... what it actually is for you that makes you feel warm, positive and purposeful, in touch with the pulse of life and the creative process ... where you are in relationship to your 'fire' and how you are expressing it.

WATCH OUT FOR ... any fear or reluctance to express your inner self, suppressing or replacing it with drugs or drink, or living it out vicariously. These are like depriving a fire of air, with deleterious effect upon your health and vitality.

'Kokorokoo' (African 'Call of Togetherness')

♎︎

A MAN TEACHING THE TRUE INNER KNOWLEDGE

✵ KNOW THYSELF ✵

✷ GENERAL INTERPRETATION

You are finding out that only through personal experience and a connection with the core and root of your very being, can real awareness and intelligence be found, thereby inspiring and guiding one's fellow creatures.

KEEP FOCUSED ON ... your natural sense of what resonates within you as being relevant and harmonious – and helpful to others ... who or what is now teaching you something of importance, and learn their lessons for they will serve you better than anything else you might be studying.

WATCH OUT FOR ... intellectual pretension, the real intention of which is merely to impress and dominate.

♥ LOVE/RELATING/SOCIAL

Unless it refers to a literal teacher–student relationship, the Oracle is showing you here that you are in a learning–teaching relationship through which you learn life's lessons most intimately. Going to a school or teacher is one thing, where there are clearly defined roles, but in a relationship such as this you are showing and learning how you really work as a personality, especially on an emotional level. Furthermore, it is often not clear who is doing the teaching and who is doing the learning. Perhaps it would be wise to ...

KEEP FOCUSED ON ... being open to teaching *and* learning with humility as the predominant attitude to such a situation ... the fact that this relationship will definitely cause you to grow.

WATCH OUT FOR ... preaching or lecturing.

♟ MONEY/WORK/CREATIVITY

Your work is involved with imparting self-knowledge or philosophical wisdom in some way, or it ought to be. Or you need to gain a deeper insight into your field of interest. The Oracle is saying that you are close to this source of important information, and as you draw from it you must pass it on. Such knowledge is priceless in one respect, but you still have to put a price on it because our society is deeply materialistic.

KEEP FOCUSED ON ... teaching what you have found most valuable ... keeping things as simple as possible, but without dumbing down so much that there ceases to be any point.

WATCH OUT FOR ... trying to teach what you do not yet fully know or follow. This will either find you embarrassingly over-stretched, or what you say or do to be irrelevant.

☯ KARMA/ATTITUDE/HEALTH

The answer to your question already exists within you, or is something that can be channelled via yourself. Life on Earth is, despite what anybody might tell you, a place of learning, and the ultimate lesson is finding out who you are. You are being given the opportunity to find out more about yourself and your inner workings and truth. It has been said that all knowledge is stored within the cells of our bodies, especially our bones. This is why we can learn a great deal about ourselves through listening to our body, be it healthy or not.

KEEP FOCUSED ON ... the voice, within or without, literal or metaphorical, and listen to what it says. This voice is also the one that can convey wisdom through your own mouth or other senses ... what you feel in your bones.

WATCH OUT FOR ... thinking that there is only one 'answer', or that any one person has it.

'The further one travels, the less one knows'

THE IDEALS OF A MAN ABUNDANTLY CRYSTALLIZED

☆ ENERGY FOLLOWS THOUGHT ☆

 GENERAL INTERPRETATION

What we want – be it worthy or sheer fantasy, comes back to us as reality and experience. So the more clear, accurate and appropriate our vision of a better life is, then the more likely it is to be fulfilled.

KEEP FOCUSED ON ... building and working out with your imagination what you ideally want or want to be (something the British in WWII called 'imagineering', an expression coined to encourage resourcefulness and inventiveness) and then discovering and developing the very best that you can be, and what you are supposed to be ... making your question to the Oracle very clear – so its response will be.

WATCH OUT FOR ... frustration and failure through expecting too much or too little, or resisting any expectation at all for fear of failure.

 MONEY/WORK/CREATIVITY

This refers to aspiration as opposed to ambition, to vocation rather than mere occupation. Material reward has to take second place to making your ideals and vision of a better world a reality. Keep in mind that the world's greatest problem is being motivated mainly by the need or greed for money. Your ideals are in the process of being made real – or if not, they need to be.

KEEP FOCUSED ON ... any labour of love that you have or have in mind, for ultimately that is the only way you will find satisfaction and purpose ... continuing to pursue any ideal you have been endeavouring to realize; when the right time and conditions arrive, then your ideal will become a reality.

WATCH OUT FOR ... sticking with pointless quests or impossible projects that have been proved to be so by the test of time.

LOVE/RELATING/SOCIAL

A person or relationship that fits your ideal – or holds you as being the ideal. The wish for, or prospect, of this.

KEEP FOCUSED ON ... what exactly it is you want in a relationship, and if it has any measure of reality (that is, it is something you truly deserve, need or have in your heart), then it shall happen.

WATCH OUT FOR ... making someone or something fit your ideal when they are far from it ... pretending that you want someone merely because they want you ... getting stuck in a relationship because you have no vision of how to improve it or of having something better than it ... anyone (including yourself) who is too set in their ways or who is frozen emotionally ... what you wish for, because it may well happen!

KARMA/ATTITUDE/HEALTH

Your thoughts create the world you inhabit. Evolution, in human terms, is all Humanity's thoughts put into motion, making them real and relatively long-lasting. Clarity comes with vision and foresight; vision and foresight come with clarity.

KEEP FOCUSED ON ... nurturing and fashioning your ideals or most positive thought-forms; they are the promise the future holds, not just for you, but possibly for many ... where your heart wants to go; this poses the question of what is in your heart ... visualizing the cells of a healthy body.

WATCH OUT FOR ... holding ideals that are not realizable, are just hot air, for they will elicit derision from others and breed frustration in yourself ... fixed ideas, for they could give rise to complaints of rigidity or bloating ... negative thoughts for they will create negative situations.

'Follow the path that has heart, for in that way your treasure lies'

A WOMAN FEEDING CHICKENS AND PROTECTING THEM FROM HAWKS

☆ FOOD AND SHELTER ☆

✴ GENERAL INTERPRETATION

The nurturing and protection of the weak and defenceless, and the compassionate and courageous principles or instincts that give rise to this.

KEEP FOCUSED ON ... your wholesome sense of what being human is all about, along with the example set to others by the healthy values inherent in this sense ... the possibility that your situation (or the Oracle itself) is feeding you in some way, or protecting you from something without you knowing it, or knowing what it is protecting you from.

WATCH OUT FOR ... holding a one-sided or naive view of life that misses the point that there is a predatory streak in nearly everyone and everything ... being so over-protective/protected that you, or those in your care, can't handle the slings and arrows of life on their own.

♥ LOVE/RELATING/SOCIAL

Here is a relationship or person that is highly encouraging, supportive and protective. There is a feeding of whatever needs feeding, especially on an emotional level, but it could also be a case of being given material assistance. On the face of it, this is a very positive situation, or promises to be one.

KEEP FOCUSED ON ... gladly giving or receiving the support and security that is required or offered ... the fact that someone needs caring for and protecting.

WATCH OUT FOR ... using what you give to another as an emotional lever or means of control, or, conversely, falling into this 'bird in a gilded cage' trap. Such an arrangement may work for a time, but it is inherently divisive as it undermines mutual respect ... over-protectiveness, for this conceals a weakness of one's own.

MONEY/WORK/CREATIVITY

Any kind of work or activity that involves giving or getting a form of nourishment or security is well-starred here. Then again, the 'chickens' could refer to people, projects, resources or investments in your care, that have to be regularly and constantly attended to or worked upon.

KEEP FOCUSED ON ... maintaining your interests and all will be well, barring the occasional and inevitable attack from some aggressive quarter. Everything depends on how watchful and resourceful you are. Getting and accepting professional assistance is a good, possibly essential, course of action ... becoming strong enough to fend for yourself; paradoxically, it could be the 'hawk' in you that is best at this.

WATCH OUT FOR ... vulnerable or under-capitalized areas of business or financial interests; leaving them open to attack, especially from 'hawkish' elements.

☯ KARMA/ATTITUDE/HEALTH

Health will benefit from a pure and regular diet, and from prevention through protection (physical or psychic) against harmful elements. Karmically, there is the necessity and duty of protecting and caring for something or someone, or a number of others.

KEEP FOCUSED ON ... making a priority of your designated or chosen role as provider/protector; in this way you will not only do it well, but also avoid wearing yourself out because of a resistance to it (possibly unconscious). Such a role carries considerable spiritual 'brownie points', but avoid making this your motivation ... allowing yourself to be helped if such is freely given.

WATCH OUT FOR ... stress and strain being occupational hazards when it comes to giving care ... being too solicitous and not allowing others to help themselves as a blind to admitting to your own helplessness.

'And the strong shall protect the weak'

A BLAZING FIREPLACE IN A DESERTED HOME

☆ WELCOME WHERE NEEDED ☆

⊛ GENERAL INTERPRETATION

The force of life that illuminates and warms us, whether we are aware of it or not. The generosity and comfort that are implicit in life. Being with someone in spirit if not in the flesh.

KEEP FOCUSED ON ... keeping one's spirits up at all costs, even though there may not appear to be any point. Ask the Oracle for help here if need be ... creating or maintaining a disposition that is ever ready to warm and reassure others ... what your supply is (what you have to offer) and set about finding who or what is in need of it.

WATCH OUT FOR ... wasteful and indiscriminate, if well-meaning, activity.

♡ LOVE/RELATING/SOCIAL

You do your very best to welcome others into your private world, but something still seems to be missing, seems to go awry. Even when you have on offer all the best that money can buy and that your heart can give, it still doesn't seem enough.

KEEP FOCUSED ON ... the fact that one thing which truly satisfies is allowing significant others into your most vulnerable and unsure spaces, instead of paying so much attention to theirs.

WATCH OUT FOR ... lavishing affection and attention on anyone who does not appreciate them. This could be reflecting the fact that you do not appreciate yourself enough and feel you have to give more than you should in order to be loved back, or you want to stop them from seeing parts you think are unlovable ... throwing yourself away on anyone who does not love you for what you are.

MONEY/WORK/CREATIVITY

The warmth and creativity you possess are not being made the best of or attracting what you deserve. This could be because you are not aware of this.

KEEP FOCUSED ON ... what it is about you that is not technically essential to the job, but sets you apart from others of similar occupations. There is a spiritual or emotional factor that you need to identify or make more of, such as bringing warmth and reassurance to your customers and co-workers ... putting your heart into your job, for this is what is needed ... matching the supply to the demand.

WATCH OUT FOR ... the possibility that your job does not provide scope for your more enterprising and energetic qualities ... putting in more energy than you get back ... wasting your talents on those who do not fully appreciate them.

☯ KARMA/ATTITUDE/HEALTH

This images wasted energy or being ever hospitable, despite it all – it could be hard to decide which it is. Having to be deliberately creative rather than being able to fall back on your usual routine or traditional roles. For example, women who cannot have children must find some more conscious creative outlet.

KEEP FOCUSED ON ... what it is that consistently 'burns' hot inside you, but as yet has no 'audience' or 'customers'. Recognize that you are going to have to let people into your space in order to validate and encourage what you have to offer or, initially, just get the measure of it.

WATCH OUT FOR ... hiding your light under a bushel, and the frustration that is caused by wanting to be seen and not wanting to be seen at the same time. Trust your inner fire or spirit to burn on, to attract what makes sense of it all.

'Keep the Home-fires burning,/While your hearts are yearning,
Though your lads are far away/They dream of Home'

♎

THREE OLD MASTERS HANGING IN AN ART GALLERY

☆ A QUESTION OF VALUE ☆

✦ GENERAL INTERPRETATION

The number three should be taken as whatever it means to you personally, but it can be seen to represent the threefold nature of personality: physical, emotional and mental. So, we could understand this Symbol to mean a highly evolved expression of these aspects of personality. Furthermore, they are paraded in an appropriate and optimum place, such as presenting the right thing at the right time to the right person. An important point is that the value of the object of your concern is entirely intrinsic or relative to what is important to you as a person.

KEEP FOCUSED ON ... what you *feel* to be of worth, as distinct from thinking something has worth because you have somehow been led to believe it has ... acquiring suitable insurance.

WATCH OUT FOR ... an unhealthy reverence for what was once worthy of respect, but which is now simply outmoded.

♡ LOVE/RELATING/SOCIAL

Great care and love are present in this relationship or person – or at least, if you wish the relationship to last, great care and love must be bestowed on it. Perhaps there is an issue of taste or preference here.

KEEP FOCUSED ON ... what truly has value for you with regard to your relationship, or your own or someone else's nature ... creating and maintaining your relationship as being utterly original, something entire unto itself, comparing it to nothing else.

WATCH OUT FOR ... resting on your laurels by just expecting a relationship or the people involved to thrive or get by on past merits and performance ... depending too much on appearances and culturally ingrained ideas of what a 'valid relationship' is supposed to be.

MONEY/WORK/CREATIVITY

Your work is of high, even classic, quality; it may have a value that cannot readily be assessed in ordinary terms. You have great assets, but whether you realize them or let them increase in value could be the question.

KEEP FOCUSED ON ... recognizing that your standards and performance are high, and primarily aesthetic, with the view to preserving them but not being too precious or neurotic about them ... the probability that your business and its practice have a long and esteemed tradition that is something you can naturally draw on ... keeping your 'act' clean and polished.

WATCH OUT FOR ... the possibility that how you value something might be entirely different to how someone else does; this might be an issue that needs clarifying before going forward, otherwise a conflict of interests could sabotage things ... letting matters 'gather dust' in any way.

✪ KARMA/ATTITUDE/HEALTH

Living is an art. This Symbol can be seen as a 'trilogy of lifetimes', which is a way of grasping the meaning of the most important of them – the present one – bearing in mind that a 'lifetime' could also be regarded as any period within this lifetime. For example, paint a picture or get an impression of what you were in your previous two 'lifetimes', or, of what you were 'last', what you want or are likely to be 'next', and what you are in this one. Health is fundamentally sound, but must be carefully maintained and protected, especially if age is an issue.

KEEP FOCUSED ON ... what has gone before as in the images of ancestors that are portrayed in places with an established history ... each lifetime as being a testament to having done your very best ... living a healthy life physically (diet and exercise), emotionally (being in tune with feelings) and mentally (study and work).

WATCH OUT FOR ... neglecting your past.

'To know your most stable and positive self, identify the three best things about yourself'

A CANOE APPROACHING SAFETY THROUGH DANGEROUS WATERS

☆ CLIFFHANGER ☆

✸ GENERAL INTERPRETATION

This Symbol is obviously saying that you are almost in the clear – *almost*. A classic Libran case of keeping your balance under stress. Your situation may involve the acceptance of risk as a means to salvation.

KEEP FOCUSED ON ... your salvation, or whatever it is you are after, as it is in sight ... being prepared to brave emotional conflicts and storms ... not losing your cool, keeping your eye on the ball; then you are bound eventually to reach that state of harmony and security.

WATCH OUT FOR ... courage bordering on the foolhardy, or any reckless act ... leaving too much to chance ... panicking – don't rock the boat.

♥ LOVE/RELATING/SOCIAL

Hang on in there! The turbulent or frustrating time that you are going through will take you to a more peaceful and harmonious place. It is also likely that this was the only way to reach a realization or understanding.

KEEP FOCUSED ON ... keeping 'upright' or righting yourself as you go. It doesn't matter that you get a bit hurt, look a fool or get emotionally overwhelmed; the important thing is that you will come through feeling far more at ease with your relationship(s).

WATCH OUT FOR ... complicating or jeopardizing matters unnecessarily – your situation is precarious enough as it is ... making the emotional waters choppier than they are by over-reacting.

♟ MONEY/WORK/CREATIVITY

Your troubles will soon be over, but they are not over yet. There are still a number of issues, visible or not, that could catch you out. You have got this far and you are still afloat (if a bit wet!), so ...

KEEP FOCUSED ON ... carrying on as you have been doing, for such assiduousness and conscientiousness will take you the distance ... dealing with each obstacle as it comes, and once negotiated leave it behind, freeing your strength and attention for the next one. It won't be long now.

WATCH OUT FOR ... those not so obvious snags that may be still around, but don't allow yourself to be spooked. You are supposed to make it.

☯ KARMA/ATTITUDE/HEALTH

At last, after a length of time struggling with adversity, there is an end in sight. Highly welcome and positive as this Symbol is, it must be born in mind that you are only *approaching* safety, so ...

KEEP FOCUSED ON ... the situation as it is, rather than as it looks as if it soon will be. You could still capsize if you relax your grip or attention at this final stage ... developing or maintaining emotional self-reliance for negotiating life's difficulties ... staying the course of any kind of health treatment you are undergoing ... using the current of events to carry you along; using minimal effort to stay upright and on course.

WATCH OUT FOR ... any temptations to take it easy until you are absolutely sure you are in the clear, home and dry.

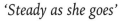

'Steady as she goes'

♎

A PROFESSOR PEERING OVER HIS GLASSES

☆ THE FAVOUR OF AUTHORITY ☆

✦ GENERAL INTERPRETATION

This image has a strong implication of the greater mind, or of one who has a measure of authority, condescending to look up from what he or she is doing to see to the needs or questions of the lesser mind or of one under that authority. There is not necessarily any haughtiness or better person/lesser person here, because the seniority is well-established. Indeed, seen here is a benign and tactful way of conveying such authority.

KEEP FOCUSED ON ... closing your eyes and looking upwards (without moving your head). This increases alpha activity in the brain, which effectively shifts one from rational to intuitive thinking and perception.

WATCH OUT FOR ... academic superciliousness or intellectual snobbery; this can stop one from seeing clearly, especially on an emotional level.

♥ LOVE/RELATING/SOCIAL

If one person is felt to have the intellectual authority, then the other probably has the emotional authority. It is possible, but unlikely, that one person has both. The issue here is one of expressing or accepting this authority with grace, and not feeling put out by it.

KEEP FOCUSED ON ... the fact that, despite what you might think, you feel this authority in you or over you ... taking responsibility for how you express it if you are the one who has it ... recognizing and benefiting from the weight of influence that another has over you.

WATCH OUT FOR ... feeling dominated or intimidated by anyone, for this is a sign that it is your own sense of inferiority that is the problem, not their perceived sense of superiority ... overlooking feelings in favour of logic, for such dryness fails to relate to others properly.

MONEY/WORK/CREATIVITY

The issues of how one thinks and perceives, and of how one exercises or responds to authority are essential to the success or nature of your current occupational or financial concerns. Recognizing who or what really has the authority is the first important step. Finding favour with it or exercising it is the next.

KEEP FOCUSED ON ... every so often looking up or taking a break from what you are doing – perhaps to hear what someone else has to say – and then you will see more and be better equipped for the job ... the disciplined specialization in your chosen subject, for this will lead to honour and respect.

WATCH OUT FOR ... being distracted by anything or anyone that does not merit your attention ... thinking that everything you do has to 'make sense' or has a 'right or wrong' answer; it may be more a case of just doing what pleases or feels right.

☯ KARMA/ATTITUDE/HEALTH

This images a necessary shift in one's perception and thinking. This may apply to a health issue or simply to the way you interpret what the Oracle is telling you. It could also refer to the authority of Fate itself, which could be saying, 'You can have/do such-and-such when or if I say you can.'

KEEP FOCUSED ON ... the object of your enquiry, and the Oracle's reply to it, with an intuitive rather than a logical eye, with lateral rather than literal thinking ... that there is something or someone that gives the 'yea or nay' to what you can and cannot do or have in life, and that respecting this is the first step towards finding favour with it.

WATCH OUT FOR ... not seeing the trees for the forest – what is actually happening by insisting on only seeing what you want to happen or think ought to happen.

'True authority can pause from itself'

MINERS EMERGING FROM A MINE

☆ FROM DARKNESS INTO LIGHT ☆

✪ GENERAL INTERPRETATION

After much labouring and feeling about in the dark, things at last come out into the open and you can see what it was all about, what the lie of the land is.

KEEP FOCUSED ON ... how events will reveal what the score is ... the prospect of relief or celebration resulting from the hard-won extraction of what is priceless from what is deep, dark and dangerous.

WATCH OUT FOR ... trying to gain something ahead of its time ... escaping into superficiality in a bid to avoid your deeper feelings and responsibilities ... staying stuck down in your darker thoughts and spaces when it is time to come out into the light of day.

♥ LOVE/RELATING/SOCIAL

A relationship or person that only offers up its best through delving into its deepest and darkest recesses. The strong sense of camaraderie that is born of such trials and intimacy. Matters clearing up after a crisis or misunderstanding.

KEEP FOCUSED ON ... surfacing all issues concerning yourself, or between one person and another ... drawing one another out with love and acceptance, and not being judgemental.

WATCH OUT FOR ... how you could be unconsciously bringing your own shadows and personal issues into the world outside and then wondering why other people appear murky ... feeling alone and misunderstood because you are buried in your own self-pity and your feelings of being cut off.

♟ MONEY/WORK/CREATIVITY

Coming out of the woods financially or something you have been working at behind the scenes now begins to bring results – or soon will. There may be the suggestion of the aversion of disaster here, or a lesson concerning it.

KEEP FOCUSED ON ... bringing to the surface what you have worked so hard on. This could mean that you sense something of great value 'down there' and must employ whatever means available to access, process or express it ... ensuring that safety and security measures are properly installed and observed.

WATCH OUT FOR ... depressing, hard or dirty work for little reward. You may have to 'down tools' or make some sort of stand rather than put up with such a dire situation any longer.

☯ KARMA/ATTITUDE/HEALTH

It is by coming through dark and difficult times that we find our own true power and transform from something lesser into something greater. Such an occasion is here or is approaching. The benefits of depth psychology or any kind of deep therapy.

KEEP FOCUSED ON ... the light and whatever is 'above' you. The natural direction is one of emerging from being buried or trapped into a state where everything is above-board, where there is no need for being covert or suspicious and there is the possibility of reunion with others ... coming clean.

WATCH OUT FOR ... missing the opportunity to be open and free, because you have grown 'accustomed to the dark', it suits you to be an 'unknown'. This would be a retrograde step, like cutting off your nose to spite your face.

'The trust comes with the dirt, depth and darkness'

CHILDREN BLOWING SOAP BUBBLES

✫ A SENSE OF WONDER ✫

⚙ GENERAL INTERPRETATION

A time or situation that offers or calls for a simple and innocent fascination with those little things in life that are an engaging combination of Nature's wonders and human ingenuity. This is not really a time for earnest consideration or practical endeavour, but to dream dreams that could in time become the inspiration for something more substantial.

KEEP FOCUSED ON ... connecting with your childlike imagination and spontaneous playfulness; this is a delight and relief, to yourself and others, from the mundanity of life ... the 'rainbow effect' or magical qualities of whatever or whoever concerns you.

WATCH OUT FOR ... unremitting or inappropriate fantasizing ... expecting anything firm or predictable in the near future.

♡ LOVE/RELATING/SOCIAL

This is strongly indicative of a relationship or person that may be gentle, childlike or enchanting, but lacks in substance and reliability. If that person is you, then you may or may not be inclined to admit it. If you do not want your bubble rudely burst ...

KEEP FOCUSED ON ... the advice and opinions of those who are more practical and grounded than you and who you can genuinely trust with your delicate and romantic emotions ... protecting the vulnerability and innocence of your inner child, or someone else's, or of an actual child, who could indeed be seen as a dream made flesh.

WATCH OUT FOR ... bursting another's bubble too readily; if you are that close it could make you cry too ... the fact that your fantasies will encounter reality just as a bubble collapses when it touches the earth.

🏆 MONEY/WORK/CREATIVITY

Creatively speaking, this Symbol is encouraging you to follow up on your ideas, give them more substance than they have at present, and perfect your skills. Then and only then will you know their worth or material potential. Bubbles are ideas (air) given physical or emotional significance (soapy water). On a purely practical, financial level, it is saying that you are in danger of investing in a pipe dream, or relying on someone or something that will not last or will not deliver soon enough. On the other hand, it may be that you don't need to be quite so hard-headed.

KEEP FOCUSED ON ... developing your ideas, flexing your imagination's muscles to the point where your 'bubbles' are recognized as something of worth ... being clear about the financial situation, making it firm, and not budging from your resolve.

WATCH OUT FOR ... notions posing as realities.

☯ KARMA/ATTITUDE/HEALTH

Here we could be experiencing the effects of escapist or childhood fantasies, or unrealized dreams from an earlier time. Although the 'bubbles' may be insubstantial and unrealistic, they do symbolize subtle yet important notions that leave an impression, rather like the mark left by a burst bubble. Such a mark could be a scar if it has to do with a dream being dashed or something fragile having been abused.

KEEP FOCUSED ON ... the nature or meaning of dreams for they are a testament to the beauty and magic of your immortal soul ... never losing a sense of wonder, or on regaining it if you feel you have lost it. (*See also* 'Self Talk', page 463.)

WATCH OUT FOR ... getting lost in whimsical memories or longings without connecting to exactly what they *really* remind you of, rather than what initially you think they remind you of.

'Fortune's always hiding, I've looked ev'rywhere
I'm forever blowing bubbles, pretty bubbles in the air'

A NOON SIESTA

☆ TAKE A BREAK ☆

☼ GENERAL INTERPRETATION

Occasioned or called for is the withdrawal from the hurly-burly of everyday life that is traditional and acceptable in certain areas of thought and attitude. It does, however, presuppose an early start to the day – such rest must be prefaced or accompanied by effort and discipline. A short sleep.

KEEP FOCUSED ON ... the idea that if you know when and how to withdraw from the external world, you perform very well when you are in it ... giving yourself a break from whatever is concerning you, taking a step back from it all to see the whole picture. You may even be forced to do this.

WATCH OUT FOR ... an opportunistic laziness that simply wastes time and energy.

♥ LOVE/RELATING/SOCIAL

Every relationship needs to take a break every so often – even if only for a few hours. Such breaks can sometimes be unconsciously imposed, such as with a 'temporary separation' occurs when things have got too 'hot'. They can also take the form of being without a partner altogether as one re-gathers one's emotional energies. Alternatively, this Symbol could be suggesting that one should withdraw from pondering or fretting over a relationship that seems inadequate or questionable.

KEEP FOCUSED ON ... being apart as a natural process whereby emotional equilibrium and perspective can be re-established. 'Absence makes the heart grow fonder'.

WATCH OUT FOR ... putting off or closing your eyes to issues of real and obvious concern.

MONEY/WORK/CREATIVITY

The need for giving and taking breaks from work, or from any particular work issue or work problem when it seems to be defeating you. We can often ...

KEEP FOCUSED ON ... on something more efficiently by 'sleeping on it'. Also, dreams can supply us with solutions to which the conscious mind is blind.

WATCH OUT FOR ... laziness, for this is an all too common version of 'taking a break'. Laziness has many reasons behind it, not least a lack of confidence or direction. Then again, it can be a reaction to the excessive busy-ness of our workaday world ... the opposite of this – workaholism. This derives from either a punishing work schedule that is born of the illusion of being indispensable and an inability to delegate, or from a means of leaving no gaps for emotional issues to make themselves felt.

♄ KARMA/ATTITUDE/HEALTH

This Symbol is referring to meditation or a similar form of withdrawal from the external world of ego and commerce. We are not supposed to be continually engaged with the stresses of this world throughout the daylight hours. But this is saying that your withdrawal should not just be from work but from the stress of being 'on-line' all the time, something which is often born of a neurotic need for control. Withdrawal will refresh you, and go some way towards relieving stress-related complaints. The significance of the Sun is alluded to here, noon being its highpoint in the sky, suggesting Solar Meditation, an appropriately aligning and revitalizing 'noon siesta' (*see* pages 467–8). In any way you like or choose, take a break from the habits or patterns that benumb and frustrate.

'There the wicked cease from troubling, and there the weary be at rest'

CIRCULAR PATHS

☆ RELIABILITY OR GOING NOWHERE ☆

✴ GENERAL INTERPRETATION

Routine or repetitive activity that ensures thoroughness and familiarity. Knowing one's ground, but not going over it more than one has to. Learning from one's mistakes. Circulating. Doing the rounds. Coming back to where you were before.

KEEP FOCUSED ON ... your ability or need to keep focused on any given issue until you have mastered it or exhausted any outworn elements that appertain to it ... appreciating the reliability, thoroughness and effectiveness that stem from this.

WATCH OUT FOR ... going nowhere as a result of getting stuck in a rut ... the aimlessness or obsessiveness of habit and addiction ... flogging a dead horse.

♥ LOVE/RELATING/SOCIAL

A relationship, social round or manner of relating that has an established pattern – or the need for such. Conversely, if a relationship is unsatisfactory then change the way you relate.

KEEP FOCUSED ON ... the regular reassurance and predictability that this situation obviously has going for it ... the comfort that you can draw from knowing that matters will soon revert to their usual, steady and familiar state after any disillusionment or distress ... frequently reassuring and comforting each other.

WATCH OUT FOR ... becoming addicted to stale or habitual ways of interpreting, responding or relating to the object of your enquiry, otherwise you will only fix yourself in an unreal and unproductive position. If need be, take a break from this boring or rigid behaviour or lifestyle.

MONEY/WORK/CREATIVITY

A regular job with a regular pay cheque and, possibly, a repetitive form of work. The schedules and routines of working life, or cycles of activity and rest, profit and loss, creativity and recreation, or a lack of inspiration. Track record. Method.

KEEP FOCUSED ON ... the advantages of being part of a cyclical process, the fact that through putting in a regular amount of time and effort targets are reached and profits are made ... the good results you have had in the past.

WATCH OUT FOR ... becoming fixed on dull and unstimulating drudgery ... getting nowhere with something or someone that is out of your control ... never finishing a job for fear of it not being 'perfect' ... identifying and eliminating any stale or negative pattern.

☯ KARMA/ATTITUDE/HEALTH

Regular sleep, food, diet and exercise is the obvious recipe for a healthy life, mind and body. Daily rituals such as yoga, prayer or meditation are also important – especially for the state of your soul.

KEEP FOCUSED ON ... the fact that all of life is cyclical, and that each cycle is affected by other cycles ... the certainty that through tirelessly going over an issue it will eventually be resolved ... the central reason for your involvement with the object of your enquiry, for this will centre *you* ... changing your ways if you wish to change your life ... cycles and planetary influences.

WATCH OUT FOR ... ignoring these regular needs of the body for it will eventually lead to a malfunctioning body ... leaving things undone for they will only have to be dealt with later, possibly in more difficult circumstances ... becoming bored.

'What goes around comes around'

A BOAT-LANDING WASHED AWAY

✧ ENTROPY ✧

❋ GENERAL INTERPRETATION

You are finding out that in time Nature undoes all that we humans devise for our own convenience, thus posing a need either for constant maintenance, or to not expect to find things as they were. Nothing lasts forever. This may refer literally to a home or harbour that is no longer tenable or available.

KEEP FOCUSED ON ... being aware of life's inherent unpredictability, and then you can go to meet it with ever-increasing powers of improvisation and spontaneity ... the fact that it is probably time to move on and that a new 'mooring' will be, or needs to be, found – a better one than the last.

WATCH OUT FOR ... hopelessness born of indecision ... hanging on to a dream or anything that is past its sell-by date.

♡ LOVE/RELATING/SOCIAL

Without constant and regular upkeep, any relationship is liable to weaken, until eventually it drifts apart and then there is no longer any point of emotional access. On the other hand, it can be the upkeep itself that proves to be emotionally exhausting.

KEEP FOCUSED ON ... maintaining relationships through any means that are available to you. If this is difficult emotionally, try holding an image of the person in your mind's eye at least once a day, sending them loving and caring thoughts and feelings. This will forge a psychic link which you will both eventually feel the benefit of – but you must make it a regular 'transmission'.

WATCH OUT FOR ... wearing yourself out by relating to anyone with whom there is only a tenuous link; give and respond minimally – what you can afford.

♛ MONEY/WORK/CREATIVITY

Nothing needs upkeep as much as material things. The object of your concern has been, or is going to be, subject to dissolution or winding down.

KEEP FOCUSED ON ... keeping intact anyone or anything that is useful to you and yours. Keep the wheels well oiled if you wish things to continue, for degenerative forces are looming.

WATCH OUT FOR ... missing opportunities through assuming that they will always be there ... cutting your losses when demise, recession or liquidation is unavoidable.

☯ KARMA/ATTITUDE/HEALTH

This is symbolic of the waters of Fate washing away what was hitherto a relatively secure and reliable aspect of your life. This may have occurred through an imperceptible erosion over time, or it could have been a 'cyclone' that wiped it out overnight. In any event ...

KEEP FOCUSED ON ... accepting the fact that all things must pass, outlive their usefulness, fall into disrepair or fade away. In some cases this can be a kindness ... making repairs only where and when they are clearly feasible and practical.

WATCH OUT FOR ... hanging on to situations or attitudes that are precarious or based purely on a misguided sentiment.

*'... the great globe itself,/Yea, all which it inherit, shall dissolve
And, like this insubstantial pageant faded,/Leave not a rack behind'*

A RETIRED SEA CAPTAIN

☆ REFLECTION AND RECOLLECTION ☆

✦ GENERAL INTERPRETATION

Now is the time for reflecting on the adventures that you have made out in the wide wild world that can give rise to wisdom born of experience and possibly a creative portrayal of your exploits.

KEEP FOCUSED ON ... developing or drawing on a relaxed and worldly awareness that is born of experience and that provides the necessary poise and point of view that can entertain and enlighten yourself and others who are less familiar with the ways or mysteries of life.

WATCH OUT FOR ... dreams of past glories and exploits when coupled with the frustrated desire to relive them ... premature withdrawal from what still requires your input.

♥ LOVE/RELATING/SOCIAL

Having grown tired of the tempestuous emotions of intimate relating or intense social involvement, a more passive, laid-back or mature kind of relationship or way of relating is sought after or called for.

KEEP FOCUSED ON ... the inner, more spiritual dimensions and values of relating; without this, life would be more relaxed but stagnant, safe but meaningless ... making a study of your inner being and processes, enabling you to attract a better kind of relationship and social life in the future, or improve them in the present.

WATCH OUT FOR ... retirement or retreat from emotional involvement as an escape from your own demons, from an unwillingness to confront your own shortcomings.

♟ MONEY/WORK/CREATIVITY

The object of your enquiry requires deep reflection and consideration in its own right. Alternatively, the object itself has passed a peak and is in decline. Either way, contemplating its nature will reveal the truth of the matter. Possibly retirement itself.

KEEP FOCUSED ON ... the track record that you or the issue of your concern possesses, for this should reveal the answer, or at least part of it ... trends, figures, graphs and such ... using any wealth of experience in your field.

WATCH OUT FOR ... living in the past when an up-to-date outlook and style is required ... losing heart or giving up on something just because the going has got rough.

☯ KARMA/ATTITUDE/HEALTH

Following a period of hectic living upon the high seas of life, one is now allowed to withdraw to contemplate, meditate and reflect on what it all means. Such a retirement could pose an unavoidable return to whatever it was that was being escaped from on 'dry land' – Earthly responsibilities.

KEEP FOCUSED ON ... the feelings inside you. If they are peaceful and fulfilled, then you may rest assured that you have a deserved retirement, be it permanent or temporary. If there is still turmoil, guilt or restlessness within, then you must discover what lies behind such feelings and see to them. Ask the Oracle about *this*.

WATCH OUT FOR ... using your natural ability to withdraw from things solely as a means of not having to bother contributing something others could benefit from – even if it is just a laid-back demeanour or a tale to tell

'To love, and bear: to hope till Hope creates/From its own wreck the thing it contemplates'

♎

TWO MEN PLACED UNDER ARREST

☆ JUST DESERTS ☆

❂ GENERAL INTERPRETATION

Removal of troublesome elements from circulation. The necessity that one remains responsible for one's thoughts and deeds, and that one's inner reality is in accord with that of society's rules or values. The doubling of an image in symbolism means a certain issue is now coming into consciousness and must be dealt with. However, it could also literally mean that one of more (men or women) are stopped or restrained.

KEEP FOCUSED ON ... cultivating a healthy conscience that earns the respect of yourself and others; your conscience is only too aware of what can result from transgressing its own laws.

WATCH OUT FOR ... ineptitude in relating to and dealing with the world at large that attracts limitations or directives imposed from without because none had been imposed from within.

♡ LOVE/RELATING/SOCIAL

A karmic relationship. This is the coming together of two people so that they are forced to contend with life issues or personality traits, longstanding patterns and deep-seated roots. Alternatively, there is the image here of being denied a normal relationship until a lesson has been learnt. Also the possibility of the trials that homosexuality poses.

KEEP FOCUSED ON ... whatever it is that you feel you are being deprived of in relationship terms, for this is the key to discovering what needs 'correcting'. For example, if you have a history of being possessive, then eventually you will find yourself without the person you want.

WATCH OUT FOR ... being limited or coerced by others because you have not imposed any demands or limitations on yourself.

♔ MONEY/WORK/CREATIVITY

Certain figures or practices in your working life are no longer viable or free to continue. You can take this as being just unfortunate, or recognize that your fate is calling your attention to the need for a radical change in the way you go about your occupation, in the nature of the occupation itself, or in how you deal with or acquire money. So ...

KEEP FOCUSED ON ... what these missing or troublesome parts are, as they indicate the cause of the problem or the nature of the change being called for. For example, shortage of your type of work could mean the need to upgrade, retrain, branch out, diversify or be more flexible.

WATCH OUT FOR ... 'occupational recidivism' – going back to the same old ways or questionable lines of work that you have allowed to imprison you simply because they are the devil you know.

☯ KARMA/ATTITUDE/HEALTH

Karmic dues or issues that are ripe for the dealing with are what this time is all about. 'Just Deserts' stresses the fact that whatever happens just had to happen for it is rightly deserved. Whether one is guilty or innocent, the experience of being 'arrested', of Fate catching up with you, still has to be experienced and addressed. What is important is that you ...

KEEP FOCUSED ON ... what it is that you need to have a good look at, possibly finding your freedom curtailed until you do so and take a corrective measure or new path in life ... studying and listening to your conscience, and then acting on it ... being rid of negative ideas.

WATCH OUT FOR ... thinking that whatever happens is merely 'bad luck'. Every occurrence has a cause in the form of a thought or feeling that you once had, and then acted on or not ... being made to feel guilty when you are not.

'Conscience is thoroughly well-bred and soon leaves off talking to those who do not wish to hear it'

A GANG OF ROBBERS IN HIDING

☆ UNACCEPTABILITY ☆

⚙ GENERAL INTERPRETATION

Having to resort to antisocial methods in order to survive, and the consequences that this recourse brings. However, there could be a Robin Hood interpretation here – that is, operating in a covert manner in order to destabilize an oppressive regime and help those afflicted by that regime. What you are dealing with here is either unacceptable to the status quo, or it is the status quo that is unacceptable, or both.

KEEP FOCUSED ON ... your alertness to every threat against freedom and true individuality ... any kind of 'behind-the scenes' activity that's serves the common good ... being clear about the validity of your principles, otherwise you could find yourself 'in hiding' indefinitely.

WATCH OUT FOR ... an outright lack of honesty and respect for one's fellow beings.

❤ LOVE/RELATING/SOCIAL

This Symbol suggests either a lack of faith in one's ability to find or make a secure relationship, or a lack of faith in one's own inner hero/heroine. These two 'lacks' could well be linked. Fear of not being accepted.

KEEP FOCUSED ON ... what it is in you or your past that makes you distrustful or fearful of commitment, because these feelings will attract situations that appear to justify them ... believing in the part of you that wants to be the noble and generous partner or individual who selflessly makes a mission out of championing the oppressed ... showing your true feelings, then, sooner or later, they'll be accepted.

WATCH OUT FOR ... being paranoid and suspicious about what you think might be going on behind your back – or feeling guilty about what you are doing behind someone else's back.

MONEY/WORK/CREATIVITY

If this isn't referring to an element in your work or financial life that is secretly undermining or conspiring against you, then it is pointing to something about yourself that is doing the same thing – for instance, a reluctance to play by the rules, not paying your way, not wanting to put in the necessary effort or investment to attain what you are after, or harbouring ideas and values that progressively set the 'powers that be' against you.

KEEP FOCUSED ON ... being above-board in all your dealings, unless your interests are by their very nature aimed at subverting a negative regime. You will have to be very honest and clear about which applies to you.

WATCH OUT FOR ... shady dealings of any kind, for they will eventually backfire on you ... anything or anyone that does not have your true interests at heart.

☯ KARMA/ATTITUDE/HEALTH

Something negative and potentially harmful that is temporarily out of circulation – or is it waiting in ambush? This could be one's own guilty conscience or unlaid ghosts, and one is anxiously lying low for fear of being found out for some past misdemeanour. Or, lack of faith or wrong thinking could be denying one grace, robbing one of peace of mind. Then again, what is plaguing you could be an entity or group that has long played and fed upon the fears of Humanity as a whole.

KEEP FOCUSED ON ... any kind of wrongdoing which is on your conscience and make amends for it as you see fit ... how it is may be the collective condition of the world that is the problem; yet seeing to one's own bad karma would still be the best remedy ... physical, possibly hidden, complaints stemming from a similar condition of guilt.

WATCH OUT FOR ... denial and repression.

'What you don't know can hurt you'

A JEWISH RABBI

☆ TRUE TO TRADITION ☆

✴ GENERAL INTERPRETATION

Occasioned or called for here is a complete adherence and dedication to a set of eternal values or longstanding tradition or belief system. A set of laws that guide, enable and maintain one's individual integrity, especially when alienated or in a wilderness of some kind. The importance of obeying such laws. The good fortune that extends from keeping to a tradition.

KEEP FOCUSED ON ... your ability to minister to the needs of your community through employing the insights and knowledge provided by the great souls upon whose shoulders you stand and who provide you with peace and security.

WATCH OUT FOR ... an air of superiority or piety that repels rather than attracts ... giving off a heavy presence that is more oppressive than it is uplifting or guiding.

♥ LOVE/RELATING/SOCIAL

What you have, or require, are some principles or vows that guide your relationships and relating in a way that is tailored to your idiosyncrasies. If you have some particular tradition or pattern that has been already established, this may be what you (should) adhere to. So ...

KEEP FOCUSED ON ... whatever it is that has worked especially well for you in the past. If this is not apparent, then seeking out such a thing should meet with success. This may well take the form of an individual, such as a counsellor or priest. Or create your own contract or set of rules.

WATCH OUT FOR ... trying to live and relate by rules that are not really suited to you personally, or trying to live and relate without any consciously constructed and observed rules at all.

MONEY/WORK/CREATIVITY

Your work is, or should be, concerned with expounding some theory, teaching or philosophy. Money and the making of it is seen here as an utter necessity. As Samuel Johnson said, 'No man but a blockhead ever wrote, except for money.' In other words, outside of family and emotional relationships, it would be unwise to spend one's time and energy without suitable reward.

KEEP FOCUSED ON ... how it is the basic need and oppression that you feel within you and around you that qualifies you for the task in hand, and enables you to make a good profit or, at least, survive in the world ... whatever is, or should be, your policy for living in the material world.

WATCH OUT FOR ... bending the rules to accommodate any kind of business practice or justify any kind of creative expression.

☯ KARMA/ATTITUDE/HEALTH

Your spiritual life and health are dependent upon some deep and profound set of beliefs and guidelines that go way back in time. This may literally involve the Judaic tradition or, more esoterically, the Qabala.

KEEP FOCUSED ON ... following, discovering or devising rituals or beliefs that create and maintain a connection with a matrix of spiritual guidance and support ... contriving or finding special diets to ensure better health ... a 'manifesto for living' – or create one if need be.

WATCH OUT FOR ... persecuting or being persecuted. Being singled out may be the unavoidable consequence of being unusual or peculiarly aware of certain truths of life. It may fall to you personally to take some special responsibility for those in your care.

'Whom the Lord loveth He chasteneth'

A CROWD ON A BEACH

☆ IN THE RAW ☆

✹ GENERAL INTERPRETATION

Here is a situation where people are stripped of their masks and disguises. This stripping away creates a natural sense of connectedness, enabling everyone to be themselves in a basic fashion. They feel free just to watch, sunbathe, exercise, play and parade sexually in a relatively unselfconscious way. Herd instinct, with the plusses and minuses that this implies. Basic appeal.

KEEP FOCUSED ON ... creating or maintaining the openness and ingenuousness that allows others to relax and feel a part of whatever is happening ... the fact that very few people are 'perfect' when seen in the raw ... beating them or joining them, but not oscillating between the two.

WATCH OUT FOR ... a fearful inclination to lose oneself in the crowd, thereby dulling your individual position and expression ... fear of exposure.

🏆 MONEY/WORK/CREATIVITY

Your work and success depend on or appeal to whatever or whoever is seeking a communion with Nature or the Unconscious, or on any kind of captive audience where needs have to be met or goods or services taken to the customer.

KEEP FOCUSED ON ... the secret of any success to do with connecting with or cashing in on whatever appeals to the masses ... the 'Crowd on a Beach' as a clue to what kind of market you are aiming at – for example, something that makes one stand out from the crowd yet at the same time makes one feel part of it.

WATCH OUT FOR ... obvious areas of doubt or difficulty, such as seasonal factors or the lack of demand for certain items and services.

♥ LOVE/RELATING/SOCIAL

Here is an emotional or social situation where a 'return to Nature' is called for. A typical beach scene is a wonderful example and symbol of how relaxed and unselfconscious people become when side by side, partially or totally naked. So ...

KEEP FOCUSED ON ... the fact that it is perfectly natural to expose yourself and, indeed, others and thereby get closer to one or more people ... that everyone has something to show and something to hide ... that you are human, no more and no less.

WATCH OUT FOR ... being afraid of being seen – the chances are that no one will even notice. Nothing draws attention to itself as much as self-consciousness; this poses the possibility of unconsciously needing to have something noticed or made conscious.

☯ KARMA/ATTITUDE/HEALTH

This Symbol perfectly represents how we are caught between the secrets and urges of the Unconscious (the sea) and the conventions and securities of the Conscious or Known (dry land). What will happen and what we want to happen may or may not be the same thing. There is also the notion that as we originally came from the ocean, and the shoreline has a common and binding significance for us – making us feel as one. Possible congestion.

KEEP FOCUSED ON ... whatever it is about the object of your enquiry that is subject to the forces of the Unconscious and to feeling, or not feeling, a sense of belonging. This will guide you with regards to the outcome of it, or a suitable approach to it.

WATCH OUT FOR ... any sense of exclusivity – it could exclude you in more ways than you'd like.

'Et in Arcadia ego' (And I too came from a time and place closer to Nature)

♎

A CHILD GIVING BIRDS A DRINK AT A FOUNTAIN

☆ NATURAL AND INFINITE SUPPLY ☆

 GENERAL INTERPRETATION

Here is the source of innocence and beauty that naturally and directly feeds the soul and spirit, the mind and body. Innocence refreshes spirit, and spirit refreshes innocence. The soul and body should be given what they need.

KEEP FOCUSED ON ... your spontaneously creative concern for the welfare of and communion among all living things, bearing witness to your own sweet soul. (*See also* 'Self Talk', page 463.)

WATCH OUT FOR ... a naivety that appeals, but does not survive the harsher realities of life.

 LOVE/RELATING/SOCIAL

Beyond all the complications of relating in a confused and modern society lies the simplicity of a natural generosity of spirit, of giving another what they need – something which has to do with the child in one person recognizing the child in the other, and whatever its needs are.

KEEP FOCUSED ON ... what it is in another that is thirsty for what you have to offer – probably their soul, whether they know it or not ... your source of supply, what it takes to keep it flowing, and that it depends ultimately on something beyond your control. If it is there to be given, then give it freely. If it is not there, then you cannot give it.

WATCH OUT FOR ... being sapped by anyone with neurotic needs and who does not recognize your own or Nature's limitations.

 MONEY/WORK/CREATIVITY

It is your role to refresh others with anything that represents the Water of Life – anything that makes a basic requirement available to people. This could be physical or spiritual food. Money is no problem as long as you believe you will get what you need when you need it, and you do the same for others in need when you can.

KEEP FOCUSED ON ... providing essentials in the spirit of the simple pleasure of knowing that you are part of a natural chain of supply.

WATCH OUT FOR ... becoming motivated by anything other than this simple and innocent cycle of supply and demand, such as stockpiling or being mainly profit-motivated.

☯ **KARMA/ATTITUDE/HEALTH**

Recognizing that Life and Nature will always sustain you as long as you maintain your innocence and a simplicity of requirements. Recognizing that you have the ability to help those who cannot help themselves.

KEEP FOCUSED ON ... learning to trust in Natural Supply, that there is no more and no less to go round than there ever was; it keeps rotating and recycling ... believing that if your needs are simple they will be simply and gladly met.

WATCH OUT FOR ... giving to others what is not natural, even though their desire for it might be great ... symptoms of lack of faith in Natural Supply, such as wanting more than you really need, worrying that you won't get it, and suffering from the stress of such worry. Such stress can create anxieties and manifest in physical ailments such as back problems.

'Nature looks after Her own'

CHANTICLEER

❊ NEW DAY – NEW YOU ❊

❊ GENERAL INTERPRETATION

The cockerel in the French tale that announces the new day – and possibly thinks that he is actually creating it! The sense of what is about to be. So, you now have the chance to make a new start regarding the object of your enquiry, to make a declaration of intent, to inaugurate, to launch. The time is teeming with possibilities, so rejoice in this rather than being overwhelmed by seeing only the snags.

KEEP FOCUSED ON ... creating and maintaining an enthusiasm for what each day brings. This will help to win others over to whatever you wish to do or attain ... waking others up to what turns you on, but ...

WATCH OUT FOR ... outright and annoying egocentricity. This is called solipsism – believing that life is only an extension of yourself, and that no one else has anything to do with it.

♡ LOVE/RELATING/SOCIAL

A new relationship or lease of life for a relationship is there for the asking. Your broader social life can also be made new by the same means – that is, simply announcing to yourself and those who can or should hear that that is your intention. In so doing, you effectively set in motion a number of events that create a 'new day'.

KEEP FOCUSED ON ... the opportunity to create this 'new day' in your love life and social life by matching your desire for it with exuberant activity and a proclamation of intent.

WATCH OUT FOR ... believing that it is all down to you alone, and then getting others' backs up as you insist on doing everything your own way. The Oracle is saying the 'new day' is coming of its own accord, as surely as the Sun rises – just meet it.

♛ MONEY/WORK/CREATIVITY

Work and finances are approaching or at a point of new departure. Possibly even a new vocation is calling. Your ideas are very much in tune with Now and how things shall be. You are an awakener.

KEEP FOCUSED ON ... the actual thrust and urgency that is inherent in the feeling of embarking on a new venture or way of doing things. This will both guide you and give you the forward push to get past any discouragement or inevitable difficulties. The cockerel is after all a male, yang symbol and brooks no resistance from those less convinced or motivated – be it from others or from within your own being.

WATCH OUT FOR ... overlooking or steaming through considerations that at first appear to oppose or inhibit your enthusiasm, for they could be essential to your continued progress.

☯ KARMA/ATTITUDE/HEALTH

We make our lives with our thoughts, feelings, deeds and karma. Your birth chart symbolizes all this potential and heralds the 'new day' that is your very life at the moment of birth.

KEEP FOCUSED ON ... the sheer enthusiasm that you have for your own existence at any given moment; if you cannot find any, then search for it until you do. Pretending to be a cockerel crowing is an effective, almost yogic way of getting in touch with the primal exuberance which is present in all of us by virtue of being alive.

WATCH OUT FOR ... if you cannot 'crow', then you are afraid or unsure of your own life force. It is only negative experiences and voices that insinuate that you don't have anything to crow about. A cockerel simply crows because it feels alive for yet another day on Earth.

'Behold, I make all things new'

♎

A THIRD WING ON THE LEFT SIDE OF A BUTTERFLY

☆ MUTATION ☆

 GENERAL INTERPRETATION

Encountered or in the offing is the extra intuition or brilliance of mind that is a spin-off from successfully undergoing a transformation. Alternatively, being in possession of an extra faculty – maybe as a compensation for an imperfection elsewhere.

KEEP FOCUSED ON ... the fact that when acquiring or going for something above and beyond the usual, initially you have to carry more, try harder, and even be regarded as a bit odd.

WATCH OUT FOR ... discarding that which at first appears to be strange or an intrusion – it could be a blessing in disguise.

LOVE/RELATING/SOCIAL

A relationship that has a dimension to it, or missing from it, that can be seen as either a burden or blessing. This may imply a third party intruding upon an existing relationship, but do not jump to this conclusion without checking out the facts.

KEEP FOCUSED ON ... what this 'extra wing' represents – it could have value or it could prove to be an aberration ... ruthlessly cutting out anything or anyone leeching you.

WATCH OUT FOR ... making comparisons, especially when someone or something is an unknown factor ... disowning an awkward aspect to a relationship that really belongs to you; if anything is bothering you and cannot be shaken off, this implies that there is something you are not 'owning' about yourself that you are projecting on to another. What is it?

MONEY/WORK/CREATIVITY

You have something in process that might look very unlikely to others – and even to yourself – but then you are attempting to accomplish something that has not been done before.

KEEP FOCUSED ON ... any extraordinary talent that sets you apart from the rest, even though it can make you feel a freak or out on a limb ... your most closely held ideals; the pain you feel and the effort you make are commensurate with what you hold dear.

WATCH OUT FOR ... signs that what you have in mind is a very long shot, and that it is becoming a waste of your time and energy. But be very sure before giving up.

KARMA/ATTITUDE/HEALTH

Health issues resulting from excessive mental control should be seen as an imperative to transform one's lifestyle. Overall, this Symbol indicates unfinished business that is going to be a burden until you have confronted and assimilated what it means, ultimately transforming it into something beautiful, useful, or both.

KEEP FOCUSED ON ... the possibility that this 'burden' could in fact be a creative project or relationship that you never finished, saw through, or made the most of. It now appears out of place, unwelcome even, but you must find its truth and assets – although they may need 'dusting off', they are there.

WATCH OUT FOR ... rejecting what you find odd or distasteful, for it will only come back to haunt you again and again. Lay your ghosts.

'An asset when seen as an affliction becomes an affliction'

♎︎

INFORMATION IN THE SYMBOL OF AN AUTUMN LEAF

☆ ULTIMATE REASSURANCE ☆

✳ GENERAL INTERPRETATION

The unmitigated promise that as surely as the life force will recede, it will also return. Generally speaking, paying attention to Nature's signs and the inevitability of seasonal change. Literally speaking, the reward gained through intense and intuitive study of Nature and her processes and seasons.

KEEP FOCUSED ON ... maintaining a faith that all will go well so long as natural desires and worthwhile goals are pursued. You may have to ponder the issue and your feelings deeply in order to do so ... closely studying whatever is before you, and it will tell you what you wish to know – and maybe what you don't. This will be an unalterable fact that you would do well to accept and gain intelligence from.

WATCH OUT FOR ... making more of things than they merit ... over-interpreting 'signs and omens'.

♥ LOVE/RELATING/SOCIAL

Libra is the Sign of Relationship and it heralds in Autumn. This says that becoming involved with anyone necessitates the ultimate death of selfish indulgence and an intense sense of beauty and significance. And a relationship is a symbol in itself, as it shows us much about life and ourselves. There are as many relationships as there are Autumn leaves; each one is unique and must be studied and experienced closely in order to absorb the richness of its meaning.

KEEP FOCUSED ON ... what a person or relationship represents to you in order to understand why it or them is in your life.

WATCH OUT FOR ... superficial appraisal or anything or anyone, for you could be attaching too much or too little importance to them.

MONEY/WORK/CREATIVITY

What you need to know about the market, finances, prospects or ideas is available if you take a balanced and holistic view of the current state of affairs. It would seem that something has reached a point that precedes a decline or a turning inwards in order to contemplate what you have going for you or where you are headed.

KEEP FOCUSED ON ... the object of your concern in as detached a way as possible until you see the true nature and inner meaning of the matter, and the direction it wants to proceed.

WATCH OUT FOR ... putting too much store by anything that is on the way out or is of a strictly seasonal or short-lasting nature, unless this is precisely what you are banking upon.

☯ KARMA/ATTITUDE/HEALTH

The Autumn of life or what appears to be a bleak prospect could be what concerns you. But everything depends upon how you read the situation, so ...

KEEP FOCUSED ON ... interpreting your life situations in terms of what they represent to you as you would in interpreting a dream, or in using the Oracle, rather than by merely working things out logically or from surface appearances ... what any ailment means in terms of it reflecting a negative lifestyle or attitude, the altering of which would positively affect your health ... seeing your current situation as a definite season or turning point that is bound to eventually bring about some kind of rebirth or renewal.

WATCH OUT FOR ... condemning yourself to a 'winter of discontent' because of a reluctance to change with the times.

'To see the world in a grain of sand/And heaven in a flower
Hold infinity in the palm of your hand/And eternity in an hour'

AN EAGLE AND A LARGE WHITE DOVE TURNING INTO ONE ANOTHER

☆ BALANCING EXTREMES ☆

GENERAL INTERPRETATION

Managing to use and express, when appropriate, aspects of life or yourself that are apparently diametrically opposed. This Symbol speaks of the aggressive, predatory and creative dynamic on the one hand, and of the passive, peace-loving perspective, on the other.

KEEP FOCUSED ON ... using or developing your ability to change swiftly from one mode of expression to another, thereby commanding a positive and efficient response from others. This is made possible through a disciplined sureness of the fulcrum of your own being ... being familiar with and accepting both sides of a situation/person.

WATCH OUT FOR ... creating disasters as a result of fluctuating between aggression and meekness of disposition ... resisting the alternation between extremes, for this is what creates manic behaviour.

MONEY/WORK/CREATIVITY

It would seem that you have two or more ways of working or making money and they seem to be incompatible. Actually, they are not; they are complimenting one another, balancing one another out – possibly through a transitional stage. The secret is to ...

KEEP FOCUSED ON ... adjusting and responding according to the state of affairs or demands of the moment or customer ... the possibility that things are in a state of flux because a working policy, method or style that is being sought after. By staying with this process things will eventually find a formula and balance that is better than ever ... organize your working situation so that it allows for extremes.

WATCH OUT FOR ... thinking that you have to be one thing to all people. This would deny the fact that you are versatile and multi-talented.

♥ LOVE/RELATING/SOCIAL

The relationship or social situation calls for a typically Libran balancing act as you cater to opposing needs and dispositions. The Oracle implies that you can be successful in this for the Eagle and Dove are seen to be interchanging without too much difficulty. But this is not a certainty, so you best ...

KEEP FOCUSED ON ... the fact that there *are* these opposing elements in play, be it within a relationship, a group or a person ... the mercurial and oscillating nature of things as being stimulating and self-balancing rather than threatening and destabilizing ... rolling with the punches and responding appropriately; going with the flow or counterbalancing extremes.

WATCH OUT FOR ... trying to fix anything or anyone (including yourself) into one mode of behaviour – that would be asking for trouble.

KARMA/ATTITUDE/HEALTH

Life itself is created by the interplay of opposites – male and female, day and night, for example. The present moment can also be seen as the point balanced between the extremes of past and future, be they near or distant. The trouble is that we forget this basic process, probably because it *is* so basic. So ...

KEEP FOCUSED ON ... how one kind of life, time or experience gives way to its opposite: anger–reconciliation; war–peace; busy-ness–boredom; good times=bad times; these are just a few of a multitude of examples. In the final reckoning, what we have taken is equal to what we have given. This is a bit like riding a bicycle – you have to keep moving to stay upright.

WATCH OUT FOR ... not allowing inconsistencies of character; they are what make one interesting; denying them can create tension and inhibition.

'We make war that we may live in peace'

AN AEROPLANE HOVERING OVERHEAD

✳ IN ABEYANCE ✳

✸ GENERAL INTERPRETATION

Emphasized here is the need for and advantage of achieving a detached perspective, seeing things in terms of a larger process. You are in a state that is 'hovering', in that you have not decided anything one way or the other, and are somehow suspended, observing the lie of the land. In this situation your own state is not that easy to identify, which can be an advantage right now. Sitting something out.

KEEP FOCUSED ON ... calmly contemplating the issue; you then grasp the real significance of things ... putting some distance between yourself and the object of your concern until you get a better idea of what it poses or means to you.

WATCH OUT FOR ... a reluctance to get involved in down-to-earth reality, leading to indifference and inertia ... being out of touch and not really enjoying it or feeling right.

♡ LOVE/RELATING/SOCIAL

Either this describes someone who is hard to reach emotionally or a situation that requires you to take a step back from things. In the first case it could simply pose a shyness or reluctance to commit, or looking for a place to 'land', that is, someone to commit to. In the second case, it may need to be borne in mind that being too available can be unattractive and lacking in mystery.

KEEP FOCUSED ON ... the fact that, if you are the one 'in the air', you cannot stay aloft forever, and the longer you put off committing the slimmer your chances are of a safe or satisfactory 'landing'. If you are the one 'on the ground'; bide your time, knowing that what you want has to come around eventually.

WATCH OUT FOR ... getting stuck in 'icy altitudes' of emotional dissociation if you are 'in the air', or being boringly, misguidedly reliable, if you are 'on the ground'.

♕ MONEY/WORK/CREATIVITY

Matters are 'hanging' at present and so it is difficult to make out what's what or how things are shaping up. If your business involves some kind of survey, surveillance or aerial view, then this Symbol is saying that this is favourable.

KEEP FOCUSED ON ... the fact that if things appear not to be moving, they are really; it is just that they look that way from where you are currently situated ... observing how circumstances develop and then making a decision or an important move ... broadening your scope in order to find a new field, situation or direction if that is what you are after ... surveying the scene or job market.

WATCH OUT FOR ... being unavailable in some way, or for too long, as business depends on maintaining contacts ... being too idealistic or ambitious in your choice or method of work, for this could be frustrating and counter-productive.

♄ KARMA/ATTITUDE/HEALTH

Past experiences can be such that one is unwilling to live a life on Earth; one is always just a spectator as this avoids the heaviness and intimacy that being on Earth involves. Such dissociation can also mean that one is not properly 'in one's body', out of touch with one's senses and the practicalities of life. Unless this Symbol is alluding to the fact that you have managed to transcend some issue, which is a possibility, then you need to ...

KEEP FOCUSED ON ... precisely what it is that you are afraid of experiencing and telling yourself that the reason for it is in the past and that now you can live things in a new way, your way.

WATCH OUT FOR ... being denied what you want simply because you are not making yourself available to whatever that might be ... devitalization of the physical body for fear of living a physical life.

'Then I felt like some watcher in the skies/When a new planet swims into its ken'

♎

A MAN IN THE MIDST OF BRIGHTENING INFLUENCES

☆ HALCYON DAYS ☆

 GENERAL INTERPRETATION

Rewarding experiences and benevolent people. More to the point, the decidedly upbeat attitude to life that actively attracts these things. Plain sailing and inspiring views.

KEEP FOCUSED ON ... making the most of the situation – they don't come much better than this ... the more creative or positive side of the situation, because it is most certainly there ... the object or person of your concern as being in a good place – they soon will be if they are not already ... the certainty that if things have been dark and difficult, the light is returning; things will be on the up, if they are not so already.

WATCH OUT FOR ... refusing to see life's unavoidable snags ... being or becoming complacent or smug, otherwise you'll look round one day and find no one is there.

 MONEY/WORK/CREATIVITY

An inspiring and consequently productive environment or state of mind is indicated here. Financial aid or advice is available for the asking. Creatively speaking, you are on the right track; the Muse is with you.

KEEP FOCUSED ON ... whoever or whatever gives you a feeling of making it, of being connected, of being uplifted and uplifting ... being a source of support, guidance or inspiration – because that is what you are supposed to be and you can rest assured that you can deliver the goods.

WATCH OUT FOR ... feeling jealous or resentful if the 'Man In The Midst Of Brightening Influences' appears not to be you. He or she is there to enlighten, not to put you in the shade!

❤ **LOVE/RELATING/SOCIAL**

A relationship or social situation that allows you to shine, and that does the same for others as well. Someone who is the life and soul of the party. A warm and positive relationship or person.

KEEP FOCUSED ON ... shedding light and giving warmth wherever it is needed – because you certainly have it. Or someone does!

WATCH OUT FOR ... depending too much on others for positive help and input ... not appreciating what is bright and loving about your partner or social milieu ... doubting or putting a price or condition on the sunny effect you have on others ... the outside possibility that this Symbol is saying that this 'brightness' is what is needed in your love and social life.

KARMA/ATTITUDE/HEALTH

You are in touch with a very positive and loving plane, energy or being. What you are, or have been after spiritually, is now close at hand.

KEEP FOCUSED ON ... whatever or whoever 'has the light' for you, and it will be delivered, found, bestowed ... imagining what or who would give you a feeling of warmth or enlightenment ... the feeling or fact that you are being helped.

WATCH OUT FOR ... being 'polarized in the light', only seeing what you want to see, insisting that everything is easy, wonderful and beautiful. Much as this is the case at higher levels of consciousness, it is not so at lower levels, which is where most of us are for most of the time. It can be peculiarly deluding not seeing one's own or another's shadow.

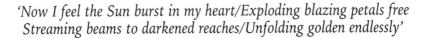

*'Now I feel the Sun burst in my heart/Exploding blazing petals free
Streaming beams to darkened reaches/Unfolding golden endlessly'*

LIBRA 29 DEGREES

HUMANITY SEEKING TO BRIDGE THE SPAN OF KNOWLEDGE

MENTAL EVOLUTION

GENERAL INTERPRETATION

Whatever it is that you are concerned with is forming a vital link in a chain or process, even though you may not yet be aware of it. This bridge takes one forward as an individual and contributes to taking society and civilization into the next era or phase of evolution.

KEEP FOCUSED ON ... your constructive ability to contribute towards a meaningful and wondrous end, and guide or point others towards it ... the fact that you are not alone in your humanitarian endeavours ... following the process.

WATCH OUT FOR ... frustrated attempts to achieve what is not possible in terms of time or resources – or, at least, what you believe is not possible because you think you are on your own ... living solely in your head when you should actually be doing something.

LOVE/RELATING/SOCIAL

What we think, feel, say and do affects others more than we are usually aware. Every thought, emotion, word and deed of each individual is what creates or furthers a relationship. Because of this process, the relationship subtly feeds and changes each of us. As relationships evolve, so do the individuals involved. Involvement and evolvement promote and quicken one another. So ...

KEEP FOCUSED ON ... being true to yourself and your own path, then the other person can reciprocate appropriately. Harmonizing with another is desirable, but trying to fit too much to their (imagined) requirements can get confusing.

WATCH OUT FOR ... assuming that you know how a relationship will unfold and then creating issues or problems that only exist in your mistaken projection of where you think it's going.

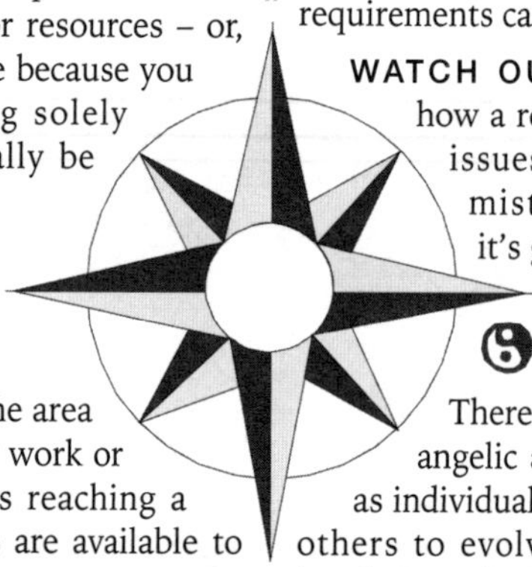

MONEY/WORK/CREATIVITY

You are in the process of getting from one area of endeavour to another: this takes your work or creative issues a stage further towards reaching a long-term or distant destination. Funds are available to carry you over.

KEEP FOCUSED ON ... how your efforts and achievements are the bolts and girders that make up the bridge into the future of your field of interest ... the fact that others are also helping to construct this bridge, and they will be able to use it and follow you along it, be inspired by it, and refine it ... the creative process where one idea and its expression leads to another.

WATCH OUT FOR ... giving up because you cannot see how your task can be achieved. It can't by you alone; it is being accomplished by you and many others – but possibly you are doing your part all *on* your own, for the time being.

KARMA/ATTITUDE/HEALTH

There are two forces that play upon humanity: angelic and devic. The Angels help us to evolve as individual human beings, and then we in turn help others to evolve. The devas or fairies are forces of involution who keep the material realm of Nature intact, building and rebuilding it wherever and whenever necessary – hopefully with our co-operation. Humanity is the bridge between these two realms, between Heaven and Earth.

KEEP FOCUSED ON ... making sure that you are as in touch with your body as you are with your spirit, and vice versa, and that each part of you is included and nothing left out, such as your inner child (*see* page 464) ... healing and creating understanding.

WATCH OUT FOR ... missing the point of being in touch with Angels or devas. Failing to extend and risk yourself to bridge the gulf with their help is like having a building crew and not building anything.

'Everything serves to further'

THREE MOUNDS OF KNOWLEDGE ON A PHILOSOPHER'S HEAD

✵ HOLISTIC AWARENESS ✵

✹ GENERAL INTERPRETATION

The understanding, consideration and expression of any life issue at three levels – such as the esoteric Rays of Love, Power and Intelligence; the Holy Trinity of Father, Son and Holy Ghost; the threefold reality of Physical, Emotional and Mental; the threefold decision-making process that has to satisfy 'I can', 'I must' and 'I will'; or any other trinity which seems appropriate or meaningful to you. So this Symbol counsels you to ponder the object of your concern very carefully, and ...

KEEP FOCUSED ON ... whether or not your situation or course of action is satisfactory on any three levels. When it is, you will have the answer or key to your question ... something happening three times, for that is a confirmation.

WATCH OUT FOR ... intellectual concepts only, for they can amount to little or nothing.

♡ LOVE/RELATING/SOCIAL

To have knowledge and intelligence is one thing – to be able to relate is another thing entirely. One may have a theory of how to relate, or know what one should do or say in order to have a better love or social life, but whether one does or says it, and in the right way, is another matter. Saying 'I think I love you' is not the same as 'I love you', anymore than saying 'I love you' is actually *loving you*.

KEEP FOCUSED ON ... what it is that the other person actually needs rather than what you think they need ... behaving or responding as you *feel* you ought rather than as you *think* you ought to ... creating mutual understanding, a shared philosophy of life, or a set of rules.

WATCH OUT FOR ... getting stuck with how you think a relationship or social set-up *ought* to be, instead of relating to how it *actually* is.

⚕ MONEY/WORK/CREATIVITY

The material sphere of life lends itself to working things out in one's head – in fact its stability and productivity depends upon it. This Symbol also indicates receiving or amounting to something with regard to the field of your endeavour, especially if it is of the cerebral kind or if it deals in the giving of advice.

KEEP FOCUSED ON ... the facts and resources that are in your possession, and this will give you the answer you are after ... putting your excellent mind to the job in hand, and then nothing can stop you ... accumulating enough material or information to create the desired effect.

WATCH OUT FOR ... being too lofty-minded, intellectual or academic, for unless that is in your actual field, you will go over others' heads and fail to gain appreciation or popularity ... getting stuck in your head with ideas and intentions only. All you'll get is a sore head.

☯ KARMA/ATTITUDE/HEALTH

You have got to a point of completion with respect to the nature of your concern. However, what often coincides with a state of completion is a state of exhaustion. This is especially so when one does not appreciate that something is finished with, that one is, so to speak, dragging around the corpse of whatever it is that is dead. This could be with regard to a relationship, a belief, an attitude of mind, a job, or (true to the Symbol) living too much in your head. If you do not know what it is, you will discover it if you ...

KEEP FOCUSED ON ... whatever it is that is giving you cause for concern. For instance, if something doesn't make sense, it could be because your way of thinking about things has to change. A health condition would also indicate the completion or exhaustion of something.

WATCH OUT FOR ... wearing yourself out looking for a comprehensive 'answer' because there isn't one!

'I think, therefore I am – or I think I am'

THE SABIAN SYMBOLS OF
SCORPIO

Either directly, or in a subtle way, all these Symbols are concerned with the following qualities, or with situations that involve or call for them:

DEATH

DELVING/SPYING

DEPTH

DESIRE

HARMONY THROUGH CONFLICT

THE HIDDEN (OCCULT)

INTIMACY

INTRIGUE

POWER

SEXUALITY

TAX AND INHERITANCE

TRANSFORMATION

A SIGHTSEEING BUS

☆ LOOK AND SEE ☆

☀ GENERAL INTERPRETATION

Suggested here is a pleasant and convenient manner of orientating oneself and perusing what's on offer. At the same time, this puts one neatly in touch with one's fellow travellers by sharing with them the culture common to the area, or what you have in common. Or you could simply be in the midst of a passing show.

KEEP FOCUSED ON ... familiarizing yourself with your environment, or other people with the world they live in, thereby creating an intimacy with faces and places ... orientating oneself by knowing, in relation to where you are, the cardinal points, the nearest water, the nature of the soil, and suchlike.

WATCH OUT FOR ... an impersonal, profit-motivated approach towards interacting with others and the environment that is dis-enchanting or even disastrous.

♥ LOVE/RELATING/SOCIAL

Looking around and finding out what's on offer socially, romantically or sexually. Everything that is happening now is with a view to finding a mate, or discovering a group with whom you can identify as you pass through life, taking in the scenery, sharing your feelings about it all.

KEEP FOCUSED ON ... the fact that we are all seeing and being seen, as is evidently intended.

WATCH OUT FOR ... just being a passenger in a relationship, or believing you are one just because you are the more passive partner ... feeling estranged or self-conscious, for this would point to the possibility that you regard yourself as either above others or below them. You are neither – just afraid of being a normal human being. Even though you might have good reason, you have got to join the throng sooner or later.

MONEY/WORK/CREATIVITY

Unless your line of work or business intention has to do with some kind of guided tour (in which case this is an auspicious oracle) then you are probably on the look out for what is available or what suits you. The Oracle is saying that it is through doing this that you will eventually find what you are after. Creatively, you may be gathering material and ideas. Commercially or financially, you could be finding out what works or sells.

KEEP FOCUSED ON ... and be mindful of the nature of what it is you are involved in. In this way you become more and more au fait with it, and better and better at it. Try out different rides, ranges and approaches.

WATCH OUT FOR ... always looking for jobs, ideas or opportunities but never following them up. If this is the case you'll need to get on your feet and do something about it.

☯ KARMA/ATTITUDE/HEALTH

This Symbol is telling you that life is allowing you to view what's available so that you eventually know what to do or get, where to go, which way to go. You may be reacquainting yourself with something from your past with a view to taking it up where you left off. For health, keep moving, busy and watchful.

KEEP FOCUSED ON ... enjoying the ride or whatever experience you are going through, for it is in this way that you will take on board what is most meaningful and useful to you. Then later you can make your decision or plan ... those around you, for they have something in common with you on an essential level; they are in the same boat as you – but in what respect? ... your 'guide'.

WATCH OUT FOR ... always being an observer and never a doer ... thinking that you have not got a life because you are currently assessing what life means.

'Befriending others eliminates alienation'

A BROKEN BOTTLE AND SPILLED PERFUME

☆ EMOTIONAL EVOCATION ☆

 ### GENERAL INTERPRETATION

This Symbol has a dramatic ring to it that brings forth a number of possibly poignant images and associations – ones that will be remembered for some time to come. A tragedy and its aftermath, an emotional outburst and its consequences, or an accident causing the loss of something precious. But such eventualities are life and Fate, making us aware of what is in store for us, or what we have been storing up and now must be released.

KEEP FOCUSED ON ... the respect and reverence that you express so appropriately and subtly with regard to any emotional upset. This in itself helps to heal any wounds related to such an incident.

WATCH OUT FOR ... a careless attitude towards finer feelings that insidiously pervades your sense of well-being, or rather, lack of it.

♡ LOVE/RELATING/SOCIAL

Here is a situation or person that elicits powerful emotional responses by breaking the shell in which such feelings are contained or hidden. They may or may not mean to do this, but it is still something that was waiting to happen in order that strong and important feelings be revealed, recognized and revered.

KEEP FOCUSED ON ... the feelings of the people involved, including yourself, for they are what are truly important now ... how intimacy depends on certain home truths being revealed and shared, and how this can be initially painful.

WATCH OUT FOR ... being upset by the lesser considerations of convention, image, physical looks and whether or not it 'makes sense' ... ignoring uncomfortable feelings; they won't go away because they are expressly there to remind you of something emotionally significant.

 ### MONEY/WORK/CREATIVITY

A mistake or carelessness has resulted in, or may result in, a loss of some kind – such as money, income, job, opportunity or ideas. However, creatively this Symbol could be viewed as suggesting a dramatic theme or breakthrough.

KEEP FOCUSED ON ... damage limitation and identifying what caused the 'accident' in the first place. There is no use crying over spilt milk, but the 'bottles' better be looked after in future ... how a dramatic device is essential as far as grabbing and keeping attention is concerned ... anything that is going wrong and make the necessary changes before it is too late.

WATCH OUT FOR ... any accident that could be waiting to happen. However, try not to get neurotic about this – or the accident could result from that.

 ### KARMA/ATTITUDE/HEALTH

Loss and suffering are, it seems, central to the experience of Earth life. So-called 'accidents of fate' occur in order to remind us what 'scent' we are on the trail of – or what is on our trail. In other words, your situation is one whereby you are being made aware of the contents of your soul and its karma. Health-wise, this Symbol could be referring to a 'leaky aura' that is due to having a damaged etheric body. This is the invisible envelope that encases, energizes and protects the physical body and which, when disturbed by trauma, can leave one too open to emotional and physical infections.

KEEP FOCUSED ON ... how 'trailing clouds of glory do we come', that we all have something evocative and beautiful within us that we may have to be shocked into remembering ... sealing your aura.

WATCH OUT FOR ... signs of a damaged aura, and repair and maintain.

'When the heart weeps for what it has lost, the soul laughs for what it has found'

A HOUSE RAISING

☆ COMMUNAL CONSTRUCTIVENESS ☆

⚙ GENERAL INTERPRETATION

Occasioned or called for here is common enterprise and the joy and accomplishment that goes with it. Others come to your aid regarding your situation or dilemma. Strength in numbers. A good image here is one in the film *Witness*, where all the Amish community build newlyweds a home in one day. Cryptically speaking, this Symbol could refer to some kind of domestic ruckus.

KEEP FOCUSED ON ... your uncanny knack for getting others to bend to a task that benefits them solely because they are made to feel that something is worthwhile and fun to do. This in turn motivates them towards a more personal endeavour ... the fact that you are not on your own ... keeping the peace.

WATCH OUT FOR ... neurotic dependence on others for support or approval.

♥ LOVE/RELATING/SOCIAL

Something new is in the making, disrupting and influencing all social and emotional involvements. Setting up home.

KEEP FOCUSED ON ... working together to build your relationship to last; enlisting the help of others to this end ... the idea that you are one of many who is building a new society with a new set of values and taboos ... any ability you have to construct something that serves everyone concerned, and to make sure they contribute too ... sharing your most private feelings.

WATCH OUT FOR ... beating yourself up because you feel there is something about you that doesn't make the grade; it is better to view it in terms of how the collective values that you are a product of affect – but don't blame society for your own shortcomings ... being too self-contained.

⚛ MONEY/WORK/CREATIVITY

Clearly, the issue is one of collective effort or enterprise, such as a co-operative, and the satisfaction, economy and success that can arise from this. This could also refer to benefit derived from several opinions or types of expertise.

KEEP FOCUSED ON ... the spirit of co-operation among those concerned; improve and encourage this if necessary ... the fact that you do not have everything it takes to make a success; you are one of a number of parts making up an effective whole ... seeking out the help that is available.

WATCH OUT FOR ... situations where there is no 'architect' or 'master builder' because then any communal effort would be liable to become chaotic. Everyone must know their role, one which suits their temperament and abilities ... the weakest link in the chain, for that is as strong as the whole will be.

☯ KARMA/ATTITUDE/HEALTH

Human evolution can be seen as the collective building of a gigantic team, each with his or her own role in this enterprise, the 'human project'.

KEEP FOCUSED ON ... determining one's role in the human project, taking necessary steps to adopt it and become proficient in it ... making a difference ... the wonderful idea that when enough people are doing what they are supposed to be doing, then the whole of humanity will shift into a higher gear ... healing in your own circle.

WATCH OUT FOR ... being a square peg in a round hole, something or someone being where they shouldn't be, or feeling that you are just a unit lost in the midst of the grey mass of humanity ... leaving up to others what you should be doing yourself; depending on the state ... blaming the general state of affairs for not getting your act together.

'Many hands make light work'

A YOUTH HOLDING A LIGHTED CANDLE

☆ AS SURE AS IS PURE ☆

✴ GENERAL INTERPRETATION

Here is a true sense of what leads and illuminates the way; hope in its purest and most positive form; a desire to be free of distracting, polluting or disturbing thoughts and feelings. However, naivety could be a problem.

KEEP FOCUSED ON ... your reliable and consistent sense of what is good and worthwhile ... whatever it is that holds your attention, for that will lead you safely towards your goal ... your sense of what is sacred or holy and holding it up to guide and illumine others.

WATCH OUT FOR ... a vacuous or simplistic approach towards matters ... becoming caught up in youthful ideals when there are more adult responsibilities or realistic considerations calling for your attention ... withholding light and love, or casting a shadow over someone or something.

♥ LOVE/RELATING/SOCIAL

Here is a love nature or relationship which is strongly under the influence of youthful ideals. This can light and lead the way or, conversely, be romantic or illusory. This could also include a precious or controlling nature for fear of that 'light' being snuffed out.

KEEP FOCUSED ON ... the real 'light' in your relationships or social life, and go about preserving it, following it, being true to it. Then you will 'see the light' ... the love or attraction that still shines between you, especially at the times when it might 'flicker' ... eliminating whatever eclipses the light.

WATCH OUT FOR ... carrying the torch for someone when the light has gone out ... naively puritanical expressions and interpretations of love, relating and loved ones ... the effects of disappointment in youth.

⚜ MONEY/WORK/CREATIVITY

Your efforts here are significant and worthwhile but are not dynamic enough to be effective. Then again, a single candle can be highly significant in a dark place.

KEEP FOCUSED ON ... keeping alight your original ideals in the face of a world that is slow to appreciate them ... whatever it is about you that others look to for hope and guidance, and which highlights their potential and brings it out into the open ... using your energy and ideas to ignite projects or inspire other people ... being careful with your finances until they stabilize – they then eventually will.

WATCH OUT FOR ... the wind of change or any other unexpected disturbance that could snuff out your candle or, at least, cause it to gutter. In other words, carefully protect your interests ... being precious or mean materially.

☯ KARMA/ATTITUDE/HEALTH

This is highly suggestive of classic meditation upon a candle flame. This Symbol is counselling you to adopt a meditation technique, or simply to contemplate the significance of the light that is your life. Karmically, here is something that you have to keep alive and remain true to, especially through difficult times, or you will get lost. The source of vitality is the source of all health.

KEEP FOCUSED ON ... whatever is the essential life-giving, hope-inspiring and illuminating quality, for this will guide you and show you how to improve your outlook and health, and those of others also ... shedding light wherever it is needed.

WATCH OUT FOR ... being idealistic or wildly hopeful when obviously (to others, at least) you are just holding 'a candle to the Sun', attempting to maintain your ego's stance against a superior power, intelligence or situation.

'How far that little candle throws his beams! So shines a good deed in a naughty world'

A MASSIVE, ROCKY SHORE

✫ DEMARCATION ✫

✸ GENERAL INTERPRETATION

Nature's way of protecting her boundaries between one element and another, suggesting that your situation is one where there is a considerable degree of self-containment, or that is what is called for.

KEEP FOCUSED ON ... the reassurance that you gain from accepting your limitations, and the wondrous impression you can give from knowing your own ground ... creating and being proud of your own space, so that it is not assailed or invaded by destructive elements.

WATCH OUT FOR ... making what is valuable in yourself inaccessible to others ... letting your personal boundaries be eroded away by a misguided or neurotic need to be accepted, or by sublimating this need with drugs, alcohol or any other 'gap filler'.

♥ LOVE/RELATING/SOCIAL

Either this is referring to a relationship that is a law unto itself, with very few others getting close or understanding it, or it refers to an individual who is so self-contained and emotionally embattled that no one can reach them. Generally speaking, the need to define boundaries and limits of intimacy – who you let into your space, and how far.

KEEP FOCUSED ON ... finding a way to reach the other person, and allowing yourself to be reached ... whatever it is that is inhibiting closeness and the trust that goes with this, and then find a way of dissolving it ... the way in which you depend upon one another, for there is the key to finding a channel of approach, a 'landfall'.

WATCH OUT FOR ... jeopardizing yourself or others through forcing or resisting intimacy.

MONEY/WORK/CREATIVITY

A case of having to thrash out a fair deal or to establish who owns or is responsible for what – or who is entitled to it.

KEEP FOCUSED ON ... your position and worth as against the position and worth of the other party. One of you may be the one who holds the purse-strings, manages the material affairs and is more in touch with the world or market-place; the other the more free, creative and inspirational force. Both of you have advantages and limitations that complement one another, that must be respected.

WATCH OUT FOR ... giving in too easily, or holding out too stubbornly ... being so practical that it restricts your imagination, or so dreamy that it is of no practical or commercial use.

☯ KARMA/ATTITUDE/HEALTH

This strongly emphasizes the necessity of the body's natural defences against any kind of intrusion, and of maintaining one's own psychic space. Conversely, it warns against the loneliness or disease arising from being too heavily defended.

KEEP FOCUSED ON ... the absolute right to resist intrusion into your domain by anyone or anything. This right precedes any other consideration, otherwise your mental, emotional and physical health could suffer or break down.

WATCH OUT FOR ... neurotic or karmic reasons for not allowing anyone closer to you. You may still be defending yourself against an enemy that has long ceased to exist, other than in your memory or imagination. Health-wise, this could give rise to excess fat or fluid retention.

'This fortress built by Nature for herself/Against infection and the hand of war'

A GOLD RUSH

☆ THE PURSUIT OF HAPPINESS ☆

 GENERAL INTERPRETATION

There is now present the opportunity and urge to discover and make something of life and yourself, something that is initially hidden and hard to reach. But there exists at least the promise of great wealth. A willingness not to settle for the lot of most people and to stake a claim to a better life.

KEEP FOCUSED ON … your instinctive dedication to the unseen potentials of everyday existence … what it is that has real, reliable and lasting value – and pursue it.

WATCH OUT FOR … being blinded to important considerations because of being too intent on what you see as the main objective … outright greed and amoral opportunism, charged with ridiculous expectations – your fears are in direct proportion to your desires … losing what is of real value in pursuit of something of only notional value.

 MONEY/WORK/CREATIVITY

The material world implies 'gold rush' for everything about it is geared to the drive for wealth and affluence. At a basic level, this Symbol says that you have got the idea, so you should believe that the gaining of material wealth and status is what happiness is primarily all about. Then again, the 'gold' may be artistic inspiration, the seeking of which is a story and journey in itself (*see* Karma opposite).

KEEP FOCUSED ON … what you are after, the 'gold' – for the 'rush' suggests that this is the case. Assuming that this is all you are after, then there is no problem to address; just keep rushing after the gold. However …

WATCH OUT FOR … the fact that 'money can't buy you love' or health, or anything else that a capitalist philosophy tends to overlook.

 LOVE/RELATING/SOCIAL

You and your partner or group are passionately searching for a better love or social life. Or you may be avidly looking for a person with whom to strike lucky and find the perfect match, through whom your own life is elevated to a better condition. All of this is perfectly acceptable and natural, except that there is the inherent danger of not seeing what you've already got, owing to a desire to get what you believe you need.

KEEP FOCUSED ON … what it is that actually brings you happiness. This may take some inner adjustment and remembering, for the world itself has imposed its own glamorous and illusory idea of what creates happiness … looking for the best.

WATCH OUT FOR … romantic illusions and mistaking lust for love, or looking in another for what can only be found in yourself.

 KARMA/ATTITUDE/HEALTH

The 'gold' that you are after is the wealth that is health or inner peace and richness – the two are probably interconnected. This is akin to the alchemist's quest to turn base metal into gold, which means going from the lower, animal or egotistical state to the higher, spiritual or enlightened state.

KEEP FOCUSED ON … your interior state if you wish to know what it is that is in need of conversion from 'lead' to 'gold'. In other words, if you overlook something base in yourself you are never going to transform it, and this would be reflected in any disease or discontent … the 'gold' of love and generosity of spirit, for this will illuminate and eventually convert the 'lead'.

WATCH OUT FOR … the very desire to 'go for gold' or enlightenment, for this can prevent you from finding it or receiving it. Likewise, the stress of ill health can worsen the complaint.

'All that glitters is not gold'

DEEP-SEA DIVERS

☆ PLUMBING AND DELVING ☆

 GENERAL INTERPRETATION

Going or sinking to the depths, especially emotional ones, in order to uncover root causes and the real potential of life – whether you know it or not at the time. Investigating anything that lies beneath surface appearances or in the unconscious is auspicious.

KEEP FOCUSED ON ... your desire to reach what is most genuine and authentic concerning other people, objects and events, thereby bringing to the surface the truth of the matter ... using the Oracle to delve deeper into your issue.

WATCH OUT FOR ... the self-justification of loneliness ... a paranoid inability to accept anything at face value.

 LOVE/RELATING/SOCIAL

The intimacy stakes, which demand the death of any wrong thinking or defensive systems that inhibit the closeness we crave. These 'deaths' can be painful as these deeply-entrenched psychological complexes resist access and transformation. This is a battle between what one wants and what one fears.

KEEP FOCUSED ON ... the fact that for intimacy to occur, one's feelings have to go deeper than the complexes, the desire for closeness has to be stronger than the fear of it. One may have to take the plunge and hit the bottom in order to realize this.

WATCH OUT FOR ... being too intense for too long, this will merely exhaust you and create problems; you have to come up for air every so often!

 MONEY/WORK/CREATIVITY

If your work entails depth investigation or treatment of some kind, then this is an auspicious oracle and you should take note of the plusses and minuses given here overall. Generally speaking, it is saying that you are having to dig down deep within yourself or into your resources in order to reach and attain what you are after.

KEEP FOCUSED ON ... getting to the very root of any problem, ruthlessly confronting anyone or anything in yourself or your situation that could be creating problems at a fundamental level ... whatever gives you or those around you the deepest or most genuine satisfaction, and promote and maximize that.

WATCH OUT FOR ... superficial answers or methods, for they just won't wash ... wasting too much time and energy on unlikely 'treasure hunts'.

KARMA/ATTITUDE/HEALTH

The causes of certain things (the object of your enquiry probably being one of them) lie very deep in the unconscious. So, if you want to contact them, you will need to find a means of getting down there. This will firstly involve a willingness to go to those depths. It may also require having 'weights' attached, which means using a method where there is 'no turning back', that does not allow you to wriggle out of the situation or rationalize it away. All of the above would also apply to a health issue, and that a form of investigation was necessary.

KEEP FOCUSED ON ... what you feel to be at the very core of your being, and attempt to get as close to (knowing) it as possible.

WATCH OUT FOR ... becoming obsessed with the object of your concern; don't be too hard on yourself.

'Errors, like straws, upon the surface flow;/He who would search for pearls must dive below'

THE MOON SHINING ACROSS A LAKE

☆ THE POWER OF RESPONSIVENESS ☆

 GENERAL INTERPRETATION

Reflecting upon what is already a reflection in itself; the unconscious is being presented to you through some medium or other, such as this Oracle. This can be fascinating or confusing, especially if you are trying to reduce your concern to an intellectual formula. Any emotional occasion that has as its essence an intimate awareness of the soul of the matter. The magic of Nature and the inspiration it evokes.

KEEP FOCUSED ON ... the state of your feelings regarding the object of your enquiry; through keeping still within, you will discover that you have an appropriate response to the inner dimensions of people and things.

WATCH OUT FOR ... a morbid preoccupation with the emotional side of life ... reflecting endlessly on something that you mistakenly think has a finite 'answer'.

 LOVE/RELATING/SOCIAL

Every person or situation we encounter is a reflection of ourselves and our state at that time. The Symbol could also be referring to someone who is lunar – soulful, female, reflective – who embodies, dramatizes or intensifies your own emotional nature. Definite emotional interaction.

KEEP FOCUSED ON ... looking at what you are 'putting out' if you wish to understand and deal with what you are getting back. For example, being too tolerant will ultimately attract someone you cannot stand ... enjoying and making good use of the psychic sensitivity between yourself and another; they will pick up your thoughts and feelings.

WATCH OUT FOR ... branding another with negative traits when they are just reflecting yours.

 MONEY/WORK/CREATIVITY

Your work is all a matter of imagination – preferably creative imagination – be it your own or someone else's. As such, it is subject to the Creative Process, which means that the ideas and images that issue from the imagination are given form through whatever medium seems appropriate at the time. And as time goes by, the various scenes and acts of your 'play' are revealed as they unfold.

KEEP FOCUSED ON ... letting the Process reveal in its own manner and time whatever is due to be revealed and given form. All you have to do is be still and stay with the Process. It will eventually be revealed. But ...

WATCH OUT FOR ... impatiently pushing for things that are either not there or not yet there. The 'lake' can only reflect/give form to whatever the Moon or Unconscious happens to be doing, something which is outside of our control.

 KARMA/ATTITUDE/HEALTH

What we ourselves are at any given time, sooner or later comes back at us. In fact, one could say that a whole lifetime is our soul (Moon) manifesting (shining) as our Earthly personality and reality (lake). Because of this phenomenon, we often transfer or displace feelings, qualities and urges of our own onto someone such as a doctor, a therapist or anyone who appears to be able to express what we are suppressing. Or, we can ...

KEEP FOCUSED ON ... how everything and everyone merge and mesh so perfectly that it is seen to be beautiful, uplifting and enchanting.

WATCH OUT FOR ... ruffling the surface of your mind and feelings, so not being able to understand or respond appropriately to whatever you are involved with. If you feel disturbed and are not aware of being so, you will see disturbance in what lies about you.

'Is it me, or is it thee?'

DENTAL WORK

✳ MAINTENANCE AND TENACITY ✳

 GENERAL INTERPRETATION

A time or situation calling for regeneration and the creation of constant demand through regularly ensuring that what needs taking care of *is* taken care of.

KEEP FOCUSED ON ... dealing with what is decaying or out of alignment, or is about to get that way ... finding the self-discipline that is essential for stability and welfare, in spite of a lack of appreciation of your efforts ... being decisive ... accepting some pain now as being necessary to avoid more pain later.

WATCH OUT FOR ... a *feeling* of inadequacy that insidiously degenerates into *real* inadequacy ... allowing things to go to seed ... cutting corners, for you will find there is no such thing as a shortcut with regard to the object of your concern.

 LOVE/RELATING/SOCIAL

Every relationship has to be fed and maintained if it is not to fall into stagnation or become mere habit or hard slog. Someone who requires ongoing attention and commitment.

KEEP FOCUSED ON ... regularly reviewing and inspecting your relationships ... confronting yourself or others with any issues that are making life awkward or difficult, even though it may hurt to do so. Great pain can be prevented now with relatively little pain ... extricating yourself from an abusive or painful relationship, but only as a last resort; the gap created could be painful too.

WATCH OUT FOR ... any reluctance to address your problems or fulfil your responsibilities (*see* Karma below); left till later they will need deep and drastic measures that may possibly leave permanent damage.

 MONEY/WORK/CREATIVITY

Whatever is ailing or broken, now needs fixing. This also applies to the way you work. Study any plans or prospects carefully before embarking on them because they will entail constant attention and more work than you'd wish for. Financially, a regular income and checking of expenditure is required. Creatively speaking, spadework rather than inspiration is on the cards.

KEEP FOCUSED ON ... meticulously checking every aspect of your product and each stage of your procedure. This will pay off eventually, just as long as you are conscientious and persistent.

WATCH OUT FOR ... weariness brought on by the sheer drudge of it all. Unfortunately, at times one just has to push on through difficult patches. Depending on how much was left undone previously, such a slog will not last too long.

⑨ **KARMA/ATTITUDE/HEALTH**

Saturn, the planet that governs teeth in astrology is also the one that rules karma. So this Symbol is saying that some kind of reparation is due, and if overlooked matters will only get worse.

KEEP FOCUSED ON ... getting on with sorting out whatever needs sorting out, seeing a suitable health practitioner if need be ... the fact that when a duty has at last been seen to, little will be needed to maintain matters – and you could be free of the need to do so altogether.

WATCH OUT FOR ... moaning about, or evading, the responsibilities that come your way; they are there to be met and that's all there is to it; neglecting them would build up a heavy debt to be paid off later ... polluting and decadent aspects of modern life, or of one's own attitude, that undermine the very fabric of one's well-being.

'Does the road lead up-hill all the way?/Yes, to the very end
Does the day's journey take the whole long day?/From morn to night, my friend'

A FELLOWSHIP SUPPER

☆ KINDRED SPIRITS ☆

 GENERAL INTERPRETATION

Being once again where you belong in terms of place, the people you are with, and what you are doing – and the celebration that this involves. The importance of being a part of a group in which everyone is sympathetic to, and accepting of, each others' traits. In this atmosphere the experiences of life may be properly and thoroughly processed and digested.

KEEP FOCUSED ON ... the healthy sharing of thoughts and feelings that keep you and others clean of mind, body and spirit ... heartily including in everyone who is a part of your life.

WATCH OUT FOR ... elitist or aimless commingling that completely misses the point of human gatherings ... being partisan or leaving out those who should be made to feel welcome.

 LOVE/RELATING/SOCIAL

Being (back) with who you belong with. Your relationships need and thrive on regular social input, as do the individuals within them. This feeds the spirit and makes new connections that stimulate you socially and romantically. The Oracle smiles on any gathering of like-minded individuals.

KEEP FOCUSED ON ... those people you most like to be with, for they indicate where you should be and what you are happiest doing ... creating or attending social gatherings and occasions wherever and whenever possible.

WATCH OUT FOR ... keeping yourself too much to yourself, for this could cause you or your relationships to stagnate ... gatherings that have no real purpose, but are just habit and no longer please or mean much.

MONEY/WORK/CREATIVITY

Any pursuit or enterprise that brings people together in the name of a shared vision or sentiment is favoured here, or it is where you are bound. You may also further the object of your concern through being with people who are after the same thing. Friendliness and conviviality promote good feelings and subsequent success.

KEEP FOCUSED ON ... immersing yourself in group activity, somewhere you can share and digest, thereby getting feedback and motivation ... catering to the needs of the group you identify with or wish to reach ... accessing the social side of your profession, for it is a case of who you know rather than just what you know, as well as getting into the swim of things.

WATCH OUT FOR ... limiting yourself to an exclusive area or public – unless that is precisely what you are interested in ... going it alone.

KARMA/ATTITUDE/HEALTH

Here is a civilized reconvening of old ties and associations. Touching base. You find yourself in familiar territory, perhaps after years, even lifetimes, away in some other area. Or simply the reassurance and confirmation of something already established.

KEEP FOCUSED ON ... immersing yourself in pastimes, feelings, ideas and groups that resonate with your deepest concerns. You will then find yourself at peace, ensconced in the sense that you are where you ought to be.

WATCH OUT FOR ... things not being quite as they were or as you remembered them, or insisting on them being how you think you want them to be. You may need to go through a phase of adjustment until you re-establish those old links ... being disenchanted as a result of expecting too much.

'Birds of a feather flock together'

A DROWNING MAN RESCUED

☆ REDEMPTION ☆

GENERAL INTERPRETATION

A very positive oracle, for it suggests sure delivery from a precarious or ominous situation. When close to death or in crisis, the meaning of (one's) life is potently at hand. Accidents of fate carry vital messages that can be powerfully redirecting as long as a basic enthusiasm for life is present and maintained.

KEEP FOCUSED ON ... your strong sense of survival and will to live, furthered and intensified by the very dilemmas that it attracts.

WATCH OUT FOR ... being prone to panicky reactions; these could prevent or destroy the very thing you are after, or hurt those close to you ... the truth of the saying, 'Those that don't ask, don't get'.

♥ LOVE/RELATING/SOCIAL

As water represents emotion, this Symbol carries a critical message. On the surface, it says that emotional rescue is on its way or has already arrived. At a deeper level it is suggesting a number of other things, such as you being in an emotionally sticky situation but not allowing yourself to be rescued; being frightened of drowning or inundated by your own or someone else's feelings; being a victim in relationships and always having to be rescued.

KEEP FOCUSED ON ... what pride or conditioning you are clinging to that prevents another from saving you ... tracking down what in your past gave you a fear of deep involvement ... learning how to 'swim' or deal with your emotions more yourself.

WATCH OUT FOR ... not genuinely admitting to your emotional state, for no one will know how you feel.

MONEY/WORK/CREATIVITY

If you have been in difficulty, professionally or financially, something or someone is about to help you out, if they haven't already done so. Alternatively, this Symbol is saying that whatever you have in mind will rescue you, in the sense of making you feel more worthwhile and useful – so go for it.

KEEP FOCUSED ON ... making sure that someone has shouted 'Man overboard!' – that it has been announced to the appropriate quarter that you are in need of assistance; this could just be by prayer ... making sure that yourself or others have room to breathe.

WATCH OUT FOR ... not recognizing offers of help ... refusing them out of a misguided sense of pride, or thinking that something easier or better may chance along. It may, but what would you do if you were actually drowning?

☉ KARMA/ATTITUDE/HEALTH

You, or the object of your enquiry, are now in a position to be delivered or released from whatever has been confining, suffocating or threatening you. The only condition is that you recognize your need, and surrender to the aid that will meet it. There is also the possibility of having to understand why you got into such straits in the first place.

KEEP FOCUSED ON ... anyone or anything that is a sign of this deliverance, gently cling to it, and allow it to show you the way back to 'dry land' or the stability and reunion you are after ... any crisis or method that can reveal vitally significant experiences – mostly relating to the past.

WATCH OUT FOR ... forever following or attracting lost causes; they are probably your own unlooked at needs or weaknesses, projected on to others or the world at large.

'I was much too far out all my life/And not waving but drowning'

AN EMBASSY BALL

☆ FORMAL DISPLAY ☆

GENERAL INTERPRETATION

A traditional and dramatic process whereby social rank is paraded and assessed before what is regarded as the established social elite or upwardly mobile. Getting seen in the right places.

KEEP FOCUSED ON ... mustering yourself in a manner that wins acclaim and self-esteem in the eyes of your peers ... laying down or following whatever rules pave the way for a more spontaneous and personal commingling and advancement.

WATCH OUT FOR ... pomposity and snobbishness ... being politically correct to the point of being a nonentity with no opinion of your own, being powerless, listened to by no one ... getting stuck in a pleasurable but meaningless habit or social round, that could degrade you rather than raise you up.

LOVE/RELATING/SOCIAL

If one wishes to get what one wants socially, sexually or romantically, or even if one wants to merely get by with a minimum of difficulty or embarrassment – then sometimes one has to 'play the game'. This means following certain rules and procedures.

KEEP FOCUSED ON ... mastering whatever rules or rituals are required in order to find favour or satisfaction, or simply pass muster. This could be learning the rules of etiquette, what is fashionable, Tantric sex or whatever is the 'form' regarding your area of concern ... being genuine and sincere if you do not wish to 'play the game'.

WATCH OUT FOR ... assuming that you can just do as you please. Nothing is actually stopping you, but can you get along without support from others? ... losing yourself amid meaningless social conventions.

MONEY/WORK/CREATIVITY

Nearly all professions or financial systems have some kind of hierarchy. Whether one likes it or not, there is always someone or something above you who says 'yea or nay' to whatever you are offering or doing, and decides what the criteria are, what the market is. If you wish to be a success in this world, in all but exceptional cases you have to do something that conforms to what this hierarchy likes and approves of.

KEEP FOCUSED ON ... creating and maintaining useful contacts ... what area of the market interests you, establishing what it is after and endeavouring to supply it – with a dash of your own uniqueness thrown in, otherwise you or your creation will eventually be seen for the mere contrivance it is.

WATCH OUT FOR ... sycophancy, boot-licking.

KARMA/ATTITUDE/HEALTH

Here this Symbol denotes a karma of privilege, of moving in high and powerful circles. This also means that higher standards than usual have to be maintained while one's 'karmic calibre' is assessed. It also poses the possibility of rejecting or being rejected by those in high circles. A feeling of being an outcast or rebel would be a sign of this release or fall from grace – depending on how you view it.

KEEP FOCUSED ON ... upholding and developing the spiritually and morally sound values that this karmic stream has inculcated into you. For example, dignity and good health ... using your position to help who or what appeals to you.

WATCH OUT FOR ... clinging to the questionable values of this karmic stream, such as snobbishness and using one's position to get out of personal responsibilities ... being in a lowly position now because of having transgressed previously.

'To meet the right faces, be in the right places'

AN INVENTOR EXPERIMENTING

☆ TRIAL AND ERROR ☆

 GENERAL INTERPRETATION

You are finding out what works for you. This entails being wholeheartedly reliant on your own resources and ingenuity, with little or no regard to the limiting opinions and scope of conventionality or of others who cannot see what you can.

KEEP FOCUSED ON ... the open-mindedness that enables you to discover dimensions of experience that are closed to most people ... the possibility that your use of the Oracle is itself an experiment as you make a bid to determine the nature of the materials, circumstances and people that you are involved with.

WATCH OUT FOR ... any eccentric preoccupations with the inconsequential which are driven by fanciful thinking or delusions of grandeur.

 LOVE/RELATING/SOCIAL

Although deliberately approaching relationships and emotional issues in a clinical or experimental way could be regarded as inappropriate or distasteful, if we are honest, we do go through certain relationships or ways of relating with a view to finding the right 'formula' for, or 'chemistry' between, ourselves and others. In fact, in order to keep troublesome and damaging emotions under control, it is a good idea to ...

KEEP FOCUSED ON ... establishing a degree of objectivity as you look for what works for you emotionally, socially or romantically. It is also important that you identify where you could be going wrong, and learn from it ... getting there.

WATCH OUT FOR ... playing with another's feelings; one day this could blow up in your face.

 MONEY/WORK/CREATIVITY

You are in the process of finding out what works for you. To impose on yourself or others a neurotic need to get everything right at once would be asking for trouble, and probably the very failure you fear. The 'back to the drawing board' scenario is a statistical likelihood, as is arranging and rearranging your finances until they balance out or show a profit.

KEEP FOCUSED ON ... the nature of the Creative Process, that one thing leads to another, and then another, until the whole picture eventually takes shape.

WATCH OUT FOR ... forcing the facts to fit what you want to be the case when you know deep down they don't ... trying to achieve what only leads to ridicule and more frustration because it is not yet achievable.

KARMA/ATTITUDE/HEALTH

Every human being could be said to be an experiment in the gigantic laboratory called Life, Nature and Planet Earth. We could then view the 'inventor' as God, Evolution or the Creator. We could also see ourselves as expressions of God and Evolution, or as co-creators. It can also be helpful to ...

KEEP FOCUSED ON ... the certainty that one day you will find the 'solution', providing you stay on the case and maintain a degree of detachment ... the fact that fortunate accidents can happen if you keep at it (Sir Alexander Fleming discovered penicillin by chance).

WATCH OUT FOR ... going 'mad' owing to the mistaken idea that you can achieve something that which the Laws of Nature herself will not permit. If you do manage to transgress or get round these Laws in pursuit of your dream, there will be hell to pay – a nightmare, in fact.

'There are no mistakes except the ones you do not learn from'

TELEPHONE LINEMEN AT WORK

✵ MAKING GOOD CONNECTIONS ✵

 GENERAL INTERPRETATION

The creation and maintenance of all forms of communication, including those that are hidden or underestimated. Everything is being done to make, mend or improve communications; to put things across clearly, simply and swiftly.

KEEP FOCUSED ON ... making sure a message gets through ... acquiring or maintaining the ability to keep the one in touch with the many, and the many in touch with the one ... whatever message is trying to get through, or is on its way.

WATCH OUT FOR ... a preoccupation with intrigue, rumour or gossip ... taking in incomplete or erroneous information ... imagining that the 'phone' is being tapped or there are 'voices in the head' when really there is a message trying to come through.

♥ LOVE/RELATING/SOCIAL

Attempts are being made to improve or repair communication, the life-blood of healthy relationships. For this to meet with success – each party getting through to the other – it requires equal effort from both sides. This involves give and take, being prepared to listen. One person sometimes needs to meet the other more than half way when the other is having trouble expressing what they really mean or feel.

KEEP FOCUSED ON ... keeping open lines of communication, especially emotionally; others are helping you here, even though you may not be aware of it ... appreciating any attempt made to keep in touch ... the new ties that are replacing the old ones ... just making that call!

WATCH OUT FOR ... pulling the plug too soon, perhaps because there is something you do not want to hear.

MONEY/WORK/CREATIVITY

In these times of mass media and information technology, this Symbol takes on a powerful significance. It is simply saying that whatever lines of communication are important to you must be kept in good working order. This Symbol is also affirming and encouraging any industry associated with communications.

KEEP FOCUSED ON ... the probability that communications are improving, or need improving ... what is happening in the world of communications generally and in your own sphere in particular ... keeping abreast of the latest developments in this field, for things are moving ahead all the time.

WATCH OUT FOR ... failure to connect, for this could be at the root of any problem, and it is now in a position to be put right ... wrong thinking or ideas.

KARMA/ATTITUDE/HEALTH

Every so often, the way we perceive or communicate has to be overhauled, but it may take a crisis or serious breakdown in communication to make this known to us. Certain forms of communication, such as the nervous system in the body, may reflect an issue of something vital being garbled or not getting through.

KEEP FOCUSED ON ... maintaining an 'in-touchness' within you or with the world around you, and with spiritual agencies ... the probability that rectification of this is underway, but you must help it along, and trust it ... receiving the Call.

WATCH OUT FOR ... not getting the messages that your life or body is sending you ... denying certain aspects to your personality, giving rise to complaints, such as deafness or tinnitus, or dissociation.

'It's good to talk'

CHILDREN PLAYING AROUND FIVE MOUNDS OF SAND

☆ CHILD–ADULT INTERACTION ☆

GENERAL INTERPRETATION

Hopefully you are interacting with the challenges that life presents you in a spontaneous and innocent way, thereby creating a valid and rewarding lifestyle. Alternatively, there is the prospect of having children and the responsibilities that they incur. Or, seeing how the passage of time is inexorably set against remaining a child or in a childlike state.

KEEP FOCUSED ON ... your adventurous and childlike streak, for this helps to take life beyond the humdrum and into a more magical realm of being ... a playful attitude to the challenges and difficulties that life presents (*see* Karma below) ... having fun as a means of dealing with heavy issues.

WATCH OUT FOR ... pointless and indulgent dabbling ... procrastination, for this will make everyday problems insurmountable.

MONEY/WORK/CREATIVITY

Either you have a situation that has got too bogged down in its own theories and agendas and so needs an injection of playfulness, honesty and spontaneity to jazz it up, or there is an immature and unworldly element on the loose that requires greater earnestness and seriousness, especially when it comes to financial management.

KEEP FOCUSED ON ... finding elements or people who are free and creative and young at heart to breath freshness and spontaneity into an over-earnest and analytical situation ... introducing professionalism and business acumen into a set-up which is too impetuous and immature ... cheerfully surmounting difficulties and thereby satisfying your ambitions.

WATCH OUT FOR ... the humdrum ... the chaotic.

♥ LOVE/RELATING/SOCIAL

This Symbol raises the whole issue of how the emotional and intellectual, the child and the adult, interact in relationships. Most conflicts can be traced back to getting one's lines crossed in this respect. One person will be wanting a feeling response and instead they receive an analysis or solution; someone's trying to be practical in the face of another being excessively emotional.

KEEP FOCUSED ON ... who wants what – emotional or intellectual input? Once you know this you must feed or be fed what is wanted – or expect to be frustrated.

WATCH OUT FOR ... spouting some theory when a person just wants you to say, 'There, there, then', or being friendly and sentimental when someone is in need of hard facts or practical advice. That someone could be you.

KARMA/ATTITUDE/HEALTH

The number 5 is representative of the planet Saturn, the energies of which are serious, practical and ordered, but can also be depressive and decidedly unplayful. And so, this indicates that the child (literal or inner) and the adult (literal or inner) have to learn to relate, or the child will feel sad and oppressed, and the adult will feel played up and out of control.

KEEP FOCUSED ON ... a method called Self Talk where you give a name to your inner child and a name to your adult and get them both to talk to one another (*see* page 464).

WATCH OUT FOR ... the vicious circle created by feeling low (child) and then condemning it (adult) ... back problems owing to lack of support.

'Any system ... that shocks the mind of a child cannot be a true system'

A GIRL'S FACE BREAKING INTO A SMILE

☆ SHINING THROUGH ☆

✺ GENERAL INTERPRETATION

On the face of it, here is a favourable outlook. But this Symbol also stresses that happiness is not so much something you 'get' as something that is attracted by an internal state, such as the magic of personality that can transcend all difficulties and win through with a sense of unbounded joy. People are prepared to do or give up a lot when such a positive atmosphere is being generated.

KEEP FOCUSED ON ... a natural sense that everything and everyone is, not just has, a spirit, and that the spirit will inevitably shine through ... thinking bright thoughts.

WATCH OUT FOR ... embarrassment or social ineptitude owing to a naive assumption that you can get by on just a smile ... the transitory nature of a happy mood or prospect – so don't break out the champagne until you are sure.

♡ LOVE/RELATING/SOCIAL

Here you have a relationship or individual that is a happy one, or promises to be so as a result of whatever is the nature of your enquiry or course of action, simply because of a positive attitude and upbeat personality. A pleasing encounter. A strong alternative to this is that an injection of a positive mood or appearance is what is required to 'save the day'.

KEEP FOCUSED ON ... making others happy, especially through radiating a warmth of feeling ... putting on a happy face and being cheerful, even though you feel you are dying inside.

WATCH OUT FOR ... moping around and feeling sorry for yourself, for this will have the opposite of the desired effect ... being deluded into thinking that things are all right when they are not ... smugness; this is a 'false smile' just waiting to be wiped from one's face.

♆ MONEY/WORK/CREATIVITY

Happiness breeds success. If you are happy in your work you will do that work well; if you are happy with your creations, then others will be happy with them too, or, at least, they will create a positive feeling that encourages you to carry on.

KEEP FOCUSED ON ... doing whatever you have to do with the feeling that wherever you are and whatever you are doing is right for you – and it will be ... pursuing creative ventures with the main aim of self-amusement.

WATCH OUT FOR ... kidding yourself that everything in the garden is lovely when it is patently not. For an accurate picture of one's situation, seek out dissenters as well as followers.

☯ KARMA/ATTITUDE/HEALTH

Good news, possibly out of the blue. Health-wise, it is proven that smiling is good for you, and not just psychologically – it actually improves or promotes physical health. Karmically, a happy and healthy disposition is indicated.

KEEP FOCUSED ON ... the object of your concern with an attitude of something shining inwardly and outwardly; actually wearing a smile will help this along ... the principle that one has the power to choose how you want to be – and now more than ever. Laugh and the world laughs with you ... someone's eyes if you wish to see whether they really are happy or not, or merely just 'all right'.

WATCH OUT FOR ... superficial or pretentious displays of well-being or good nature. One has to find something genuinely to smile about, even if it is only the sky being blue.

'Count your blessings one by one ... They will light your heart with happiness'

A WOMAN THE FATHER OF HER OWN CHILD

☆ RESOURCEFULNESS ☆

✴ GENERAL INTERPRETATION

Not only a literal depiction of a single parent, this also symbolizes the authority and capability that is hard won as the result of a loss or crisis. The necessity of having to find in oneself what was possibly lacking in the quarter where it was expected.

KEEP FOCUSED ON ... your sheer grit and ability to provide both everyday nurture and long-term spiritual guidance – then you will win through ... just doing what has to be done.

WATCH OUT FOR ... unnecessary, self-defeating, even masochistic independence ... taking responsibility for too much; ask yourself why you are doing this – it could be for reasons of needing to control everyone and everything around you ... feeling put upon, as this will actually weaken you when you have no choice but to 'carry that load'.

♥ LOVE/RELATING/SOCIAL

This Symbol poses a number of distinct possibilities: one parent having the children because of separation; a person who is taking care of their partner almost as if they are a child; an 'unequal' relationship, which is really a case of one person being stronger in practice than the other.

KEEP FOCUSED ON ... putting the needs of your children first ... the possibility that you are in need of mothering/fathering, so should not presume to be more independent than you are ... why you are doing the 'carrying': because you care or are stronger, or because it is a means of feeling more secure and in control? Or both?

WATCH OUT FOR ... projecting your inner child onto your own child or partner (*see* Karma below) ... thinking you are carrying someone when in fact they could be carrying you.

♟ MONEY/WORK/CREATIVITY

Having to be both homemaker and bread-winner, or having to do everything because of a shortage of staff and funds, or because you are a one-person business. If you are in the business of caring for children or the child in others, then this is an auspicious oracle.

KEEP FOCUSED ON ... the fact that it is only you who can do what has to be done, and because of this your eventual achievement will be truly remarkable.

WATCH OUT FOR ... refusing help when it is offered because of a misguided sense of pride. Your business or creation might be your 'baby', but as it gets bigger (as babies do) you need others to help you carry it ... an inability to delegate, your own inner child could manifest as treating co-workers as children and having constantly to supervise them.

☯ KARMA/ATTITUDE/HEALTH

Here is the karma of having to be strong in the face of a demanding situation because you appear to be having to do more than your share, or do what you are not apparently equipped for. This strongly points to the issue of the inner child and how it falls to one to parent oneself as a result of the 'real thing' being lacking in childhood or a previous lifetime.

KEEP FOCUSED ON ... using the Self Talk method (*see* page 463) if you feel you have an inner child problem, that is, you feel frightened or weak inside in some way ... unconditionally and unstintingly caring for whoever is obviously in need of your care.

WATCH OUT FOR ... feeling bitter and resentful about your lot, for this would only perpetuate it ... indulging or over-protecting others.

'At a certain point in one's development it is necessary to be both father and mother to oneself'

A WOODS RICH IN AUTUMN COLOUR

☆ THE GLORY OF TRANSITION ☆

✿ GENERAL INTERPRETATION

The intense significance that characterizes a critical point in any cycle of development. Possibly you are involved in part of a significant and poignant process of transformation, that holds the prospect of 'wintering' until the 'spring' of rebirth arrives. If your question has some reference to time, this Symbol may well be indicating this is 'autumn'.

KEEP FOCUSED ON ... the high degree of success that you achieve through investing yourself in any area of true interest.

WATCH OUT FOR ... imbuing any given situation with more significance than it merits with the consequence of being disappointed ... making a crisis out of a drama.

♥ LOVE/RELATING/SOCIAL

There is great poignancy here because it is saying that something has reached its peak and so must decline. But it may be back later. Equally, this could be a time when relating or a relationship is going through a peak of intensity – be it high or low – in order that it may transform into something else.

KEEP FOCUSED ON ... the process of transition that is occurring without trying to escape from it, diminish or rationalize it. Something has to die for something new to be born on the other side, so endure, enjoy and wonder at the sheer intensity of it all.

WATCH OUT FOR ... romanticizing, in the sense of trying to freeze a 'high' in time; this would make things unreal and brittle, leading to disillusionment.

♆ MONEY/WORK/CREATIVITY

In commercial and financial terms we could be looking at something that has a seasonal quality to it. Then again, something may have reached a peak and we would need to make provision for a decline. Creatively speaking, it is more likely to be saying that the object of your concern has a rich, vivid and evocative quality about it. This could also be the glow of success or abundance that you are enjoying, with a strong hint that you should soon go about feathering your nest, or take advantage of whatever's in the offing.

KEEP FOCUSED ON ... reading the signs of the time and do whatever necessary to 'gather in the harvest' or 'prepare the ground' for the future.

WATCH OUT FOR ... missing this moment of abundance – it will not last forever.

☯ KARMA/ATTITUDE/HEALTH

A time of vividness and intensity – a peak experience perhaps – that is supercharged with the inevitability that it is about to disappear. It is as if Life or the situation is saying that death or dormancy is not far off, but it will be back. In human terms, we talk of the 'autumn of life' and this could have an important relevance to your question.

KEEP FOCUSED ON ... respecting or having feelings of awe for anything or anyone that is approaching a point of seeming decay, which is actually a bright and intense preface to death, be it literal or metaphorical.

WATCH OUT FOR ... missing the potency and poignancy of what is going on in your life or, sadder still, seeing it as something depressing and foreboding.

'If there wasn't death, I think you couldn't go on'

A PARROT LISTENING AND THEN TALKING

☆ ATTUNEMENT AND ACCLIMATIZATION ☆

GENERAL INTERPRETATION

Occasioned or called for here is the basic human function that enables an individual to tune into the sights and sounds of the world, then integrate and communicate them, eventually becoming fluent and in possession of real ability. Simon says. Recording or replication of any kind.

KEEP FOCUSED ON ... your ability to respond to circumstances in an appropriate, even amusing way that helps give cohesion and direction to your efforts, or the efforts of others ... studying and researching your subject matter for this will lead to good results.

WATCH OUT FOR ... an inappropriate or formulaic response to others or to work that fails to further matters.

♥ LOVE/RELATING/SOCIAL

Repetitive scenarios, oppressive and boring though they may be, serve to teach us something important about how to relate, how to appreciate and be appreciated, how to understand and be understood. What is being shown that needs to be known, rather than simply reacted to?

KEEP FOCUSED ON ... listening carefully to one another ... the fact that you and another are learning something from each other, and that the lesson will be repeated until it is ... the essence of what your relationship is telling you, comprehending its meaning, then make it clear to yourself or another, and put it into action.

WATCH OUT FOR ... caging others or yourself into some rigid role, causing you to squawk or to feel dull and uncomfortably ruffled.

⚕ MONEY/WORK/CREATIVITY

Success depends upon your ability to respond to situations and demands in an appropriate fashion, to give what is expected. Procedures will have to be gone over again and again until they are made one's own, performed as second nature or known by heart. Question and answer occupations are well-starred.

KEEP FOCUSED ON ... receiving and putting across the necessary sound bites, the punch lines, the appreciable product or idea ... obtaining professional advice and acting upon it, passing it on ... introducing variety to offset any drudge.

WATCH OUT FOR ... merely sticking to formulas, clichés or copying others, for interest will wane quite quickly ... doing anything 'parrot fashion' for it lacks conviction and is unconvincing ... any job that has a significant boredom factor.

☯ KARMA/ATTITUDE/HEALTH

Stressed here is the importance of finding and listening to the inner voice, then being true to it in your own life and translating what it tells you into the everyday world in a meaningful way.

KEEP FOCUSED ON ... whatever it is that has a genuine meaning for you, not just what you have been led to believe ... affirming to yourself repeatedly, 'I can do this' and 'I can do that' ... an appreciation of the depth of meaning and emotion surrounding the issue of your concern.

WATCH OUT FOR ... following too closely any doctrine or knowledge that has been fed to you and expressing it too literally or rigidly, for it will constrain rather than guide, hypnotize rather than inspire ... listening to habitual inner voices saying, 'I can't do this' and 'I can't do that'. Silence them!

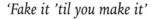

'Fake it 'til you make it'

A WOMAN DRAWING TWO DARK CURTAINS ASIDE

✠ FATE REVEALING THE TRUTH ✠

 GENERAL INTERPRETATION

Fate or intuition piercing the dense or sinister veils that conceal the deeper and profound truths which have resisted superficial acceptance or observation. Whatever your (proposed) course of action is at present, it will reveal to you what you have been hiding from or looking for, liberating you in the process.

KEEP FOCUSED ON ... your uncompromising desire to get to the real causes behind surface appearances as this will change a situation for the better ... the fact that fears have to be faced and dealt with sooner or later.

WATCH OUT FOR ... resisting confrontational situations that you think you are not yet ready for – the Oracle says you now have to be ... exposing flaws in others instead of those in yourself ... paying lip service to the truth by revealing what is of little significance for even less effect.

 MONEY/WORK/CREATIVITY

If your work is concerned with anything that has to do with exposing the truth of a matter, then the Oracle is approving of it and stressing the great benefits that ensue from such efforts. The Oracle is, after all, doing just this! Alternatively, the Oracle could be referring to something in your professional or financial affairs that is blocking progress or withholding vital information.

KEEP FOCUSED ON ... rooting out whatever it is that is in the way of your seeing or getting what you are after. Help is at hand to accomplish this, but you will first have to show willing. For example, writers may not know what ideas are coming through until they write.

WATCH OUT FOR ... creating intrigues and manipulative devices – although they may work initially, they are creating a minefield for the future.

♡ **LOVE/RELATING/SOCIAL**

Intimacy or living at close quarters with anyone is bound to bring out in us any resistance to such intimacy. But this merely mirrors whatever it is within our own personality that we are afraid of getting close to and dealing with. Scorpio is the Sign of both Death and Intimacy because something in us has to die, like the fear of being exposed, if we are to attain the greater intimacy that is so craved.

KEEP FOCUSED ON ... identifying your own fears or dubious intentions before seeing or dealing with them in another ... the fact that the darker the 'darkness', the brighter will be whatever it is concealing ... how the truth *will* out.

WATCH OUT FOR ... your hates and fears regarding a person or relationship for they point the finger at your shadow and the chinks in your armour.

☯ **KARMA/ATTITUDE/HEALTH**

There exists in human and personal history many damaging events and distortions of the truth. Karmically speaking, human and personal history are one and the same, and so we are all subject to these sins of the past – Man's inhumanity to Man. Here is a time when such sins must be discovered and exposed. They have attained critical mass and are doing harm in the present; they are ripe for identification and dispersal.

KEEP FOCUSED ON ... courageously revealing (to yourself) whatever your 'dark secret' is, and this will release you from whatever fears and shadows imprison or inhibit you, thereby healing you.

WATCH OUT FOR ... the possibility that a physical complaint that is suffered (along with its treatment) stems from a deep dark cause (and the failure to look at that cause).

'In time we hate that which we often fear'

A SOLDIER DERELICT IN DUTY

☆ A QUESTION OF CONSCIENCE ☆

✴ GENERAL INTERPRETATION

The question of to who or what one owes true allegiance, and then facing the consequences of decisions made in respect of this. Having to find the right motivation.

KEEP FOCUSED ON ... an uncompromising response to your innermost values and beliefs ... being true to the dictates of your conscience, possibly in opposition to convention ... listening to advice that promotes the more demanding course rather than the easy way out. Who is the braver soldier: the deserter who refuses to kill other human beings, or the soldier who is 'only doing his duty'?

WATCH OUT FOR ... moral weakness in the face of tests of true character, or simply not having your heart in it ... not taking heed of what the Oracle tells you or has already told you.

♥ LOVE/RELATING/SOCIAL

A sense of responsibility in relationships is like the backbone is to the body. Without this a relationship will eventually collapse. In your current situation, you need to distinguish between 'good soldiers' and 'bad soldiers' (*see* General Interpretation).

KEEP FOCUSED ON ... being a good soldier, someone who proves themselves to be honest and reliable, possessing principles and keeping to them ... having to do something that goes 'beyond the call of duty', paying no regard to what seems to be purely your own interests.

WATCH OUT FOR ... bad soldiers, being involved with those who lack emotional courage and commitment – or being one yourself. This is what the Oracle is directly warning about.

MONEY/WORK/CREATIVITY

There are no excuses when it comes to falling short of what the material world demands of us. On a personal level, one can evade one's responsibilities and get away with it. But in the 'real world' of 'machines and men' you can only argue so far with things such as a rejection slip, a bank statement or an officer of the law. That is, unless you hold a Higher Power or Inner Truth to be your Reality and Law, in which case you have to be stronger and more honest than most, but your fortunes will come to you through these channels. If this is the case, you need to ...

KEEP FOCUSED ON ... making a priority of what you have to do, rather than what you get out of it materially. Yet, at the same time ...

WATCH OUT FOR ... 'rendering unto Caesar what are Caesar's, and unto God what are God's'.

☯ KARMA/ATTITUDE/HEALTH

Karma and duty are inseparable. They both mean 'what is due'. Your situation therefore has everything to do with knowing what is due and performing it. In effect, whatever the subject matter of your question, the Oracle is saying that it has to do with karmic duty. It is therefore inescapable since you can evade or avoid it now if you like, but it'll only come back to be sorted out later – possibly as a health condition.

KEEP FOCUSED ON ... finding the ways, means and courage to do what you know in your heart you have to do ... keeping to any health regimen that is necessary ... making up for past failings.

WATCH OUT FOR ... the ego's way of making something spiritual seem easy and glamorous at first, so that when you realize it is not, it is dropped altogether; this is why the peace and love movement of the 1960s faltered and declined.

'Lock the door, bolt the hatch, and the rain and wind will rust the latch away. You cannot escape'

HUNTERS STARTING OUT FOR DUCKS

☆ HUNT OR BE HUNTED ☆

✳ GENERAL INTERPRETATION

The time calls for the basic drive to go out into the 'wild', the 'jungle' of life, to get what is needed to sustain life, and also to provide an outlet for this drive. You don't necessarily know what you are going to 'bag' until you are out there – or in there if it is something internal. This could simply be saying that you are new to something, so don't have unrealistic expectations.

KEEP FOCUSED ON ... the natural and uncomplicated desire to go for whatever is required, born of a sense of the right to do ... whatever it is you are trying to get, hit or locate; this is the only way you are going to be successful.

WATCH OUT FOR ... preying on those weaker than yourself, be they human or otherwise, or being a 'sitting duck' yourself.

♡ LOVE/RELATING/SOCIAL

This could simply be about looking for a mate, with all the persistence and chance that it entails. Or it could suggest a hunter and the hunted, a predator and the prey. It could even be reciprocal, with each person taking turns to chase or chastise, snipe or snap at the other. Whether one or both of you relish this set-up or hate it, could be a question here.

KEEP FOCUSED ON ... accepting that there is this predator–prey dynamic and that you must create a balance of power ... whether or not what is going on is harming anyone. If you think it is then you are bound to do something about it, such as leave or make a stand.

WATCH OUT FOR ... being an aggressor or a victim or patsy ... the fact that there is a predatory streak in most people.

MONEY/WORK/CREATIVITY

You have just set out, or are thinking of setting out, on some venture. You must tell yourself that it's early days yet and whether you like it or not, it's a dog-eat-dog world out there and it would be best to acclimatize yourself to this fact. Is what you are after in sufficient demand? Are you being hunted – and for the right reasons, at the right time? Remember, an oracle is not an accountant or a feasibility study.

KEEP FOCUSED ON ... going for whatever you see as 'fair game', an objective or market that will 'feed' you and yours, enabling you to survive and prosper ... the fact that you don't know until you've tried.

WATCH OUT FOR ... wantonly or vindictively using others to satisfy a base desire or to make you feel 'king or queen of the castle' ... being the hunted rather than the hunter.

☯ KARMA/ATTITUDE/HEALTH

Indicated here is a conflict concerning finer feelings versus basic needs, desires versus fears, freedom versus limitation, ambition versus capability, and spirituality versus materialism. The ultimate karmic law is that of balance, which would have us be harmless, yet at the same time not be so soft that we get harmed in the process.

KEEP FOCUSED ON ... the probability that the situation is either calling you to toughen up or soften up – or a balance of both, depending upon the circumstances ... hunting down what is vulnerable in yourself, like your inner child, before someone else does. You must care for it, they may not (see 'Self Talk', page 463).

WATCH OUT FOR ... being a 'lame duck' or victim because that would be asking for more punishment, which could eventually take the form of physical complaints or damage ... 'petty tyrants' who try to oppress you; never let them do so.

And a-hunting we will go

A BUNNY METAMORPHOSED INTO A FAIRY

☆ ETHEREAL POWER ☆

 GENERAL INTERPRETATION

The inevitability that over-sensitivity or raw libido has to graduate into something more refined. Also, timidity that has to evolve into psychic sensitivity. Alternatively, a child or childlike person who becomes one with their own dreams or departs into another world.

KEEP FOCUSED ON ... promoting the ability to make what others might regard as childish imaginings into something real and enchanting ... allowing sexual instincts naturally and harmlessly to have their way until a spontaneous inclination arises towards finer feelings and expressions of sensuality and desire.

WATCH OUT FOR ... impotency or perversion as signs of repressing rather than refining sexual energy ... immature flights of fancy that are damaging to the integrity of the personality.

LOVE/RELATING/SOCIAL

Here is a childlike or sexually active and uninhibited person or relationship that has now moved on, or is about to. The childlike person (or actual child) is on their way to seeing things more spiritually, but they may become rather twee or fey in the process. The sexually oriented individual, whether they know it or not, is tired of being dragged about by their genitals and is looking for a more satisfactory means of expressing their essential creative energy.

KEEP FOCUSED ON ... facilitating or being facilitated with this transformation from the childlike to the soulful, from a basic to a subtle expression of sexuality.

WATCH OUT FOR ... not recognizing this transformative shift ... being forcibly sexless.

MONEY/WORK/CREATIVITY

You used to be quite immature with regard to the material world, but now you have moved on to seeing it as the area in which you can make known your spiritual or creative ideals.

KEEP FOCUSED ON ... the fact that this process is relatively unusual and can be beset with problems. Most people go from being a child in the world to an ego in the world, whereas you have gone or are going from a child to a spiritual being. Your criteria of success are therefore different from others in that making your point is more important than making money.

WATCH OUT FOR ... feeling inadequate because you are evaluating yourself in terms of how much material power you do not have, rather than in terms of how much truth and beauty you are bringing into the world.

KARMA/ATTITUDE/HEALTH

Your life and being is shifting, or has already shifted, into a subtler or spiritual mode. This can pose many things: eating finer, possibly vegetarian, food; recognizing that your physical health is largely determined by your lifestyle and etheric body; identifying your ideals and living up to them.

KEEP FOCUSED ON ... how you may be called to heal yourself or another through influencing these vital energies in ways, such as hands-on healing, yoga, meditation, reiki, diet and making a healthier living and environment ... following your ideals.

WATCH OUT FOR ... any inclination to backslide into old indulgent ways – but then again do not overindulge in the new ones either. It is very difficult making this transition when the toing and froing of the natural progression is not recognized.

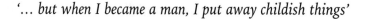

'... but when I became a man, I put away childish things'

CROWDS COMING TO THE MOUNTAIN TO LISTEN TO ONE MAN

☆ PULLING POWER ☆

 GENERAL INTERPRETATION

The charisma that is able to draw people to itself. Because of the strong allusion to Jesus' Sermon on the Mount, this Symbol implies a spiritual message that best drives or uses such charisma.

KEEP FOCUSED ON ... the power that you have, be it speech or another talent, that impresses others to strive towards the realization of the higher and better in themselves and others. This point must be made in a practical and uncompromising way that does not fail to reach the hearts and minds of those concerned ... finding or seeing the healer or teacher ... whatever gets under your skin or creates goose bumps.

WATCH OUT FOR ... a flair for self-expression which is let down by an inner lack of substance, the gullibility that this is initially met with, and the disillusionment that it ultimately encounters.

 MONEY/WORK/CREATIVITY

You definitely have something that others want or need at a fundamental and possibly non-material level; or, at least, this is the nature of your concern. In other words, everything depends upon it having and maintaining this basic appeal.

KEEP FOCUSED ON ... whatever is uplifting to the human spirit, and de-emphasizing how things look from a purely commercial standpoint ... longer-term goals, for they are what will guide you on ... the fact that you have what it takes to succeed.

WATCH OUT FOR ... using tricks to gain wealth or popularity. This could work, but there is the potential for 'selling one's soul to the devil'. Success won in this way eventually leads to being uncomfortably stuck with the low standards of the propaganda that got you there.

♥ **LOVE/RELATING/SOCIAL**

Your social life or relationships tend to revolve around, or are strongly influenced by, someone or something with charismatic appeal. This could apply to yourself, your partner, what you feel you need, a celebrity or the nature of your milieu. Everything depends on whether or not such charisma is merited or wisely bestowed.

KEEP FOCUSED ON ... whatever it is about yourself, someone or something else that has such a strong appeal; then ask yourself what it has actually attracted or done for anyone. If it has had a lasting beneficial effect then you can rest assured that it will continue to do so. However ...

WATCH OUT FOR ... being seduced by 'spin' to the extent that you lose sight of what is real and valid. You may need to get free of this to realize its falsity.

☯ **KARMA/ATTITUDE/HEALTH**

This Symbol can be referring to what is known as a 'peak experience', where one is powerfully put in touch with a higher reality that is normally outside of and beyond the everyday. This also points to the recognition of the spiritual as ultimately having more authority and meaning than the material.

KEEP FOCUSED ON ... what it is that appeals to your deepest sense of truth and beauty, something probably characterized by there being no easy route ... giving to others what any epiphany or peak experience has given you.

WATCH OUT FOR ... any come down after such peaks – it will pass as you get yourself grounded ... having to do anything that has to set up an 'enemy' in order to look or feel better about itself. For example, Adolf Hitler had the charisma, but he appealed evilly to latent racism to gain power over the masses.

'You are what you attract; the more you attract, the more careful you must be of what you are'

AN X-RAY

☆ LOOKING INTO AND SEEING THROUGH ☆

GENERAL INTERPRETATION

The situation requires that you appreciate that the truth of the matter can be revealed through concentration, insight or synchronicity. Then again, there may be an 'X factor' in play, which means that the truth of the matter may evade you until the time is right.

KEEP FOCUSED ON ... of what it is that you wish to see the hidden cause, reality or meaning ... the possibility that discovering what you wish to know is dependent on a genuine desire *to* know.

WATCH OUT FOR ... being seen through or the paranoia born of the mistaken impression that others can see what you can – or naively allowing them to do so ... a fear of knowing the truth of the matter, for this will either distort or disallow your perception of it.

LOVE/RELATING/SOCIAL

You are involved in an extremely intense and intimate relationship or set of relationships. This does not mean that any of them is sexual, although they may well be, but just that the innermost parts of each of your personalities are deeply in touch with each other. Possibly no one consciously knows what these parts are, but there may be someone here who has a strong psychological insight. It could be you.

KEEP FOCUSED ON ... discovering exactly what these innermost parts comprise; left unlooked at, or only experienced emotionally, uncomfortable sensations of control and manipulation will persist ... the root causes of strife or pleasure.

WATCH OUT FOR ... trying to sidestep or skim over current issues; they must be seen through to a definite conclusion or understanding.

MONEY/WORK/CREATIVITY

How something or someone works, needs looking into so you have a thorough understanding of the pros and cons of the situation. Also, the issue in question needs persisting with, and true motivations determining, if a successful development is to be achieved.

KEEP FOCUSED ON ... the facts and figures, especially the less obvious ones, until you feel equipped with enough information to make your next move or decision ... contacting the nucleus of what you wish to express, or your efforts will be frustrated.

WATCH OUT FOR ... drawing conclusions when you are only in possession of superficial details ... the fact that the object of your concern has the ability to look deeply into your affairs, hence the importance of looking into the dealings you have with them or it.

KARMA/ATTITUDE/HEALTH

In the context of health, this Symbol can be taken literally in that it refers you to X-rays or the need for them. Then again it could be entreating you to look at the deeper, underlying psychological causes for a physical complaint – something which the Oracle itself can help you with, so ask again if need be.

KEEP FOCUSED ON ... looking beyond surface appearances to the core meaning and original cause of the object of your enquiry, for, by their very nature, this is what the psychological or spiritual levels themselves are concerned with.

WATCH OUT FOR ... forming an idea or opinion without understanding the intricacies of what you are dealing with. This would be like a non-medical person analysing an X-ray – not very reliable and possibly dangerous. Don't pretend to be a medical, occult or psychological 'expert'.

'The truth which makes men free is for the most part the truth which men prefer not to hear'

INDIANS MAKING CAMP

✧ SECURITY THROUGH ATTUNEMENT ✧

 GENERAL INTERPRETATION

The situation produces or calls for an ability to establish security and provide for you and yours wherever and whenever. This is particularly the case when you find yourself in a strange or hostile environment.

KEEP FOCUSED ON ... familiarizing yourself with the customs, vibrations and practical facilities of the 'territory' that you are concerned with, where you need to feel safe and at ease ... your gut instincts concerning the places or faces you are involved with ... allowing time for settling in and acclimatizing yourself.

WATCH OUT FOR ... a manipulative or naive sense of opportunism that is bound to backfire on itself eventually.

 LOVE/RELATING/SOCIAL

This could mean that you are in the process of making yourself comfortable in, or familiar with, a social or romantic set-up. Or someone might be doing this with you. Basically, you are equipped to put yourself and anyone else at their ease, as long as you ...

KEEP FOCUSED ON ... feeling out or making clear what is acceptable and unacceptable, reassuring or threatening, accommodating or inhospitable ... how safe you feel in the presence of the person(s) concerned, for this indicates how safe any developments will be.

WATCH OUT FOR ... invading the space of others or allowing your own to be invaded. Such invasions will usually create insecurity or animosity, making it hard to win (back) ease and confidence.

 MONEY/WORK/CREATIVITY

Whoever or whatever you are involved with or working on requires that you feel at home; perhaps there is the need for a degree of personal familiarity to help things proceed or to achieve objectives. This could mean a sensitive take-over.

KEEP FOCUSED ON ... knowing your pitch ... allowing the time and space necessary to get used to new practices, rules, styles and standards ... familiarizing yourself with the facts and figures ... creating or discovering a positive working environment, a job you feel at home with ... creatively, 'writing what you know', that is, doing what comes from personal experience.

WATCH OUT FOR ... alienating or presuming on anyone or anything that is not familiar with what you are or make ... trying to be something or someone you are not ... contriving rather than creating.

KARMA/ATTITUDE/HEALTH

At a spiritual or psychological level there is now a need to tune into the spirits or psychological attitudes that inhabit the area in which you find yourself. The medicine man of a tribe would establish contact with these spirits, asking for their permission and/or protection. Health-wise, feeling secure at a spiritual level can be highly important, otherwise one is forever on one's guard, no matter how secure one might be mentally, materially or emotionally.

KEEP FOCUSED ON ... discovering or devising a method that creates security for the soul. This could entail the use of psychic protection, affirmation or a therapy such as soul retrieval.

WATCH OUT FOR ... paranoia or overuse of the intellect to keep tabs on everything, giving rise to complaints such as migraine, insomnia or panic attacks.

'The Earth is all the home I have,/The heavens my wide roof-tree'

A MILITARY BAND ON THE MARCH

✫ ALTOGETHER NOW! ✫

✹ GENERAL INTERPRETATION

The call to join or support a movement that has great and far-flung objectives that would take one beyond the ordinary pace and values of everyday life. The martial aspect to this Symbol need not be taken literally, but 'March' derives from Mars (the co-ruler of Scorpio), and in astrological symbolism this means taking a decisive and irrevocable step towards something, making it happen, mobilizing what one has towards an end.

KEEP FOCUSED ON ... your flair for encouraging and inspiring others to pursue higher goals, and thereby gaining a greater sense of satisfaction, while making it clear that sacrifices will have to be made.

WATCH OUT FOR ... making an irresponsible appeal to others' boredom, neuroses or dreams, or being impelled or seduced by one's own.

♥ LOVE/RELATING/SOCIAL

Being carried along by a tide of emotion and desire, off towards a challenging situation where you have to show the courage to overcome whatever it is that assails you or blocks the path to romantic, sexual, emotional or social harmony.

KEEP FOCUSED ON ... the fact that you will join or have already joined with one or many who share similar ideals or lifestyles. Therefore, lesser considerations and petty complaints should not be allowed to interfere with your common purpose and the collective morale that makes this achievement possible.

WATCH OUT FOR ... 'all's fair in love and war', so steel yourself for ups and downs, disagreements and frictions, remembering that the greatest harmony is gained through enduring and seeing through conflicts.

♆ MONEY/WORK/CREATIVITY

There is, or needs to be, a movement or trend calling you to the 'front' of whatever your field of concern happens to be. Then again, it could be that your role is that of enlisting others to a cause. In both cases, a sense of 'play' should be inherent in the work and there needs to be a strong passion or conviction behind what you do. Only true glory wins over false.

KEEP FOCUSED ON ... any end that truly inspires and goes beyond the petty drudgery of workaday life ... a sense that what you are doing is contributing to the 'war effort', that is, whatever is needed to overcome a common adversity ... your noblest intentions.

WATCH OUT FOR ... embarking on enterprises that mainly have glory and profit as their ends, or a misguided sense of idealism or loyalty as their motive and justification.

☯ KARMA/ATTITUDE/HEALTH

There are events and predicaments in life that are put there to exhort us to make a greater effort, to involve ourselves in a cause that goes beyond our limited little lives. This Symbol is saying that there is a greater adventure calling you, yet it is entirely up to you whether you follow that call, or feel up to it. In the end, it depends on whether an inexplicable urge seizes you and launches you into a new chapter of your life.

KEEP FOCUSED ON ... the fact that life is a series of battles and you have to rally yourself and others to overthrow a common enemy – this may be internal or an illness or weakness – and meet whatever challenges are thrown at you. Also, being prepared to endure hardship and apparent injustice.

WATCH OUT FOR ... gung-ho ventures or beliefs.

'C'est la guerre' (That's war for you)

THE KING OF THE FAIRIES APPROACHING HIS DOMAIN

☆ COMING BACK INTO YOUR POWER ☆

✪ GENERAL INTERPRETATION

The King of the Fairies could be regarded as the invisible sovereign of one's own being, the part of you that is your psychic centre, like the nerve centre or heart of any system. As such, it commands all your thoughts and feelings. This particularly positive Symbol informs you that, with respect to the object of your enquiry, you are coming home to what it is really all about, and so things will be begin to fall more and more into place.

KEEP FOCUSED ON ... framing life's affairs in a more romantic or spiritual context and this will have a commanding effect on those around you.

WATCH OUT FOR ... an unreal sense of superiority ... presuming success as being automatic – you are not arriving yet, just approaching.

♥ LOVE/RELATING/SOCIAL

You're very close to what you are after, yet, ironically, you were never really that far away. Perhaps you were not looking in the right direction. 'Fairies' or the invisible qualities of love and loved ones can only be seen when we allow the obscuring fog of the ego's fears and desires to drop from our eyes.

KEEP FOCUSED ON ... whatever it is that gives a fine but definite feeling of being at home with the person(s) in question. It is this inner sense of ease and connectedness that really matters, not what might appear as more conventionally acceptable or desirable.

WATCH OUT FOR ... not believing in 'fairies', those finer, more genuine aspects of emotion and related-ness ... past disillusionment making you cynical about the magic of real love.

⚘ MONEY/WORK/CREATIVITY

The nature of your work is coming back to the point it originally set out from; whatever was closest to your heart in the first place is what you are once more drawn to. Any line of work that appeals to people's fantasies, longings or dreams is well-starred. This Symbol could also be referring to the return of something or someone of great spiritual value.

KEEP FOCUSED ON ... heading towards whatever it is you have in mind, and you will get a progressively stronger 'signal'. In other words, you are getting nearer and nearer the source of your inspiration, supply or reward. You only need to carry on in the same direction.

WATCH OUT FOR ... being distracted by logical or market-driven values for they will lead you away from your path 'home', frustrating and delaying what is inevitable and giving you cause for regret.

☯ KARMA/ATTITUDE/HEALTH

You are returning to a more complete and healthy state of being from a less desirable one. For example, at some point in their lives many people have been traumatized out of their physical body into a state known as 'dissociation', a condition that is like an electrical appliance not being properly plugged in. Esoterically, this is the energy or etheric body (which vitalizes you) being out of alignment with the physical body.

KEEP FOCUSED ON ... the fact that being in charge of yourself is an entirely internal affair concerned with the realms of imagination and psychological or spiritual connectedness.

WATCH OUT FOR ... not recognizing or being in touch with your spirit or psychic centre, for all health and well-being springs from there. The innermost may often manifest outermost, like skin.

'What I had been seeking all this time was present all around me'

AN INDIAN SQUAW PLEADING TO THE CHIEF FOR THE LIVES OF HER CHILDREN

☆ CREATURE OR CREATOR ☆

☀ GENERAL INTERPRETATION

Being in a situation where one has to appeal to a higher authority – be it human or divine – to protect or further what is closest to one's heart, even if this means putting oneself in an apparently lowly position. Indeed, this might be an important condition of receiving such help or guidance.

KEEP FOCUSED ON ... championing your creations, or whoever or whatever needs championing ... your sense of priorities, for then all will go well ... the truth that sometimes we have to be driven to our knees to find out what really has value in our lives.

WATCH OUT FOR ... being in a weak and vulnerable position as a result of investing power where it is not deserved ... overselling yourself, losing respect or demeaning yourself ... being too sub-servient regarding the object of your enquiry, for you could lose your sense of free will.

♥ LOVE/RELATING/SOCIAL

This Symbol is imaging or predicting a rather dire situation where someone is in a position to grant, or not grant something that is extremely important to another person. One is moved to wonder what could have got the first person into such a powerless position in the first place – and what are the creations or charges whose fate is so vulnerable to the choice, opinion or whim of another.

KEEP FOCUSED ON ... what it is about yourself or someone else that has allowed you or them to fall too much under another person's spell ... treating desperation with compassion.

WATCH OUT FOR ... investing anyone with a power over you that is dependent upon you not believing in your own creative will and right to be ... power plays that are a call for help.

♆ MONEY/WORK/CREATIVITY

The material world, whether we like it or not, is based upon a hierarchy or power structure. As such, the value and fate of whatever we do or create is subject to the judgement of whoever is 'above' us. This could be one's boss, publisher, producer, director, any kind of official or authority figure, or one's customers. This is fair enough, but it is important to ...

KEEP FOCUSED ON ... the fact that such people are merely human and so are not infallible ... 'hawking your wares' passionately.

WATCH OUT FOR ... believing that any figure of authority is worth grovelling to – that is, unless you are simply playing the game in order to get what you want. Even so, such a loss of dignity could play into their hands because, deep down, you'd know you were demeaning yourself.

☯ KARMA/ATTITUDE/HEALTH

Here we have a karmic or health situation that is concerned with issues of power and creativity, or, simply, creative power. Those who create are part of the very fabric of Creation itself, and have some degree of power to influence their own and others' lives; they are co-creators with God. Those who do not create are merely 'creatures', the 'created', and are subject to the will of the 'creators'.

KEEP FOCUSED ON ... what you are or want to be – creator or creature, doer or done to, one who *makes* life happen or one who feels life is something that happens *to* them ... the fact that the only thing that has absolute power, short of the Sun and Nature, is whatever you believe has it. Whole countries can be subject to such beliefs.

WATCH OUT FOR ... abusing power if you are a creator ... being at the mercy of others, for that would mean you were a creature.

'Every country has the government it deserves'

THE HALLOWEEN JESTER

✫ MAKING LIGHT OF THE DARK ✫

⚛ GENERAL INTERPRETATION

Here you have, or need to have, a playful disregard for what can seem an authority or superstition that cannot be questioned. This serves simultaneously to placate supernatural forces or anything that is spooking you or others, and to free you from cumbersome taboos.

KEEP FOCUSED ON ... the transformative effect on outlook and mood that is released when you allow artlessness and innocence to be the natural part of your personality that it is.

WATCH OUT FOR ... being a fool to yourself – or making a fool of yourself – as a consequence of taking yourself too seriously ... not taking something that actually merits it seriously enough, such as the occult or a discarnate entity ... not taking the Oracle seriously, for then it will appear not to take you seriously either.

♡ LOVE/RELATING/SOCIAL

Relationships, astrologically governed as they are by Libra, are all a matter of balance. Scorpio, following Libra, 'ups the ante' and introduces the heavier ingredients of sexual intimacy and shared possessions – one has to be very careful about taking such things lightly. At the same time, one shouldn't get too heavy about them either.

KEEP FOCUSED ON ... taking others as seriously as you would like to be taken yourself ... introducing levity where and when it is acceptable and appropriate.

WATCH OUT FOR ... taking lightly the effects of sexual interaction, because consciously or not, this tends to show up people's weaknesses – something that should be taken very seriously.

⚱ MONEY/WORK/CREATIVITY

The situation calls for the integration of interests or considerations that may on the face of it appear incongruous. But it is this very merging or working in parallel that comes up with the goods. This Symbol could also be referring to balancing out the business side of things with a measure of informality. Equally, though, it could be a case of not being business-like enough, and letting personal feelings get in the way. If humour is your game, especially the irreverent kind, then this is an auspicious oracle.

KEEP FOCUSED ON ... creating a balance or fusion between whatever elements or extremes you are involved with.

WATCH OUT FOR ... not getting down to the serious business of organization, price structures, debt collection, taxes and so on. Some things are just never meant to be funny.

☯ KARMA/ATTITUDE/HEALTH

A theme of this Symbol is the coexisting of extremes – such as flippancy and passion, intensity and lightness, darkness and light – and it could be said that the quality of one period or lifetime acts as a balance to the preceding one. This process continues while we seek to integrate one with the other.

KEEP FOCUSED ON ... maintaining or mustering a cheerful, humorous air for this will dispel 'bad spirits' or gloomy moods, and do wonders for your psychological health. In turn, this also benefits your physical well-being ... psychically protecting yourself.

WATCH OUT FOR ... giggling or being flippant and fidgety when one is frightened of the unknown or supernatural when it would be advantageous to concentrate and get to know it and use it – or simply avoid it.

'It is better to appear a fool than it is to be one'

THE SABIAN SYMBOLS OF
SAGITTARIUS

Either directly, or in a subtle way, all these Symbols are concerned with the following qualities, or with situations that involve or call for them:

EXPANSION/EXPANSIVENESS

FAITH

GREAT THINGS

HIGHER EDUCATION

HIGHER MIND VERSUS LIBIDO

JOY

LAW

LEGS

OPPORTUNITY

PHILOSOPHY

POSITIVITY

RELIGION/BELIEF

SPORT

TRAVEL

A GRAND ARMY OF THE REPUBLIC CAMPFIRE

☆ THE SPIRIT OF REUNION ☆

❂ GENERAL INTERPRETATION

The celebratory recall of whatever it might be that gives a strong sense of group purpose and strength in the face of common oppressors, be they from the past or in the present. For reunion to be lasting it must go through stages of integration into your life as it is at present.

KEEP FOCUSED ON ... your cheerful and ongoing ability to bring together kindred spirits, thus making for an even stronger sense of accord ... re-energizing old allegiances, but keeping things in perspective ... stoking up interest in the object of your concern ... remembering who you are.

WATCH OUT FOR ... an out of touch and self-congratulatory sense of communion with others of like mind ... letting old ties eclipse present ones through a misguided blend of sentiment, exclusivity and enthusiasm.

🏆 MONEY/WORK/CREATIVITY

It has been said, disparagingly by some, that it is not what you know but who you know. This Symbol is stressing the positive side of using your past connections, experiences or pursuits, and possibly regenerating them in order to further your career or to support you in your material situation.

KEEP FOCUSED ON ... the importance of convening with those who share your professional or political interests in order to create security and to keep you informed of latest developments ... reviving past methods and lines, but considering them carefully and reasonably before investing too much time, energy or money in them.

WATCH OUT FOR ... using the old boy/girl network as a substitute for actual capability, for this could prove embarrassing, or worse, at a later date ... putting past priorities in front of current ones.

♥ LOVE/RELATING/SOCIAL

Whatever the situation, this Symbol is a call to come together with others, or one other in particular. If this is not necessarily predicting an actual reunion of some kind, it is encouraging you to be optimistic about doing whatever you can to create such a thing. Your dilemma might have to do with the fact that you do not take steps to do this, but choose instead to stay in uncomfortable isolation.

KEEP FOCUSED ON ... reuniting with anyone who has a common background or history to your own, being enthusiastic about them and coming to terms with them – to forgive and forget if need be ... sharing past memories.

WATCH OUT FOR ... nursing resentments – remember that 'misery loves company' ... thinking that having a common enemy will create a positive bond with others for very long.

☯ KARMA/ATTITUDE/HEALTH

Reunion here can mean the regrouping of a number of people who are on the same 'soul-flight', or a sense of having met someone before, or another kind of karmic re-encounter. This can evoke both bright and dark memories and feelings, so ...

KEEP FOCUSED ON ... seeing and experiencing reunions with others as unavoidable meetings with your own history, for they are very important to your present and future development and well-being ... letting bygones be bygones and creating a sense of comradeship; we are all souls struggling along the path; the main cause for celebration is that we have survived, the main cause for regret is for those who have not. Both should bring us closer.

WATCH OUT FOR ... the surfacing of real issues such as wounds (received or inflicted) that have been re-opened or have not healed properly.

'To meet again by a fleeting chance/With the Bells of Time all chiming
In our hearts and minds,/Reason drowned by rhyme'

THE OCEAN COVERED IN WHITE CAPS

☆ STIRRING STUFF ☆

 GENERAL INTERPRETATION

The eternity of wonders that excite the soul, and the implied necessity that these should be channelled and focused in a personal and meaningful way. The prospect of something thrilling or exhilarating, and possibly feeling disturbed by it so not seeing it clearly. Fleeting opportunities to be grasped.

KEEP FOCUSED ON ... a childlike and spontaneous enjoyment of all that life throws at you and presents you with ... being a calming influence where necessary ... accepting hiccups and doubts as being part of the process.

WATCH OUT FOR ... an aimless, haphazard and possibly hysterical temperament, be it in yourself or others, giving rise to more worries or excitement than the situation merits ... making wild guesses, perhaps with regard to interpreting what the Oracle is trying to tell you.

 LOVE/RELATING/SOCIAL

We often need a relationship, or something within a relationship, that stimulates our deeper feelings, thereby making our lives and relationships more interesting and fulfilling. Something could be in the air that is going to do just this – whip up the surface of your emotional life. Flirtatiousness.

KEEP FOCUSED ON ... enjoying the thrill of the experience of feeling, but also focusing on the deeper emotional issues to stabilize matters ... making small changes.

WATCH OUT FOR ... having reservations concerning emotional upsets because this could prevent a relationship from developing or happening at all ... going for frothy people or relationships; going merely for the thrill and then finding nothing deeper or longer lasting, or something deeper than you bargained for.

 MONEY/WORK/CREATIVITY

By surveying the whole scene relating to the object of your concern, you will see significant points where you can gain access, measure or purchase. Much depends on making a personal contact in order to hook the bigger fish or reach a wider market. Starting with a small idea that you like, it can develop into something bigger with a wider appeal. Playing the field.

KEEP FOCUSED ON ... the fact that the masses love little things ... that a good idea or product is only as good as its distribution ... creating distinct points of interest that draw attention to the whole ... making a lot out of a little, or a little out of a lot.

WATCH OUT FOR ... cheap ideas or gimmicky products for they will be gone in an instant, giving rise to very little of worth unless you can make a great deal of them at once.

 KARMA/ATTITUDE/HEALTH

Our own, relatively small and insignificant, personal lives and feelings, although seemingly more prominent than global concerns and mass emotions, are actually influenced by them. An earthquake creating strife and death the other side of the world affects us in subtle ways, as too does our deep and distant past.

KEEP FOCUSED ON ... how you can plumb deeper emotions through teasing out the surface ones ... the bigger emotional picture in order to make more sense of your personal position.

WATCH OUT FOR ... rationalizing away your unknown depths for they are the underlying reason for any surface disturbances ... feeling overwhelmed by the world around you when really it is a personal issue that you are feeling and displacing onto that mass situation – then saying how terrible it is that you cannot do anything about! This is the path to emotional chaos.

'I am for ever walking upon these shores, betwixt the sand and foam. The high tide will erase my footprints, and the wind will blow away the foam. But the sea and the shore will remain for ever'

TWO MEN PLAYING CHESS

☆ TIME FOR TACTICS ☆

❂ GENERAL INTERPRETATION

A time for testing and proving the intellectual faculties of retentive memory, step-by-step planning and tactics, or the testing of anything. Implied here is the necessity and opportunity to out-manoeuvre anything or anyone that is attempting to do the same to you.

KEEP FOCUSED ON ... your healthy sense of intellectual and psychological contest that rewards you with a sense of proficiency and authority ... psyching out a difficult adversary rather than using direct confrontation.

WATCH OUT FOR ... a scheming and suspicious mentality that creates its own enemies and pitfalls ... blundering into situations, hoping for the best, being impulsive rather than thinking ahead.

♥ LOVE/RELATING/SOCIAL

This is a time when emotions must not be allowed to take over. You could be dealing with someone who is quite cool and calculating, coming from their head rather than their heart; it might even be you. Possibly a homosexual confrontation with ulterior motives, or any relationship where the interaction is mainly or exclusively cerebral.

KEEP FOCUSED ON ... identifying and protecting who and what is most important to you (king and queen) ... playing for time if needs be ... developing or using an established skill with regard to relating or lovemaking.

WATCH OUT FOR ... playing games or for someone trying to catch you out, emotionally blackmail you, compromise or trap you ... being paranoid and needlessly suspicious or calculating.

MONEY/WORK/CREATIVITY

Your situation is being, or should be, worked out by thrashing out an agreement, fighting or bidding for something, or through business or artistic skills and values pitting themselves against the problem. The actual outcome is not that predictable, as is often the case where tests or competitions are concerned, for everything is down to individual form and judgement.

KEEP FOCUSED ON ... simply doing your very best, through concentrating on the job in hand ... waiting for the result with as much equanimity as possible if it is out of your hands ... plotting out all the various scenarios in order to have ready your best move ... helping 'key players' in whatever way is legal or practical.

WATCH OUT FOR ... leaving things to chance ... underestimating your opponent.

☯ KARMA/ATTITUDE/HEALTH

Something is being fought out here – hopefully, in your head. This could be quite taxing, depending upon who or what your adversary is. In truth, your opponent probably represents a suspect part of your own personality that is in conflict with your better nature. Such an inner conflict could play itself out as inner tension, or a condition caused by this. In any event ...

KEEP FOCUSED ON ... your best interests and those of everyone else concerned, and sacrifice any lesser desires or considerations. To do this you will have to be quite ruthless (mainly with yourself) and know what side you are playing on.

WATCH OUT FOR ... crafty feints or flanking manoeuvres, that is, your lower nature getting one over on you when you are not concentrating on doing the right thing, or are not sure what that is.

'Plots, true or false, are necessary things,/To raise up commonwealths and ruin kings'

A LITTLE CHILD LEARNING TO WALK

✧ ONE STEP AT A TIME ✧

 GENERAL INTERPRETATION

The natural process of learning something primary and essential. Possibly a steep learning curve, particularly if it is a case of being a 'late developer' who did not acquire a basic ability when they were supposed to.

KEEP FOCUSED ON ... making spontaneous efforts to reach out for experience and independence ... the vital importance of patience and encouragement, to yourself and others ... the certainty of achieving your goal because, with rare exceptions, you are naturally destined to do so.

WATCH OUT FOR ... remaining stuck at one level of capability ... holding on to others too much for support, for you will never learn that way ... trying to run before being able to walk.

 LOVE/RELATING/SOCIAL

A relationship where one or both of you has to learn a basic skill in relating or in another sphere of living which affects you both. Alternatively, you could be in a relationship that is still trying to find its feet, and as such this requires mutual faith and encouragement.

KEEP FOCUSED ON ... the fact that one day, probably quite soon, you will be up and running in a healthy relationship just so long as you are able to maintain the will and determination to get there ... the wonderful feelings that come with making a break-through, no matter how small ... encouraging one another – always.

WATCH OUT FOR ... expecting yourself or another to be perfect or whatever you think they or you ought to be ... pressurizing or letting yourself be pressurized.

 MONEY/WORK/CREATIVITY

You are probably on a steep learning curve or trying to get back on your feet again. A new vista of endeavour could be presenting itself to you, but it is early days yet.

KEEP FOCUSED ON ... how the Creative Process develops in much the same way as anything else – through definite stages that inexorably proceed towards their goal. However, it won't if it is hurried, or if you forget that such progress starts in a wobbly and meandering fashion rather than a straight unwavering line ... setting yourself reachable targets ... investing in the future.

WATCH OUT FOR ... towering ambitions, because they will not be sustained throughout the time it takes to realize them ... spending more than you can afford.

KARMA/ATTITUDE/HEALTH

It is as if you are having 'to become as a little child' in order to learn or relearn something that you let go to seed, abused or took for granted in the past. This could also entail building up the muscle, literally or figuratively, in order to do so.

KEEP FOCUSED ON ... the fact that you are at the beginning of something, and that the step up from the top of the 'second division' is the bottom of the 'first division' ... ensuring you have the necessary handholds to facilitate your progress ... the importance, and the power, of humility.

WATCH OUT FOR ... precipitous behaviour ... impatience or taking the easy way out ... depending too much on the efforts of others ... remaining forever a victim, or at a childlike or childish level of behaviour.

'More haste, less speed'

AN OLD OWL UP IN A TREE

☆ NATURAL WISDOM ☆

✸ GENERAL INTERPRETATION

Occasioned or called for is a knowledge born of the long and patient observation of Nature and her organic ways. One image here is that of the 'teacher' who is trying to tell you something – probably to wait and see, to be philosophical, but most of all to learn properly, with study and reflection, possibly into the night. And when the 'getting of wisdom' is your fate, yours could be an unusual life-path.

KEEP FOCUSED ON ... using your natural aplomb that allows you to see things for what they are, how they work, how to relate to them, and how to make the best of them ... how wisdom is not just knowledge, but the correct and judicious use of it, laced with an emotional awareness.

WATCH OUT FOR ... aloofness regarding a superior trait or situation, that sours any real pleasure or respect it could bring.

♡ LOVE/RELATING/SOCIAL

This is referring to wisdom in relating, and in choice of a partner or social milieu. The basis for this is having a firm sense of one's own authority and authenticity.

KEEP FOCUSED ON ... what is natural and good in others rather than anything merely glamorous or superficial ... that whatever you are going through is teaching you something profoundly important, something which will serve you wonderfully well in times to come.

WATCH OUT FOR ... continually seeking approval from others because it can become a requirement which is a bottomless pit and they will eventually give up on you ... feeling superior to others for this will alienate you, get you rejected.

MONEY/WORK/CREATIVITY

The object of your concern is a mentally sound course or project. It has an integrity born of long and patient study, particularly with regard to areas that have to do with the world of intuition and the unconscious. Wisdom is wealth here rather than money, which can actually forestall or blind you to wisdom.

KEEP FOCUSED ON ... the fact that wise advice or ideas are always relevant and appropriate to the habitat or demography of your interest or concern ... being wise about your business if 'wisdom' is what your business is about.

WATCH OUT FOR ... lofty words and ideas that are incomprehensible to those 'on the floor', that is, the general public or average worker ... being disheartened or distracted by the brighter, more glamorous success of others.

☯ KARMA/ATTITUDE/HEALTH

The gaining of wisdom as a part of life's course and experience. This can mean deep suffering as the only way that such wisdom be acquired. One has to agonize and make oneself vulnerable, sometimes finding oneself alone or out on a limb.

KEEP FOCUSED ON ... the more profound reasons for whatever is the object of your concern ... explanations that have their roots lying deep in the past or unconscious ... seeking out and taking heed of someone who has superior knowledge about the subject matter of your question ... using intuition first and foremost – 'Owl hasn't exactly got Brain, but he Knows Things'.

WATCH OUT FOR ... settling for easy answers or solutions ... going against the laws of Nature ... believing that you have all the answers.

'Wisdom denotes the pursuing of the best ends by the best means'

A GAME OF CRICKET

☆ PLAYING THE GAME ☆

✷ GENERAL INTERPRETATION

Here is (a need for) a set of rules or conditions that provides the development and proving ground for a particular skill. Indeed, observing and maintaining these conditions is an integral part of the skill. An 'umpire' or impartial judge may be needed to decide matters.

KEEP FOCUSED ON ... whatever life sets before you as a game with a definite set of rules. Set about finding out what those rules are so you might excel, or at least not get caught out ... keeping a 'straight bat', that is, playing things cautiously and correctly, protecting where you are vulnerable and not taking any unnecessary chances ... any game you know well and seeing how it can be used as a metaphor for how to live.

WATCH OUT FOR ... letting prevailing conditions defeat or restrict you, rather than taking time to see what those conditions pose and how they work.

✷ MONEY/WORK/CREATIVITY

The world of commerce, fashion and art have definite practices and ideas as to what is 'in' or 'out' with regard to the market place and public taste. If you wish to be materially or creatively successful then you have to observe the rules of the game and act accordingly. This means that you are advised to ...

KEEP FOCUSED ON ... the correct way of going about anything at the present, such as being interviewed, studying for an exam, submitting your work, writing a letter or learning a technique.

WATCH OUT FOR ... being *too* confined by the apparent rules of the game, especially if what you are doing is endeavouring to be original or maverick. But you would have to be prepared to be excluded from the establishment, for in their eyes it wouldn't be cricket.

♡ LOVE/RELATING/SOCIAL

Organizing relationships and relating according to a set of rules, either devised by convention or your own predilections. This takes a degree of impersonal objectivity, so it may not come easily if you are the more emotional type. This in itself might be a very good reason for having some ground rules.

KEEP FOCUSED ON ... what positions or roles each person is best suited to and defer to them as and when the occasion demands. For example, one person may be good at dealing with money while the other is better at dealing with people.

WATCH OUT FOR ... hiding behind social rules because of an inability to show how you feel – never mind if it appears to be 'bad form' ... being too competitive rather than operating as a team ... underestimating others.

☯ KARMA/ATTITUDE/HEALTH

Here we are reminded that a life is a 'game', part of a life an 'innings'. Your role at any given time is one of 'batting' or 'bowling' – actively pursuing something; 'fielding' – catching whatever opportunity or responsibility comes your way; and knowing your 'position' – simply awaiting your turn to 'bat' or 'bowl'. Above all, there are the rules which are the karmic laws of reaping what you sow, and the biological laws of health, so it is best to ...

KEEP FOCUSED ON ... *playing*, for that is what games are all about! ... the way you play the game more than whether you are winning it or not.

WATCH OUT FOR ... anyone who is not playing by the rules, deliberately or otherwise. If this is the case, withdraw from the field of play until they see the error of their ways, rather than frustrating yourself trying to force them to play by the rules.

'For when the One Great Scorer comes to mark against your name,
He writes – not that you won or lost – but how you played the Game'

CUPID KNOCKING AT THE DOOR

✫ ANSWER TO YOUR DREAMS ✫

⊛ GENERAL INTERPRETATION

Opportunity is presenting itself to your apparently incurable appetite for entering into relationships or schemes that appeal to your sense of and longing for a more exquisite, pleasurable and meaningful existence. Yet, although the object of your concern could be the 'Answer to your dreams', this is ultimately an injunction to follow the call of your heart if ever you wish to satisfy its desires. So …

KEEP FOCUSED ON … your enthusiastic readiness to risk heartache and being made a fool of for the depth and richness of intimate experiences … believing in the power of love.

WATCH OUT FOR … self-deception born of lust or immaturity … enticement; you may be about to be set up, or already have been – but only because you cannot be made to submit to the call of your emotions in any other way.

♡ LOVE/RELATING/SOCIAL

Cupid, God of Love and Desire, shoots his dart and we fall in love – and into the happiness and pain, excitement and confusion, that this engenders. Presently, he could be making you an offer – can you refuse? You may already be in the throes of an intimate relationship, and those 'secondary' arrows that inflict love's bittersweet twists and turns are now being felt.

KEEP FOCUSED ON … accepting that you are involved with someone on an emotional level, and that struggling only makes wounds more sore … showing love, responding to love lovingly – then no pain! … what pricks in your heart, and respond *with* your heart.

WATCH OUT FOR … mistaking desire for love, as it makes for impulsiveness when you should be patient … where you find it hard to give or receive love, for that is where Cupid's wounds go septic.

⚚ MONEY/WORK/CREATIVITY

Here, this Symbol simply says that you have the opportunity to attain what you are after, providing you are also willing to experience the ups and downs, thrills and disappointments that go with pursuing your dream. This opportunity could take any number of forms, but financial assistance could be one of them. Any kind of pursuit that creates opportunity is well-starred.

KEEP FOCUSED ON … challenges and difficulties being part and parcel of upholding what you believe is valid or valuable … that ultimately what you do is a labour of love, and that to focus merely on the material aspect of it would be misleading, if not actually undermining.

WATCH OUT FOR … greed and satisfaction of desire at any cost, for there would be a subtle twist that would undo all your efforts and dash your dreams.

♋ KARMA/ATTITUDE/HEALTH

It is the story of Cupid's own love life that is relevant here, for it sheds light upon why he plays tricks upon us, causing us to suffer in the name of love. By one of his tricks, his paramour, Psyche, was made to stay with him in a magical palace on condition that she never saw him in the light. Doubt and suspicion were sown in her mind by her jealous sisters, and she looked at him by candlelight while he was asleep. He awoke and abandoned her, leaving her to many terrors and trials. Finally, she overcame them all, was rejoined with Cupid and made immortal. (Check out this story in full!)

KEEP FOCUSED ON … attaining, through thick and thin, whatever your soul craves (Psyche means *soul*), and you will eventually do so, forever.

WATCH OUT FOR … the monsters of envy, doubt, jealousy and avarice … demanding guarantees, not trusting what your heart alone can see.

'Falling in love/Now that's doing something!'

ROCKS AND THINGS FORMING THEREIN

☆ **FAITH IN FATE** ☆

 GENERAL INTERPRETATION

In the darkest and most impenetrable recesses, knowledge, creations and new abilities are developing. All this implies that one should have faith that life brings forth whatever is needed to sustain itself. So, don't rock the boat.

KEEP FOCUSED ON ... the conviction that you are the matrix for all possibilities relevant to your growth, thereby giving rise to continued nurture and eventual prosperity ... nurturing the 'new you' that is growing inside.

WATCH OUT FOR ... getting muddled as a result of interfering in the natural unfolding of things, forcing issues, letting things go to seed ... the intrusion of, or contact with, hard and cold people or things; take measures to avoid or protect yourself against them.

 LOVE/RELATING/SOCIAL

You cannot directly influence the situation at present; you cannot accelerate it, slow it down, make it happen or prevent it from happening. Thoughts and feelings abound that are too complex or inaccessible to do anything with, other than let them unfold – painful or pleasurable as this may be.

KEEP FOCUSED ON ... keeping as composed and neutral as possible with regard to the issue concerning you ... any positive thoughts and feelings you have, for they will create a good 'psychical connection' that attracts the best outcome.

WATCH OUT FOR ... forcing issues or interfering with things that will sort themselves out eventually ... any mistaken ideas you might have about being able to manipulate things towards a desired end. Any such intrusive activity would only confuse matters or make them worse.

 MONEY/WORK/CREATIVITY

Rest assured that something of worth is taking shape, even though you may not be clear what it will be. Everything and everyone has a part to play in the object of your enquiry. Creatively speaking, ideas are forming unconsciously as you go about your usual business. It helps to ...

KEEP FOCUSED ON ... giving encouragement to and having faith in whatever or whoever is relevant to your situation. Only fertilize the process when it is required, and weed out any negative or unnecessary elements. As a rule of thumb, just let things proceed as they are.

WATCH OUT FOR ... signs that things are not developing as they should, and then take steps to correct matters. However, if they have reached a critical point you may just have to ride the storm.

KARMA/ATTITUDE/HEALTH

Something is happening that is outside your consciousness or control. The perfect metaphor for this, which could even be a reality, is that of being pregnant. An embryo forms in accordance with elements that have been set in motion previously, including sperm fertilizing the egg, and the karma of the incarnating soul. One cannot directly influence this other than by invasive means. On the other hand, if you ...

KEEP FOCUSED ON ... making a strict priority out of creating a good atmosphere and consuming the right 'foods', then the healthy formation of the 'baby' will be greatly assisted. In other words, respecting any process that has been set in motion, like this 'gestation', and surrounding it with 'good vibrations' will ensure a happy and healthy result.

WATCH OUT FOR ... and resist anything that goes against the grain of natural development.

'Let Nature take Her course'

A MOTHER WITH CHILDREN ON THE STAIRS

☆ PROGRESSIVE CARE ☆

✳ GENERAL INTERPRETATION

This is a Symbol of nurture and evolution combined – helping others to progress in life. More literally, it evokes the poignancy of bringing up children, with overtones symbolized here of waiting for father's return, or of the denouement of a domestic drama. Simply putting the children to bed or bringing them down to breakfast to start a new day.

KEEP FOCUSED ON ... your readiness to care for those in need in times of growth or transition, or because they cannot yet fend for themselves.

WATCH OUT FOR ... unnecessary fretting which can create the very problems it anticipates ... childish behaviour: put it away if it is your own for it will inhibit progress; set a mature example if it is somebody else's.

♡ LOVE/RELATING/SOCIAL

A healthy relationship or society depends on simultaneously furthering and caring for one another. One of you may be the 'parent' and the other the 'child' – of course, this may actually be the case. Either way, one person may be there to help the other to a point where they become independent of the helper. But the helper will also evolve in doing this. Occasionally, such an arrangement of helping and evolving can last and last, providing it is agreeable to all concerned.

KEEP FOCUSED ON ... cultivating a selfless attitude if you are the 'parent', and an independent one if you are the 'child'.

WATCH OUT FOR ... creating co-dependency, that is, a set-up that feeds off each other's insecurities, giving rise to eventual resentment.

⚚ MONEY/WORK/CREATIVITY

Young ideas or new products have to be carefully nurtured through their early stages, before being 'put to bed' or let loose in the world. Similarly, financing such projects can be down to making an investment in the future. So it is imperative that you ...

KEEP FOCUSED ON ... the weaker elements, and either strengthen or eliminate them ... the stronger elements, and put them to the fore ... promoting and investing in any activity that helps others to get started with their interests.

WATCH OUT FOR ... spoon-feeding others for longer than is necessary or throwing good money after bad.

☯ KARMA/ATTITUDE/HEALTH

This Symbol points to the profoundly important issue of how a parent or carer, particularly but not exclusively the mother, provides security and promotes personal evolution – or not, as the case may be. Health-wise, this Symbol recommends the most advanced and natural type of healthcare. (*See* also Self Talk, page 463.)

KEEP FOCUSED ON ... encouraging progress and independence in whoever needs them, while at the same time always being there for support when it is genuinely needed ... the idea that progress itself is nurturing, or is in need of it.

WATCH OUT FOR ... signs that one is compromised by feelings of being denied security if one becomes independent. This could be the result of controlling, judgemental or conditional parenting, but in the end you have to 'climb the stairs' of life on your own.

'If You Love Somebody Set Them Free'

A GOLDEN-HAIRED GODDESS OF OPPORTUNITY

☆ THE WORLD IS YOUR OYSTER ☆

 GENERAL INTERPRETATION

You now most certainly have the God-given opportunity to attain what you wish. If this is not in any way apparent at the moment, then this Symbol is entreating you to be aware that something good comes out of everything.

KEEP FOCUSED ON ... your positive thinking and open-heartedness that attracts all manner of wealth and wonder ... being alive to the fact that life is what one makes it, especially when your potential is grasped and realized.

WATCH OUT FOR ... a false optimism that only recognizes the truly good when all vain imitations have been exhausted ... what might seem difficult or unwelcome at first, is probably a blessing in disguise.

 LOVE/RELATING/SOCIAL

This is describing a social or emotional connection of some worth that should definitely be followed up and kept true to. However, 'an opportunity' is not usually a way in which a relationship or romantic connection is described without sounding a bit mercenary. That is, not unless you ...

KEEP FOCUSED ON ... the possibility that such a relationship is there to improve you (and each other) in some way. It just may be a chance to have fun together, but it is more likely that there is an emotional or spiritual goal asking to be achieved in this relationship. Or someone close to you could be setting you free.

WATCH OUT FOR ... making yourself or another out to be more than they are or are able to live up to. Glamorizing someone or a relationship invariably has only one outcome – disappointment.

MONEY/WORK/CREATIVITY

Here is an offer you cannot or should not refuse. However, any opportunity is only that – an opening, a chance, a beginning, potential in the raw. It is entirely up to you what you make of it as time goes by, possibly in the face of setbacks that are commensurate with the opportunity at hand. There is no such thing as a free lunch.

KEEP FOCUSED ON ... being open and receptive to what is available to you, both from without, in the form of material offers, and from within, in terms of ideas and talents.

WATCH OUT FOR ... anything shaky or tacky about what is on offer. Promising or attractive as it might seem, it could just be gilt, so if you have any doubts scratch the surface and see what it's really made of.

KARMA/ATTITUDE/HEALTH

The word 'opportunity' literally means 'before a harbour'. So you are on the verge of a new chapter or passage in your life, with all the possibilities and adventures that this poses. You have it all stretching or laid out before you.

KEEP FOCUSED ON ... embracing or going forward into all that life is now offering you, probably appertaining to the question you are asking the Oracle ... the possibility that something will have to go, be left behind, in order to lay claim to opportunity and a new life. This may take a while, with opportunity beckoning from afar.

WATCH OUT FOR ... not seeing, ignoring, or rationalizing away what life is offering you, because it does not conform with your idea of what a 'golden opportunity' should look like. Think it's a mirage for long enough and it will be.

'God loveth a cheerful giver'

THE LAMP OF PHYSICAL ENLIGHTENMENT AT THE LEFT TEMPLE

☆ BODY WISDOM ☆

⚙ GENERAL INTERPRETATION

This decidedly esoteric Symbol is referring to one's body as the key to enlightenment, and that one needs to take an intuitive leap to experience it as such. This is seen in a limited way as 'body language'.

KEEP FOCUSED ON ... your body as the real field of all life activity. Those 'religious scientists', the Mayans of Southern Mexico, called the human body *winclil*, which means 'vibratory root or vessel'. This means that our souls come down to Earth into our bodies which are, as it were, rooted *in* the Earth. We then vibrate or resonate like transmitter/receivers between Heaven and Earth.

WATCH OUT FOR ... accepting the commonly conceived idea of the human body as being a bag or skin with a person locked inside it, merely trying to get from A to B unscathed. It is far more than that.

♡ LOVE/RELATING/SOCIAL

Your relationship can be better understood by viewing it in terms of its actual physical circumstances and experiences rather than the circumstances that you *think* it is in or *ought* to be in.

KEEP FOCUSED ON ... how your body feels towards another body – without lust or analytical thought getting in the way – for this is the real key to understanding here ... experiencing one another, or yourself, as primarily physical beings. Using a Taoist or Tantric method to facilitate this ... how spontaneous physical responses reflect your earliest physical and thereby emotional responses to life itself, and vice versa. Feelings of rejection attract feelings of rejection.

WATCH OUT FOR ... getting stuck with only a rational idea of what a relationship means ... rejecting or ignoring what your body is telling you.

♛ MONEY/WORK/CREATIVITY

Any kind of work that sees the physical body as something more than just organic tissue, and which promotes psychological well-being is favoured here (*see* Karma opposite). Physically engaging with the object of your enquiry will tell you all you need to know.

KEEP FOCUSED ON ... your material state as being a reflection of your inner state ... throwing yourself physically into your work rather than just thinking about it ... taking a break and doing something physical if your work is entirely cerebral or sedentary.

WATCH OUT FOR ... feeling poor on the inside for this will probably attract very little from the outside ... work and the pursuit of material gain blinding you to the state of your body.

♐ KARMA/ATTITUDE/HEALTH

Our bodies are the vehicles in which we explore and live a life. Therefore, the type of life we live has a great deal to do with the type and health of the body we have. For example, if you were travelling across country, a four-wheel drive would be preferable, but if you drove it fast and hard over too many bumps it would soon be in need of repair. To stay in touch with your body, to keep it healthy and receive its wisdom ...

KEEP FOCUSED ON ... practices and disciplines such as tai chi, Alexander technique and yoga. The Mayan method of 'embodiment' is also highly effective as it uses an 'energy language' describing your 'vibratory signature' or soul's purpose that the body then translates through a kind of mime. (Details obtainable from author – *see* page 470.)

WATCH OUT FOR ... physical signs of emotional, mental or psychical states ... not being earthed.

'The body is the temple of the soul'

A FLAG THAT TURNS INTO AN EAGLE THAT CROWS

☆ REASON TO REJOICE ☆

✿ GENERAL INTERPRETATION

You have accomplished something and have cause to celebrate it and make it known. This is one of a pair of similar Sabian Symbols, the other being Aquarius 9 – 'A Flag Turned Into An Eagle', the difference being that this seems to have gone beyond 'Potential Made Real' and is proclaiming its attainment, rejoicing in it – or is merely boasting about it.

KEEP FOCUSED ON ... being able to walk your talk, and the difficulties and accolades that accompany this ... the fact that you prove and discover yourself by doing rather than just thinking or saying.

WATCH OUT FOR ... high-flown aims or people, that only find expression as spoken intentions rather than as substantial achievements, or that persistently dine out on past glories.

♥ LOVE/RELATING/SOCIAL

When you discover the love or emotional/physical experience you had always dreamt of, there is an urge to shout it from the rooftops. Something to sing about, to be very pleased with. One should try not to overdo this 'celebration' for it could break the very spell that you are rejoicing in.

KEEP FOCUSED ON ... the actual nature of the other person, as much as you are focused on how you are feeling yourself ... what it is that created or gave you the pleasure, and keep your eye on that, look after that.

WATCH OUT FOR ... elation or jubilation becoming a blind to the reality of the situation as a whole ... promising or bragging, but not doing ... trying to maintain an emotional or sexual high with the consequence that the natural comedown seems worse than it is.

⚚ MONEY/WORK/CREATIVITY

A good idea that could be made real but may be in danger of giving an unsuitable impression, one that is beneath itself. Your idea or product is great, but everything depends on how you pitch it or sell it, and to whom. For example, overstating can repel and understating can be overlooked.

KEEP FOCUSED ON ... being as great, good, rich, efficient or popular as you would like to be, and distributing any such good fortune downwards – to those less fortunate ... following your ideal and making it known.

WATCH OUT FOR ... others who might have an investment in 'seeing the mighty fallen', for making too much of yourself – your possessions or creations could attract this very thing ... striking too high a profile for you may get shot down, or find it hard or impossible to live up to.

☯ KARMA/ATTITUDE/HEALTH

This involves that subtle aspect of human nature whereby a victory can be attained through a proclaimed intention that you have to live up to, but it can also be soured or momentary because you become too full of yourself. Alternatively, if one has a strong sense of something coming into being, like a 'new age' or some such vision of the future, then it needs to be broadcast far and wide.

KEEP FOCUSED ON ... the essence of what makes you feel good, powerful, knowledgeable or in some way above and beyond the common awareness of life ... getting things off your chest.

WATCH OUT FOR ... signs that any misfortune stems originally from not walking one's talk, or from any feelings of resentment and anger one might have towards someone else who has or has not put their money where their mouth is.

'For whosoever exalteth himself shall be abased; and he that humbleth himself shall be exalted'

A WIDOW'S PAST BROUGHT TO LIGHT

☆ OUT OF THE CLOSET ☆

✴ GENERAL INTERPRETATION

Perhaps this patently enigmatic Symbol should first of all be regarded as representing just that – an enigma. Undertones of redemption or scandal could be an issue. This would depend on how in touch you are with your feelings and past actions, and how honest you are concerning them. So …

KEEP FOCUSED ON … baring your deepest feelings, thereby relieving and enlightening yourself – and giving others the courage to do so … the probability that there is at present considerable sympathy for your position; now would be a good time to get something off your chest, to curry understanding, to expect acceptance.

WATCH OUT FOR … the denial of certain home truths that perpetuate difficulties and discomfort.

♥ LOVE/RELATING/SOCIAL

Something is making someone aware of an emotional truth that hitherto has escaped them – or that they avoided, consciously or unconsciously. Now, or in the recent past or near future, this truth is laid bare. Initially, it can be very painful or embarrassing to have one's deepest feelings or seemingly shady past brought to the surface, but great relief and openness follows. In turn, such a denouement can be the very thing that paves the way for a happier love and social life. Just so long as you …

KEEP FOCUSED ON … the precise feeling, or what you have learned, regarding the issue currently concerning or upsetting you or someone else. This will tell you all you need to know.

WATCH OUT FOR … burying your head in the sand – again! … any cause for regret.

⚒ MONEY/WORK/CREATIVITY

The past has a habit of catching up with us, not least regarding business dealings and ingrained working habits. They can go unnoticed for quite a time, but inevitably something brings them into the open or shows them up to be harmful, or not very positive, where once they were effective. This could also refer to an intrigue around work or money that is blowing up in one's face. There is a chance that what has been 'brought to light' is positive, but you should know for sure whether it is or not. Ask the Oracle again if you do not.

KEEP FOCUSED ON … any areas that need revising, reworking or overhauling and do so before awkward turns to disastrous.

WATCH OUT FOR … anything shady or sloppy, compromising or illegal, and do whatever is necessary to put matters back in shape or in the clear.

☯ KARMA/ATTITUDE/HEALTH

Something from your past, be it of this lifetime or a previous one, has at last been made known. This can pose a number of reactions, depending on what the 'something' is. Implied here is also the issue of loss, along with the sympathy and support that goes with it. Whatever the case, the important thing is to …

KEEP FOCUSED ON … the fact that what is in the open, can no longer haunt you in the same way. As long as you accept what is now apparent, you can learn and benefit from it; it may even be spiritually enriching or emotionally releasing … the idea that what's gone is gone; it need not affect your present too much if you let it go.

WATCH OUT FOR … refusing to acknowledge, accept or own up to what is now (being) made known. This would be like ignoring a health symptom.

'Those who cannot remember the past are condemned to repeat it'

THE PYRAMIDS AND THE SPHINX

☆ MYSTERIES AND RIDDLES ☆

✦ GENERAL INTERPRETATION

The mysteries of the past and of other planes of reality, along with the questions that cannot be answered easily or in a normal way. A feeling of awe or serious long-term enquiry is called for. Being still and majestic.

KEEP FOCUSED ON ... the fact that life on Earth is a mysterious affair that has deep and powerful origins, and thus commands awe and respect ... getting on with whatever you have to do in the spirit of knowing that you will one day fulfil your destiny, a greater purpose, as long as you keep on keeping on ... discovering or being true to your greater or spiritual purpose.

WATCH OUT FOR ... the abuse or misuse of power, or an ignorance of the real significance of wondrous things ... accepting quick or superficial answers as being sufficient; obviously they are not.

♥ LOVE/RELATING/SOCIAL

A relationship that has its roots steeped in deep feelings and history, probably in a way that you cannot fathom. Because of this, it is very compelling and you feel forced to live it out, regardless of any difficulty or pain involved. Ties that go back so far exercise a pull on us that just cannot be resisted.

KEEP FOCUSED ON ... the probability that this relationship or situation is serving an important purpose on a soul or emotional level, and that being true to it will benefit all concerned in ways that currently you can only guess at ... letting go of wanting quick fixes, or expecting desires to be met immediately.

WATCH OUT FOR ... emotionally exhausting yourself by trying to resolve issues that probably only time will resolve.

⚜ MONEY/WORK/CREATIVITY

If not actually a case of archaeology or investigating the past, there is great wealth close at hand. It all depends on how you look at your current situation and what you think you want to gain from it.

KEEP FOCUSED ON ... what really has value. Is it a quick return involving possibly dubious methods, or is it something priceless in that it has an intrinsic and eternal value? ... being a testament or raising a monument to higher creative or economic values that will last and last, setting an example to others as how to conduct affairs ... building something worthwhile.

WATCH OUT FOR ... being distracted by what has no real bearing on your long-term concerns ... being motivated by greed; you may get what you think you want, and then be cursed by guilt or always being on the run from something.

⚅ KARMA/ATTITUDE/HEALTH

Literally, this Symbol could be referring to Ancient Egyptian things, such as past lives there, or using the power of pyramids for healing. It could also be referring to the Occult. Then there is the Riddle of the Sphinx to consider.

KEEP FOCUSED ON ... in what way if any the object of your concern could be affected by or connected to such things as death cults, deep and powerful ties, or any profound ideas and feelings that seem to stem from ancient times.

WATCH OUT FOR ... frustrating yourself by trying to gain answers to questions that have none or that you are not equipped to understand. In the myth, the Hero on his Quest is stopped by the Sphinx and asked the Riddle. Wanting to impress this half-lion and half-woman creature, he ponders and ponders, while his real quest goes unattended to. Proceed with the business in hand.

'Go walk' (injunction to traveller inscribed on pyramid)

THE GROUNDHOG LOOKING FOR ITS SHADOW

☆ PREDICTION AND PROJECTION ☆

☀ GENERAL INTERPRETATION

The search for a sign of what is to be, especially as might affect general welfare – the Symbol refers to a yearly custom in Poughkeepsie NY, which has to do with predicting the weather. Implicit in this is a tongue-in-cheek quality of possibly mocking something, for instance, soothsaying, which was ever a candidate for this. In the end, all prediction is merely the extension or projection of one's past and present into the future.

KEEP FOCUSED ON ... what you cast before you, then take responsibility for it, and you will see your way forward ever more clearly.

WATCH OUT FOR ... being reluctant to see your own weaknesses and pettiness, then projecting them on others, only to find yourself hemmed in by what you do not like (about yourself) coming back as external reality ... getting anxious about dubious predictions.

⚷ MONEY/WORK/CREATIVITY

The groundhog can be seen as symbolizing what is most earthy and materialistic. This area of life must be viewed with the possibility in mind of greed and manipulation casting their shadows, or of you earnestly trying to find out where you are going, be it right or wrong, and if there is any light at the end of the tunnel.

KEEP FOCUSED ON ... determining any ideas, products or policies that are creating, or have created, profit and satisfaction for all and sundry. Continue with these and expand on them; maintain your most positive outlook, and all will be well.

WATCH OUT FOR ... any ideas, products or policies that are creating, or have created, profit and satisfaction for the few at the expense of the many, or that have not created, or are not creating, any profit or satisfaction at all. Eliminate these, think again, and all will be well.

♥ LOVE/RELATING/SOCIAL

One of the most powerful psychological phenomena in human relations is that of Shadow Projection, where we project onto another what we fear or cannot accept as being a part of our own personality. This is the 'original sin' of relating for it perpetuates and intensifies dislikes and misunderstandings, and it is behind many a falling out and separation. We then find ourselves presented with the same irritating trait in another person because again we are having reflected back at us what is actually our own.

KEEP FOCUSED ON ... owning and taking back only your *own* shadow (this is called 'introjection'), then the other person's projections will find no purchase on you.

WATCH OUT FOR ... any obsessive dislike you have for someone, for more than likely they are catching your shadow, reflecting your own dread – or vice versa (*see* Karma below).

☯ KARMA/ATTITUDE/HEALTH

Imagine life as a movie theatre where you are the projector and your life as it appears to happen to you is what you project on to the screen. Your karma is the film that gets fed through the projector; your attitude is the lens of how you see and are seen. So, it is the light and shadow of your own being or unconscious that you behold as happening to you. Viewed in this way, you can see that what you ...

KEEP FOCUSED ON ... is therefore entirely up to you, and will become your reality ... shedding light as love or awareness on what or who is around you and their shadows will diminish or disappear altogether. On the other hand ...

WATCH OUT FOR ... projecting your fears, distrust, need to control or anything else negative onto the world, future or those around you, for they will appear just as fearsome, untrustworthy, controlling, chaos-producing or sick-making.

*'If you hate a person, you hate something in him that is part of yourself.
What isn't part of ourselves doesn't disturb us'*

SEAGULLS WATCHING A SHIP

☆ AN EYE ON OPPORTUNITY ☆

✷ GENERAL INTERPRETATION

Be assured that there will always be something to sustain you, as long as you keep an eye out for the main chance. Where are you in relationship to what you are after? Are you 'on the case', focused and determined regarding what you need? Or do you just watch and wait but never go for it, always keeping your distance, allowing yourself to be upstaged by others? Do you readily recycle your waste or excess materials for the benefit of others? Or are you hanging on to what you no longer need but would be useful or vital to others?

KEEP FOCUSED ON ... being ever alert to what life can offer and provide; you can then live modestly but happily ... being persistent, even a bit pushy, in acquiring what you need.

WATCH OUT FOR ... grubbing around, accepting scraps as being sufficient.

♡ LOVE/RELATING/SOCIAL

Opportunism in love and relating can seem inappropriate – cold and calculating even. But in the natural world we see that the mating game is all about looking for opportunity and seizing it, or of making oneself into an opportunity. And when a relationship is up and running, to be honest, this opportunism still persists.

KEEP FOCUSED ON ... giving or getting what is going to best sustain you and others ... the symbiosis that exists between people as being quite natural, as long as it is consciously seen to be fair.

WATCH OUT FOR ... advantage being taken of the weaker or needier person, for this can lead to a serious imbalance and mutual disdain ... 'poverty consciousness' where a poor sense of self-worth means that one accepts less than one should.

♆ MONEY/WORK/CREATIVITY

Apart from having an eye for opportunity, which is essential to any form of creativity, productivity or looking for work and money, this Symbol also points to the importance of recycling and being environmentally friendly or in league with Nature in some way. It also means that keeping an eye open for advancement, be it for yourself or others, is important to progress.

KEEP FOCUSED ON ... what the main resources are, either for yourself or others, and make a point of accessing and utilizing them – 'buzzing' others occasionally if necessary ... the fact that what is 'rubbish' to you may be highly valuable to others.

WATCH OUT FOR ... undervaluing yourself and accepting less than you are worth ... being profligate or uneconomical ... expecting handouts always to be available ... amoral opportunism in yourself or another.

☯ KARMA/ATTITUDE/HEALTH

We can see here both the hovering needy and the natural and acceptable scavenging that is necessary to life. We also see those who give what they do not need to them. The point is that there is a fine balance between graciously giving and receiving and being made to feel a beggar or begged upon, be it in a physical, emotional, mental or spiritual way.

KEEP FOCUSED ON ... feeling entitled to what you need and making it known in a dignified and justified manner ... bestowing upon others what they need and you don't, without any kind of condition; with the understanding that such giving and receiving serves to uphold the natural order of things.

WATCH OUT FOR ... letting a need become an addiction or an affliction, or seeing one as such ... being preyed upon by negative energies (vampirism).

'Where observation is concerned, chance favours only the prepared mind'

AN EASTER SUNRISE SERVICE

✵ REVERENCE FOR RESURRECTION ✵

⊛ GENERAL INTERPRETATION

Occasioned or called for here is the honouring of the belief that everyone will eventually be redeemed, maintained by the certainty and promise of everlasting and self-renewing life – especially through suffering. Doing whatever is necessary to revert the body to its previous state.

KEEP FOCUSED ON ... suffering, and the giving of something of lesser importance for the sake of something of greater importance ... an unusual sense of immortality and of the Christ within and without; an ability to express this with humility and to relate to it with joy ... making sacrifices that you trust will ultimately prove justified and worthwhile ... the fact that a crucifixion or crisis has to come before a resurrection.

WATCH OUT FOR ... formal observance but little or no personal awareness of what 'dying on the cross' means.

♥ LOVE/RELATING/SOCIAL

A great deal depends on your belief that the relationship that concerns you can and will be revived and restored to its former or a better condition. Such resurrection would also apply to the individual members of that relationship, for they will naturally benefit from the reunion. But the Oracle is not predicting or assuring you of this, only stressing that this is what will happen if you really believe it will, and live and act in a way that is a constant testament to that belief.

KEEP FOCUSED ON ... eradicating any thought, act or feeling that gets in the way of love, compassion and understanding ... constantly revering that aspect of each person involved that is seeking to be reborn through the trials of relationship, whether they know it or not.

WATCH OUT FOR ... expecting things to improve or turn around if one's whole heart is not in it.

⊽ MONEY/WORK/CREATIVITY

You go through certain crises – in the form of such mundane things as meetings, presentations, interviews, creative blocks or cash flow problems – in order that you eventually enjoy a regeneration of whatever is the object of your concern.

KEEP FOCUSED ON ... religiously pursuing the regeneration of what matters to you, even performing a regular ritual to this end ... the fact that your suffering for your art or business is worth it, as long as it has an end that endures, that it is in the name of an ideal that goes beyond mere getting and spending.

WATCH OUT FOR ... paying lip service to higher reason for doing what you do when your motivations and ambitions are merely self-serving.

♋ KARMA/ATTITUDE/HEALTH

That death is not an end but a beginning is the simple interpretation of the Resurrection, a concept common to many religions, not just Christianity, which unlike most others holds that the physical body is resurrected. In any event, in symbolic terms it is saying that there has to be the death of something for the new to rise. So ...

KEEP FOCUSED ON ... whatever it is in you, probably as a result of negative past conditioning, that needs to 'die' in order for something new and regenerated to come into being ... how your active belief in the process of death and rebirth acts as an inspiration to those around you.

WATCH OUT FOR ... a messiah complex where you or someone else believes that they have Christ-like qualities when really they are just suffering delusions of grandeur as an escape from reality.

'Si Dieu n'existait pas, il faudrait l'inventer'
(If God did not exist, it would be necessary to invent Him)

TINY CHILDREN IN SUNBONNETS

☆ PROTECTION OF INNOCENCE ☆

 GENERAL INTERPRETATION

Protection is afforded to the weak or vulnerable parts of ourselves, other creatures, and anything else of a delicate nature, in order that they might live and grow free from care. Sagittarius as a Sign is usually regarded as being far from protective as it is essentially adventurous and risk-taking, but the point here is precisely that if one is new to an exploit, make sure that you are properly equipped and shielded from unnecessary harm.

KEEP FOCUSED ON ... a sweetness of concern that enchants others and allows them to feel safe so they can reveal their own better nature.

WATCH OUT FOR ... an overweening concern that inevitably exacerbates the sensitivity it is seeking to shield. The State, and consequently society, can be seen to do this in its preoccupation with institutionalized 'nannying', political correctness and unnecessary litigation.

 MONEY/WORK/CREATIVITY

Any form of work that protects one from the harm that life can inflict is favoured here, as too are realistic forms of insurance of life, limb and property. This also extends to ensuring the security of work and workers themselves. Creatively speaking, one has to live a bit dangerously in order to get anywhere. Artists and entrepreneurs, by their very nature have to gamble.

KEEP FOCUSED ON ... the fact that there can be a trade-off between what you wish to gain materially or creatively and what you stand to lose in terms of exposing yourself to market forces or the forces of the imagination (have you got what it takes?).

WATCH OUT FOR ... being too fussy or too challenging.

♡ **LOVE/RELATING/SOCIAL**

Here is a position where you or others are in need of a protective relationship or need protecting from a relationship, or at least aspects of it, that are a bit too 'grown-up' for them to deal with yet. More simply, in order to have fun and play within a relationship one needs to feel safe from intrusion and the glare of external elements.

KEEP FOCUSED ON ... who it is that needs protection – someone does. It may be your own inner child or someone else's (see 'Self Talk', page 463) ... the possibility that growing emotionally sometimes necessitates being protected emotionally.

WATCH OUT FOR ... anyone being forever the child when it comes to the harsh facts of life and its emotional realities. Over-concern will perpetuate the very anxieties it seeks to protect you from.

 KARMA/ATTITUDE/HEALTH

There is the literal interpretation of screening off harmful UV rays. Symbolically though, this alludes to the fact that in the early stages of psychological and spiritual discovery, one has to be very careful not to bite off more that one can chew. Astrologically, the Sun is *the* creative force and can either quicken or burn, whereas the Moon screens the Sun, protects us from being exposed too soon to the truth and core of life, and this includes the harshness of certain egos.

KEEP FOCUSED ON ... ensuring that everyone has the necessary awareness of and protection against what they are getting themselves into.

WATCH OUT FOR ... being exposed to facts and forces that can be threatening to a safer and well-known, but possibly limited, viewpoint.

'Protection and caution should facilitate steady growth, but not inhibit it'

PELICANS MOVING THEIR HABITAT

☆ SELFLESS MOTIVATION ☆

❄ GENERAL INTERPRETATION

Taking into consideration what is peculiar about pelicans in particular – that they carry their young in their beak pouch and are said to feed them on their own flesh when food is scarce – we can say that this Symbol has to do with great originality and self-sacrifice with regard to the manner of caring for others. If it becomes necessary to 'up-sticks', then that course will be readily taken in the selfless interest of one's charges.

KEEP FOCUSED ON ... your own or someone else's knack for making an advantageous move or change for the good of the whole, born of a minimum of self-concern, but depending greatly upon a strong sense of the bigger picture.

WATCH OUT FOR ... leaving an area of difficulty as a result of the victim within not being able to stand their ground. Nevertheless, survival is still the priority here.

♡ LOVE/RELATING/SOCIAL

The way in which you relate is moving, or is having to move, towards the selfless, in terms of unconditional love and universal interests. The relationship(s) or person(s) in question make this inevitable, unavoidable and desirable – particularly if the question involves domestic matters.

KEEP FOCUSED ON ... the emotional priorities of others and make them your priorities ... the physical needs of others and make them your needs ... making personal sacrifices for the good of the relationships ... any selfishness in others as being a call for you to be selfless. Be as the pelican with its young, carrying and giving naturally, unquestioningly.

WATCH OUT FOR ... extending yourself to others to a point where you are too weak to care for them.

⚘ MONEY/WORK/CREATIVITY

For a personal reason, possibly concerning your environmental or emotional concerns, you feel the need to make a radical move regarding your career. Or you need to remind yourself that the type of work you do is in the name of something more than personal security and a pay cheque – or it ought to be.

KEEP FOCUSED ON ... and be guided by your most fundamental and heartfelt principles ... the progressive nature of your work; how you aim to further the interests of others, often at great expense to yourself ... issues regarding basic survival, and be guided by them.

WATCH OUT FOR ... giving in to the 'opposition' without putting up a fight. At the same time, be prepared to meet them halfway if necessary, especially if there is an area of common concern.

☯ KARMA/ATTITUDE/HEALTH

The ultimate and most valid reason for making a move or a change originates from a deep-seated urge to improve the general welfare. Furthermore, such motivation is self-sustaining, because it has such a fundamental interest in the survival and furtherance of what really matters. In other words, it has the power of Nature and Fate backing it up. This is the position you are currently in, or in which you best see yourself.

KEEP FOCUSED ON ... adopting an attitude of mind that is open to change for reasons of improving the general health and welfare of those close to you and who come after you, especially with regard to environmental conditions.

WATCH OUT FOR ... sapping yourself in the name of collective concerns to the point that your health begins to suffer.

'L'amor che muove il sole e l'altre stelle' (The love that moves the Sun and the other stars)

MEN CUTTING THROUGH ICE

☆ MAKING A DIFFERENCE ☆

 GENERAL INTERPRETATION

Making a lasting impression. Making the effort to obtain something that is both useful and unique – ice can last a very short time or help preserve something else for a very long time. But it is hard work for which you have to brace yourself.

KEEP FOCUSED ON ... developing and maintaining an energetic and resourceful nature that enables you to deliver the goods ... the need to keep things cool, and to keep one's cool ... the possibility that you have to enter an area which is 'cold' in some way, so you will have to be pretty 'hot', sharp or strong.

WATCH OUT FOR ... labouring to produce something for rewards that can all too easily slip from one's grasp ... making life unnecessarily hard for yourself.

 LOVE/RELATING/SOCIAL

It looks as if someone has got to take the initiative and say or do something that breaks a deadlock or the ice, introduces some warmth and vigour into a situation, relationship or an individual's emotional life, that has gone cold.

KEEP FOCUSED ON ... the fact that either you have it in you to turn things around, to get things back on the right emotional track, or you are the one who is being cold and unforgiving, with only your hurt feelings to keep you warm ... coming from a genuinely warm and loving place if it is down to you to get that ice melted.

WATCH OUT FOR ... not feeling anything as a justification for being afraid to feel (in need of thawing out) ... stubbornly refusing to allow another's attempts to get through or make amends.

 MONEY/WORK/CREATIVITY

Getting something out of 'cold storage', or putting it 'on ice'. This would entail hard work in the first case, and maybe a hard choice in the second. Nonetheless, a situation where some action is called for.

KEEP FOCUSED ON ... what you really wish to gain from such a dramatic and demanding course of action; what would merit it. It could be a case of needs must ... the necessity of the right tools and expertise, and some hardship, and then there will be nothing that cannot be accomplished or dealt with ... discovering hidden or latent talents ... the job in hand.

WATCH OUT FOR ... leaving others to do the dirty work, especially when they haven't been properly rewarded ... distractions or energy drawn by issues that do not matter ... shooting yourself in the foot.

KARMA/ATTITUDE/HEALTH

Discovering something that has remained dormant for a very long time, like a mammoth in frozen tundra. The question becomes whether to thaw it out to make it usable (or would it just become a mess), or leave it as it is. But then again, whatever it is that has 'lain dormant' may already be in the process of being laid bare, thawed out or revived.

KEEP FOCUSED ON ... the fact that what has long been frozen, unusable or unexpressed has now begun a process whereby it can eventually be put to use and find expression.

WATCH OUT FOR ... letting things slide back to the way they were for fear of being seen to be your own person. Apart from missing the opportunity to free yourself or others, you could be setting yourself up for a health condition born of fear and rigidity at a later date.

'When the going gets tough, the tough get going'

A CHILD AND A DOG WITH BORROWED EYEGLASSES

☆ THE PLAY OF ILLUSION ☆

✸ GENERAL INTERPRETATION

The curious fact that the world and human society is only what we make it or see it to be, and that between one level and another there are only the differences that one arbitrarily chooses. Because of this, what is originally clear-sighted and purely intuitive is in danger of becoming unnecessarily adjusted or misused.

KEEP FOCUSED ON ... developing or tuning in to your unusual ability to see what is really happening, at the same time appreciating the value of humour or quirkiness in your view of any situation ... what is self-evidently true even though it may not be technically correct.

WATCH OUT FOR ... a basic distortion of reality as a result of a childish or childhood misperception, or of not having one's own individual point of view ... putting things where they do not belong ... giving or getting the wrong impression.

♡ LOVE/RELATING/SOCIAL

Pretence and make-believe are valuable and enjoyable aspects of loving and relating, except when everyone is not included in the 'fantasy'. Also, childish behaviour or memories can prevent one from seeing what is really happening or how one is being treated.

KEEP FOCUSED ON ... seeing someone for who they really are as distinct from who one wants them to be or fears them to be ... reassuring others in a heartfelt manner – then you will all see more clearly, feel more secure ... seeing matters through someone's else's eyes.

WATCH OUT FOR ... misplaced loyalty, especially when unmet childhood needs are clouding one's judgement ... not seeing the situation properly; not *wanting* to see it properly.

MONEY/WORK/CREATIVITY

The critical factor here is whether it is a case of your having an unusual way of looking at things which has a certain charm about it, or one of your insisting on seeing things through rose-tinted spectacles, or trying to be something that you are not, or are not ready for. Possibly something you are attached to for personal reasons is clouding the issue.

KEEP FOCUSED ON ... seeing things through to a point where it is clear and obvious what the score is ... playful and childlike use of imagination, something which should be evidenced by having no fixed goals, agendas or ambitions.

WATCH OUT FOR ... whose opinion or viewpoint you heed concerning the object of your enquiry – it could be biased, have a false sense of loyalty, have ulterior motives, or be born of a fear of your reaction ... thinking everyone has got it wrong but you, as this would be a sign that the opposite is the case (they're right, you're wrong).

☯ KARMA/ATTITUDE/HEALTH

Your situation is dogged by a misperception, perhaps born of a longstanding illusion that has been carried over from an earlier time. The catch-22 here is that the distortion of how and why things are, could prevent you from seeing that things *are* distorted! And so you carry on looking at it from every angle except the right one.

KEEP FOCUSED ON ... the desire to know the truth of the matter *free* from any fears of what you think you do not want to see, hear or know. Only in seeing things as they truly are will you see the answer, the reason or the way (*see also* 'Self Talk', page 463).

WATCH OUT FOR ... thinking that it is wrong to be wrong. Everyone and everything was originally perfect and appropriate, but because of a great deception, we started to veil the truth. One only has to remove the veil, take the 'wool from one's eyes', and all will be clear again.

'The truth hurts, but the truth shall set you free'

A CHINESE LAUNDRY

☆ HUMBLE SERVICE ☆

GENERAL INTERPRETATION

A service to the community which is not, at least at first, accepted as part of that community – even though it has standards that are higher than average. Dealing with things personally, as distinct from using a 'conveyor-belt' process.

KEEP FOCUSED ON ... your ability for holding to your own values and customs with dignity in an environment or situation that may scorn or ridicule them – or even seek to destroy them ... developing the art of inscrutability.

WATCH OUT FOR ... inappropriate behaviour as a result of feeling out of one's element or of being elitist ... getting ideas above oneself.

♥ LOVE/RELATING/SOCIAL

An individual, or two or more individuals, who are isolated within the social environment they find themselves. Or an individual who feels alien to, or alienated by, another. Awkwardness or animosity can arise from such things, unless a subtle style is adopted and a useful role performed.

KEEP FOCUSED ON ... maintaining a correct distance from whoever is the object of your concern, but without appearing rejecting or aloof. This has the effect of keeping a person sweet, while at the same time attracting them with your enigmatic style ... keeping yourself to yourself if extreme difficulties are to be avoided ... helping those who are socially challenged or inept.

WATCH OUT FOR ... assuming airs and graces, or taking risks, when you are in a vulnerable position ... branding any other as inferior.

⚜ MONEY/WORK/CREATIVITY

The work you do has to be executed in the spirit of service – and a service that is possibly not properly appreciated, at least initially. Any kind of service that cleans or purifies is auspicious.

KEEP FOCUSED ON ... getting the best results by cleaning or dealing with things personally rather than leaving it to an impersonal method ... carrying on with what you are doing, maintaining your high standards in whatever way you can ... using traditional, maybe literally Oriental, means to attain your goals.

WATCH OUT FOR ... reacting hotly to any disapproval of your methods or products, for they are above average; this is the very reason why they may be attacked. In time, quality will out ... being taken to the cleaners ... expanding to the point of losing sight of your essential nature.

☯ KARMA/ATTITUDE/HEALTH

It behoves you to be of service to your community or an individual in a manner that has deeply rooted traditions, or that respects them. Such service is the most effective way of balancing karma, redressing past sins of omission or commission. Health-wise, this Symbol could be referring to a cleansing method or ritual, be it to body or aura. Chinese medicine?

KEEP FOCUSED ON ... cultivating an unemotional but convincing aura that is born of inner conviction ... a non-egotistical way of making your point, for this is probably the only way you are going to do so successfully ... cultivating humility, reducing your demands and self-importance to a minimum.

WATCH OUT FOR ... being obsessed with hygiene or your way of doing things: such obsessions are pollutants or repellents in themselves.

'Give us grace to persevere'

IMMIGRANTS ENTERING

☆ INFLUX AND RELOCATION ☆

☀ GENERAL INTERPRETATION

Being prepared to risk all one has and the threat of alienation in order to obtain a brand new start. Conversely, something or someone entering your life that you are unfamiliar with.

KEEP FOCUSED ON ... developing a sense that the world is your home, along with the broadmindedness and bigheartedness that this implies and engenders ... the fact that it is natural to feel anxious when faced with the unknown – indeed, it is designed to sharpen your wits when they need to be more acute ... extending a welcome to whoever or whatever is in need of it. Put yourself in their shoes.

WATCH OUT FOR ... making a misguided move because of an unawareness that the capacity for failure or lack of integration will travel with you ... xenophobia, a cardinal sin against Humanity.

♔ MONEY/WORK/CREATIVITY

New ideas, resources or personnel are coming in, or are needed. Or you are attempting to enter a new field of activity. Possibly both.

KEEP FOCUSED ON ... being open to the inclusion of 'new blood' ... making sure that you approach your objective in the manner laid down by whoever or whatever comprises that objective.

WATCH OUT FOR ... being indiscriminate with regard to what you incorporate or entertain with respect to this 'new blood', perhaps out of a mistaken sense of political correctness.

♥ LOVE/RELATING/SOCIAL

The process of getting to know one another more intimately, or a case of someone who is new to a particular type of relationship or social situation. Or some new factor has entered into an existing relationship, making you more aware of how you feel. It may well be necessary to ...

KEEP FOCUSED ON ... accommodating or bearing with either yourself or others while you or they become accustomed to what is acceptable and understandable ... exactly how you feel and where your true allegiances lie.

WATCH OUT FOR ... any habits, conditions or attitudes that aggravate or offend. Limit them if they are your own; be helpful and tolerant if they are someone else's ... comparing the 'new' with the 'old' and labouring under the illusion that one is better than the other.

☯ KARMA/ATTITUDE/HEALTH

Here, this Symbol is suggestive of the migration of souls, and how the world can seem alien to some and familiar to others when they first 'arrive'. One's attitude to such a new venture can make the difference between the 'natives' feeling that one is sapping the general welfare or contributing towards it. It is very important to ...

KEEP FOCUSED ON ... acclimatizing yourself to your environment, learning its customs and language, or finding a group that you can relate to because it has similar roots and habits to your own ... the idea that today's 'aliens' are tomorrow's 'citizens'.

WATCH OUT FOR ... feeling intimidated by any unknown factors, especially regarding health. After all, the unknown is just that until suspicions are confirmed or facts proven.

'When in Rome, do as the Romans do'

A BLUEBIRD STANDING AT THE DOOR OF A HOUSE

☆ PERSONALLY AUSPICIOUS ☆

✹ GENERAL INTERPRETATION

Behold the magic and beauty of spirit that is so close to home and constantly offering opportunity and guidance in the signs and omens that everyday reality is so rich in – if we care to look. On an inner or personal level at least, this is an oracle of good fortune entering your life.

KEEP FOCUSED ON ... your essential faith and the goodwill that radiates from it, for it lights the way for both yourself and others ... the nature of the spirit world as being one that transcends the ego, ultimately one has to surrender to this.

WATCH OUT FOR ... an over-optimism that is blind to the details and practicalities of life ... missing something special about you that anyone close to you would be aware of ... 'hippie crap', fanciful ideas, new-age nonsense.

♥ LOVE/RELATING/SOCIAL

This images an extremely personal, special and spiritually-oriented relationship. Whatever it has going for it is somewhat rarefied – as is the connection between you both. There is also the possibility of it being something more of the imagination than something that the world at large would be aware of. Beauty and poignancy.

KEEP FOCUSED ON ... those aspects of the relationship, person or group that appeal to the most idealistic and soulful aspects of your own being. There is a fine connection here, but paradoxically, its strength lies in its delicacy.

WATCH OUT FOR ... presuming too much on such a person, relationship or group. Any value or meaning is entirely down to your finer understanding and appreciation.

⚚ MONEY/WORK/CREATIVITY

This is an auspicious oracle, and domestic issues are under a particularly beneficial influence, but the qualification 'personally' auspicious does not necessarily mean 'professionally'. In other words, the object of your enquiry is well-starred from a private point of view but not necessarily publicly.

KEEP FOCUSED ON ... whatever is the object of your concern, as its personal significance for and to you is very high ... activities and interests that are close to home or get you 'where you live'; they have a potential for the future that is subtle and far-reaching, but possibly not what you assume.

WATCH OUT FOR ... over-commercialization and ambitiousness with regard to your ideas or creations because their validity depends on their spiritual qualities rather than their material worth.

☯ KARMA/ATTITUDE/HEALTH

This Symbol is saying that a point has been reached when it has been personally brought home to you – by a sign, coincidence, condition or encounter – that life is a spiritual affair and must be lived as such from now on. Any bird, but especially a bluebird, is a spiritual messenger and go-between, and you would be wise to follow its intimations. So ...

KEEP FOCUSED ON ... trusting your spirit to influence those (including yourself) who cross your threshold – literally or into your personal space ... something or someone wonderful and beautiful you have inside of you or close to home, possibly that you have not been fully appreciating up to now ... any further signs, omens or dreams that are trying to tell you something significant.

WATCH OUT FOR ... over-interpreting signs, or imagining 'signs and portents' where there aren't any.

'Mister bluebird on my shoulder/It's the truth, it's actch'll/Ev'rything is satisfactch'll'

A CHUBBY BOY ON A HOBBY HORSE

☆ MAKE-BELIEVE OR PET SUBJECT ☆

❋ GENERAL INTERPRETATION

A fullness of life that is characterized by a desire for growth and expansion, and modelled upon one's heroes and dreams. Being allowed to explore one's dreams and ambitions with the support being given from some quarter.

KEEP FOCUSED ON ... your determination to make real the adventure that life always promised to be, and the sense of fulfilment that it brings ... making full use of the golden opportunity that is being given you to further yourself and enjoy yourself at the same time.

WATCH OUT FOR ... a puffed-up sense of self that is blind to the ridicule it attracts and to the fact that it does not get you very far ... being spoilt to the point of not knowing the reality that is bound to descend on you at some point ... indulging in self-indulgence.

♥ LOVE/RELATING/SOCIAL

You, or somebody else, is in an indulgent or indulged position that allows you or them to do as they please, to follow your/their own personal pursuits and pastimes. Or it could be referring to a relationship where one or both of you (or more if it is a group) are just playing at it – perhaps with a view to getting on with the real thing later, or just horsing around. Innocent and enthusiastic sexuality. Whatever the case, there is quite a bit of fun to be had here. But you would be advised to ...

KEEP FOCUSED ON ... how the relationships will develop in the future when things get more real, when more commitment is called for, when extra responsibilities start to make demands.

WATCH OUT FOR ... being lulled into a false sense of security – and not noticing someone else's needs or emotional state until it is too late.

⚜ MONEY/WORK/CREATIVITY

The area of your concern is either at an experimental stage, or it is a specialized field of interest – you will know which because they are quite distinct. Then again, it could be a combination of the two, like breaking into a specialized field. Whatever the case, it is your enthusiasm for it that is the important determining factor. Financially, it would seem quite advantageous, such as being sponsored or patronized.

KEEP FOCUSED ON ... the preparation or training that is required. Do this enthusiastically and you will have no cause for regret, setting yourself up for a good position at a later stage.

WATCH OUT FOR ... certain points being missed or overlooked as a result of inexperience or being too specialized. There needs to be someone watching over what is happening for things to proceed safely or productively.

☯ KARMA/ATTITUDE/HEALTH

Your current situation is best viewed with the useful and thought-provoking attitude to life that everything we do or that happens to us is a preparation for something to come. The better we do in this 'training ground' the better it'll be for that time ahead, be it in this life or in another one. Furthermore, living in this spirit affords one a certain protection. This is because Fate or Spirit smiles upon those who adopt what is essentially a modest and positive attitude to life.

KEEP FOCUSED ON ... aspiring to be a better person, and working and playing towards it.

WATCH OUT FOR ... presuming upon special privileges as being unconditional or indefinite; you only have them because you *do not* greedily presume upon them ... becoming obsessed with the object of your concern for this will drive away good fortune and make you ill, or even more ill.

'Practice makes perfect'

A FLAG-BEARER

☆ WHAT YOU STAND FOR ☆

 GENERAL INTERPRETATION

What is at stake here is those things you are prepared to die for, make yourself vulnerable for. You are looked to as an example of something positive, significant and brave, as someone for whom the following or upholding of ideals goes beyond personal safety and petty values. If you feel this does not apply to you, then perhaps it is time to make it do so – determine what you stand for.

KEEP FOCUSED ON ... rallying to your own cause, what is important to you ... your willingness to sacrifice the lesser for the greater, and being an example of this ... designing your own personal flag. Try it. It's fun!

WATCH OUT FOR ... empty show and demands for false credit ... exposing yourself to attack for something you do not really believe in ... taking more than you can bear without good reason.

 MONEY/WORK/CREATIVITY

Your enterprise or situation has, or needs to have, something or someone who represents all that it stands for, works so hard for. This 'flagship' may not be profitable in a strictly material sense, but it is what inspires you and others to forge on through hard times, and on to the good times.

KEEP FOCUSED ON ... what your aspirations and long-term goals are or, better still, the reasons that you do what you do that goes beyond merely making a living. There are agencies and individuals who are available to help projects that are 'charitable', officially or otherwise ... rallying yourself and co-workers to the 'cause'.

WATCH OUT FOR ... confusing your ambitions with your aspirations. The former need a hard-headed and practical approach, whereas the latter require vision and solidarity. The object of your concern is probably the latter.

♡ LOVE/RELATING/SOCIAL

A relationship or individual without a moral code or backbone is liable to collapse. Often it is a case of one person depending on the other for a value or purpose, which is okay as far as it goes. But possibly one of the main reasons or advantages of relationships is the forming of some standard that you *both* share and bear. Someone 'to die for'?

KEEP FOCUSED ON ... the values that you share with one another, and build on them ... setting an example of what you believe love and relationships are about and you will attract what you want and need ... believing in yourself.

WATCH OUT FOR ... expecting yourself or the other person always to be the one that holds things together or shows the way forward ... there being no common morality, for this will result in disarray and eventual separation.

☯ KARMA/ATTITUDE/HEALTH

You are bearing up, or are being encouraged to do so. You have got a grip on the central principles of what concerns you, or you need to do so if you feel weak or purposeless. As a consequence of courageously upholding something, you are protected by forces that share those principles, both on inner and outer planes of existence.

KEEP FOCUSED ON ... creating an objective regarding your spiritual life or health, that you are prepared to move Heaven and Earth to attain ... what you are fighting or suffering for; there is most definitely something ... creating an image in your mind's eye that inspires and exhorts you – and others too ... rallying yourself, or on whatever or whoever rallies and inspires you.

WATCH OUT FOR ... problems of feeling directionless or unsupported – these may manifest as back problems, exhaustion or lethargy.

'We must arrive at the correct standpoint ourselves, for only from this vantage can we work correctly'

A SCULPTOR

✵ SHAPING THINGS ✵

 GENERAL INTERPRETATION

You are moulding your life and experience into something of enduring significance. We all have a set of expectations that we consciously or unconsciously endeavour to realize, whether they are positive or negative. What happens is up to you.

KEEP FOCUSED ON ... how it is that your strongest convictions (should) give rise to lasting impressions ... how things and people tend to live out our expectations of them ... letting life shape *you* sometimes, just to see how it feels and what happens ... how hard graft is often unavoidable.

WATCH OUT FOR ... a cold and self-contained style of living that is blind to life's ever-changing nature ... fearful or rigid expectations born of a need to control, for they could become real; try not having any agenda at all concerning what you regard as difficult people and situations.

 MONEY/WORK/CREATIVITY

You have the raw materials or resources for making whatever it is you wish to make or do. Everything now depends upon your will and skill and those of others who you are involved with. This Symbol aptly depicts the very nature and process of material achievement – going from raw material to finished product.

KEEP FOCUSED ON ... the character of the materials or people you are working with; keep true to them; choose them well ... the fact that realizing an idea takes time, hard work and discipline ... making sure that you have the right tools or methods, and a suitable work environment ... being patient and steady.

WATCH OUT FOR ... wasting time and materials through lack of skill or vision ... being so ruthlessly bent on realizing your goal that you overlook the input or needs of those around you; they may not be there when you need them at a later date.

♥ LOVE/RELATING/SOCIAL

This could describe one person moulding the other in a relationship – or how the relationship itself is moulding one or both people, or is moulded by them. The question is whether that moulding is for better or worse, undergone consciously and willingly, or against one's will, possibly without even knowing it's going on. Some manipulation happens in all close relationships and can be decidedly positive. However ...

KEEP FOCUSED ON ... what your intentions and motives are if you are doing, or thinking of doing, the moulding ... if you are being moulded by the other person; if it's to your liking, then well and good.

WATCH OUT FOR ... any kind of negative manipulation and firmly resist it. Strangely, this may be happening to make you more your own person.

☯ KARMA/ATTITUDE/HEALTH

The shape of things to come. This is determined by deliberate and random acts; the very way in which the Oracle itself works is a mixture of deliberately asking it a question, picking cards or throwing dice, and receiving a randomly selected result. Like the sculptor, the combination of your will and skill (hands/tools) interacting with Fate and your environment (clay, wood and stone) produces an end result which may or may not be true to life.

KEEP FOCUSED ON ... the way in which you are shaping your life – and the way in which life is shaping you – if you wish to get some idea of how things will turn out ... concentrating on what you ask the Oracle; then the more precise and helpful will be the reply.

WATCH OUT FOR ... what you are putting out into the world in the form of fears and negative expectations, for this will shape your world.

'The drop of rain maketh a hole in the stone, not by violence, but by oft falling'

AN OLD BRIDGE OVER A BEAUTIFUL STREAM

☆ ESTABLISHING TRANSITION ☆

❋ GENERAL INTERPRETATION

You have here, or are recommended to find, a traditional means of successfully accomplishing something, which at the same time is elegant and pleasing to all concerned. The Symbol may also be saying that a way is being offered to you to get from one state or place to another. A crossing-over.

KEEP FOCUSED ON ... a natural setting or means for dealing with or staging your issue ... the value of traditional or longstanding qualities, for they can achieve your ends simply and admirably.

WATCH OUT FOR ... getting stuck with sentimental ideas and connections, habits and haunts that are no longer practical, even though they may have served you well once and still seem quaint ... mistaking a means of getting to a place for the place itself.

♥ LOVE/RELATING/SOCIAL

Whatever the state of the emotions that flow between you and another person, there is a means of transcending them or finding a way of connecting that is pleasing and useful to you both. If there is some divide between you, then you can provide some means by which you can reconnect. Then again, perhaps this is a longstanding relationship, or one from the past, that is experiencing a reunion – or is simply being remembered, with a sense of its charm and beauty.

KEEP FOCUSED ON ... the link that you have with others, or one other in particular, with a view to seeing if that connection is (still) viable.

WATCH OUT FOR ... relationships that are only ornamental or fancy, where the practical, day-to-day connection is not, or is no longer, present.

♛ MONEY/WORK/CREATIVITY

A sound idea or product, rooted in popular sentiment. This Symbol stresses the importance of keeping to traditional or organic methods and lines. It also indicates that in order to progress and get to a new area of endeavour you need to cross over to that new area, learning as you go what is on offer and what is required of you. Financially, some kind of bridging loan or fund is in the offing, or could be sought out if necessary.

KEEP FOCUSED ON ... the fact that there is a way of getting where you want to get to. The means have been laid down already. Follow this route, making any repairs and adjustments – if and when you need them.

WATCH OUT FOR ... sticking to old ideas and practices purely for sentimental reasons, unless sentiment is your business.

☯ KARMA/ATTITUDE/HEALTH

This Symbol is an image that says everything and nothing; it could just be a picture-postcard memory frozen in time, or it could be a real connection to a feeling or time with whatever is going on now. Then again, it could be an image of a link with someone or something that needs to be kept open and in use until it is needed.

KEEP FOCUSED ON ... this Symbol in your mind's eye and note what you see happening there. Is it dried up and lifeless, or is it flowing and active? You may have to wait a while, or have a number of visualizations, until you see what is happening. Eventually this image will tell you what you need to know. Similarly, this image can tell you something concerning a state of health – is something stuck or flowing freely?

WATCH OUT FOR ... assuming something is all right just because it looks all right at a cursory glance.

'Have nothing in your house that you do not know to be useful, or believe to be beautiful'

A FAT BOY MOWING A LAWN

☆ A NEED TO TRIM DOWN ☆

✴ GENERAL INTERPRETATION

The necessity of encouraging those who are disinclined to knuckle down to everyday tasks that maintain the basic fabric of our world and society. Doing one's best in this respect, even when one's physical state is inadequate, possibly as a result of this disinclination – laziness or indulgence.

KEEP FOCUSED ON ... having a spirit that is stronger than the flesh as this enables you to make that flesh (physical involvement) more effective, both for yourself and others ... exercising your mind-power to attain the desired effect, because you can ... self-respect and motivation, and tending to something that needs doing.

WATCH OUT FOR ... inefficiency as a result of insufficient and perfunctory input (which could apply to the way you are using the Oracle itself), or because of keeping up appearances only.

♥ LOVE/RELATING/SOCIAL

There appears to be grudging willingness to keep up social appearances, or to go through the motions of being committed in order to keep a relationship in shape. It also suggests that a way or style is available which is beneficial to both your relationship and yourself.

KEEP FOCUSED ON ... what aspects of yourself or your relationship need regular attention and maintenance, and give it gladly ... grooming, reducing or cutting down whatever is necessary to improve your relationship or relationship prospects.

WATCH OUT FOR ... one person making all the effort in a relationship, especially when they are the one who is carrying the most. Then again, this just might be an unavoidable necessity ... being a slob, or being victim to a slob.

♆ MONEY/WORK/CREATIVITY

Being met or called for here is a need to downsize, to cut costs or to shape your ideas or product so that they are more attractive or useable. Lazy or inefficient workers or practices.

KEEP FOCUSED ON ... motivating and encouraging those who are reluctant or feckless ... finding ways of making unattractive tasks look more worthwhile, or by pointing out their sheer necessity ... making it clear that failure to maintain output or keep to a steady and organized routine will suffer the consequences ... appreciating that cutting back is good for growth.

WATCH OUT FOR ... bad economics or ergonomics, for these are the root problems ... wasting unacceptable amounts of time and energy on anything or anyone that is not pulling their weight, or that is not rewarding enough.

☯ KARMA/ATTITUDE/HEALTH

This is alluding to any condition that is in need of being reduced, such as fat or any other kind of unwanted growth or tissue. It could also refer to cutting the ego down to size as well, or anything else excessive. Equally, there is the implication that a course is only being pursued because someone else said so, rather than because you really want to – a situation that needs looking at in itself.

KEEP FOCUSED ON ... the fact that this method or approach has only a temporary effect and would have to be repeated regularly. For a more lasting effect you will have to get to the root of the matter ... breaking a vicious circle through force of will.

WATCH OUT FOR ... a combination of being overweight and of overexertion. Get back in shape slowly over time to avoid even more stress.

'Less is more'

THE POPE

☆ MORAL RESPONSIBILITY ☆

🌞 GENERAL INTERPRETATION

As a symbol in itself, this represents the embodiment and expression of the highest point in a (religious) hierarchy. It suggests that your situation involves taking a form of (moral) high ground, fitting in with a long-established (catholic or Catholic) structure, and very probably having to forego what may be regarded as a normal lifestyle.

KEEP FOCUSED ON ... how willing you are to sacrifice your personal concerns for the sake of the whole and the long-term goals concerned ... how and in what way you are the one others look to for guidance or as an unimpeachable example of how to behave.

WATCH OUT FOR ... getting caught up in something that you cannot live up to ... being involved with or the victim of a disastrous blend of power and hypocrisy.

❤ LOVE/RELATING/SOCIAL

Here is a relationship or individual that is having to not take sides, yet at the same time adheres to a very definite set of principles. If that person is you, then you will be tried and tried again as to your position and the example you set to others.

KEEP FOCUSED ON ... being consistent in the manner you conduct yourself ... being true to love itself – something which may sometimes involve appearing not to be 'true' to the loved ones ... conducting yourself in a manner that you imagine some revered figure – such as Jesus, Buddha or Krishna – would do in a similar situation.

WATCH OUT FOR ... saying one thing and doing another for this will not create any respect, respect being vital to welfare here ... being pompous and holier-than-thou, as this would smack of being emotionally or physically inept.

MONEY/WORK/CREATIVITY

What is important here is your higher reason for doing anything. Financial matters greatly depend upon straight dealing – even in the way you *think* about them. Possibly you are entertaining, are having to fill a position that carries great responsibility, or one that involves finding or referring to some individual in a position of great power.

KEEP FOCUSED ON ... the worth and validity of your own credentials and those of anyone you are entrusting yourself to ... whether or not you can positively justify any position you take up, because you may be sure that it will be rigorously tested.

WATCH OUT FOR ... any doubts you may have; there will be very little room for them ... serving two masters – you could wind up being split in two.

☯ KARMA/ATTITUDE/HEALTH

Definite, even quite rigid, spiritual values characterize your path. The rewards and security that can accompany long-held faith and lasting service to an ideal.

KEEP FOCUSED ON ... determining or keeping to a distinct code of ethics ... the importance of suffering for what you hold dear, for this is probably the most reliable validation of it ... how your beliefs are furthered through them being tested ... the paradox that 'high-ness' is evidenced by lowliness ... pure living for a healthy life.

WATCH OUT FOR ... being too black and white in your philosophy when there is a sizeable grey area to consider – probably within your own make-up or behaviour ... condemning others when you should be scrutinizing yourself ... health problems caused by being too ascetic.

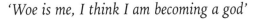

'Woe is me, I think I am becoming a god'

THE SABIAN SYMBOLS OF
CAPRICORN

Either directly, or in a subtle way, all these Symbols are concerned with the following qualities, or with situations that involve or call for them:

AMBITION

AUTHORITY

BUILDING

BUSINESS/MATERIAL WORLD

COMMAND

CONTROL

LIMITATION

OBJECTIVITY

ORDER

ORGANIZATION

OUTSIDE WORLD

PATRIARCHY

POLITICS

PROFESSION(ALISM)

REALISM

RESPONSIBILITY

STATUS

STRUCTURE

WORLDLY SUCCESS

AN INDIAN CHIEF DEMANDING RECOGNITION

☆ A QUESTION OF AUTHORITY ☆

GENERAL INTERPRETATION

The situation calls for (a figure of) leadership and authority. In turn, this demands a sense of absolute integrity which will not rest until everything and everyone concerned conforms to its standards and requirements, and heeds what it says.

KEEP FOCUSED ON ... long-held principles and actions for they elicit respect both from those who follow and who oppose you ... striving to understand and obey what the Oracle is telling you concerning the truth of the matter, and using it properly (*see* page 4) ... earning recognition.

WATCH OUT FOR ... any arrogance, or ignorance of hard cold facts, for they are in time bound to lead to humiliation or confusion ... attention seeking – and what it is trying to draw attention towards.

MONEY/WORK/CREATIVITY

This Symbol is very appropriate for the first degree of Capricorn, as it is the Sign of the Chief, of worldly recognition and success. It is saying that you have what it takes to be accomplished in your chosen field or current endeavour. But it is also saying that by putting yourself 'up there' you will find what you are made of, rather than just boasting, hoping or wondering about it.

KEEP FOCUSED ON ... the fact that you are the 'chief' in this situation in that it all comes down to you. By attempting to prove yourself, you are actually doing something that deserves credit and that reaps valuable experience and rewards.

WATCH OUT FOR ... others who may vie with you for power and supremacy; such is the nature of 'demanding recognition' as it invites competition ... self-effacement born of the fear of being ridiculed, probably by yourself, because this would attract that very thing.

LOVE/RELATING/SOCIAL

Someone is feeling that they are not being recognized, valued and respected for who they are in a relationship or social set-up. Therefore they are having to get in touch with their own sense of strength and self-esteem in order to accomplish and recognize this. Perhaps they first need to recognize this very thing – that they must value and respect themselves before anyone else will.

KEEP FOCUSED ON ... and hold dear what you or others have of genuine worth and usefulness, not forgetting to take into account those more 'invisible assets' such as compassion, consideration, and effort made relative to ability.

WATCH OUT FOR ... overly dramatic and heated displays and protests, justifiable though they may be, for these smack of not being sure of your position and worth.

KARMA/ATTITUDE/HEALTH

The word 'authority' derives from the same Latin word as 'author', *auctor* – one who increases or produces. Throughout lifetimes, or certain stages of them, we build on our ability to do just this; we become more and more the *authors* of our own life stories. And so one's life is like a film, the directing of which determines how it does in the world and in our own eyes, and in the next life.

KEEP FOCUSED ON ... the fact that you are the architect of your own fate, and that your health can also be a testament to how well you are producing that epic called your life, and how well you are promoting the star which is your own personality ... how such expertise is the accumulation of effort, learning, courage and the recognition of your higher self and those spiritual betters that guide and encourage us.

WATCH OUT FOR ... expecting only the good and not the bad to be recognized. That's *not* good.

'Experto credite' (*Trust one who has gone through it*)

THREE STAINED-GLASS WINDOWS, ONE DAMAGED BY BOMBARDMENT

☆ RESTORING THE WHOLE ☆

GENERAL INTERPRETATION

The point here is that what is beautiful and/or reverential is also vulnerable to attack. Of the trinity of personality (mental, emotional and physical), or of any other set of three, such as Father, Son and Holy Ghost, or the three esoteric Rays of Power, Love and Intelligence, there is always the likelihood that one of them is frail, or vulnerable due to ignorance, inexperience, abuse or misunderstanding. It is as if some part is not as it should be, and needs seeing to.

KEEP FOCUSED ON ... the awareness you have of the divine qualities of life and how they easily get corrupted by the way of the world; this entreats you to uphold them ... setting about restoring or reintroducing such qualities.

WATCH OUT FOR ... leaning on one's stronger traits while scorning the weaknesses in others that actually reflect one's own.

MONEY/WORK/CREATIVITY

Something is in need of repair, replacement or restoration, and now is the time to see to it. Alternatively, there is a part or person in your operation that is not functioning as well as they should; they must be identified and the problem addressed.

KEEP FOCUSED ON ... seeing to the above, and then your product, project, financial status or working life will be restored to its former glory ... any kind of pre-emptive measure that will forestall the damage that could be done ... identifying and strengthening any weak points regarding the object of your concern.

WATCH OUT FOR ... trying to repair what is beyond it – but only when you are absolutely sure that this is the only option.

LOVE/RELATING/SOCIAL

A beautiful relationship or social set-up that is marred by there being a flaw or damage done to it. This could be a sin of commission – such as one person having an affair – or omission – such as a negative show of commitment. This 'damage' could be on an unsaid or unconscious level that has not yet been identified, but that is spoiling the relationship as a whole.

KEEP FOCUSED ON ... what it is, now or in the past, that is giving rise to discontent or insecurity on the part of one or more of you; then track back to the original cause and repair the damage ... the original love and beauty of the relationship, for this is the reason for making the effort to make amends and let go of old hurts ... doing all restoration *lovingly*.

WATCH OUT FOR ... doing more damage while you attempt to heal rifts, sort out old problems.

KARMA/ATTITUDE/HEALTH

This is essentially about damage done to faith, of the abuse of or disregard for something holy or divine. This could relate to a personal faith or a religious denomination. It could also refer to a weak aspect to one's health or mental–emotional–physical system. The result of past trauma on the present.

KEEP FOCUSED ON ... whatever aspect of the object of your concern is dysfunctional, misunderstood or poorly expressed. For example, a bad mental attitude can eventually affect physical health, and denying some past misdeed could lie heavily on one's conscience ... admitting, healing, forgiving or atoning for any such shortcoming ... the truth and wonder of any life function or general true spiritual teaching.

WATCH OUT FOR ... feeling guilty and (self-) destructive behaviour rather than forgiving yourself and others.

'Praise my soul, the King of Heaven;/To His feet thy tribute bring.
Ransomed, healed, restored, forgiven,/Who like me His praise should sing'

THE HUMAN SOUL RECEPTIVE TO GROWTH AND UNDERSTANDING

☆ OPENNESS ☆

⚙ GENERAL INTERPRETATION

Here you have the essence of the female or yin aspect of self and life, in the sense of being entirely open to the experiences that it attracts. The vulnerability that goes along with this is taken as a small price to pay for the enormous rewards and achievements that can be attained.

KEEP FOCUSED ON ... being open to receive your rightful rewards and opportunities; contrary to the proverb, it is just as important to be able to receive as it is to give ... the yearning and hunger of your soul that ensures that eventually it will be satisfied, but not necessarily in the way that you currently imagine.

WATCH OUT FOR ... it being a case of all feeling but no action when this is necessary ... raising 'reasonable' objections or setting conditions when really one is afraid of being made to feel.

♥ LOVE/RELATING/SOCIAL

All too often, owing to our desire to get what we think we want and to be understood – and out of our fears of not being so – we overlook the fact that the other person has similar desires and fears as well. So, this Symbol is reminding you to ...

KEEP FOCUSED ON ... the fact that everyone is sensitive and receptive, whether they show it or not. So, send good thoughts and loving feelings, healing and blessings, to others and they will pick them up. The more receptive you are to others, the more receptive they'll be to you ... trusting that eventually you and they will know what needs to be known.

WATCH OUT FOR ... entertaining negative or aggressive thoughts about anyone, for they will receive them and then act out the very things that you have thought.

⚛ MONEY/WORK/CREATIVITY

If your concern is of a creative nature then this Symbol reassures you that you are well-positioned for receiving whatever impressions, ideas or inspiration you need to further your endeavours. Money and job issues are areas where spiritual values can be sorely tried or even out of place. If this is the case ...

KEEP FOCUSED ON ... trying to accept whatever your situation is in the faith that its direction and meaning will be revealed in due course ... the probability that the public, or whoever is your concern, is now receptive to your product or idea, or they will be as much as you are yourself.

WATCH OUT FOR ... being too sensitive and too understanding in areas where a more worldly awareness and hard-edged approach is needed. You may have to be in that world even though you are not of it. Either get some body armour or look for a more sympathetic working environment.

☯ KARMA/ATTITUDE/HEALTH

This marks a very important point in your development, especially spiritually. Most of the problems people have with their lives are down to their egos, or the egos of others reflecting their own, eclipsing the light of the soul and thereby blocking understanding. Here, however, that Point of Return has been reached, where you take the long but inevitable path back to your divine source, essential being and ultimate accord.

KEEP FOCUSED ON ... the fact that this Point of Return is also the Point of No Return because once you have perceived or experienced the nature of the soul there is no more turning back than there would be if you had found your long lost love ... using whatever spiritual subjects and practices that have helped you so far.

WATCH OUT FOR ... thinking that the Path of Return, that living the Life of Soul, is easy. It is more difficult than the 'normal' ego life, but infinitely more satisfying and meaningful.

'There is one thing stronger than all the armies in the world; and that is an idea whose time has come'

A PARTY ENTERING A LARGE CANOE

☆ COMMON FATE ☆

GENERAL INTERPRETATION

Being, or about to be, inextricably involved with a number of others. This could mean a form of group enterprise and the preparation, processing and commitment that its successful launch and continuance entails.

KEEP FOCUSED ON ... using or developing your talent for organizing others in such a way that they all pull together and reach the desired goal ... making sure that you and everyone concerned 'knows their place' and sticks to what they are in a position to do best ... how important your 'shipmates' are to you.

WATCH OUT FOR ... not knowing where you stand, and the instability that this can attract ... rocking the boat ... being antisocial and not wanting to fit in – someday you could wind up stranded.

LOVE/RELATING/SOCIAL

You are on an emotional voyage of discovery with all the thrills and spills, the ups and downs that this engenders. If there are just two of you then it may be important to realize that you are part of something greater than just a couple; there are probably others who are somehow caught up in your relationship. You need to ...

KEEP FOCUSED ON ... what you are all doing together; ask yourself how it got started, for this is a prime clue to why it is happening.

WATCH OUT FOR ... trying to 'throw overboard' anyone or anything that appears not to belong; they are 'on board' for a reason that cannot simply be jettisoned. This sharing of fate means that people have to pull together, be made to find their place and fit in. If anyone jumps ship of their own accord or falls overboard, then so be it.

MONEY/WORK/CREATIVITY

This images an enterprise or project that depends greatly upon the individuals, ideas or products conforming to a collective aim. What is stressed is the importance of co-operation, possibly in a confined space, which could mean a limitation of some sort, such as funds, time or, literally, space. Creatively, finding some kind of accord is the essential ingredient for success.

KEEP FOCUSED ON ... keeping every part of your project 'shipshape' – even if it entails some hardship – for this is the prerequisite for achieving your goal and for staying afloat.

WATCH OUT FOR ... not really wanting to be or get involved, for once things are underway it may not be that easy to pull out. If you have already enlisted for the 'voyage' and it is not going how you wanted, then see it all as a learning experience.

KARMA/ATTITUDE/HEALTH

We have come together with certain people in certain circumstances as part of our fate. We are destined to be involved with each other for deep and far-reaching reasons. Health-wise, you could see the various parts of your life and personality as having to operate in harmony with one another, and that the efficacy of this would be reflected in the various parts of your body.

KEEP FOCUSED ON ... any part of your body that is playing up, for it might represent an aspect of your being that is not pulling its weight, is not being a happy or willing member of the 'crew', or is in some way reluctant or unable to stay the course ... who is the 'captain', that is, the part of you that is keeping the other parts' spirits up, their hands to their tasks, and is headed in the right direction for a worthwhile purpose.

WATCH OUT FOR ... mutinous attitudes that do not recognize the need for discipline and hardship.

'We are all in the same boat'

INDIANS ROWING A CANOE AND DANCING A WAR DANCE

☆ DRUMMING UP ENTHUSIASM ☆

 GENERAL INTERPRETATION

The call to action and arms that is basic to any creative enterprise – or the defence of that enterprise. The primitive, tribal streak in personality that equips one to gather together those of like mind to overcome a common enemy, especially one that is purblind and greedy for power.

KEEP FOCUSED ON ... what is necessary in terms of positive thinking and enthusiasm to reach a goal ... maintaining a positive attitude and pursuing enterprising activities, for they are what contribute to the likelihood of success.

WATCH OUT FOR ... aggressiveness that stirs up chaos and results in upset ... intimidation: guard against it in yourself or others ... violent emotions: quell them or channel them in a worthwhile direction.

♥ **LOVE/RELATING/SOCIAL**

On a one-to-one level this Symbol is saying that emotions are being aroused and juices are flowing. With regard to a group, the feel for a common purpose and goal is strong, or is in the process of being made so.

KEEP FOCUSED ON ... the most fundamental drives and feelings that give relationships momentum, such as the loves and hates of those concerned. In this way one can stir others up and attract them to your cause or person ... having a common goal that transcends your differences.

WATCH OUT FOR ... getting into hot water more than you emotionally bargained for. Those most basic and powerful feelings that are being played upon cannot just be turned off once they have been aroused – be it in yourself or others ... upsetting each other needlessly.

 MONEY/WORK/CREATIVITY

We see here a marshalling of forces, talents and resources – or the need for it. Your idea or product, if it is concerned with a kind of mobilization towards an ideal is very well-starred, it is getting off on the right foot. Implied here is the prospect of suffering a loss or making an investment for the sake of a gain.

KEEP FOCUSED ON ... getting all your forces and resources to head in the same direction, in the spirit of an enterprise that defends anything which is close to Earth, or that embodies a noble tradition in the face of overly materialistic forces.

WATCH OUT FOR ... bulldozing anything or anyone that gets in your way – that is unless it is genuinely a case of them or you ... arousing enmity in others, especially when they are more powerful than you.

☯ **KARMA/ATTITUDE/HEALTH**

Overcoming tyrannical forces that were set in motion in the past, and gathering brave and spirited souls to assist in such an enterprise. In the shadow of the great tragedy that was the destruction or disempowerment of a noble, natural and spiritual expression of being human, we now have to summon the courage and faith that is necessary to stop the rot, redeem the sins of our forefathers, and fight for a true civilization that respects planet Earth and all that exists upon Her.

KEEP FOCUSED ON ... the idea that you are one of the 'Indians' and that the 'canoe' is the vehicle of faith and feelings that will carry you through the rough waters between now and a better future, and that the 'war dance' is any activity or words that drum up the enthusiasm in you and others to meet any challenge set before you.

WATCH OUT FOR ... getting carried away on some ill-considered, self-righteous crusade.

'A desperate disease requires a dangerous remedy'

A DARK ARCHWAY AND TEN LOGS AT THE BOTTOM

☆ SUPPLY AND DEMAND ☆

❋ GENERAL INTERPRETATION

The juxtaposition of the unknown and foreboding (dark archway) with something so ordinary, practical and precise as the fuel (ten logs) suggests an awareness of yet to be discovered realities, and the preparedness for meeting them. Or, with the logs being 'at the bottom', it is suggested that we get what we need once we have got to a place where we really do need it. Hence the Supply follows the encountering of the Demand, and not necessarily the other way around.

KEEP FOCUSED ON ... fearlessness coupled with a readiness for any eventuality, making for intrepid leadership and the discovery of what one needs to have or know.

WATCH OUT FOR ... an anxiety about the unknown, possibly born of past failures.

♥ LOVE/RELATING/SOCIAL

This poses the darker recesses or more difficult emotional passages that intimate relationships inevitably include. Such experiences can be anything from emotionally gruelling to sexually intriguing. The point is that, whatever they are, they reveal to us something that was previously unknown to us, and which potentially is a highly valuable emotional or sexual experience.

KEEP FOCUSED ON ... the fact that there is something vital for you to discover about life and yourself in the midst of whatever is the object of your concern, even though it might appear to be hell, darkly compelling or just plain unavoidable. And as you go through it all, you gain and eliminate as required.

WATCH OUT FOR ... taking anything lightly that happens now; it is deep, powerful and serious.

♟ MONEY/WORK/CREATIVITY

Whatever is before you now, it is preparedness that is most important. If what you are enquiring about has already past, in fact it is your preparedness (or lack of it) which will inform you of how you will fare. Creatively speaking, what is stressed is the importance of groundwork and of readying your materials, conceiving your plot, plan or pitch. Then when you step into the unknown territory – the realms of your imagination – you will receive and express what you find there with deftness and ease.

KEEP FOCUSED ON ... the idea that who or what may be intimidating you is not as they seem. As you venture onwards, you find talents and resources you didn't know you had – and nor would you if you were not facing your fears and doubts.

WATCH OUT FOR ... just staying where you are because of those doubts and fears.

☯ KARMA/ATTITUDE/HEALTH

Here is a difficult patch that will eventually produce something to your advantage once you get to the bottom of it. Implied here is also the possibility of encountering a real fear, ingrained in childhood or from earlier. Through engaging and dealing with whatever it is, you not only free yourself from that fear, but gain something into the bargain.

KEEP FOCUSED ON ... those areas of life that frighten, intimidate or fascinate you, possibly in spite of the fact that the weaker side of your personality doesn't want you to ... the help, resources and positive influences that are at hand.

WATCH OUT FOR ... being immobilized by indecision, or thinking that what is unknown is 'bad'. Simply by getting to know what it is, it ceases to be unknown and becomes something whose value is as great as the fear you initially felt.

'Confronting what you fear provides what you need'

A VEILED PROPHET OF POWER

☆ INSCRUTABLE INFLUENCE ☆

 GENERAL INTERPRETATION

Something profound that is not obvious from its appearance, but is felt at a deep inner level. Alternatively, the Oracle could be saying that the future is powerful but not easily penetrated or discernible – at the moment anyway. If this is the case, you are going to have to use the Oracle again and again until you gain the insight you want, or find the question you really want to ask.

KEEP FOCUSED ON ... using intuitive awareness of what captures people's imaginations or sense of seriousness ... sending out bright thoughts and feelings to others, bearing in mind that they may not be recognized or appreciated at first ... the deepest, most hidden reasons for what concerns you.

WATCH OUT FOR ... an affected sense or neurotic anticipation of mystery and foreboding.

♥ LOVE/RELATING/SOCIAL

Here is a relationship or person that is captivating or exercises a strong pull, but it is not quite clear where it will all lead. There are deep connections here; it is quite mystifying as to what it all poses and, therefore, how to relate. If you are on your own, perhaps it is saying that others find you hard to get through to, too intense, and therefore they are put off or intimidated.

KEEP FOCUSED ON ... the mere fact that there is no easily perceived answer here. All you can do is follow the sense that something fateful is going on – with caution ... being genuine.

WATCH OUT FOR ... getting in too deep too quickly; wait until you have a clearer view of how things are panning out ... being seduced or conned.

MONEY/WORK/CREATIVITY

You are dealing with an idea, product, person or information that has great potential for future profit and influence. Then again, it could blow up in your face if you let things get out of control, or do not closely monitor all developments. Also, any kind of vague predictions concerning your fortunes or finances should be taken with a pinch of salt until it is plainly proven that things really are taking off. If your line of work actually involves the prediction of anything, then this could be very auspicious, but you could still get your fingers burnt – but that is an occupational hazard.

KEEP FOCUSED ON ... what it is that you are hoping to gain and, more importantly, how much you want to gain it. There is a danger here of being blinded by ambition and not seeing what you are getting yourself into.

WATCH OUT FOR ... being taken advantage of by anything or anyone that flatters your ego.

KARMA/ATTITUDE/HEALTH

Whether it is yourself or someone else who is perceived as the 'Veiled Prophet Of Power', the question is whether you or they are the genuine article. More simply, it could be that you are now moving into a profound and critical stage of your life, especially with regard to your spiritual path in life. Health-wise, you may be dealing with a powerful element or healer. Whatever the case ...

KEEP FOCUSED ON ... how matters develop stage by stage, monitoring everything very carefully ... making sure that the use of psychic or religious insights are for the good of the whole, and not one person in particular ... trusting your influence without being too obvious about it, 'Veil your light but still shine'.

WATCH OUT FOR ... submitting to any kind of treatment that induces trance. Check the credentials or side effects of anyone or anything ... how any others involved have been affected.

'A prophet is not without honour, save in his own country, and in his own house'

BIRDS IN THE HOUSE SINGING HAPPILY

☆ LIFT UP YOUR HEART ☆

 GENERAL INTERPRETATION

Your situation is filled with the spirit of life itself. Every aspect of it is imbued with the essence that brought it into being: the beauty and wholesomeness of Nature herself. Happy thoughts make for a happy life. Or, you need to discern and appreciate these very things. Domestic bliss, possibly.

KEEP FOCUSED ON ... your consistent urge to put everything and everyone joyfully to use and thereby bring out the best in them ... the saying 'Charity begins at home'; fill yourself, and where you live, with positive and good feelings, thoughts, images and sounds.

WATCH OUT FOR ... twittering complacency or shallow conceit ... a lack of genuine joy in your life and the lives of those around you.

 LOVE/RELATING/SOCIAL

Pleasure and satisfaction are confirmed or predicted here, but the accent is on the contentment that comes more from a personal or private connection or occasion, rather than something of a glamorous or external nature – a candlelit dinner rather than a night out on the tiles. The general message is that happiness is where you find it, that you create it and take it with you wherever you go.

KEEP FOCUSED ON ... how you make sweet music together, and then anything you build together will be secure, happy and creative ... the spiritual link you have with another or others, for this is the fount of true happiness together.

WATCH OUT FOR ... seeking abroad or externally, the good time you are more likely to find at home or within your heart.

 MONEY/WORK/CREATIVITY

The work you do best, that is most suited to you, is the work you are happy doing. And if you are happy doing your work, then the material reward for it does not need to be too much of a priority. A happy work environment is an efficient and productive one. Also, being happy at work can depend on being happy at home and in your personal life, for the peak of a mountain rests upon its base. Creatively, you are on to a good thing. Materially, you have assets you may not have noticed. Music itself is well-starred.

KEEP FOCUSED ON ... cultivating within yourself and those with whom you work a feeling of well-being that stems from a sense of common purpose or of your work's spiritual significance.

WATCH OUT FOR ... neglecting your personal life and substituting it with work or money(-making).

KARMA/ATTITUDE/HEALTH

Genuine happiness and a sense of joy is infectious. It spreads to everyone in your sphere. There is something about you or your situation that is favourable at a simple and essential level – like singing in the bath.

KEEP FOCUSED ON ... whatever it is that prompts in you or others a feeling of light-heartedness. Whatever it is will act like a homing signal that unerringly leads you back to a positive place in your heart and soul ... actually singing for the sake of it, which is to let out what may be trapped inside you.

WATCH OUT FOR ... a false sense of joy that is based on selfish escapism and a lack of awareness rather than being alive to something beautiful and special in yourself and the world.

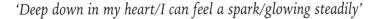

'Deep down in my heart/I can feel a spark/glowing steadily'

AN ANGEL CARRYING A HARP

☆ UPLIFT THROUGH ATTUNEMENT ☆

✹ GENERAL INTERPRETATION

The Divine is expressing itself to the human senses via whatever means come naturally, be it words, dance, healing, pictures or music itself. Other ways of tuning into and requesting assistance include meditation, visualization, and listening for/to one's inner voice.

KEEP FOCUSED ON ... your creative talent that inspires others to raise their consciousness ... the beautiful idea that we humans are the 'harps' or instruments that the Angels play on or express themselves through, and that support us in our times of need.

WATCH OUT FOR ... fanciful imaginings and spiritual pretensions ... seeing adversity merely as adversity when really it is telling you that you can and should seek help.

♥ LOVE/RELATING/SOCIAL

You have, or have the opportunity to have, a beautiful and harmonious relationship; one where you make music together, literally or figuratively. You have someone or something 'up there' who acts as a 'tuning fork', keeping you, your partner or group subtly in touch with one another – possibly in pursuit of a spiritual purpose.

KEEP FOCUSED ON ... whatever you regard as your highest guiding principles in relating to others ... the fact that you *do* have divine help with your relationships, and that you only have to believe in it, relate to it, and call it up.

WATCH OUT FOR ... being smug regarding your fine sense of togetherness or combined purpose, for this would necessarily lower your vibration and may cause you to lose temporarily your divine connection.

MONEY/WORK/CREATIVITY

Something or someone on a higher level is helping and guiding your business or creations. This may seem out of place in the material world of down-to-earth Capricorn, but it must be remembered that truly it is the sign of the Sea-Goat: it is half earthy climber and half mystical, in touch with other dimensions or inner planes of reality. So ...

KEEP FOCUSED ON ... the idea that you need not fear collapse or loss just so long as you become or stay attuned to an 'angel' or higher helper. You are helped and supported more when you *believe* that you are, so conduct your affairs with this idea firmly in mind.

WATCH OUT FOR ... being put off by the philistine non-believers who inhabit the world of business and commerce. They may be good at functioning in the material sphere, but this is because *that* is what *they* believe in.

☯ KARMA/ATTITUDE/HEALTH

You most definitely have a 'connection to the spirits', whether you know it or not. However, the harp signifies that angelic or higher help is something that is better and more accessible when you are consciously attuned to and in sympathy with it. The Divine is trying to catch your attention for it wishes to express itself through and to you – especially if this is for healing of any kind.

KEEP FOCUSED ON ... feeling a part of a spiritual hierarchy, in that you are part of a team with its members working on (and from) different levels or planes of reality. Humanity is said to be the Middle Kingdom, mediating between the higher (angelic) and lower (animal) realms ... keeping healthy by staying attuned.

WATCH OUT FOR ... not being in touch with your angelic helpers because they cannot dynamically intervene unless asked or allowed to.

'It came upon the midnight clear,/That glorious song of old,
From Angels bending near the earth/To touch their harps of gold'

AN ALBATROSS FEEDING FROM THE HAND

☆ CONNECTION TO THE SPIRITS ☆

GENERAL INTERPRETATION

In evidence here is a wonderfully trusting relationship with those elements of life that have spiritual significance in that they look over and guide us in a subtle way that must not be violated. Here is a good omen for whatever is the object of your enquiry. This is based on the fact that sailors hold that harming an albatross brings bad luck, which may have something to do with these big birds being so tame and friendly on dry land, so alluding to returning home safely. Appealing to the soul of anything or anyone to whom you feel some tie.

KEEP FOCUSED ON ... staying attuned to whatever you feel has a subtle influence over your welfare and that of others close to you.

WATCH OUT FOR ... reading more into things than is actually so, or simply misusing intuition ... being out of tune with the Spirit in the Sky.

MONEY/WORK/CREATIVITY

Your occupational, domestic and financial security are presently in the lap of the gods, or dependent on your respect of forces and agencies that are unseen or that you have no control over. The Oracle says you do have this link, but it is not something you should presume upon indefinitely or without constant mindfulness of the delicate or subtle relationship you have with them. A strong Capricornian alternative to this is that, like the albatross, you achieve your objective because you eat and sleep on the job, until you do so.

KEEP FOCUSED ON ... cultivating your link with whatever you regard as having an overview of, or influence over, your situation – then all will be well ... seeing and valuing the true inner purpose of what you are doing.

WATCH OUT FOR ... biting the hand that feeds.

LOVE/RELATING/SOCIAL

There are often aspects to a relationship of which we are totally or partially unaware, but which are critical to the welfare of that relationship. Sadly, we are sometimes not made aware of them until the relationship ends or suffers estrangement. We then pine and crave for the return of that subtle and previously overlooked quality. So ...

KEEP FOCUSED ON ... aspects of your relationships that are seen to be vitally significant when they are not so available. This may entail imagining, or experiencing, a situation where you are without your partner or friend, and being honest and aware enough about how you identify and admit to your feelings.

WATCH OUT FOR ... taking the 'invisible' assets of another for granted ... hanging on to a misguided sense of loyalty.

KARMA/ATTITUDE/HEALTH

This Symbol is reminiscent of the fact that people suffering from depression experience a distinct uplift when in the presence of dolphins. Human interaction with other species and realms is a mysterious thing. An explanation of this has to rest with the subtler or etheric aspects of human existence. This implies that how we fare and how we feel is dependent upon how our auras interact with others, and how some creatures are so intricately and intimately a part of the greater whole that they seem directly to affect us as well.

KEEP FOCUSED ON ... your relationship and experiences with non-human messengers and what they are trying to tell you.

WATCH OUT FOR ... 'over-interpreting' omens ... sheer superstition.

'He prayeth best that loveth best/All things both great and small'

A LARGE GROUP OF PHEASANTS

✮ NATURE VERSUS EXPLOITATION ✮

✸ GENERAL INTERPRETATION

The issue here refers to any social group as an instinctual mass that can be seen either as a unit of safety and natural order, or as a vulnerable state that invites exploitation, or that lacks individuality or originality.

KEEP FOCUSED ON ... your sense of how to gather people together for a cultural, political, religious or creative purpose – or being a valid member of such a group ... finding a balance between the natural and the man-made.

WATCH OUT FOR ... sacrificing individual values for the comfort of convention ... ignoring the group's values if you want to be part of it, or appeal to it ... succumbing to the group values if you don't want to be part of the crowd ... being part of the system and not being recognized as having a soul.

♥ LOVE/RELATING/SOCIAL

How any individual, relationship or group fits into society as a whole. The question arises as to whether the larger whole has values and pursuits which support or appeal to the individual. Is society exploiting one or in sympathy? The issue could be one of natural appetites against man-made ones that are demeaning or destructive. At best, a closeness born of natural drives that is undisturbed by those elements that are actually using or pitted against these drives.

KEEP FOCUSED ON ... what the 'group' means to you in the context of your question, because it is this that holds the key to satisfying or disenchanting you.

WATCH OUT FOR ... any practice or pursuit that is motivated by something that you find hard to justify in your heart of hearts; it will come to nothing – or worse.

⚜ MONEY/WORK/CREATIVITY

Here is a large resource – the general public or a big corporation or institution – open to having its nature and instincts exploited and profited from. It may be that you are a part of this resource – if so, read the following in terms of being on the receiving end ...

KEEP FOCUSED ON ... considering the welfare or nature of whatever or whoever you are wishing to benefit (from) ... getting your ends to justify your means ... the importance of your own integrity and safety ... whatever advantages there might be in anonymity, in being a small fish in a big pond.

WATCH OUT FOR ... exploiting or being exploited, especially when or where greed is posing as need ... getting buried in the values of an organization or state where your own worth is not recognized.

☯ KARMA/ATTITUDE/HEALTH

The connotation here is one of the natural proliferation of something, or of its demise due to exploitation or a lack of caring forethought. 'Large groups of pheasants' are, after all, bred to be killed for human food or 'sport'.

KEEP FOCUSED ON ... your own innermost feelings and values ... breaking out of situations that are inhibiting your expression and freedom ... the various parts of your life and being, keeping them rounded, tended to, protected and secure.

WATCH OUT FOR ... being sucked into a group or mass that is unaware of what it actually is, or what is in store for it – 'lambs to the slaughter' ... being part of anything unnatural, that destabilizes the whole ... the possibility that there is not necessarily 'safety in numbers'.

'We are all but pawns in the game of life'

A STUDENT OF NATURE LECTURING

☆ THE THEORY OF WHOLESOMENESS ☆

⚙ GENERAL INTERPRETATION

Everything conspires to make you true to your own nature. Learning or imparting how things are ordered in a harmonious and functional fashion. This is particularly with regard to comparing how you or anything else works with the way Nature herself works – that everything has its 'season'.

KEEP FOCUSED ON ... your profound sense of organic rightness, especially where a particular design or course of action is concerned ... the nature of all the people or elements involved, for then you will see the whole clearly ... what is natural.

WATCH OUT FOR ... a lopsided assessment of your issue owing to an overuse of scientific objectivity ... going against a natural or wholesome way of being ... imposing your own subjective viewpoint.

♥ LOVE/RELATING/SOCIAL

A close to the earth and studious relationship or person is represented here. There is an emphasis upon the wholesome and intellectual. This is fine as far as it goes, but the emotional or intuitive aspect could well be weak or dysfunctional.

KEEP FOCUSED ON ... leaving things more or less as they are, if you do not wish to rock the boat. If you do wish to make waves and changes, you will have to take responsibility for them eventually.

WATCH OUT FOR ... not taking into consideration the emotional or psychological dimensions, for a purely scientific or logical theory would be inapplicable and therefore ineffectual ... boring or haranguing others with the 'facts' when they are more concerned with feelings.

⚘ MONEY/WORK/CREATIVITY

Your function in the world is one of informing others how best to go about their business, be that living in general, business or a specialized field of endeavour. Your method and philosophy is decidedly 'organic' in that you (should) trust your career and means of expression to unwind and develop, rather than launch a grand project without going through the necessary 'organic' steps.

KEEP FOCUSED ON ... what comes naturally to you so that you do not feel you are pretending in any way ... ideas and feelings that have spontaneously arisen rather than ones you think you 'should' think and feel.

WATCH OUT FOR ... paying too much attention to voices – be they internal or external – that would have you be, or feel you are, not as Nature intended.

☯ KARMA/ATTITUDE/HEALTH

This is strongly alluding to a natural form of health or way of living. So, one's diet and outlook should be as pure and free from pollutants as possible. Then again, such a regimen can be taken too far, and find you living your life according to fads posing as facts.

KEEP FOCUSED ON ... the way that creatures approach the business of living, acquiring what is needed and no more ... defending your space only when it is invaded ... keeping clean without being overly fastidious ... the voice within you that feels natural and calm, unassuming and unimposing.

WATCH OUT FOR ... assuming that you have all the answers when you have not studied all the facets of a given subject ... boring or bothering others with your 'natural remedies' or one-sided theories that are not really borne out by the facts. Check out those facts.

'Nature does nothing without purpose or uselessly'

A FIRE WORSHIPPER

☆ PASSION AND RESPECT ☆

 GENERAL INTERPRETATION

A passionate situation, but passion is a double-edged sword. Is it giving cause for joy or grief? Basically, the element of Fire represents the Spirit; it is the vital energy of life itself, driving everyone and everything. Right now you are experiencing it in some way that may need adjusting or redirecting.

KEEP FOCUSED ON ... the 'positive spirit' of the position you are currently in. Raw energy on its own can be troublesome and one needs to know what it can do that is creative, enjoyable and good. A fire can heat and brighten up a home – or burn it down. If you cannot identify what 'good' can be done with your passion or life energy, then ...

WATCH OUT FOR ... it could be dangerous, and probably needs damping down or dissipating if you are to see clearly (what the Oracle is telling you?).

MONEY/WORK/CREATIVITY

The accent here is on creativity, making what you want. It also points to the fact that you have sound basic resources in the form of ideas or workmanship, so that funds can always be drummed up. In both cases, what matters is that you ...

KEEP FOCUSED ON ... paying frequent respect to the Creative Process and creative elements, to your imagination and ambition, to co-workers, and to the whole process of commercial interaction ... what 'burns' most within you or is spreading and catching on externally, then nurture and invest in that.

WATCH OUT FOR ... getting carried away with enthusiasm or ambition, overestimating your resources or abilities. Respect for your creative or business passions also means respecting limitations – or observing them.

LOVE/RELATING/SOCIAL

Passionate feelings or sexual urges are being experienced. This Symbol is saying that one must respect these feelings, and neither let them have their way totally with you, nor suppress or ignore them.

KEEP FOCUSED ON ... expressing your passionate feelings in a way that is *mutually* satisfying, which may entail exploring what is suggested in the Karma section ... the spirit of other individuals and a mutual respect will arise, and consequently an accord or bond.

WATCH OUT FOR ... worshipping or denying the object of your passion (or passion itself). In the first case, you would be asking for a 'burn-out' where one person feels overwhelmed and either leaves or cools; in the second case denial is a form of disrespect which would invite more trouble ... failure or disrespect as a result of being too tentative or lily-livered.

KARMA/ATTITUDE/HEALTH

We are talking here of the inner strength that is born of an inviolable tie with the creative power of the universe itself, and the high achievement that this may give rise to in terms of divine realization. Esoterically, it is referring to the *chi*, inner fire or *kundalini* energy that vitalizes and courses through all life. Controlling or removing blocks to this energy is of primary importance. This can be achieved through various methods where you ...

KEEP FOCUSED ON ... the flow of the energy itself. Such methods include tai chi, kundalini yoga, Taoism or Tantra, or simply by allowing your 'fires' to ascend through your body as if it were an iron chimney, not attaching yourself to them or analysing them, but just letting them fly up into the sky or back to the Sun from whence they came.

WATCH OUT FOR ... any 'hot' reactions in your body such as fever, inflammation or hot flushes.

'Do not play with fire if you do not wish to get burnt'

AN ANCIENT BAS-RELIEF CARVED IN GRANITE

✦ LASTING LEGACY ✦

✹ GENERAL INTERPRETATION

Something that is here to stay for a considerable time, characterized by a sense of conviction and significance. This Symbol also suggests an historical fact or artefact representing a philosophy and set of values that may be significant today; possibly more so than those of our own culture.

KEEP FOCUSED ON ... your ability to leave your mark and create a true and lasting impression ... attaining and maintaining a state of stillness and coolness that is only moved by the weighty or profound ... drawing comfort and guidance from the eternal verities. For example, the bird song I hear now is as I heard it when I was a child, and as my forebears heard it.

WATCH OUT FOR ... meaningless and suffocating limitation through excessive reliance on tradition or on outworn values.

♥ LOVE/RELATING/SOCIAL

A reliable, rock-steady type of person or relationship that will last and last – or that already has. On the face of it this is a good thing, but there can be the danger of it becoming dull or meaningless. There is also the issue of making lasting impressions or preserving a social set-up.

KEEP FOCUSED ON ... what has lasting value and seeking to preserve it, even if this entails making a few sacrifices ... the lasting qualities of a person or relationship, for they will eventually outweigh the more glamorous or superficial aspects ... staying in touch with what your relationship or social life stands for, and revamping it if necessary.

WATCH OUT FOR ... letting tradition and the 'devil you know' pose as 'love' or become a substitute for a vital and self-renewing relationship ... being compromised by other's squabbles.

MONEY/WORK/CREATIVITY

You are dealing, or are being advised to deal, with something or someone that has long been established. This could be a product or business practice, an artistic style or a financial institution. It could also be one's personal record with respect to professional and financial matters that is the issue. What has lasted *will* last.

KEEP FOCUSED ON ... those elements that have proved themselves through time to be lasting and reliable ... the meaning and significance of your concern, for they may have been lost along the way ... promoting and preserving what truly has worth and appeal according to its track record, while discarding any unnecessary facets.

WATCH OUT FOR ... adhering to ideas or standards because they have been cast in stone.

☯ KARMA/ATTITUDE/HEALTH

There are elements of our karma that have been there – and may continue to be so – for a very long time, be they good or bad. It could be regarded as a priority to ...

KEEP FOCUSED ON ... identifying what the long-standing elements of our karma are, and seek to draw from and perpetuate the good, and learn from and expiate the bad ... what you would like to leave behind at the end of this life as a lasting impression of your personality and testament to that life.

WATCH OUT FOR ... the 'Ozymandias Syndrome' where it is thought that one's status or legacy will last through all eternity, that you live for ever, when in fact everything returns to sand and dust ... rigidity of mind, for this can give rise to rigidity of body ... ignoring or indulging longstanding negative karma; this will simply prolong its existence.

*'Lives of great men all remind us/We can make our lives sublime,
And, departing, leave behind us/Footprints on the sands of time'*

MANY TOYS IN THE CHILDREN'S WARD OF A HOSPITAL

☆ TENDER LOVING CARE ☆

⚙ GENERAL INTERPRETATION

Occasioned or called for here is the fundamental kindness and generosity that is or should be shown to those who have been disadvantaged through no apparent fault of their own, or who are in genuine need of care and accommodation. However, considering that this is a Saturnine, Capricornian Symbol and that hospitals have to have rules, such care has to be tempered with discipline and a setting of limits. 'Tough love', if necessary.

KEEP FOCUSED ON ... your ability to develop your own and others' potentials, and take care of their needs, despite any setback that Fate might have dished out.

WATCH OUT FOR ... giving into an idle and irresponsible reliance on whatever service or materials have been handed out to you.

♡ LOVE/RELATING/SOCIAL

Here we have a person, relationship or social scenario that requires or engenders a special kind of attention. One or more individuals may be afflicted in some way, temporarily or indefinitely, hence the need for such caring devotion. Any of this may involve a child or children – or someone who is childlike.

KEEP FOCUSED ON ... providing whatever can console or distract attention away from distress ... exactly where a talent for tender loving care is needed – and developing it if it doesn't come naturally.

WATCH OUT FOR ... toying with another's affection, or having your own toyed with ... any point where one has to put away childish things, whatever they might be ... spoiling or being spoilt.

MONEY/WORK/CREATIVITY

The area of your concern is either in need of special care and attention to get it back on its feet, or the nature of your work is, or should be, in line with the play–recovery–healing process that this Symbol represents and blesses.

KEEP FOCUSED ON ... keeping the personal and nurturing aspect to the fore. This may seem strange for a Symbol of cool and businesslike Capricorn, but that is just the point – it is saying that sometimes in the material world such care is precisely what is required ... the auspiciousness of any kind of philanthropic work.

WATCH OUT FOR ... taking care and attention too far as this can lull yourself or others into an apathetic state. 'Toys' and 'hospitals' should not be permanent fixtures – unless of course that *is* your business.

☯ KARMA/ATTITUDE/HEALTH

This is the only Sabian Symbol that refers directly to 'hospital' and so it can either be directing you to one, or saying that the care you are receiving in one is of the very best. In any event, you have available to you everything possible for optimum recovery or support. Figuratively speaking, it is saying that after some kind of damage or crisis, you have at hand all that is needed to entertain, relieve, redeem or resurrect yourself or others.

KEEP FOCUSED ON ... meeting the needs of those who cannot help themselves ... the belief that special help is always available at one level or another ... taking full advantage of whatever help is being offered to you, if you are on the receiving end.

WATCH OUT FOR ... becoming institutionalized, dependent or out-staying your welcome ... being too soft and kind if you are the one doing the ministering; this would be counterproductive.

*'Suffer the little children to come unto me, and forbid them not:
for of such is the kingdom of God'*

BOYS AND GIRLS IN GYMNASIUM SUITS

☆ CONCERTED ENERGY ☆

❋ GENERAL INTERPRETATION

The necessary imposition of convention on the activities and relationships between males and females, or any varied group of individuals, particularly with regard to physical aspects.

KEEP FOCUSED ON ... your healthy sense of how to get the best out of male–female interaction, or any other dualism, through self-discipline or a means of organization ... egging one another on with regard to meeting any challenge that faces you.

WATCH OUT FOR ... any awkwardness with the opposite sex, or any other group different to one's own, as this is probably down to an outworn or inappropriate social attitude ... assuming that being physically fit will equip or protect you on levels other than the physical, such as emotionally, mentally and spiritually.

MONEY/WORK/CREATIVITY

Here is stressed the necessity and desirability of teamwork and co-operation in the workplace, and of the equal or complementary roles men and women play within it. Individual roles and talents are also an important factor here. A male–female partnership could be a very creative and productive team.

KEEP FOCUSED ON ... identifying and then organizing the various talents and forces within a situation or project ... fitting in with a whole or convention ... establishing what your speciality is, and practising to make it as effective as possible ... the importance of training and discipline.

WATCH OUT FOR ... seeing yourself or others as just cogs in the machine, sacrificing individuality merely for the sake of material success.

♥ LOVE/RELATING/SOCIAL

Social or sexual etiquette is the advisable route to take now, especially in any relationship where you and others are not really playing for the same 'team'. Also, when each of the sexes knows their identity and role in a given situation with consciously agreed values and rules, then harmony and efficiency may prevail. Group sex?

KEEP FOCUSED ON ... channelling sexual energy or anger in a disciplined or socially acceptable way ... the physical side of your relationship as being a means to feeling closer and more together ... fulfilling traditional (gender) roles, if trying to be more 'liberated' is causing chaos and friction.

WATCH OUT FOR ... being solely performance orientated with regard to sex. This may initially impress or satisfy, but will eventually become a meaningless and sweaty chore ... there being no spark; a sign of being *too* conventional.

KARMA/ATTITUDE/HEALTH

With regard to health matters, this Symbol is urging you to be physically active, perhaps literally in a team or communal sport where competition or mutual encouragement is an element. Karmically, this Symbol could be alluding to the prospect or advisability of being with others who are readily recognized as belonging to what you stand or fight for, and that there is no sexual discrimination, but at the same time a certain emphasis on sexuality.

KEEP FOCUSED ON ... being among like-minded people in an active rather than purely intellectual way ... how males and females are the basic elements of the 'team' called Humanity, and that we need to strive to work and play together in a healthy and matter-of-fact fashion.

WATCH OUT FOR ... getting stuck in roles that are too closely defined or that set one faction off against the other.

'Healthy body, healthy mind – healthy mind, healthy body!'

A GIRL SURREPTITIOUSLY BATHING IN THE NUDE

☆ **SELF-CONSCIOUS REVELATION** ☆

GENERAL INTERPRETATION

A communion with Nature, or a similar activity, that is marred by an anxiety that such an act will not be understood or respected by those who are not sympathetic to it. This anxiety potently comments on the perennially narrow or lascivious attitude towards the naturalness of the human body – especially the female one.

KEEP FOCUSED ON ... being true to your natural inclinations, despite feelings of vulnerability ... encouraging others to be more open by setting an example.

WATCH OUT FOR ... a coyness that can be a liability, as it smacks of a lack of sureness of one's own purity of intent.

LOVE/RELATING/SOCIAL

This Symbol perfectly represents the dilemma of wanting to immerse oneself in an emotional relationship but at the same time being fearful of feeling vulnerable and exposed. It also says that one feels the fear and does it anyway – so natural and irresistible is the urge.

KEEP FOCUSED ON ... the exquisite pleasure and ultimate increase in confidence that goes with taking the plunge into any relationship or social occasion ... what it is you fear to reveal, such as emotional vulnerability, as this is what you are trying to overcome through such a relationship, and why you are prepared to risk it.

WATCH OUT FOR ... exposing yourself to anyone who isn't prepared to expose themselves too. Test the water a bit first ... chancing it when there really is something that you are not ready to reveal ... tempting Fate.

MONEY/WORK/CREATIVITY

Your effectiveness and success depends on your overcoming self-consciousness by doing the very thing that makes you feel self-conscious – such as doing your own thing, putting pen to paper, pushing yourself forward or asking for a raise.

KEEP FOCUSED ON ... what it is you wish to attain, while trusting that the best way of finding out the worth of something, or if it will work, is by putting it through its paces.

WATCH OUT FOR ... the self-fulfilling prophecy of saying 'I won't try for I know I won't make it/get it/hack it'.

KARMA/ATTITUDE/HEALTH

Eventually we have to contact and express our inner selves – to speak our truth. This is done awkwardly and self-consciously at first, but with every unveiling we become more used to our 'nakedness' until we actually feel empowered by it and able to express ourselves fluently.

KEEP FOCUSED ON ... identifying and eliminating the inhibitions that imprison you by surrendering to the truth that there is nothing to hide other than what some 'snake' led you to believe you had to hide. After all, it was precisely when Adam and Eve felt shameful of their nakedness that they were cast out of Paradise.

WATCH OUT FOR ... embarrassment, for the word means to feel barred or blocked by something – this must be overcome before it overcomes you.

'Feel the fear and do it anyway'

THE UNION JACK

☆ THE POWER OF ALLIANCE ☆

 GENERAL INTERPRETATION

Here is a power, influence and protection available to individuals that is way beyond what they could muster purely by their own efforts, as long as the principles of an over-riding whole or organization are conformed to. However, it should be borne in mind that a flag is merely representative of something – whether it is lived up to or not is another question.

KEEP FOCUSED ON ... a sense of benevolent and efficient order, and an ability to leave your own particular stamp on things ... accepting the order of things as they are if you cannot change it.

WATCH OUT FOR ... a domineering and patriarchal conceit that either lasts a short time in the face of a rapidly changing world, or attracts more trouble than it is worth.

 LOVE/RELATING/SOCIAL

What we have here is a relationship or social set-up that has given itself the challenge of maintaining equality of status, but in fact this requires one party to see that this ideal is adhered to. At best, this can be a happy union where everyone feels they have a part to play and a benefit to draw, but it can just be an uneasy alliance that stumbles on through thick and thin. So ...

KEEP FOCUSED ON ... letting others do things in their own way, and be graciously available when they realize that their way does not work ... establishing a fair system where it is possible to live with each other's differences ... bringing about reconciliation whenever necessary.

WATCH OUT FOR ... being taken advantage of or not respected ... putting up with the situation merely for the sake of maintaining the status quo.

 MONEY/WORK/CREATIVITY

This very Capricornian Symbol stresses the significance of organizing various parts into a whole, and most importantly that there must be a central governing body or theme, even though a certain amount of autonomy is granted to those parts. This last point is vital to the smooth running of the whole. Then everyone profits.

KEEP FOCUSED ON ... how various parts, ideas or people fit together to form something long-lasting ... upholding the principle of 'symbiotic integrity', where each part of an organization knows its unique role and nature, as well as its dependency on the other parts for presenting a powerful and united front to other organizations or market forces.

WATCH OUT FOR ... empire-building if there is trouble 'at home', for if any one part is not strong enough it could cause the rest to collapse.

 KARMA/ATTITUDE/HEALTH

In order to create and maintain integrity – be it spiritual or physical well-being – a diagram, image or mandala of such a system is required that can be referred to, prayed to, paid homage to, pledged obedience to or meditated upon. In this way it can be seen how the parts fit into the greater whole.

KEEP FOCUSED ON ... how certain elements belong together, often for obvious or natural reasons. For example, the mainland countries of England, Scotland and Wales are relatively at peace, whereas Northern Ireland across the sea, and part of another land mass, continues to be a trouble spot ... a power that is greater than your ego.

WATCH OUT FOR ... forcing together those who do not want to be together, or who want their independence ... the 'karma of imperialism' where you have to give back to those you originally took from.

'If you can't beat 'em, join 'em'

A CHILD OF ABOUT FIVE WITH A HUGE BAG OF SHOPPING

☆ BOUNTY OR BURDEN? ☆

 GENERAL INTERPRETATION

Having to bear responsibilities that are greater than age or experience would supposedly allow. Alternatively, one could be in line for a reward – probably well-earned. It should be clear, sooner or later, which is the case. Either way, this is a typically Capricornian situation of seeing a responsibility as an opportunity or a worthwhile purpose.

KEEP FOCUSED ON ... attaining or maintaining an ability to rise to the demands that material circumstances thrust upon you ... being open to receive abundance, especially if you know you have worked to deserve it.

WATCH OUT FOR ... taking on more than is possible to manage, perhaps at the expense of emotional issues, or in order to evade them ... being lumbered; not claiming your due.

 LOVE/RELATING/SOCIAL

Either you or the other person, or both of you, are experiencing the relationship as a burden of responsibility that feels more than you can carry. But as the Symbol suggests, this burden in itself contains or promises sustenance and reward.

KEEP FOCUSED ON ... the fact that you are getting stronger and better able to relate as time goes by, with each test ... trying not to allow the 'burden' outweigh the 'bounty'.

WATCH OUT FOR ... putting onto others, especially children, responsibilities that they are not equipped to bear ... letting an immature part of you take on a relationship or agreement which your better judgement knows would stretch you more than is acceptable.

 MONEY/WORK/CREATIVITY

You may be in a position that you do not feel quite up to – although the rewards are great. You could already have obtained the basic materials or ideas; you now have to sort them and set them out in the manner that is most or easy to deal with.

KEEP FOCUSED ON ... rising to the demands made on you, seeking help from those more experienced than yourself if need be ... methodically processing, organizing and itemizing the tasks you have to carry out ... the fact that you have supplies to keep you going, just so long as you keep working at things.

WATCH OUT FOR ... biting off more than you can chew ... passing the buck or a burden on to someone who is not equipped for it ... allowing the material side of life to weigh you down so much that it defeats the whole purpose of your endeavour.

KARMA/ATTITUDE/HEALTH

Looking back you can probably find a time in your past when you had to bear something that strained you, a 'strain' that you feel to this day. Perhaps some karmic debt or responsibility was thrown at you then, forcing you to grow up faster than most in some area of your life. Then again, something from the past may have been thrust upon you *now* to carry and sort out.

KEEP FOCUSED ON ... what you stand to gain from such an experience ... how problems can be solved and your health made stronger by grasping the nettle and taking on your adult responsibilities.

WATCH OUT FOR ... still seeing yourself as the child carrying around a great weight. You are now an adult with considerably more strength and awareness, which you must use without complaining – too much ... overemphasizing the material side of life for this could become a burden in itself.

'Nothing happens to anybody which he is not fitted by nature to bear'

A HIDDEN CHOIR SINGING

☆ NOUMENON ☆

 GENERAL INTERPRETATION

A phenomenon is something that can be perceived by the physical senses. A noumenon is something that you cannot quite put you finger on but know to be there because of what you intuitively sense or have inferred as being present by dint of experience. As a Symbol of Capricorn it is interesting because it points to the 'hidden' and 'mystical' side of this Sign. This is seen in the original image of Capricorn as being a Sea-Goat: half earthy climber (goat), and half watery, otherworldly or unconscious (fish).

KEEP FOCUSED ON ... being so well-attuned to your inner vision of what must or could be made real, that you enlist others to aid you and who become an integral part of its realization.

WATCH OUT FOR ... a vague sense of something special that is used to attract others, but that never quite amounts to anything.

 MONEY/WORK/CREATIVITY

This Symbol speaks of an imagination or vision that is both ordered and inspired. It is also in harmony with itself, but, more often than not, it is given the lie by external values and appearances. Whatever your concern, it has not yet found form or appreciation in the outer world of convention and commerce. You could say that it is the Spirit calling from the future to the present, or from the inside to the outside, in order that one day it may be heard or seen in all its glory.

KEEP FOCUSED ON ... giving expression to any sense you have of a new idea or vision. Initially, only share it and substantiate it with people who you know will be in sympathy with it.

WATCH OUT FOR ... expecting something so close to your heart to find immediate widespread approval, and being disappointed.

 LOVE/RELATING/SOCIAL

There is something subtle and decidedly spiritual about this relationship, other person or social set-up. There is certainly a beautiful and transporting harmony here – or at least the sense or potential of such. 'I hear music and there's no one there,/I smell blossom but the trees are bare ...'

KEEP FOCUSED ON ... living up to the sacredness or promise of whatever you feel is the essence of your relationship or desire for a relationship ... discovering what is calling to you from your hidden depths, for this is the key to the union and satisfaction you yearn for.

WATCH OUT FOR ... imagining there are finer feelings present or some special hidden bond, when there is nothing to bear this out ... one-sided or fantasized relationships ... elusive or escapist individuals.

 KARMA/ATTITUDE/HEALTH

There are memories or notions, perhaps from previous lifetimes that are like a vague but subtly influential backdrop to one's life now. These can be inspiring or haunting, and possibly of a religious nature. The 'choir' could be seen as the chakra system that, when in harmony, vitalizes and energizes the whole of the physical body.

KEEP FOCUSED ON ... your inner voice by tuning in to it, being led by it or being informed by it ... what bearing this 'choir' or inner voice has upon your current situation ... giving expression to the astral 'radio station' you have tuned into. At first it may be weak, but the more attuned you get to it, the stronger its signal will become.

WATCH OUT FOR ... ignoring internal promptings that could be useful to you ... anything that prompts you to do or say something you do not approve of yourself.

'We are all from a grander place'

A RELAY RACE

☆ TEAMWORK ☆

⚙ GENERAL INTERPRETATION

Presented or called for here is a process whereby something is achieved as a result of group effort and organization, with a sense of positive interaction and a common goal being of the essence.

KEEP FOCUSED ON ... bringing together a number of different types of people to work or play as an efficient whole ... the probability that your issue has to go through definite stages to get where it's going ... anyone who might be 'on your team', and go about helping one another.

WATCH OUT FOR ... buck-passing and being too independent, wanting to be the 'star'; or, paradoxically, lacking self-reliance ... being too much of a loner; this would be a sad misperception of your place in Humanity.

♥ LOVE/RELATING/SOCIAL

Here is pictured a healthy relationship because it functions as a team – or it ought to. It may also see itself as a part of and contributing to that greater team called society itself, making it even more healthy and stable. The people involved recognize that they complement each other, that there is no winner or leader overall – only areas in which one naturally fares better.

KEEP FOCUSED ON ... matters of the heart where feelings and loving are to the fore, while others attend to matters of the head where practicality and objectivity are called for. Head learns from heart, and heart from head, so the relationship goes from strength to strength.

WATCH OUT FOR ... seeing relating as competitive; these two things are at opposite poles.

MONEY/WORK/CREATIVITY

You are not alone in your efforts or situation. Definitely a case of strength in numbers. This could mean that you are a part of an organization that is as strong as those parts, or that you are a member of a team that may not have actually met, but which is dedicated to achieving the same goal.

KEEP FOCUSED ON ... how you and those you are teamed up with are doing their particular tasks ... that you are involved in a process through time: this could be seen as a production line or that your work is preparing the way for someone who comes after you, for instance, one artist inspiring another ... passing the sceptre of responsibility when you feel you have done all you can.

WATCH OUT FOR ... being a maverick when the situation is patently calling for group effort ... trying to do everything yourself; collapse that way lies ... hanging on when you are past it.

☯ KARMA/ATTITUDE/HEALTH

In terms of Karma this refers to how individual lifetimes can be seen as individual members of a team of lives that is running the soul's course through eternity. Viewed in this way, we can appreciate that we do not have to get it all done or all right in one go. The baton, or how well you have run, gets handed over as your karma to the next in line, which is, of course, you too, but at a more advanced stage. Health-wise, one is possibly involved in a healing process. This goes through stages such as symptom–diagnosis–treatment–prognosis–review, until one is eventually made well.

KEEP FOCUSED ON ... each lifetime or healing stage and what it means, seeing it through thoroughly, with discernment and to the best of your ability ... there being a medical team or healing group on the case.

WATCH OUT FOR ... trying to jump stages or cram more in than is possible.

'Humanity, if only it knew it, is the many striving for the one goal: Humanity'

A GENERAL ACCEPTING DEFEAT GRACEFULLY

☆ THE POWER OF SURRENDER ☆

⚙ GENERAL INTERPRETATION

How through seeing and admitting where one goes wrong, one can correct oneself and improve one's life.

KEEP FOCUSED ON ... being prepared to see matters in the light of truth rather than frustrated desire, then you will find yourself in a superior position, and being an example to others of how to attain the same ... how surrendering totally to one's fate actually protects one. (Using the Nichiren Shoshu Buddhist chant *nam-myoho-renge-kyo* is recommended here) ... accepting that there is a force greater than you.

WATCH OUT FOR ... wearing oneself out with mistaken resistance ... giving in to something which appears to have greater strength but is simply playing on one's fear or sense of inferiority.

♡ LOVE/RELATING/SOCIAL

The often unappreciated method of resolving conflict through admitting one's fault or failure – with grace. The more genuine and heartfelt such an admission is, the more profound the effect on all concerned. It could also mean the necessity of handing over the reins to one's partner or someone else, in the knowledge that this is the most practical and conflict-free course.

KEEP FOCUSED ON ... the truth of the matter. This means conceding to another and apologizing for any bad behaviour of your own. Both help to create peace.

WATCH OUT FOR ... having your better nature or a weakness of character taken advantage of. In the first case, you must challenge such behaviour; in the second case, toughen up.

MONEY/WORK/CREATIVITY

Not wasting time or resources through trying to make a success of something that is evidently not achieving its objective. On a creative level, this Symbol could mean that in order to be inspired you must put aside your closely proscribed intentions and ambitions. As they say, 'murder your little darlings' – your pet ideas. Instead, you should ...

KEEP FOCUSED ON ... allowing ideas to come through as a 'stream of consciousness', not checking that everything fits in with what you think is a good plan ... salvaging whatever you can from the wreckage, but not at the risk of incurring further damage.

WATCH OUT FOR ... mistaking 'surrender' for giving in to your own weaknesses ... not putting up some kind of fight first of all.

☯ KARMA/ATTITUDE/HEALTH

The ego's ultimate recognition that it is not really in charge and that something else is that is infinitely more powerful and aware. If you are in pain, then succumbing to it will diminish or even vanquish it. Furthermore, recognizing that wrongdoing, in yourself and others, creates, hardens or increases when fought against blow for blow.

KEEP FOCUSED ON ... something abstract or divine, such as a God or a Higher Power, to whom you may hand over your need for control, leaving that to *It* ... giving substance to the belief that through granting another power, as distinct from giving yours away, they then no longer have reason to create conflict or cause damage.

WATCH OUT FOR ... just pretending to surrender, or doing so but harbouring secret reservations, for this will instil deep distrust and perpetuate whatever strife it is you are trying so hard to avoid.

'Resist ye not evil: but whosoever shall smite thee on thy right cheek, turn to him the other also'

TWO AWARDS FOR BRAVERY IN WAR

☆ OVERCOMING THE ODDS ☆

☀ GENERAL INTERPRETATION

Something you are doing or have been doing will be regarded as an act of courage. This is effective for achieving an objective, and maintaining self-control or a certain standard against the odds. They will also be recognized by the ruling authority in your field of endeavour.

KEEP FOCUSED ON ... the respect and impact that you have from and on others because you stick to your guns in situations that would cause most people to take the easy way out.

WATCH OUT FOR ... fortitude not being recognized ... a questionable self-righteousness born of a need to be far more aware of what you are actually fighting for.

♥ LOVE/RELATING/SOCIAL

Not only enduring emotional conflicts, but winning through to a form of emotional or spiritual realization. Many cave in or look for an easy way out when the going gets tough in the relationship stakes. In these days of quick divorces, being in a minority is in itself an act of bravery. Indeed, 'bravery' in this context is simply staying the course in the face of acute emotional pain and mental confusion. If you do not appreciate that all this is worthwhile or necessary, then you soon will.

KEEP FOCUSED ON ... the truth that 'faint heart never won fair lady [or man]' ... the fact that true moral rectitude or emotional stamina is often only recognized in private, without fanfare.

WATCH OUT FOR ... overlooking such 'emotional bravery' in others.

♆ MONEY/WORK/CREATIVITY

Your efforts are being or are about to be rewarded or recognized – if not, they certainly ought to be. You are not the sort to take a back seat or who fails to fight to the last breath for what you believe in.

KEEP FOCUSED ON ... recognizing and rewarding yourself until the world, or those in authority, do so too. The doubling of the image (Two Awards) stresses the importance of being aware of your own faith, drive and ambition ... holding out until relief arrives or success is achieved.

WATCH OUT FOR ... being too gung-ho with respect to gaining your objective, for you might find that there are casualties other than those you incur that sour any victory ... craving spurious awards that are merely the product and invention of a society whose values are suspect.

☯ KARMA/ATTITUDE/HEALTH

This could simply be a karmic reward or release thanks to the grit taken to continue with your quest in the face of adversity – especially when that adversity finds you fighting your patch all alone and sometimes wondering why. With regard to your health, you are most probably made of quite stern stuff.

KEEP FOCUSED ON ... the fact that you are or have been fighting for something, and that this something is not the obvious or external kind of enemy. It may be an illness or an enemy within, such as doubt or fear, or you are fighting for a spiritual cause that has no conventional form of approval or recognition, but is viewed in the eyes of God, an inner 'judge' or anything that is deemed to have a genuine sense of what is right and true.

WATCH OUT FOR ... 'battle scars' or ailments resulting from past stresses and conflicts.

'Fortis fortuna adiuvat' (Fortune assists the brave)

A WOMAN ENTERING A CONVENT

☆ RETREAT OR ESCAPE? ☆

 GENERAL INTERPRETATION

Posed here is need to immerse oneself in a situation that focuses one's senses upon a meaningful reason for being, be it in a religious, artistic, scientific or another specific field of endeavour. This Symbol can sometimes mean that you have been trying too hard to get the answer you want (from the Oracle?) and that it is now best that you withdraw from it for a while.

KEEP FOCUSED ON ... your sense of fate or destiny that guides you and which ignores everything but your inner calling ... taking time out somewhere quiet or sacred for long enough for matters to return to normal, or to get the 'call'.

WATCH OUT FOR ... an ostensibly worthy course of action (or non-action) that is really an escape from facing life ... hiding away (your) femininity or sensitivity because of a mistaken sense of shame.

 LOVE/RELATING/SOCIAL

You or another may be in need of getting away from the emotional pressures of a relationship. You or they could be there already, which could be posing a problem, such as not finding it easy to relate in the ordinary way. There may also be a need to make contact with a spiritual dimension to your love or social life, requiring you to look at the deeper motivations and reasons where relationships are concerned.

KEEP FOCUSED ON ... retreating from the 'slings and arrows' of emotional or social interaction – but only long enough to gain a new perspective and heal any wounds.

WATCH OUT FOR ... avoiding social or emotional interaction to the point that you become ill at ease in these areas.

 MONEY/WORK/CREATIVITY

If your question is concerned primarily with the material sphere of life, then the Oracle is asking you to consider whether you should withdraw completely from whatever you are considering, or to resist retreating into obscurity for fear of failure or because you feel you cannot hack it. The material world is hard because it has no time for those who are half in and half out of it. So ...

KEEP FOCUSED ON ... giving your fullest commitment, energy and involvement to whatever you are concerned about, or take a back seat, possibly with a view to withdrawing completely.

WATCH OUT FOR ... being neither materially nor spiritually minded, unless the business concerned is expressly to do with some kind of creative dedication or spiritual devotion. But be careful that this is not just an ill-conceived escape from reality.

 KARMA/ATTITUDE/HEALTH

It is worth considering that historically the lives that most commonly have a drama to them are those of soldier, prostitute, slave, nun and monk. This Symbol is obviously referring to the last pair of these and how such a reclusive period is now affecting how you live now. It could also be saying that it is a good time to go to some kind of spiritual retreat. With regard to these ...

KEEP FOCUSED ON ... how being out of circulation for some time affects one ... what caused or is causing you to retreat or escape from the world. If it is purely for the positive purpose of getting closer to God or your inner being, then well and good, but if it is merely to escape what you cannot handle, then ...

WATCH OUT FOR ... fearful feelings about life, when you haven't actually tried to identify what your fears are.

*'Many people believe that they are attracted by God or by Nature,
when they are only repelled by man'*

AN ORIENTAL RUG DEALER

☆ THE IMPORTANCE OF PITCH ☆

⚙ GENERAL INTERPRETATION

The purveying, conveying or perpetuation of values and skills that are a result of all commercial interactions since the dawn of civilization. Apart from the basic value of something, an emphasis is placed here on there being no fixed price to anything; rather it is determined by the time, place and individuals involved. What you get for what you've got.

KEEP FOCUSED ON ... your effective employment of the facilities and goods of a modern society ... really believing in what you have to offer; without this you would not make the necessary first impression, and would be vulnerable to being undervalued.

WATCH OUT FOR ... using the system to disguise one's own moral shortcomings ... repelling interest from others as a result of overselling yourself, or being overbearingly egocentric.

♥ LOVE/RELATING/SOCIAL

Love, truly described, should not really be regarded as a 'deal' whereby one person only gives the 'love' that they feel is worth their while. However, viewed pragmatically (this is a Capricornian Symbol!), certain agreements concerning give and take, and the sharing of responsibilities have to be thrashed out in most relationships – witness the introduction of 'prenuptial agreements'. When it comes to courting, presenting one's best qualities and interacting in a flexible way is important.

KEEP FOCUSED ON ... love as being negotiable only when considering what is strictly practical, rather than emotional or spiritual. What someone is giving may not be obvious.

WATCH OUT FOR ... pricing oneself out of the running, be it too low or too high.

⚚ MONEY/WORK/CREATIVITY

Quite straightforwardly, this Symbol points to the importance of a philosophy or technique of salesmanship with regard to your situation or product. First and foremost, you have to ...

KEEP FOCUSED ON ... the fact that what you have is valuable, and, if necessary, psych yourself into really believing it. Then set about identifying exactly what comprises the necessity, desirability or essential quality of your idea, product or services. You are then able to present it in a manner that is appropriate, impressive and irresistible ... pitching yourself or your product's worth high, but not too high, and then adjust it downwards if necessary.

WATCH OUT FOR ... any doubts you might have and set about eliminating them, for they will effectively queer your pitch ... cheap or gimmicky sales techniques.

☯ KARMA/ATTITUDE/HEALTH

Oriental rugs originally had a religious or spiritual significance, yet they still cost a lot to make in terms of time, materials and expertise. So this Symbol is saying that not only do you get out what you put in, but that the amount of faith or confidence you feel regarding the object of your concern has a great deal to do with what you feel your contribution to be worth.

KEEP FOCUSED ON ... what you feel, deep down, that you have to offer, for this will inform you of what you can expect ... valuing yourself much higher and then adjusting down to a level that others can appreciate, understand or tolerate.

WATCH OUT FOR ... losing sight of the inner meaning of your life and then finding yourself feeling empty or passed by ... complaints born of a lack of appreciation of internal values.

'Costs merely register competing attractions'

A WATER SPRITE

 GENERAL INTERPRETATION

A Water Sprite or undine is the personification of the role that water plays in the Earthly scheme of things. This is something that is essential to life but because it is so elementary, it is also something whose significance can be overlooked. The object of your concern, therefore, has both obvious and not so obvious qualities about it. There is also a beguiling and subtle influence in play. It should also be remembered here that Capricorn is half-goat and half-fish, half earthy climber and half watery mystic.

KEEP FOCUSED ON ... the aspect of your nature that can enchant people and thereby direct them toward higher and better things.

WATCH OUT FOR ... ignoring, suppressing or being unaware of the emotional, metaphysical or subtle aspects of life, people or yourself.

 MONEY/WORK/CREATIVITY

The answer to your question is found by continuing with the process that you already find yourself involved in. Then again, your career could or should be concerned with putting people in touch with the hidden, emotional or mystical side of life – restoring the flow. Inscrutability – or a need for it.

KEEP FOCUSED ON ... the part played by the unconscious elements or emotional undercurrents of your situation or project; a great deal depends on being in tune with these factors. This is like keeping one's ear to the ground as you 'feel in your water' which way things are going.

WATCH OUT FOR ... attempting to define the course of events too closely; this would be like trying to determine the route a raindrop is going to take down a windowpane ... ideas or enterprises that are just scotch mist, a figment of one's imagination.

 LOVE/RELATING/SOCIAL

A person or relationship that embodies emotional mystery and whatever this might prompt the imagination to conjure up, be it fascinating or misleading, elating or frightening.

KEEP FOCUSED ON ... whether you are dealing with the enigmatic, the emotionally enlightening, the capricious or the downright contrary – or any combination of these ... being true to your own feelings, and not being fazed by those of others.

WATCH OUT FOR ... an emotional ineptitude that is irresponsible and confusing ... being led a dance by someone who is merely trying to find their own level ... emotional dysfunction in another that reflects your own ... projecting your idealistic fantasies on to someone, for they will vanish into the mist ... sidestepping the deeper reality of the situation.

KARMA/ATTITUDE/HEALTH

This Symbol is reminiscent of the Process of Universal Water (Mayan cosmology) which may be seen in the nature of a raindrop. It falls from the clouds, lands and trickles as it follows the line of least resistance, collects as larger bodies of water, evaporates to form clouds, and then the process begins again. So, this is the Principle of Flow and your situation or health depends on your letting go into the mystery of the unknown and allowing what must join to be joined, what must separate to be separated.

KEEP FOCUSED ON ... the state of your feelings, both emotional and physical. Where they are flowing, go with them. Where they are stuck or blocked, release them ... the nature of water for the answer to your question.

WATCH OUT FOR ... forgetting what you are – possibly reflected in body parts malfunctioning because they have also forgotten.

'As vapour from the sea rises up into the sky, and falls as rain, or sleet or snow, so too shall we go'

A MOUNTAIN PILGRIMAGE

☆ THE PATH IS THE GOAL ☆

⚙ GENERAL INTERPRETATION

The classic human journey of striving toward a spiritual goal, a meaningful destination. On a more mundane level, you are currently having to strive towards a desired target, but which in the process quickens in you a fusing of heart and mind, of body and soul – the very process which gets you there, and qualifies you to be there.

KEEP FOCUSED ON ... the galvanizing and blending of your heart and mind, body and soul, for it enables you to accomplish tasks which others would regard worthy of reverence – or scorn ... finding out as you go, for there is really no other way; follow the path as it unwinds.

WATCH OUT FOR ... lofty pretensions that alienate rather than inspire; neglecting those responsibilities that are of the everyday emotional kind.

♥ LOVE/RELATING/SOCIAL

Any serious relationship has its hardships and ups and downs. This is because a relationship is a journey of discovery, where the 'terrain' is strewn with emotional blocks and pitfalls that have to be negotiated. Alternatively, you may be considering such a journey on your own, outside of a relationship.

KEEP FOCUSED ON ... what it is that the relationship is teaching or showing you, and keep this 'on top' as the substance of the relationship, rather than as something more selfish ... the possibility that your partner is the rock or 'base camp' of your 'climb' and, if so, recognize and cherish them as such.

WATCH OUT FOR ... giving up because it seems to be too hard a climb and you cannot see the summit. It's worth it, and you *can* get there.

🏆 MONEY/WORK/CREATIVITY

Hard work but a worthwhile goal. Unless you have an experienced guide, then you will be learning as you go, going up several blind alleys, having a few falls.

KEEP FOCUSED ON ... each step of progress as being an achievement all its own and an essential part of getting where you want to get to ... using, where possible and appropriate, the paths that have already been laid down by those who have gone before you, using their experience and expertise. This will save time, money and energy.

WATCH OUT FOR ... those 'false peaks' where you think the goal is in sight, only to reach it and see that it is another 'peak', and then another. You'll need to inure yourself to these vagaries of ambitious ventures.

☯ KARMA/ATTITUDE/HEALTH

You are on a spiritual path, the path of discipleship and initiation. Perhaps you should take time out and get away from a world that is too much with you, going naked (literally or figuratively) into the wilderness.

KEEP FOCUSED ON ... your holy path, amid the desolation, coldness, hardness and distractions. Keep yourself *above* the petty values and differences, for they are beneath you ... carrying through to a satisfactory conclusion whatever task you have embarked on, experiencing each step as a lesson and reward in itself ... getting close to what really matters through shedding all that is superficial.

WATCH OUT FOR ... pretending to be above the mundane concerns of day-to-day life and interactions, when you are not.

'I'll pack my grip for a farewell trip/Kiss Susan-Jane goodbye at the fountain
I'm going, says I, to the Land of the Sky,/Away out on the mountain'

A LARGE AVIARY

☆ SOCIETY AND THE SYSTEM ☆

✺ GENERAL INTERPRETATION

Imaged here are the myriad facets of daily life and the individuals involved that need to be contained and organized in order to create an overall and concerted effect. An incidence of pecking order, and the need to acknowledge it.

KEEP FOCUSED ON ... your ability to define limits that allow individuals to flourish and thereby further the common welfare ... the idea that life and society are simply an extension of your own nature, with its likes and dislikes, trust and fear, order and chaos.

WATCH OUT FOR ... a bureaucratic or bird-brained attitude that reduces life to a meaningless set of categories and functions ... being confined by your fears of the outer world – or your inner world, for that matter.

♡ LOVE/RELATING/SOCIAL

To create and maintain a healthy relationship – be it between two or many people – the myriad facets, feelings, longings and sensitivities of each person have to be identified and given a place in that relationship, otherwise chaos, dissolution, fragmentation and dissonance will result.

KEEP FOCUSED ON ... the promise or opportunity that you have to become a vital part of a relationship or community ... what your role, and the role of others is in that relationship or community.

WATCH OUT FOR ... what might be regarded as a fear of confinement or loss of freedom, as this could well just be reluctance to commit or confront.

MONEY/WORK/CREATIVITY

Job description, satisfaction and profitability all depend on having a community to which to belong or to target as being suitable to your ends. This also implies that you demographically define or choose very carefully such a community or market area; then again, it may choose or have chosen you. A lot of ideas that need to be organized into a whole.

KEEP FOCUSED ON ... meeting the needs of this community and protecting your interests in it ... the Internet, for this would seem to be an obviously favourable area of endeavour or research ... limiting your interests to a known and therefore manageable area.

WATCH OUT FOR ... predators who might wish to poach or sabotage your products or ideas.

☯ KARMA/ATTITUDE/HEALTH

This images both the individual human, and Humanity as a whole. The individual is a collection of different thoughts, feelings and sensations that is contained within the body. Humanity is a number of spirits, or the human spirit itself, confined to the Earth plane. In both cases we are forced to function within that which contains us. Freedom is knowing one's limitations, and appreciating the scope that we have to explore and express potential.

KEEP FOCUSED ON ... discovering for yourself and showing others that the 'way out' is the door that takes you beyond the meaningless daily grind into a greater sense of 'being here' by making full use of what society and life have to offer.

WATCH OUT FOR ... being prey to illusions or fears of freedom ... health issues around not being integrated within yourself or your community.

'Just as the luminaries in the sky serve for the systematic division and arrangement of time, so human society and all things that really belong together must be organically arranged'

A WOMAN READING TEA LEAVES

☆ OF ORACLES AND INTUITION ☆

GENERAL INTERPRETATION

Be aware how intuition can be activated by peering long enough into any randomly produced pattern (like an inkblot), sign (like a coincidence) or image (like a dream) and seeing the meaning and information concealed therein. This Symbol could be referring to using this Oracle or a clairvoyant.

KEEP FOCUSED ON ... peering into the 'cup' – the object of your concern – until you see how things are panning out and developing, while at the same time keeping your mind free and open to suggestion, unbiased by hopes and fears ... the image of the Sabian Symbol itself and work with it until you see the answer it is trying to give you – for it is (*see* Guided Imagery, page 427) ... intuiting how things are shaping up.

WATCH OUT FOR ... being superstitious or too logical – or too literal unless it actually is so.

MONEY/WORK/CREATIVITY

Trying to find out how things are going to turn out on a material level is the most difficult kind of prediction. This is because, unlike matters that are purely personal, money and work depend upon many other people, political, cultural and economic institutions, that is, complex factors with complex and varied outcomes. Be that as it may, using an intuitive sense or future projection, that is unaffected by hopes or fears, can be very useful now, but it should only be employed as *part* of your view or plan – and not too *large* a part of it. However, if the object of your enquiry has to do with prediction of any kind, this could be regarded as a favourable Oracle. In any event ...

KEEP FOCUSED ON ... the hard facts, over and above any hunches, unless there is a sound track record of having accurate ones.

WATCH OUT FOR ... giving yourself over to whimsical premonitions of success or failure.

♥ LOVE/RELATING/SOCIAL

If you are female, believe in and use your intuition, if you are male, then listen to the female – or to your intuition. As far as having any sense of what is in store for one or both of you, simply make known what you see, but only if you are very sure of yourself or very concerned. Also, seeing a part of yourself reflected in your partner's state.

KEEP FOCUSED ON ... the possibility that informing someone what might lie ahead could help them avoid it if it is bad, or to attract it if it is good. Present your intuitive feelings in this way, rather than as a fixed or fated certainty.

WATCH OUT FOR ... being alarmist as a means of seeking attention or getting your own way ... confusing your own fears with what you think might happen; for one's fears have the power to be self-fulfilling, or are completely unfounded.

KARMA/ATTITUDE/HEALTH

The very state that you are currently in tells you all you need to know as long as you trust your own or someone else's intuition, because it is intuition that is now in play – or needs to be. Intuition is 'female' – whether you are male or female by gender – which means that you are listening to your feelings and inner promptings, unaffected by logical agendas or personal preconditions. Trusting your intuition means that you must first ...

KEEP FOCUSED ON ... what is obvious, what is right in you or in front of you, until it eventually 'talks' to you. You know the answer, but you may have to still your heart and mind in order to hear it ... taking one step at a time, which means ...

WATCH OUT FOR ... trying to see too far into the future. It cannot be assumed what 'step two' will be when it is still in the balance as to what 'step one' consists of ... believing patently fanciful or doomy predictions of any kind; take them with a pinch of salt.

'Intuition when it works is really brilliant. When it doesn't it's plain stupid'

A SECRET BUSINESS CONFERENCE

☆ CONFIDENCE AND CONFIDENTIALITY ☆

 GENERAL INTERPRETATION

Suggested here is a project that is planned or set in motion without some of those involved necessarily knowing the motives and aims that lie behind what they are doing; the reasons for that may become clearer as matters progress. Tactical or group decision-making. Taking someone into your confidence, or vice versa.

KEEP FOCUSED ON ... employing your talent for executing whatever task is set before you in a disciplined and committed fashion, even though you may not know why ... keeping matters close to your chest, especially if there are elements abroad that you do not trust ... how outcomes depend on ongoing developments.

WATCH OUT FOR ... making puppets out of people, or allowing yourself to be one ... allowing yourself to get caught up in intrigues and made vulnerable to exploitation.

 MONEY/WORK/CREATIVITY

This could literally be referring to a secret meeting and to the necessity of formulating and discussing plans and ideas in confidence, or to the fact that your work, of necessity, takes place behind the scenes. Then again, it could also be talking about what is a secret from yourself, such as the secret of what you ought to be doing work-wise, or why you have problems with money when you work hard or have a good job. In addition to what is advised in the Karma section below, try to ...

KEEP FOCUSED ON ... whatever interests you have at the deepest level of your being; what you would like to do as distinct from what you think you ought to do. A secret from ourselves is only a secret because we have been looking in the wrong quarter, or because it's not yet time for the 'secret' to be revealed. Keep looking.

WATCH OUT FOR ... deceit posing as secrecy.

 LOVE/RELATING/SOCIAL

Secrecy is essential to intimacy, whereas secretiveness can actually undermine a close bond. The former is a testament to the fact that one person trusts another with their innermost feelings and memories; the latter is when they don't and keep things to themselves, or worse, share a part of themselves in secret with someone else, possibly on a sexual basis. So, this Symbol is either describing an intimate relationship of great trust, or a situation that founders for want of allowing just one other fully into one's confidence. It also poses the issue of 'secret feelings' which need to be shared in order that they may be made known and healthily expressed.

KEEP FOCUSED ON ... gaining another's confidence and building a bond of trust.

WATCH OUT FOR ... withholding feelings you are ashamed of, for this would attract shame.

KARMA/ATTITUDE/HEALTH

On a psychological or spiritual level, this Symbol refers to the Unseen Realm from which issues much of our life and reality. It is as if there is a meeting of minds, the Board of Spiritual Directors, that convenes in the Unconscious and judges and decides what is our due. All we can do is ...

KEEP FOCUSED ON ... this deep level with such means as meditation, dreamwork, prayer, listening to the higher self/God/Higher Power/subconscious or with any other method that allows you to tap into that 'secret conference' ... following the dictates of your conscience/inner voice/better judgement.

WATCH OUT FOR ... insisting on knowing more than you are currently able or allowed to know, for the 'Board' will then not show or tell you anything at all ... 'voices in the head' that tell you things you do not agree with. Shut them out if they do come in the name of Good.

'For secrets are edgéd tools,/And must be kept from children and from fools'

THE SABIAN SYMBOLS OF
AQUARIUS

Either directly, or in a subtle way, all these Symbols are concerned with the following qualities, or with situations that involve or call for them:

ASPIRATIONS

AWAKENING

CHANGE

DETACHMENT

EVOLUTION

EXPERIMENTATION

THE FUTURE

HUMANITY

INNOVATION

LIBERTY AND LIBERATION

MIND POWER

NEW AGE

ORIGINALITY

PARADOX

PRINCIPLES

PROCESS

RIGHTS

SCIENCE AND TECHNOLOGY

UNUSUALNESS

AN OLD ADOBE MISSION

☆ THE PERSISTENCE OF FAITH ☆

 GENERAL INTERPRETATION

The persistence of faith, no matter how simple or far-flung from its origins, in the spiritual side of life and Humanity, and in a constant striving towards higher aims. And so your issue has to do with the state of your faith, and how true you are to it – especially when on a limb.

KEEP FOCUSED ON ... something that is good and old and true about you that cannot but help assist others (and yourself) in the search for lasting faith and peace, as well as with practical matters ... seeing yourself as an outpost of your own beliefs and values ... upholding worthy values and standards in situations that are particularly lacking in them.

WATCH OUT FOR ... sticking to beliefs and traditions without any attempt to reform them or express them in an original way ... helping where help is not needed or asked for.

MONEY/WORK/CREATIVITY

Your work involves, or should involve, an outreach towards a better understanding among your public, customers and co-workers. There is an idealism here that is bound to attract acute difficulties when the values of others clash with yours. But faith in what you are doing should outweigh such difficulties, making it all the more worthwhile.

KEEP FOCUSED ON ... promoting and upholding whatever you believe to have importance and lasting value.

WATCH OUT FOR ... placing yourself in a no-go or inappropriate market area, unless you have another goal in mind, such as testing the water, or seeing how your convictions hold up in the face of the world.

LOVE/RELATING/SOCIAL

Sometimes it is essential to hold out and believe in a relationship (or the prospect of one) or in another person, even though the circumstances are not encouraging. Love is tested by proving itself through time and hardship.

KEEP FOCUSED ON ... the fact that eventually you will get what you want – as long as you genuinely believe you will ... carrying the torch – but don't get burnt! ... how it is the exposing and accepting of one another's dubious and unattractive parts that truly creates a lasting bond.

WATCH OUT FOR ... fantasies concerning the object of your desire that have nothing to do with the actual facts – friends might be telling you this.

KARMA/ATTITUDE/HEALTH

Adobe is mud or dung mixed with straw. This Symbolizes the fact that faith and health often are built and depend on recycling and dealing with one's 'shit' or whatever you get stuck in. Faith and good health will persist providing one does not get entrenched in the bog of dogma or the constipation of old emotional attachments or habits. So ...

KEEP FOCUSED ON ... doing whatever is necessary to keep your faith alive, fresh and relevant to the moment while at the same time maintaining old and eternal values that have stood the test of time ... identifying, admitting, processing and eliminating longstanding emotional issues from your past.

WATCH OUT FOR ... hanging on to a belief, memory or experience that is preventing you from moving on ... finding yourself so out of touch as to become devitalized and unwell.

'A faint heart never won a fair lady ... or a good man, or anything else worth a damn'

AN UNEXPECTED THUNDERSTORM

☆ SUDDEN AWAKENING ☆

✹ GENERAL INTERPRETATION

You are encountering the fact that life always has something in store for us that we have not quite prepared for, and that it is the natural tendency of things to come to a head or crisis. Experiencing and dealing with the unexpected. A sudden upheaval and release of tension, with all the alarm and inconvenience that this might involve. But, ultimately, peace and calm will reign again.

KEEP FOCUSED ON … an internal self-quickening that keeps you on your psychological toes, ever ready to meet chance events creatively … the relief and advantages that will follow current pressures and demands.

WATCH OUT FOR … an unpredictable nature that others learn to avoid … falling prey to needless or disproportionate anxiety.

♥ LOVE/RELATING/SOCIAL

Here is a person, relationship or social situation that surprises or shocks you. Somebody's stormy temperament may be the issue, and the cause of disturbances. It may be very stimulating or quite alarming – or a mixture of both. Your concern is quite natural in the usual course of events, for every so often there has to be a release of built-up tension to clear the air or force one into an awareness of something that one would otherwise have missed.

KEEP FOCUSED ON … what state or emotion such an event or person has aroused and revealed. Take heed of what it is trying to show you, then you will be wiser and lighter.

WATCH OUT FOR … over-reacting to upsets or over-indulging in thrills. This would either wreak regrettable damage or set a trend that cannot be kept up, leading to anticlimax.

♆ MONEY/WORK/CREATIVITY

'The best laid schemes o' mice an' men/Gang aft a-gley', wrote Robert Burns – whoever you are, your plans and intentions often do not go as intended. The situation therefore calls for a rethink.

KEEP FOCUSED ON … the fact that what might appear to be a setback or disappointment can turn out to be a blessing in disguise, so continue to pursue your original goal and do not lose your nerve … the benefit of being more aware of what your goal entailed than when you first set out in pursuit of it … regathering, realigning and reorganizing as soon as the initial 'shock' has passed and you have found out why it happened.

WATCH OUT FOR … any wishful thinking or glamorous ideas that may have fogged or are fogging your perception of what the pursuit of your course or objective involves.

♅ KARMA/ATTITUDE/HEALTH

Understanding the principle of shock and the unexpected is the issue here. As with clouds gathering and differing pressures interacting, our lives accumulate emotions and conflicting urges that, if not given conscious release or expression, must find another way of doing so. Hence the abrupt explosions or revelations.

KEEP FOCUSED ON … what any shock or unpredicted outcome is trying to tell you – that it is ultimately good. You can do this by asking yourself what it is that you are not consciously expressing or have been concealing.

WATCH OUT FOR … fearing, resisting or trying to avoid the unexpected in life; this smacks of a controlling nature born of a mistrust of Fate. This can give rise to complaints arising from tension and rigidity. Trust yourself to roll with life's punches … dismissing shocks as mere accident and not seeing them as the wake-up calls they are.

'God (the truth) comes forth in the sign of The Arousing'

A DESERTER FROM THE NAVY

☆ BREAKING AWAY FROM THE NORM ☆

✸ GENERAL INTERPRETATION

What we have here is an outright rebellion against the status quo – especially with respect to what is generally regarded as morally acceptable. No matter what others think, one is driven to take the consequences as the price one pays for being true to oneself.

KEEP FOCUSED ON ... your inner sense of what is right that gives you both the courage to fly in the face of convention, and also set an example to others of a personal integrity that has its own conscience as the ultimate law-maker ... being prepared to take what comes with 'living outside the law' or being 'on the run'.

WATCH OUT FOR ... an arrogant refusal to shoulder the responsibilities incurred either by one's own choices or by society's rules, along with the psychological weakness that this engenders.

♥ LOVE/RELATING/SOCIAL

Here is a person, relationship or social situation that chooses, or is forced, to live according to a moral code that is outside of the norm. Alternatively, getting out of an oppressive relationship. In pursuing either course, be aware that you might not have the social or legal support that is generally depended upon.

KEEP FOCUSED ON ... finding sympathy and support for your cause or plight.

WATCH OUT FOR ... whether what you are involved with sits comfortably with you – if it doesn't, you will regret it for a long time ... having no moral code at all; this might appear to avoid difficulties, but it'll catch up with you eventually ... running away from emotional responsibilities.

♟ MONEY/WORK/CREATIVITY

The 'navy' here is any institution such as a corporation or the armed services, or anything which could be considered as part of the system. The situation is one of getting out of such an institution, or the need to do so. Going it alone, being self-employed or casting yourself adrift. Or *being* cast adrift, perhaps through a change of policy or circumstances.

KEEP FOCUSED ON ... the fact that whatever has found you without the usual support, such as salary and insurance, is actually helping to cut you loose from the Rat Race ... putting together your own set of rules, schedules or targets for without them you would most likely end up 'shipwrecked' ... the fact that you are your own 'captain' now.

WATCH OUT FOR ... wasting time and money as a result of 'freedom' going to your head ... a lack of discipline.

♄ KARMA/ATTITUDE/HEALTH

Most people draw their security and their identity by subscribing to the status quo. There comes a time, and this is it, when your own feelings and values can no longer conform to what you now see as restricting and blinding to the 'greater life'. This breaking away can arise from an 'accident of Fate' where conditions have become unbearable (as in *The Mutiny on The Bounty*), or as a conscious choice to follow your own path.

KEEP FOCUSED ON ... the fact that what is calling you to break away is helping to make you more your own person, which means not having the excuses to hide behind what is expected by the majority ... trying complementary health methods.

WATCH OUT FOR ... kidding yourself that you are seeking freedom when really you are avoiding a confrontation with the truth ... oversubscribing to alternative health methods.

'Two roads diverged in a wood, and I – /I took the one less travelled by'

A HINDU HEALER

 ☆ **GETTING BETTER INSIDE AND OUT** ☆

 GENERAL INTERPRETATION

Matters regarding the object of your concern will get better as long as every individual element involved is recognized for the vital part it plays in creating and maintaining the welfare of the whole. This alludes to Ayurvedic medicine or any other method of holistic healing, and to the time and discipline it takes to learn to put it into practice. Knowing how everything interconnects is the precondition to improving matters.

KEEP FOCUSED ON ... developing your flair for seeing the whole and restoring it to a better condition ... detaching yourself from the desire to be 'the healer' or 'getting a result', instead of just being part of the healing process ... being patient.

WATCH OUT FOR ... unsubstantiated claims of special gifts in order to deflect attention away from what is mistakenly regarded as inferior.

MONEY/WORK/CREATIVITY

This Symbol could be confirming your role or potential as a healer and stressing the holistic aspect of looking to every part of an individual's life in order to re-establish health. Your career, workplace or co-workers may be in need of healing in this way, and the Oracle is saying that this would meet with success. Materially speaking, apart from healthy finances reflecting healthy ideas or situations, it could also be saying, 'If you look after the pennies, the pounds will look after themselves.'

KEEP FOCUSED ON ... being guided by spiritual principles and seeing your work as a process of healing rather than being motivated purely by material gain ... using metaphysical means to attain a healthy situation, such as visualizing what is wanted or needed.

WATCH OUT FOR ... seeking fast or superficial results that will only frustrate or disappoint you.

LOVE/RELATING/SOCIAL

This describes a healing relationship, or one in need of healing. In either case, the healing has to go deep. Each person needs to know themselves as an individual, internally and externally, before they can really know another person. One or both people are drawn into this healing process, simply by being together.

KEEP FOCUSED ON ... the necessity for the acceptance of a need for healing, such as coming to terms with past hurts, forgiveness and reconciliation, or recognition of shortcomings in relating and relationships.

WATCH OUT FOR ... the parts that hurt or confuse you or another with respect to this relationship or situation; this is pointing to those parts of you that need seeing to, accepting or changing.

KARMA/ATTITUDE/HEALTH

This is expressly about the healing through, of and by the spirit, so it poses a certain denial of the material world. Essentially, this means that the object of your concern is guaranteed to get better and become whole just so long as everything is seen in a spiritual light. In other words, the spirit is originally and eternally healthy, but getting the body to align with it and its intent is the challenge. Learning this can take lifetimes.

KEEP FOCUSED ON ... the real meaning of life, as this will guide and connect you to the spirit that gave you life and that can heal and revitalize you.

WATCH OUT FOR ... the fact that no one can be healed until they themselves really wish to be healed. This entails the identification and removal of the false and illusory impressions, values and perspectives that dog us all.

'Physician, heal thyself'

A COUNCIL OF ANCESTORS

☆ THE POWER OF PRECEDENT ☆

🌑 GENERAL INTERPRETATION

The infinite spiritual well that the individual seeks integration with and approval from, and can seek and expect guidance from. A tradition whose weight and history provides a body of knowledge, wisdom and security.

KEEP FOCUSED ON ... your self-assuredness that rests on what has been handed down from your wealth of previous experience ... anything in your personal history or those of your antecedents that may have a bearing on the object of your enquiry ... how history tends to repeat itself.

WATCH OUT FOR ... stuffiness that comes from a reliance on something less authentic than one's own inner voice ... being restricted by unquestioned taboos.

♥ LOVE/RELATING/SOCIAL

Relationships or social life have created a pattern. You are attracted to similar people and situations, over and again, until you make a kind of 'tradition' out of what is positive and good, and eliminate any patterns of behaviour or mindsets that attract difficult people or destructive interactions.

KEEP FOCUSED ON ... what is loving and creative, or has about it a good feel or memory, for these could be said to be good 'ancestors', taken together forming a basis for a healthy love, family and social life.

WATCH OUT FOR ... repetitive negative reactions from yourself or weaknesses and flaws in another. These are warning signs that you are caught up in a negative pattern which could form into a group of negative 'ancestors', creating a destructive or misguided relationship.

🏆 MONEY/WORK/CREATIVITY

Your work is part of a tradition or stems from a significant lineage. The Council of Ancestors could be the board of directors, the founders or something more spiritual (which is the essential meaning of this Symbol) such as a healing tradition or a source of creative inspiration. You are placed in a position where you can obey or benefit from such a 'council' – on this plane or another.

KEEP FOCUSED ON ... the historical nature of your work and finances so far, for this will inform you as to what your 'ancestors' do and do not approve of in terms of there being a stable and healthy situation. The words 'custom' and 'customers' come from the same root.

WATCH OUT FOR ... being too hidebound or stuck in outworn methods and styles.

💲 KARMA/ATTITUDE/HEALTH

One's ancestors can be seen as spirits of dead family/clan/tribe members, or as the pageant of the previous existences of your soul. The point is that they have formed into a 'council', which means that there is some kind of organization on the inner planes, the other side or in the Unconscious. This council or gathering of unconscious elements could be there to help or guide you, or to judge or condemn you. It all depends on what you feel you are entitled to at a deep level of your being.

KEEP FOCUSED ON ... in what way you have been helped or hindered with regard to the object of your enquiry. Are you standing on the shoulders of giants, or are they putting pressure on you? Either way, you can be sure you are in intimate touch with them, and them with you.

WATCH OUT FOR ... presuming on such ancestors in any way, for it is they, not you, who hold sway.

'For my heart, the fount of ancestors old/Leaps to its part in the story being told'

A PERFORMER IN A MYSTERY PLAY

☆ **CHANNELLING OR EMBODIMENT** ☆

⚙ GENERAL INTERPRETATION

Suggested here is the enactment of inner realities, be they personal or the truths concerning life on Earth. Even though these secrets may be unknown to us, most of us feel them at some level of our being – be it ever so dimly. One can deliberately tune into such concealed and profound realities with the aid of ancient teachings, trance work or psychodrama.

KEEP FOCUSED ON ... connecting with the true significance of your own existence, and this will give you the ability to portray it in the here and now ... maintain a grip on your own identity or persona ... the saying 'Ours is not to reason why, ours is but to do or die'.

WATCH OUT FOR ... a loss of individual identity amid the fogs and fancies surrounding a so-called mystery ... being 'possessed' by anything or anyone, including your own obsessions.

♡ LOVE/RELATING/SOCIAL

At times relationships can be enchanting, at other times painfully baffling. This Symbol points to the ancient concept that we are the playthings or living expressions of the Gods, and their relationships. Astrology itself is the study and explanation of how the Gods or planets are seen to do this. Base instincts become more refined as we become more conscious of them and how we feel about them.

KEEP FOCUSED ON ... what you are feeling deep within, expressing and acting it out as gracefully and appropriately as possible ... letting the 'mystery' unfold as it will.

WATCH OUT FOR ... making a 'Greek Tragedy' out of what is happening, or thinking that you should have ready answers; it'll only frustrate you.

⚚ MONEY/WORK/CREATIVITY

The world of commerce and art is simply the expression of whatever is currently going on in the Collective Unconscious. This is our 'culture', a word that describes what things *grow* in. Whatever you are currently doing or thinking of doing is an expression of your culture, be it a great or small contribution to it. It may last a day, it may last more than a lifetime – but it still makes that contribution. Financially speaking, you are caught up, like most, in the economic state of the whole – for good or ill.

KEEP FOCUSED ON ... how much your culture would benefit from what you (propose to) do, and base your decisions on that ... using the system rather than trying to beat it.

WATCH OUT FOR ... taking things over unless you are very sure of the power of your position.

☯ KARMA/ATTITUDE/HEALTH

It would be well now to view life as emphasizing processes that go on all the time everywhere – which is why we do not usually notice them! The forces of Creation or Evolution playing themselves out in a more dramatic way than usual, enabling you to tune into what this means to you. Mythologically, this is the Gods expressing themselves through humans; psychologically, it is archetypes manifesting in human affairs and possibly in the state of one's health.

KEEP FOCUSED ON ... letting whatever is happening unfold, play itself out, while attempting to 'play your part' as well as possible. You could say that we are all 'method acting' in that we are all in the process of getting into the parts that we have chosen or been elected to play.

WATCH OUT FOR ... 'overacting', getting carried away, mystifying yourself and others, losing the plot.

'Life is not a problem to be solved but a mystery to be experienced'

A CHILD BORN OF AN EGGSHELL

✵ GOING OUT INTO THE WORLD ✵

⚙ GENERAL INTERPRETATION

Continual self-sustainment as a consequence of the sense that whatever exists always has a history and an origin that stems from, and is embedded in, a caring Universe. Also, when the sustenance from one source is all used up, then one has to go and look for some of one's own from somewhere else.

KEEP FOCUSED ON ... the conviction that whatever you want or do will be given or supported for as long as necessary ... how sheer need can galvanize you ... the fact that it is only by going beyond the known that we discover what we need.

WATCH OUT FOR ... a minimalist existence that depends solely on life's handouts ... sticking to old habits and haunts; this could seriously jeopardize your safety or security in the present, and diminish the development of your potential.

♥ LOVE/RELATING/SOCIAL

This can simply be referring to the birth and sustainment of a child, and the *natural* function of the parents to furnish the child with whatever it may need when it eventually flies the coop. Also, it could be referring to a relationship where you or another has to learn to fend for themselves – it could be both of you. This could be a 'Babes in the Wood' scenario where you must look out for one another above all else.

KEEP FOCUSED ON ... how you can sustain yourself and others when no one else is at hand to do so – be it emotionally, materially, spiritually or mentally.

WATCH OUT FOR ... 'feeding' off another unless you are sure that they are happy to let you, otherwise you may suddenly have to make out on your own.

♆ MONEY/WORK/CREATIVITY

Making full use of whatever resources are at hand. You are preparing yourself for the next stage of development – or you have already done so. Having to set out on your own, or begin a new venture, but without the same supply or support you have hitherto enjoyed.

KEEP FOCUSED ON ... whatever is at hand to keep you going for the present, but also exploring or investing in ways of bringing in more as time goes by ... the belief that you can be self-sustaining.

WATCH OUT FOR ... giving up the ghost if things do not develop as well or as swiftly as you hoped; such despondency would make you (more) vulnerable ... poverty consciousness: the feeling that you are worth less than you actually are, born of the mistaken idea that if this is true you will never 'disappoint' yourself or others.

♇ KARMA/ATTITUDE/HEALTH

You have reached a stage when you or the object of your concern must find its own safe place, with its own supply of whatever is needed. This might necessitate the relinquishing of something that is a 'shell', a sentiment rather than something more substantial or pertinent to your welfare. Such a 'shell' could also be regarded as an empty place, void of nourishment. On a more esoteric level, this Symbol images the idea of a 'new breed' who are feeding themselves, free from the negative 'food' of ideas and opinions which dogged their ancestors.

KEEP FOCUSED ON ... the vulnerability that is innate in us all ... the fact that you are now equipped to venture out into the unknown and fend for yourself – or soon will be.

WATCH OUT FOR ... depending upon something you have grown used to, for it has now gone, or is about to go.

'Cast thy bread upon the waters; for thou shalt find it after many days'

BEAUTIFULLY GOWNED WAX FIGURES

☆ LIFE'S MASQUERADE ☆

GENERAL INTERPRETATION

On the one hand, here is a focus on the form that one has to take in order to function successfully in the world. It can be a hard lesson for the idealist to realize that very few people can get through this life without 'playing the game', being a part of the masquerade. On the other hand, one can become constricted and false as a result of conforming too closely to the rules and perceived expectations of society or whatever your situation happens to be. So ...

KEEP FOCUSED ON ... outfitting yourself in the garb or 'body armour' that the world appreciates and understands – and that protects you from it – yet maintaining the individuality of mind that animates your outer display.

WATCH OUT FOR ... contemporary styles that hide a vacuity of mind, or, conversely, refusing to stoop to conquer.

♥ LOVE/RELATING/SOCIAL

Is the situation one where formal manners and charm will suffice and it pays not to be too animated? There is no point in being deep and genuine with those who do not appreciate it or find it hard to be so themselves – unless you are prepared to reach and teach. Or is the situation one that is hampered by a reluctance to let it all hang out, to show that you are a real live emotional being?

KEEP FOCUSED ON ... making the right noises and expressions in order to get by ... allowing the 'inner you' out, creatively using your personality to get across to others what you really think and feel.

WATCH OUT FOR ... being intimidated or misled by the social, cosmetic or glamorous masks of others ... barging into situations where prevailing social standards outweigh your self-confidence.

MONEY/WORK/CREATIVITY

A case of all style and no content? Or is it a case of an attractive medium or showcase waiting to find something worthy of it? Creatively speaking, this is like a good literary device in need of being used to make a good point, or interesting characters needing to be animated by good roles. Waxing lyrical.

KEEP FOCUSED ON ... breathing life into the object of your concern, for there is the promise of great success in doing this. But you won't know until you try ... matching your 'advertisement' with your 'product' ... finding new forms.

WATCH OUT FOR ... attaching too much importance to, or being overwhelmed by, the trappings or reputations of others; they are only human and have their own doubts and feelings of inadequacy ... wearing yourself out trying to be or do something that just isn't you.

☯ KARMA/ATTITUDE/HEALTH

The nameplate for this Symbol could have been 'A Need To Animate' for it suggests that the form of what you are or have is attractive, impressive or seemingly sure of itself, but in fact it has little or no soul (*anima* in Latin), little or nothing animating it; this well-established but relatively superficial form is preventing the real thing or person showing through. A situation where the personality (from *persona*, Latin for 'mask') is compromising or stifling the being within. Health conditions resulting from suppressed self-expression.

KEEP FOCUSED ON ... the Inner Dwelling Being, that is really and truly you – and accept no imitation.

WATCH OUT FOR ... passing muster with those who appear to matter, but ultimately are seen not to, and not with those who really do ... emulating someone you admire to the point of losing yourself ... being fooled by appearances.

'A little sincerity is a dangerous thing, and a great deal of it is absolutely fatal'

A FLAG TURNED INTO AN EAGLE

☆ POTENTIAL MADE REAL ☆

GENERAL INTERPRETATION

You only find out about something by living it. Your issue is an inevitability or a *fait accompli*. What remains to be done is for the transformation from idea or reputation into real power and hard fact to be maintained and lived up to. This Symbol could simply be a confirmation of whatever you have in mind. This is one of a pair of similar Sabian Symbols, the other being Sagittarius 12 – 'A Flag Turns Into An Eagle That Crows', but this one, being Aquarian, does not draw unnecessary attention to itself.

KEEP FOCUSED ON ... your ability to convert the artificial into the genuine, thanks to a forward vision that is way beyond the average ... the power of actualization, of wishing.

WATCH OUT FOR ... vain pretence; riding on the coat-tails of another.

MONEY/WORK/CREATIVITY

Whatever conventional wisdom or the consensus of opinion says, what you stand for is becoming the norm. Your innovative stance, product or idea has, or will be, what everyone regards as 'it', and it will be profitable.

KEEP FOCUSED ON ... what you believe in, and in being a testament to that; walking your talk ... the fact that actualizing what is as yet latent or at the ideas stage takes investment and commitment ... renewing ideas, policies or standards; in this way your output will be sustained, rather than declining when it has lost its initial impetus.

WATCH OUT FOR ... getting too 'comfortable' for there is the danger of insidiously and gradually reverting to something of lesser substance.

LOVE/RELATING/SOCIAL

Your ideal of a relationship or social life has become real, or is about to. This may mean that you have an opportunity to rise to the occasion, that is, you have to be as impressive or adept as others expect you to be, or you expect of yourself.

KEEP FOCUSED ON ... what it is you are becoming or want to become, for there is great power in this. If you look, you will see that this process of becoming, or developing from an idea to a reality, is under way – revealing it to be as undeniable as the Sun rising in the morning.

WATCH OUT FOR ... losing sight of the fact that you are on the up and up. If you act like you are weak when you are really in a position of strength, then you might actually become weak.

KARMA/ATTITUDE/HEALTH

An idea or possibility that has become a reality can be seen either positively or negatively. It all depends on whether you like what is now evident – or if you have taken a really good look at it. An eagle is symbolic of something positive, heroic, prophetic, visionary, all-seeing and a vanquisher of whatever the foe is at the eleventh hour. A flag simply stands for such things – a symbol of a symbol, you could say. All in all then, there is very good karma in operation here, which will continue as long as you ...

KEEP FOCUSED ON ... being a living example of the highest morals and your soundest beliefs ... the probability that any difficulties you are currently experiencing are just an 'occupational hazard' of living up to something good and true, and that such difficulties will pass.

WATCH OUT FOR ... losing heart or height.

'From strength comes more strength'

A POPULARITY THAT PROVES EPHEMERAL

☆ A NEED FOR SELF-APPROVAL ☆

GENERAL INTERPRETATION

Whether it is the fickleness of the general public or one's peer group, or whether it is simply down to not having established what has lasting value, it is the inner sense of worth that counts in the end. This is what is in the process of being discovered – by painfully discovering what has not.

KEEP FOCUSED ON ... making it clear to yourself and others what really matters in the long run ... doing things for yourself, rather than seeking the approval of those you do not respect that much, or whose approval is not really worth anything. This sets a good example.

WATCH OUT FOR ... shallow opportunism that comes to nothing ... playing to the gallery rather than coming from a set of your own inner values ... ill-founded longings or fears.

♥ LOVE/RELATING/SOCIAL

A short-lasting relationship, or an unpromising aspect to a relationship. Possibly an affair that has little mileage in it (as in a love triangle), or a relationship where one or both people feel judged.

KEEP FOCUSED ON ... those social values that have staying power ... whatever it is that was found attractive in the first place, for it may have a value that is more than merely skin deep. You may have to delve in order to find out what it is.

WATCH OUT FOR ... being enamoured with or impressed by frothy or flashy people or experiences. They could be fun, but do not invest too much of yourself in them ... hanging on to relationships that are past their sell-by date ... the likelihood that the more anyone is allowed to indulge in something shallow, the quicker they'll be tired of it.

MONEY/WORK/CREATIVITY

For some reason, that will probably become clearer as things progress, the object of your enquiry does not have an appeal or motivation that is going to last very long – either with others or your own enthusiasm.

KEEP FOCUSED ON ... finding the underlying reason for this state of affairs. You will find it as long as you are prepared to admit to any short-sightedness or misappropriation on your own part ... the idea that nothing is ever wasted; of even the most short-lived bloom there is always the seed, which goes into the making of a new idea or product ... 'writing what you know'.

WATCH OUT FOR ... flogging a dead horse as soon as it becomes apparent that that is what you have been backing or riding ... being led by the values or opinions of those you do not respect, those who are simply looking over the shoulders of others for their values and ideas.

☯ KARMA/ATTITUDE/HEALTH

Here is suggested a pattern of 'backing the wrong horse', that is, attracting or being attracted to something that has no real value in relation to your true path.

KEEP FOCUSED ON ... any quality, feeling, place or person that has an ennobling effect on you, that touches you deeply, that uplifts your soul – even if there is pain and effort involved ... your own motivations and experiences ... enthusiasm for your goal ... what you like about your own body.

WATCH OUT FOR ... situations or people that do not have any spiritual content or principles, or that lead you a dance, do not keep promises, indulge in gossip, or create needless anxiety ... people with whom you cannot be yourself, or, worse still, actively prevent you from being yourself by playing on your fears or weaknesses.

'To thine own self be true'

A MAN TÊTE-À-TÊTE WITH HIS INSPIRATION

☆ CREATIVE ATTUNEMENT ☆

GENERAL INTERPRETATION

Whatever concerns you, what really matters is the satisfaction and realization that occurs when you are aligned with and working towards something of real significance for yourself. Only in this way will be revealed true capabilities, and from them something that appeals to and benefits others as well. The importance of having a dream and following it.

KEEP FOCUSED ON ... really being 'on the case', that is, following your vocation or concentrating deeply on the object of your concern – and then nothing and nobody can stop you attaining your goal or finding what you are after.

WATCH OUT FOR ... a self-preoccupation coupled with false pretensions that ultimately amount to less than nothing ... being side-tracked by lesser considerations.

LOVE/RELATING/SOCIAL

This person or relationship is your inspiration, that is, what gives meaning to your life, stimulates you creatively, and keeps you in touch with whatever you need to be in touch with – especially on an emotional or spiritual level. Alternatively, this Symbol is saying that your inspiration could be found in a suitably stimulating relationship or social set-up.

KEEP FOCUSED ON ... those qualities that strongly influence you, challenge you, touch you, uplift you, and occasionally hurt you; they are what provide the inspiration.

WATCH OUT FOR ... thinking that inspiration should always be easy – it can be quite the contrary ... thinking someone is an inspiration to you when really they have just got you on a string, playing upon your whims and weaknesses.

MONEY/WORK/CREATIVITY

Your work moves you, so it should move others too. Conversely, unless your work inspires you it is unlikely to satisfy or reward you or do much for your colleagues, customers or audience.

KEEP FOCUSED ON ... what it is that motivated you in the first place, and stay connected or reconnect with that ... your vision, and making it real – or finding a vision if you haven't got one ... inspiring others you are working with or who are depending on you – or you on them.

WATCH OUT FOR ... confusing what inspires or moves you with what does the same to others. In other words, bear in mind that what inspires *you* is simply that.

KARMA/ATTITUDE/HEALTH

The central dynamic to a spiritual view of life is that life, collectively and individually, has a purpose. Furthermore, through discovering that spiritual purpose it is also found that there is something somewhere that sees to it that you are kept in touch with it, guided by it, inspired by it, healed by it. This may be one's muse, guide, guru, God, Channel Central, soul or higher self.

KEEP FOCUSED ON ... whatever or whoever it is that keeps you in touch with your higher purpose – and you will be all right, in good health. This may involve a technique such as meditation or prayer, creative activity or communing with Nature.

WATCH OUT FOR ... false gods or gurus, or making a conceit out of being more 'in touch' than others ... fancying yourself being 'in the know' or having 'higher connections'.

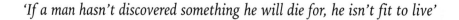

'If a man hasn't discovered something he will die for, he isn't fit to live'

PEOPLE ON STAIRS GRADUATED UPWARDS

☆ EVOLUTIONARY STATUS ☆

✵ GENERAL INTERPRETATION

In any process of development, be it great or small, there are those who are at the forefront, those who are lagging behind, and the vast majority somewhere in between. But whatever their position they are all still an integral part of the same process of evolution, moving progressively onwards.

KEEP FOCUSED ON ... your effective forward point of view, and your genuine appreciation of your own and everyone else's role in the scheme of things ... what social or cultural level you are on, or those you wish to reach or associate with, and adjust yourself and your expressions according to their standards.

WATCH OUT FOR ... losing yourself in a mistaken sense of human equality, being politically correct rather than sure of your own stance ... being too afraid of putting a foot wrong and getting nowhere.

♥ LOVE/RELATING/SOCIAL

Often we find ourselves in an 'unequal' relationship or social set-up where one individual appears to be more advanced, developed or better off than the other. This can be experienced as incompatibility, with all the problems this can entail. However ...

KEEP FOCUSED ON ... the probability that the 'less developed' individual is either more advanced in areas that are less obvious (as with 'invisible' qualities such as tolerance and compassion), or they have been put there to teach others something as they too are being taught. In the first case, identify what those 'invisible' qualities are; in the second, determine who is teaching what to who, and learn.

WATCH OUT FOR ... allowing feelings of superiority or inferiority to destabilize your relationships.

⚘ MONEY/WORK/CREATIVITY

You are on the ladder of success with respect to the object of your enquiry. Rung by rung you eventually get there, but there are some definite tips for getting there more smoothly and swiftly, and for avoiding slipping downwards or getting stuck.

KEEP FOCUSED ON ... the fact that you are headed for success, and that all you need to do is concentrate on the particular rung you are on and the one you are about to negotiate ... what appeals to the level or nature of the area you wish to reach or profit from.

WATCH OUT FOR ... having titanic ambitions and trying to take more than one step at a time; you could waste a lot of time, energy, money and opportunity that way ... being distracted or aggravated by envy of those higher up the ladder than you; they too had to climb to get there.

☯ KARMA/ATTITUDE/HEALTH

This is about knowing your own and others' places in the scheme of things. Possibly you have the karma of having to help the evolution of others.

KEEP FOCUSED ON ... teaching by being a living example of your own beliefs and standards ... how everyone concerned has a role to play regarding the object of your enquiry. There are those who are operating at lower vibrational levels and those at higher ones. Be careful you appreciate that you and others are usually operating at combinations of these. So ...

WATCH OUT FOR ... being condescending, berating, or making value judgements about yourself or others. The Sign of Aquarius is a challenge not only to making sure that egos do not get too big (hubris/arrogance), but also that they do not get too small (self-effacement) for fear of being oneself.

'Different strokes for different folks'

A BAROMETER

☆ SENSING CHANGE ☆

⊛ GENERAL INTERPRETATION

What is literally a measure or indicator of atmospheric pressure and the weather it predicts can be seen here as doing the same thing with regard to life and human issues. The Oracle itself could be regarded as a kind of symbolic barometer, with the Sabian Symbols being the readings on the dial.

KEEP FOCUSED ON ... those powers of observation and judgement you have that are intuitive, physical and automatic, and should therefore be trusted despite more logical or analytical methods of assessment ... what you feel the Oracle is telling you; you may have to 'tap' it, that is, read between the lines or make your own personal interpretation – or simply ask again.

WATCH OUT FOR ... uncertainty born of a dependence on, or over-sensitivity to, passing thoughts, moods and atmospheres.

⚷ MONEY/WORK/CREATIVITY

The nature, state or place of your work is telling you something about your own internal process. If things are unsettled then so are you; if there are changes going on there, then there are changes, or the need for them, going on with you. Alternatively, this Symbol is saying that you have to keep your ear to the ground in order to be aware of what is going on, for instance, with colleagues or the public.

KEEP FOCUSED ON ... what the 'pressures' are telling you, but do not jump to conclusions or make moves too soon. Wait until you detect a definite trend or lasting condition, then act accordingly. This means keeping a weather eye on matters as they develop day to day ... putting out feelers as to how any project could pan out.

WATCH OUT FOR ... being swayed this way and that by passing opinions, fashions and gossip. This could wrong-foot or embarrass you.

♥ LOVE/RELATING/SOCIAL

A relationship acts as a barometer that registers how we feel. And perhaps what one is telling you now is more than usually significant. Being particularly good at sensing how another person feels or where they're at – or the need to be so.

KEEP FOCUSED ON ... the fact that virtually all people, and therefore relationships, have their ups and downs, rainy days and sunny days ... the possibility that the state of a relationship or another is more an indication of how *you* are rather than how *they* are ... acting on any need for change, be it minor or major, for this will stabilize matters.

WATCH OUT FOR ... thinking that what is happening now is going to persist; it won't – at least, not unless you insist on hanging on to passing states and not going with the ebb and flow.

☯ KARMA/ATTITUDE/HEALTH

You are feeling a change approaching, or the need for one, because you have been stuck in the same conditions for too long. Health-wise, a need for some simple tests, or for keeping a record of your state of health and daily activities, looking for possible correlations.

KEEP FOCUSED ON ... reading the signs correctly: Is there too much or too little pressure, or the wrong kind of pressure? Is it increasing or decreasing, indicating that a change is going to occur naturally or inevitably? Or should you change before your back is against the wall? Consult your feelings regarding the issue once or twice a day, getting a measure of where things are headed.

WATCH OUT FOR ... letting the pressure get to you rather than you getting what it is telling you.

'Those who feel the pressure can sense the coming change'

A TRAIN ENTERING A TUNNEL

✴ LIGHT AT THE END ✴

GENERAL INTERPRETATION

The beginning or prospect of having to make it through a dark or difficult passage, which implies the need for faith that there is light at the end of the tunnel – which there always is unless it is blocked (by lack of faith). The train in this Symbol implies that it is not just an individual on the threshold of a journey, but a group or whole of which the individual is but a part.

KEEP FOCUSED ON ... having what it takes to enter into situations that demand utter resolution, and a reliance on the wisdom and courage of those who have gone before you. It is your commitment and faith that carries you through.

WATCH OUT FOR ... giving up or being intimidated because of a test of faith or nerve ... blind faith in lines of thought or activity of which you only have a theoretical knowledge.

LOVE/RELATING/SOCIAL

Possibly you are going through an emotionally trying time, and you may not be able to see an end to it – but there is. This Symbol could also describe a relationship in which two or more people have to go through a psychological process (*see* Karma below).

KEEP FOCUSED ON ... seeing the 'light' – the reason why you have had to be plunged into the situation. You may not think there is any reason, resolution or light, but there is ... hope for a better future as a result of discovering and coming to terms with the reason for your dilemma; use the Oracle again to help you discover this.

WATCH OUT FOR ... feeling too sorry for yourself, or, worse still, not understanding or working through your darkness – this is the only thing that could actually get you stuck in that tunnel.

MONEY/WORK/CREATIVITY

This looks like a bad patch with regards to cash or creative flow, seeing where you are going, or to work and money matters generally. It may be that you are caught up in a general trend such as a recession or slump. It is important that you ...

KEEP FOCUSED ON ... the fact that you will come out into the light at the other end, for it is this positive attitude that lights your way through the darkness.

WATCH OUT FOR ... losing your nerve and looking for an alternative route. At best, this could prove to be a long way round, but it could also cause you to get 'derailed' or 'shunted into the sidings'. This means that your lack of faith could cause you to lose track of where you are supposed to be headed, or that others no longer support or believe in you.

KARMA/ATTITUDE/HEALTH

This is the Night of Soul, that time when one has to confront one's greatest fears – whatever they may be. Esoterically this is called facing the Dweller on the Threshold, which, along with one's fears, includes key doubts and the darker side of your personality – and maybe someone else's. Actually, someone else's shadow could be seen as your own being projected on to the screen of life in order that you might see it.

KEEP FOCUSED ON ... penetrating the deepest and darkest recesses of your psyche so that whatever lies therein is then 'brought to light' and transformed into powers and talents, self-understanding and selfless understanding ... maintaining faith, hope and commitment, no matter what. Nothing lasts forever.

WATCH OUT FOR ... giving up, for this would be like lying down on the tracks and waiting for a train.

'Pessimism feeds off the past, optimism dines out on the future'

TWO LOVEBIRDS SITTING ON A FENCE

☆ A NEED TO AGREE TO MOVE ON ☆

 GENERAL INTERPRETATION

The simple attraction between the sexes but with the added dimension of having to change in order to get the best out of the situation. Then there is the magic created through a tender sharing on all levels of human personality: mental, emotional and physical. All the world loves a lover. Alternatively, two or more people who are constantly indecisive.

KEEP FOCUSED ON ... sustaining unequivocally a romantic and constant nature that wins loyalty and happy co-operation ... the possibility that you and your concern may simply be 'resting' before taking off again.

WATCH OUT FOR ... unrealized intimacy due to a reluctance to take the plunge into the unknown ... being easily influenced by the easily influenced.

 LOVE/RELATING/SOCIAL

Here we have a loving relationship, but it is characterized by having something about it that prevents it from moving on – possibly a form of confining circumstances or indecision, or one person waiting for the other to commit. More generally, we see here a social set-up that is harmonious and good but not quite sure where it stands.

KEEP FOCUSED ON ... abiding with and overcoming any obstacle to a happier union ... being more decisive, and acclimatizing yourselves to a decision-making process ... being committed to love and loving, rather than insisting that someone else should be committed – then you will inevitably get love and commitment.

WATCH OUT FOR ... being trapped or frozen in a situation for want of being alive to your situation, or for fear of commitment.

 MONEY/WORK/CREATIVITY

Here we have a labour of love, with all the virtues and vicissitudes that go with it. There is also the suggestion of two people being emotionally involved in a work situation – this may promote things or hold them back, depending upon how harmonious or well-managed such a relationship is. Joint finances. If your area of work involves music or anything to do with relationships, then this is auspicious – so get moving!

KEEP FOCUSED ON ... the overall, long-term goal of the object of your concern, for this should justify any sacrifices you have to make ... rooting out any dissension or disagreement as this is what stops progress.

WATCH OUT FOR ... trying in vain to mix business with pleasure. This would indicate that you are too work-orientated, or too pleasure-orientated.

KARMA/ATTITUDE/HEALTH

Before something can come together or move on there has to be closure or a decision to proceed that is not compromised by one person (or part of you) wanting one thing and the other person (or part of you) wanting another – or by simply hoping against hope. This can take the form of a third party or event that comes along to force the issue; it may ultimately be the only solution to break a deadlock.

KEEP FOCUSED ON ... only the best, most positive and creative reasons for doing something or being with someone, and settle for nothing less.

WATCH OUT FOR ... restlessness ... being 'a bird in a gilded cage' by staying with something because it is convenient and easier than confronting the unknown. Such a 'cage' can be a waste of life – for both yourself and others.

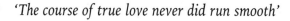

'The course of true love never did run smooth'

A BIG BUSINESSMAN AT HIS DESK

☆ POWER AND CONTROL ☆

 GENERAL INTERPRETATION

Personal stability can be gained and maintained through organizational powers. Or the object of your concern may be quite hard to attain, or out of your reach or league. You should know which – but if it were the latter, then it would be because you *assumed* it was the latter.

KEEP FOCUSED ON ... gaining or maintaining a sense of position in life that enables you to have things how you like them to be ... whether what you are concerned about is really practical or desirable, considering your position at present.

WATCH OUT FOR ... using a material position to seal you off from your emotional life ... there could be a powerful factor in play that you would not care, or would not know how, to deal with.

 LOVE/RELATING/SOCIAL

You are probably dealing with someone who uses their sense of position to get what they want, who puts something between themselves and others or who is in a state of denial so as not to make any direct emotional contact. Unless this person is you (in which case you need to be less defensive and more in touch with your feelings) ...

KEEP FOCUSED ON ... being sure of your own position and emotional standpoint ... being more under your own power and control, then they will be less able to disempower or control you ... taking a step back from the situation, then organizing yourself in a manner that is better able to deal with it.

WATCH OUT FOR ... expecting empathy where there is not likely to be any ... believing that love will win through without having to work at it.

 MONEY/WORK/CREATIVITY

Notwithstanding more spiritual or psychological realities, your fortunes presently rest on the organizational abilities and business acumen of yourself and others who are directly or indirectly concerned with the object of your enquiry.

KEEP FOCUSED ON ... the idea that your sense of position and material power enables you to attract and maintain these very things. So think like a business-person, even if you are not that kind of person as a rule ... gathering all the pertinent facts and figures and then making a decision based on them ... delegating where necessary.

WATCH OUT FOR ... the fact that you are dealing with the hard, cold facts about money, commerce and business, and so personal agendas and emotional excuses will just not wash – not for long, at any rate.

KARMA/ATTITUDE/HEALTH

The ultimate reality with regard to your health and fate is that they are down to you. Ultimately, you have to see yourself as being the 'executive' in charge of your own life and welfare.

KEEP FOCUSED ON ... seeing everything that is happening to you as being something you are directly responsible for and have some power and control over. Everything depends upon the power of thought and concentration. Your mind and your body are intimately interconnected.

WATCH OUT FOR ... leaving yourself to the mercy of those who are ostensibly in command of your situation. For example, putting yourself totally in the hands of doctors, as if your body was a car and they were mechanics ... being too airy-fairy in your spiritual pursuits; you may need to get real.

'The buck stops here'

A WATCHDOG STANDING GUARD

☆ PROTECTION OR PARANOIA? ☆

⚙ GENERAL INTERPRETATION

The basic protection and maintenance that is still necessary in a state where life and property, quality and individuality, are not always respected.

KEEP FOCUSED ON ... your firm belief in the right of all living and created things to be and feel safe, and your skill that makes a definite contribution to upholding this right ... what is not secure enough and make it so ... keeping a constant wary eye on the object of your concern, but not to the point of being obsessive.

WATCH OUT FOR ... a suspicious nature that attracts the very things it fears and prevents help from approaching ... closing the stable door after the horse has bolted ... doing anything that gives the illusion of making you feel relaxed or safe when in reality it makes you feel more vulnerable.

♥ LOVE/RELATING/SOCIAL

Here is a person or relationship that is highly protective, possibly in priority to everything else. If security in such extreme measure is what is needed, then well and good, the Oracle confirms that you have it. But the Symbol also suggests that this protectiveness is of a blinkered and instinctual nature, and as such may not recognize what is subtly on your side, or subtly against you.

KEEP FOCUSED ON ... what comprises this protectiveness, be it in yourself or another. What are its interests, values and motivations? This will tell you whether it is good, bad or just misguided ... the possibility or necessity of having to protect someone from themselves, or vice versa.

WATCH OUT FOR ... being over-protective or over-protected.

⚖ MONEY/WORK/CREATIVITY

The need to safeguard one's assets is an issue here. So too may be the necessity of sealing yourself off from unwanted distractions or demands when you are trying to perform an important task. If security is your game, then this is an auspicious oracle, as is anything that aims to give people and property a sense of security based in reality.

KEEP FOCUSED ON ... installing whatever is needed to ensure material or job security, or for personnel ... the need for copyright control.

WATCH OUT FOR ... anything or anyone that robs you of your energy or resources, taking moderate steps to stop them from doing so ... having too much security so that you do not enjoy what you have got. This would suggest that you have an emotional or spiritual insecurity that you have displaced onto your material situation ... being over-insured due to falling for a sales pitch.

☯ KARMA/ATTITUDE/HEALTH

Feeling safe from harm is one of the predominant needs of nearly every species. Physiologically this is evidenced in our immune system, psychically in our 'radar'. These networks take care of security matters adequately until one of them breaks down or becomes too hair-triggered, giving rise to the immune system turning on healthy tissue or the mind perceiving enemies where there are none.

KEEP FOCUSED ON ... recognizing that you are protected in more ways than you may appreciate at first ... using conscious means of psychic protection.

WATCH OUT FOR ... signs that your defence system is over-reaching itself, such as being overly suspicious, forgetting what you were worrying about, or physical complaints such as arthritis or protecting yourself with excess weight.

'Quis custodiet ipsos custodies?' (Who is to guard the guards themselves?)

A MAN UNMASKED

☆ TIMELY EXPOSURE ☆

✸ GENERAL INTERPRETATION

Something or someone revealing the truth, particularly about a man or the male aspects of a woman. In turn, this might imply the experience of what false or true masculinity is. Possibly an 'outing'. In general terms, this Symbol represents being stripped of one's social mask in order that the real person behind may be seen.

KEEP FOCUSED ON ... your forthright, clear and honest manner of self-expression that serves to promote greater understanding between yourself and others, and amongst those others ... the probability that as soon as everyone knows the truth, the better it will be for all concerned.

WATCH OUT FOR ... any kind of deceit, for it is about to be exposed – or may already have been ... thinking that always being nice and easy-going is a recipe for success or a peaceful life.

♥ LOVE/RELATING/SOCIAL

A group or relationship, or an individual within one, having their façade seen through or shattered. Whether this is welcome or not is another matter, but it is on the cards – so be prepared! Or possibly the issue is one concerning the necessity of this being made to happen.

KEEP FOCUSED ON ... the importance of everyone concerned benefiting from knowing the truth, even if it hurts or is embarrassing at first ... an acceptance of the way someone or something really is.

WATCH OUT FOR ... letting your mask slip indiscreetly or wantonly unmasking others, possibly for fear of being so yourself ... exposing or having exposed what is not yet ready to be seen.

♟ MONEY/WORK/CREATIVITY

Affairs are such that, for some reason, something has to be made known. This could be referring to a matter such as an office or business secret, the disclosure of financial details, or a creative strength, weakness, theme or development. The truth of a matter is made known; this is uncomfortable but necessary, so that you can rearrange your interests and express yourself freely, discover your talents. If, however, you are in the business of exposing anything, then this is an auspicious oracle.

KEEP FOCUSED ON ... keeping things as straight as possible, for if there is a rat to be smelt, it will be ... informing everyone who has the right to know ... unabashedly expressing yourself, and encouraging others to do so too.

WATCH OUT FOR ... shady dealings or false pretences ... trying to hide.

☯ KARMA/ATTITUDE/HEALTH

A denouement or exposition that serves at last to clarify and breathe fresh air into matters, or, at least, to lay bare a karmic/past issue so that it can be addressed and looked into.

KEEP FOCUSED ON ... speaking your truth, for this will cathartically remove blockages and liberate whatever is in need of liberating ... dispelling intrigues or deceptions that shun the light of day ... whatever it is that is trying to be expressed or break free – no matter what ... getting what's inside of you outside ... resolving difficulties through having the courage to experience difficulties.

WATCH OUT FOR ... maintaining or making a pretence that is hard to keep up or that is deleterious to your own or another's well-being ... inhibitions.

"'The Book of Life begins with a man and a woman in a garden" – "It ends with Revelations"'

A FOREST FIRE QUENCHED

☆ CONFLAGRATION ENDED ☆

✦ GENERAL INTERPRETATION

Successfully meeting an emergency; overcoming a disaster. Also the relief and sense of victory that follow such occasions. Something being consumed or taken over; maybe a question of what this leaves behind. Satisfying hunger and its consequences.

KEEP FOCUSED ON ... the fact that it often takes a crisis or conflagration to galvanize an individual or group into accomplishing what necessity demands ... the resolve you have that can make an advantage out of adversity, especially where emotional self-control is called for ... burning off excess fat or energy (anger) through activity and exertion.

WATCH OUT FOR ... suppression of passion, for this could do away with heartfelt meaning too ... getting your fingers burnt through using inappropriate methods or not letting things cool down first.

♡ LOVE/RELATING/SOCIAL

In emotional terms, this Symbol may be referring to the end of a crisis, row or a spent passion – either to come or that has already happened. The question is whether this is an acute or chronic case: is the drop in passion or peace a passing thing or something more long-lasting?

KEEP FOCUSED ON ... answering the above questions. This can be achieved by determining how you really feel about passion and peace. Some people need passion, whereas others prefer to keep things cooler. Do you like a roller coaster ride or a sedate stroll? More to the point, do you and the other like the same thing?

WATCH OUT FOR ... killing off passions that keep a relationship alive – in the name of peace and security ... allowing trouble spots to flare up again when they needn't.

⚜ MONEY/WORK/CREATIVITY

Most likely you are, or are about to be, breathing a sigh of relief. Whatever is bothering you will burn itself out or be sorted by whatever resources have been set this task. Then again, it could be a case of damage done; if so, don't dwell on it but take good note of what caused the problem. Also, it could just be that what was spreading – in terms of popularity or promotion – no longer is so.

KEEP FOCUSED ON ... doing all you can to stop such an event happening again if it was damaging, and getting on with rebuilding and restocking ... creating a campaign to breathe new life into things if possible and desirable, or acknowledging that 'it' has run its course.

WATCH OUT FOR ... carelessness as being the most likely culprit here, although it may have been intentional damage.

☯ KARMA/ATTITUDE/HEALTH

On the face of it, this appears to be a case of 'panic over'. However, there can be several types of reaction or aftermath when a disaster or crisis is at last over. There can be relief, but this may be mixed with grief; there can be a sense of peace and of being able to relax, but this can make one inclined to play it safe and come to a standstill. Then there is the consideration of what damage has been done. Metabolism.

KEEP FOCUSED ON ... what the 'conflagration' was, then what caused it, eradicating that cause where possible and necessary, then how it is affecting you and others now. Spiritually speaking, you may have to 'go back into the fire' to find out what 'burns' or has intense meaning for you.

WATCH OUT FOR ... areas where trouble could start up again. Consult the Oracle again if need be.

'Ashes can either fertilize what is to come or be bitter cause for regret'

A BIG WHITE DOVE, A MESSAGE BEARER

☆ GLAD TIDINGS ☆

 GENERAL INTERPRETATION

Peace shall come. A safe haven is near at hand. An end to disaster. Redemption. This Symbol assures us that the sheer beauty and integrity of life and its forces will eventually bring into manifestation what is longed for in the pure and faithful heart – be it the resolution of a personal difficulty or world peace. Like appreciating the Oracle itself, such messages are like receiving a signal from a sonar device. You cannot physically see it, but you trust the 'technology' and know it to be there.

KEEP FOCUSED ON ... the ever-present quality within yourself or others of goodness combined with an acceptance that unerringly produces positive results ... the idea that whatever happens, it will contain a valuable message.

WATCH OUT FOR ... a naive or do-gooder attitude of mind.

 MONEY/WORK/CREATIVITY

Reliable signs of matters improving. Finances stabilize or take an upturn, working conditions and relations get better, creative ideas or solutions become available. Possibly someone or something is appearing that can put things to rights, or point the way. A more pure and peaceful quality is coming into fashion.

KEEP FOCUSED ON ... offering an olive branch to anyone with whom you are in conflict, as this paves the way to mutual profit and advancement, not to mention the removal of strife and delay ... casting your bread upon the waters, making your bid, advertising your wares.

WATCH OUT FOR ... bloodymindedness; not giving in for reasons of pride and the need always to be in control ... giving up through loss of faith.

♡ **LOVE/RELATING/SOCIAL**

Someone is bringing you the emotional solace or fulfilment you have been looking for, or you are doing the same for them. On a more incidental level, whatever you are currently thinking, hearing or looking at is a good sign. A cause for rejoicing.

KEEP FOCUSED ON ... and accentuate those aspects and feelings that fill you with love, peace and optimism ... all problems as being resolvable as long as you believe in love and acceptance.

WATCH OUT FOR ... becoming preoccupied with snags or shortcomings to the point that they eclipse the real goodness that is within and around you – or soon will be ... thinking that someone, be it yourself or another, is the 'saviour'. They may well be the answer to your dreams, but that does not mean you should ascribe to them an image they cannot live up to.

KARMA/ATTITUDE/HEALTH

In many respects this Symbol is the ultimate Oracle for all questions: everything will work out eventually as long as you trust this to be the case, it is this trust that carries you through to that place and time, and attracts signs that you are on course.

KEEP FOCUSED ON ... believing in the best of possible outcomes, and that is precisely what you will get – but the whole point is that this is taken for what it is and not necessarily what you expect it to be. This *is* the message – it is up to you whether or not you receive or understand it.

WATCH OUT FOR ... refusing to recognize, believe or accept good news, or the reassurance that things will get better ... cynicism – for this would be a bit like saying that the Big White Dove was just a whitewashed crow.

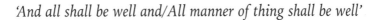

'And all shall be well and/All manner of thing shall be well'

A WOMAN DISAPPOINTED AND DISILLUSIONED

✪ EXPLODING THE MYTH ✪

✪ GENERAL INTERPRETATION

The pain and discomfort that is the result of submitting to someone or something for reasons that have to do with wrong thinking or unhealthy conditioning, and their consequently misguided inclinations. For example, marrying or working merely for status or security, only to find oneself trapped and bored.

KEEP FOCUSED ON ... the ability to learn and benefit from your mistakes ... the serious reappraisal that the situation calls for.

WATCH OUT FOR ... repeatedly suffering the consequences of faulty attitudes and habits without recognizing and correcting the conditions and patterns of behaviour that lie behind them ... believing that what you want is going to be exactly what you get.

♥ LOVE/RELATING/SOCIAL

Love and disappointment are paired only too often – but for good reason. This is because we have ideas and expectations regarding 'love' that have little to do with the real thing. We invariably enter relationships for unconscious reasons, which come under the heading of learning more about ourselves. Seeing that we usually have security, pleasure and excitement as our conscious motivations, it is not surprising that we are often disappointed and disillusioned.

KEEP FOCUSED ON ... discovering the difference between what you thought you wanted and what you really needed. You probably needed to find out what you did not want.

WATCH OUT FOR ... giving up on love, because it was not love or a lover that let you down, but just your idea of it and them. Time to look within.

MONEY/WORK/CREATIVITY

Whatever you have or had in mind is not going to pan out as profitably, easily or attractively as you expected. This does not mean to say that it is going to be an outright failure, but there are certainly going to be setbacks, rough edges to be smoothed over, or complications. If this is a new venture, teething problems will be to the fore for longer than anticipated.

KEEP FOCUSED ON ... the fact that it is your illusions and misguided (emotional) expectations concerning the object of your enquiry that the Oracle is alluding to, not necessarily the thing in itself ... each twist and turn of development – learning, refining and adjusting as you go ... strongly on any positive aspects.

WATCH OUT FOR ... banking on success at this stage in the proceedings. Don't 'give up your day job' if this isn't it.

☯ KARMA/ATTITUDE/HEALTH

This is very much a case of seeing adversity as your teacher. This seems like cold comfort, but to persist with ideas, wishes or fears that have no bearing on reality would only compound any difficulties you are already experiencing. What you have in mind is not what you imagine it to be; what you have on your plate is not what it seems.

KEEP FOCUSED ON ... reserving judgement or commitment until you can see the whole more clearly, which probably means waiting for something definite to happen one way or the other, and heeding the opinion of a trusted and impartial source ... the object of your concern in a spiritual way (as a service or a karmic duty) and it could then be seen quite differently – as enlightening or liberating.

WATCH OUT FOR ... jumping to conclusions, especially with regard to health matters.

'Both Sides Now'

A RUG PLACED ON THE FLOOR FOR CHILDREN TO PLAY

☆ CREATIVE OPPORTUNITY ☆

 GENERAL INTERPRETATION

The safety and comfort that facilitates the revealing and exploring of innocent and sensitive qualities, giving rise to the development of ideas and imagination. You now have the space and opportunity to sort out any issues or problems. As long as primary needs are taken care of, possibly for children, then there is not too much to worry about, for then they are actually quite capable of amusing or looking after themselves.

KEEP FOCUSED ON ... your special flair for creating an atmosphere where people may work and grow together in a spirit of togetherness and familiarity ... the fact that opportunity is just that – effort and dedication are needed to make something of it.

WATCH OUT FOR ... a protectiveness that can too easily create an illusion of safety, or too much comfort leading to indolence.

 MONEY/WORK/CREATIVITY

Unless this Symbol carries a direct agreement with the nature of your question (something that relates to children or security for growth, for instance), then it is stating that a growth plan or security system is under way or is favourable to your ends, so ...

KEEP FOCUSED ON ... creating opportunity and providing good conditions as a basis for further development ... giving time to, and taking great care of, anything that is in its early stages; then success is a natural likelihood, especially if you have more than one iron in the fire.

WATCH OUT FOR ... forcing progress as opposed to nurturing it.

 LOVE/RELATING/SOCIAL

Here we have a situation that has the rudimentary basis for care and concern that can lead to pleasure and the creation of something worthwhile, possibly children or the healthy development of children. There is also the implication that adults too have the chance to 'play', perhaps sexually.

KEEP FOCUSED ON ... improving the basis of any relationship, social gathering or project; then the natural inclinations of those involved stand a good chance of spontaneous fun and creativity.

WATCH OUT FOR ... leaving who or what you care about to get along on rudimentary attention and emotional investment, or leaving them to their own devices; an eye and will for constant improvement is essential ... perfunctory concern for those deserving better.

 KARMA/ATTITUDE/HEALTH

A stage has been reached when something or someone now has a chance to make up for the lack of concern that has been shown hitherto. The rug on the floor also suggests some health routine such as yoga. Provision made for recovery.

KEEP FOCUSED ON ... providing whatever is available, even if very simple, in order to improve (health) conditions ... being resourceful and inventive if, for the time being, supply is minimal ... the potential that is present.

WATCH OUT FOR ... expecting too much too soon, for conditions are conducive to better welfare, but probably only just.

'Silver and gold have I none, but such as I have give I thee'

A BIG BEAR SITTING DOWN AND WAVING ALL ITS PAWS

☆ POWER TAMED ☆

☀ GENERAL INTERPRETATION

Imaged here is the great power of the id or primitive nature when in a playful mood. This means that such lower drives can and should be acknowledged, tamed and harnessed (with good humour) in order to further whatever is regarded as worthwhile. Without the employment of what might be regarded as 'untamed' instincts, it would be a case of all ideas and no action.

KEEP FOCUSED ON ... making your good nature combine with your inner conviction and unwillingness to compromise to create a commanding aura and an impressive effect.

WATCH OUT FOR ... a dangerous element that lurks just beneath a surface display of affability. Avoid baiting anyone or anything, or rising to the bait yourself.

♥ LOVE/RELATING/SOCIAL

You are dealing here with powerful emotions or sexual desires that are in a harmless or playful mood – and this is the best way to deal with or express them. However, never lose sight of how a wrong word or move could elicit a change of mood, leading to crisis or disaster. There is also the whole issue of 'performance' to be considered.

KEEP FOCUSED ON ... any subtle or barely perceptible mood changes in yourself or others ... dealing with any emotional or sexual aversions you might have, for they could destroy a relationship or prevent one from happening ... exercising tolerance and self-control ... following natural instincts.

WATCH OUT FOR ... signs of disturbance or unusual sensitivity which can give rise to displays of unaccountable rage or hysteria.

⚕ MONEY/WORK/CREATIVITY

On the face of it your material affairs are set to be in a healthy, better than usual, state. But this is not something you should rest on your laurels about, or presume upon. A 'bear' market is one where prices are going to fall, so investing yourself or your funds in something safe is recommended. Creatively speaking, this Symbol is saying that you have a powerful and impressive idea or entity that needs to be 'tamed', that is, put into a form where it can be properly appreciated or expressed. Humour is also suggested here.

KEEP FOCUSED ON ... using wisely whatever funds or talents you have, for they have great power.

WATCH OUT FOR ... anything or anyone that has more power and influence than they know what to do with, for disappointment, unwelcome entanglements or sheer disaster could ensue.

☯ KARMA/ATTITUDE/HEALTH

Something big and powerful is surfacing from the depths of your unconscious, and whatever or whoever is in your life must adjust to it or get out of its way. Most of all, you need to familiarize yourself with it, or it could prove too difficult to handle.

KEEP FOCUSED ON ... how your urges and preferences are changing, for these are signs of a greater inner change that is taking place ... getting in touch with your raw, animal nature in a controlled or creative way – then great rewards, achievements and experiences can be yours.

WATCH OUT FOR ... playing around with the feelings of yourself or others for it could be discovered that you or they are no 'teddy bear' ... health problems or other difficulties resulting from not having taken your powers seriously enough, or even recognizing them.

'Truly great power does not degenerate into mere force but remains inwardly united with the fundamental principles of right and justice'

A MAN TURNING HIS BACK ON HIS PASSIONS AND TEACHING FROM EXPERIENCE

☆ GIVING SOMETHING BACK ☆

✺ GENERAL INTERPRETATION

A critical point in life has been reached or is approaching when one has to read the writing on the wall and follow what it says. In this way a creative, positive and permanent change in character is brought about.

KEEP FOCUSED ON ... advancing yourself through a willingness to sacrifice the lesser for the greater ... recognizing the hollowness of continuing to pursue self-indulgent goals and seeing how life is enriched by living it for others. 'Service to others is the rent you pay for your room here on Earth' (Muhammad Ali).

WATCH OUT FOR ... sanctimonious self-denial that fails in its purpose ... merely playing at leading a more selfless life, with the result that sooner or later you fall back into old and pointless ways.

♥ LOVE/RELATING/SOCIAL

Whatever is driving or preoccupying you emotionally or sexually has now reached a point where it could be destructive if you don't let go of it and pursue something more meaningful.

KEEP FOCUSED ON ... what makes love and creates life rather than what merely satisfies desires and distracts from Nature's intent ... what you have learnt from your emotional and social life so far, and giving others, possibly children, the benefit of that experience.

WATCH OUT FOR ... flogging a dead horse; withdraw and take stock of what you have learnt; this will prove useful in future ... giving in to your lower drives or cruder urges, like anger and lust – they would eventually teach you a harder lesson than you had bargained for.

♈ MONEY/WORK/CREATIVITY

What you have been doing to earn your bread is due for a change in some way. The events or feelings that give rise to this may not at first be recognized for what they are, because it may be the fate of someone else that indirectly affects yours; for example, a boss retiring to involve him or herself in charitable works. Then again, it could be you who has the 'call' away from ambition and towards something more sublime or spiritual. Or, more simply, the time has come to teach rather than do, for your experience has equipped you well for such a role.

KEEP FOCUSED ON ... the bare historical facts rather than your hopes and fears if you wish to know what the score is.

WATCH OUT FOR ... where personal hang-ups or pet projects have inveigled themselves into material or political affairs as they could prove their undoing.

☯ KARMA/ATTITUDE/HEALTH

A widespread spiritual teaching is that it is desire that creates karma and keeps us enchained to the ever-repeating cycle of birth and rebirth. And, as the I Ching says, 'Passion and reason cannot exist side by side' – one or the other has to go. A time has arrived, or is arriving, when you have the choice or necessity of 'taking the high road' (or lowly path) where powerful feelings are transmuted into something finer and put into the service of Humanity.

KEEP FOCUSED ON ... the relatively superficial, selfish and primitive nature of your desires, as compared to your aspirations. It is your aspirations that are now calling you to define them more closely and to contribute the fruits of your life or lifetimes to whoever or whatever needs them ... letting things take their course.

WATCH OUT FOR ... health problems created by the over-indulgence or suppression of your desires.

'A man who has not passed through the inferno of his passions has not overcome them'

A BUTTERFLY WITH THE RIGHT WING MORE PERFECTLY FORMED

☆ A NEED TO COMPENSATE ☆

✦ GENERAL INTERPRETATION

You are going through a transformation that demands that either you identify and use the stronger side of your personality or whatever you are considering, or you identify and develop the weaker side. More precisely, your analytical (right) side is more developed than the intuitive (left) side, posing a need to redress the balance. Equally, it could be that your rational, logical perception is being developed or emphasized to another level entirely, as with, for example, computer technology.

KEEP FOCUSED ON ... making the most of what is unusual about yourself, especially during critical periods of development or transformation.

WATCH OUT FOR ... lopsidedness created by not finding or taking up a challenge ... not getting the message owing to being too analytical/literal rather than intuitive/metaphorical.

♡ LOVE/RELATING/SOCIAL

A transformative relationship is imaged here, with the person with the logical (right-body = left-brain) being in a better or more powerful position than the other person who is intuitive (left-body = right-brain). Alternatively, the situation could be one where through approaching emotional matters too intellectually things get bogged down or never get started at all. In any event, some give and take is required, perhaps the strong person back-peddling to give the other a chance to come up to par. Logic makes way for intuition.

KEEP FOCUSED ON ... making sure that imbalances are graciously compensated for.

WATCH OUT FOR ... thinking superseding feeling.

⚜ MONEY/WORK/CREATIVITY

If your line of work is to do with logic and practical order, then you can be sure that you have a 'good hand' and are coming from a position of power – if only because the business or material world is currently based on this convention. Then again, for this very reason you could be underplaying the intuitive or creative side of matters with the result that things just don't get off the ground.

KEEP FOCUSED ON ... emphasizing or giving rein to the more spontaneous and creative elements of whatever you are considering. You can rely on the practical or technical side to look after itself, simply because it is so well developed.

WATCH OUT FOR ... merely employing those parts that are already functioning well and are up and running for this could lead to a serious state of imbalance ... a one-sided view of things giving a false impression.

☯ KARMA/ATTITUDE/HEALTH

During any process of transformation there is usually going to be a distortion or mutation before something is perfected. More particularly, the process could be one of going from a purely instinctual/biological impulse (left) to a more conscious/cerebral awareness (right). This Symbol implies that the object of your concern is at such a stage: it is on its way somewhere but it may appear out of kilter or worse than it was in the first place.

KEEP FOCUSED ON ... what are obviously your stronger, probably cerebral, attributes, and use them to compensate for what appears to be lacking – a bit like flying a plane when one engine is malfunctioning ... working on the weaker side so that it can 'catch up' ... what exactly is the imbalance within you, for this is the root cause (especially of a health condition).

WATCH OUT FOR ... regarding any imbalance or malfunction as permanent – it's not, it's in passage.

'Increase that which is too small, and decrease that which is too great'

A HYMDROMETER

☆ INSTINCTUAL EVALUATION ☆

✺ GENERAL INTERPRETATION

A hydrometer is an instrument which measures the specific gravity of any given substance by comparing its weight to an equal volume of water, so it symbolizes the real quality and value of a given person, object or situation as measured against an eternal or elementary constant. In short, gut instinct.

KEEP FOCUSED ON ... your acute sense of whatever you consciously choose to involve yourself in, for this in turn clarifies matters for everyone concerned ... how you personally feel about the object of your concern rather than by using a more objective assessment.

WATCH OUT FOR ... a reluctance or inability to contribute, even though you know exactly what is required ... overreacting to everything rather than using self-control.

♡ LOVE/RELATING/SOCIAL

A relationship in which each person experiences their individual emotional truths and realities acutely, for each person accurately mirrors the other.

KEEP FOCUSED ON ... trusting or developing your ability to sense the weight and importance of what is going on emotionally, and thereby responding appropriately without too little or too much emotional investment or response ... seeing yourself simply as a registration of whatever the emotional problem or situation is, which necessitates freeing yourself from childish reactions to such things.

WATCH OUT FOR ... thinking that being detached to the point of not caring is being aware of the real situation, for this would be like taking a measurement and not actually reading or comprehending it.

♆ MONEY/WORK/CREATIVITY

You probably have your finger firmly on the pulse of whoever or whatever it is you wish to be 'reading' or assessing. Empathy here is strong, so working with people is well-starred.

KEEP FOCUSED ON ... making sure you keep the 'reading' or assessment regularly updated and consider whatever global or market forces are influencing it at any given time. This is rather like a sailor taking 'soundings' to gauge the depth of a channel being navigated ... listening to your gut feelings, for they are often the most appropriate measure of something.

WATCH OUT FOR ... always believing what the figures or pundits tell you. Remember, 'there are three kinds of lie: lies, damned lies and statistics' (Benjamin Disraeli).

☯ KARMA/ATTITUDE/HEALTH

The weight of one's karma, particularly the responsibility born of such. Here is emphasized the importance of assessing one's life, and any incident in it, in the context of a far greater whole. For example, one could view an experience as one of millions taking place in one of millions of lives.

KEEP FOCUSED ON ... the truth that your fate is inseparable from what and who you are ... immersing yourself in whatever your life presents you with, for only then will you know your true feelings and reactions regarding it ... an impartial, humble, but genuine response to all things, especially the object of your current concern.

WATCH OUT FOR ... judging a person when you have not experienced what they have, or judging a situation when you have not experienced it yourself.

'Man is the measure of all things'

AN ANCIENT POTTERY BOWL FILLED WITH VIOLETS

☆ CONSTANCY OF SOUL ☆

 GENERAL INTERPRETATION

The situation is a testament to, or calls one to be mindful of, the constancy of refreshing sentiments that spring from the heart. Through all trials and tribulations there persists something pure and true that reminds and assures one that it is all ultimately worthwhile, that some things are sacred.

KEEP FOCUSED ON ... the deep-seated feeling that is consistent in saying that there is an eternal goodness to the human spirit. The refreshment that this brings ... whatever reminds you of something sublime and deeply significant – this will be your guiding principle ... a prevailing influence, within or without, that can be relied upon to guide and inspire.

WATCH OUT FOR ... aesthetically pleasing but ultimately insincere displays.

 LOVE/RELATING/SOCIAL

The person or relationship in question here is to be relied upon utterly. However, as this Symbol has everything to do with the soul and modesty, you may need to view it in that light in order to appreciate fully that you are blessed with long-lasting love and commitment, and have nothing to worry about, in spite of the vagaries of human nature.

KEEP FOCUSED ON ... the fact that at a deep level you and your partner or group have a soul connection that underlies and goes beyond what might appear as passing difficulties and disagreements. If you are alone, this too is blessed with a modesty and purity of purpose that should not be eclipsed by lesser considerations.

WATCH OUT FOR ... doubting the rightness of your position by expecting something more showy or glamorous in your emotional life.

 MONEY/WORK/CREATIVITY

This patently spiritual Symbol, in the context of the material sphere of life, refers to the importance of introducing or maintaining a spiritual quality to one's work, co-workers and financial dealings. If you are concerned about being able to make it materially as you pursue a spiritual course, then you are forgetting that the spirit will sustain you as long as you remain in touch with it. If your work is concerned with helping others to keep in touch with spiritual issues, then the Oracle blesses and confirms your course.

KEEP FOCUSED ON ... the sentiments of heart and soul in all your dealings, even though they feel easily crushed or disregarded. It is the very persistency of such sentiments that is their strength.

WATCH OUT FOR ... making false offerings to God, Spirit or a Higher Power by paying them lip-service, just as trappings of spirituality.

 KARMA/ATTITUDE/HEALTH

Violets are symbolic of spirituality, pure and simple. That they are contained in a vessel points to the soul that animates the physical body. So, this Symbol is saying that the object of your concern has to do with, or can benefit from, spiritual or energetic healing, or any religious or magical ceremony. This includes dreamwork, meditation and hatha yoga, or birth itself.

KEEP FOCUSED ON ... how the soul or spirit feels within the body. This will answer your question and possibly resolve any problem ... this Symbol's image, internally or externally, and you will gain a connection with the eternal peace that exists within, it being redolent of one's pure origin, and possibly of some spiritual tradition.

WATCH OUT FOR ... missing out on this through not appreciating its subtlety and poignancy.

'The Soul is the Believer, with Memory so old./The Soul is the Believer, as Mind and Body show'

A TREE FELLED AND SAWED

☆ USE OR ABUSE? ☆

GENERAL INTERPRETATION

A sharp polarization between Man's healthy interaction with and utilization of Nature's resources, and a wanton abuse of them. In more everyday terms, this Symbol simply suggests good workmanship and preparedness, having got to a particular stage in an orderly process. A need to mature.

KEEP FOCUSED ON ... being industrious and maintaining a down-to-earth efficiency ... doing credit to the raw materials that have been laboriously made ready; this may be a case of it being better to use something rather than let it go to waste ... making more of what you have.

WATCH OUT FOR ... a disregard for others and the environment that is supposedly justified by short-term benefits and a sense of satisfaction ... jumping or hurrying natural stages or processes.

MONEY/WORK/CREATIVITY

You have the raw materials in terms of ability or resources. All that remains is that you put them to good use. You have the potential for making money. However, the ecological/environmental consideration is strongly emphasized here, and this would include doing right by the hearts and minds of those that your work will reach.

KEEP FOCUSED ON ... making sure that what you do is economical in every sense of the word; that resources can be recycled or replaced; that there is a real call for what you have in mind ... allowing things to 'season', ripen and mature before using them or acting on them.

WATCH OUT FOR ... the cardinal sin of modern life which is the 'take, make and throw away' abuse of natural materials, also taking advantage of people's weaknesses in the pursuit of financial gain ... premature use of resources.

LOVE/RELATING/SOCIAL

Having reached or got past the first basic objective in a relationship – that of finding a mate and adjusting to each other – we are now ready to embark upon creating a more 'finished product', such as being a social entity, and raising a family. Whatever this might be, it involves the further discovery of our feelings for one another.

KEEP FOCUSED ON ... the basic values you hold as a couple and endeavouring to make more of them, to refine and polish them, working continually to improve them, ultimately holding them up to others as an example.

WATCH OUT FOR ... getting stuck at a primitive level of relating, for the finer points will not be able to find a means of expression, and the relationship will rot, falling into disuse or abuse, communication getting cut short by distrust.

KARMA/ATTITUDE/HEALTH

Something that you prepared (for) in the past, and can now make good use of. Taking radical action towards the raw materials of the psyche and Nature. What you have here are the basic materials you need for a new life and pioneering adventure.

KEEP FOCUSED ON ... choosing very carefully whatever it is that you wish to say or do with respect to the object of your concern, because once you have got so far there'll be no way of going back ... weighing objectively what is natural and what is not; whether what you get out of what you are doing merits the cost of it in physical or mental health terms or in natural resources.

WATCH OUT FOR ... waste of past efforts or resources ... using resources at your disposal indiscriminately, as merely a show of power, or worse still, an abuse or disuse of it.

'I think that I shall never see/A poem lovely as a tree'

A BUTTERFLY EMERGING FROM A CHRYSALIS

✥ METAMORPHOSIS ✥

✳ GENERAL INTERPRETATION

After a period of dormancy, a new situation or sense of being emerges. It is also implied that there was another stage before the one of dormancy, and a stage before that, and so on. You, or the object of your enquiry, are involved in a natural process of transformation and are now at the point where one stage inexorably gives way to the next. Metaphorically, you are going from crawling to flying.

KEEP FOCUSED ON ... your innate awareness of the promise of renewed life and the wonders of continuing creation ... whatever it is that you are struggling to be free of, for this will certainly happen one day.

WATCH OUT FOR ... staying put in spite of a call to the new – this would leave you neither as you were, nor as you are supposed to be.

♡ LOVE/RELATING/SOCIAL

There is nothing like a certain type of relationship or personality for transporting us from one style of living and being to another. It has often been said, 'I didn't know I was alive until I met you'. This Symbol says that you, and probably the other person too, are in (line for) such an awakening relationship.

KEEP FOCUSED ON ... the fact that what you are going through now is a small but significant part of a bigger cycle of growth and transformation, and that freedom and beauty are central to the whole process.

WATCH OUT FOR ... the struggles and conflicts that result from the parts of yourself or another that are 'old' and 'asleep', resisting or not recognizing the changes that are called for by being in this relationship.

MONEY/WORK/CREATIVITY

Some aspect of your working life or material situation is going through a natural and irresistible change for the better. Creatively and financially, after a period that has been short on inspiration or funds, you are now emerging into a period that is happily characterized by increased mobility and scope, fruitfulness and advantage.

KEEP FOCUSED ON ... the wonderful opportunities and improved conditions that are just around the corner, for these are what the present changes are heralding ... negotiating and seeing through any changes, for they are the keys to progress and ultimate success.

WATCH OUT FOR ... having doubts about your real and latent abilities, for only such doubts can prevent you from making this positive transition.

☯ KARMA/ATTITUDE/HEALTH

You are at that important but critical stage where you struggle from one phase of development to another. In comparison to the stage you are now entering, you were to all intents and purposes 'asleep' to the object of your concern. For example, hitherto you may have automatically subscribed to the values and beliefs of your culture, but now you are striving to develop your own philosophy and concepts. All you need do is ...

KEEP FOCUSED ON ... what it is about you that is gradually unfolding, where you are bound, and the means of getting there ... letting the process of liberation continue as it will ... what other transformations have occurred.

WATCH OUT FOR ... old and apparently comfortable ideas and habits sticking to you, trying to lay claim to you and preventing you from moving on toward your destiny and a better life.

'Change, Life's only constant'

THE FIELD OF ARDATH IN BLOOM

☆ SACRED SPACE ☆

 GENERAL INTERPRETATION

The mystic meadow of ancient Babylon, re-created by Marie Corelli, may be seen to represent the perennial renewal of the beautiful and the good, even in the midst of strife and corruption.

KEEP FOCUSED ON ... the source within you that continually guides, motivates and refreshes both yourself and others ... the respect and protection of the inviolable core of your being that no one can enter without your express permission. Respecting the same in others.

WATCH OUT FOR ... retreating from responsibility into fantasy.

 LOVE/RELATING/SOCIAL

There is either something undeniably blithe and tranquil about your relationship and manner of relating, or there is a need to find such a feeling within, to retreat in order to restore yourself, and then bring you and your relationship to this tranquil state.

KEEP FOCUSED ON ... whatever you have between you that resonates with a deep sense of peace and renewal. If you cannot find such a thing, or do not believe that it exists, then you must either suspend your disbelief until you have located it, or resign yourself to emotional or spiritual bankruptcy.

WATCH OUT FOR ... imagining that everything in the garden is lovely when really there are some weeds and illusions to get rid of.

 MONEY/WORK/CREATIVITY

There is here a wonderful prospect of wealth and growth, of beauty and inspiration. Escapism or a mystical search may be the nature of your quest or product.

KEEP FOCUSED ON ... whatever it is that appeals on a profound or dreamy level ... an awareness of the emotional and mental inscape of those you wish to reach or appeal to.

WATCH OUT FOR ... attempting to cater to something which is a fantasy of yours rather than a need or quality of others.

KARMA/ATTITUDE/HEALTH

This Symbol calls you to be reminded of a deep memory of a better, more beautiful and peaceful time and place. It is also saying that it is available to be visualized or called upon as an inner sanctuary that no one can disturb, or as a power source, or a means to heal any negative condition in the present.

KEEP FOCUSED ON ... that beautiful and peaceful image within – or go somewhere that reminds you of it – and be replenished, pacified and reassured.

WATCH OUT FOR ... beguiling images becoming an escape from the real day-to-day world that we have to contend with, for this could turn beauty into discontent and peace into unrest ... giving in to any kind of addiction because of impatience or a fear of looking within, as going there is inevitable.

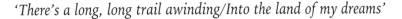

'There's a long, long trail awinding/Into the land of my dreams'

THE SABIAN SYMBOLS OF
PISCES

Either directly, or in a subtle way, all these Symbols are concerned with the following qualities, or with situations that involve or call for them:

COMPASSION

HEALING

IMAGINATION

LONGING

MUSIC

MYSTERY

MYSTICISM

SACRIFICE

SELFLESSNESS

SENSITIVITY

SPIRITUALITY

SUFFERING

THE SEA

VISION

A PUBLIC MARKET

☆ MEETING GROUND ☆

✳ GENERAL INTERPRETATION

You are in the market place of life, where the various types of people in different walks of life meet and exchange what they have to offer. Such a time and a place is therefore the acid test of worth. Before buyer meets seller, the worth of anything is purely notional.

KEEP FOCUSED ON ... your ability to make the most of what society has to offer, to tune into its needs and foibles, and subsequently bring benefit to both it and yourself ... getting involved with this meeting of all types of people; in this way you will find what you are fundamentally made of ... the fact that this meeting place is always there for you to make use of.

WATCH OUT FOR ... either getting lost in and intimidated by the hurly-burly of life, being taken advantage of – or taking mercenary advantage of it. You may need to protect yourself in some way.

♡ LOVE/RELATING/SOCIAL

Here this Symbol either suggests a person or relationship too mercenary for love to exist in, or it is saying that you can find what you are looking for by wholeheartedly immersing yourself in a relationship, or in whatever society has to offer.

KEEP FOCUSED ON ... what field you are most likely to find who or what you want ... the consolation that, if you feel at a loss, there are 'plenty of other fish in the sea'.

WATCH OUT FOR ... treating others as objects you can buy, for this implies that you do not feel worth much as a person yourself ... 'going to market' with inflated expectations based on a faulty assessment of your own eligibility ... doing badly by underplaying your hand ... a 'pig in a poke' – 'buying' without inspecting the 'goods' first.

♆ MONEY/WORK/CREATIVITY

This Symbol is clearly mostly concerned with this section in that it refers to market forces, the likes and dislikes of the person in the street, price structures, promotion and bargaining. Although it could be read as an affirmation of your item's worth, or the fact that your situation is a straightforward matter of ascertaining worth, it could be asking you to ...

KEEP FOCUSED ON ... how the public would receive your product or idea on a street level, how you could make them aware of it and get it to them, and whether the money people would back it. Ask the Oracle these questions.

WATCH OUT FOR ... the fact that you are dealing here with the status quo where commercialism is concerned. In other words, you are dealing with something that is essentially conservative in its tastes and practical in its outlook, and there is little room for sentimentalism or idealism.

☯ KARMA/ATTITUDE/HEALTH

The public market can be seen here as a place of reckoning. This fits being the first degree of Pisces, the Sign of Karma itself, for karma is just that – a reckoning that is implemented by actually being in the world of people and things. Whatever the object of your enquiry, its time of reckoning has come: accounts must be settled, any rewards or honours bestowed.

KEEP FOCUSED ON ... the fact that the market place of life with its commingling of all and sundry is always a place of gain – even if you only gain the knowledge that what you are or have is wanting, for what better way is there to know for sure?

WATCH OUT FOR ... allowing the weight of the past or a fear of the future to inhibit you unnecessarily. It is better to submit yourself to judgement or assessment by God and Life and be the wiser for it, rather than live in fear with only regret and uncertainty as your particular 'reckoning'.

'Grace is given of God, but knowledge is bought in the market'

A SQUIRREL HIDING FROM HUNTERS

✵ SELF-PRESERVATION ✵

 GENERAL INTERPRETATION

In order to preserve a way of life, especially a delicate one, it is necessary to find the line of least resistance. This Symbol may also be telling you that you are pursuing an answer from the Oracle in a fashion that is too intent upon getting the answer you want – the true answer will retreat out of sight until you are in a more sensitive and receptive frame of mind.

KEEP FOCUSED ON ... or develop an animal cunning that perfectly protects and augments your sensitive creative interior.

WATCH OUT FOR ... a reluctance to face one's inner demons ... hounding anything or anyone in a bid to get what you think you want ... the possibility that you do not want to know the true answer to your question ... feeling persecuted – if so, ask why that is.

♡ **LOVE/RELATING/SOCIAL**

The more sensitive, delicate or vulnerable facets of your personality (must) now protect themselves from the predatory or rougher elements of society. In personal relationships this can mean that one person is in a weaker position or has to be low-key in order to avoid embarrassment or injury.

KEEP FOCUSED ON ... any possible areas where you are socially or emotionally vulnerable and set about putting yourself out of harm's way. Bear in mind that your own vulnerability may be manifesting in the state of your partner – so protect them ... the fact that by being reserved you can bring out qualities that are usually hidden in others.

WATCH OUT FOR ... playing the victim in any way, for this attracts the very aggression you fear (see Karma below) ... how insecure aspects of yourself and others will avoid intimacy.

 MONEY/WORK/CREATIVITY

Your personality, idea or product is not presently strong enough to contend with the material world of commerce and competition – at least not directly. You may have some fine point that has to be developed and given a stronger identity before it can stand up for itself. In the meantime ...

KEEP FOCUSED ON ... using or developing the charm and finer points of yourself or the object of your concern, for these are its current strengths.

WATCH OUT FOR ... being intimidated by the tougher and more established players in the arena of your concern. Your protection lies in being true to yourself, even though you may have to learn this the hard way by being exposed to direct competition with a very different sort of creature to yourself ... being so fearful of the world that you pay for safety with boredom and a lack of fulfilment.

 KARMA/ATTITUDE/HEALTH

We are dealing here with shyness, tentativeness and a fear of being seen. There are two ways of looking at this – either one is genuinely in a weak position and it is wise to lie low and hide from superior or threatening forces, or one finds that being a trembling wallflower is a way of avoiding the fact that perceived weaknesses are really just one's dread of showing others one's darker or more aggressive side, for fear of not being liked or approved of.

KEEP FOCUSED ON ... seeking or providing a safe place or protection from harmful elements, be they people, thoughts, bacteria or the environment.

WATCH OUT FOR ... being a victim of the habit of being a victim. Squirrels are hunted mainly because they are seen as vermin – victims are unconsciously seen as undermining the 'tribe' and as such are to be eliminated or made to toughen up.

'Discretion is the better part of valour'

A PETRIFIED FOREST

☆ LASTING IMPRESSIONS ☆

✴ GENERAL INTERPRETATION

This is a particularly Piscean Symbol because it is mysterious and ancient, and it is not what it appears to be. A petrified forest is not simply trees that have turned to stone – or rather it is exactly that, but not in the way that animal bones fossilize. Here, the cells of the wood have been invaded by minerals, in effect replacing the form of the tree with a silica or calcite replica of it. Hence, 'lasting impressions' or illusions, rather than permanence itself.

KEEP FOCUSED ON ... your sense of continuity and resourcefulness for this enables you, after a fashion, to leave your mark ... on the object of your concern until it crystallizes, comes clear.

WATCH OUT FOR ... indolence, congestion or inertia as a result of sticking to outworn ideas or values ... entertaining fixed views or ideas.

MONEY/WORK/CREATIVITY

Apart from the Oracle saying that the type of work you do best is concerned with old records and memories, it could also be saying that certain elements and practices are embedded in the way you work and the manner you make or regard money. If such long-held practices profit you, then well and good. However, there is an indication that something is stuck in the past or frozen in time, and while this may be impressive it is a bit of a white elephant. So ...

KEEP FOCUSED ON ... how you can make the most of longstanding assets and styles, but be ruthless in rooting out any 'dinosaurs' – in the form of ideas, products, methods or personnel – that are clogging up the works. Endeavour to do this without throwing the baby out with the bathwater, that is, while still preserving and drawing from healthy traditions.

WATCH OUT FOR ... becoming institutionalized.

♡ LOVE/RELATING/SOCIAL

Certain people get under our skin and make a lasting impression upon us, whether they are still with us or not. Whether we enjoy or dislike this effect they have on us is the question. The key to answering it is to ...

KEEP FOCUSED ON ... what positive aspects of your relationship have lasted, for they are what will carry you both on through ... what has life and potential, and feed and follow that.

WATCH OUT FOR ... any feelings you have for another that are not growing or going anywhere, and then detach from those feelings and stop feeding them. Leave them merely as inert testaments to what was, or they'll just be negative thoughts that have no place in a healthy relationship ... wasting too much time or energy on people and relationships when they are too set in their ways.

☯ KARMA/ATTITUDE/HEALTH

This Symbol is representative of ancient karma itself: the memory and effects created by an impression lodged on our souls at a point in the past. The event has passed, but the effect is still with you in the form of the object of your enquiry. Whatever this is, it will stay as it is until it is properly dealt with, but by the same token, it need not be with you forever.

KEEP FOCUSED ON ... the possibility that a process or growth is being put on hold until you deliberately correct the matter, possibly by changing your attitude toward it ... being active and positive, if the problem is one of inertia, over-passivity or the result of such.

WATCH OUT FOR ... merely waiting for something to get better or change; you could turn to stone before that happened ... clinging on to a fearful or negative idea of the object of your concern, for this would only perpetuate it.

'The tree becomes the Earth with the full consent of the tree,
and I surrender my life to you who sustained me'

HEAVY TRAFFIC ON A NARROW ISTHMUS

☆ STAYING WITH THE PROCESS ☆

 GENERAL INTERPRETATION

You are caught up in a teeming profusion of things, people and ideas to such an extent where it seems that the environment or yourself can barely sustain it. The problem of keeping matters moving, flowing and in process.

KEEP FOCUSED ON ... simply waiting, or how you can facilitate the flow of events and experiences going in an organized fashion, or maintain calm and good spirits until things get through, come into the open.

WATCH OUT FOR ... a bottleneck or impasse caused by a reluctance to process various items and confront certain emotions ... trying to find a shortcut – there isn't one ... taking on too much, in view of your resources ... thinking too much, it is counterproductive. Just be.

MONEY/WORK/CREATIVITY

Too much going on for the space, resources or channels provided. The system works, but it could work a lot better – and more happily – if improvements were made to the methods of processing. Creatively, this is like having too many ideas and thoughts to be packaged suitably or expressed satisfactorily in the current medium. However, time and resources may mean that you have to continue to wait it out and be patient in inadequate conditions.

KEEP FOCUSED ON ... looking ahead to a time and place when circumstances will be more suitable ... making the best of a bad job, perhaps with a spirit of optimism prevailing against tough conditions or a bad atmosphere.

WATCH OUT FOR ... making matters worse by making a fuss when there is nothing that can practically be done.

♡ LOVE/RELATING/SOCIAL

There are a lot of thoughts and feelings you have to confront and deal with, but it will all be worth it. It is only a matter of time and patience. This could involve someone who is heavy going who will just have to learn, and be treated with patience.

KEEP FOCUSED ON ... 'policing' the difficult straits you are currently in by knowing what your duty is and not taking another's reactions personally. You are perfectly aware that if everyone keeps their cool and sits things out, matters will free up.

WATCH OUT FOR ... letting frustrations and communication difficulties get to you. A liberating outcome is assured, but the measure of mutual happiness and harmony are not; they depend upon how you handle your tempers now ... such impasses becoming a regular thing. If they are, avoid what causes them.

KARMA/ATTITUDE/HEALTH

Too many things are happening at the same time, possibly as a result of some of them not being dealt with when they should have been. Consequently, your life is stuck and cluttered in some area. It will eventually become clear, but when and in what state you will be in is another question. Healthwise, such tardiness or inhibition could manifest as problems such as constipation, congestion or constriction.

KEEP FOCUSED ON ... accepting the inevitable ... having more faith in what lies ahead, that things will become clear ... processing stuff from the past that has now built up to critical proportions.

WATCH OUT FOR ... trying to keep tabs on everything, for that will just slow things down ... any resentment or reluctance to speak your truth, for that will inhibit you, get you more stuck.

'The inevitability of gradualness'

A CHURCH BAZAAR

☆ RAISING FUNDS FOR GOOD CAUSES ☆

GENERAL INTERPRETATION

Literally, raising funds – ostensibly for a good cause. More generally, it is pointing to the gentle and convenient amenities that can be created by a co-operative and altruistic spirit.

KEEP FOCUSED ON ... any flair for combining a sense of supply with a sense of need that has no profit motive other than maintaining the supply and meeting the need.

WATCH OUT FOR ... ineffectual philanthropy that profits no one – materially or spiritually.

LOVE/RELATING/SOCIAL

Whatever is in need of support or resurrection is the theme here. Most relationships engender a situation where one, both or more are in need of charity. This can sometimes appear unromantic or unsexy, and so inadequacy can become regarded as a liability and unwelcome. Extending oneself for the benefit of another is more worthy of the term 'love' than many other expressions of the word, as too is graciously receiving this benefit.

KEEP FOCUSED ON ... the benign, gentle and comforting side of relating ... the familiar and parochial over the deep and profound.

WATCH OUT FOR ... not emphasizing enough the sexual side of a relationship (possibly for fear of encountering it), for this could lead to frustration and disappointment.

MONEY/WORK/CREATIVITY

Your occupation and finances would appear to be of a charitable sort or of a small-scale homespun nature. Or at least, the emphasis is on doing something for a worthy cause rather than something that is purely profit-motivated. A case of art for art's sake, literally or figuratively. Having money as a motivation could inhibit creative flow or repel a softer, friendlier feel to one's endeavours. The exception would be one where material reward itself is seen as a means to the continued furtherance of a spiritual cause. But, as a general rule ...

KEEP FOCUSED ON ... working and attracting funds for reasons that go beyond selfish ambition.

WATCH OUT FOR ... underselling just because it seems vulgar or inappropriate in the circumstances. It should be born in mind that, up to a point, the end justifies the means.

KARMA/ATTITUDE/HEALTH

On the face of it, here is a gentle and well-intentioned situation resulting from something or someone of a similar nature. There is a suggestion of good deeds and good causes attracting peace and sustainment. At a deeper level, we could be said to be using a mild form of commerce towards spiritual ends. This in itself implies a situation where funds are not forthcoming from an official source, but have to be raised by donation from the community. So this Symbol also points to the fact that the State does not support the Church – rightly or wrongly – which in turn means that spiritual endeavour, or health, cannot depend upon the normal or material scheme of things for its continuance.

KEEP FOCUSED ON ... supporting whatever appeals to your sense of compassion or justice.

WATCH OUT FOR ... a lack of charity.

'Put your money where your mouth is'

OFFICERS ON DRESS PARADE

✫ DISPLAY OF EXCELLENCE ✫

 GENERAL INTERPRETATION

The grand display of what is seen to command the protection of our culture and way of life. Feeling you are on display – in particular, to be judged. Having your better qualities tested and proven.

KEEP FOCUSED ON ... a dignity of bearing that impresses others with a sense of excellence and impeccable values ... taking pride in performing the responsibilities imposed on you ... the 'right stuff' you are made of and being able to 'cut it'.

WATCH OUT FOR ... a stiff and possibly outdated expression of authority and moral rectitude ... the way things are turned out giving the lie to how they actually are ... anything obviously unsatisfactory in the manner of looks or maintenance of equipment.

 LOVE/RELATING/SOCIAL

The situation requires that you look your very best and show what you are made of – be this in terms of your genuine and innermost feelings or simply looking your best for someone you care about and wish to attract.

KEEP FOCUSED ON ... the inner man or woman, something that is evident from the look in the eye or in quiet acts of kindness rather than something sensational or superficial ... teaching by being a shining example of what you stand for if you wish to influence someone.

WATCH OUT FOR ... being taken in by appearances, particularly when they are dazzling ... anything that could be regarded as 'conduct unbecoming' or failing to measure up to the justifiable expectations of others – or your own high standards.

 MONEY/WORK/CREATIVITY

You are dealing here with the highest echelons of your field of endeavour. Only the best quality will find any place or favour. Expenditure could well be higher than usual, with something having to be put up in the first place as a show of calibre.

KEEP FOCUSED ON ... creating as impressive and polished a presentation as possible. Without this, any more intrinsic quality won't get a look in ... drawing your inspiration, support and values from higher levels, be it your superiors, your muse or your god ... putting up the best that you have to offer.

WATCH OUT FOR ... being outclassed while avoiding being intimidated by who or what appears to be way above you.

KARMA/ATTITUDE/HEALTH

This poses the question of whether something is a tradition that glorifies war and aggression or that ennobles what is necessary for the protection of the weak and keeps an eye on the qualities of those who lead. Health-wise, this indicates a thorough inspection – or the need for one.

KEEP FOCUSED ON ... what 'glory' really is, and accept no substitute ... getting the very best medical care ... what good deeds have been done as the only real testament of worth ... being true to your highest ideals and values ... what is 'high', for it will support and guide you.

WATCH OUT FOR ... simply looking good as an indication of good health; how you feel on the inside could be an issue ... false prophets ... fancy credentials; are they genuine and do they count for much?

'Rank imposes obligation'

A CROSS LYING ON ROCKS

☆ ACCOUNTABILITY ☆

✦ GENERAL INTERPRETATION

Whatever is divine or holy in one is in danger of being discarded or given up on in the face of a world that is apt to ridicule such idealism. But it is this very sense of something higher and greater that is able to transform the world into a better place. We must be prepared to put our shoulder to the task.

KEEP FOCUSED ON ... your consistent expression of there being a higher purpose to life that is born of a sense of spiritual values and duties ... regenerating your faith that things will ultimately be for the better, mainly because of the sacrifices you are making or have made.

WATCH OUT FOR ... giving up, hopelessness, being feeble.

♥ LOVE/RELATING/SOCIAL

We are often tempted to avoid or escape from a relationship or person regarded as a burden.

KEEP FOCUSED ON ... taking responsibility for choices and actions. Failing to do this is bound to find you presented with the same problem, possibly with another person ... ascertaining who is responsible for what in a relationship or social situation, and making sure that each lives up to it – especially yourself.

WATCH OUT FOR ... forsaking anyone who is important to you, including anyone who is a great responsibility to you – or even an embarrassment – as they shall remain so until you honour them and do right by them ... carrying burdens for another which they can and must eventually carry themselves.

♟ MONEY/WORK/CREATIVITY

This is about doing whatever you do *in the name of* something higher and better, or in the name of whatever sentiment you hold dear. This could well be a labour of love. Although material reward may be minimal or temporarily non-existent, job satisfaction more than compensates. However, doing your job for no more than selfish or financial reasons will eventually find you a slave to whatever or whoever you work for, or a victim of its lack of real meaning or direction.

KEEP FOCUSED ON ... discovering nobler and more wonderful reasons for the work you do, or if you cannot do that, change your line of work or who you work for. If you have no work it is for the same reason, you have lost sight of the right reason for having a job – so find it; ask the Oracle.

WATCH OUT FOR ... having your devotion or commitment taken advantage of ... being poorly rewarded.

☯ KARMA/ATTITUDE/HEALTH

This suggests an abandoned or bankrupt faith, and whatever burden goes with it. Eventually this poses finding a higher reason for what one does and then taking it up again, or holding yourself accountable to something greater than yourself, or for a karmic debt and doing your duty by it.

KEEP FOCUSED ON ... what any suffering signifies, for therein lies the key to your issue. Physical pain or complaint is your unconscious mind's way of telling you that you have to carry your load even if you have avoided taking up a challenge or cause consciously. It would be better to ascertain what your 'cross' is and bear it deliberately, gladly and creatively, as opposed to bearing it as apparently meaningless pain ... what else a cross might mean regarding your question.

WATCH OUT FOR ... the possibility that you no longer need carry a cross – but be very sure of this.

'... before the rooster crows today, you will deny three times that you know me'

A GIRL BLOWING A BUGLE

☆ THE CALL OF THE FEMININE ☆

 GENERAL INTERPRETATION

The situation engenders a call to rally 'female' forces, to muster resources and potential, based on an intuitive feeling rather than a logically defined objective. This may be in order to achieve an important or momentous goal that is only dimly conceived at present – but very much on the way all the same. This is akin to a woman being newly pregnant, or better still, being aware of this on conception.

KEEP FOCUSED ON ... putting energy into whatever you and others feel strongly about and that has a ring of significance, into the realization of a vision, or meeting some future need ... believing and making known your hunches and instincts.

WATCH OUT FOR ... an attitude that is blind to the fact that not everyone has the same interests and priorities ... hysterical fears or desires.

♡ LOVE/RELATING/SOCIAL

Attention is being called to the role of the female in society or in a particular relationship. It may be you who is having to make that call or who is having to attend to it.

KEEP FOCUSED ON ... the values and contributions that the feminine brings to the situation or relationship. This may involve something that is freely given or a sympathetic response, and as such can be overlooked ... being awake to what your feelings are telling you, and following them ... proactive femininity – deliberately making it known to yourself and others what feminine qualities are, and consciously expressing them.

WATCH OUT FOR ... undervaluing or overlooking 'invisible assets' such as being accommodating, compassionate, pleasant or obliging.

 MONEY/WORK/CREATIVITY

Weighing the pros and cons of whatever concerns you could be missing the point. What is important now is the freshness and overall feel about your project, product, situation or idea. The actual objective may be far-flung, but you should be 'pregnant' with the feeling that it is going somewhere, even if it takes generations or many attempts to get there. Enterprises that are concerned with, say, the female take on war or abuses of Nature are well-starred here, but the same long-term, intuitive, visionary view needs to be incorporated.

KEEP FOCUSED ON ... rallying yourself and others to the 'cause', and reminding yourself and others what that cause is about ... whatever or whoever inspires you, that keeps you alive to what you and others are doing.

WATCH OUT FOR ... being carried away by overly subjective, misinformed or ill-timed enthusiasm.

⊛ KARMA/ATTITUDE/HEALTH

Female forces are being aroused in some way, for good or ill. This could mean anything from the forces of intuition to the power of hormones. Being made available is an awareness of the two major aspects of the feminine: mother and lover – and possibly a balance needs to be struck between the two. Karmically, the time has arrived when the female power is in the ascendant, which means that the best and the worst of motherhood and female sexuality is being made known to us.

KEEP FOCUSED ON ... seeing femininity as being basically good, and what is 'bad' is often just branded that way by males who feel threatened by the innate supremacy of the feminine.

WATCH OUT FOR ... oestrogen/progesterone levels and balance ... pollution of the environment.

'Consider her ways, and be wise'

A JOCKEY

☆ POSITIONING ONESELF ☆

✱ GENERAL INTERPRETATION

Occasioned or called for here is the skill, courage and determination necessary to achieve a position in life against stiff competition. Commanding one's animal drives could also be a factor here. Implicit is the necessity of competition as a challenge to win or overcome, and the fact that in the end it is all down to you.

KEEP FOCUSED ON ... your good-natured drive to prove yourself in the field of human endeavour – and to 'keep your seat' ... the 'form' of the object of your concern, for this will tell you much you want to know.

WATCH OUT FOR ... a cruel and hard-bitten ambition to succeed at any cost ... not playing by the rules (there are some) – you could get disqualified.

♥ LOVE/RELATING/SOCIAL

A possible scenario is that you or another are competing for the affections of someone else. This could be a conventional love triangle, a case of a parent being jealous of their child's partner for the attention they receive, or any such competitive set-up. Or simply trying to win a social position or the object of one's desire.

KEEP FOCUSED ON ... the fact that love and rivalry are linked, at least from a primitive standpoint ... the question of which is the better man or woman – time and effort will tell ... not being unnerved by the competition.

WATCH OUT FOR ... pursuing someone merely because you like the chase; do you actually want to commit to them? If not, your victory would be hollow and embarrassing, not to say cruel.

♕ MONEY/WORK/CREATIVITY

We see here a highly competitive world where everyone is out for themselves. There is also the ever-present possibility of questionable or illegal goings on.

KEEP FOCUSED ON ... keeping your weight down, if you want to stay in the race; in other words, do with less ... being more ambitious and ruthless, but only if the end really justify the means ... the possibility that you are coming up on the outside – that is, you'll win in the long run.

WATCH OUT FOR ... what kind of race you are in – a horse race, the human race or the rat race? Is all this jockeying for position worth it to your body and soul ... falling, for no matter how lucky or skilled you are there is always the possibility of an accident – something which causes you to question what you are doing and where you are heading ... being deliberately cut up or boxed in by someone after the same thing as you.

☯ KARMA/ATTITUDE/HEALTH

The race that is life itself – an endless race, which cannot be won, as such. The important thing is that you are only as good as your 'form' or karma of good deeds and sins of commission and omission. However, supreme effort and courage can always win the day, surprising the expectations of the majority. An outsider can always win or at least make a good showing.

KEEP FOCUSED ON ... disciplining and pacing yourself ... developing poise and stamina ... maintaining your correct weight ... positioning yourself for a breakthrough at a later stage ... assessing your chances through past form ... the finishing post or whatever is your overall objective in life.

WATCH OUT FOR ... antagonizing others, for they could balk or unseat you later on.

'May the best man or woman win'

AN AVIATOR IN THE CLOUDS

☆ POOR VISIBILITY ☆

✸ GENERAL INTERPRETATION

Being in a position where you, or the object of your enquiry, cannot be seen clearly, yet at the same time there is the potential of gaining a far better perspective when current doubts or obscuring conditions disperse. Because of this, the Oracle may not be able to help you right now, so try again later. But read on, all the same.

KEEP FOCUSED ON ... your capacity for seeing individual matters in relation to the whole and being guided by long-term goals.

WATCH OUT FOR ... the fact that by dint of circumstance you are not in full possession of the facts ... an aloofness that helps and impresses no one, and that means no one is aware of your isolation ... thinking you are sailing above your problems when really you are lost in them, or evading them.

♥ LOVE/RELATING/SOCIAL

Emotional fog and mental pollution in the form of confused, conflicting feelings and poor communication and awareness are dogging your love, social or domestic life. However, it will eventually clear up. This Symbol could also refer to someone who is aloof and hard to reach or confused emotionally, or is deluded.

KEEP FOCUSED ON ... rising above the fog and pollution by not allowing yourself to be sucked into conflicts and demands (either from others or yourself) for what is erroneously thought to be needed or wanted ... discovering emotional independence by putting yourself in a neutral position.

WATCH OUT FOR ... trying to force a solution – you will just get more lost, confused and agitated ... anything obscuring the truth.

♟ MONEY/WORK/CREATIVITY

Flying by the seat of one's pants could be what the Oracle says you are doing here, or you are having to proceed with a minimum of information, input or feedback until the 'clouds' clear.

KEEP FOCUSED ON ... having or maintaining a strong sense of direction, no matter what assails you ... clarifying matters, or waiting for them to clear up, before making any decision or move ... obtaining whatever is available to navigate you through difficulties, such as professional expertise of some kind.

WATCH OUT FOR ... it being a case of your own doubts or refusal to see being the 'clouds' that are confusing or blocking your progress ... blocking tactics and intrigues that are preventing you from seeing what is happening.

☯ KARMA/ATTITUDE/HEALTH

It is often not clear where one is or where one is headed, but one is proceeding all the same. At times like this it is advisable to 'fly by instruments only' – any means from intuition to this Oracle that you regard as 'ground or mission control'. Using one's usual means of perception – believing what appears to be happening – could be misleading. At a more evolved level, this Symbol is referring to transcendental powers of perceiving and comprehending the plan of life on Earth, with a view to helping solve mankind's problems, seeing through its illusions, being free of its polluting ways.

KEEP FOCUSED ON ... whatever now is right in front of you that you have some control over; doing and using this will carry you safely through.

WATCH OUT FOR ... thinking the Oracle can answer all health questions; just see a practitioner.

'Obstacles are those frightful things you see when you take your eyes off your goal'

MEN SEEKING ILLUMINATION

☆ ON THE PATH ☆

⚙ GENERAL INTERPRETATION

Firstly, here is someone who is genuinely looking – or a situation that is calling – for self-knowledge and enlightenment. Then there is the point that there is such a thing as 'illumination' and that Humanity, collectively and individually, has long been seeking it. At any one time, far fewer people are seeking illumination than are not; the Path of seeking illumination has to go against the grain of conventional life and denies us of its comforts and illusory assurances. The Path involves discipline and hardship.

KEEP FOCUSED ON ... developing a firm yet gentle nature through discovering and expressing the higher qualities of yourself and human nature.

WATCH OUT FOR ... any pretence of spirituality ... anything that needlessly darkens the Path, while still confronting your own darkness.

❤ LOVE/RELATING/SOCIAL

Whether it is known or not, this relationship – or your social life generally – is making you more aware of who you are as an individual. This would also be the case if you were not involved in a relationship at all. However, many of us are forced to seek illumination through relationships because at dark and critical points it is only through love, understanding and self-knowledge that a relationship can find light and harmony at all – and find a way through the shadows that a relationship, or being alone, may cast.

KEEP FOCUSED ON ... whoever you are involved with in the knowledge that they are showing you something important ... a partner as your greatest teacher.

WATCH OUT FOR ... blaming others for anything; they are simply catching your shadow.

⚒ MONEY/WORK/CREATIVITY

Your work may engender ideas or values that are too elevated or rarefied for the 'man in the street'. Yours could be a specialized field in that it seeks to shed light on matters that many would prefer to leave in the dark, or would simply not appreciate or recognize. On a more mundane note, this Symbol could be saying that you will find out what you need to find out when the time comes for it to be known – like the result of an interview, for example.

KEEP FOCUSED ON ... seeking to find a way that enlightens those who need it – this could also include yourself; persevering in this when things are looking dim.

WATCH OUT FOR ... trying to illuminate others when you have not yet found illumination yourself, or when you are no further down the Path than they are.

☯ KARMA/ATTITUDE/HEALTH

'Master, how can I walk a peaceful path when the world is so unpeaceful?' 'Peace lies not in the world, Grasshopper, but in the man who walks the path.' This dialogue between Caine and his guru from the TV series *Kung Fu* beautifully illustrates what is involved in discipleship, and in seeking truth and peace, and in being a living example of them.

KEEP FOCUSED ON ... the fact that the reality of your life is entirely self-created, including how much of it you leave, consciously or unconsciously, to the powers of Creation ... *allowing* yourself to be illuminated as much as, if not more than, actually *seeking* to be so ... the fact that the process of seeking a health cure is integral *to* the cure.

WATCH OUT FOR ... expecting a Damascene experience of sudden enlightenment ... 'spiritual bypassing', being into mystical and spiritual things as a blind to very real personality problems.

'Know thyself'

AN EXAMINATION OF INITIATES

☆ SPECIAL TESTS ☆

GENERAL INTERPRETATION

The demand that higher than usual standards are met, and that there is a conscious awareness that all things can be viewed in terms of a spiritual purpose. Having to do something original. Then again, this Symbol may be referring to any examination.

KEEP FOCUSED ON ... a way of living that is governed only by definite principles ... finding a way to allay anxiety regarding results, as this can sabotage one's efforts – with the exception of not having studied or practised sufficiently.

WATCH OUT FOR ... a false sense of superiority or exclusivity that is characterized by taking oneself too seriously ... using nerves as an excuse for failure, when something such as lack of discipline is the more likely culprit.

LOVE/RELATING/SOCIAL

Relationships here are in aid of the 'making of love' itself. This means that one or more people are aspiring to be selflessly concerned for others in the name of loyalty, and furthering evolution for the one and the many. More often than not such relationships will entail crises and catharses as one or more people are stripped of self-interest, and decadent lifestyles or attitudes are 'burned off'. Examinations passed take one to a higher level of living and loving.

KEEP FOCUSED ON ... any emotional conflicts as being challenges to identify and process negative emotions; this is an exercise of higher reasoning whereby conflicts are seen as the death throes of emotional attachments and sexual fixations.

WATCH OUT FOR ... projecting one's own issues onto another, projection being one of the key causes of strife and misunderstanding.

MONEY/WORK/CREATIVITY

Your work has, or should have, a spiritual connotation or purpose. As such it will test you in more ways than simply being 'spiritual', for it will call you to do something mundane and 'un-spiritual' in order to keep you materially. At the same time, your art or principles have to take precedence over money matters. So ...

KEEP FOCUSED ON ... being materially-minded only when needs must, having two jobs if necessary, in order to function in the *business* of living, being *in* the world of commerce but not *of* it ... your spiritual intent as being a long-term goal that has as its purpose the meeting of a collective need which is not purely material.

WATCH OUT FOR ... being seduced by the 'glamour' of doing something 'spiritual', because this will blind you to the hard work and dedication that is required of you.

KARMA/ATTITUDE/HEALTH

Initiation is the means by which an individual takes a more direct root to enlightenment. There are various types of initiation, depending on the esoteric tradition. Considering the background of the creators of the Sabian Symbols, initiation here is probably described by Theosophy, and the reader is referred to the writings of Alice Bailey, Dr Douglas Baker and Dion Fortune. Drawing this Symbol would imply that you are going through a process of initiation, and so should ...

KEEP FOCUSED ON ... the idea that you are learning to see and live life at a causal level, that you are the architect of your own life and fate ... seeing through illusions and self-deceptions.

WATCH OUT FOR ... licentiousness and gluttony, abusing alcohol and drugs, for these are like sand in the petrol tank of a car. They slow you down and eventually destroy the vehicle (your body) itself.

'Divine indifference ... signifies the refusal to be identified with anything save the spiritual reality'

A SWORD IN A MUSEUM

☆ BATTLES OVER ☆

⊛ GENERAL INTERPRETATION

This is a testament to courage in the field of battle or, more particularly, in a situation where the odds are definitely not in one's favour. Also implied here is the personal story behind such bravery, and which sets a multi-layered example to those who follow. Acts of heroism. Martial arts.

KEEP FOCUSED ON ... summoning or maintaining your grit and determination which serve to show others that nothing can defeat the human spirit ... not struggling or taking issue any more; then the conflict recedes into the past ... drawing from past achievements or dusting off things of proven value to serve you or others now.

WATCH OUT FOR ... having an attitude of mind or way of life that is not only hard-edged or aggressive, but also irrelevant or outmoded.

♥ LOVE/RELATING/SOCIAL

Either an end to a conflict or a need to bury the hatchet is imaged here. Letting matters drop and the forgiveness that this necessitates, probably also involving forgiving and being kind to yourself.

KEEP FOCUSED ON ... seeing aggression and argumentativeness as things of the past ... emphasizing and expressing love and understanding ... quelling anger and redirecting it into something more productive than taking issue with those close to you.

WATCH OUT FOR ... harking back to past wounds or conflicts, victories or defeats. This may give one a sense of justification, but it just provokes animosity and perpetuates strife.

⚒ MONEY/WORK/CREATIVITY

Merit accumulated in the past is what now serves you in the present. For instance, having an impressive CV or sales record now provides offers and opportunities, opens doors and gains approval. This could also be saying that there is no longer any need for aggressive tactics where work and acquiring money are concerned.

KEEP FOCUSED ON ... what has served you well or gained credit previously, for this will now enable you to win others over or reach your objective. Whether or not you have to be as forceful as before could be a question; your reputation may now go before you, precluding the need for pushing so hard.

WATCH OUT FOR ... assuming that all past glories have a relevance to the present. Fashions and the market values may have changed, so making past successes irrelevant, or even damning.

☯ KARMA/ATTITUDE/HEALTH

Any problems or conflicts in question are behind you, or soon will be. The difficulties that have gone before may now serve as a reminder that many, if not all, differences are illusions created by your internal conflicts and foolish regrets. This is evidenced by not being able to remember what a past fuss was all about. Then again, the battle may be over, but not the war. All the same ...

KEEP FOCUSED ON ... sorting out any conflicts with words and arbitration, or any other means rather than outright or veiled aggression. 'To jaw-jaw is always better than to war-war' as Sir Winston Churchill said back in 1954.

WATCH OUT FOR ... 'hanging up your spurs' or declining to take issue when confrontation or direct action is the only course to sorting things out.

'Little girl ... Sometime they'll give a war and nobody will come'

A LADY IN FOX FUR

☆ BEWITCHED, BOTHERED AND BEWILDERED ☆

✹ GENERAL INTERPRETATION

In the context of fashion during the period the Sabian Symbols were conceived (1920s), this Symbol could be said to represent a curious blend of sophistication and barbarity, taste and tastelessness, thus giving rise to a dramatic and arresting style. There is something about your situation that calls for this sort of attention – or is grabbing attention in this way. Enigma strikes.

KEEP FOCUSED ON ... your ability to combine contrasting elements to create a very effective impression ... being alive to contradictory elements and what they pose and elicit.

WATCH OUT FOR ... sensitivity posing as its opposite ... getting ensnared or confused by something or someone that has more impact than substance or meaning ... using the Oracle too much or indiscriminately; it'll muddy the waters.

♥ LOVE/RELATING/SOCIAL

Here is a relationship, individual or manner of relating that is not what it seems, doubts its worth, or is a minefield of conflicting needs and desires (*see* Karma below). There is animal magnetism here – perhaps a *femme fatale* or foxy lady.

KEEP FOCUSED ON ... treading very carefully, feeling your way for slippery patches or where you could find yourself in hot water ... the reason why you are allowing yourself to be seduced and beguiled, or why you are being seductive and beguiling.

WATCH OUT FOR ... treachery or danger, while at the same time avoiding being paranoid about it ... what you are after, or what is after you, being more trouble than it is worth. Then again, this might be the only way to get you involved in the emotional mysteries of life and love.

♟ MONEY/WORK/CREATIVITY

For success, the emphasis here is, or needs to be, on style. At the same time, there could be a danger of losing sight of the real value of something due to covering it up with too much. Hype and spin have their place, but can be counterproductive. Financially, cunning is in order – but not so much that you wind up foxing yourself and those that really need to know.

KEEP FOCUSED ON ... creating an impression that is eye-catching, powerful and possibly controversial ... making sure that you are able to maintain an image, and not let it slip.

WATCH OUT FOR ... artifice or conflicting interests creating trouble ... abusing animal rights or the environment ... trying to possess beauty or art, or it could bite the hand that feeds – or is it a case of shooting yourself in the foot?

☯ KARMA/ATTITUDE/HEALTH

Here is something that has to do with the link between sexuality and defensiveness. These two predominant human drives interweave through time, giving rise, for instance, to allure on the one hand and shyness on the other. At some point these mutually antagonizing but attracting elements need to be identified and unravelled, straightened out. Perhaps there is the need to express or receive warmth, but some sacrifice has to be made. The complexities of femaleness, such as attractiveness having to integrate with protective-ness, could be an issue, perhaps on a health level, such as frigidity or hormonal imbalance, for example.

KEEP FOCUSED ON ... the possibility that you may have to get baffled or hurt some more before you start to sort matters out.

WATCH OUT FOR ... being seen, sooner or later, for what you are behind any disguise.

'I expect that Woman will be the last thing civilized by Man'

AN OFFICER PREPARING TO DRILL HIS MEN

☆ A NEED FOR ORDER ☆

☀ GENERAL INTERPRETATION

You are, or should be, involved with the contemplation of what resources are available and how they must be organized, trained and disciplined in order that an effective impression may be made, secured and maintained – and that ultimate victory be achieved.

KEEP FOCUSED ON ... the rare ability you have to keep in focus an overall vision and intent in the face of potential danger or ridicule.

WATCH OUT FOR ... where, why and how there is resistance to authority or doing things in a conventional way. This would give cause for concern, and eventually create disorder and, worse still, prove unreliable in the face of real enemies or difficulties ... slavery to a formality that is part of something essentially destructive, or at least going nowhere.

MONEY/WORK/CREATIVITY

You are, or ought to be, organizing your talents and resources for maximum efficiency. Success depends upon strategy, discipline and organization. Without these ingredients your enterprise or state will, as is the natural order of things, sink to its lowest common denominator of efficiency.

KEEP FOCUSED ON ... your objectives and organize everything and everyone towards achieving them ... creating and maintaining a chain of command and a list of priorities ... making a feasibility study of whatever plans you have in mind ... assuming command.

WATCH OUT FOR ... being all order and ambition with no areas of playfulness and respite, or leeway given for natural appetites and inclinations. These must be limited rather than eradicated, for a lack of them would incite rebellion or inefficiency; too many would lead to disintegration.

♥ LOVE/RELATING/SOCIAL

The situation is as it is because there is a necessity for discipline and order being imposed on one or both of you, or on the group concerned. This first requires that you know how best to go about this – instilling discipline and order requires that you be disciplined and ordered yourself.

KEEP FOCUSED ON ... the nature of all the parts or aspects of the person or persons of your concern; be firm, cautious and somewhat distanced from those difficult or rebellious parts until they begin to fall into line, while favouring and appealing to those parts that are positive and co-operative.

WATCH OUT FOR ... awkward or errant parts for they may have to be allowed to consume themselves, learn through their own hard lessons in the school of life, maybe outside of the relationship ... being too strict or regimented.

☯ KARMA/ATTITUDE/HEALTH

Essentially this Symbol is referring to the various parts of a personality (sub-personalities) and how it is vitally important that there is a central part (the higher self) governing these sub-personalities. When one or more of these is not pulling its weight or acting as part of the team that makes up your personality as a whole, then the whole and its life and relationships suffer. For example, if one part of you wants to indulge too much, another part of you, such as your waistline and health, could suffer.

KEEP FOCUSED ON ... the likelihood that a lack of discipline or integration may have been in existence for a long time, so must have its root causes identified and examined, and must be granted time and patience in putting it right ... exercising mind over matter.

WATCH OUT FOR ... being too hard on yourself for this will have an adverse effect.

'A chain is only as strong as its weakest link'

THE FLOW OF INSPIRATION

☆ THE LINE OF LEAST RESISTANCE ☆

 GENERAL INTERPRETATION

Creativity, vitality and profound meaning stream forth from the psychical source of one's being when the minimum of effort is made and the ego is aligned with it in order to tap it. The Line Of Least Resistance is not merely taking the easy way out; it is accepting whatever you think or feel as being all right and allowing its expression, facilitated by disregarding or, rather, 'flowing over' any judgement or criticism from yourself or others – water off a duck's back. Flow means acceptance.

KEEP FOCUSED ON ... what everyone benefiting from your being in tune with whatever Nature or Spirit is calling for, in spite of lesser but tempting considerations – or the ego's fears and desires.

WATCH OUT FOR ... delusions of ease and awareness, and a lack of discipline ... whatever is too steep a learning curve, for it won't happen.

♥ LOVE/RELATING/SOCIAL

This Symbol could be referring to an inspiring, creative or uplifting person, relationship or social event – or it could be saying that a Line Of Least Resistance has to be found to make it work or tolerable. In the first case, well and good – but the second case demands that, for the time being at least, one has to find the path that just allows yourself and others to ebb or flow, according to their own wishes and disposition.

KEEP FOCUSED ON ... avoiding conflict or confrontation ... accepting things as they are, then feelings and moods will eventually free up, returning the current of events to an acceptable state ... being in tune with one another.

WATCH OUT FOR ... trying to force resolution, agreement or closure for this would worsen matters and entrench you more uncomfortably.

MONEY/WORK/CREATIVITY

This is about having, maintaining or needing cash flow or creative flow – or being on a roll. Being 'in flow' in the sense of being in the swim of things so as to create and be open to opportunity could also be an issue. The keys here are to ...

KEEP FOCUSED ON ... working through whatever needs it even though it might be boring, turgid and *un*inspiring; this is simply a blockage to flow that can and must be dissolved ... appreciating that income/inflow is dependent upon output/outflow, which means not only that you are as generous to give as you are open to receive, but also that investment should, in a direct fashion, further and maintain input ... not forcing solutions, let them come in their own time.

WATCH OUT FOR ... hanging on to money or being miserly for this blocks the flow more than anything ... clinging to ideas that do not work.

KARMA/ATTITUDE/HEALTH

Every human being is a channel, a receiver/transmitter for whatever the satellite dish of our senses and imagination is picking up. Likewise, our life or lifetimes can be seen as a continuous stream, with material existence being the banks of that life-stream. Health and quality of life depend on keeping this stream flowing freely through original creative expression and dissolving any blockages to flow that have been created by inhibitions resulting from fear (of ridicule) or ignorance of the fact that you are indeed a channel for inspiration and sensitivity.

KEEP FOCUSED ON ... allowing yourself to talk, act, paint, play, sing, laugh, cry, shout, rave or write whenever and in whatever way you want to, with or without others knowing about it.

WATCH OUT FOR ... censoring in any way what wants to come through you as words or actions.

'I'm swimming in the river, with the river swimming in me'

AN EASTER PARADE

☆ STEPPING OUT ☆

 GENERAL INTERPRETATION

The display of whatever is believed to be one's best qualities, in the spirit of each individual being a part of a greater whole. Having seen what you are made of, particularly in the moral sense.

KEEP FOCUSED ON ... your profound sense of occasion and the contributing roles that you and others play within it, thereby inspiring all to a greater sense of moment and community. What satisfies is feeling involved with something greater than just yourself ... putting your best foot forward ... just observing, if unsure ... taking steps to make your situation clear or known.

WATCH OUT FOR ... a preoccupation with the needs of self or fashion that misses the point of a collective event or of being one amongst many, or failing to get to the underlying cause or meaning of what is concerning you.

 MONEY/WORK/CREATIVITY

Whatever you have going for you is as nothing if it is not advertised and made available. On the other hand, putting your best foot forward in an imaginative and regular fashion will progressively attract the custom and acclaim you are after. With this proviso, this Symbol implies that your 'line' is very much on its way to success.

KEEP FOCUSED ON ... your most suitable and appealing qualities, and then make them known; from the feedback you get make adjustments to whatever needs it, and emphasize whatever hits the spot with others ... how stage by stage you reach your objective ... using topical events as opportunities to promote your interests.

WATCH OUT FOR ... superficial appeal rather than something that grabs people at a grassroots level ... making unnecessary sacrifices.

♥ **LOVE/RELATING/SOCIAL**

Any occasion where amusement, stimulation, a mate, or a sense of belonging is sought. Most people are socially opportunistic or competitive, rather than entering into an occasion with a sense of the deeper, more spiritual reasons for its existence.

KEEP FOCUSED ON ... finding out what you really want from your social or love life, and then pursuing it ardently; Easter was originally to do with Spring, when the sap begins to rise (*see* Karma below). The religious connotation confused this, but often making some sacrifice is the only way to relate appropriately.

WATCH OUT FOR ... entering into things with only a vague intention or a fanciful expectation, for you will be disappointed ... seeking to be on display when you are unsure or self-conscious; this would prove uncomfortable and the opposite of what you hoped for.

 KARMA/ATTITUDE/HEALTH

This is a surprisingly complex Symbol because the original meaning of Easter came from the word *oestrus*, sexual heat or impulse, and from *Eostre*, the goddess whose festival was held at the Spring Equinox. Then it was commandeered by the Christians to celebrate the resurrection of Christ. This was followed by the Easter Parade itself, which turned the whole thing into a social or fashion event. The common meaning here is therefore one of emerging or re-emerging, or just stepping out. So this is a birth of a new time or cycle, but what you think that means can make the difference between being a profound rebirth or a superficial attempt at being noticed for what you have to offer.

KEEP FOCUSED ON ... renewing yourself.

WATCH OUT FOR ... being stuck in a meaningless convention, or your own emptiness, for this could prove damaging to who you really are or wish to become ... 'Oestrogen Dominance'.

'Blossom by blossom the Spring begins'

A GIGANTIC TENT

☆ THE ARENA OF LIFE ☆

 GENERAL INTERPRETATION

This Symbol calls attention to the travelling show that is the ever self-conscious representation of all that life can be; dramatizing and bringing into intense focus all that is, and thereby enabling us to display our skills and our shortcomings.

KEEP FOCUSED ON ... identifying the part you play in the 'ring of life' and putting everything you've got into it ... the fact that the show must go on ... your situation as taking place in as large a context as possible – then you will get things into perspective.

WATCH OUT FOR ... inappropriate showmanship, hokum or over-ambition ... taking anything too personally for your situation is best viewed and experienced in the sense of life being long and big, and one's place in it of passing significance.

 MONEY/WORK/CREATIVITY

The circuses and fairs at which one might display your wares or seek them out. This could be a stand at a trade fair or the Internet, and this Symbol blesses and encourages any such enterprise or the use of one. Great possibilities, exalting prospects.

KEEP FOCUSED ON ... thinking big, and that there is plenty of room for all, be they buyer or seller, artist or audience ... making full use of the enormous potential that is available to you ... what is holding everything up, even though it may not be part of the 'show' itself (like 'guy ropes') ... advertising and publicity.

WATCH OUT FOR ... having too little to offer, or too small a canvas to paint your vision on ... making great plans while not paying attention to the details.

 LOVE/RELATING/SOCIAL

A generous and accommodating style or big-hearted person is imaged here. Or there is the need to approach social or romantic matters in a spirit of largesse. There is possibly more to the situation than you are yet aware.

KEEP FOCUSED ON ... the emotional life for the tragicomedy that it so often is. Make allowances for all manner of eventualities and moods ... the fact that there are elements in life you can control and those you cannot ... letting life and love live itself.

WATCH OUT FOR ... overreacting or being too dramatic for this could blow things out of proportion, creating the very disaster you are anxious of ... driving yourself into a frenzy trying to predict every possibility ... being or feeling hollow for want of emotional sincerity, enthusiasm or commitment.

KARMA/ATTITUDE/HEALTH

In the show that is life, human beings, as Shakespeare said '... have their exits and their entrances;/And one man in his time plays many parts,/His acts being seven ages'. Your situation calls you to adopt this attitude, otherwise you are in danger of attaching too much importance to yourself on the one hand, or too little on the other.

KEEP FOCUSED ON ... all your lives and all the experiences within those lives as being an endless tapestry, the meaning of which is only gained by taking a step back from it.

WATCH OUT FOR ... feeling that you account for nothing, or that life is a big and empty affair. Sometimes it might seem that way, but that is possibly because you are not entering into the spirit of things, or because you believe the show is over. The show is never over; there are just pauses between the various acts.

'All the world's a stage,/And all the men and woman merely players'

A MASTER INSTRUCTING HIS PUPIL

☆ ON GUIDING AND BEING GUIDED ☆

☀ GENERAL INTERPRETATION

Through the situation, you are being taught, subtly or obviously, something you need to learn that will take you forward. But, as it is said, when one is ready for something to happen, only then will it happen. Such readiness may not be conscious.

KEEP FOCUSED ON ... seeking out the advice or knowledge you need; it is out there waiting for you to find it. If you do not know what you are supposed to be learning, then ask the Oracle again ... practising what you preach, walking your talk, being true to what you say or believe is true.

WATCH OUT FOR ... forever studying but never doing ... teachers who do not practise what they preach, or are in some other way not to be respected. This does not mean to say they cannot be merely human – supposing that they *are* human.

♥ LOVE/RELATING/SOCIAL

Every relationship has the potential to be a teaching and learning experience, but this one most definitely is. Furthermore, one or both of you should be aware of this. This counsels you to decide in what areas one of you is 'master' and the other 'pupil', and to grant, with grace, authority where it is due.

KEEP FOCUSED ON ... what the relationship is telling you about you and your life – and act upon it ... that such a teacher–pupil relationship could be spiritual ... learning from each other, and developing the humility that makes this possible. There is always something we need to learn.

WATCH OUT FOR ... people who keep telling you what to do, say or be, but do not live up to their own advice or criteria ... 'lecturing' for it smacks of self-righteousness and a lack of grace.

⚘ MONEY/WORK/CREATIVITY

Whether it is literally or figuratively a case of being in a teaching–learning situation, this Symbol is a strong confirmation of the rightness of the auspiciousness of the situation. It is instructing you to obey and be true to whatever you are teaching or being taught, and to who is doing the teaching and the learning.

KEEP FOCUSED ON ... the probability that we teach what we wish to know, and that those we are teaching are teaching us something too. In this way our knowledge and methods are always fresh and effective ... your Muse, whoever or whatever inspires you and shows you what form to give things ... learning what you need to learn; teaching what (you) must be taught.

WATCH OUT FOR ... pomposity or an air of intel-lectual superiority, for this distances us from those we are trying to reach, or whatever is trying to reach us.

☯ KARMA/ATTITUDE/HEALTH

This is one of the most direct and literal Sabian Symbols. It is important to recognize that someone is learning or hearing something that they need to learn or hear, and that they should bow to the authority of whoever is doing the teaching. Equally, someone is there doing the teaching and the telling, and they should recognize the fact.

KEEP FOCUSED ON ... whatever teachings inspire you, and give form to them, be a good example of them ... trusting what rings true, what has respect and admiration.

WATCH OUT FOR ... thinking you have the answer when you have not yet acknowledged that you have a burning question ... ignoring or not recognizing your teacher, for possibly they cannot or will not always be there for you ... false gurus.

'When the student is ready, the master appears'

A TABLE SET FOR AN EVENING MEAL

☆ ULTIMATE SATISFACTION ☆

 GENERAL INTERPRETATION

Apart from there being a more personal interpretation here (for mealtimes do have very particular associations for different people) this speaks of the prospect of reward and repose that comes at the end of any period of effort or activity.

KEEP FOCUSED ON ... your sensitivity to the innate pleasure and reassurance that humans draw from simple and familiar formalities ... making good preparation for whatever you have in mind; this is the key to success.

WATCH OUT FOR ... obscuring what the Oracle is trying to tell you by overlaying it with too fixed an idea or expectation of what you think its reply should be, or of what is going to happen as a consequence (of the object of your concern).

 LOVE/RELATING/SOCIAL

Everything is in place for a rewarding relationship to occur – but this could just be a case of your expectations. In other words, the Symbol gives no indication that any 'food' or 'guests' are on the way, just that there is a readiness and anticipation of them. So ...

KEEP FOCUSED ON ... making yourself as attractive and available as possible ... what experience and effort you have had or put in with regard to your love and social life as this should give you some indication of what to expect.

WATCH OUT FOR ... having too 'set' an idea of what kind of relationship you deserve or are involved in; the contrast between this and the reality could find you mistaken, disappointed or making too tall an order for Fate or another to fill ... idly hoping for something to 'crop up', you could get very hungry that way!

 MONEY/WORK/CREATIVITY

The fruits of our labours are naturally dependent on those labours. There is also the indication of inheritance here, in the sense that provision has been made, and when the time comes the 'food' shall be served. Practically speaking, it is saying that you have the tools and plans ready, and possibly the product too, and now you are waiting to see who comes to buy.

KEEP FOCUSED ON ... making sure that the groundwork is done thoroughly and efficiently, and then you can expect the rest to follow. Effort will eventually be amply rewarded.

WATCH OUT FOR ... being over-prepared, for this can inhibit or confuse a natural flow of events ... preparing without knowing what you are actually preparing for; this can be an enormous waste of time and effort.

 KARMA/ATTITUDE/HEALTH

As the 'evening' is symbolic of the end of a cycle, in this context we are looking at preparing ourselves for it, making ready for whatever or whoever relates to such a time. There is even a suggestion of a 'last supper' here. Apart from this, the Oracle is saying that an eventuality has been made ready for, and so you can expect some form of realization or denouement. Health-wise, a definite diet is being suggested or approved of, and that perhaps it should be made a ritual of so that it might be more attractive and effective.

KEEP FOCUSED ON ... the belief that a place has been made ready for you, meaning that ultimately all will be well, all is set out as it should be in the light of this certainty.

WATCH OUT FOR ... expecting closure, success or fulfilment when only a perfunctory input has been made, or a diet not kept to.

'Thou shalt prepare a table before me against them that trouble me ... and my cup shall be full'

A LITTLE WHITE LAMB, A CHILD AND A CHINESE SERVANT

☆ PURITY, INNOCENCE AND WATCHFULNESS ☆

✹ GENERAL INTERPRETATION

A basic and sensuous curiosity, overseen by something or someone who is objective and aware of the vagaries of life, making for a special experience or result, a particularly immediate sense of what is actually happening.

KEEP FOCUSED ON ... creating a blend of guileless simplicity and a mature gentle awareness ... making the most of your potentials, which are evidently considerable, not least because you are modest about them ... monitoring or taking care of anything or anyone that is vulnerable to being taken advantage of or losing its way.

WATCH OUT FOR ... a naivety that needs to recognize its essential value if it is to avoid feeling victimized and disempowered ... any kind of perverting influence that distorts or abuses childlike innocence and purity of intent.

♡ LOVE/RELATING/SOCIAL

There are elements to your situation that can appear diverse and unrelated. When viewed from a more enlightened perspective though, they fit together perfectly, complementing and supporting one another, and revealing something quite special. To enjoy this infinitely more positive scenario ...

KEEP FOCUSED ON ... the inner or 'soul' qualities of those involved rather than mere personality traits ... respecting the softness and childlike qualities of whoever you are concerned with, while at the same time unobtrusively monitoring what is going on ... relating in a spontaneous and helpful fashion, for this is bound to bring out the best in everyone.

WATCH OUT FOR ... viewing what is happening through cynical or resentful eyes.

♟ MONEY/WORK/CREATIVITY

The images in this Symbol would seem out of place in the world of ambition and money, implying that what you have in mind has little place in, or chance of succeeding with, such things – or that you are trying, or need to try, to inject simplicity and guilelessness into the work and financial sphere. On a literal level, any occupations or enterprises that have purification or selfless service as their predominant theme are well-starred.

KEEP FOCUSED ON ... introducing or pursuing charitable works or non-profit motivated activities, wherever possible ... being motivated by the purest of values; creatively this would mean being inspired by noble values rather than by the lower ones that may be those of the market-place.

WATCH OUT FOR ... prostituting yourself, your art or your principles for the sake of making a profit ... being an 'innocent abroad'.

☯ KARMA/ATTITUDE/HEALTH

Pure, or at least, purer living is indicated or recommended here, be it for purposes of health, spirituality or both. There is also the suggestion of Oriental or non-allopathic medicine. There is a profound beauty in innocence and simplicity, and this quality is present or available to you. Also available is a modest wisdom, or a wisdom through being modest.

KEEP FOCUSED ON ... aligning yourself to a whole-souled purpose ... meditating or pondering on the image of this Symbol for this would put you in touch with what it is that you need to heal or further your current concern.

WATCH OUT FOR ... being sucked in or polluted by influences that the figures in this Symbol would naturally shy away from ... believing that being puritanical, squeaky clean or spiritual in a merely intellectual way is going to get you or anyone else closer to God.

'Childlike simplicity is both precious and powerful – and must be guarded well'

A MAN BRINGING DOWN THE NEW LAW FROM SINAI

☆ MODERN MORAL CODE ☆

 GENERAL INTERPRETATION

This Symbol obviously alludes to Moses receiving the Ten Commandments, as written in the Old Testament. The introduction and enforcement of these laws were necessary to bring the Children of Israel into line at a critical time in their history. Whatever is your situation now, it is in need of firm and definite guidelines.

KEEP FOCUSED ON ... any scriptures that you feel have value for you and yours. Feel free to amend them with certain reservations; for example 'Honour thy father and mother' from the Ten Commandments should not give them carte blanche to do what they want and get away with inadequate care, cruelty, hypocrisy, emotional blackmail or any other poisonous parental 'sin'.

WATCH OUT FOR ... any principles based more on control and fear than on order and love.

 LOVE/RELATING/SOCIAL

The decline of traditional and universally accepted values since the beginning of the Twentieth Century often finds us with emotional or domestic dilemmas that hitherto would not have arisen – or at least, there would have been a ready solution to them, like it or not. We need to rediscover or invent for ourselves a moral code that lays down the laws and limitations necessary for a more stable emotional life.

KEEP FOCUSED ON ... determining, agreeing upon and setting down certain principles which make it clear what is expected of whom. Such principles must take precedence over everything else, otherwise the exercise is worthless. In other words, anyone not abiding by your agreed code jeopardizes their normal rights and privileges within a relationship.

WATCH OUT FOR ... being too flexible or rigid.

 MONEY/WORK/CREATIVITY

A new system or legislature is at hand and you must either conform to it or challenge it. What you do depends greatly on your own innermost values and convictions. Then again, a new product or market situation could be making an opportunity for you. If it is you who is introducing something new, especially if there is a moral element to it, then be prepared for hard work in putting it across. If valid it will eventually prevail.

KEEP FOCUSED ON ... the whole lie of the land with respect to the object of your concern, for something is coming down that is going to bear on it in an important way ... having and being true to a code of practice.

WATCH OUT FOR ... trying to serve two masters – at least, for too long – for this will ultimately find you out of favour with both of them.

 KARMA/ATTITUDE/HEALTH

As if in answer to the need for guiding principles, someone or something may now appear on the scene to introduce these very things. Through striving against great odds to reach heights of awareness and true morality, an authority combined with humility and reverence is attained – and dispensed to those ready to receive. It may be falling to you to discover such principles and put them forward. For well-being and health, this Symbol is referring to the need for a strict regimen, and that it must be kept to if it is going to be effective.

KEEP FOCUSED ON ... your selfless sense of service and order born of an urge to further the ultimate uplift of all within your reach.

WATCH OUT FOR ... self-righteousness leading to megalomania ... anyone (including yourself) who thinks they have all the answers.

'Without limitations there comes chaos'

SPIRITIST PHENOMENA

☆ IS THERE ANYBODY THERE? ☆

 GENERAL INTERPRETATION

The subtler reality that penetrates the one we live in day to day, that can offer us guidance and consolation, or that frightens us and so limits our lives. Ghosts, fairies and spirit guides exist for those who have the sensitivity to perceive them.

KEEP FOCUSED ON ... the part of you that is pure 'receiver', that is purely a channel for whatever is presently passing through or is drawn to your space ... what is happening inside you, for therein lies the answers to your questions.

WATCH OUT FOR ... fanciful and irrational notions that may attract the very dilemmas they are attempting to evade ... wasting time and energy looking on the outside for what exists only on the inside. The body is more than just physical.

 LOVE/RELATING/SOCIAL

You have to be very careful in the assessment of the object of your enquiry. The person involved (and this could mean you) is prone to being caught up with romantic expectations and illusions of love and life rather than something more real and substantial. If this is to your taste, then enter that mist, but be aware that this is all it may be. Alternatively, this could be a relationship specifically concerned with psychic pursuits, or it should be handled in a metaphysical way.

KEEP FOCUSED ON ... the finest and most sentimental aspects of the relationship or person, honouring them for their soulful, otherworldly qualities. But ...

WATCH OUT FOR ... committing yourself or your possessions until there is a substantial show of commitment from the other party.

 MONEY/WORK/CREATIVITY

Possibly you are giving form to something from the 'other side', channelling material from another plane of existence, or literally involved with mediumistic work. The Oracle could be said to be favouring such activities, but it is also probably urging you to be guarded against believing that what you are doing is utterly reliable or extraordinary in some way. It may well be, but if you are not sure, ask the Oracle.

KEEP FOCUSED ON ... the effects that your work has upon others. If it is positive, then that is all the proof you need that you and your 'contacts' are genuine.

WATCH OUT FOR ... going overboard with metaphysical energies on the one hand, or cynically discounting them on the other. See how they run, then form an opinion.

KARMA/ATTITUDE/HEALTH

This Symbol patently refers to subtle and psychic realms of existence, and urges you to view the object of your enquiry in that light. In terms of karma, we as beings are 'spiritist phenomena' in that we are spirits manifesting in the physical world. Our attitudes send out subtle impressions to the world around us, and also come back to us as subtle impressions. The state of our souls, and how firmly ensconced they are in our bodies, has everything to do with how healthy we feel or are.

KEEP FOCUSED ON ... in what way the 'other side' relates to the object of your enquiry, for it is trying to tell you something about it ... fruitful areas of search such as soul retrieval, regression, psychic surgery and discarnate doctors.

WATCH OUT FOR ... the reliability and credentials of anyone you choose to be involved with in respect of such psychical work.

'We are such stuff/As dreams are made on, and our little life/Is rounded with a sleep'

AN INHABITED ISLAND

✧ FILLED WITH LIFE ✧

 GENERAL INTERPRETATION

Ultimately it is a matter of free choice as to what one fills one's life with, and how one governs it. The surrounding circumstances are of course owed deep consideration, but ultimately they are beyond one's total understanding and control, and therefore have to be accepted for the mystery they are and left to their own devices. It is better by far to …

KEEP FOCUSED ON … whatever area of endeavour you do have some direct influence upon and interest in … the possibility of achievement and satisfaction born of a creative sense of opportunity and practical ability.

WATCH OUT FOR … complacency and apathy, possibly born of exclusiveness or a sad lack of enthusiasm … letting in 'unwelcome aliens', that is, anything that disturbs or saps you, that is just 'not you' … being over-defensive, insular.

 LOVE/RELATING/SOCIAL

Any relationship, be it with one or many people, can be regarded as a rich opportunity to develop and discover yourself and realize your potentials. It also entails learning how to coexist, which in turn means making allowances for one another and sharing resources. This Symbol is saying that you are becoming more socially integrated and active – or at least have the opportunity to.

KEEP FOCUSED ON … befriending and co-operating with others as much as possible … seeing others as being the same as you, in that they have similar hopes and fears.

WATCH OUT FOR … harbouring feelings of alienation, envy or resentment, for they create a feedback from others that can be perceived as hostile, perpetuating those very feelings and the uncomfortable situation that they attract.

 MONEY/WORK/CREATIVITY

You have a lot going for you here – at least potentially. This Symbol could also be referring to something ready-made that you are considering. Whatever the case, there is a wealth of talent and resources here, but you may have to be tactful and respectful in your manner of accessing it and making use of it. Some kind of co-operative would be auspicious.

KEEP FOCUSED ON … the layout of the object of your concern and how the various parts all function together – or not, as the case may be … allowing everything to reveal its nature and role, and come together organically in their own time, according to their own natures and inclinations … what works, allowing it to carry on that way … setting an example.

WATCH OUT FOR … imposing an overall plan or organization without knowing the nature of the various parts, or your part in it.

 KARMA/ATTITUDE/HEALTH

You 'populate' your mind and body with whatever you choose. If you do not do this, it may be invaded by something that is not 'you', such as viruses and bacteria, or negative feelings about life and others. Then again, anything that you experience could be seen as being 'you'. The critical factor is what you *make* of it, for this is ultimately and entirely up *to* you.

KEEP FOCUSED ON … making whatever you think or feel, particularly with regard to the object of your enquiry, into what you *like* and that serves your physical and psychological well-being … drawing a map of your 'island', populating it with whatever you feel is there or ought to be there, and rejecting whatever you think and feel should not be there … respecting all forms of life.

WATCH OUT FOR … entertaining ideas or feelings that do not belong in your true state of being.

'No man is an island, entire of itself'

THE PURGING OF THE PRIESTHOOD

☆ STOPPING THE ROT ☆

GENERAL INTERPRETATION

The situation is designed to purge you or others of egotistical drives and reactions. Undergoing a process of purification. The inevitable collapse that befalls those who pervert the truth in the name of upholding it. Although such a demise may be a long time in the coming, it does so because corruption ultimately corrupts itself, and because (being) a seeker after truth makes sure of this.

KEEP FOCUSED ON ... your avid and devoted commitment to dispelling anything that obscures the truth – be it in yourself or others ... the process of purification that is under way; somehow or the other, you must accept it and facilitate it ... putting a stop to longstanding negative practices.

WATCH OUT FOR ... wearing a hair shirt or being holier-than-thou ... anything that pollutes or perverts, and resist it.

MONEY/WORK/CREATIVITY

The Oracle is favouring any endeavour that has an interest in restoring to the world the natural and humanitarian element, be it on a global or local scale. The Oracle is disfavouring anything that has dubious content or intentions that are entirely self-interested or profit-motivated, or has a dubious political agenda.

KEEP FOCUSED ON ... being a part of the movement that promotes natural living, that introduces sound and healthy ideas, that is kind and compassionate, and that reveals the wrongs done to Humanity, the natural world and the feminine, and brings any perpetrators to book.

WATCH OUT FOR ... there is a process of global purification going on, courtesy of human, divine and natural agencies. Any political, professional or environmental malpractice will eventually be found out or will create disaster for all concerned.

♥ LOVE/RELATING/SOCIAL

It is extremely rare for two or more people to come together and there being no issues arising that have deep and dark origins. The nature of the issue in this case is one of power and belief – the power that one or more people believe or do not believe they have. Powerful emotions such as anger and morbid fears, desires or needs, are what have to be identified, dealt with and eliminated if they are not going to be destructive.

KEEP FOCUSED ON ... what it is in your own nature or behaviour that is wrong – thinking you are always right is at the root of the problem ... being ruthlessly honest with yourself.

WATCH OUT FOR ... feelings of rage mixed with self-righteousness – for you can be sure that either you are victim, oppressor or both, and such traits must be got rid of before they inflict (more) damage.

KARMA/ATTITUDE/HEALTH

'Priesthood' means any authority, originally male but not always, that holds sway, profoundly influencing the minds and bodies of the people. Here it is the negative influence we are talking about, and this can be anything from the literal case of perverted religious indoctrination to the political/scientific pollution of our planet, and thereby the destabilization of our minds and bodies.

KEEP FOCUSED ON ... identifying any destabilizing influence – be it in the environment, or your own physical body or karma – and eliminate it through activism, service, diet or atonement.

WATCH OUT FOR ... what you take into your mind through any media that is materially or politically motivated, or take into your body by way of chemically processed foods and other toxic substances. Boycott anyone or anything that fosters or perpetuates such activities and crimes.

'Pave your mind with stones of truth, keep every corner clear and bright'

A NEW MOON THAT DIVIDES ITS INFLUENCES

☆ HORSES FOR COURSES ☆

✺ GENERAL INTERPRETATION

What is new or significant can have decidedly different, even antipathetic, meanings for different groups or individuals. Being at the beginning of a new phase can find you split in two or more ways, forcing you to determine your priorities, or create a division of labour.

KEEP FOCUSED ON ... what matters to you most of all, and make that your priority, with anything else being disregarded or given considerably less significance. Then again, you may have to make a number of priorities ... being able to tune into the subtle inclinations or predilections of various types of people or ideas, and thereby create accord between them.

WATCH OUT FOR ... ambivalence or downright hypocrisy ... trying to 'have your cake and eat it' and then 'falling between two stools'.

♥ LOVE/RELATING/SOCIAL

The paradox of harmony in life and relationships is that it is sometimes found in each individual begging to differ, rather than insisting on being the same. Something has occurred, or is about to occur, that makes it necessary to appreciate such a paradox. You may find that the whole of your love or social life stands or falls by taking on board this significant point. When this has not been realized or understood, which may be the case here, such unaccepted differences can accumulate to a point of separation.

KEEP FOCUSED ON ... being true to 'live and let live', either in your current relationship or a future one, and then you will find true harmony.

WATCH OUT FOR ... the possibility that what you disagree with in another is what you are not sure of, or do not accept, in yourself.

MONEY/WORK/CREATIVITY

You are at a new point of departure in your career. Your nascent position in life entails various ideas and directions that cannot be forced to a conclusion ahead of a natural process of development. All you can do is ...

KEEP FOCUSED ON ... the various seeds and strands that are sprouting and burgeoning, ever watchful of which way they want to go. A New Moon is at first invisible, but then slowly and inexorably it waxes through Crescent to Full ... allowing what might appear to be unlikely ideas or combinations of ideas to unfold, without judging them to be one thing or the other ... being eclectic, that is, selecting, borrowing and choosing the best out of everything.

WATCH OUT FOR ... being aloof or self-critical for this would inhibit the flow of ideas or cash ... conflicts of interest; let them sort themselves out.

☯ KARMA/ATTITUDE/HEALTH

Like any birth, the new situation that you find yourself in can have its complications. This one does because it is rather like twins in the womb (something inside of you) fighting for who is going to be born first. This creates discomfort, alarm and delays. But all the little streams eventually merge and make one river.

KEEP FOCUSED ON ... allowing one or the other (idea, feeling, thought or person) to go first, take precedence, for it does not matter which, so long as they are released *now*. The drama can then play itself out rather than being left as an inner conflict which could create an emotional or physical problem. A thing cannot begin to unfold until it is allowed to.

WATCH OUT FOR ... signs of conflict and indecision. These will be in the form of feeling or being compromised, stuck, congested, constipated, blocked, unsure, doubtful, fearful or confused.

'Let the winds of the heavens dance between you'

A HARVEST MOON

☆ **REAP WHAT YOU SOW** ☆

 ### GENERAL INTERPRETATION

Occasioned or called for is an instinctual awareness not only of the abundance and fruitfulness of Nature, but also that effort and timing are vital ingredients with respect to benefiting from what is currently concerning you. Literally, the Harvest Moon is the Full Moon nearest the Autumnal Equinox.

KEEP FOCUSED ON ... the symbolism of any Full Moon, which is the maximum illumination of unconscious or emotional issues; the Harvest Moon is the most poignant of them all ... a fine appreciation of produce and worldly goods, as well as an ability to attract them for the benefit of all ... co-operating with Fate.

WATCH OUT FOR ... feeling that you have hit the jackpot just because a lot appears to be happening; the question is not 'How much?' but more 'What?' and 'Why?'

♥ LOVE/RELATING/SOCIAL

This is a so-called 'karmic relationship'. This means that it can include anything from meeting your soul mate to meeting your own emotional issues full on, whether you know what they are or not. The whole point here is that they are now being presented to you.

KEEP FOCUSED ON ... the emotional and practical implications of your relationships, for they are immensely powerful, important and full of potential for joy and pain, enlightenment and confusion ... what originally caused your current situation, for therein lies the answer or resolution.

WATCH OUT FOR ... falling under the illusion that a soul mate, or anyone you feel strongly for, is immediately going to bring you happiness and joy ... excessive sentimentality, for this would blind you to the reality of the situation, possibly incurring the loss of something valuable.

 ### MONEY/WORK/CREATIVITY

You are now in a position to see the fruits of your labours, or to set about making the most of them, tying things up in manageable bundles, getting products or ideas into a place where they can be stored or worked on in a safe and secure environment.

KEEP FOCUSED ON ... where and how you have worked hard and diligently, for reward is bound to come from there ... an awareness of the best and the worst, the profitable and the useless, the wheat and the chaff. Such knowledge is gold indeed.

WATCH OUT FOR ... counting your chickens before they've hatched; spending or using what you think you have got before thoroughly assessing it, seeing it with your own eyes ... bitter harvests, that is misfortunes that are no fault of your own, but which contain an important lesson ... being bitter about bitter harvests.

⊙ KARMA/ATTITUDE/HEALTH

This is the essence of karma itself, or more particularly, it emphasizes the fullness of the consequences of any previous action or set of actions, or lack of them. Getting what you deserve, be it good, bad or indifferent.

KEEP FOCUSED ON ... what has happened so far regarding the issue at stake, for all you wish to know, feel or have can be drawn from that ... saying, doing and thinking what is most positive with respect to the object of your concern, for this will eventually produce a wonderful effect or outcome ... what you feel you are in line for with a sense of acceptance.

WATCH OUT FOR ... saying, doing or thinking anything that you may regret, because this would be a case of 'sowing the wind and reaping the whirlwind' ... resting on your laurels before the job is done (the harvest home).

'And the lives of a man are strung like pearls on the thread of his spirit'

A FERTILE GARDEN UNDER THE FULL MOON

☆ POTENTIAL ABUNDANCE ☆

☀ GENERAL INTERPRETATION

An abundance or plenitude is imaged here, or at least there is the prospect of it. This may have its source in an unseen realm such as the imagination or as a reward for good deeds performed in the past. It also suggests that these rewards are experienced in the soft light of regular and unassuming activity, rather than the glaring light of spectacular activity. More esoterically, this Symbol points to the abundance contained within our dreams, for everything originally issues from there – the subconscious.

KEEP FOCUSED ON ... your never-ending supply, that is dependent only on your keeping your supply flowing.

WATCH OUT FOR ... wallowing in possessions ... a lack of awareness of potential wealth.

♥ LOVE/RELATING/SOCIAL

There are great possibilities in this person or relationship. All that is required is that the potential is realized. This is achieved through involvement and commitment, through 'planting' good feelings and ideas into the rich 'soil' which is that potential. Firstly, however, you need to ...

KEEP FOCUSED ON ... the nature of the potential of this relationship or person so that you might behold this goodness. Then you will know how to relate to it, get the best from it. Very much a case of getting out exactly what you put in – be they 'weeds' or 'roses'.

WATCH OUT FOR ... expecting what you want to appear overnight ... getting carried away with romantic or dramatic feelings, be they ecstasy or panic, for sooner or later both will fade into the common light of day.

MONEY/WORK/CREATIVITY

The potential for development and success is enormous here. The only thing that could stop your venture from being productive and profitable would be a failure to recognize and appreciate the great scope and opportunity that lies before you.

KEEP FOCUSED ON ... whatever is going on in your own imagination, and on the talents of those around you; these are clues that you should follow up. The cross-pollination and germination of ideas will then proceed apace, as too will the pooling of funds ... investing in whatever you feel is worth it, because it is – and some.

WATCH OUT FOR ... the abundance of ideas and opportunity itself being a problem. Simply start with one idea or product and the rest will follow and proliferate naturally ... the fact that such potential for abundance does not last forever; in fact, the possibilities are already in decline – so act now!

☯ KARMA/ATTITUDE/HEALTH

The time is ripe for you to make far more out of your life or, at least, to take in and appreciate what the fullness of life is, what possibilities are open to you, and then begin to partake of what it has to offer. Even though you might be in the midst of complications and dramas, this *is* life, *your* life.

KEEP FOCUSED ON ... this aspect of your reality, that it is an adventure wanting to happen, that whatever is happening is rich and eventful – or has the potential to be so if you surrender to it, let life live you rather than you trying to control life. In this respect ...

WATCH OUT FOR ... what chaos, frustration or boredom can mean in your life, for they are the result of not embracing or recognizing life's potential, possibly owing to a fear of the unknown, or to hanging on to old sterile attitudes and patterns of behaviour.

'There is no wealth but life'

A PRISM

☆ THE ONE AND THE MANY ☆

 GENERAL INTERPRETATION

Demonstrating fundamental and self-evident truths, such as the fact that white light breaks down into the visible spectrum of seven colours. Also, how the one can be seen in the many, and the many seen in the one; how everyone is the same but different – *'In lak'ech'*, as the Mayans greet, 'I am another (like) yourself.'

KEEP FOCUSED ON ... attaining a clarity of judgement and simplicity of expression that is a wonder to behold ... breaking down the issue of your concern into component parts and thereby understanding it better. Conversely, finding out how the various parts go to make up a whole.

WATCH OUT FOR ... stating the obvious to an extent that misses the point ... losing sight of something by reducing it down to meaning-less parts, such as reducing a rose to a heap of petals.

 MONEY/WORK/CREATIVITY

There is something or someone that is the 'originating factor'. You could call this the first principle, the inventor or artist, the founder. This 'originating factor' then got or gets broken down into various themes, branches, styles, offshoots and derivations. It is important therefore to ...

KEEP FOCUSED ON ... the precise nature of the 'originator factor', and then you will become clearer as to how it should be taking shape and organizing into meaningful, profitable and satisfactory individual parts or facets. In effect, you are being a prism, or you are finding someone else who acts as one, as an organizer of the many into the one, into an integrated whole, where each part knows what colour they are, what their job or role is supposed to be, and how they correspond to and with one another.

 LOVE/RELATING/SOCIAL

Here is a relationship or person that can reveal or expose definite traits of character that go to make up the individuals involved. Or it could be imaging a group that represents certain distinct qualities, yet is well integrated.

KEEP FOCUSED ON ... discerning what part you play in contributing to the relationship or group, for you most certainly do. What 'colours' are you? ... how certain qualities of other people complement your own, even though, or because, they sometimes contrast one another.

WATCH OUT FOR ... falling prey to the common illusion that a person or a relationship is only what they appear to be when you have explored and got to know a number of their shades. There is always an extra quality that is 'off the visible spectrum'. This is the mystery of personality.

KARMA/ATTITUDE/HEALTH

Esoterically, the breaking down of clear light into the colours of the spectrum symbolizes how pure spirit manifests as the various aspects or planes of being. In turn, these colours correspond to the energy centres or chakras. This Symbol suggests you ...

KEEP FOCUSED ON ... each of your chakras and visualize them as the following colours as a means of tuning, toning, realigning and revivifying them: Crown = Violet; Brow = Indigo; Throat = Blue; Heart = Green; Stomach = Yellow; Abdomen = Orange; Groin = Red. Then imagine a prism above your head, and visualize all the colours converging on the prism and coming out above it as clear light. You can then reverse the process, visualizing the clear light descending through the prism and breaking down into the spectrum. In the process you will discover less vibrant chakras which correspond to parts that need to be tuned or colour-intensified.

'To what is One, sages give many a title'

THE GREAT STONEFACE

☆ THE POWER OF VISION ☆

 GENERAL INTERPRETATION

This refers to the story by Nathaniel Hawthorne where a majestic rock formation resembling a face is seen by a boy as his ideal of greatness, and as the boy grows up he begins to look like it. So, the formative power of ideals and aspiration. Emulation.

KEEP FOCUSED ON ... your capacity to choose a creative objective, grow towards it and achieve it ... the fact that you have to believe in something and pursue it in order to find out whether or not it is attainable ... how through growing towards anything you and your vision develop and change accordingly.

WATCH OUT FOR ... trying to emulate the greatness of others at the expense of not being yourself ... casting expectations in stone for this means you would not be open to making the adjustments that would enable you to realize those plans.

 LOVE/RELATING/SOCIAL

Whatever you want a relationship to be like is what it shall become or be like. However, what you 'want' is often more unconscious than you would like to think, so the relationship you get is actually 'ideal' in that it perfectly fits your real, rather than supposed, idea of the right person or social situation. So ...

KEEP FOCUSED ON ... what you like or love about the other person, for that reflects what is positive about yourself, whereas what you dislike about them tells you what facets of your own personality must be reshaped, chipped off or smoothed down.

WATCH OUT FOR ... trying to make a person or relationship 'fit' your supposed 'ideal', then finding that they don't live up to it, simply because it was neurotic or too romantic ... 'stony-faced' people – best meet stone with stone, or with great compassion.

 MONEY/WORK/CREATIVITY

You have to have or create a goal in order to aim for it. If you have a goal, then this Symbol urges you to keep striving towards its realization, for it is as real as you make it. If you have not got a goal, then you must create one, or ask for something or someone to help you define it.

KEEP FOCUSED ON ... the precise features of what it is you wish to attain, and then you will find a way to do so ... some form of role model, and then emulate their positive characteristics – for example, if 'determination' is one of your role model's defining qualities, then *be* determined.

WATCH OUT FOR ... titanic aspirations for yourself that have no hope of realization, as evidenced by the lack of any impartial support for them.

 KARMA/ATTITUDE/HEALTH

Something which you have been striving towards for a long time breeds a complex array of feelings – from anxiety and despair to renewed hope, from sticking to your guns to occasionally having to put your progress on hold until the way is open again. Whatever the case ...

KEEP FOCUSED ON ... the essential nature of your original intention, only adjusting it temporarily or, if a certain alteration is unavoidable; never give in to hopelessness or doubt ... holding a better, healthier state of body or affairs firmly in your mind's eye.

WATCH OUT FOR ... being too rigid or stubborn in your outlook or beliefs when this may be based upon inner doubt or a fear of change ... false gods.

'To strive, to seek, to find, and not to yield'

✳

PART III

MAKING THE MOST OF THE ORACLE

TRACKING AND TRIANGULATION

ere are methods of using *The Astrological Oracle* that give you more comprehensive answers or guidance.

⁂ ORACLE STORMING

⁂ UPDATING

⁂ BASIC TRIANGULATION

⁂ THE MAGIC OF THE TRIANGLE

⁂ PROPOSITION-OPPOSITION-RESOLUTION

⁂ THE TIMELINE

⁂
TRACKING

There are two methods of Tracking:

ORACLE STORMING

Here one uses the Oracle deliberately to establish a satisfactory point of view, emotional stance or direction to take by casting for as many Sabian Symbols as it takes. This is rather like being 'at sea' somewhere, somehow, so you plot a course from Oracle reading to Oracle reading until you arrive at a conclusion or point of clarity. One client likened Oracle Storming to having 'Conversations with God'.

EXAMPLE: BE TRUE
A teacher friend had got to a point in his career where he was no longer sure of himself in terms of continuing to be the kind of teacher he always had been.

1ST CASTING – He had some idea of what he wanted to do but he was in a fog of confusion most of the time. He asked for a Reality Check on his situation and received from the Oracle, Cancer 10 – 'A Large Diamond Not Completely Cut'. This told him that there was an ideal that he was not bringing to fruition. His teaching had started as a vocation but had become stuck merely as a function because he was not nurturing (Cancer) his ideal.

2ND CASTING – He then asked, 'What is this unfinished facet, this task still to be done?'. He drew Gemini 21 – 'A Labour Demonstration'. This made him think that if he was making a protest about the state of teaching it would be concerning his view that education was being governed by an arbitrary set of standards and on an equally arbitrary set of levels. It was concerned with instruction (putting something into the student) rather than education (leading something out of the student). Note here that Gemini governs secondary education, his field. The Oracle was now beginning to 'heat him up', make him more aware of what truly motivated him.

3RD CASTING – Enthused, he then asked, 'What is my tool to help me perform this task?' To this the Oracle replied through Aries 4 – 'Two Lovers Strolling Through A Secluded Walk'. At first, this appeared incongruous (despite the Nameplate 'Being True To Your Path'!), but I asked what his immediate association was – always the best key to a direct understanding of any symbol. It made him think of his young partner, and how their unusual relationship had found them ostracized and isolated. Furthermore, she could not appreciate his current state of confusion, and just wanted him to carry on as before – another problem in its own right. We had previously pondered on the fact that a diamond needs something equally hard to cut it. His partner was that equally hard edge (they both have strong personalities), a worthy opponent – the tool, no less. And note that Aries governs Weapons and Tools. It was taken further to a realization that she was representing his own reluctance to make a change. If nothing else, at this stage he was enlightened in realizing how the two problem areas were so elegantly connected. However, his reluctance to change and pursue his ideal was still resisting what the Oracle was telling him.

4TH CASTING – And so he asked, 'To what ultimate purpose was all this in aid of?' The Oracle came back with Libra 6 – 'The Ideals Of A Man Abundantly Crystallized'. This was startlingly impressive! Here was a Sabian Symbol talking about 'ideals', a 'man', and a 'crystal' alluding to the diamond of first question/answer. There was also the double meaning of making something clear and real (crystallization). The Oracle was really talking to him – even his name was Chris!

5TH CASTING – But, as is so often the case, he was still reluctant to take on board what it was saying to him, that he should follow his ideal – of education as opposed to instruction – and, starting from this first step of radical commitment, make it real. And so he asked, 'What is this ideal that I am supposed to be making real?' He drew his two cards, 10♥ and K♣, the 10th Degree of Cancer, the very one he received first of all – 'A Large Diamond Not Completely Cut'. This was affirmation and confirmation of the most clear kind – crystal clear.

Whether or not he follows this course so lucidly laid out by the Oracle has yet to be seen, but to me at least it is obvious what his destiny is.

UPDATING

This is rather like having the Oracle pilot you through a difficult passage, and where the circumstances are liable to be changing frequently – rather like nautical 'sounding'. You may throw or draw for a new Sabian Symbol at regular intervals, varying from every few minutes if something is 'going down' right there and then, to longer intervals of every hour or every day or longer, depending upon how protracted the issue concerned happens to be. Such 'bulletins' can be very helpful and consoling – and quite fascinating in their accuracy.

TRIANGULATION

When you don't know where you are geographically, you find two points at some distance from where you stand, locate them on the map, and then using the compass, locate your own position on the map. This is called Triangulation – or to put it another way, 'When you're in a fix, get a fix!' With the Astrological Oracle there are four Triangulation Methods:

BASIC TRIANGULATION

This is the simplest method and sees yourself as the first point of the triangle, i.e., where you are, and drawing cards or throwing dice for the other two points.

EXAMPLE
A friend felt very unsure of where he stood financially. He had prospects but it was not clear if they would breed positive results. He first drew two cards that translated as the 16th Degree of Leo, and then two more that gave the 20th Degree of Leo. His first 'fix' was therefore 'Sunshine Just After A Storm' which was making it very clear that things would come out right after his bad patch. The second 'fix' was 'The Zuni Sun Worshippers', which was strongly confirming his 'sunny' prospects, giving cause for rejoicing and thanks, providing he found favour in the right places and in the right way. (Astrological note: the Sun is the planetary ruler of Leo). All this came to pass.

THE MAGIC OF THE TRIANGLE
Another method of Triangulation is to select three different degrees or Sabian Symbols. You may see these three points as different but related aspects of the issue concerned, thereby clarifying your position. Write down your intuitive findings.

EXAMPLE
A client was in a difficult and limiting live-in relationship where he and his partner were living with a third party, and upon being told astrologically that the coming Spring was a time of change for both he and his partner, he asked what that time boded for him and her. He received the following three degrees/Symbols:

1 **Leo 14 –** 'The Human Soul Awaiting Opportunity For Expression'

2 **Aries 22 –** 'The Gate To The Garden Of Desire'

3 **Pisces 4 –** 'Heavy Traffic On A Narrow Isthmus'

After interpreting the Symbols intuitively and analytically, and reading the texts, one should then summarize or indicate what each point is and means for you. My client came up with this:

1 **Leo 14 –** Awaiting release and free expression. INNER CERTAINTY of doing this.

2 **Aries 22 –** Threshold of DELIGHT is THERE, it is COMING.

3 **Pisces 4 –** Problem of trying to maintain flow and keep one's cool. CONGESTION is dealt with by STAYING WITH THE PROCESS.

Then contemplate the triangle of Symbols and the interactive meaning of them – which he did as follows:

There is here a certainty of going through the gate to greater and freer expression, or a situation that would allow such freedom. In the meantime there is this bottle-neck of congestion, and although it can be anyone's guess when any tailback will clear, it implies that Spring is the time of the 'gate', for Aries is the Sign of Spring. As it turned out, come that Spring he and his partner were still in the 'jam' but lived more in the faith of knowing that it would one day clear, and that counting to ten and not reacting was a good policy while waiting for it to do so. (This method and its example are taken further in 'Advanced Readings' on page 427).

PROPOSITION–OPPOSITION–RESOLUTION

This involves seeing your issue, and three answers to it, in terms of:

1 **Proposition** This gives a reading of how what you are proposing to do, or what is in store for you, measures up in the eyes of the Oracle. Once you have drawn or thrown the Sabian Symbol for this it is advisable to read the General Heading of any or all of the four categories of interpretation.

2 **Opposition** This shows what is getting in the way of what you are proposing to do or attain. Read the 'Watch Out For' approaches of any or all categories.

3 **Resolution** This gives you a way of surmounting difficulties and/or most easily attaining your objective or resolving the problem. Read the 'Keep Focused Upon' approaches of any or all categories.

EXAMPLE

A man wanted to know if he was capable of 'hands-on' healing his partner of an ailment. He cast the following Oracles:

1 **Proposition: Gemini 5** – 'A Radical Magazine'. Interpreted as: Doing something radical, with inner conviction, a crusade, ignoring the conventional medical approach of this not being possible.

2 **Opposition: Sagittarius 12** – 'A Flag That Turns Into An Eagle That Crows'. Interpreted as: Intention only, not walking one's talk. (Astrological note: Sagittarius is the opposite sign to Gemini, his proposition Symbol, *see* Zodiac layout on page 8).

3 **Resolution: Virgo 1** – 'A Man's Head'. Interpreted as: A statement of self to be relied upon; simply being who

and what you are. (Virgo is the Sign of health, and also the Sun-Sign of the man asking the question.)

In the event, he did not do what he intended – for that is all it was, an intention. However, simply being himself on a day-to-day basis was what his partner actually found healing and supportive.

THE TIMELINE

Here one simply draws Sabian Symbols for the Past, Present and Future with regard to the object of one's concern, such as a relationship, project or physical condition.

EXAMPLE

A friend was quite daring in that he asked about the Past–Present–Future of his life as a whole. He got:

1 **Past Scorpio 3** – 'A House-Raising'. He recognized this as how he had always had to rely on the assistance of others to help make his way in life, particularly with regard to accommodation, and that he was always ready to help others too.

2 **Present Sagittarius 1** – 'A Grand Army Of The Republic Campfire'. All his friends from the past, who were part of this pattern of mutual assistance, were now closer than ever, and frequently in touch even though spread around the country, and they made special occasions out of such gatherings. This Symbol brought home to him, quite emotionally, the remembrance of who he was and what was important to him. He was also currently in the process of putting together his past encounters and experiences in the form of a creative project. He felt he was presently remembering who he was.

3 **Future Cancer 9** – 'A Tiny Nude Miss Reaching In The Water For A Fish'. This was particularly poignant for he felt that at last he was on the brink of really 'finding within yourself, rather than without, that part you feel is missing' to paraphrase a line in the Karma section. (Astrological note: This was also the degree of Saturn in his own birth chart, and he was just coming up to his second Saturn Return, really beginning to deal with a lifelong creative objective and emotional issues which this Symbol represented to him.

You can use The Timeline over any time frame you choose. For instance, you could look at the last six months, the present month, and the coming year.

ADVANCED READINGS

GUIDED IMAGERY

Ultimately, this is the best way of using the Sabian Symbols because, in effect, the method puts you *en rapport* with the same realm that the Sabian Symbols themselves spring from – the unconscious or super-conscious mind. It involves being put, or putting yourself, into a relaxed and receptive state of body and mind. The optimum times to spend the 15–20 minutes practising this are during the two periods of the day when the human organism is, or wants to be, in this state – around 11am and between 4 and 5pm. Traditionally, we treat these times as coffee or tea breaks, to relax and refresh ourselves, but also to be perked up by these beverages in order to counter the natural urge to go into semi-sleep mode. One could regard this as another one of humanity's foolish departures from natural living.

Either record the spoken induction, which is given below, or get someone you trust with your inner spaces to speak it to you. This should be done in a slow, gentle and monotonous voice. First of all, ensure that you are warm and comfortable and unlikely to be disturbed for somewhat more than the 15–20 minutes. Also, feel reassured that should your attention be required else-where, you will open your eyes, feel alert, and as if you'd just had a daydream – which essentially is how you could view this exercise. Now pose your question and cast the Oracle in the usual way, and ascertain the Sabian Symbol that you are going to use as your guiding image. Then,

with eyes closed, listen to the taped or spoken induction that goes like this:

> 'Notice the place upon which … you are resting … allow yourself a sense of sinking a little … into that place … Notice how this gives you support … in a way that is right for you … and every part of you … And you are breathing … would breathing like to become a little slower and deeper … or would breathing, which happens by itself, like to stay the same … as you wonder about [SABIAN SYMBOL] … allowing this image to just 'come' … almost as if *it* is coming to you … letting this image unfold as it will … through space and time … And you can safely observe just what this image wants you to know … and this knowing may want to come to you as feelings, memories or other images … simply allowing whatever needs to come … all by itself … revealing itself in that way that is important to you … The feelings, memories and images continue … especially in a surprising, unexpected, and changing way'

Stay with this for up to 20 minutes (but do not hurry to complete), and subsequently dip into it naturally as time goes by. In time, you will find that you can place yourself in this relaxed and suggestible state at will, and go through the Guided Imagery quite spontaneously.

EXAMPLE

This comes from the first of many Sabian Symbol workshops run by myself and a friend, professional hypnotherapist Sally Stubbs, to whom I am very grateful for giving the above induction. A tall woman of around 30 with wonderful red hair offered to be the first to experience the Sabian Symbol Guided Imagery. She was made comfortable and induced with words similar to the above. Her selected Sabian Symbol was Sagittarius 10 – 'A Golden-Haired Goddess Of Opportunity'. As is commonly the case, there were some moments before anything appeared to happen. Then she became tearful. This, or some other show of feelings, is usually a good sign, because it means that one's emotional or astral body is being accessed or stimulated, one is being put in touch with the higher reality of whatever your situation happens to be. She then told us that she was on a long sandy beach with no one on it but a figure in the distance coming towards her. She described the Golden-Haired Goddess as she came closer – long tresses blowing in the wind and wrapping around her body. The Goddess was smiling at her intently and reassuringly. The woman then revealed to us that her husband had died quite recently and she had been feeling lost and depressed. The Goddess told her that he was all right, and that he wanted her to make full use of her life in every way, socially and professionally. All this took longer to transpire than it has taken to recount it here, for she went into what she felt her opportunities were, things which previously had been blocked and obscured by the emotional limbo in which her husband's untimely death had left her. Eventually she saw the Goddess recede into the distance, and she opened her eyes, smiling, relieved, uplifted – and amazed. Needless to say, all of us there were also very moved.

Although it was not necessary in this case, it can help to have someone prompt and encourage you through the experience. Preferably, this should be someone with experience in hypnosis, trance work or counselling, and this method is highly recommended to anyone involved in this sort of work. Also, Guided Imagery can be especially enlightening in answer to an open question.

BIRTH CHARTS

This requires that you or another person has a knowledge of astrology extending to being familiar with where the planets are in your personal birth chart, and with transits and aspects. (*See also* 'Interpreting Birth Charts' on page 432 where it is shown how to apply the Sabian Symbols directly to a birth chart rather than casting the Oracle to get the Symbols.)

EXAMPLE 1

An artist friend was going through a bit of a crisis in his career and he wanted to know if he had the 'inner knowledge' to teach and create in his own right rather than just be a part of an organization. This was marked astrologically by transiting Pluto squaring his natal Moon in Pisces in the Tenth House. To this the Oracle gave him Pisces 26 – 'A New Moon That Divides Its Influences'. First

of all this was strongly 'agreeing', for here was a 'Moon' in Pisces that had 'a conflict of interests' or a compromising influence, like twins fighting for first birth, with delays in delivery. It also assured him that he was at a new beginning and that things would unfold as the Moon waxed.

We noted that this conflict of interests was mirrored in his chart by having the natal Moon in Opposition to Venus and Saturn in Virgo. He felt that whereas his Moon in Pisces had all the inspiration and talent to go it alone, those critical Virgo planets would be saying who was he kidding in thinking he could become an independent filmmaker at over 50 years of age. He tracked this point by asking the Oracle to zoom in on this. He got Aries 12 – 'A Flock Of Wild Geese' which said to him: follow your instincts, the magnets in your head, migrate to more suitable climes; it was still a matter of teamwork and not just you, find your soul flight (or you already have), and at the right time you will know when to take off. (Instincts are ruled by the Moon).

EXAMPLE 2

This was regarding the question from one of my clients: 'When will there be an end to my bad karma, plus any information about paying it off?' The reply to this was Cancer 30 – 'A Daughter Of The American Revolution'. Apart from indicating in the Symbol itself that he will have done so when he has managed to connect with and express his feminine side more, it then was seen in his chart that this degree was the very last degree to be contained in his Twelfth House, the House of Karma itself. So, not only did the Oracle allude to the fact that all things Cancerian described his karmic due (the whole of that Sign being contained in his Twelfth House), but also that he was indeed very near the end of paying off that karma, Cancer 30 being the last degree of it. The next one is the first degree of Leo, his Ascendant or Rising Sign, the point of emergence from out of previous conditions. Note how by using a chart and the Oracle in this way a method of determining *timing* is developed.

VISUAL AIDS

By drawing, either freehand or onto a Zodiac wheel, you can gain a greater insight into a situation. This is because drawing and intuition are both right-brain functions, they feed one another, and so convey something helpful that logical deduction alone may not be able to. If you refer back to 'The Magic of Triangles' (*see* page 425), the example given was greatly facilitated by arranging the three Symbols on the Zodiac wheel (a blank of which can be found on page 469). Bear in mind that there are thirty degrees to each Sign and that the first degree proceeds to the thirtieth in an anticlockwise direction (note that here the Zodiac is orientated in the conventional manner, as opposed to the sideways reflection on the cover and page 8). Label each point of the triangle with a brief summary of its meaning, and join them all up with lines.

EXAMPLE
His example looked like this:

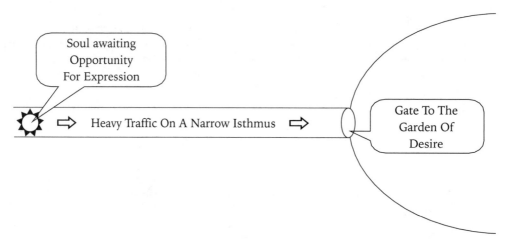

He also drew the image above that was highly interesting considering that the partner in question was somewhat of a mother figure to him, and that the 'Gate to The Garden of Desire' could be seen as going in either direction, depending on one's perspective!

USING THE ASTROLOGICAL ORACLE WITH ANOTHER ORACLE

Sometimes when using an oracle, the meaning is not clear enough – or we simply don't believe what it is telling us – so we like to ask for a second 'professional opinion'.

EXAMPLE
In one case, a client of mine had asked the Chinese oracle, the *I Ching*, about the prospects of creative success. The *I Ching* had given her Hexagram 63 – 'After Completion/ Already Fording' moving to Hexagram 37 – 'The Family/ Dwelling People'. This counselled that fruition was already under way but if she dithered or doubted her inner feelings of conviction then it would come to naught or even founder. The image here was of being some way across a ford, and of the futility of giving up when you were half way across.

My client was pleased with this reading, but still was not quite reassured, and so she asked the Astrological Oracle to comment upon the *I Ching* reading. As there were two hexagrams, she decided to triangulate, by picking two Sabian Symbols. She received the 9th Degree of Capricorn and the 9th Degree of Scorpio. The first one is 'An Angel Carrying A Harp' – saying that the Divine is expressing itself to you through the *I Ching*, and therefore you can trust what it is saying. The image was intuitively embellished

by her through seeing the Angel carrying its Harp above its head as it went through the ford. The second Sabian Symbol was 'Dental Work'. This confirmed the necessity of continual attention to what she was doing and not giving up or resting on her laurels, otherwise decay could set in.

Of course, one can use the Astrological Oracle first and then some other oracle.

SPREADS

As with the Tarot or any other set of divination cards where certain 'spreads' or layouts of cards are used, you may also use any spread of your choice with the Astrological Oracle, picking a Sabian Symbol in the usual way for each placement.

ASPECTS

'Aspects' in astrology are angular relationships that are formed between one planet or point and another in a chart. According to the angle made they denote certain qualities of interaction. How they are used in interpreting charts is not within the scope of this book, but we can use them with the Astrological Oracle in the following way.

You can only use this method when you have asked more than one question in a session, such as in Triangulation or Oracle Storming, *and* you get the *same degree Number* recurring for two or more questions/Sabian Symbols received. This is best demonstrated with an Example and by referring to this simplified summary of the five Major Aspects and their qualities as applied to the Astrological Oracle.

Aspect Name	No. of Degrees Apart	No. of Signs Apart*	Qualities
Conjunction	0	Same Sign	Intensifying, Confirming
Opposition	180	Opposite Signs or 6 Signs apart	Opposing, Confronting or Compensating, Direction-giving
Square	90	At Right Angles or 3 Signs apart	Challenging, Confusing or Compromising
Trine	120	Of same Element or 4 Signs apart	Supporting, Alleviating or Easing
Sextile	60	Complementary or 2 Signs apart	Supporting with effort

* See the Zodiac Wheel on page 469 in order to determine this.

EXAMPLE

A man was concerned about his elderly mother, and simply asked of her fate. He received Aquarius 22 – 'A Rug Placed On The Floor For Children To Play'. This told that caring provision would (have to) be made for her in a sort of ad hoc way, in the home, rather than being sent to a home. This was meaningful because she was becoming more and more childlike, but as she was 'difficult' and inclined to control him, out-and-out 'care' on his part was complicated. So, he asked for help concerning this dilemma. He obtained Scorpio 22 Degrees – 'Hunters Starting Out For Ducks'.

Now this was where this Aspect method became a possibility: the repeating of the same Degree number – 22, and, as seen in the above table, the two Signs concerned being three Signs apart, a Square Aspect, accurately described as Challenging, Confusing or Compromising. The Sabian Symbol of Scorpio 22 spelt out the necessity of being tough if need be, and not to be or feel 'hunted' himself.

Finally, he asked how could all this be resolved or how it would turn out. To this he again received 22 degrees of a Sign, this time Libra, which is the same Element, Air, as the first Symbol received, Aquarius, thereby a Supporting, Alleviating or Easing influence. Libra 22 is 'A Child Giving Birds A Drink At A Fountain' which showed perfectly for him that the child in him, and the child of his mother, would find it in himself to readily give what was needed, with trust in supply providing supply.

Naturally, such coincidence of degree numbers will not occur too often, but when it does it serves not only to emphasize a clear and precise path or fate, but it also opens up a whole new way of seeing and using the Sabian Symbols for anyone suitably intuitive or informed. For example, personally, I have a very 'heavy' Mercury at Virgo 16, sometimes giving rise to a far too busy and analytical mind. In addition to using the Sabian Symbol of Virgo 16 itself, by taking a look at the degree furthest away from it, that is, the opposite degree at Pisces 16, I find the compensatory 'Flow Of Inspiration' balm to my besieged brain!

SCHOOLING CONSCIOUSNESS

This is not so much an advanced reading as an advanced level of understanding the effect that the Oracle can have upon you. The first chapter ends on a section called 'Divination and Science' (*see* page 5) where *archetypes* are alluded to – the Jungian dynamics of the psyche. Viewed in this way, it can be appreciated that the Oracle is able to train your inner being and attitude to become more positive and aligned with your true path. Progressively then, you become more fulfilled, satisfied and aware, while allaying the confusion, anxiety and inner conflict that are products of being on the wrong track or having an inappropriate attitude or idea of life and yourself. This could be likened to combing tangles out of hair, washing it, and leaving it naturally vital and abundant – or tuning an engine so that it runs more smoothly and economically.

Schooling your consciousness in this way takes some time to accomplish, or even to notice a difference. Not only is the process truly worth it, but also it is facilitated through simply being aware of it happening, or merely of the possibility of it happening.

FURTHER WAYS OF USING
THE ASTROLOGICAL ORACLE

❋ INTERPRETING BIRTH CHARTS
❋ A SABIAN SYMBOL FOR EACH YEAR OF YOUR LIFE
❋ SABIAN SYMBOL WALKS
❋ GROUP SESSIONS
❋ A BOOK OF WISDOM

INTERPRETING
BIRTH CHARTS

This was originally how the Sabian Symbols were used, and is still the most common way that astrologers use them. The Sun, Moon and planets in your Birth Chart, as well as important points such as your Ascendant, are all placed on individual degrees of the Zodiac, and so each one of these heavenly bodies will have a Sabian Symbol according to the degree at which it is placed. For someone who is not well-versed in the technicalities of astrology it would be difficult to work out these degrees. But once your Birth Chart has been calculated accurately, you should not have too much trouble reading off these planet/degree positions.

However, there is one very important point to bear in mind when doing this. If, for example, you found you had your Moon at 28 Degrees and 46 minutes of Aries, then this would mean that it was at the 29th Degree of Aries, *not* at the 28th Degree of Aries. Why this is can be understood if you had a planet at 0 degrees and 25 minutes of, say, Virgo. This would mean that you looked up the Sabian Symbol for the 1st Degree of Virgo – there could not be a degree before the First degree. Similarly, clock time is measured in the same way, with, say, 0.25 am occurring during the first hour of the day.

Having discovered what your Symbols are, they can then be looked at and interpreted in terms of the Planet concerned. In the context of this book, we can see all the Sabian Symbols that correspond to the Planets in your

Birth Chart as being the answers to the questions you unconsciously asked of the Oracle through each Planet at the moment of your birth. And so, here are the kind of questions each Planet would be asking of you, or you of it:

YOUR SUN

- 'What is my life essentially going to be all about?'
- 'What is my life purpose and what have I got to accomplish it?'
- 'What is my central spiritual intent this lifetime?'
- 'What is the key to or nature of my father?'

YOUR MOON

- 'What is the nature of my soul and feelings?'
- 'What do I possess on an emotional level to help myself and others along?'
- 'Where and how do I find security and a sense of true belonging?'
- 'What is the nature of my predispositions and instincts?'
- 'What is the key to or nature of my mother?'

YOUR MERCURY

- 'What kind of intellect and perception do I have?'
- 'How do I best work effectively and avoid anxiety?'
- 'How may I best communicate?'

YOUR VENUS

- 'What kind of love life do I have?'
- 'How can I best relate to others?'
- 'How do I value myself and things around me?'
- 'What is the nature of my femininity, or the kind of femininity I am attracted to?'
- 'What is my key to happiness?'

YOUR MARS

- 'How do I best mobilize and assert myself?'
- 'What is the nature of my sexual and personal drive?'
- 'What is the nature of my masculinity, or the kind of masculinity I am attracted to?'

YOUR JUPITER

- *'What is the nature of my faith and belief?'*
- *'How can I best live life positively and optimistically?'*

YOUR SATURN

- *'What am I learning in this life time?'*
- *'What do I probably have difficulty with?'*
- *'What is the nature of my responsibility and karma?'*

YOUR URANUS*

- *'What is the nature of my intuitive ability?'*
- *'What faculty am I and my soul group helping to evolve?'*

YOUR NEPTUNE*

- *'Where and how do I find a sense of peace and universality?'*
- *'What is the nature of my sensitivity and psychic awareness, or illusions and blind-spots?'*

YOUR PLUTO*

- *'What are my regenerative powers and deepest qualities?'*
- *'What is the nature of my convictions or obsessions?'*

YOUR ASCENDANT

(the degree for this is only reliable if birth time is known to be exact)

- *'How do I go to meet life; what is my process of becoming?'*
- *'What is the window through which I see life and through which life sees me?'*

YOUR MIDHEAVEN

(the degree for this is only reliable if birth time is known to be exact)

- *'What is the nature of my career and material purpose?'*
- *'What do I amount to in the world, and how can I do so?'*

YOUR NORTHERN LUNAR NODE

- *'What are my present karmic conditions and intentions (the "bow-wave" of personality vessel)?'*
- *'How do I find my self in-sync with my social and cultural trends and milieu?'*

YOUR SOUTHERN LUNAR NODE

- *'What are my previous karmic conditions that I should progressively leave behind (the "wash" of personality vessel)?'*
- *'Where do I find my self out of sync with my social and cultural trends and milieu?'*

* These planetary positions may only be generational and not so specific or meaningful to your own personality – but they could be.

EXAMPLE

My own Moon is at Aries 29 – 'A Celestial Choir Singing'. Apart from a more subjective interpretation regarding this and the answer to the above five questions to or from my Moon, my two professions are music and astrology. Furthermore, my Moon is in the Tenth House, which governs career or professional status.

SOME FAMOUS EXAMPLES

Check out these people and events and see how they expressed their Sabian Symbols, but bear in mind that Sabian Symbols are usually best understood subjectively by the person themselves.

ADOLF HITLER *Moon:* Capricorn 7 – 'A Veiled Prophet Of Power'.

BILL CLINTON ('The Come-back Kid') *Sun:* Leo 27 – 'Daybreak'; *Venus:* Libra 12 – 'Miners Emerging From A Mine'.

CARL GUSTAV JUNG *Moon:* Taurus 16 – 'An Old Man Attempting Vainly To Reveal The Mysteries'.

CHALLENGER SHUTTLE DISASTER *Uranus* (space-flight/accidents/glitches): Sagittarius 21 – 'A Child And A Dog With Borrowed Eyeglasses'.

CHERNOBYL *Uranus* (rules radioactivity): Sagittarius 23 – 'Immigrants Entering' (*see* Nameplate).

DALAI LAMA'S ESCAPE FROM TIBET *Pluto:* Virgo 3 – 'Two Angels Bringing Protection'; *Saturn:* Capricorn 7 – 'A Veiled Prophet Of Power'.

EVA BRAUN *Sun:* Aquarius 16 – 'A Big Businessman At His Desk' (*see* Love/Relating/Social).

GEORGE W. BUSH *Sun:* Cancer 14 – 'A Very Old Man Facing A Vast Dark Space To The North-East' (*see also* United States of America); *Saturn* (rules presidents): Cancer 27 – 'A Storm In A Canyon'.

MAHATMA GANDHI *Moon:* Leo 20 – 'The Zuni Sun Worshippers'.

MAO TSE-TUNG *Sun:* Capricorn 5 – 'Indians Rowing A Canoe And Dancing A War Dance'.

MIKHAIL GORBACHEV *Sun:* Pisces 11 – 'Men Seeking Illumination'; *Saturn:* Capricorn 21 – 'A Relay Race' (he was very much part of the stage by stage process of his country's liberation).

MUHAMMAD ALI *Mars* (the fighter): Taurus 4 – 'The Rainbow's Pot Of Gold'; *Ascendant:* Leo 1 – 'A Case Of Apoplexy'.

NOSTRADAMUS *Uranus* (astrology/prediction): Pisces 10
– 'An Aviator In The Clouds' (*see* Karma section).

PADDINGTON RAIL DISASTER *Mercury* (signal failure):
Scorpio 1 – 'A Sightseeing Bus' (*see* General
Interpretation/Watch Out For – accident was due to
cost-cutting).

PEARL HARBOR *Sun*: Sagittarius 16 – 'Seagulls Watching
A Ship'; *Saturn*: Taurus 24 – 'A Mounted Indian With
Scalp Locks'; *Neptune*: Virgo 30 – 'A False Call
Unheard In Attention To Immediate Service'.

POWER CUT (WORLD'S BIGGEST, CANADA MARCH
13TH 1989) *Uranus* (electricity/accidents): Capricorn 6
– 'A Dark Archway And Ten Logs At The Bottom';
Saturn and Neptune (the conjunction of these two
planets on this degree was a major astrological event);
Capricorn 13 – 'A Fire Worshipper' (power-cut was
caused by a Solar storm).

PRINCE CHARLES *Sun*: Scorpio 23 – 'A Bunny Metamorphosed Into A Fairy'.

PRINCESS DIANA *Sun*: Cancer 10 – 'A Large Diamond
Not Completely Cut'; *Moon*: Aquarius 26 –
'A Hydrometer'; *Pluto*: Virgo 7 – 'A Harem'.

UNITED STATES OF AMERICA *Sun*: Cancer 14 – 'A Very
Old Man Facing A Vast Dark Space To The North-
East' (*see also* George W. Bush).

WORLD TRADE CENTRE ATTACK *Mars* (war/aggression):
Capricorn 2 – 'Three Stained-Glass Windows, One
Damaged By Bombardment'; *Ascendant* (Significator)
at moment G.W. Bush was informed (9.05 am EST):
Libra 19 – 'A Gang of Robbers In Hiding'.

YURI GAGARIN *Uranus* (space-flight/accidents): Aries 26
– 'A Man Possessed Of More Gifts Than He Can Hold'.

A SABIAN SYMBOL FOR
EACH YEAR OF YOUR LIFE

In astrology there is something called your Progressed
Sun. Its position symbolizes a year in your life according
to the degree it is travelling through at the time in
question. As a rule this year will not go from birthday to
birthday or from January to December (although it
might), and may gradually shift forward or back as your
life progresses. These start dates and end dates to your
Progressed Sun year are easily worked out by someone
with astrological know-how.

EXAMPLE
A client of mine was going through a year where her
Progressed Sun was travelling through the 22nd Degree of
Capricorn, the Sabian Symbol for which is – 'A General
Accepting Defeat Gracefully'. This she recognized as a
confession she had to make in the face of an adversary,
and more significantly, the admission that she had been
trying, misguidedly, to achieve or prove a certain
something for many years. When she dropped this false
objective, her true objective then became clear. The
following year/degree, which in her case began in March,
was Capricorn 23 – 'Two Awards For Bravery In War' when
she found herself getting a better position in life and
earning more as a result of her efforts, not to mention the
foregoing confession, as well as overcoming the emotional
conditions that had prevailed previously and given rise to
the false motivation.

SABIAN SYMBOL WALKS

This is literally an exercise in synchronicity for those
who have access to an astrological computer program or
who can erect a horoscope by hand. Draw up Charts for
each hour, on the hour, of your walk, and note down the
Sabian Symbol for the degree rising for each chart/hour
(you can do this for shorter or longer intervals if you
wish). Then look for a representation of that Sabian
Symbol at that time as you walk. A friend and I went for
one of these walks, with the first hour commencing at
noon, about five minutes into our walk along one side of
a river valley. I looked at the chart for this hour which
had the Ascendant at Capricorn 3 – 'The Human Soul
Receptive To Growth And Understanding'. Upon reading
this out loud to my friend, two buzzards flew up from
the undergrowth immediately to our right and proceeded
up the valley, veering left up a gully about a mile away.
Suitably inspired we followed their route! With such an
auspicious beginning, we encountered highly significant
sightings to match each Sabian Symbol on the five hours
of our walk. But the last was the most fascinating.
We had got to a spot overlooking two lakes and it being
five o'clock we looked up the last Symbol: Aries 27 –
'A Lost Opportunity Regained In The Imagination'.
Try as we might, we could not see anything to match this
Symbol, and eventually, somewhat disappointed, we
headed home. When we got back, my friend found his

beloved black astrakhan hat was missing. 'Aha!' we thought, 'that's what's "lost".' So early next morning – my friend was leaving that day – we set out to retrieve his hat from our last spot. But after looking for about half an hour we had to concede that it was not there. Some hours later, after I had returned from the station where my friend had caught his train home, I sat and pondered this last Symbol. As I was doing so I saw a black cloth object under some magazines on the sideboard. I leapt up and grabbed it – but it was just our black tea cosy. But then I pondered a bit more – that tea cosy is usually kept in a certain drawer. I went for it – and there was his astrakhan hat! My partner had unconsciously tidied it away, thinking it was the tea cosy, quite soon after we had first returned from our walk the previous day.

Another remarkable example of how the Sabian Symbols are in sync with the cosmos was occasioned by a walk we went on that lasted longer than we had expected, so we did not have a Symbol for the Ascendant for that time. It was 5 pm and my partner and I were sitting on a wall looking at a stone circle (Castlerigg in Cumbria, UK) feeling very close. When I got back and calculated the Symbol for then it turned out to be Aquarius 15 – 'Two Lovebirds Sitting On A Fence'! This also happens to be the Symbol for the Sun in my partner's birth chart.

GROUP SESSIONS

Getting together with two or more people and looking at the issues of one or more of those present with the aid of the Astrological Oracle can be very enlightening – not least of all because it is often easier for someone other than oneself to see what is being said. The pooling of awareness in this way is also quite bonding for any group for it reveals the deeper thoughts, feelings and life conditions of those involved. Highly recommended – and sometimes highly amusing too!

A BOOK OF WISDOM

As the existence and channelling of cosmic order and intelligence is intrinsic to the origin and interpretation of the Sabian Symbols and the Astrological Oracle, it follows that they can be regarded as a source or expression of wisdom. As such, just browsing and studying them will be enlightening, uplifting and highly interesting. You can do this in a more applied fashion by looking for relevant words or subjects of interest in the Sign subject matter (see The Sabian Symbols Index, page 26; The Nameplates, page 440; The Quotes, page 445; and The Sabian Symbols Search Index, page 456).

✳

APPENDIX

1

USING DICE TO CAST
THE ASTROLOGICAL ORACLE

The using of dice to cast the Oracle derives more directly from the bones or stones that were originally employed when oracles first came into existence a long, long time ago. They are not only more authentic, but are more random in their given result, whereas cards can get marked with wear and tear, and shuffling is not always that thorough. Initially, it seems a little more complex than using cards, but ultimately it is simpler and quicker. An aspect to dice that I personally like is that I can invest more psychic energy into the actual throwing.

USING ONE DIE

To help understand this system, we will use a working example.

THROWING FOR THE DEGREE
Throw the die. In our example **3** is thrown. Looking at the table opposite, check against possible throws in the top-left panel headed FIRST THROW for the selection of 6 degrees you are to throw for next.

3 = 13–18 Degrees

[**Note:** If you get a **6** for the first throw, as this is 'Void of Course'. This means that the Oracle cannot or will not answer your question at this time because your attitude is incorrect, you are not focused enough on the question, or there is no case to answer (a future event does not happen). So, 'dig' deeper with more focus, if necessary rephrasing your question, and then throw the die again. If you throw a **6** for a second time, repeat and then try again. If you throw a **6** for a third time, it's a case of 'three strikes and you're out'. For a reason best known to the Oracle, the question is inappropriate or irrelevant at this time or could be answered in some other way. Of course, you are free to override this rule, but you probably won't get a satisfactory answer.]

Throw the die for a second time. This time **5** is thrown. Look at the top-right panel headed SECOND THROW and find the number which you have just thrown. Below this there are given five possible degrees (5, 11, 17, 23, 29). Only one of these will fall in the range you achieved with your first throw (13–18). So, your degree number is:

17 Degrees

THROWING FOR THE SIGN
Throw the die for a third time. Now **4** is thrown. Looking at the table, in the bottom-left panel headed THIRD THROW. If you throw an Odd number (1, 3 or 5), your next throw will be to select from the Yang/Male Signs (Aries, Gemini, Leo, Libra, Sagittarius or Aquarius). If you throw an Even number (2, 4 or 6), your next throw will be to select from the Yin/Female Signs (Taurus, Cancer, Virgo, Scorpio, Capricorn or Pisces). Since you have thrown 4, you will next be selecting from Yin/Female Signs.

Throw the die for the fourth and last time. You have thrown **2**. Look in the panel headed FOURTH THROW in the column headed **2**, the corresponding Yin/Female sign is **Cancer**.

THE RESULT
Put the Degree and Sign together and you have:

Cancer 17 Degrees

By looking at the Sabian Symbols Index (*see* page 26), you find that the Sabian Symbol for Cancer 17 Degrees is 'The Germ Grows Into Knowledge And Life'.

DEGREE	FIRST THROW			SECOND THROW					
				1	2	3	4	5	6
	1	= 1–6	→	1	2	3	4	5	6
	2	= 7–12	→	7	8	9	10	11	12
	3	= 13–18	→	13	14	15	16	17	18
	4	= 19–24	→	19	20	21	22	23	24
	5	= 25–30	→	25	26	27	28	29	30
	6	THROW AGAIN							

SIGN	THIRD THROW		FOURTH THROW					
			1	2	3	4	5	6
	Odd number (1, 3 or 5) → Yang/Male		Ari	Gem	Leo	Lib	Sag	Aqu
	Even number (2, 4 or 6) → Yin/Female		Tau	Can	Vir	Sco	Cap	Pis

USING TWO DICE*

For this you need two dice of different colours. Supposing you have a red die and a green die; the red one becomes your FIRST THROW, and the green one becomes your SECOND THROW. The point is that you can throw them together. Then use the table in exactly the same way as before.

[Again, if the first throw (or red die) is a **6**, it is 'Void of Course' (*see* above).]

FIRST THROW

If you throw: **red 2** and **green 3**, this would mean you had selected the 9th degree, as the **2** signifies a degree in the range 7–12, and the **3** determines that the degree number is **9**.

SECOND THROW

If you throw: **red 4** and **green 2**, this would mean that you had selected Cancer, as an **even** number signifies a yin sign and the **2** determines the sign to be Cancer.

So, you would have **Cancer 9 Degrees**, the Sabian Symbol of which is 'A Tiny Nude Miss Reaching In The Water For A Fish'.

USING FOUR DICE*

If you can get hold of four dice all of different colours or sizes, then you can obtain your Degree and Sign all in one throw. Supposing you have a red, a green, a blue and a white die. The red can be the first throw, the green the second throw, the blue the third, and the white die can be the fourth throw. Using the table in the same way as above, we obtain the Degree and Sign.

If you throw: **red 4**, **green 1**, **blue 4** and **white 5**, then the degree would be **19** and the Sign would be **Capricorn**.

So you would have **Capricorn 19 Degrees**, the Sabian Symbol for which is 'A Child Of About Five With A Huge Bag Of Shopping'.

* WARNING – Because when using two or four dice the casting of the Oracle is a lot quicker, there is a danger of not focusing enough on your question. I therefore strongly suggest that some ritual is used when using more than one die.

2
✳
THE NAMEPLATES

THE NAMEPLATES OF ARIES

1 Emerging Potential
2 Raise A Laugh
3 Character Is Destiny
4 Be True (To Your Path)
5 On Standby
6 Accentuate The Positive
7 Division Of Labour
8 Inspired Vigour
9 Insight Through Clarity
10 Upgrade And Re-Presentation
11 Sovereignty Of Being
12 Natural Timing And Sense of Direction
13 Averting Disaster
14 The Urge To Evolve
15 The Threads Of Life
16 Supernatural Attunement
17 Sobriety Or Denial?
18 Much Needed Rest
19 Elevated Overview
20 Nurture Of The Needful
21 Fight The Good Fight
22 The Pleasure–Pain Principle
23 Important Burden
24 Receptive To Reward
25 Everything Is Going To Be All Right
26 Spoilt For Choice
27 The Power Of Visualization
28 Who To Be True To?
29 Cosmic Attunement
30 Mother Nature's Bosom

THE NAMEPLATES OF TAURUS

1 Natural Inclination
2 Discharge Of Tension
3 Coming Up Roses
4 Promise Of Reward
5 A Need To Let Go
6 Healing Splits
7 Absence Of Agenda
8 The Need To Get Unstuck
9 Time To Celebrate
10 Selfless Service
11 Cultivation Of Worth
12 Just Looking
13 Carry That Load
14 Primal Playpower
15 Style As Protection
16 No Quick Fix Or Easy Answer
17 Left Brain Versus Right Brain
18 Clearing Air And Getting Rid
19 Virgin Territory
20 The Transitory
21 And So It Is Written
22 Peace And Goodwill
23 Store Of Great Worth
24 Seizing Power
25 Pleasing Order
26 Passion And Skill
27 Modest Or Menial?
28 Timely Reward
29 Co-operation
30 Inherent Wealth And Privilege

THE NAMEPLATES OF GEMINI

1 Lucidity Through Transparency
2 Goodness Unseen
3 Classical Style And Form
4 Ritual and Renewal
5 Rooting Out And Rooting For
6 Probing And Prospecting
7 Source And Refreshment
8 Organized Protest
9 Equipped To Conquer

10 To Take Or Not To Take Control
11 Tomorrow Never Knows
12 Righteous Self-Expression
13 Virtuosity
14 Psychic Rapport
15 Open Discussion
16 Emancipation
17 Mind Over Matter
18 Otherness And Synchronicity
19 Ancient Wisdom
20 The Choice Is Yours
21 Rightful Reward
22 Commingling
23 Pre-Flight Nerves
24 Youthful Exuberance
25 Necessary Eradication Only
26 Dormant Power
27 Ingenuousness
28 Honest Admission
29 Eclecticism
30 Attractive Display

THE NAMEPLATES OF CANCER

1 Turning Point
2 Hung Up Or On Hold?
3 Rugged Individuality
4 No Contest?
5 Superior Power
6 Making Provision
7 Supernature
8 Children In The World
9 Emotional Appeal
10 Almost There
11 Seeming Insincerity
12 Unique Promise
13 Acceptance And Assertion
14 Desolation To Consolation
15 Positive Indulgence
16 Morphogenetic Field
17 Quickening Process
18 Basic Survival
19 Joined In Heaven
20 Living The Myth
21 Fervour Plus Control
22 Patience And Composure
23 Of Like Mind
24 The Eternal Triangle

25 Dramatic Portent
26 Recreation And Relaxation
27 Necessary Intensification
28 Radical Humanitarianism
29 Divine Arbitration
30 The Feminine Unbound

THE NAMEPLATES OF LEO

1 Fit To Burst
2 Loss Of Power
3 Makeover
4 Stiff Upper Lip
5 On The Brink
6 Then And Now
7 Cosmic Order
8 Sowing Revolution
9 The Breath Of Life
10 Starting Afresh
11 Freedom From Care
12 Sophisticated Ease
13 Restless Contemplation
14 Inner Certainty
15 Ongoing Story
16 All's Well That Ends Well
17 Natural Harmony
18 The Science Of Interaction
19 Creative Co-operation
20 Creating Favour
21 Getting In A Flap
22 The Message
23 Feel The Force
24 Pauper Or King?
25 Staying Power
26 The Covenant
27 New Beginnings
28 The Great And The Small
29 Otherworldliness
30 Trust Or Naivety

THE NAMEPLATES OF VIRGO

1 The Importance Of Identity
2 The Upholding Of Faith
3 Taken Care Of
4 Integration
5 In Your Dreams
6 Progress Through Repetition
7 Subjugation Or Security

THE NAMEPLATES OF PISCES

3

※

THE QUOTES

ARIES

1 'Our birth is but a sleep and a forgetting:/The soul that rises with us, our life's Star,/Hath had elsewhere its setting,/And cometh from afar:' – William Wordsworth from *Ode. Recollections of Immortality in Early Childhood* (1807) st.5

2 'A sense of humour is a sense of proportion' – Kahlil Gibran from *Sand and Foam* (1927)

3 'What you are is what you're going to be' – Author from *Just a Little Love* (1975 song)

4 'Two's company, three's a crowd' – Proverb

5 'Be here now' – Ram Dass, title of his 1971 book

6 'Always look on the bright side of life' – Eric Idle from the song of that title from the film *The Life of Brian*

7 'Delegation is the secret of success' – Saying

8 'He who binds to himself a joy doth the wingéd life destroy/But he who kisses the joy as it flies, lives in Eternity's sunrise' – William Blake from *MS Note-Book* p.99 Several Questions Answered

9 'Only a man devoted to complete inner sincerity can know the future' – Mo Dsi from *The Doctrine of the Mean*

10 'They that drink of the old wine have no place for the new' – Proverb

11 'Rule yourself or be ruled over' – Author from *Do It Yourself Astrology* (1996) Saturn in Leo

12 'To everything there is a season, and a time to every purpose under heaven' – *Ecclesiastes* ch.1, v.14

13 'Trust in Allah, but tie up your camel' – Anon (Arabic?)

14 'Life is a sexually transmitted disease' – Anon. Graffito found on London Underground from D.J. Enright (ed.) *Faber Book of Fevers and Frets* (1989) p.345

15 'Upon our dignity's seed we weave and gaze away,/With 'voidance vanquished we no longer plead or dwell in our dismay' – Anon from *Enterada*

16 'Those who cannot see the Unseen are like radios stuck on one waveband' – Author

17 'Moral indignation is jealousy with a halo' – H.G. Wells from *The Wife of Sir Isaac Harman* (1914) ch.9, sect.2

18 'Sleep, come unto me. Stay/While I might mend/My violated vehicle/O sleep, stay with me/Until dawn' – Author from *Sleep* (1987 poem)

19 'We carry within us the wonders we seek without us' Sir Thomas Browne from *Religio Medici* (1643) pt.1, sct.1

20 'He rained down manna for the people to eat, He gave them the grain of heaven' – *Psalm 78*, v.24

21 'Courage is not simply one of the virtues, but the form of every virtue at its testing point' – Palinurus (Cyril Connolly) from *The Unquiet Grave*. Nameplate: 'Fight the good fight with all thy might' – John Samuel Bewley Monsell from 1863 hymn of that title

22 'Strange, the desire for certain pleasures is a part of my pain' – Kahlil Gibran from *Sand and Foam* (1927) p.8

23 'Thus does the superior man live with the great mass: he veils his light but still shines' – *I Ching* (trans. Richard Wilhelm) hexagram 36. 'Superior man' means the higher or spiritual aspect of one's being

24 'It's an ill wind that blows nobody any good' – Proverb

25 'A promise made is a debt unpaid, and the trail has its own stern code' – Robert W. Service from *The Cremation of Sam McGee* (1907)

26 'Stop wanting, start having' – Sam Reifler from *I Ching*

27 'Happiness is not an ideal of reason but of imagination' – Immanuel Kant from *Fundamental Principles of the Metaphysics of Ethics* (1785) sect.2 (trans. T.K. Abbott)

28 'Commercialism is doing well that which should not be done at all' – Gore Vidal in *The Listener* 7 August 1975, p.168

29 'A band of angels coming after me, coming for to carry me home' – Anon from *Swing Low Sweet Chariot* (Negro spiritual c.1850)

30 'From troubles of the world/I turn to ducks/Beautiful comical things' – F.W. Harvey from *Ducks* (1919)

TAURUS

1 'Flow like a flower, fall like a shower' – Author from *Let Me Get Along With You* (1975 song)

2 'A little alarm now and then keeps life from stagnation' – Fanny Burney from *Camilla* (1796) bk.3, ch.11

3 'I'm taking one step at a time/And I'll rest every seven,/For it's a mighty long climb/On your way up to heaven' – Author from *Mind's Eye's Blue Star-Way* (1975 song)

4 'Hope springs eternal in the human breast:/Man never Is, but always To be blest' – Alexander Pope from *An Essay on Man* Epistle 1 (1733) ln.95

5 'O death where is thy sting? O grave, where is thy victory?' – *I Corinthians* ch.15, v.55

6 'Why did the chicken cross the road? Because it wanted to get to the other side' – Old riddle

7 'In transparency, worlds are created' – Ariel Spilsbury and Michael Bryner from *The Mayan Oracle* (flyleaf)

8 'Appeal to Heaven when only Heaven can help you' – Author

9 'Oh Christmas Tree, oh Christmas Tree, with faithful leaves unchanging' – from the English version of *O Tannenbaum* by E. Anschutz (1819)

10 'He who would do good to another, must do so in minute particulars' – William Blake from *Jerusalem* (1815) 'Chapter 3' plate 55, ln.60

11 'Let us cultivate our garden' – Voltaire

12 'Are we in fact, more accurately speaking, condemned to choose?' – Ernesto Spinelli from *Demystifying Therapy*

13 'I might formulate it as an affirmation of things as they are; an unconditional "yes" to that which is, without subjective protests' – Carl Jung, on what came to him following a near death experience during a life-threatening illness, from *Memories, Dreams and Reflections*

14 'Lo, I receive the gifts thou bringest me – Life, and more life, in fullest ecstasy. I am the Moon, the Moon that draweth thee, I am the waiting earth that needeth thee. Come unto me, Great Pan, come unto me!' – Dion Fortune from *The Goat-Foot God, The Rite of Pan*

15 'May I address myself to me so the eye inside my head might see' – Author from *Spark* (1985 poem)

16 'Genius is only a greater aptitude for patience' – Comte de Buffon from H. de Seychelles *Voyage à Montbar* (1803) p.15

17 'Jack Spratt could eat no fat, his wife could eat no lean/And so between them both they licked the platter clean' – Anon from old nursery rhyme

18 'Slowly the poison the whole blood stream fills./It is not the effort, nor the failure tires./The waste remains, the waste remains and kills' – William Empson from *Missing Dates* (1935)

19 'Atlantis will rise, Babylon will fall' – Author

20 'All things must pass' – Proverb (Indian?)

21 'The moving finger writes, and, having writ, moves on' – Edward Fitzgerald from *The Rubaiyat of Omar Khayyam* st.51

22 'Peace be unto you' – *St. Luke* ch.4, v.36

23 'Money is like muck, not good except it be spread' – Francis Bacon from *Essays* (1625) 'Of Seditions and Troubles'

24 '*Dum loquimur, fugerit invida/Aetas: carpe diem, quam minimum credula postero*' (While we're talking, envious time is fleeing: seize the day, put no trust in the future) – Horace from *Odes* bk.1, no.7, ln.27

25 'Now I was young and easy under the apple boughs/About the lilting house and happy as the grass was green' – Dylan Thomas from *Fern Hill* (1946)

26 'If music be the food of love, play on' – William Shakespeare from *Twelfth Night*, act 1, sc.1, ln.1

27 'Before enlightenment: chop wood, carry water. After enlightenment: chop wood, carry water' – Zen injunction

28 'A woman is like a man's shadow. Walk away from it and it will follow you; follow it and it will walk away' – French adage. This can also be read as: 'A man is like a woman's shadow …'

29 'Life without industry is guilt, and industry without art is brutality' – John Ruskin from *Lectures on Art* (1870) Lecture 3 'The Relation of Art to Morals' sect.5

30 'True style and pedigree need never vaunt themselves; they are plain for all to see' – Author

GEMINI

1 'I used to feel a stranger to how most things appeared to be,/But now it's 'coming clear to me, I was a stranger to myself' – Author from *Can You Find A Home* (1974 song)

2 'Blessed be' – Wiccan entreaty

3 'Art follows Nature' – This Symbol tends to answer the old question of 'Does Nature follow Art, or Art follow Nature?' by stating that the best man-made things are based upon Nature's shapes and proportions

4 'The magic and the beauty are still to be found/If you can spy a bluebird's wing' – Author from *Bluebird's Wing* (1975 song)

5 'Today's radicals are tomorrow's conservatives' – adaptation of Hannah Arendt's 'The most radical revolutionary will become a conservative on the day after the revolution' from the *New Yorker* 12 September 1970, p.88

6 'Seek and ye shall find' – *St. Matthew* ch.7, v.7

7 'The town may change, but the well does not' – *I Ching* (trans. Richard Wilhelm) hexagram 48

8 'A riot is at bottom the language of the unheard' – Martin Luther King from *Where Do We Go From Here?* (1967) ch.4

9 'Bring me my arrows of desire' by William Blake from *Milton* (1805–1810) preface

10 'I claim not to have controlled events, but confess plainly that events have controlled me' – Abraham Lincoln in Letter to A.G. Hodges, 4 April 1864 in R.P. Dasler (ed.) *Collected Works* (1953) vol. 7

11 'The proof of the pudding is in the eating' – Proverb

12 'No one can make you feel inferior without your consent' – Eleanor Roosevelt in *Catholic Digest* August 1960, p.102

13 'Genius does what it must, and Talent does what it can' – Owen Meredith (Earl of Lytton) from *Last Words of a Sensitive Second-Rate Poet* (1868)

14 '[Without telepathy] A lie will go round the world while the truth is pulling its boots on' – (Adapted) Old proverb, from *Gems from Spurgeon* (1859) p.74 by C.H. Spurgeon

15 'Nothing is closed to openness' – Author

16 'The argument of the broken window pane is the most valuable argument in modern politics' – Emmeline Pankhurst in G. Dangerfield's *The Strange Death of Liberal England* (1936) pt.2, ch.3, sect.4

17 'Look to your health; and if you have it, praise God, and value it next to a good conscience' – Izaak Walton from *The Compleat Angler* (1653) pt.1, ch.4

18 'A paradox is the truth standing on its head to attract attention' – *The Cynic's Encyclopaedia* (1922)

19 'What's past is prologue' – William Shakespeare from *The Tempest*, act 1, sc.2, ln.405

20 'Help yourself, and heaven will help you' – Jean de la Fontaine from *Fables,* bk.6 (1668) 'Le Chartier Embourbé'

21 'By their works you shall know them' – adaptation of 'By their fruits ye shall know them' from *St. Matthew*, ch.7, v.20

22 'Will you, won't you, will you, won't you, will you join the dance?' – Lewis Carroll from *Alice's Adventures in Wonderland* (1865) ch.10

23 'When you gotta go, you gotta go' – Saying

24 'Hail to thee, blithe Spirit!' – Percy Bysshe Shelley from *To a Skylark* (1819)

25 'What's green is growing, what is not is dying' – Anon

26 'The darkest hour is just before dawn' – Saying

27 'O born in days when wits were fresh and clear … before this strange disease of modern life' – Matthew Arnold from *The Scholar-Gypsy* (1853) ln.201

28 'Sometimes one has to get to zero before you know the score' – Author

29 'All originality is simply an improvement or variation upon an ancient or natural theme' – Author

30 'Love built on beauty, soon as beauty, dies' – John Donne from *Elegies*, 'The Anagram' (c.1595)

CANCER

1 'As one door closes, another one opens' – Anon

2 'Negative Capability, that is when a man is capable of being in uncertainties, mysteries, doubts, without any irritable reaching after fact and reason' – John Keats from Letter to George and Thomas Keats, 21 December 1817, in H.E. Rollins (ed.) *Letters* (1958) vol.1

3 'My heart is a lonely hunter that hunts on a lonely hill' – Fiona McLeod (William Sharp) from *The Lonely Hunter* (1896) st.6

4 'Actions speak louder than words' – Proverb

5 'Woe be to them that resist their fate' – Author

6 'Hasten to the needs of our children's children's children' – Author's adaptation of Moody Blues album title *For Our Children's Children's Children*

7 'There never was a merry world since the fairies left off dancing, and the Parson left conjuring' – John Selden from *Table Talk* (1689) 'Parson'

8 'If the cap fits, then wear it – but do not if it does not' – Anon, with addition by author

9 'The innocent and the beautiful have no enemy but time' – William Butler Yeats from *In Memory of Eva Gore Booth and Con Markiewicz* (1933)

10 'Spirituality completes us. The idea of a search for the soul presumes that the ordinary man and ordinary woman are, in a manner of speaking, "unfinished" ' – Harry R. Moody from *The Five Stages of the Soul*, p.32

11 'Very sorry can't come. Lie follows by post' – Lord Charles Beresford (1846–1919) in telegraphed message to the Prince of Wales on being summoned to dine at the eleventh hour

12 'The hand that rocks the cradle/Is the hand that rules the world' – William Ross Wallace from *What rules the world* (1865)

13 'Life is not a case of either Fate or Free Will – but a case of Both' – Author – 'Speak softly and carry a big stick; you will go far' – Theodore Roosevelt from a speech given April 3rd 1903 (quoting an 'old adage')

14 '*Nil desperandum*' (Never despair) – Horace from *Odes*, bk.2, no.2, ln.102

15 'The road of excess leads to the palace of wisdom' – William Blake from *The Marriage of Heaven and Hell* (1790–93), 'Proverbs of Hell'

16 'What you are is what you get' – Author

17 'Large streams from little fountains flow/Tall oaks from little acorns grow' – David Everett from *Lines Written for a School Declamation* (aged 7)

18 'Back to basics' – Common phrase, slogan adopted by John Major's Tory Party in the UK during the 1990s, but rather poorly expressed and understood

19 'Thou wilt never make from others the One which thou seekest except first there be made one thing of thyself' – Gerhard Dorn, mediaeval alchemist

20 'Gather ye rosebuds while ye may,/Old Time is still a-flying:/And this same flower that smiles today,/Tomorrow will be dying' – Robert Herrick from *To the Virgins, to Make Much of Time* (1648)

21 'Prosperity doth best discover vice, but adversity doth best discover virtue' – Francis Bacon from *Essays* (1625) 'Of Adversity'

22 'Time and tide wait for no man' – Proverb

23 'If you steal from one author, it's plagiarism; if you steal from many, it's research' – Wilson Mizner from *The Legendary Mizners* by A. Johnston (1953) ch.4

24 'There were three of us in this marriage, so it was a bit crowded' – Diana, Princess of Wales from a 1998 television interview

25 'Unless you see miraculous signs and wonders, you will not believe' – *St. John* ch.4, v.48

26 '*Trahit sua quemque voluptas*' (Everyone is dragged on by their favourite pleasure) – Virgil from *Ecologues* no.2, ln.65

27 'Most human beings are too lazy, fearful or enclosed to wake up without the help of some kind of alarm' – Author

28 'Her ways are ways of gentleness and all her paths are Peace' – Sir Cecil Spring-Rice from *I Vow to Thee, My Country* (1918). See also *Proverbs* ch.3, v.17

29 'Oh, East is East, and West is West, and never the twain shall meet,/Till Earth and Sky stand presently at God's great Judgement Seat' – Rudyard Kipling from *The Ballad of East and West* (1892)

30 'Men do, women are' – William James

LEO

1 'An atheist is a man who has no invisible means of support' – John Buchan from H.E. Fosdick *On Being a Real Person* (1943) ch.10

2 'I get my energy by getting rid of it, by constantly expending it, by not hanging on to it' – Dr Douglas Baker, an expansion upon something he once said

3 'Change what is on the inside and you change what is on the outside' – Author from *Do It Yourself Astrology* p.2

4 'God and devil are fighting there, and the battlefield is the heart of man' – Fedor Dostoevsky from *The Brothers Karamazov* (1879–80) bk.3, ch.3

5 'Nothing ventured, nothing gained' – Proverb

6 '*Si jeunesse savait; si viellesse pouvait*' (If youth knew; if age could) – Henri Estienne from *Les Prémices* (1594) bk.4, epigram 4

7 'As above, so below' – Hermes Trismegistus

8 'Stir It Up!' – Jimmy Cliff from song of that title

9 'Life is what you make it' – Anon

10 'Tomorrow to fresh woods, and pastures new' – John Milton from *Lycidas* (1638) ln.193; Karma/ Attitude/Health: '*En ma fin git mon commencement*' (In my end is my beginning) – Mary Queen of Scots (1542–87), her motto

11 'Rhythm and rhyme make a dance out of time' – Author

12 'Recreation should be an invitation to inspiration' – Author

13 'The mass of men lead lives of quiet desperation'

– Henry David Thoreau from *Walden* (1854) 'Economy' in *Writings* vol.2, p.8

14 'Call the world if you please "The vale of soul-making"' – John Keats from a letter to George and Georgiana Keats, 24th October 1818 in H.E. Rollins (ed.) *Letters* (1958) vol.2

15 'Trailing clouds of glory do we come/From God, who is our home' – William Wordsworth from *Ode. Recollections of Immortality in Early Childhood* (1807) st.5

16 'Take away my demons and you take away my angels' – Danté Alighieri

17 'It's the singer not the song' – Anon, from a West Indian calypso

18 'Transformation, that's the name of the game' – Author, after the song *Multiplication*

19 'Recipe for life: Enjoy where you are and who you are with' – Author

20 'The Sun is God' – William Turner, the painter's last words

21 'Whatever you do, don't panic' – Saying

22 'The medium is the message, and the message is the medium'– Author's extension of 'The medium is the message' by Marshall McLuhan from *Understanding Media* (1964) ch.1 (title)

23 'Life is like riding a bicycle; keep going or you fall over' – Author

24 'I was unhappy because I had no shoes. Then I saw someone who had no feet' – Indian saying

25 'Human life is everywhere a state in which much is to be endured, and little to be enjoyed' – Samuel Johnson from *Rasselas* (1759) ch.11

26 'My heart leaps up when I behold/A rainbow in the sky./So it was when my life began;/So it is now I am a man' – William Wordsworth from *My heart leaps up when I behold* (1807); Karma/Attitude/Health: 'God gave Noah the rainbow Sign,/No more water, the fire next time' – Anon from *Home in that Rock* (Negro spiritual)

27 'Morning has broken'– Eleanor Farjeon from *A Morning Song (for the First Day of Spring)* (1957)

28 'Pecking order is universal' – Author

29 'I guess I don't know really who I am,/A struggling bard or a king from Iran, But there's no one else I'd rather be,/I'd just like to be a better me' – Robert Noel Byron from *I am Mary Shelley* (1977) by Barbara Lynne Devlin

30 'With nothing to hide, you are free to express who you truly are' – Author

VIRGO

1 'I am that I am' – Exodus 7:1

2 'Faith is believing what you know ain't so' – Mark Twain

3 'Talk of angels and you hear their wings' – Dion Fortune from *Demon Lover* p.183

4 'We must learn to live together as brothers or perish together as fools' – Martin Luther King from speech at St. Louis, 22 March 1964; in *St. Louis Despatch* 23 March 1964

5 'A dream not considered is like a letter from God left unopened' – Gnostic proverb

6 'If at first you don't succeed, try, try, and try again' – Saying

7 'It is a strange desire to seek power and to lose liberty' – Francis Bacon from *Essays* (1625) 'Of Great Place'

8 'Let's face the music and dance' – Irving Berlin from 1936 song of that title

9 'No fate but what you make' – James Cameron from the film *Terminator 2 – Judgement Day*

10 'A problem shared is a problem halved' – Saying

11 'A slavish bondage to parents cramps every faculty of the mind' – Mary Wollstonecraft from *A Vindication of the Rights of Woman* (1792) ch.11

12 'Every harlot was a virgin once' – William Blake from *For the Sexes: The Gates of Paradise* 'To the Accuser who is The God of This World' (epilogue); Karma/Attitude/Health: 'Do not judge, or you too will be judged' *St. Matthew* ch.7, v.1, 'Why do you look at the speck of sawdust in your brother's eye and pay no attention to the plank in your own eye?' *St. Matthew* ch.7, v.3

13 'You're either part of the solution or you're part of the problem' – Eldridge Cleaver from speech given in San Francisco, 1968, in R. Scheer Eldridge Cleaver, *Post Prison Writings and Speeches* (1969) p.32

14 'The family – that dear octopus from whose tentacles we never quite escape' – Dodie Smith from *Dear Octopus* (1936) p.120

15 'If a job is worth doing, it is worth doing well' – Anon

16 'There's only one golden rule/Let outside what's inside of you' – Author from *Way Down South* (1974 song)

17 'And then more torrents of fire and shit/A feast of blaming and resentment/Framed in Honesty's great expanding infinity/Accommodating all our dread' – Author from *Let's Cough Up The Bile* (1988 poem)

18 'Be careful what you wish for – you might just get it!' – Anon

19 *'Es irrt der Mensch, so lang er strebt'* (Man will err, while yet he strives) – Johann Wolfgang von Goethe from *Faust* pt.1 (1808) *'Prolog in Himmel'*

20 'A rolling stone gathers no moss' – Anon

21 'I do not wish them (women) to have power over men; but over themselves' – Mary Wollstonecraft from *A Vindication of the Rights of Women* (1792) ch.4

22 'Truth is the cry of all, but the game of the few' – Bishop George Berkeley from *Siris* (1744) para.368

23 'Let him that hath understanding count the number of the beast: for it is the number of a man' – *Revelation* ch.13, v.18

24 'He who departs from innocence, what does he come to? Heaven's will and blessing do not go with his deeds' – Confucius, comment upon hexagram 25 of *I Ching* (trans. Richard Wilhelm); General Interpretation: 'Mary had a little lamb,/Its fleece as white as snow,/And everywhere that Mary went the lamb was sure to go' – Sarah Josepha Hale from *Poems for Our Children* (1830) 'Mary's Little Lamb'

25 'Though lovers be lost, love shall not; and death shall have no dominion' – Dylan Thomas from *And death shall have no dominion* (1936)

26 'Yea, though I walk through the valley of the shadow of death, I will fear no evil; for thou art with me; thy rod and thy staff comfort me' – *Psalm* 23, v.4

27 'A sacrifice of the higher element that produces an increase of the lower is called an out-and-out increase: it indicates the spirit that alone has the power to help the world' – *I Ching* (trans. Richard Wilhelm) hexagram 42

28 'You Don't Pull No Punches, But You Can't Push The River' – song title from Van Morrison's *Veedon Fleece* (1974). By kind permission of Van Morrison and Warner Chappell Music Inc.

29 'The answer lies within' – Anon

30 'Concentration is the secret of success' – Author

LIBRA

1 'What does not kill me makes me stronger' – Johann Wolfgang von Goethe

2 'A thousand mile journey begins with the first step' – Proverb

3 'The ebbing tide of night gave place to the flood of daybreak and all creation rejoiced' – Dion Fortune from *The Demon Lover* (1929)

4 'Kokorokoo' (the African/Ghanaian 'Call of Togetherness') – from song of that title by Osibisa

5 'The further one travels, the less one knows' – Lao-Tzu from *Tao Te Ching*

6 'Follow the path that has heart, for in that way your treasure lies' adaptation of 'Where your treasure is, there your heart will be also' – *St. Matthew* ch.6, v.21

7 'And the strong shall protect the weak' – Anon, possibly contraction of what is said in *Psalm* 12, v.5

8 'Keep the Home-fires burning,/While your hearts are yearning,/Though your lads are far away/They dream of Home' – Lena Guilbert Ford from *Till the Boys Come Home* (1914 song, music by Ivor Novello)

9 'To know your most stable and positive self, identify the three best things about yourself' – Author

10 'Steady as she goes' – Nautical expression

11 'True authority can pause from itself' – Author

12 'The trust comes with the dirt, depth and darkness' – Author

13 'Fortune's always hiding, I've looked ev'rywhere. I'm forever blowing bubbles, pretty bubbles in the air' – Jaan Kenbrovin and John William Kellette from *I'm Forever Blowing Bubbles* (1919 song)

14 'There the wicked cease from troubling, and there the weary be at rest' – *Job* ch.3, v.17

15 'What goes around comes around' – Anon

16 '... the great globe itself,/Yea, all which it inherit, shall dissolve/And, like this insubstantial pageant faded,/Leave not a rack behind' – William Shakespeare from *The Tempest* act 4, sc.1

17 'To love, and bear: to hope till Hope creates/From its own wreck the thing it contemplates' – Percy Bysshe Shelley from *Prometheus Unbound* (1820) act 4, ln.573

18 'Conscience is thoroughly well-bred and soon leaves off talking to those who do not wish to hear it' – Samuel Butler from *Further Extracts from Notebooks* (1934) p.279

19 'What you don't know <u>can</u> hurt you' – Author's inversion of popular but illusory saying

20 'Whom the Lord loveth He chasteneth' – *Hebrews* ch.12, v.6; Money/Work/Creativity: 'No man but a blockhead ever wrote, except for money' – Samuel Johnson from James Boswell's *The Life of Samuel Johnson* vol.3, p.19 (April 5, 1776)

21 'Et in Arcadia ego' (And I too came from a time and place closer to Nature) – Tomb inscription of disputed meaning; the one given here being based upon the idea or memory that Arcadia in Ancient Greece was a land of people simply and blissfully in tune with Nature; Pan himself is said to have come from there

22 'Nature looks after Her own' – Anon

23 'Behold, I make all things new' – *Revelation* ch.22, v.2

24 'An asset when seen as an affliction becomes an affliction' – Author

25 'To see the world in a grain of sand/And heaven in a flower/Hold infinity in the palm of your hand/And eternity in an hour' – William Blake from *Auguries of Innocence* (1803) ln.1

26 'We make war that we may live in peace' – Aristophanes from *Nicomachean Ethics* bk.10, 1177B 5–6 (trans. M. Oswald)

27 'Then I felt like some watcher in the skies/When a new planet swims into its ken' – John Keats from *On First Looking into Chapman's Homer* (1817)

28 'Now I feel the Sun burst in my heart/Exploding blazing petals free/Streaming beams to darkened reaches/Unfolding golden endlessly' – Author from *The Sun* (1994 poem)

29 'Everything serves to further' – *I Ching* (trans. Richard Wilhelm) oft used injunction

30 'I think, therefore I am – or I think I am' – after Rene Descartes' 'Cogito, ergo sum' from *Les Discours de la méthode* (1637) pt.4

SCORPIO

1 'Befriending others eliminates alienation' – Author

2 'When the heart weeps for what it has lost, the soul laughs for what it has found' – Anon

3 'Many hands make light work' – Anon

4 'How far that little candle throws his beams! So shines a good deed in a naughty world' – William Shakespeare from *The Merchant of Venice* act 5, sc.1, ln.90

5 'This fortress built by Nature for herself/Against infection and the hand of war' – William Shakespeare from *Richard II* act 2, sc.1, ln.40

6 'All that glitters is not gold' – from 'Not all that tempts your wand'ring eyes/And heedless hearts, is lawful prize;/Nor all, that glisters, gold' – Thomas Gray from *Ode on the Death of a Favourite Cat* (1748)

7 'Errors, like straws, upon the surface flow;/He who would search for pearls must dive below' – John Dryden from *All for Love* (1678) prologue

8 'Is it me, or is it thee?' – Anon (Shakespeare?)

9 'Does the road lead up-hill all the way?/Yes, to the very end/Does the day's journey take the whole long day?/From morn to night, my friend' – Christina Rossetti from *Up-Hill* (1862)

10 'Birds of a feather flock together' – Proverb

11 'I was much too far out all my life/And not waving but drowning' – Stevie Smith from *Not Waving But Drowning* (poem)

12 'To meet the right faces, be in the right places' – Author

13 'There are no mistakes except the ones you do not learn from' – Author

14 'It's good to talk' – British Telecom advertising slogan

15 'Any system of religion that has any thing in it that shocks the mind of a child cannot be a true system' – Thomas Paine from *The Age of Reason* pt.1 (1794) p.20

16 'Count your blessings one by one/When all appears and day has just begun/They will light your heart with happiness/Make each hour bright and bring you gladness' – Edith Temple and Richard Morgan from *Count Your Blessings* sung by Josef Locke (1948)

17 'At a certain point in one's development it is necessary to be both father and mother to oneself' – Author

18 'If there wasn't death, I think you couldn't go on' – Stevie Smith in the *Observer*, 9 November 1969, p.21

19 'Fake it 'til you make it' – Anon

20 'In time we hate that which we often fear' – William Shakespeare from *Anthony and Cleopatra* act 1, sc.3, ln.12

21 'Lock the door, bolt the hatch, and the rain and wind will rust the latch away. You cannot escape' – Author from *To Live Eternally* (1975 song)

22 'And a-hunting we will go' – Anon

23 'When I was a child, I spoke as a child, I understood as a child, I thought as a child: but when I became a man, I put away childish things' – *I Corinthians* ch.13, v.11

24 'You are what you attract; the more you attract, the more careful you must be of what you are' – Author

25 'The truth which makes men free is for the most part the truth which men prefer not to hear' – Herbert Agar from *A Time for Greatness* (1942) ch.7

26 'The Earth is all the home I have,/The heavens my wide roof-tree' – W.E. Ayrtoun from *The Wandering Jew* (1867) ln.49

27 'C'est la guerre' (That's war for you) – French saying

28 'What I had been seeking all this time was present all around me' – Harry Moody from *The Five Stages of the Soul* (1997) p.299

29 'Every country has the government it deserves' – Joseph de Maistre from *Letters et Opuscules Inedits* (1851) vol.1, letter 53 (15 August 1811)

30 'It is better to appear a fool than it is to be one' – Author from *Do It Yourself Astrology* (1996) Mercury in Capricorn

SAGITTARIUS

1 'To meet again by a fleeting chance/With the Bells of Time all chiming/In our hearts and minds,/Reason drowned by rhyme' – Author from *Venus* (1994 song)

2 'I am for ever walking upon these shores,/Betwixt the sand and foam./The high tide will erase my footprints,/And the wind will blow away the foam./But the sea and the shore will remain/For ever' – Kahlil Gibran from *Sand and Foam* (1927) p.1

3 'Plots, true or false, are necessary things,/To raise up commonwealths and ruin kings' – John Dryden from *Absalom and Achitophel* (1681) pt.1, ln.7

4 'More haste, less speed' – Anon

5 'Wisdom denotes the pursuing of the best ends by the best means' – Francis Hutcheson from *Enquiry into the Original of our Ideas of Beauty and Virtue* (1725) Treatise 1, sect.5, subsect.15; Karma/Attitude/Health: 'Owl hasn't exactly got Brain, but he Knows Things' – A.A. Milne from *Winnie the Pooh* (1926) ch.9

6 'For when the One Great Scorer comes to mark against your name/He writes – not that you won or lost – but how you played the Game' – Grantland Rice from *Alumnus Football* (1941)

7 'Falling in love/Now that's doing something!' – Ansari, Sufi poet (c.1300)

8 'Let Nature take Her course' – Saying

9 'If You Love Somebody Set Them Free' – Sting from the song of that title from *The Dream of Blue Turtles*

10 'God loveth a cheerful giver' – *II Corinthians* ch.9, v.7

11 'The body is the temple of the soul' – Anon

12 'For whosoever exalteth himself shall be abased; and he that humbleth himself shall be exalted' – *St. Luke* ch.14, v.11 (see also *St. Matthew* ch.23, v.12)

13 'Those who cannot remember the past are condemned to repeat it' – George Santayana from *The Life of Reason* (1905) vol.1, ch.12

14 'Go walk' – injunction to traveller inscribed on pyramid

15 'If you hate a person, you hate something in him that is part of yourself. What isn't part of ourselves doesn't disturb us' – Hermann Hesse from *Demian* (1919) ch.6

16 'Where observation is concerned, chance favours only the prepared mind' – Louis Pasteur from Address, 7 December 1854; in R. Vallery-Radot, *La Vie de Pasteur* (1900) ch.4

17 'Si Dieu n'existait pas, il faudrait l'inventer' (If God did not exist, it would be necessary to invent Him) – Voltaire from *Epitres* #96 'A l'Auteur du livre des trois imposteurs'

18 'Protection and caution should facilitate steady growth, but not inhibit it' – Author

19 'L'amor che muove il sole e l'altre stelle' (The love that moves the Sun and the other stars) – Dante Aligheri from *Divina Commedia* 'Paradiso' canto 33, ln.145

20 'When the going gets tough, the tough get going' – Joseph P. Kennedy in J.H.Cutler *Honey Fitz* (1962) p.291 (also attributed to Knute Rockne)

21 'The truth hurts, but the truth shall set you free' – Combination of popular saying and what Jesus Christ says in *St. John* ch.8, v.32

22 'Give us grace to persevere' – Percy Dearmer from *Jesu, good above all other* (1906 hymn)

23 'When in Rome, do as the Romans do' – St. Ambrose from *St. Augustine: Letters* vol.1 'Letter 54 to Januarius (AD circa 400)

24 'Mister bluebird on my shoulder/It's the truth, it's actch'll/Ev'rything is satisfactch'll' – by Ray Gilbert from *Zip-A-Dee-Doo-Dah* (1945 song from the film *Song of the South*, music by Allie Wrubel)

25 'Practice makes perfect' – Proverb

26 'We must arrive at the correct standpoint ourselves, for only from this vantage can we work correctly' – *I Ching* (trans. Richard Wilhelm) hexagram 64

27 'The drop of rain maketh a hole in the stone, not by violence, but by oft falling' – Hugh Latimer from Second Sermon preached before the King's Majesty (19 April 1549)

28 'Have nothing in your house that you do not know to be useful, or believe to be beautiful' – William Morris

from *Hopes and Fears for Art* (1882) 'Making the best of It'

29 'Less is more' – Proverb

30 'Woe is me, I think I am becoming a god' – Emperor Vespasian, when fatally ill, from Suetonius *Lives of the Caesars* Vespasian sect.23, subsect.4

CAPRICORN

1 *'Experto credite'* (Trust one who has gone through it) – Virgil from *Aeneid* bk.9, ln.641

2 'Praise my soul, the King of Heaven;/To his feet thy tribute bring/Ransomed, healed, restored, forgiven,/Who like me his praise should sing' – Henry Francis Lyte from *Praise, my soul, the King of Heaven* (1834 hymn)

3 'There is one thing stronger than all the armies in the world; and that is an idea whose time has come' – Anon from *Nation* 15 April 1943

4 'We are all in the same boat' – Saying

5 'A desperate disease requires a dangerous remedy' – Guy Fawkes on 6 November 1605

6 'Confronting what you fear provides what you need' – Author

7 'A prophet is not without honour, save in his own country, and in his own house' – *St. Matthew* ch.13, v.57; Karma/Attitude/Health: 'Veil your light but still shine'; *I Ching* (trans. Richard Wilhelm) hexagram 36

8 'Deep down in my heart/I can feel a spark/glowing steadily' – Author from *Just a Little Love* (1975 song)

9 'It came upon the midnight clear,/That glorious song of old,/From Angels bending near the earth/To touch their harps of gold' – Edmund Hamilton Sears from *The Christian Register* (1850) 'That Glorious Song of Old'

10 'He prayeth best that loveth best/All things both great and small' – Samuel Taylor Coleridge from *The Rime of the Ancient Mariner* (1798) pt.7

11 'We are all but pawns in the game of life' – Author

12 'Nature does nothing without purpose or uselessly' – Aristotle from *Politics* bk.1, 1256b

13 'Do not play with fire if you do not wish to get burnt' – Saying

14 'Lives of great men all remind us/We can make our lives sublime,/And, departing, leave behind us/Footprints on the sands of time' – Henry Wadsworth Longfellow from *A Psalm of Life* (1838)

15 'Suffer the little children to come unto me, and forbid them not: for of such is the kingdom of God' – *St. Mark* ch.10, v.14

16 'Healthy body, healthy mind – healthy mind, healthy body too, possibly more so!' – Saying/Author

17 'Feel the fear and do it anyway' – Susan Jeffers from her book of that title

18 'If you can't beat 'em, join 'em' – Anon

19 'Nothing happens to anybody which he is not fitted by nature to bear' – Marcus Aurelius from *Meditations* bk.5, sect.18

20 'We are all from a grander place' – Anon; Love/Relating/Social: 'I hear music and there's no-one there,/I smell blossom but the trees are bare ...' – Irving Berlin, *You're Just In Love* from 'Call me Madam'

21 'Humanity, if only it knew it, is the many striving for the one goal: Humanity' – Author

22 'Resist ye not evil: but whosoever shall smite thee on thy right cheek, turn to him the other also' – *St. Matthew* ch.5, v.14

23 *'Fortis fortuna adiuvat'* (Fortune favours/assists the brave) – Terence from *Phormio* l.203

24 'Many people believe that they are attracted by God or by Nature, when they are only repelled by man' – Dean Inge from *More Lay Thoughts of a Dean* (1931) pt.4, ch.1

25 'Costs merely register competing attractions' – Frank H. Night from *Risk, Uncertainty and Profit* (1921) p.159

26 'As vapour from the sea rises up into the sky, and falls as rain, or sleet or snow, so too shall we go' – Author from *Do It Yourself Life Plan Astrology* p.286, ln.18

27 'I'll pack my grip for a farewell trip/Kiss Susan-Jane goodbye at the fountain/I'm going, says I, to the Land of the Sky,/Away out on the mountain' – Jimmie Rodgers from *Away out on the Mountain* (1927 Song)

28 'Just as the luminaries in the sky serve for the systematic division and arrangement of time, so human society and all things that really belong together must be organically arranged' – *I Ching* (trans. Richard Wilhelm) hexagram 13

29 'Intuition when it works is really brilliant. When it doesn't it's plain stupid' – Anon. Written on the page of a day-to-day desk calendar the day the author left work to become an astrologer

30 'For secrets are edgéd tools,/And must be kept from children and from fools' – John Dryden from *Sir Martin Mar-All* (1667) act 2, sc.2

AQUARIUS

1 'A faint heart never won a fair lady ... or a good man, or anything else worth a damn' – Anon/Author

2 'God comes forth in the sign of The Arousing' – *I Ching* (trans. Richard Wilhelm) hexagram 51

3 'Two roads diverged in a wood, and I –/I took the one less travelled by/And that made all the difference' – Robert Frost from *The Road Not Taken* (1916)

4 'Physician, heal thyself' – *St. Luke* ch.4, v.23

5 'All I know is the blood running in my veins/Thrills me, exhorts me, again and again,/For my heart, the fount of ancestors old/Leaps to its part in the story being told' – Author from *Jupiter* (1994 poem)

6 'Life is not a problem to be solved but a mystery to be experienced' – Albert Einstein

7 'Cast thy bread upon the waters; for thou thy shalt find it after many days' – *Ecclesiastes* ch.11, v.1

8 'A little sincerity is a dangerous thing, and a great deal of it is absolutely fatal' – Oscar Wilde from *Intentions* (1891) 'The Critic as Artist' pt.2

9 'From strength comes more strength' – Anon/Author

10 'To thine own self be true' – William Shakespeare from *Hamlet* act 1, sc.3, ln.76

11 'If a man hasn't discovered something he will die for, he isn't fit to live' – Martin Luther King from speech in Detroit, 23 June 1963; in J. Bishop *The Days of Martin Luther King* (1971) ch.4

12 'Different strokes for different folks' – Anon

13 'Those who feel the pressure can sense the coming change' – Author

14 'Pessimism feeds off the past, optimism dines out on the future' – Author

15 'The course of true love never did run smooth' – William Shakespeare from *A Midsummer Night's Dream* act 1, sc.1, ln.3

16 'The buck stops here' – Harry S. Truman, unattributed motto on his desk

17 '*Quis custodiet ipsos custodies?*' (Who is to guard the guards themselves?) – Juvenal from *Satires* no.6, l.347

18 '"The Book of Life begins with a man and a woman in a garden" – "It ends with Revelations [sic]"' – Oscar Wilde from *A Woman of No Importance* (1893). Lord Illingworth to Mrs Allonby, and her reply

19 'Ashes can either fertilize what is to come or be bitter cause for regret' – Author

20 'And all shall be well and/All manner of thing shall be well/When the tongues of flame are in-folded/Into the crowned knot of fire/And the fire and the rose are one' – T.S. Eliot from *Four Quartets* 'Little Gidding' (1942) pt.5. Also, 'Sin is behovely, but all shall be well and all shall be well and all manner of things shall be well' – Julian of Norwich from *Revelations of Divine Love* (the long text – after 1416) ch.27, Revelation 13

21 'Both Sides Now' – Joni Mitchell. Remember/listen to the lyrics of this song

22 'Silver and gold have I none, but such as I have give I thee' – *Acts of the Apostles* ch.3, v.6

23 'Truly great power does not degenerate into mere force but remains inwardly united with the fundamental principles of right and justice' – *I Ching* (trans. Richard Wilhelm) hexagram 34

24 'A man who has not passed through the inferno of his passions has not overcome them' – Carl Gustav Jung from *Memories, Dreams and Reflections* (1962) ch.9

25 'Increase that which is too small, and decrease that which is too great' – Author, after 'Every valley shall be exalted, and every mountain and hill shall be made low; and the crooked shall be made straight, and the rough places plain' from *Isaiah* ch.40, v.4

26 'Man is the measure of all things' – Protagoras in Plato's *Theaetetus*

27 'The Soul is the Believer, with Memory so old/The Soul is the Believer, as Mind and Body show' – Author from *The Soul is the Believer* (1974 song)

28 'I think that I shall never see/A poem lovely as a tree' – Joyce Kilmer from *Trees* (1914)

29 'And so now the Moon has arrived at this instant/At this Time we had hoped for, feared, and expected/For the Moon's ever Change, Life's only constant/For Change is all that She ever reflected' – Author from *Dark Moon* (1994 poem)

30 'There's a long, long trail awinding/Into the land of my dreams' – Stoddard King from *There's a Long, Long Trail* (1913 song)

PISCES

1 'Grace is given of God, but knowledge is bought in the market' – Arthur Hugh Clough from *The Bothie of Tober-na-Vuolich* (1848) pt.4, ln.149

2 'Discretion is the better part of valour' – Proverb

3 'The tree becomes the Earth with the full consent of the tree, and I surrender my life to you who sustained

me' – Robert Benson, client and friend, uttered in response to this Symbol

4 'The inevitability of gradualness' – Sidney Webb (Baron Passfield) from *The Labour Party on the Threshold*, Fabian Tract no.207, 1923, p.11

5 'Put your money where your mouth is' – Colloquialism

6 'Rank imposes obligation' – Meaning of the motto *Noblesse oblige*

7 '… before the rooster crows today, you will deny three times that you know me' – *St. Luke* ch.22, v.34 (what Jesus utters to his disciple Peter shortly before he is arrested to be crucified, and which comes to pass)

8 'Consider her ways, and be wise' – *Proverbs* ch.6, v.6

9 'May the best man or woman win' – Anon

10 'Obstacles are those frightful things you see when you take your eyes off your goal' – Hannah More

11 'Know thyself' – Anon. Inscribed on the temple of Apollo at Delphi; Plato ascribed it to the Seven Wise Men

12 'Divine indifference … signifies the refusal to be identified with anything save the spiritual reality' – The Tibetan/Alice Bailey from *Glamour: A World Problem* p.262

13 'Little girl … Sometime they'll give a war and nobody will come' – Carl Sandburg from *The People, Yes* (1936)

14 'I expect that Woman will be the last thing civilized by Man' – George Meredith from *The Ordeal of Richard Feverel* (1859) ch.1

15 'A chain is only as strong as its weakest link' – Anon

16 'I'm swimming in the river, with the river swimming in me' – Author from *Swimming In The River* (1974 song)

17 'Blossom by blossom the Spring begins' – Algernon Swinburne from *Atalanta in Calydon* (1865) chorus 'When the hounds of spring'

18 'All the world's a stage,/And all the men and woman merely players:/They have their exits and their entrances;/And one man in his time plays many parts,/His acts being seven ages.' – William Shakespeare from *As You Like It* act 2, sc.7, ln.34

19 'When the student is ready, the master appears' – *I Ching* (trans. Richard Wilhelm) hexagram 4

20 'Thou shalt prepare a table before me against them that trouble me … and my cup shall be full' – *Psalm 23*, v.4 from the Book of Common Prayer

21 'Childlike simplicity is both precious and powerful – and must be guarded well' – Author

22 'Without limitations there comes chaos' – Author, after 'In human life too the individual achieves significance through discrimination and the setting of limits' from *I Ching* (trans. Richard Wilhelm) hexagram 60

23 'We are such stuff/As dreams are made on, and our little life/Is rounded with sleep' – William Shakespeare from *The Tempest* act 4, sc.1

24 'No man is an island, entire of itself' – John Donne from *Devotions upon Emergent Occasions* (1624) 'Meditation XVII'

25 'Pave your mind with stones of truth, keep every corner clear and bright' – Author from *Love, Is Your Heart Aching?* (1975 song)

26 'Let the winds of the heavens dance between you' – Kahlil Gibran from *The Prophet* (1923)

27 'And the lives of a man are strung like pearls on the thread of his spirit' – 'The Priest of the Moon' from *The Sea Priestess* by Dion Fortune, or 'Be not deceived; God is not mocked: for whatsoever a man soweth, that shall he also reap' – *Galatians* ch.6, v.7

28 'There is no wealth but life' – John Ruskin from *Unto this Last* (1862) Essay 4, p.156

29 'To what is One, sages give many a title' – Ancient Hindu principle

30 'To strive, to seek, to find, and not to yield' – Alfred Lord Tennyson from *Ulysses* (1842) ln.67

4

✳

THE SABIAN SYMBOLS SEARCH INDEX

This listing enables you to find a Sabian Symbol you know contains a certain word but cannot remember the Symbol itself, or to check how often a certain word occurs overall when weighing odds or for general interest. Insignificant words have not been listed.

Abundantly – lib 6
Accepting – cap 22
Adobe – aqu 1
Airplane – gem 10, lib 27
Albatross – cap 10
American – can 30
Ancestors – aqu 5
Ancient – tau 30, cap 14, aqu 27
Angel – cap 9
Angels – vir 3
Animal – vir 23
Apoplexy – leo 1
Approaching – lib 10, sco 28
Archaic – gem 19
Archway – cap 6
Ardath – aqu 30
Arguing – can 4
Arms – vir 22
Army – sag 1
Arrest – lib 18
Arrows – gem 9
Art – lib 9
Aspiration – vir 11
Asserting – gem 12
Attempting – tau 16
Attention – vir 30
Audience – ari 28
Automobile – vir 20, can 5
Autumn – lib 25, sco 18
Aviary – cap 28
Aviator – pis 10
Awaiting – can 22, leo 14
Awards – cap 23

Baby – can 12

Back – aqu 24
Bag – tau 18, cap 19
Baggage – tau 13
Bald-headed – vir 28
Ball – sco 12
Band – sco 27
Bankrupt – gem 28
Bareback – leo 23
Barn – gem 22
Barometer – aqu 13
Basketball – vir 21
Bas-relief – cap 14
Bathing – gem 30, cap 17
Battle – tau 17
Bazaar – pis 5
Beach – lib 21
Beads – tau 27
Bear – aqu 23
Bearer – aqu 20
Beauties – gem 30
Beautiful – sag 28
Beautifully – aqu 8
Big – aqu 16, aqu 20, aqu 23
Birds – ari 20, can 6, leo 28, lib 22, cap 8
Bit – can 24
Black – vir 4
Blanket – ari 15
Blazing – lib 8
Bloom – aqu 30
Blowers – leo 9
Blowing – ari 24, lib 13, pis 8
Bluebird – sag 24
Board – vir 18
Boat – gem 1

Boat-landing – lib 16
Bobbed – leo 3
Bolshevik – leo 8
Bomb – ari 13
Bombardment – cap 2
Book – tau 21
Born – aqu 7
Borrowed – sag 21
Bottle – sco 2
Bottom – cap 6
Bowl – aqu 27
Boxer – ari 21
Boy – vir 11, vir 26, sag 25, sag 29
Boys – cap 16
Bravery – cap 23
Breaking – sco 16
Bride – vir 12
Bridge – tau 6, lib 29, sag 28
Brightening – lib 28
Brightly – ari 6
Broken – sco 2
Brood – ari 30
Bubbles – lib 13
Bugle – pis 8
Built – tau 6
Bundled – can 3
Bunny – sco 23
Bus – sco 1
Business – cap 30
Businessman – aqu 16
Butterfly – lib 1, lib 24, aqu 25, aqu 29

Cafeteria – gem 20
Call – vir 30

Camel – leo 25
Cameo – ari 3
Camp – sco 26
Campfire – lib 4, sag 1
Candle – sco 4
Canoe – lib 10, cap 4, cap 5
Caps – sag 2
Captain – leo 13, lib 17
Caravan – vir 20
Carpet – ari 19
Carrier – leo 22
Carrying – ari 23, cap 9
Carved – cap 14
Case – leo 1
Cat – can 4
Celestial – ari 29
Censer – vir 26
Ceremony – can 19
Changed – lib 3
Chanticleer – lib 23
Chemistry – leo 18
Chess – sag 3
Chickens – leo 21, lib 7
Chicks – can 18
Chief – sco 29, cap 1
Child – vir 4, lib 22, sco 17, sag 4,
    sag 21, cap 19, aqu 7
Children – tau 14, gem 15, gem 24,
    leo 11, vir 4, lib 13, sco 15, sco
    29, sag 9, sag 18, aqu 22
Children's – cap 15
Chinese – gem 18, can 12, sag 22,
    pis 21
Choir – ari 29, leo 17, cap 20
Christmas – tau 9
Chrysalis – aqu 29
Chubby – sag 25
Church – leo 17, pis 5
Circular – lib 15
Clear – tau 1
Clothes – can 8
Clouds – tau 20, pis 10
Clown – can 11
Coat – vir 22
Cobblers – tau 29
Coiling – ari 14
Colouring – sco 18

Colours – ari 23
Comedian – ari 2
Coming – gem 27
Completely – can 10
Conference – cap 30
Constellations – leo 7
Contentment – can 26
Continent – tau 19
Convent – cap 24
Conversation – gem 14
Cornucopia – ari 24
Council – aqu 5
Country – ari 3, ari 11
Covered – sag 2
Cricket – sag 6
Cross – tau 10, vir 2, pis 7
Crossing – leo 25
Crowd – lib 21
Crowds – sco 24
Crows – sag 12
Crystal – ari 8
Crystallized – lib 6
Cupid – sag 7
Curtain – ari 24
Curtains – sco 20
Cut – can 10
Cutting – sag 20

Damaged – cap 2
Dames – vir 27
Dance – gem 22, cap 5
Dancing – ari 16, vir 8, cap 5
Dangerous – lib 10
Dark – can 14, can 25, sco 20, cap 6
Dart – lib 1
Daughter – can 30
Dawn – lib 3
Day – lib 3
Daybreak – leo 27
Dealer – cap 25
Declared – gem 28
Decorated – tau 9
Deep – sco 7
Deer – can 3, leo 4
Defeat – cap 22
Demanding – cap 1
Demonstration – gem 21

Dental – sco 9
Derelict – sco 21
Desert – leo 25
Deserted – lib 8
Deserter – aqu 3
Desire – ari 22
Desk – aqu 16
Devas – ari 16
Dew – leo 10
Diamond – can 10
Disappointed – ari 28, aqu 21
Disillusioned – aqu 21
Displayed – can 1
Dissolved – gem 17
Divers – sco 7
Divides – pis 26
Dog – sag 7, sag 21
Domain – sco 28
Door – sag 24
Double – ari 25
Dove – tau 22, lib 26, aqu 20
Drawing – vir 9, sco 20
Dreaming – vir 5
Dress – pis 6
Dressed – can 8, leo 4
Drill – pis 15
Drilling – gem 6
Drink – lib 22
Drowning – sco 11
Duck – ari 30
Ducks – sco 29
Dutch – gem 15
Duty – sco 21

Eagle – lib 26, sag 12, aqu 9
Early – leo 10
East – ari 8
Easter – sag 17, pis 17
Edge – leo 5
Eggshell – aqu 7
Electrical – tau 2
Embassy – sco 12
Embraces – ari 1
Emerging – lib 12, aqu 29
Empty – ari 18
Enjoyed – can 15
Enlightenment – sag 11

Entering – ari 21, sag 23, cap 4, cap 24, aqu 14
Entertaining – ari 2
Ephemeral – aqu 10
Epidemic – leo 2
Eruption – vir 17
Evening – leo 12, pis 20
Everything – lib 3
Examination – pis 12
Experience – gem 11, aqu 24
Experimenting – sco 13
Explosion – ari 13
Expressing – ari 7
Expression – leo 14
Eyeglasses – sag 21

Face – sco 16
Facing – ari 8, can 14, can 24
Fairies – can 7, vir 5, sco 28
Fairy – sco 23
Falling – gem 10
False – vir 30
Family – vir 14
Fat – sag 29
Father – sco 17
Feeding – ari 20, lib 7, cap 10
Felled – aqu 28
Fellowship – sco 10
Fence – aqu 15
Fertile – pis 28
Field – aqu 30
Figures – aqu 8
Filled – aqu 27
Filling – gem 2
Finger – tau 21
Fire – cap 13, aqu 19
Fireplace – lib 8
First – gem 29, vir 8
Fish – can 9
Five – sco 15, cap 19
Flag – can 1, vir 25, sag 12, aqu 9
Flag-bearer – sag 26
Fledglings – gem 23
Flexed – can 13
Flock – ari 12
Floor – aqu 22
Flow – pis 16

Flowers – tau 11
Flying – ari 8
Folded – leo 4
Forest – gem 27, aqu 19, pis 3
Formally – leo 4
Formations – leo 5
Formed – tau 19, aqu 25
Forming – sag 8
Forms – ari 10
Fountain – lib 22
Fox – pis 14
Frost – gem 26
Full – gem 9, pis 28
Fur – can 3, pis 14
Furled – can 1
Furtively – gem 2
Futurist – vir 9

Gaining – vir 29
Gallery – lib 9
Game – can 6, sag 6
Gang – lib 19
Garden – ari 22, gem 3, pis 28
Gate – ari 22
Gazer – ari 9
Geese – ari 12
General – cap 22
Germ – can 17
Gifts – ari 26
Gigantic – pis 18
Girl – ari 20, leo 6, cap 17, pis 8
Girl's – sco 16
Girls – cap 16
Girls' – vir 21
Giving – lib 22
Glass – leo 9
Glass-bottomed – gem 1
Glasses – lib 11
Goddess – sag 10
Gold – tau 4, sco 6
Golden-haired – sag 10
Gondoliers – can 20
Gorge – tau 6
Gowned – aqu 8
Gracefully – cap 22
Graduated – aqu 12
Grand – sag 1

Grande – vir 27
Granite – cap 14
Grave – tau 5
Great – gem 13, pis 30
Grimaces – can 11
Groping – tau 14
Groundhog – sag 15
Group – ari 2, can 15, lib 4, cap 11
Grows – can 17
Growth – cap 3
Guard – aqu 17
Gulls – sag 16
Gymnasium – cap 16
Gypsy – gem 27

Habitat – sag 19
Hair – leo 3
Half-mast – vir 25
Halloween – sco 30
Hammock – ari 18
Hand – can 13, vir 13, cap 10
Handkerchief – vir 15
Handling – tau 13
Hanging – lib 9
Happily – cap 8
Happiness – can 26
Haranguing – gem 16
Harem – vir 7
Harp – cap 9
Harvest – pis 27
Haste – tau 20
Hat – ari 8, tau 15
Hawks – lib 7
Head – gem 17, vir 1, lib 30
Heads – vir 10
Healer – aqu 4
Health – gem 17
Heavy – ari 23, pis 4
Hen – can 18
Hidden – cap 20
Hiding – lib 19
High – gem 23
Hindu – aqu 4
Hobby – sag 25
Hold – ari 26
Holding – tau 18, sco 4
Holly – gem 4

Home – lib 8
Horns – leo 4
Horse – sag 25
Hospital – cap 15
House – sag 24, cap 8
Houseboat – leo 19
House-raising – sco 3
Hovering – lib 27
Huge – leo 11, cap 19
Human – leo 14, cap 3
Humanity – lib 29
Hunters – sco 22
Hydrometer – aqu 26
Hysteria – vir 13
Ice – gem 24, sag 20

Ideals – lib 6
Illumination – pis 11
Imagination – ari 27
Immediate – vir 30
Immigrants – sag 23
Indian – ari 15, tau 24, sco 29, cap 1
Indians – sco 26, cap 5
Industrial – gem 8
Influences – lib 28, pis 26
Information – lib 25
Inhabited – pis 24
Initiates – pis 12
Inner – lib 5
Inspiration – aqu 11, pis 16
Instructing – pis 19
Instruction – vir 8
Intoxicated – leo 21
Inventor – sco 13
Island – pis 24
Isthmus – pis 4

Jack – cap 18
Jester – sco 30
Jewellery – tau 23
Jewish – lib 20
Jockey – pis 9

King – sco 28
Knocking – sag 7
Knowledge – can 17, vir 29, lib 5,
    lib 29, lib 30

Labour – gem 21
Lady – pis 14
Lake – sco 8
Lamb – vir 24
Lamp – sag 11
Large – ari 8, ari 28, tau 25, gem 19,
    can 10, leo 25, leo 28, vir 2,
    lib 26, cap 4, cap 11, cap 28
Laundry – sag 22
Law – pis 22
Lawn – tau 30, leo 12, sag 29
Leading – can 3
Leaf – lib 25
Learning – sag 4
Lecturing – cap 12
Left – lib 24, sag 11
Letter – leo 30
Level – can 2
Life – can 17
Light – lib 2, sag 13
Lighted – sco 4
Limb – leo 28
Linemen – sco 14
Listen – sco 24
Listening – sco 19
Lit – ari 6
Literary – can 23
Little – leo 28, sag 4, pis 21
Lives – sco 29
Load – ari 23
Locks – tau 24
Logs – cap 6
Looking – vir 10, sag 15
Lost – ari 27
Lovebirds – aqu 15
Lovers – ari 4
Luxury – can 26
Lying – pis 7

Magazine – gem 5
Magic – ari 19
Man – ari 3, ari 7, ari 10, ari 14,
    ari 26, tau 13, tau 15, tau 16,
    gem 25, gem 28, can 2, can 3,
    can 14, can 16, leo 4, leo 24,
    vir 5, vir 9, vir 28, vir 29,
    lib 5, lib 6, lib 28, sco 11,

sco 24, aqu 11, aqu 18, aqu 24,
    pis 22
Man's – vir 1
Mantle – can 25
Manuscript – can 16
Many – leo 28, cap 15
March – sco 27
Market – pis 1
Marriage – can 19
Mary – vir 24
Massive – sco 5
Master – pis 19
Masters – lib 9
Mature – tau 28
Meal – pis 20
Meeting – can 23
Men – gem 18, can 24, lib 18, sag 3,
    sag 20, pis 11, pis 15
Mentality – gem 17
Mermaid – leo 29
Merry-go-round – vir 6
Message – can 12, aqu 20
Metamorphosed – sco 23
Military – sco 27
Mine – lib 12
Miners – lib 12
Miss – can 9
Mission – aqu 1
Mistletoe – gem 4
Mockingbird – gem 29
Modern – can 28
Moon – sco 8, pis 26, pis 27, pis 28
Moonlit – can 7
Morning – leo 10
Mother – vir 11, sag 9
Moulded – vir 11
Mounds – lib 30, sco 15
Mountain – tau 1, sco 24, cap 27
Mounted – tau 24
Mouse – can 4
Moving – sag 19
Mowing – sag 29
Muffled – tau 15
Mumps – leo 2
Muse – can 29
Museum – pis 13
Musician – gem 13

Mysteries – tau 16
Mystery – aqu 6

Narrow – pis 4
Nature – cap 12
Navy – aqu 3
Nest – gem 23
Nests – can 6
Net – ari 24
New – ari 10, gem 11, lib 3, pis 22,
    pis 26
Newly – tau 19
Night – can 7
Nonvested – leo 17
Noon – lib 14
Northeast – can 14
Nude – can 9, cap 17
Nurse – tau 10
Nursing – can 12

Oak – leo 11
Ocean – sag 2
Officer – pis 15
Officers – pis 6
Oil – gem 6
Old – ari 10, tau 16, can 14, leo 13,
    lib 9, sag 15, sag 28, aqu 1
Old-fashioned – gem 7, leo 6
One – ari 6, can 13, lib 26, sco 24,
    cap 2
Open – tau 5, tau 21
Opportunity – ari 27, leo 14, sag 10
Orang-utan – vir 16
Oriental – cap 25
Ornamental – vir 15
Ouija – vir 18
Outline – ari 3
Overeaten – can 15
Owl – sag 5

Pageant – leo 15
Palms – gem 25
Paper – vir 29
Parade – can 8, pis 6, pis 17
Parading – tau 30
Park – tau 25
Parrot – sco 19

Party – leo 12, leo 19, cap 4
Passions – aqu 24
Past – sag 13
Pastel – ari 23
Path – gem 11
Paths – lib 15
Paws – aqu 23
Peacock – tau 30
Peering – lib 11
Pelicans – sag 19
People – can 15, can 26, aqu 12
Perfect – lib 1
Perfectly – aqu 25
Performer – aqu 6
Performing – can 19
Perfume – sco 2
Petrified – pis 3
Pheasants – cap 11
Phenomena – pis 23
Philosopher's – lib 30
Physical – sag 11
Piano – gem 13
Pigeon – leo 22
Pilgrimage – cap 27
Place – can 2
Placed – lib 18, aqu 22
Play – aqu 6, aqu 22
Playing – tau 14, vir 4, sco 15, sag 3
Pleading – sco 29
Pocahontas – can 28
Pointing – tau 21
Political – vir 13
Pond – ari 30
Pope – sag 30
Popularity – aqu 10
Possessed – ari 26
Pot – tau 24
Power – cap 7
Precipice – leo 5
Preparing – pis 15
President – ari 11
Priest – can 19
Priesthood – pis 25
Prim – ari 17
Prima donna – can 21
Prism – pis 29
Professor – lib 11

Profile – ari 3
Prominent – can 13
Promise – ari 25
Propagandist – leo 8
Prophet – cap 7
Protecting – lib 7
Protection – vir 3
Proves – aqu 10
Public – tau 25, pis 1
Pupil – pis 19
Purging – pis 25
Pursued – tau 28
Pyramids – sag 14

Quenched – aqu 19
Quiver – gem 9

Rabbi – lib 20
Rabbits – can 8
Race – vir 19, lib 2, cap 21
Radical – gem 5
Rainbow – leo 26
Rainbow's – tau 24
Rakish – tau 15
Reaching – can 9
Reading – can 26, vir 29, cap 29
Realism – gem 11
Realms – ari 7
Receptive – cap 3
Recognition – cap 1
Red – tau 10
Regained – ari 27
Relay – cap 21
Republic – sag 1
Rescued – sco 11
Reveal – tau 16
Revolution – can 30
Rich – sco 18
Rider – leo 23
Right – can 25, aqu 25
Ring – ari 21
Rises – ari 1
Robbers – lib 19
Rock – leo 5
Rocking – leo 13
Rocks – sag 8, pis 7
Rocky – sco 5

Romance – tau 28
Rowing – cap 5
Royal – vir 22
Rug – cap 25, aqu 22
Rush – sco 6

Safety – lib 10
Sailboat – can 22
Samaria – tau 7
Sand – sco 15
Santa Claus – gem 2
Saucily – gem 12
Sawed – aqu 28
Scalp – tau 24
Scratching – can 18
Scroll – can 16
Sculptor – sag 27
Sea – leo 13, lib 17, sco 7, sag 16
Seal – ari 1
Secluded – ari 4
Secret – vir 29, cap 30
Seeking – lib 29, pis 11
Selling – tau 27
Senorita – tau 26
Serenade – can 20
Serenading – tau 26
Serpent – ari 14
Servant – pis 21
Service – vir 30, sag 17
Set – pis 20
Setting – ari 16
Seventh – lib 2
Shadow – can 25, sag 15
Shadows – vir 10
Shaggy – can 3
Shellfish – tau 14
Shining – sco 8
Ship – sag 16
Shop – tau 23
Shopping – cap 19
Shore – sco 5
Shoulder – can 25
Side – ari 6, lib 24
Siesta – lib 14
Sight-seeing – sco 1
Silk – tau 15
Sinai – pis 22

Singing – ari 29, can 21, cap 8, cap 20
Sitting – aqu 15, aqu 23
Sixth – lib 2
Skating – gem 24
Sky – leo 7
Sleigh – tau 8
Slightly – can 13
Smile – sco 16
Snatched – vir 12
Snow – tau 8
Soap – lib 13
Society – can 23
Sofas – can 26
Soldier – sco 21
Soul – leo 14, cap 3
South – can 24
Space – can 14
Span – lib 29
Spaniard – tau 26
Sphinx – sag 14
Spilled – sco 2
Spinsters – ari 17
Spiritist – pis 23
Spring – gem 29
Sprinkling – tau 11
Sprite – cap 26
Square – ari 6, can 16
Squaw – tau 27, sco 29
Stained-glass – cap 2
Stairs – sag 9, aqu 12
Standing – sag 24, aqu 17
Starting out – sco 22
Still – gem 1
Stockings – gem 2
Stoneface – pis 30
Storm – tau 2, leo 16
Stream – tau 1, sag 28
Streamers – ari 8
Strike – gem 8
Strolling – ari 4
Strong – vir 13
Student – cap 12
Successfully – ari 7
Suddenly – can 25
Suffragist – gem 16
Suits – cap 16

Sun – ari 16, leo 20
Sunbonnets – sag 18
Sunlit – can 24
Sunrise – sag 17
Sunshine – leo 16
Supper – sco 10
Supplanting – vir 13
Surreptitiously – cap 17
Suspended – can 2
Swimming – vir 19
Swing – leo 11
Sword – pis 13
Swords – tau 17
Symbol – lib 25
Symbols – ari 10

Table – gem 29, pis 20
Talking – gem 15, gem 18, sco 19
Tea – vir 27
Tea leaves – cap 29
Teacher – leo 18
Teaching – ari 10, lib 5, aqu 24
Team – vir 21
Telepathy – gem 14
Telephone – sco 14
Temple – sag 11
Ten – cap 6
Tent – pis 18
Tête-à-Tête – aqu 11
Things – sag 8
Third – lib 24
Three – gem 23, lib 9, lib 30, cap 2
Thrown – can 25
Thumb – can 13
Thunderstorm – aqu 2
Tiny – can 9, sag 18
Topsy – gem 12
Torches – tau 17
Toys – cap 15
Traffic – pis 4
Train – can 5, aqu 14
Trainer – vir 23
Transmuted – lib 2
Tree – tau 9, gem 23, leo 11, leo 28, vir 14, sag 5, aqu 28
Triangle – ari 5
Trimming – gem 25

Troubled – tau 22
True – lib 5
Tuileries – gem 3
Tunnel – aqu 14
Turned into – aqu 9
Turning – aqu 24
Turning into – lib 26
Turns into – sag 12
Twins – can 29
Two – ari 4, ari 7, ari 17, tau 29,
    gem 15, gem 18, can 7, can 24,
    vir 3, vir 10, lib 18, sco 20, sag 3,
    cap 23, aqu 15

Understanding – cap 3
Unexpected – aqu 2
Unfurled – can 1
Unheard – vir 30
Union – cap 18
Unkempt – leo 24
Unmasked – aqu 18
Unsealed – leo 30
Unsuccessful – ari 13
Untidy – leo 24
Upraised – vir 2
Up-to-date – leo 6
Upwards – aqu 12

Vainly – tau 16
Valuable – ari 23
Vast – can 2, can 14
Veil – vir 12
Veiled – ari 23, cap 7
Vessel – can 1, can 14
Violets – aqu 27
Volcano – vir 17
Volume – gem 19

Walk – ari 4, sag 4
War – cap 5, cap 23
Ward – cap 15
Washed away – lib 16
Watchdog – aqu 17
Watching – sag 16
Water – ari 1, gem 1, can 9, cap 26
Waters – tau 22, lib 10
Waving – aqu 23
Wax – aqu 8
Weaving – ari 15
Weighing – can 29
Well – gem 7
Well-kept – tau 25
White – tau 22, vir 2, vir 4, vir 24,
    lib 26, sag 2, aqu 20, pis 21
Widow – tau 5

Widow's – sag 13
Wild – ari 12
Wind – tau 20
Window – ari 24, tau 18
Windows – cap 2
Window-shoppers – tau 12
Wing – lib 24, aqu 25
Wings – ari 5
Winter – ari 20, gem 26
Woman – ari 1, ari 14, ari 23, tau 7,
    tau 11, tau 18, tau 28, gem 16,
    can 12, can 22, can 24, leo 3,
    lib 7, sco 17, sco 20, cap 24, cap
    29, aqu 21
Woods – gem 26, sco 18
Work – sco 9, sco 14
Working – tau 29
Worshipper – cap 13
Worshippers – leo 20
Wrecked – can 5

X-ray – sco 25

Young – ari 20
Youth – sco 4

Zuni – leo 20

5

SELF TALK

This technique enables you to identify two highly important dimensions of your personality – the Inner Child and the Adult. Having identified them you are then able to develop and regenerate them, and build a loving relationship between the two, through the Inner Dialogue that is Self Talk. The Child within you represents your past and all its influences, good and bad. It manifests as your reactions and emotions. The Adult is the thinking, rational expression of yourself. Nowadays, the interaction between the two tends to be mostly negative – for example, you feel low (Child) so you condemn yourself (Adult), this makes the Child feel worse, so more condemnation follows. This vicious circle persists year after year and, combined with the negative input of others, creates a bedrock of fear and mistrust that can blight one's life. This goes on unconsciously, like corrupted computer software that you have not yet detected, consistently messing up what you do and want to do. Self Talk not only debugs this program, but upgrades it into something that positively improves the quality of your life. A positively functioning Inner Child brings spontaneity, playfulness, creativity and a sense of wonder into one's life. A positive Adult makes for a more secure and effective personality. Each then serves, rather than disserves, the other.

TECHNIQUE AND PRACTICE

1 Name your Inner Child and Adult. The Adult will usually have the name you go by in your normal outer life, as it is the Adult that deals with the outer world – astrologically, this is Saturn. The Inner Child – astrologically the Moon – usually has the name you were called as a child. If not, choose or make one up that has an endearing quality about it. In my own case, Lyn is my Adult and Lynny is my Inner Child.

Adding 'y' or 'ie' to your Adult name, or abbreviating it, commonly does the trick. It will help a great deal if you have a picture of yourself as a child – keep it somewhere safe and near at hand.

2 Whenever you FEEL something that troubles you, this is your Inner Child trying to tell you something. This is when it needs SUPPORT from the Adult. Whenever you are BEING or DOING something negative, it is your Adult malfunctioning. This is because it needs APPRECIATION from your Inner Child. This can be a catch-22 situation, but as a rule it falls to the Adult to be RESPONSIBLE and make the first step to repair the relationship. In other words, the critical element here is exercising your will to get the Adult to support your Inner Child, and then eventually, when your Inner Child feels that the Adult cares, it will open up and show its appreciation. So, CARE = TRUST = APPRECIATION = CARE. This interaction is demonstrated and expanded on in the Example and Guide below. However, the overall theme that needs to persist is one where the Adult is, one way or another, saying to the Child, 'I Recognize You; I Believe In You; I Accept You Just As You Are; I Support You; I Love You', and where the Child is, one way or the other, saying to the Adult, 'I Trust You; I Feel Secure With You; I Appreciate You; I Love You.' In effect, Self Talk helps re-parenting the Child in a positive manner, and making the parent or Adult stronger in the process.

3 Learn to relate to the Inner Child and Adult as real living beings within yourself. Always address them by name – especially the Child. As the Adult, imagine how you would relate in a positive manner to an actual child, particularly one that was your own. For instance, you wouldn't want to ignore him or her (a sign of the Negative Adult), especially when they need you for some reason, nor would you leave them

unattended for too long. The terrible truth is that most people do not know, or have forgotten, that their Inner Child is there. During the course of the day, get into the habit of frequently acknowledging and chatting with your Inner Child. Give him or her a regular smile or wink. Feel the difference that this makes. If you feel silly doing this, then that is a sign that your Adult is denying your Child.

4   Use Self Talk whenever you are troubled or to sort out any problem – eventually you can use it for purely amusing or creative ends, as interactions with children often are. It helps to make a routine of it, so try to use it first thing when you wake up, and when you go to bed. Go to sleep embracing your Inner Child.

EXAMPLE INNER DIALOGUE

One wakes up *feeling* insecure and anxious about being able to hack it through the day, let alone your whole life. This is the Inner Child – children usually wake up first, remember. In response to this the 'negative' Adult might just say 'Tough – let's just get on with it', or instead might go back to sleep, or toss and turn fitfully and wind up getting out of the wrong side of bed. In all three of these possible reactions (of which there are many), the Adult has ignored or not recognized how the Child is feeling. In response to this the Child may sulk (giving rise to a 'stiff upper lip' from the Adult and a continuing negative mood throughout the day), escape into fantasy (going back to sleep), or feel angry and throw a tantrum (hence the tossing and turning and a subsequently bad day). However, with Self Talk, it could go something like this:

Adult (in response to feeling of insecurity and anxiety) – '[child's name], what's troubling you? I'm sure I can help, whatever it is.'

Child (tight-lipped) – 'Don't know. Frightened.'

Adult (concerned) – 'What are you frightened of?'

Child (spontaneously) – 'Having nowhere to live.'

Adult (genuinely a bit puzzled, but not making the Child feel silly – that would be fatal) – 'How could that happen, [child's name]?'

Child (after some time, which the Adult must always give) – 'Not enough money.'

Adult (recognizing that money should not be the Child's concern, but theirs) – 'Don't you worry your little head about that. You can trust me to see that we have enough money, one way or the other.'

This is a critical point in the Inner Dialogue where the Adult has to affirm to themselves that they can do what they are supposed to do – deal with the outer world, something which the Adult may have to work on 'in their own time'. The significant factor here is that if the Child does not feel supported or reassured by the Adult, then its feelings of insecurity will leak through to the Adult, effectively sabotaging their ability to deal with the material world. If the Child believes that nothing can be done to relieve the situation, material or otherwise, then that belief is subconsciously passed on to the Adult. But when the Adult is *being* the Adult, it can be objective and do whatever is necessary to secure the situation, and in a manner that does not jeopardize the Child's welfare (such as breaking the law).

Child – 'Are you sure, [adult's name]?'

Adult – 'Of course I am sure [child's name]. I care about you too much to let you down. Do you feel better now?'

Child – 'Yes, thank you. I think you're great.'

Adult – (feeling touched and inspired by the Child's trust and admiration) – 'Thank you. I love you very much.'

The outcome of this Inner Dialogue is the obvious benefit of the Adult and the Child making each other feel better about themselves and the situation. It must be remembered that Rome was not built in a day. The Child will need constant reassurance and the Adult will need frequently reminding that they are the Adult, and that they are capable as such.

There are many different kinds of scenario. In all cases one must persist with the Inner Dialogue, really get into it like an actor getting into a part. Let it unfold and reveal it's own story, and not give up because the Adult cannot be bothered or the Child does not respond or talk as readily as the impatient Adult would like. Such impatience can often be reflecting the Child's desperation. As the relationship develops and strengthens, so will you.

A GUIDE TO SELF TALK

THE INNER CHILD		THE ADULT	
needs SUPPORT expresses itself through FEELINGS EMOTIONS THE RIGHT BRAIN THE UNCONSCIOUS MIND		needs APPRECIATION expresses itself through THOUGHTS WORDS THE LEFT BRAIN THE CONSCIOUS MIND	
WHEN YOU ARE FEELING:		**WHEN YOU ARE BEING:**	
Appreciative Cheeky Creative Cute Dreamy Emotional Enthusiastic Free Fun loving Guileless Illogical Imaginative Innocent Instinctive Intuitive Open Passionate Playful Receptive Spontaneous Subjective Suggestible Truthful	Angry Anxious Embarrassed Frightened Frustrated Guilty Inadequate Inferior Insecure Jealous Lonely Moody Naive Negative Nervous Rejected Selfish Self-Pity Threatened Unsupported Vulnerable Weak Worthless	Active Articulate Assertive Compassionate Confident Decisive Direct Disciplined Firm Guiding In Charge Logical Objective Positive Rational Reasonable Reassuring Responsible Secure Strategic Strong Supportive Wise	Boring Clinical Cold Controlling Critical Destructive Dismissive Facetious Impatient Irresponsible Mean Needling Oppressive Punishing Repressive Resentful Rigid Sarcastic Scornful Suspicious Supercilious Uncaring Undermining
your POSITIVE CHILD is showing or telling you something	your NEGATIVE CHILD is in need of your Positive Adult	your POSITIVE ADULT is functioning well	your NEGATIVE ADULT needs appreciation from your Positive Child

SOME BENEFITS OF SELF TALK

Positive Transformation	Self Love	Emotional Release
Problem Solving at Root	Left/Right Brain Integration	End to Inner Conflict
Increased Efficiency/Creativity	Spiritual Unfoldment	Healthy Family Life
Elimination of Addictiveness	Inner Stability	Positive Relationships

THE HIGHER SELF

In contemplating and contacting the Inner Child and Adult it should soon become apparent that there is a third 'entity' present within you. This entity is aware of the condition of both the Child and Adult, and is concerned with their welfare. This is your Higher Self and it is likely that at some point it will be needed to arbitrate between the Child and Adult when they are 'not talking to each another'. The Higher Self is like a psychological diplomat; it also has connections to 'high places', that is, wisdom and higher intelligence (*see* Solar Meditation). Simply by recognizing when your Higher Self is present, you can bring it into play to help with your interior situation, and then, ultimately, the exterior situation.

WRITTEN INNER DIALOGUE

An effective and intriguing way of getting the Inner Child and Adult to communicate is to write the Adult's questions and remarks on the right-hand side of a page with your right hand, and the Inner Child's feelings and expressions on the left-hand side of the same page with your left hand. Reverse the sides and hands if you are left-handed. You will be amazed at what you find your Child writing – and don't try to make his or her writing that neat or legible; it is a child's writing after all.

* I am grateful to my friend, professional hypnotherapist Ian Brown, for assisting me in the writing of this section.

6

SOLAR MEDITATION

After following and using *The Astrological Oracle* for some time you may find that you are in need of a spiritual discipline and exercise that connects you further with the Solar intelligence from which the Sabian Symbols themselves spring. At first, I was loath to put forward my own meditation/ritual – a Mayan Solar Meditation that has chanting to the Sun as its basic theme, using the Mayan word for the Sun – because I do not like to impose my own spiritual practices on others. So, I asked the Astrological Oracle whether this would be a good thing to do. The Oracle responded with Libra 28 – 'A Man In The Midst Of Brightening Influences'. This had to be an agreement!

BASIC THEME

This basic theme constitutes the essentials of the session and should not be departed from in any way, but it may be elaborated on and embellished in any way that spontaneously and creatively occurs to you. Seat yourself comfortably, facing the actual Sun if possible, but this is not essential and it is not always practical. *Practise only during daylight hours!*

The Mayan word for the Sun is K'IN. It is pronounced with a hard, clicking 'K' as if you were saying 'kick' without sounding the 'i'. Physically, the back of your tongue slaps against your soft palate (the back of the roof of your mouth). This 'K' is followed, as smoothly as possible, by the 'I' which sounds like 'EEEEE'. Finally, the 'N' is sounded in the normal way, but is elongated: 'NNNNN'.

K'EEEEEEENNNNNNNN

I find it helps to sound this word with a pout, as if you were blowing a kiss to the Sun! The sound then travels from the back of the mouth to the front with ease.

One single chant takes one whole exhalation, allotting as much time and breath to the 'N' as the 'I'. This is important when you consider the onomatopoeic way the word is made up:

K represents the ignition of the Sun;

I represents its light and heat travelling;

N represents it settling upon whatever it reaches.

Chant K'IN seven, thirteen or twenty times. You may repeat these rounds as many times as you like, just as long as you keep to these multiples. Centre yourself and be still before and after.

ROUNDS OF CHANTING

Here are suggested three rounds of chanting, but, within the ritual of the Basic Theme, you can devise you own.

FIRST ROUND

Chant K'IN to the Pleiades (the Seven Sisters, or 'seven stars in the sky'). This resonates with your higher levels of tuning and vibration, the Pleiades being a star cluster of the highest spiritual significance. It is appropriate to chant at as high a pitch as you can, which will be in falsetto if you are male. Centre – be still – sense the greater pattern of existence.

SECOND ROUND

Chant K'IN to the Sun itself. This is pitched at an octave below the high note of the first set. This chant is for 'all your relations', which means anyone or anything that you wish to send solar energy to. This is unconditional love, so avoid any thoughts or feelings other than compassionate ones, and the name and image of who/what you are chanting/sending to. Centre – be still – oneness.

THIRD ROUND

This round is for yourself. This time you chant an octave below the previous one, so it should be quite deep and resonant. This is so you *feel* the chant (around your solar plexus) more than you hear it. Also, in order to internalize it further, close your mouth in the middle and at the very end of the chant. Close your eyes too, if you wish. In effect, it will sound like this:

K'EEEEEEEmmmmmmmmEEEEEEENNNNNNNmmmmmmmm

Make sure that you keep your tongue connected to the front of the roof of your mouth when your mouth is closed (mmmmmmmm) at the end. This is important for your tongue is a switch that completes a circuit of energy that goes up the spine, down through the mouth, and down the front of the body to start again at the groin. While performing this round of K'IN, make sure that you think of and nurture yourself only. Centre – be still – I AM THAT I AM.

This completes the essentials of this Solar Meditation.

CUSTOMIZING YOUR SOLAR MEDITATION

Here are some suggestions as to how to make your Solar Meditation a personal event that is aesthetically pleasing and invokes a feeling of being with your own sense of divine presence.

- ❉ Start by making your own 'temple'. This can be a mat with a symmetrical Indian/Mexican design; this allows you to arrange and align objects and focus thoughts. Remember that your body is the temple of your Soul.
- ❉ Some form of physical exercise or discipline such as yoga or tai chi is recommended as a preparation for meditation as it relaxes the body. You can do this on the mat.
- ❉ Use oils of some kind (essential, Aura Soma, etc) in a way which feels to be good for you.

- ❉ A form of yogic breathing is very good for stilling and empowering you prior to your meditation.
- ❉ First Set – Chant to each of the Seven Sisters (the Pleiades). If chanting seven times, breathe in each star, and then chant to it.
- ❉ Second Set – Breathe in the light of the candle flame, the solar icon or the Sun itself if outdoors, and then chant out to it. The solar icon could have seven, thirteen or twenty rays to chant to.
- ❉ Put your hands together and bow before and after each set.
- ❉ Music – Use partly, throughout, or not at all. Atmospheric sound effects can invoke a heightened sense of awareness. It is best to choose music that acts as a drone to your chanting.
- ❉ Arranging sacredly or personally significant objects on and around your mat gives a sense of being in a special divine place of your own for a special divine time of your own. If you want to partake of the divine in your life, then as with food at mealtimes, you best make it regular and pleasing to the taste. Some basic items are: a candle burning, perhaps of a shape and colour that resonates with you, in a special holder; incense of your choice; a solar icon or model; a picture of the Pleiades (available in astronomy books and planetariums, maybe enlarged and mounted on card).
- ❉ The Solar Meditation can be varied enormously (thus allaying that common enemy of meditation: boredom) through using the Mayan/Dreamspell Calendar, for this has different statements, meanings, images, colours, smells and mudras for each day of the 260-day calendar cycle. For further information, contact the author using the addresses given on page 470.

After the three sets you may find it easy to be in quiet meditation for a period. Close in a formal way: Bow, extinguish candle, remove any ceremonial jewellery, return objects to places if need be. Do not rush off into everyday life if you can help it.

7

*

THE ZODIAC WHEEL

(photocopy to use)

FURTHER RESOURCES

If you wish to take your interest in astrology further, I recommend that you contact:

AUSTRALIA
Federation of Australian Astrologers
Lynda Hill
20 Harley Road
Avalon NSW 2107

Tel: + 61-2-918-9539
e-mail: lyndah@bigpond.com

CANADA
Association Canadiennes des Astrologues Franscophones
Denise Chrzanwska
CP 1715, Succ 'B'
Montreal HSB 3LB

Tel: + 1-514-831-4153
Fax: + 1-514-521-1502

Astrolinguistics Institute
Anne Black
2182 Cubbon Drive
Victoria, BC V8R 1R5

Tel: + 1-604-370-1874
Fax: + 1-604-370-1891
e-mail: ablack@islandnet.com

INTERNET
The Astrological Oracle
www.thorsons.com
(Thorsons Publishers)

Sabian Assembly
www.sabian.org

Lyn Birkbeck
www.lynbirkbeck.com

NEW ZEALAND
Astrological Society of New Zealand
Joy Dowler
5266 Wellesley Street
Auckland 1003

Astrological Foundation Inc.
Hamish Saunders
41 New North Road
Eden Terrace
Auckland 1003

Tel/Fax: + 64-9-373-5304

SOUTH AFRICA
Astrological Society of South Africa
Cynthia Thorburn
PO Box 2968
Rivonia 2128

Tel: + 27-11-864-1436

UNITED KINGDOM
The Astrological Association
396 Caledonian Road
London N1 1DN

Tel: + 20-7700-6479

USA
American Federation of Astrologers
Robert Cooper
PO Box 22040
Tempe
AZ 85285-2040

Tel: + 602-838-1751
Fax: + 602-838-8293
e-mail: afa@astrologers.com

Association for Astrological Networking
8306 Wilshire Blvd.
Suite 537
Beverly Hills
CA 90211

Please address any queries or correspondence for Lyn Birkbeck (enclosing SAE if from UK) to:

Lyn Birkbeck (TAO)
c/o Thorsons,
77–85 Fulham Palace Road,
London W6 8JB, UK

or e-mail:

lynbirkbeck@talk21.com

✳ RECOMMENDED READING

The following books are recommended as companions to *The Astrological Oracle*:

An Astrological Mandala by Dane Rudhyar (Random House Inc., New York, 1973)

A Dictionary of Symbols by Tom Chetwynd (Paladin Books, London, 1982)

Do It Yourself Astrology by Lyn Birkbeck (Element Books, 1996)

Do It Yourself Relationship Astrology by Lyn Birkbeck (Element Books, 1999)

Do It Yourself Life Plan Astrology by Lyn Birkbeck (Element Books, 2000)

A Guide to the I Ching by Carol Anthony (Anthony Press, Stowe, Mass, 1988)

Man and His Symbols by C.G. Jung (Arkana, 1990)

The Sabian Symbols in Astrology by Dr. Marc Edmund Jones (Aurora Press, Santa Fe, 1993)

The Wordsworth Dictionary of Symbolism by Hans Biedermann (Wordsworth Editions Ltd., Ware, 1996)

The I Ching translated by Richard Wilhelm (Routledge & Kegan Paul, London, 1968)